The Routledge Handbook of Tourism Research

The Routledge Handbook of Tourism Research is a compendium of some of the most relevant issues affecting tourism development today. The topics addressed in this book provide some new thinking for those involved in tourism research. This book takes the reader from the beginnings of tourism research to a discussion of emerging forms of tourism and selected examples of tourism development. The underlying theoretical dimensions are reviewed, analysed and discussed from a number of perspectives. This book brings together leading researchers, many of whom are members of the International Academy for the Study of Tourism, to discuss tourism today and its future.

The works included in this volume are diverse, in terms of geographical context, research methodology, root discipline, and perspective. This book represents studies based in Europe, North America, Oceania and Asia. Research methodologies include both quantitative and qualitative. Both macro and micro issues are discussed from the economic, psychological, sociological, political science, marketing, and other perspectives, which reflect the interdisciplinary nature of tourism studies.

This book is divided into six parts. Part 1 considers the foundations for tourism research. Part 2 discusses the implications for destination management and Part 3 discusses planning for tourism development. Part 4 covers human capital for tourism development. Part 5 evaluates emerging forms of tourism and finally Part 6 offers insights into tourism evolution.

The book offers the reader a comprehensive synthesis of this field, conveying the latest thinking and research. The text will provide an invaluable resource for all those with an interest in tourism research. This is essential reading for students, researchers and academics of tourism as well as those of related studies, in particular leisure, hospitality and development studies.

Cathy H. C. Hsu is a Professor and Associate Dean in the School of Hotel and Tourism Management at the Hong Kong Polytechnic University.

William C. Gartner is a Professor of Applied Economics at the University of Minnesota, USA.

The Routledge Handbook of Tourism Research

Edited by
Cathy H. C. Hsu
and William C. Gartner

LONDON AND NEW YORK

First published 2012
by Routledge
2 Park Square, Milton Park, Abingdon, Oxon OX14 4RN

Simultaneously published in the USA and Canada
by Routledge
711 Third Avenue, New York, NY 10017

Routledge is an imprint of the Taylor & Francis Group, an informa business

© 2012 Cathy H. C. Hsu and William C. Gartner

The right of Cathy H. C. Hsu and William C. Gartner to be identified as
editors of this work has been asserted by them in accordance with the
Copyright, Designs and Patents Act 1988.

British Library Cataloguing in Publication Data
A catalogue record for this book is available from the British Library

Library of Congress Cataloging in Publication Data
A catalog record for this book has been requested

ISBN: 978-0-7890-3704-6 (hbk)
ISBN: 978-0-2031-2328-7 (ebk)

Typeset in Bembo
by Cenveo Publisher Services

Printed and bound by CPI Group (UK) Ltd, Croydon, CR0 4YY

Contents

Contents

Contents

Contents

Contents

Contents

List of figures

List of tables

Notes on the editors

Cathy H. C. Hsu, PhD, is a Professor and Associate Dean in the School of Hotel and Tourism Management at The Hong Kong Polytechnic University. She is a member of the International Academy for the Study of Tourism. Her research foci have been tourism destination marketing, tourist behaviours, service quality and the economic and social impacts of casino gaming. She has edited four books and authored five books, with over 180 refereed journal and proceedings publications. She is the editor-in-chief of the *Journal of Teaching in Travel and Tourism* and serves on eight journal editorial boards.

William C. Gartner, PhD, is a Professor of Applied Economics at the University of Minnesota. Dr Gartner has conducted numerous research studies in the area of tourism image development, seasonal home impacts, tourism marketing and methods for tourism research. He serves on the editorial board of numerous journals, and has been the Secretary, Vice President, President and Board Chair for the International Academy for the Study of Tourism. He is the author of numerous tourism articles published in professional journals and two books, *Tourism Development: Principles, Processes and Policies*, Wiley and Sons, and *Trends in Outdoor Recreation, Leisure and Tourism*, CABI.

Notes on the contributors

Julio Aramberri is Dean of the Faculty of Languages and Cultural Studies at Hoa Sen University (Saigon, Vietnam). Until 2009 he was Professor of Tourism at Drexel University (Philedelphia). Before that, he worked 15 years for Turespaña (Tourist Office of Spain) where he was the CEO between 1987 and 1990. From 1964 to 1984 he taught Sociology at Universidad Complutense (Madrid). He has authored or co-authored 8 books and more than 40 papers on general sociology, tourism theory and tourism development and marketing.

Jigang Bao is the Dean of the School of Tourism and Assistant to the President, Sun Yat-sen University, People's Republic of China. He is the Chair of the Commission on the Geography of Tourism, the Geographical Society of China. His research interests include tourism geography, theme park, tourism planning, urban tourism, tourism impacts and community tourism. Dr Bao is the author of the textbook *Geography of Tourism* (in Chinese) which has sold over 100,000 copies since 1993.

Lyn Batchelor is a Senior Lecturer in Enterprise at the University of Chichester in England. Her research interests include critical management studies and resistance through individual identity regulation. Lyn is also publishing on the impact of mobile phone use in the workplace, as well as researching the impact of MSc and MBA courses on entrepreneurialism and the management of innovation in business.

Tom Baum is Professor of International Tourism and Hospitality Management in the University of Strathclyde, Glasgow. His research interests are in the area of people and work within hospitality and tourism, with a particular focus on planning and development, and he has published 7 books and over 100 scientific papers in this field. Tom is a Fellow of the International Academy for the Study of Tourism.

Richard Butler is Emeritus Professor of International Tourism at the University of Strathclyde, in Glasgow, Scotland. A geographer, he spent thirty years at the University of Western Ontario (Canada) and eight years at the University of Surrey, moving to Scotland in 2005. He is a past president of the International Academy for the Study of Tourism and his main research interests are the destination development process, sustainability and impacts of tourism, and tourism in remote areas and islands.

Liping A. Cai is Professor and Director of Purdue Tourism and Hospitality Research Center. His research and consulting experiences include destination image and branding, rural tourism development including guest and host relationships, and visitors' behavioural and psychographic profiles. He has conducted over 30 industry projects for destination communities and a variety of tourism businesses, and published over 100 refereed papers.

Erik Cohen is George S. Wise Professor of Sociology (emeritus) at the Department of Sociology and Anthropology, The Hebrew University of Jerusalem. He conducted research in Israel, Peru, the Pacific Islands, and Thailand. He is the author of more than 160 publications. His recent books include: *Thai Tourism: Hill Tribes, Islands and Open-ended Prostitution*, *The Commercialized Crafts of Thailand*, *The Chinese Vegetarian Festival in Phuket*, *Contemporary Tourism: Diversity and Change*, and *Israeli Backpackers and Their Society*.

Malcolm Cooper is Vice President (Research) and Professor of Tourism Management at Ritsumeikan Asia Pacific University, Beppu, Japan. He is a specialist in tourism and environmental management and city planning, and has published widely in these fields. He has worked in the environmental planning and tourism management areas in the public sector in Australia and New Zealand. He has been a consultant to the Governments of China and Vietnam as well as privately and is a corresponding editor for *Annals of Tourism Research*.

Geoffrey I. Crouch is a Professor of Tourism Policy and Marketing in the La Trobe Business School. His research interests include tourism marketing, destination marketing and competitiveness, tourist choice modelling, tourism psychology and consumer behaviour, and space tourism. He is co-editor-in-chief of the journal *Tourism Analysis* and is an elected Fellow and Treasurer of the *International Academy for the Study of Tourism*.

Graham M. S. Dann became initially interested in tourism while he was lecturing in sociology at the University of the West Indies, Barbados. Having subsequently published widely in the specialist areas of tourism motivation and promotion, he is a founder member of the International Academy for the Study of Tourism and of the research committee on international tourism of the International Sociological Association. On the editorial boards of three leading tourism journals he is currently Professor Emeritus of Tourism at Finnmark University College, Norway.

Frances Devine is a Lecturer of Hospitality in the School of Hospitality and Tourism Management, University of Ulster, Northern Ireland. Frances was a manager with the Compass Group in Northern Ireland before joining the university as a lecturer concentrating on Human Resources and Organisational Studies. Her research focuses on new trends in human resource management in hospitality and tourism, presently focusing on cultural diversity.

Timothy Devinney is Professor and Director of the Centre for Corporate Change at the Australian Graduate School of Management, University of New South Wales. He has interests in choice modelling and information acceleration.

Jeremy S. Eades is Professor of Asia Pacific Studies at Ritsumeikan Asia Pacific University, researching the impact of globalization on the Asia Pacific region. His most recent books are *The Making of Anthropology in East and Southeast Asia* (co-edited with Shinji Yamashita and Joseph Bosco, Berghahn Press, 2005) and *The 'Big Bang' in Japanese Higher Education* (edited with Roger Goodman, Yumiko Hada, Trans Pacific Press, 2005).

Sheryl Marie Elliott is associate professor at the George Washington University, School of Business, Department of Tourism and Hospitality Management. She serves as the coordinator for the undergraduate programs in Sport, Event and Hospitality Management. Dr. Elliott has written extensively on development, culture and ecological aspects of tourism. She was a founding member of the Pan American Federation of Tourism and Hospitality School, and currently serves as a governor appointed tourism expert on the Maryland Heritage Area Authority.

Donald Getz is Professor of Tourism and Hospitality Management, School of Tourism, at the University of Queensland. Professor Getz has authored a number of books and teaches, conducts research, writes and consults in the field of tourism and hospitality management. He is a leading scholar and proponent of event management and event tourism. Related areas of expertise include destination and resort management and marketing, family business and entrepreneurship, rural tourism, impact assessment, consumer research and special-interest travel.

Alison M. Gill is an Associate Dean and Professor in the Faculty of Arts at Simon Fraser University in British Columbia, Canada. Her research as a geographer has focused particularly on understanding the role of community in resort settings and exploring processes of change in small communities impacted by tourism. This includes the influence of local politics and the role of community organizations in effecting change.

Anton Gosar is a professor and Dean of the Department of Geography at University of Primorska in the dynamic port-town Koper-Capodistria in Slovenia/EU. He is also the President of the Commission on Political Geography of the IGU (International Geographical Union). Professional work included studies on tourism geography, political geography and population geography. In 2005 he was awarded Ambassador of Science by the Government of Slovenia and in 2006 named Honorary Member of the Austrian Geographic Society.

Donald E. Hawkins is Eisenhower Professor of Tourism Policy, Professor of Tourism Studies, and Research Professor of Medicine at The George Washington University. He is the author or editor of more than 100 articles and books including: *Tourism in Contemporary Society*, *Ecotourism Planning and Management* and *Turismo Venezuela*. He is also the founding editor of the *Journal of Leisure Research* and serves on the editorial board of *Tourism Management*. He received the Ulysses Prize for tourism scholarship from the UNWTO in 2003.

Cathy H. C. Hsu is Professor in the School of Hotel and Tourism Management at Hong Kong Polytechnic University. Her research foci have been tourism destination marketing, tourist behaviors, service quality, and the economic and social impacts of casino gaming. She has edited four books and authored five books, with over 180 refereed journal and proceedings publications. She is the editor-in-chief of the *Journal of Teaching in Travel and Tourism* and serves on eight journal editorial boards.

Hanan Kattara is on the faculty of the University of Alexandria in Egypt. A specialist in human resource management, she has written extensively on the management and operation of hotels in Egypt.

Hai-yan Kong is a lecturer in the School of Business, Shandong University at Weihai, and Ph.D student of School of Hotel and Tourism Management, The Hong Kong Polytechnic

University. Haiyan has 11 years of working experience in the travel and hotel industry. Her research focuses on human resources management. She has co-authored 2 books and published over 20 papers in academic and professional journals.

Patrick T. Long is the Director of the Center for Sustainable Tourism, Division of Research and Graduate Studies, East Carolina University. The Center manages an interdisciplinary Master of Science in Sustainable Tourism, conducts industry-related research, and provides consultation to businesses and communities. His current scholarship focuses on sustainable practices in tourism, tourism impacts, tourism planning and policy strategies and host community adjustments to tourism development.

Jordan J. Louviere is Professor of Marketing and Co-Director of the Centre for the Study of Choice (CenSoC) at the University of Technology, Sydney. His area of expertise is conjoint analysis and consumer choice modeling, and the design and analysis of discrete choice experiments.

Julia Marcoux is a graduate of the School of Resource and Environmental Management at Simon Fraser University in British Columbia, Canada. While completing a Master's in Resource and Environmental Management, she was a researcher in the University's Centre for Tourism Policy and Research. The primary focus of her work was on examining the factors influencing relationships between tourism corporations and community stakeholders.

Gianna Moscardo has been a member of the academic staff of the School of Business at James Cook University since February 2002. Her main research interests are regional tourism development, community attitudes towards tourism, tourist behaviour and interpretation. To date she has authored or co-authored more than 160 refereed international research publications.

Peter Murphy is an Emeritus Professor in the La Trobe Business School within that university's Faculty of Business, Economics and Law. He has been a member of the IAST for many years. Although his research focus has remained on community tourism it has evolved into various strands. One strand is to explore how resorts may become development growth poles for certain communities by serving local and society's needs.

Wilson Osoro is Director of Studies in Utalii College, Nairobi, Kenya. Utalii College is a leading institution of hospitality and tourism education in sub-Saharan Africa and has an international reputation for its teaching, research and consultancy.

Douglas G. Pearce is Professor of Tourism Management in the Victoria Management School, Victoria University of Wellington, New Zealand. Email: douglas.pearce@vuw.ac.nz. His chapter forms part of a major project he has been leading on tourism distribution channels in New Zealand funded by the Foundation for Research, Science and Technology. His other research interests include urban tourism, planning and development, tourism organizations, and the spatial structure of tourism.

Philip L. Pearce holds degrees in psychology and education from the University of Adelaide and a Doctorate from the University of Oxford. He has interests in tourist behaviour, especially in tourist motivation, experience design and evaluation of visitor experiences. He also writes and researches in tourism education, specialist markets such as backpackers, and impacts of tourism. He is the Foundation Professor of Tourism at James Cook University and has been a member of the International Academy for the Study of Tourism since its inception.

Richard R. Perdue is Professor and Head of the Department of Hospitality and Tourism Management in the Pamplin College of Business at Virginia Polytechnic Institute and State University. He is an elected Fellow of the International Academy for the Study of Tourism, where he currently serves as president. He is also editor of the *Journal of Travel Research* and serves on numerous other editorial boards. His current research is focused on sustainable tourism development and marketing in the resort environments.

Roslyn Russell is a Professor in the School of Economics, Finance and Marketing at RMIT University in Melbourne. Roslyn's research in tourism has been in the area of destination development. Roslyn's primary contribution was the application of the principles of chaos theory to the theories of destination development. Roslyn has also explored the role of entrepreneurs in the economic evolution of tourism destinations.

Egon Smeral is an economist at the Austrian Institute of Economic Research (WIFO) in Vienna and teaches at the Universities of Innsbruck and Vienna, Austria. Areas of research are applied economic theory and politics, tourism forecasting and modelling, impact analysis and Tourism Satellite Accounts, designing and evaluating tourism policies programmes, and marketing strategies. He is a coordinating editor of *Annals of Tourism Research*, regional editor for Central and Eastern Europe of *Tourism Review*, and a member of three other journal editorial boards.

Stephen L. J. Smith is Professor of Recreation and Leisure Studies, and Director of the Master's Program in Tourism Policy and Planning at the University of Waterloo, Waterloo, Ontario. His interests include tourism statistics, tourism economics, destination marketing, and culinary tourism.

Haiyan Song is Chair Professor of Tourism in the School of Hotel and Tourism Management at the Hong Kong Polytechnic University. His research interests include tourism demand forecasting, tourism impact assessment, competition issues in tourism and applied econometrics. He has published widely in such journals as *Journal of Travel Research*, *Tourism Management*, *Journal of Hospitality and Tourism Research*, *Journal of Applied Econometrics* and *International Journal of Forecasting*.

Botao Su is a PhD student (Urban Geography) at Centre of Urban Planning & Environmental Management, The University of Hong Kong. He obtained his Master's degree from the Center of Tourism Planning and Research, Sun Yat-sen University.

Rivanda Meira Teixeira is a Professor in Federal University of Paraná, Brazil and acquired her PhD from Cranfield School of Management, England. In 2001 she was involved in a research project on small business in the hospitality sector in collaboration with The Scottish Hotel School, University of Strathclyde, in Scotland. Her main research interests are: small business, entrepreneurship and human resources in tourism.

Lindsay W. Turner is Professor of Econometrics and International Trade in the School of International Business at Victoria University, Australia. He is a member of the boards of Tourism Economics, the Journal of Travel Research and the advisory board of China Tourism Research. He has published over 15 books and 100 journal articles. He is specialized in tourism forecasting, tourism economics and Asian cultural studies.

Linda Venturoni is President of Venturoni Surveys & Research, Inc., Dillon, Colorado. In this capacity she conducts community surveys, data analysis, special studies, needs assessments, and trend analysis for mountain resort communities. Her current research focuses on transitions in mountain communities: resort economies and their secondary effects, most specifically the social and economic impacts of second home development.

Chau Jo Vu is a Senior Lecturer in the Faculty of Business and Law at Victoria University, Melbourne. Her research interests include tourism economics and forecasting, applied quantitative data analysis, and financial econometrics. She has published in journals such as the *Journal of Tourism Research, Tourism and Hospitality Research*, and *Tourism Economics*.

Boris Vukonić is the Dean of the Business School for Tourism and Hotel Management 'Utilus' in Zagreb. His area of specialisation is policy of tourism development, marketing in tourism and the travel agencies operations. His publications include more than 150 journal and 80 conference papers. He is an author of 25 books and monographs (four of them with co-authors). He has worked as a tourism expert for the UNDP and UNWTO in Bangladesh, Guyana, Afghanistan, Tanzania, Zanzibar, India, and Egypt.

Geoffrey Wall is Professor of Geography at the University of Waterloo, Canada. His research interests focus upon understanding the implications of tourism of different types for destinations with different characteristics and the associated planning implications. He has extensive experience in Asia and has directed environmental projects in China.

Yang Wang trained as an engineer at Tongji University in Shanghai and completed graduate degrees in the School of Planning at the University of Waterloo, Canada. She has interests in community development and is currently a planner with EBA Engineering Consultants Ltd and is based in Calgary, Alberta, Canada.

Allan M. Williams is Professor of Tourism and Mobility Studies at the University of Surrey. He is interested in the relationship between mobility and economic development, tourism and migration, and tourism innovation. Associate Editor of *Tourism Geographies,* he is also the co-author or co-editor of eight books on tourism, including *Tourism and Tourism Spaces* (Sage 2004) and *Tourism Innovation* (Routledge 2008).

Peter W. Williams is Director of the Centre for Tourism Policy and Research, and a Professor in the School of Resource and a Professor in the School of Environmental Management at Simon Fraser University in British Columbia Canada. His research focuses primarily on policy and planning issues related to sustainable tourism development in rural and resort regions. Most of this work lays at the interface between public policy and corporate strategy.

Stephen F. Witt is an Emeritus Professor (Tourism Forecasting) in the Faculty of Business, Economics and Law at the University of Surrey, UK and a consultant to the Pacific Asia Travel

Association (PATA) based in Bangkok, Thailand. His main research interests are econometric modeling of international tourism demand, and assessment of the accuracy of different forecasting methods within the tourism context.

Kevin K. F. Wong is a Senior Lecturer in the School of Professional Education and Executive Development (SPEED) at the Hong Kong Polytechnic University. He has published extensively in reputable journals such as *Journal of Travel Research*, *Tourism Management*, *Journal of Hospitality and Tourism Research* and *Asia Pacific Journal of Tourism Research*. His research interest is in the areas of tourism demand forecasting, impact of tourism, services management and competitive issues.

Kong-Yew Wong holds a PhD in Tourism Economics from the University of Strathclyde, is a faculty member of Taylor's School of Hospitality and Tourism, Malaysia. His research and publication is in the areas of trade and industrial policy, and economic impact evaluation. Kong-Yew has assisted in national tourism policy decisions in Malaysia, and abroad.

Yanjun Xie is Professor of tourism in the School of Tourism and Hotel Management, Dongbei University of Finance and Economics, China. As the author of a number of widely acknowledged books published in China, he has gained a reputation of being a serious tourism scholar. His research interests include theoretical studies of tourism, tourist experience, methodology of tourism. His articles (including published in Annals of Tourism Research) have a wide influence in the society of tourism research in China.

Honggang Xu is a professor at the School of Tourism Management, Sun Yat-Sen University, China. She obtained her doctoral degree in Urban Planning from Asian Institute of Technology. Her research interests include tourism resource management, tourism planning, regional tourism development and system dynamics.

Na Xu is a graduate of the School of Resource and Environmental Management at Simon Fraser University in British Columbia, Canada. While completing her Master's in Resource and Environmental Management, she worked as a researcher in the University's Centre for Tourism Policy and Research. The primary focus of her investigations focused on examining the factors influencing relationships between non-governmental organizations and tourism corporations.

Shinji Yamashita is Professor of Cultural Anthropology at the University of Tokyo. His research focuses on international tourism and transnational migration in the Asia-Pacific region. His books include *Globalization in Southeast Asia* (co-edited with J.S. Eades, Berghahn Books, 2003), *Bali and Beyond* (translated by J.S. Eades, Berghahn Books, 2003), and *The Making of Anthropology in East and Southeast Asia* (co-edited with Joseph Bosco and J.S. Eades, Berghahn Books, 2004).

Introduction

A compendium of papers addressing tourism research is bound to be as diverse as the field of tourism studies. The papers in this book reflect that diversity but remain connected to core disciplines that comprise the foundation of tourism studies research. The authors in this book have been publishing in tourism and related journals for many years, and their insights into particular research issues are enlightening. The topics covered in this book range from a review of the earliest tourism research, often published in a language other than English, to specific case studies addressing particular issues. In the next few pages, brief descriptions of these papers are provided, along with insights into their role in the continuing evolution of tourism studies research.

This book is divided into six main parts. Part I naturally focuses on the foundations of tourism research. It is from the work presented here that the next five sections emerge. Part II focuses on destination development and management and the current research guiding that topic. Part III is more specific to destination planning. Here readers will find other ways of looking at the local planning process, as the different political systems one finds around the world lead to different planning paradigms and the research that must be conducted to support those planning schemes. Part IV addresses the human capital dimension of tourism development with some interesting reviews of knowledge transfer, including how to measure its effectiveness, and the role of research in decision-making within the family-run small tourism dependent businesses. Part V includes specific case studies that show the relationship between research and expected outcomes from development path selection. Part VI makes an in-depth examination of tourism development examples from both mature and emerging markets. Challenges and opportunities are presented for the various destinations and markets; further research needs are also highlighted.

Part I Foundations for tourism research

Few new scholars, or for that matter many of the experienced ones, have a good grasp of early tourism studies research. This is not to say that the published works in academic journals are without a strong foundation, but that often some of the earliest scholarly investigations on a particular subject are missing from reference cited lists. Often this is because the original language of the published work may be overlooked. In an English-dominated field some of the best research published in another language does not make it into a literature review. In Chapter 1 Vukonić does an excellent job of not only citing some of this early work published in different languages, but relates that work to research, on the same subject, being conducted today. It is an essential read for novice and accomplished tourism scholars alike.

Aramberri and Xie (Chapter 2) examine some of the political forces that shape the world of tourism as we know it today. They also focus on the world's emerging international market – China – as an example of how policy is used as a driving force for tourism development. Their analysis of domestic versus international tourism flows questions the over-reliance on research that examines international markets, when most of today's tourism is of a domestic or regional nature.

Dann (Chapter 3) looks at the influence of new technology between the tourist and destination promoters and managers. The influence of webblogs (blogs) and communication techniques are contained within this chapter. For students of image research this chapter examines the changes in technology on the process of destination image formation, which promises to be a fertile field of study in the coming years.

Pearce (D.) (Chapter 4) provides a detailed view of the tourism distribution channel. This is essential reading for those interested in tourism development or marketing research issues. Product alone cannot create successful or sustainable tourism development. How the distribution channels work and how they are manipulated by destinations is a necessary ingredient for success.

Smith (Chapter 5) ends this foundation section. With a discussion on the issues of tourism barriers, Smith concludes that barriers are often region or country specific and require different approaches to how they influence tourism development. A number of interesting research issues are offered to the readers of this chapter.

Part II Implications for destination management

Forecasting tourism arrivals has become an active area of inquiry in recent years. Yet, even with all the publications on this subject, forecasting techniques remain somewhat of a mystery to new scholars to this field. In Chapter 6, Song, Wong and Witt provide a thorough overview of basic forecasting techniques for tourism arrivals. In this chapter the authors examine the 'what if' of substitute destinations, as with all forecasting studies, there is always a 'what if'.

Continuing the 'what if' theme of tourism forecasting research, Turner, Vu and Witt (Chapter 7) discuss how to include exogenous shocks within tourism forecasting equations. This is an especially relevant research area considering tourism flow disruptions caused by terrorism, SARS and natural disasters in recent years.

Smeral (Chapter 8), also a noted forecaster, provides a provocative look at funding for tourism marketing efforts. In recent years more of the burden of destination marketing is being borne by the private sector. Yet Smeral, using economic analysis, shows that publicly funded tourism marketing efforts are not only more effective but also provide a wider range of benefits to more beneficiaries. Given the current trend towards more private sector control of destination marketing, the research presented here is a foundation piece for more work in this area.

Butler and Russell (Chapter 9) take a good look at how country images benefit from the unique culture of a particular country. The example they explore is the benefit to tourism awareness that the concept of royalty has brought to the British Isles over the years. An interesting question, not explored in this chapter but for future researchers to contemplate, is whether the concept of royalty has similar effects in other culturally distinct countries.

Long, Perdue and Venturoni (Chapter 10) close this section by suggesting, through their research findings, that destination development is not all about the attraction base. In their study, resort development in the western United States is examined from a real estate rather than a visitor attendance perspective. Their findings would seem to indicate that real estate value and investment potential are much more influential in deciding resort development paths than visitor arrivals. The study of land value as a determinant of development path is an understudied area in tourism studies. This chapter will hopefully stimulate more interest in studying destination development as something other than simply a product of the attraction base.

Part III Planning for tourism development

China has lately received increasing attention as it emerges as a regional and, soon to be, international tourism generating market. Yet China is also on an expanding internal tourism development path as it prepares for increasing international arrivals and a burgeoning domestic market. The domestic market, especially, has been expanding at a rapid rate. Tourism planning in China is the focus of Chapter 11 (Xu, Bao and Su) and Chapter 12 (Wang and Wall). Xu, Bao and Su set the stage by discussing what tourism planning means within the Chinese context, and Wall and Wang provide a comparison between Western planning models and those used in China. The differences are significant and should be understood by those interested in the tourism planning process as well as researchers who examine the impacts from these different approaches.

Chapter 13 (P. Williams, Gill, Marcoux and Xu) is a primer on stakeholder analysis. Tourism development often brings competing interests to the bargaining table. This chapter discusses what it means to obtain a 'social licence' to operate and how competing interests can find common ground. Researchers studying the dynamics of tourism development will be able to use this chapter for foundational material.

Hawkins and Elliott (Chapter 14) also focus on stakeholder analysis, but their approach focuses exclusively on the expert opinion or 'Delphi process'. This chapter provides a thorough examination of what seems to work and what does not when using this process.

Chapter 15 (Moscardo) provides a new look at studying tourist/local impacts. Moscardo discusses how to use visual imagery, created by host populations, to uncover issues related to the present level of tourism development found within a community. As a new technique for studying socio–cultural impacts, it provides a different dimension from the usual ways of studying the issue of guest/host interactions.

Part IV Human capital for tourism development

Technological change and how it affects tourism development is a 'hot' area of research. Yet successful tourism development, whether at the destination or firm level, still relies on the efficient and friendly delivery of human services. At the destination level, many firms are of the small family business variety and thus personal family decisions affect business decisions. At the larger firm level, knowledge transfer to pass on the corporate culture and the 'how to get things done' skills are essential for success. Chapter 16 (A. Williams) and Chapter 17 (Baum, Devine, Kattara, Kong, Osoro, Teixeira and Wong) directly address the issues of knowledge transfer. Taken together, these chapters will provide excellent discussion material for scholars in this area, as the authors do draw the same conclusions. The issue of knowledge transfer is so important to long-term success that, as the different opinions expressed in these chapters would lead one to believe, much more work on the human capital dimension, especially in the area of knowledge transfer, is needed.

Getz and Batchelor (Chapter 18) focus on the family decision-making structure of small businesses. Families, as Getz and Batchelor conclude, do not always make decisions related to revenue generation. Quality of life issues are also relevant. The findings in this chapter would seem to indicate that tourism development efforts that fill in the shoulder seasons or expand tourism arrivals may not be consistent with the goals of a family run business. For many destinations that are dominated by family-run businesses the findings suggest additional research in this area is warranted.

Part V Emerging forms of tourism

Part V provides some case studies that examine tourism development issues around the world. The mass tourism model dominates development thinking today. Yet 'niche tourism' is increasing in popularity as travellers identify more and more with their chosen activity preferences, leading to the creation of speciality markets. Some of these forms of tourism have assumed distinctive names to more easily identify themselves to their markets. In Chapter 19 Pearce (P.) identifies his understanding of 'Entertainment tourism' and how it may be formed. In the process of analysing this market segment, he provides an excellent example of how to study these 'new' forms of tourism.

Cohen (Chapter 20) continues his tradition of introducing new ideas of how to examine tourist use patterns. In the process he introduces and analyses what he terms 'extreme tourism'. Numerous implications to guide future thinking on the subject are provided.

Chapter 21 (Murphy) takes a different look at new forms of tourism. By examining the evolution of resort development, he may be suggesting that what is new is really something old in new packaging. At the very basis of any new form of tourism may be something that has been there all along, but is just evolving according to economic and social change.

The last chapter of this part introduces a new form of transportation that in itself is an attraction. Crouch, Devinney and Louviere (Chapter 22) take us off planet Earth and into the realm of space tourism. Although space may seem unaccessible to those with less than US $20 million to spend, the future of touristic use of space is just around the corner. Crouch et al. examine the basis for this forecast and in the process outlines how basic economics will influence the development of new forms of tourism.

Part VI Insights into tourism evolution

In addition to the different forms of tourism discussed in Part V, tourist behaviours and flows, as well as the evolution of tourism development in various geographic regions, are investigated by chapters included in the final part of the book. Examples of evolution discussed include ecotourism in East Malaysia; tourist flows in the Balkans; tourism demand among the gradually aging Japanese; and the emerging Chinese senior travellers.

Chapter 23 Yamashita examines tourism development in Sabah, Malaysia, with a focus on how ecotourism is practised. Numerous sources, including qualitative field research, were used to understand the type of tourism development, and surrounding issues, that Sabah is experiencing. Gosar (Chapter 24), on the other hand, uses quantitative data to analyse tourist flows throughout the Balkans after the breakup of Yugoslavia. Although the physical plant for tourism remained essentially intact, new political divisions changed tourist flow patterns.

Chapters 25 and 26 both review tourism evolution in the context of the aging population of a particular Asian country, though each has a very different twist and outlook. Cooper and Eades (Chapter 25) bring attention to declining tourism destinations in Japan. The implications of demand declines are rarely studied and this chapter gives insights into how competition evolves when dealing with declining markets. The chapter discusses a different approach to destination development. Chapter 26 by Hsu, Wong and Cai provides an insight into the most dominant emerging market as we move through the twenty-first century. The focus of this final chapter of the book is on the senior market in China, which is a relatively new but substantial market, and is growing larger every year. Research is very important in understanding this emerging market force.

Summary

This tourism research handbook is a compendium of some of the most relevant issues affecting tourism development today. The topics addressed in this book provide some new thinking for those contemplating research in tourism studies. From the foundational aspects, to new techniques, to new challenges to old ways of thinking are just some of the tourism research contributions contained in this book.

The works included in this volume are diverse, in terms of geographical context, research methodology, root discipline, and perspective. This book represents studies based in Europe, North America, Oceania and Asia. Research methodologies include both quantitative and qualitative. Both macro and micro issues are discussed from economic, psychological, sociological, political science, marketing and other perspectives, which reflect the interdisciplinary nature of tourism studies.

This is a unique collection of materials from well-established tourism researchers around the world. By publishing this handbook, the International Academy for the Study of Tourism wishes to provide the readers with new ideas to guide tourism research. We hope that you, the readers, are inspired and challenged to move forward on tourism research, which will benefit the tourism industry in its future development.

Cathy H. C. Hsu
William C. Gartner
April, 2012

Part I
Foundations for tourism research

1

An outline of the history of tourism theory

Source material (for future research)

Boris Vukonić

Introduction

By reflecting on past events, we can gain a better understanding how we have become what we are. Using the tourism terminology, we can say that it is the way for better understanding of the essence of tourism movements and tourism industry. As an area of human activity, tourism has a history extending back to the early eighteenth century. So is the case with tourism knowledge or tourism theory. In this context this chapter covers the period from the initial stages of scientific research on tourism until the end of the twentieth century. Specifically the purpose of this chapter is to provide a series of reflections on aspects of the development of tourism knowledge in order not to avoid or forget the importance of any development stages the tourism theory was going through.

Some basic introductory theoretical issues

In all the historical texts on tourism, theorists have faced a number of questions at the very beginning of their work. Without resolving at least part of these questions, it is difficult to talk about any topic related to tourism. As a notion, tourism appeared and became a subject of discussion after tourist traffic had already been recorded in many areas and countries, and much after the time that people had started displaying an interest in travelling for hedonistic reasons. In this process, the word 'tourist' appeared earlier than 'tourism', and this shows that the sequence of events concerning the phenomenon of tourism and its theoretical explanation was different from what we would expect. Naturally, there is also the question about the time period where we should search for the roots of tourism and from when it would be theoretically correct to discuss it, as this will temporally define the period that this chapter deals with. Regardless of which period we choose, it would not be right to exclude the periods and theoretical works which precede the phenomenon of so-called modern tourism. According to recent research and opinion, theorists mainly agree that the period of modern tourism began with Thomas Cook's first organised journey in 1841, an event which the World Tourism Organisation also used when deciding on 1991 as the 150th anniversary of world tourism. Of course, there are those who disagree. Among them, the majority see the beginning of tourism in the Grand Tour.

It seems reasonable to conclude that the periods that preceded these events can only be considered as the forerunners of tourism, or as phenomena similar to tourism, so the theoretical views and works that appeared in those periods should be seen and accepted in that context too. Because of the number and serious nature of the works published in this period, we simply have to include them in a historical retrospective of tourism theory, and even more so on account of their content. The seriousness of arguments which speak in favour of the first thesis convinced me that the Grand Tour was only one of the phases in which phenomena similar to tourism started to appear, but one which, according to today's views of the modern tourism phenomenon, cannot be considered as tourism.

In this context, an overview of the phenomena related to tourism and the theory on tourism would be presented in two basic chapters: the first one deals with the phenomena similar to tourism and their accompanying theoretical works, while the second treats the unique tourism phenomenon, from the first instances of organised travel until the end of the twentieth century. In both cases, the development of tourism and tourism theory underwent different phases in these long periods, which, although not the focus of this work, will be included as a general framework for the particular works and the theses they proposed. In fact, without briefly looking at the phenomena and events in their social, political, economic and other relevant contexts, it is difficult to talk about the topics that tourism theory is interested in, and it is especially difficult to understand the true meaning of the theoretical views from different periods and different parts of the world.

However, the following has to be said too. An obsession of almost everybody in today's world is to be the first, the biggest, the best. This seems to be true of the entire world and all human activities, including science. When it comes to human sciences the situation is somewhat more complicated as it is usually difficult to be certain when and where a scientific opinion first appeared or when and where a scientific paper of some kind was published. The large-scale production, or more precisely, the hyper production of scientific and quasi-scientific works on world tourism makes the search for truth even more complicated. But, it is important to make a record of the people who were among the first, if not the very first, to discuss and write about tourism. All the work that followed is only the deepening, supplementing and correcting of the same subject matter. That work is equally valuable and original, and can bring the same kind of fame to those involved in it, and who search for arguments in order to correct other people's views. This overview will deal only with the works published in the form of expert books. It is not the intention to underestimate the value of papers published in professional journals, but they are so numerous that it was impossible to cover them fully, especially in this initial historical analysis of tourism theory. There were a large number of such papers published over the last decades of the twentieth century that were particularly significant for the development of scientific research and for the theory of tourism. However, their most important ideas were later published in book form, and it was through that medium that they have found their way into the list of works and authors relevant to this chapter.

It is the whole truth that science does not tolerate alibis. Referring to 'certain' or 'unforeseen' circumstances means searching for an alibi for one's work, and suggests an inability to explore a phenomenon objectively or fully. However, consciously not accepting such a risk, it would mean something even less acceptable: scientific arrogance. We are referring to the period entitled 'the period of scientific flourishing' in this historical overview, from the 1980s to the beginning of the twenty-first century. It has become impossible to follow present-day mass scientific production, when several thousand titles are published every calendar year worldwide. Still, it is certainly possible to discover the pioneers of tourism theory and give them their rightful place in the history of scientific thought on tourism. Also, while it is easier to follow the events in one's own geographical vicinity, that too is becoming increasingly difficult, if not impossible. So, the scientists listed here are not a complete overview of present-day world tourism theory. I chose to follow my own subjective criteria and I mention only those authors and works which I believe have created a milestone in world tourism theory, without intending to belittle the scientific efforts and results of thousands of other scientists who deal with and explore different aspects of world tourism.

Periodisation

The aim of this chapter is not to discuss the periodisation of tourism and tourism science. However, in a historical overview such as this, where some kind of periodisation of the phenomenon in question is required, it is essential to touch upon the basic assumptions from which the sequence of relevant events is to be analysed. In their writing about different periods in the development of tourism and scientific tourism thought, different authors have used various starting points. Periodisation has consequently always been based on the independent and subjective attitudes of particular authors, and this initial attitude was usually different for each of them, especially as the conditions in which they lived and worked were not the same everywhere. They often had a different scientific background as well. This explains the differences in the attempts to come up with a single, universally accepted and well-argued overview of the entire era of world tourism.

However, the chronology of events itself is not as important for the understanding of tourism as the explanations of the chronology and the events themselves, including their geographical, political or economic context. The periodisation of tourism becomes meaningful only when we look at the development of tourism in its context, and explore the interaction of different interconnected factors. This then allows us to determine both our own level of development and the level of tourism development. This overview of the history of tourism theory was based on some main criteria where two groups prevailed: the chronology of events; and, for the last period (because of the large-scale scientific production), different authors' topics of interest.

The period of the phenomena which preceded the emergence of tourism

Tourism and travel are interdependent notions. Since tourism cannot exist without travel, some theorists – placing greater importance on travel – have referred to tourism in, for example, Ancient Egypt, Greece, the Roman Empire and the Middle Ages. However, travel in these historical periods did not and could not have the character of tourism. Tourism as a new social phenomenon did not appear until the conditions were right, and this did not happen until the middle of the nineteenth century. The thesis which wrongly defines travel as tourism partly comes from the interesting notion of the traveller which was created in the period of European Humanism, and whose motive for travelling was similar to that of the modern tourist. Driven by cultural and scientific impulses, these travellers visited cultural and scientific centres around the world. This is probably why world travellers such as Montaigne (1533–92) or Marco Polo (c. 1254–1324) are often mentioned as the first tourists. An attempt has even been made to present Montaigne's travel book *Journal de voyage* (published in 1774) as the first scientific tourism book. Today's theoretical attitudes are very clear when they say that neither these nor similar travellers or explorers from the past can be considered tourists, and neither can the later explorers on Kon-Tiki, or the conquerors of the Himalayas.

The sixteenth century is also interesting because of the work of Thomas Mun (1571–1641). Mun, who was a mercantilist by orientation, was considered by later theorists (such as F.W. Ogilvie, Kurt Krapf, P.W. Titzhoff) to have created the first theory in which tourism was an invisible export. Mun's book was written in 1630 as a petition of the East India Company to the British Parliament, and was published posthumously in 1664. The only German copy of Thomas Mun's book is kept in the Library of the University in Kiel; one of several copies of the book in Great Britain is in the British Museum Library. It is true that Mun wrote about services and their influence on the balance of payments, mentioning for the first time the 'expences of travailers' as a form of service which should be taken into consideration when working out the balance of payments. In order to consistently develop his theory on their influence on the balance of payments, in both its assets and liabilities sections, Mun juxtaposes the expenses of travellers in England with the expenses of English nationals abroad. He named these expenses 'petty things'. This research rectified the previous belief that it had been G.J. Göschen who had in 1861 first presented the theoretical assumption of tourism being an invisible export in his book *Theory of Foreign Exchange*. Extensive research on Thomas Mun's work was carried out by the German theorist Peter W. Titzhoff (1964).

However, all this is not enough to ascribe scientific status to the research of tourism in the sixteenth century In his foreword to G. Carone's (1959) book *Il Turismo nell'Economia Internazionale*, Kurt Krapf pointed out that the visits of individual foreigners to England at that time were in essence the same as those of modern foreign tourists, with the obvious difference in the size of the traffic, and, consequently, the significance of that traffic.

The seventeenth century is also sometimes mentioned because of another phenomenon, the Grand Tour, suggested by some to have been the beginning of world tourism. The Grand Tour mainly involved young British and other European upper-class young men. It was interrupted by the 30 Years War (1618–48), which ravaged almost the entire European continent, and again by the Napoleonic Wars in the late-eighteenth century, but it continued until the middle of the nineteenth century. Texts on the Grand Tour not only contained a wealth of information and rich detail, but their serious content made them resemble scientific works on tourism. The names of authors who wrote about the Grand Tour in that period make the thesis that it is the beginning of tourism development even more appealing. One of these famous texts is the dialogue between the Earl of Shaftsbury and the philosopher John Locke (1632–1704), which was published in 1764 as 'Dialogues on the Use of Foreign Travel' by Bishop Hurd in one of his treatises. According to Lickorish and Kershaw (1958), the *Travel Trade* was extensively described by the historian J. W. Stoye, who, in 1952, published his treatise 'English travellers abroad: their influence in English society and politics'. This work was followed by a number of individual papers published in different professional journals worldwide.

Romanticism is another historical period which placed great importance on travel as a source of knowledge for different areas of life. Travel was then undertaken by writers, poets, philosophers, painters and so on. Still, from today's perspective on the emergence of tourism, J.J. Rousseau, Goethe, Chateaubriand, Schopenhauer, Nodier, Stendahl, Byron, Helly, Merimee, George Sand, Heine, Dumas, A. De Musset and many other authors cannot be considered primarily as tourists, but they can certainly be seen as some of the early travellers in world history. The joint name for their journeys – *Les voyages romantiques* – clearly testifies to their 'travelling' motives. Pierre Defert, a doyen of scientific tourism theory in France and Europe, later wrote about this:

> It is likely that there will always be both 'travellers' and 'tourists', without social geography confusing them. A difference should be made among travel, exploration, observation

(reconnoitring) of a particular environment, and tourism, which requires this environment to be organised for a specific purpose and for mass visits of a certain size and duration.

(Defert, 1958, 1960)

There is yet another important reason why we cannot talk about the existence of tourism in earlier historical periods. This reason is related to the concept of free time, which is one of the basic requirements for the development of tourism. It was not until after the First World War that workers' unions managed to win the right to an 8-hour working day; at the beginning of the nineteenth century the working day lasted between 14 and 16 hours, reducing to 10 hours at the end of the century. This was then followed by a struggle for paid overtime, and then for a paid annual holiday. The first law concerning a paid annual holiday was passed in France on 20 June 1936, just before the Second World War. Even so, the already popular non-lucrative form of travel, which started in the middle of the nineteenth century, caused certain changes in those places which were visited by tourists and prompted the first analyses of the consequences of these visits. For this reason, the middle of the nineteenth century is the most appropriate time to consider the emergence of tourism as a modern-day phenomenon.

The later nineteenth century: the first real theoretical works on tourism

The first four works which are referred to as the beginning of expert literature were written in the three European countries where, statistically, tourist traffic was heaviest at the time: Austria, Switzerland and Italy. It was the need to make a statistical record of the new phenomenon of tourism that was the main content of these first works on tourism theory.

The first two works are the two treatises written by a Johann Angerer from Austria, entitled '*Das Fremdenwessen im Deutschen Südtirol*' and '*Statistischer Bericht der Handels-und Gewerbekammer in Bozen*', both written in 1881. Two years later, Guyer-Freuler (1884) wrote his treatise *Das Hotelwesen* in Switzerland. In Austria, one of the most productive tourism experts of his day, Josef Stradner (1890), published his work 'Die Förderung des Fremdenverkehrs' in *Kulturbilder aus der Steiermark*, in Graz. Only a few years later, Guyer-Freuler (1895) published his *Beiträge zur Statistik des Fremdenverkehrs in der Schweiz* in Zurich, and, Luigi Bodo (1899) from Italy published an article entitled 'Sul movimento dei forestieri in Italia e sul denaro che vi spendono', in the journal *Giornalle degli Economisti*.

Therefore, we have at our disposal an insight into the work of individuals who all made a significant contribution to tourism theory. So, at a time when tourism as a general phenomenon was not yet being discussed, its development was being looked into on a regional level, which seems somewhat absurd.

Still, from the perspective of tourism theory and history, two events which took place in Graz, Austria, were significant for this period. The first one was a meeting in April 1884, concerning the promotion of tourism in the Alpine regions of Austria ('*Delegirtentag zur Förderung des Fremdenverkehrs in den österreichischen Alpenländern*'). Ten years later, in 1894, the first congress for the promotion of tourism in the Alpine regions of Austria was held ('*1 Congress zur Hebung des Fremdenverkehrs in den österreichischen Alpenländern*'). The materials and treatises from both were later taken as the foundation for the study of tourism. One of the most famous tourism theorists, Kurt Krapf (1957), thought that the relevance of these works was unquestionable and that many of the ideas that were put forward 'could not have been formulated better today'. He also said: 'It is enough to make one feel embarrassed, as it may seem that many modern-day theoretical insights are nothing but a reproduction of plans and suggestions from the past'. His words are still topical today.

Other topics discussed at these meetings included the valorisation of natural resources through tourism, tourism as an activity which economically stimulates underdeveloped areas, tourism as export, the relationship of demand and supply in tourism, the revenue that the state can raise through tourism from taxes and fees, the influence that prices can have on tourist traffic (physically and financially), the seasonal problems in tourism development and the need for a better statistical record of tourism. It is also interesting that the development outside the European continent was discussed, with Egypt being considered as a possible place for the development of tourism.

The beginning of the twentieth century to the end of the First World War

The end of the nineteenth and the beginning of the twentieth century were marked by unprecedented industrial development, as well as major social changes and the restructuring of society. In this context, it seems unreal that it was in 1900 that a large economic crisis started (lasting until 1903), as a result of social changes, the strengthening of monopolist capital and a widespread desire for political (military) supremacy. Man's restless spirit and many new discoveries were among the reasons for travelling to become a form of leisure. Central Europe provided the best conditions for tourism travel, as this area was the most peaceful. Switzerland soon became a fully fledged tourism destination, and this was proven by the increasing number of authors who analysed the effects of such travel on tourism regions and countries.

Apart from the above-mentioned Guyer-Freuler, the regional effects of tourism in Switzerland were also explored by Robert Just (1907) in *Die Gemeinde Arose, ihr Wirtschaftsleben vor und seit dem Fremdenverkehr*, Hermann Gurtner (1916) and W. Zollinger (1916), who wrote about tourism and its possible influence on the country's balance of payments. Both of these works were entitled *Fremdenverkehr und Zalungsbilanz*. Another interesting treatise was written by Werberg Karl Müller (1908), who published it under the title *Das Hotelwesen und der Fremdenverkehr in der Schweiz*. In Austria, tourism was dealt with by Josef Stradner, Franz Bartsch, Paul Mechter and Hermann von Schullern zu Schrattenhofen. These authors were mainly concerned with macroeconomic issues, such as the national economy and its relationship with tourism. Most numerous are the authors from Germany such as Leo Woerl, Fridrich Zahn, Friedrich Zahn, Paul E. Damm, Max Buschel, Gustav Ströhmefeld, Otto Kamp Karl Köhne and Maximillian Krauss, and this is puzzling because Germany was not a popular tourism destination at that time. The Germans themselves, although later among the biggest tourism travellers, did not then travel for tourism purposes. What is not surprising, on the other hand, is the subject matter of these authors' works, as many of them explain the role and the effects of the spa, at that time the most common destination for tourists in central Europe. Among tourism theorists, for the first time there is mention of B. Stringer (1912) and M. Avancini (1913) from Italy, L. Auscher (1916) from France, and Edmond Picard from Belgium. Of these, Stringer is particularly interesting because of his study of the influence of tourism on Italy's foreign trade balance. Also, the Frenchman Auscher dealt with what was then a bizarre, but, as it later turned out, prophetic theme: the influence of the car on the development of tourism (*Le tourisme en automobile*).

The continuous growth of world tourism was slowed down and largely stopped by the First World War, but this was to be expected considering the geographical areas which were mostly affected by the war. The war was mainly fought on the European continent, where tourism had evolved most, and where most expert literature on tourism had been published. It is not surprising, then, that the war and the post-war period remained relatively unproductive in terms of written theoretical work on tourism.

The period between the two world wars

As mentioned above, the First World War almost completely halted European tourism (and this, at the time, meant world tourism). However, the war also brought something positive – it gave people immense energy, which manifested itself in a general desire for life, a freer and happier existence than the one experienced before the war. This energy was partly channelled into increasingly widespread tourism travel and the transformation of certain tourism areas into target destinations, all with tourism being economically motivated. Tourism's influence on a country's balance of payments was the first tourism-related question dealt with in the treatises of T. Geering, E. Gebert and F. Demeuth in the 1920s (Mihalič, 2002).

All of this heightened interest in tourism as an economic activity, which relatively soon after the war assumed a leading role in a different and more successful economic life. This caused significant changes in tourism theory and gave an impetus to research and the scientific aspects of theoretical work. In 1930, *Arhiv*, a paper of the specialised institute for tourism, Forschungsinstitut fur den Fremdenverkehr, was first published. The academic community had great expectations of the Institute's work, and the *Arhiv* was meant to take the role of a determined, competent bearer of the research results of European scientific institutions. Unfortunately, the coming to power of the social democrats in Germany was the reason that in 1935 the Institute ceased its activity. The initiative in tourism research was taken over by the Italians, mainly the fascinating Angelo Mariotti, who was a very prolific and authoritative author. His range of interest was very wide, from microeconomic to macroeconomic topics. His first book *L'industria del forestiero in Italia: Economica e politica del Turismo* appeared in 1923. However, it was a different Italian author, G. Tabacchi (1934), who wrote the first economic work on tourism theory, a work entitled *Turismo ed Economia*. It was the first attempt to give a summary view of tourism's full role in the national economy. In the same area of interest are the works of M. Troisi (1940a, 1940b) *Nozione economica di Turismo* and *Prime line di una teoria della rendita turistica*. The second of these works is particularly interesting because the author tried to give the first theoretical explanation of tourism revenue. Among the others, there was B. Belotti (1919), who wrote about tourism law, A. Niceforo (1923) about tourist traffic in Italy, and M. Avancini (1925, 1939) and R. Benini (1926), who dealt with statistical problems in keeping records of tourism traffic.

At this time, Germany was developing a German school of tourism theory, with numerous authors and works. The leading German authors at that time were R. Glücksmann, Wilhelm Morgenroth, M. Klafkowski, Arthur Bormann, F. Oppenheimer, etc. Still the most prolific writers on economic topics, these authors now turned their attention for the first time to new, sociological topics. Morgenroth's (1927) article 'Fremdenverkehr' published in *Handwörterbuch der Staatswissenschaften* was at the time of its publication as well as later one of the most frequently quoted articles on tourism. A similar fate was shared by Arthur Bormann's (1931) work *Die Lehre vom Fremdenverkehr*, as well as Glücksmann's (1935) *Fremdenverkehrskunde*. The economic aspects of tourism were also mainly dealt with by Karl Thiess, Ronnefeld Bodo, Kurt Brenner, D. Tremohlen, E. Dietel, W. Mahleberg, E. Sutter, A. Rockstroh and Friedrich Drosihn.

As far as the topics they wrote about are concerned, Austrian experts were not very different from the German authors. An especially prolific writer was Erich Gebert, who mainly studied the macroeconomic consequences of tourism development, in particular the influence of tourism on the national balance of payments. Interestingly enough, some of the Austrian tourism experts dealt with problems of promotion, which was an area rarely or not at all covered in the works of authors from other countries. Promotion was written about by Wilhelm Krieger (1933) and Fritz Jaeger (1936).

The United Nations first tackled the questions of state interventionism in tourism in 1936, demanding countries not to impede tourist visits to foreign destinations. This was an understandable reaction to an objection made by less-developed countries which had already realised the possible role of tourism in general economic development, especially as most of the countries in question did not have other relevant resources for development.

General living and working conditions in Switzerland resulted in a different view of world events, especially economic ones, and Swiss tourism experts were more versatile in their works, exploring different aspects of tourism, but still putting the greatest emphasis on economic issues. The Swiss experts demonstrated an interest in different macroeconomic topics concerning tourism in general or its specific economic sectors (the hotel industry, traffic), and for the first time we find texts on the relationship between culture and tourism. An author who wrote about this topic was Franz Heinemann. The authors who, on the other hand, dealt with economic topics were the following: Hermann Gurtner, Julius Landmann, Franz Seiler, Max Gafner and H. Gölden. The authors E. Barberini (1929) and Fausto Pedrotta (1939) wrote about the problems of the hotel industry, and the Association of Swiss Banks published a text entitled *Le tourisme et l'industrie hôtelière en Suisse*.

French authors, apart from L. Auscher who had already been active in the field, included C. Gide (1928) and his remarkable work *L'importance économique du tourisme*. As a co-author with G. Rozet, Auscher was one of the first to look at the topic of urbanism in tourism (*Urbanisme et tourisme*) which was later to become interesting both theoretically and in practical terms (Auscher and Rozet, 1920). Tourism as a new branch of the economy was written about by E. Chaix, while the previous history of France's tourism was covered by G. Baraud.

It may be of interest that in England, the country where we find the original forms of organised tourism, theorists interested in exploring the tourism phenomenon appeared relatively late. In the period between the two wars, the English published two very well-founded works, one written by F.W. Ogilvie (1933), entitled *The Tourist Movement*, and the other, *The Tourist Industry*, was written by A.J. Norval (1936). Since their publication, these books have been considered as essential reading for the study of tourism both within and outside England.

In terms of their content, the theoretical works from this time introduced a series of novelties. Of particular interest was the debate on tourist spending and its rules, as well as its particular features. Great importance was placed on explanations of the effects of tourism spending, which had an influence on a large number of economic branches and sectors. Another greatly discussed topic was the possibility that tourism might bring about economic balance between areas and countries with different economic potential and level of economic development through a spilling over of its revenue to other areas. The general discussions on tourism spending also introduced the topics of its structure, the size of the budget for tourism, and the related topic of tourists' daily spending.

The end of this period was marked by three authors and their major works, which became the principal works of tourism theory in the world. Troisi (1940a) wrote *Nozione economica di turismo* in Bari, and Hunziker and Krapf (1940) wrote and published *Grundriss der Allgemeine Fremdenverkehrslehre* in Zürich. These were the first comprehensive systematic works on tourism, where the influence of tourism on the national economy is conclusively proved for the first time. The authors showed that, with regard to the characteristics of the national or international tourism movement, tourism could have a positive or negative influence on the size of national product. They also pointed out that the redistribution of national income in the case of domestic tourism generally has less significance for the national economy than the revenue from foreign tourists' spending which is included in the national income of the receptive tourism country. The true significance of these works became clear only after the Second World War.

Period after the Second World War: a time of intense theoretical work

It is logical to expect a period of half a century to be too long to have the same characteristics throughout and to be seen as a single historical period of development. This is why it makes sense to divide such a period into smaller segments, distinguishable from each other because of the specific characteristics that general tourism development then had. There can be a great many different criteria for such a division, and here there is the question of the general economic and political situation in different time periods and in different parts of the world. Although tourism is certainly a global phenomenon, the level of its development in different geographical areas and in different periods differs in terms of the intensity of tourism traffic and in its effect.

The rapid growth of tourism after the Second World War was reflected in an increased amount of research work on tourism and the large-scale production of expert and scientific works. In Great Britain, Elizabeth Brunner (1945) produced a major work, *Holiday Making and the Holiday Trades*. Krapf and Hunziker's theoretical views gained even more significance after they founded the first international association of tourism theorists, AIEST (Association internationale des experts du tourisme). From the start, the annual meetings (congresses) of the Association and the theoretical works it published became the foundation for scientific insights into world tourism. The above-mentioned authors did not stop working together, but worked independently as well. As a result, Kurt Krapf (1953) wrote a widely quoted work *Die touristische Konsum: Ein Beitrag zur Lehre von der Konsumption*, and Walter Hunziker (1959) wrote a comprehensive work *Betriebswirtschaftslehre des Fremdenverkehrs*, and a number of shorter articles.

Somewhat earlier Prof Paul Bernecker (1956) published *Die Stellung des Fremdenverkehrs im Liestungssystem der Wirtschaft* in Vienna, in which he, much like in his later work *Der Fremdenverkehr und seine Betriebe und Betriebswirtschaftliche Ordnungsprobleme der Fremdenverkehrsbetriebe* (Bernecker, 1959), opposed some of Hunziker's theoretical explanations, in particular those concerning the existence of 'tourism companies' and the 'economics of tourism companies'. Bernecker disproves the existence of such companies and argues that all the economic entities in tourism fit within an already existing system of companies.

Views similar to Bernecker's were also propounded by G. Walterspiel (1956) and H. Joschke (1953). In *Jahrbuch für Fremdenverkehr*, Walterspiel wrote and published in instalments an extensive work entitled 'Grundlagen der Betriebswirtschaftslehre des Fremdenverkehrsbetriebs'. In the same journal three years earlier, Joschke published a paper entitled 'Beitrag zur theoretischen Analyse des Fremdenverkehrsangebote'. Both authors argue that even though tourists use commodity and non-commodity services provided by companies in different branches, this does not mean that these companies, in this way, become companies of the same kind (or of the same branch). Their opinion is shared by Walter Thoms (1952), who published the article 'Die Arten und der Charakter des Fremdenverkehrsbetriebs' in the book *Handbuch für Fremdenverkehrsbetriebe*. Here Thoms explains how the names of real and potential consumers cannot determine the relevant economic characteristics of individual companies, but, rather, the economic characteristics and names of companies are given and defined by economic science.

In this period immediately after the war, and for some time after, one of the significant interests of theorists was to define the tourism phenomenon itself, as theorists realised that an imprecise definition causes difficulties in thinking about tourism, in keeping statistical records, and in having a general understanding of tourism as a social phenomenon. Hunziker and Krapf (1942) proposed a definition which was accepted at the time by tourism experts, AIEST members:

> On comprend par tourisme l'ensemble des rapports et des phénomènes résultant du voyage et du séjour de non-résidents en tant que ce séjour ne crée pas un établissement durable et

ne découle pas non plus d'une activité lucrative. (We understand by tourism the sum of the relationships and phenomena arising from the travel and stay of non–residents, insofar as they do not lead to permanent residence and are not connected with any earning activity.)

Prof. Walter Hunziker remained an authority until his death. Switzerland had other distinguished scientists, such as Claude Kaspar, M. Baud-Bovy, P.H. Jaccard, J.-Ch. Bürky, Jost Krippendorf, Hans Peter Schmidhauser and J. Charvát.

Even in the early years after the war it became obvious that certain countries and their experts approached tourism development in a particular way, according to the country's developmental needs. French theorists, for example, first started to look at regional development and planning. This came from France's need to bring the tourist development of the Mediterranean coast back on track, after the destruction it had suffered during the war. In this period, and for a relatively long time after, tourism theory in France and Europe was influenced by a group of scientists led by Pierre Defert and Vincent Planque, and which included Simone Troisgros, Roger Ballossier, René Baretje, Henri Barre, Pierre Lainé, Jacques Durand and Hubert Delestrée. The reason this research had a dominantly geographical focus was that it involved a large number of experts who specialised in geography, as well as regional planning, which had hardly been written about in Europe before. Later, focusing on the aims of France's developmental policy at that time, the policy of tourism development devoted its efforts to the mountainous part of the country (Haute Savoie) and to the restructuring of health tourism centres, including spas. At this point French experts turned to these problems in their works.

The same happened in other countries as well. German theorists, for instance, stayed focused on two main areas: microeconomic problems (the economics of tourism companies) and macroeconomic problems related to the influence of tourism on the national economy. German scientists had always had an interest in microeconomics, but a part of their interest then turned to tourism economics and the economics of tourist companies. The most distinguished members of the German school were Alfred Koch, Hans Ludwig Zankl, Günter Menges, Eberhard Gugg, each of whom was specialised in a particular area.

Italy continued with tourism research and the publishing of scientific works, but with relatively fewer influential authors than before. The best known Italian experts at the time were Luciano Merlo (who published the first book on marketing in Italy's tourism), Alberto Sessa (quite a prolific author with a wide scope of interest) and the circle of theorists from the University in Florence, gathered around Professor Piero Barucci (who focused particularly on regional development).

English theorists remained interested in general topics, but they founded a special higher education institution in Guildford near London, whose area of specialisation was tourism research and education. Such an orientation allowed for the development of great tourism experts, such as Slavo Medlik, Brayan Archer, A.J. Burkart, V.T.C. Middleton, who developed tourism research to an admirable level. If we also mention L.J. Lickorish and A.G. Kerhow, as well as some other theorists, such as Louis Erdi and D.T. Jeffries, we can see that Great Britain had a very impressive group of scientists in the 1950s, which resulted in the publishing of several important books on general and specific tourism topics.

Among Austrian tourism theorists, the most distinguished, besides Paul Bernecker, were Anton Würzl, Helmut Zolles, and Harald Langer-Hansel. Each of them had his own area of specialisation, conforming to the general level of tourism development, and also to the specific interests of Austria.

However, other European countries, especially those where emissive or receptive forms of tourism were more markedly present, had their own authors with prominent works. This is especially true of Spain, whose authoritative tourism theorists were José Ignacio de Arrillaga y Sanchez and J. Vila Fradera. The rapid and intense tourism development on the Spanish Mediterranean coast required more precise theoretical research and explanations for the topics which were associated with it.

Prominent theorists from other European countries included Arthur Haulot and Norbert Vanhove from Belgium, Ejler Alkjaer from Denmark, M.C. Tideman from the Netherlands, and a group of Eastern European scientists. Most distinguished among them were Srđan Marković, Dragutin Alfier, Ivan Antunac, Slobodan Unković, Janez Planina and Milan Mazi from former Yugoslavia, Oleg Rogalevski and Krysztof Przeclawski from Poland, A. Guéorguiev from Bulgaria, László Kovács from Hungary, and František Prikril and Jiri Kašpara from the Czech Republic. Srđan Marković and his wife Zora wrote one of the first books in the area of tourism economics in the world, entitled *Tourism Economics* (Marković and Marković, 1972).

The 1960s saw the publication of the first serious works of American tourism experts. Their appearance is connected with the beginnings of the discussion on tourism's multiplier effects. Back in 1958, in their book *The Travel Trade*, the British theorists L. J. Lickorish and A. G. Kershaw pointed to the interesting research results on the multiplier effects of foreign tourism spending, conducted by the Hawaii Visitors' Bureau (Lickorish and Kershaw, 1958). A more serious theoretical attempt was that of H.G. Clement (1961) under the title *The Future of Tourism in the Pacific and Far East*. Kurt Krapf (1962) drew attention to this work in his article 'Le tourisme, facteur de l'economie moderne', published in AIEST's official paper *Revue de Tourisme*. This marked the beginning of a long discussion, which is still continuing, in which proponents and opponents of the idea of the multiplier effects in tourism took turns in voicing their views. This especially goes for the mathematical model used by Clement. Clement referred to the links with the Kahn-Keynes's multiplier of national income, but he never explicitly quoted those links, and only mentioned P.A. Samuelson, which gave additional arguments to those who did not agree with the application of the model as presented by Clement. Especially severe in their criticism of Clement's multiplier were Karl Lewitt and Iqbal Gulati, John Bryden and Mike Faber, Herbert Vanhove, Albert Schmidt, Bryan Archer, Robert Erbes, Pierre Defert, Rene Baretje, and later theorists, such as Ivan Antunac, Mathieson and Wall. The bulk of the criticism referred to the work of M. Zinder, one of Clement's associates, who wrote *The Future of Tourism in the Eastern Caribbean,* applying Clement's multiplier method. The multiplier debate involved, for the first time, along with European writers, American authors as the interpreters and/or critics of the tourism theory, even though the majority of American authors acted primarily as economic theorists, explaining the irregularities in the mathematical operations and the model in general.

During the 1960s and 1970s, tourism experts from outside Europe appeared with their works. Among them, the first were Wahab et al. (1976) from Egypt and Francis M. Peltier from Canada.

One of the areas that interested tourism experts was the research of tourism demand, and the forecasting method in particular. How relevant this question still is today is illustrated by D. Frechtling's (2001) *Forecasting Tourism Demand: Methods and Strategies*, or the chapter written by Witt and Martin (1989), entitled 'Demand forecasting in tourism and recreation' in the book *Progress in Tourism, Recreation and Hospitality Management* (edited by C.P. Cooper). There is an extensive list of authors and works in this field today.

In the 1970s, there were a number of events important for history and the social sciences, which triggered off a change in tourism theorists' interest and focused their research on the novelties which these events brought. The large-scale world production of consumer goods and the growing issue of their promotion eliminated the interest of the economy in production which had existed for centuries and directed it to the sale and promotion of goods. This resulted in a new theoretical view of economics: marketing. At the same time, tourism's continuous growth resulted in unprecedented rates of supply and demand. The increasing involvement of thousands of new places and localities throughout the world in tourism brought about universal competitiveness, which prompted tourism to implement marketing. European theorists in particular turned to marketing, as it diverted tourism theorists' attention from their usual and over-researched topics for at least a couple of decades.

The first treatise on the possible application of marketing in tourism was written by the Spanish theorist José Ignacio de Arrillaga y Sanchez, who would later become the Spanish tourism minister. His treatise appeared under the name 'Marketing de los mercados turisticos' (Arrillaga, 1971). However, the real interest of experts was sparked by Krippendorf (1971) *Marketing et tourisme*. It is interesting that, already in 1971, the former IUOTO – now the World Tourism Organisation (UNWTO) – organised its 5th International Travel Research Seminar in Nassau, Bahamas, on the topic of The Changing World of Travel Marketing. With this, marketing definitely entered the area of tourism, both as a theoretical and a practical topic.

Somewhat later, V.T.C. Middleton (1979) published his article 'Tourism Marketing: Product Implications', which was followed by several similar works on tourism marketing by authors from other European countries. Middleton's major work is considered to be the one co-authored with J. Clarke (Middleton and Clarke, 2000). However, it was Middleton's article which opened a new area of interest for tourism theorists – the question of the tourism product. This issue was later discussed in a number of articles, while chapters on the tourism product appear in almost all the books that were later written on tourism marketing. What is also interesting is that at the very beginning of the 1970s, AIEST devoted its 23rd Congress (in 1973) to the topic of 'Tourisme et marketing'. This topic was later explored by an especially large number of American authors, such as T. Levitt, A.M. Morrison, R.T Reilly, R.D. Reid, C.D. Coffman, P.G. Davidoff, D.S. Davidoff, D. Foster, as well as authors from other countries. Interesting works by non-American authors included Dieter Hebestreit's (1975) *Touristik-Marketing*, Jean-Jacques Schwarz's (1976) 'Dynamique du Tourisme et Marketing', a major work in this field *Marketing for Leisure and Tourism* by M. E. Morgan (1996), *Tourism Marketing and Management Handbook* by Stephen Witt and Luiz Moutinho (Witt and Moutinho, 1989), and Walter Freyer's (1997) *Tourismus: Marketing*. Only in the 1990s did the leader of marketing theory, Philip Kotler, with co-authors, publish a work on tourism marketing, *Marketing for Hospitality and Tourism* (Kotler et al., 1996).

American theorists did not turn to general tourism topics until the early 1970s. Among the first was the joint work of the authors Robert McIntosh and Charles Goeldner (McIntosh and Goeldner, 1972), entitled *Tourism: Principles, Practices, Philosophies*, which became a general course book for American students who wanted to learn more about tourism. A book of the same title but significantly different appeared as an independent work by Robert McIntosh (1972). This period in America saw the publishing of several works concerned with general tourism subjects. Works on tourism came from Carlton Van Doren, Donald Lundberg, J.A. Patmore, etc. There were more authors, however, who explored particular topics, since US tourism was seen only as a business. Hugh De Santis, therefore, wrote about travel agencies as the leaders of travel democratisation in the world, D.E. Lundberg studied the hotel and restaurant business, and a number of works on tourism and the hotel industry were published in the professional journals of ASTA (American Society of Travel Agents), Travel Weekly, UIOTO, USA Travel Data Center and so on. Similar texts were also published by state institutions, such as the US Department of Commerce, US Department of Employment, US Department of Interior. S.R. Waters began publishing his *Travel Industry World Yearbook: The Big Picture*, which for the first time included not only a statistical analysis, but also extensive comments by the author regarding the changes in world tourism.

By the 1970s, France already had a wide range of works about different aspects of tourism development. Apart from Rene Baretje and Pierre Defert, younger authors such as Marc Boyer were focusing on economic questions of tourism development. Still, the biggest turn in theoretical considerations of tourism came from an entirely practical tourism project: Languedoc Roussillon. This programme of tourism construction, until then the biggest in the world, intrigued many French and world tourism experts. It involved, on the one hand, a completely new approach to the construction of tourism regions, especially from the point of view of the state's intervention in tourism development, which had not existed to such a degree until then, and, on the other hand, it introduced practical novelties, particularly in the architecture of tourism facilities. All of this prompted authors from different countries to publish works which were the first to tackle regional planning as a main prerequisite for tourism development.

These views should have been of special interest to American authors, as tourism by that time had not fully gained the 'right of citizenship', and state administration did not yet have a great interest in it. American authors began dealing with these issues almost 15 years later, when Clare Gunn (1979) first published *Tourism Planning*, followed by *Vacationscape: Designing Tourist Regions* (Gunn, 1988). This initiated a period of long and productive research work in which a number of experts worked more intensively on the general idea of tourism development and planning. An exception to this was Charles Gearing's (Gearing et al., 1976) book, *Planning for Tourism Development*. These theoretical considerations led to the forming of the tourism destination theory, which attracted a great deal of interest from authors in the last decade of the twentieth century. Two works deserve special mention here, *Tourism and Recreation Development: A Handbook of Physical Planning* by Fred Lawson and Manuel Baud-Bovy (Lawson and Baud-Bovy, 1977), and *Tourism Planning: an Integrated Planning and Development Approach* by E. Inskeep (1991). But the crucial work on this subject was written by Brent Ritchie and Geoffrey Crouch (Ritchie and Crouch, 2003), and titled *The Competitive Destination*.

There is another work written in the early 1970s that should not be overlooked in a chronology of world scientific theory on tourism. A. J. Burkart and S. Medlik (Burkart and Medlik, 1974) published the first edition of their book *Tourism: Past, Present and Future*, which, much like Hunziker and Krapf's work in the 1940s, freshened up general tourism theory, and took into consideration the different changes the world had gone through, in particular the changes in the development of the tourism phenomenon. This was also a major source for the new generations of students who were studying at a growing number of higher education institutions which specialised in tourism, so this book in fact became the first general tourism course book for a large part of Europe and the world.

It can be safely said that the area of tourism which has been researched and written about the most is the aspect of economics, or, rather, the economic implications and impact of tourism development.

In the same way that marketing dominated theoretical works in the 1970s, 'sociological and cultural pollution', the problem of environmental protection and the need to raise ecological awareness, became the focus of tourism works in the 1980s and 1990s. Of course, even before this there had been works which warned of the problem of ecological pollution caused by tourism development (such as the work of Arthur Haulot). No matter how perverse it may sound, by pointing out the negative effects of tourism development, sociologists and ecologist have perhaps done more for the popularisation of tourism than 'classical' tourism theorists! Tourism theory, which for a long time had focused on the economic features and consequences of tourism development, turned its attention in the 1980s and 1990s to social problems. An introduction to this may be found in Eric Cohen's (1979) text, 'Rethinking the Sociology of Tourism', which was published in the *Annals of Tourism Research*. However, this mainly positively charged work was followed by texts which attacked the tourism phenomenon, proclaiming it as asocial, irritating to local people, a-cultural, and, in a word, unacceptable as part of 'the new society' which modern civilisation was striving for. Cohen was also responsible for one of the first classifications of tourists.

The negative attitudes to tourism first appeared in Louis Turner and John Ash's (Turner and Ash, 1975) work *The Golden Hordes*, Dean MacCannell's (1976) *The Tourist: A New Theory of the Leisure Class* and Emanuel De Kadt's (1976) *Tourism: Passport to Development?* Turner and Ash made interesting observations on tourism destinations as the 'pleasure periphery', and the existence of a 'tourist belt' which surrounds the world's industrial zones. However, they turned their observation into an accusation that the 'global pleasure periphery is emerging where the rich of the world relax and intermingle'. An attempt to find some kind of objective grounding for these severe and one-sided views, whose main flaw was generalisations made from particular phenomena and events, was made by Valene Smith (1977) in her anthropological analysis of tourism, entitled *Hosts and Guests*. Fred Bosselman (1978) did something similar in his work *In the Wake of the Tourist*. Although still pointing out the negative impact of tourism development, these authors offer a number of positive examples in order to balance the theoretical views on the effects of world tourism. Still, the introductory discussion of tourism's real problems, with an emphasis on cultural and ecological issues, was certainly the book that marked a turning point in contemporary world tourism literature: Krippendorf (1986) *Die Ferienmenschen: Für ein neues Verständnis von Freizeit und reisen.*

In this context, another topic became prominent in world theoretical literature in the 1980s. Although seen from a somewhat different perspective, a number of authors, especially American ones, became interested in the centre–periphery relationships in tourism. In this relationship, T. Hoivik and T. Heiberg, W. Husbands, A. Mathieson and G. Wall, P.E. Murphy and S. Smith perceived links between the metropolitan centres (the centre) and tourism areas (the periphery), and observed the different implications in the economic, traffic, sociological, regional planning and many other sectors. These views attracted a large following over the next few years, resulting in an impressive number of works from different tourism experts worldwide.

The economic conditions and the impact of tourism development clearly remained a major theme in tourism theory. There was a remarkable amount of writing in this highly complex field, and some of the early works have already been mentioned. Interestingly enough, the topic of tourism economics had not been dealt with in any integrated way in so-called Western literature until the end of the twentieth century. This was probably a consequence of tourism in America and Australia being considered as a separate business, rather than a sector of activities with an influence on national development and GDP. On the other hand, in socialist countries such as Yugoslavia, Romania, Czechoslovakia and Bulgaria, which were generally less economically developed, but very active in the tourism sphere, the awareness of tourism's impact on the national economy was very high. If for nothing else, the problem of currency non-convertibility was certainly one of the reasons why the relationship of these countries to the tourism sector was different, as tourism significantly facilitated the acquisition of foreign currency. This is why in these countries works on tourism economics, or books similarly entitled, contain the theoretical postulates on tourism and a wide range of theses on the economic implications of tourism development. In former Yugoslavia, for example, in the short period between 1972 and 1975, five authors published books entitled *Tourism Economics*. Among them, the most famous authors were professors Janez Planina, Srđan Marković and Slobodan Unković. Similar works from Eastern Europe were those by such writers as Jiři Kašpar and Jaromir Holubov from Czechoslovakia, Horst Uebel from East Germany, A. Gueorguiev from Bulgaria and A. Kolacsek from Hungary.

In the Western world, only a few books carried the name 'tourism economics' at the time, and in the US there were none. In Europe, there were a few exceptions, such as *Economia del Turismo* by the Italian author Franco Paloscia (1965), *Aspects économiques du tourisme* by the French authors Baretje and Defert (1972), *Elements of Tourism Economics* by Albeto Sessa (1983) from Italy and *Economie touristique* by Gerard Guibilato (1983) from Switzerland. The first works on this topic appeared in Western countries in the final decade of the twentieth century, such as Bull (1991) *The Economics of Travel and Tourism,* Lundberg et al. (1995) *Tourism Economics,* Sinclair and Stabler's (1997) *The Economics of Tourism,* and Jose Marsano Delgado's (2003) *Economia del Turismo,* ended with *The Economics of Tourism Destinations* by Norbert Vanhove (2005), one of the best European economic experts in the world of tourism. From this we can see that this part of the world also started observing tourism from a macroeconomic perspective, treating it as a part of the national economy, and exploring what impact tourism as a sector had on GDP. Interesting research in this field was carried out by Wieslav Alejziak from Poland, who, writing in 1999 about the economic implications of tourism, advocated the creation of a new discipline – touristics! And finally, in 2004, a scientific debate in France discussed 'tourismology' as a new discipline, whose name attempted to suggest its fully fledged scientific character. The debate was triggered off by a book written by Jean-Michel Hoerner (2005), *La science du tourisme: Précis franco anglais de tourismologie.*

The problems of tourism development in developing countries was a 'new' topic extensively explored by tourism experts in the late 1970s and early 1980s. This topic came from the question about the dependence of particular countries' economies on the success of tourism development. This key question raised a series of follow-up questions. Among the first authors to tackle this topic was Alberto Sessa, who, in 1970, had already published a smaller study entitled *Tourism as a Factor of Progress in the Economy of Developing Countries,* and soon after him came L. Turner (1976) with his article 'The international division of leisure: Tourism and the Third World', R. E. Wood (1979) with 'Tourism and Underdevelopment in South East Asia', and D. Harrison (1992) with *Tourism and the Less Developed Countries.* UIOTO and OECD both dedicated an edition of their journals to this topic, and these associations organised seminars on the subject of tourism in underdeveloped countries. A number of authors, mainly from America, discussed tourism as a cause of developing countries' dependence on developed ones, including Turner, T.L. Hills and J. Lundgren, T. T. Heiberg, C.Wu, A. Mathieseon and G. Wall, P.A. Wellings and J. Crush, S.G. Britton. Among them, Britton was very clear in pointing out that underdeveloped countries were exploited not only by foreign capital, but also by 'local dominant capitalist firms', which had a negative impact on the economic, as well as the political and sociological, life of such countries. This area was dealt with by a number of authors, such as J. Monk and C. Alexander (1986), D.B. Miller and J. Branson (1989), P.B. Lerch and D.E. Levy (1990), D.E. Levy and P.B. Lerch (1991) and P.F. Wilkinson and W. Pratiwi (1995).

Discussion of tourism as a factor of regional development had started at the beginning of tourism development following the Second World War. One of the first to write about this was W. Christaller (1963) who discussed tourism as a means for achieving regional economic development, particularly in peripheral regions which benefited economically from tourists from richer central zones and metropolitan areas. A number of other authors dealt with the same topic over the next couple of years. Tourism is mentioned as an equally promising development strategy for both urban areas (Beauregard, 1998) and rural areas (Sharpley and Sharpley, 1997).

Especially interesting was the thesis about tourism as a factor for creating growth poles, aimed at stimulating regional development (Oppermann and Chon, 1997). These were the theoretical postulates on which Mexico and Spain founded their national tourism development policies and carried out numerous regional tourism projects (e.g. Cancun in Mexico, and the so-called 'zone urbanisation' in Spain). This involved a strategy of selecting economically relatively marginal areas which had appropriate basic tourism resources, and then stimulating their regional development. Of course, the literature mentions and analyses a larger number of regional development models, especially those which focus on the benefits for the local community. Emphasis was also placed on the role of the state and the ruling political ideology, treated in fact by many authors, including C. M. Hall (1994), Ioannides (1995) and Elliott (1997). The message of all this research is significant: peripheral regions should not expect to have the most benefit from regional tourism development (Pack and Sinclair, 1995).

That this is a global problem and a global topic is shown in Aisner and Plüss's (1983) book *La ruée vers le soleil*; similar works appeared in other world languages as well. However, the issue of underdevelopment is not solely an economic one, and neither are the consequences of tourism development. Consequently, theory shifted its focus to the issue of culture and environmental protection. The large number of authors who wrote about this include Vargniol (1975) *La planification du tourisme dans les pays en voie de développement: l'exemple de la Côte-d'Ivoire*, Vielhaber and Aderhold (1981) *Tourismus in Entwicklungsländer*, and John Leo (1988) *Tourism and Development in the Third World*. In addition, the relevance that these questions had in developing countries brought authors from these countries to the world scientific scene for the first time. They include the Mexican author A. Garcia de Fuentes (1979) *Cancun: Turismo y sudesarrollo regional*, the Argentinean E. Galeano (1971) *Las venas abiertas de America Latina*, E. Ntanyungu and F. N'Duhirahe (1981) *Tourisme et dépendance: Le Cas de l'Afrique noir*, and Tej Vir Singh et al. (1989) *Towards Appropriate Tourism: The Case of Developing Countries*.

Within the subject of third world countries, another interesting research area appeared – the relationship of religion and tourism. The most famous works published on this topic at the time were O'Grady (1981) *Third World Stopover: The Tourism Debate*, the paper, 'Ecumenical Coalition on Third World Tourism', and Vukonić (1995) *Tourism and Religion*.

In this period, European authors published their first works on an important economic subject in the field of tourism: tour operators. Particular interest in this field existed in Germany and Great Britain, two countries in which tour operators as travel organisers had the biggest influence on the development of these countries' emissive tourism, which is the largest in the world in terms of the number of tourists. This topic raised interest in other countries, particularly receptive ones, in which tour operators have a dominant role in the development of tourism. The first major work in this field had been published somewhat earlier, in 1974. *Touristik Marketing* (Hebestreit, 1975) connected what was then marketing's main area of interest with the work of tour operators. The problem of tour operators was later explored by a number of theorists, such as Mundt (1993), who published a comprehensive work entitled *Reiseveranstaltung*, and Neveka Čavlek (1998) in *Tour Operators and World Tourism*, unfortunately for the international expert public published only in Croatian. Still, many more works on tour operators have been published in professional journals in all the main world languages.

Before the closing remarks on the development of tourism theory at the end of the twentieth century, this overview would not be complete if it failed to mention the works published at the annual conferences of tourism associations. These works give us an insight into all the different theoretical opinions, and their publication has created a firm foundation for the study of the tourism phenomenon (and the history of tourism theory). A series of such journals has continuously been published by AIEST (Association Internationale d'Experts Scientifiques du Tourisme), and now numbers 46 books from 54 AIEST congresses. The works deal with practically all the relevant theoretical problems. A few that have arisen in the past 15 years are property, globalisation, quality management, destination management, marketing, tourism policy, culture, tourism growth and global competitiveness, air traffic, sport, and small and medium-sized companies in tourism. Similar work has been done by other national and international tourism organisations, such as TTRA (Travel and Tourism Research Association), ATLAS (European Association for Tourism and Leisure Studies), etc. In the last 15 years, the American association IMDA (International Management Development Association) has also included tourism topics at its annual conferences, and has published the conference papers in its journal. Irregular, but particularly significant, has been the publishing activity of the World Tourism Organisation, which has published different studies and classic course-book materials (such as Cooper et al. (1996) *Educating the Educators*). Similarly, IAST (International Academy for the Study of Tourism), founded 1989, has published a number of books about different tourism topics, especially topics presented at the organisation's annual conferences.

It is difficult to study authors in the latter part of the twentieth century according to their geographical and national origins, or to use the same criteria to discuss the interests of particular tourism theorists. The world has started living intensely within its global framework, in which interest for different topics has become universal, and a strong flow of information provides the authors, regardless of where they live and work, with enough information to discuss their joint topics. Instead of listing as many works from this period as possible, only the major works representative of the theoretical work in the last 20 years of the twentieth century will be mentioned here.

Among these, an important place belongs to *Tourists, Travellers and Pilgrims* (Hindley, 1983), *The Travel Industry* (Gee et al., 1989), *Tourismus: Einführung in die Fremdenverkehrsökonomie* (Freyer, 1990), *Managing Tourism* (Medlik, 1991), *Reiseveranstaltung* (Mundt, 1993), *Tourismus-Management* (Haedrich, 1983), *Travel, Tourism and Hospitality Research: A Handbook for Managers and Researchers* (Ritchie and Goeldner, 1994), *Resorts: Management and Operations* (Mill, 1995), *Change in Tourism* (Butler and Pearce, 1995), *Tourismus* (Freyer, 1995), *Management von Destinationen und Tourismusorganisationen* (Bieger, 1996), *Tourism Development: Principles, Processes, and Policies* (Gartner, 1996), *L'Invention du tourisme* (Boyer, 1996), *Tourismus: Eine systematische Einführung – Analyse und Prognosen* (Opaschowski, 1996), *Tourisme, Touristes, Sociétes* (Michel, 1998), *Entrepreneurship in the Hospitality, Tourism and Leisure Industries* (Morrison et al., 1999), *Tourism: Principles, Practices, Philosophies* (Goeldner et al., 2000).

A number of authors dealt with specific areas of tourism interest, such as the psychology of travel (J. Reason, 1974: 'Man in Motion: the Psychology of Travel'), tourism's anthropological aspects (Turner and Turner, 1978: *Image and Pilgrimage in Christian Culture*), the psychology of tourist consumers (P. L. Pearce, 1982: *The Social Psychology of Tourist Behaviour*), legal issues regarding package holidays (Nelson-Jones and Stewart, 1993: *Practical Guide to Package Holiday Law and Contracts*), the relationship of religion and tourism (Boris Vukonić, 1995: *Tourism and Religion*; Myra Shackley, 2001: *Managing Sacred Sites*), urban tourism (S. Page, 1995: *Urban Tourism*), the relationship of public policy and tourism (C.M. Hall, 1995: *Tourism and Public Policy*), the sociolinguistic issues of tourism (Graham Dann, 1996: *The Language of Tourism*), consumer behaviour (Pizam and Mansfield, 1999: *Consumer Behaviour in Travel and Tourism*), the relationship of tourism and ecology (Müller and Flügel, 1999: *Tourismus und Ökologie*), tourism ethics (Smith and Duffy, 2003: *The Ethics of Tourism Development*), the control of companies in the tourist industry (H. Huber, 2000: *Controlling im Hotel- und Restaurantbetrieb*).

Another author, whose work does not focus on the usual theoretical topics, but which belongs to a group of widely read papers published in the late twentieth century with great influence on people's general attitudes towards tourism and its development, is John Naisbitt (1994), whose book *Global Paradox* has had sales of several million copies. In one of the chapters, this well-founded and informed analysis gives a detailed overview of the development of the tourism phenomenon, especially some of its dynamic segments, such as air traffic and the tour operator business.

These different discussions on tourism's influence on the development of underdeveloped countries led, almost simultaneously, to the discussion of a new area of interest – what kind of tourism do we really want, what kind of tourism are we willing to accept as an option for development, what sacrifices are we willing to make for such a development? In other words, these were primarily questions on how to protect oneself from the negative effects of mass tourism, but they were also questions about a different kind of tourism – so-called alternative tourism as a possible solution (Smith and Eadington, 1992: *Tourism Alternatives*). The work of American authors dominated this field once again. However, even in the first discussions it became clear that the phrase 'alternative tourism' neither explained what was meant, nor what was understood by it. This is why other phrases, such as 'responsible tourism', 'soft tourism', '*sanfter tourismus*' and 'sustainable tourism' were created. The authors who were among the first to write about this new form of tourism were R.W. Butler, J.G. Nelson, G. Wall, J. Brohman, B. Bramwell and B. Lane. When talking about theoretical works on tourism today, this topic remains one of the leading areas of interest.

World tourism theory in the 1990s and later focused on the topic of management. The first books on this subject were *Introduction to Management in the Hospitality Industry* by Tom Powers (1992), and *Management im Tourismus* by Clode Kaspar (1994). Other significant works include *Progress in Tourism, Recreation and Hospitality Management* by Cooper and Lockwood (1994), *International Hospitality Management* by Teare and Olsen (1992), *Tourist Destination Management* by E. Laws (1995), *Management von Tourismusunternehmen* by Torsten Kirstges (1994), *Tourisikmanagement 1 and 2* by W. Pompl (1998), *Tourism Management* by Weaver and Lawton (2000), *Strategic Management in Tourism* by L. Moutinho (2000), *Tourism Management: Towards the New Millennium* by Ryan and Page (2000), and *Internationales Tourismus-management* by Pompl and Lieb (2002). Apart from a general discussion on management in tourism, an increasing number of works have been published on the subject of management in specific sectors or activities present in tourism today. Some of them are *Festivals, Special Events and Tourism* by D. Getz (1991), *Festival and Special Event Management* by McDonnell, Allen, and O'Toole (1999), *Resorts: management and operation* by Robert C. Mill (2008), *The Airline Business in the 21st Century* by R. Doganis (2001), and *Sport Tourism: Fitness Information Technology* by Douglas M. Turco et al. (2002).

Among the last topics to dominate the interest of world tourism theorists are two which are drastically different in their content and ideology: the relationship between tourism and culture on the one hand, and tourism and turbulent political changes and, especially, terrorism on the other. While it is difficult to say whether or not it is better that more works are written about the first of these topics, the relationship of culture and tourism is certainly often discussed and written about in scientific papers. One of the first who in a scientific paper examined and discussed factors which both constitute and influence the tourist culture was Jafar Jafari (1987). One of the first books in this area was Eddystone Nabel's (1983) *Tourism and Culture: A Comparative Prospective*. Among the many other works in this field are *The Tourist-Historic City* by Ashworth and Tunbridge (1990), *Tourism and Heritage Attractions* by Richard Prentice (1993), *Tourism and Culture: Image, Identity and Marketing* by Robinson et al. (1994), *Vendre le tourisme culturel* by Josquin Barré (1995), *Managing Quality Cultural Tourism* by P. Boniface (1995), *Tourisme et patrimoine* by Valéry Patin (1997), *Tourism and Heritage Relationships: Global,*

National and Local Perspectives by Robinson et al. (2000), *Issues in Cultural Tourism Studies* by M. Smith (2003).

Scientific work on political instability and its influence on the development of world tourism has had fewer pages devoted to it, although it has been particularly present in the media, as well as in professional tourism journals. A few authors from this field have produced work which can be considered as pioneering. One of the first who indicated the problem of safety in tourism was A. Stutts (1990) in his book *The Travel Safety Handbook*. Five years later (in 1995), the General Assembly of World Tourism Organisation in Cairo was devoted to the question of crisis management. At the Assembly, a report entitled 'Crisis Management' was delivered by R. Leaf. Other authors who specialised in this area were Colin Michael Hall (1994: *Tourism and Politics*), and Dallen Timothy (2001: *Tourism and Political Boundaries*). Michael Hall, Dallen Timothy and David Timothy Duval were editors of the book *Safety and Security in Tourism* (Hall et al., 2003) in which a range of scholars from all over the world highlighting the vulnerability of the tourism sector to changes in safety and security, especially after the recent terrorist attacks in the United States. The specific subject of air traffic safety was explored by D. Phipps (1991: *The Management of Aviation Security*), and security in international tourism in general by Pizam and Mansfield (1995: *Tourism, Crime and International Security Issues*). Generally speaking, professional journals are much more widespread these days than expert books, as they appear almost at the same time as the phenomena which influence the development of tourism. This can be well illustrated by the success and charisma of Jafar Jafari's *Annals of Tourism Research*, amongst others such as *Tourism Management, Tourism Economics,* which have become compulsory reading in the discussions of contemporary tourism topics.

And, finally, let us consider the tourism subject with which mankind has entered the third millennium: crisis management. Resulting from turbulent political world events at the start of the twenty-first century, the increasingly important topic of management of crisis situations in tourism has become not only a relevant theoretical subject, but a highly practical topic, which is of interest to the tourism industry throughout the world. Among the works which have been published in this field until now, particularly interesting have been the books *Managing Tourism Crises* by Sönmez et al. (1994), *Krisenmanagement im Tourismus* by A. Dreyer (2001), and *Crisis Management in the Tourism Industry* by Dirk Glaesser (2003).

As in the earlier periods, theorists today do not write just about the hottest topics, but deal with almost all subject areas. Nowadays, the most numerous are course books, but their authors also deserve the most criticism. The published course books are often so similar that it is difficult to see the reason for their publication, apart from the author's and/or the publisher's direct commercial interest. However, this should not discourage young researchers and lecturers from presenting themselves to the public. Every such work has at least some originality in its treatment of a particular tourism phenomenon, and that in itself is enough for these works to be taken into consideration. Also, these works are a guarantee that the scientific interest in tourism is not waning and that tourism theory need not worry about its future.

A rich source of theoretical papers, already mentioned, is the professional journal *Annals of Tourism Research*, first published 1973, which has been the leading tourism journal for many years and is in itself a real encyclopaedia of theoretical insights and knowledge. Special mention should be made of the topics covered, which are relevant, up to date and novel, and, by turning theoretical material into current conjectural information, they influence the formation of scientific theses in almost all areas in the scientific study of tourism. The French *Cahiers du Tourisme*, a well-known series, published by R. Baretje from CHET, Aix-en-Provence, was an important and unavoidable source of tourism knowledge in this part of the world for decades.

Boris Vukonić

Instead of a conclusion

Focusing both on pioneering works in the specific areas of interest of different authors and on the works whose ideas were significant for a particular period of tourism theory this article was intended to be an important source of credible information regarding the antecedents of modern tourism scholarship. Such a task can hardly be fully performed because of the limited availability of literature on the one hand and the large-scale production of expert literature on tourism in the past 30 years and more on the other, especially in the languages of smaller nations. This is the reason why some authors and their works are absent from this overview, even though they may be very significant for a particular country or tourism theory as a whole. This failure was not intentional, and especially was not a result of an idea to lessen the significance and the role of any theorist anywhere in the world.

This article had also the intention to inspire other world tourism theorists, IAST members in particular, to expand this material in order to develop a more comprehensive study of present-day world tourism theory and the history of theoretical insights in tourism from their beginnings until today.

Bibliography

Aisner, P. and Plüss, C. (1983) *La rueé vers le soleil: le tourisme à destination du tiers monde* (The rush to the sun: Tourism to the third world). Paris: L'Harmattan

Arrillaga, J. I. (1971) 'Marketing de los mercados turisticos' (Marketing of tourism markets). *Estudios turisticos*, 31, 5–29

Ashworth, G. J. and Tunbridge, J. E. (1990) *The tourist-historic city*. Chicester: John Wiley and Sons

Auscher, L. (1916) *Le Tourisme en automobile* (Touring by car). Paris

—— and Rozet, G. (1920) *Urbanisme et Tourisme* (Urbanism and tourism). Paris

Avancini, M. (1913) *Il traffico turistico esaminato alla luce delle indagini statistiche* (The examination of tourism flows in light of statistical investigation). Roma

—— (1925) *Entita e svolgimento del traffico turistico in Italia* (Entity and development of tourism flows in Italy). Roma

—— (1939) *Statistica turistica* (Tourism statistics). Milano

Barberini, E. (1929) 'L'industrie hôtelière et tourisme en Suisse' (The hotel industry and tourism in Switzerland). Saint Maurice

Baretje, R. and Defert, P. (1972) *Aspects économiques du tourisme* (Economic aspects of tourism). Paris: Editions Berger-Levrault

Barré, J. (1995) *Vendre le tourisme culturel* (Selling cultural tourism). Paris: Economica

Beauregard, Robert A. (1998) 'Tourism and economic development policy in US urban areas', in D. Ioannides and E.G. Debbage (eds) *The economic geography of the tourist industry: A supply-side analysis*. London: Routledge

Belotti, B. (1919) *Il diritto turistico nella legge, nella dottrine e nella giurispreudenza* (Tourism regulation in law, doctrine and jurisprudence). Milano

Benini, R. (1926) *Sulla Riforma dei metodi di calcolo dei movimento turistico* (On reforms of methods of calculating tourism flows). Roma

Bernecker, P. (1956) *Die Stellung des Fremdenverkehrs im Leistungssystem der Wirtschaft* (The role of tourism in the economic system). Vienna

—— (1959) *Der Fremdenverkehr und seine Betriebe und Betriebswirtschaftliche Ordnungsprobleme der Fremdenverkehrsbetriebe* (Tourism, its enterprises and microeconomic regulatory problems of tourism enterprises)

Bieger, T. (1996) *Management von Destinationen und Tourismusorganisationen* (Management of destinations and tourism organisations). Munich: Oldenbourg Verlag

Bodo, L. (1899) 'Sul movimento dei forestieri in Italia e sul denaro che vi spendono' (On the movement of foreigners and the money they spend in Italy). *Giornalle degli Economisti*

Boniface, P. (1995) *Managing quality cultural tourism*. London: Routledge

Bormann, A. (1931) *Die Lehre vom Fremdenverkehr* (The study of tourism). Berlin: Ein Grundriß

Bosselman, F. (1978) *In the wake of the tourist*. Washington DC: The Conservation Foundation

Boyer, M. (1996) *L'Invention du Tourisme* (The invention of tourism). Paris: Découvertes-Gallimard

Brunner, E. (1945) *Holiday making and the holiday trades*. Oxford: Oxford University Press

Bull, A. (1991) *The economics of travel and tourism*. Melbourne: Pitman

Burkart, A. J. and Medlik, S. (1974) *Tourism: Past, present and future*. London: Heinemann

Butler, R. W. and Pearce, D. (eds) (1995) *Change in tourism: people, places, processes*. London: Routledge

Carone, G. (1959) *Il Turismo nell'Economia Internazionale* (Tourism in the international economy). Milano

Čavlek, N. (1998) *Turoperatori i svjetski turizam* (Tour operators and world tourism). Zagreb: Golden Marketing

Christaller, W. (1963) 'Some considerations of tourism location in Europe: The peripheral Regions – underdeveloped countries – recreation areas'. *Papers in Regional Science*, 12(1), 95–105

Clement, H. G. (1961) *The future of tourism in the Pacific and Far East*. Washington DC: US Department of Commerce

Cohen, E. (1979) 'Rethinking the sociology of tourism'. *Annals of Tourism Research*, 6(1), 18–35

Cooper, C. P. and Lockwood, A. (1994) *Progress in tourism recreation and hospitality management*. Chicester, England: John Wiley and Sons

Cooper, C. P., Shepherd, R. and Westlake, J. (1996) *Educating the Educators in Tourism: A Manual of Tourism and Hospitality Education* (Tourism Education and Training Series) Guildford: UNWTO and University of Surrey

Dann, G. (1996) *The language of tourism: A sociolinguistic perspective*. Wallingford, England: CAB International

De Kadt, E. (1976) *Tourism: Passport to development?* Oxford: Oxford University Press

Defert, P. (1958) 'Quelques repères historiques du tourisme moderne' (Some historical landmarks in modern tourism). *Revue de Tourisme*, 1

—— (1960) *Pour une politique du Tourisme en France* (For a policy of tourism in France). Paris

Delgado, J. M. (2003) *Economia del Turismo* (Economics of tourism). Lima: Escuela Profesional de Turismo y Hoteleria

Doganis, R. (2001) *The airline business in the 21st Century*. London: Routledge

Dreyer, A. (2001) *Krisenmanagement im Tourismus* (Crisis management in tourism). Munich: Oldenbourg

Elliott, J. (1997) *Tourism: Policies and public sector management*. London: Routledge

Frechtling, D. C. (2001) *Forecasting tourism demand: Methods and strategies*. Oxford: Butterworth-Heinemann

Freyer, W. (1990) *Tourismus: Einführung in die Fremdenverkehrsökonomie* (Tourism: Introduction to the economics of tourism). Munich: Oldenbourg Verlag

—— (1995) *Tourismus* (Tourism). Munich: Oldenbourg

—— (1997) *Tourismus: Marketing* (Tourism marketing). Munich: Oldenbourg

de Fuentes, A. G. (1979) *Cancun: Turismo y sudesarrollo regional*. Mexico City: Universidad Nacional Autónoma de México, Instituto de Geografía

Galeano, E. (1971) *Las venas abiertas de America Latina*. Havana: Casa de las Americas

Gartner, W. (1996) *Tourism development: Principles, processes, and policies*. New York: Van Nostrand Reinhold

Gearing, C. E., Swart W. W. and Var, T. (1976) *Planning for tourism development*. New York: Praeger Publisher

Gee, C., Makens, J. C. and Choy, D. J. L. (1989) *The Travel Industry*. New York: Van Nostrand Reinhold

Getz, D. (1991) *Festivals, Special Events and Tourism*. New York: Van Nostrand Reinhold

Gide, C. (1928) *L'importance economique du Tourisme* (The economic importance of tourism)

Glaesser, D. (2003) *Crisis management in the tourism industry*. Oxford, England: Butterworth-Heinemann

Glücksmann, R. (1935) *Fremdenverkehrskunde* (Tourism studies). Bern

Goeldner, C., Ritchie, B. and McIntosh, R. (2000) *Tourism: Principles, practices, philosophies*. New York: John Wiley and Sons

Guibilato, G. (1983) *Economie touristique* (Economics of tourism). Denges, Switzerland: Editions Delta and Spes SA

Gunn, C. (1979) *Tourism planning*. New York: Crane Russak

—— (1988) *Vacationscape: Designing tourist regions*. New York: Van Nostrand Reinhold.

Gurtner, H. (1916) *Fremdenverkehr und Zahlungsbilanz* (Tourism and the balance of payments)

Guyer-Freuler, E. (1884) *Das Hotelwesen* (The hotel sector). Zürich: Druck von Orell Füssli

—— (1895) *Beiträge zur Statistik des Fremdenverkehrs in der Schweiz* (Contributions to the statistics on tourism in Switzerland). Zürich

Haedrich, G. (1983) *Tourismus-management* (Tourism management). Berlin: Walter De Gruyter

Hall, C. M. (1994) *Tourism and politics: Policy, power and place*. Chichester: John Wiley and Sons

—— (1995) *Tourism and public policy*. London: Routledge.

——, Timothy, D. J. and Duval, T. D. (eds) (2003) *Safety and security in tourism: Relationships, management, and marketing*. New York: Haworth Hospitality Press

Harrison, D. (1992) *Tourism and the less developed countries*. London: Belhaven Press

Hebestreit, D. (1975) *Touristik Marketing* (Tourism marketing). Berlin: Berlin-Verlag

Hindley, G. (1983) *Tourists, Travellers and Pilgrims*. London: Hutchinson

Hoerner, J. M. (2005) *La science du tourisme: Précis franco anglais de tourismologie* (The science of tourism: An Anglo-French summary of tourism studies). Baixas: Balzac Editeur

Huber, H. (2000) *Controlling im Hotel- und Restaurantbetrieb: Ein Leitfaden fur kleine und mttelstandische Unlernehmen*, Wien: Ueberreuter Wirtschaft

Hunziker, W. (1959) *Betriebswirtschaftslehre des Fremdenverkehrs* (Microeconomics of tourism). Bern

—— and Krapf, K. (1942) *Grundriss der allgemeine Fremdenverkehrslehre* (General studies in tourism). Zürich: Polygraphischer Verlag AG

Inskeep, E. (1991) *Tourism planning: An integrated planning and development approach*. New York: Van Nostrand Reinhold

Ioannides, D. (1995) 'Strengthening the ties between tourism and economic geography: A theoretical agenda'. *Professional Geographer*, 47(1), 49–60

Jaeger, F. (1936) *Werbung im Fremdenverkehr* (Advertising in tourism). Innsbruck

Jafari, J. (1987) 'Tourism models: The sociocultural aspects'. *Tourism Management*, 8(2), 151–59

Joschke, H. (1953) 'Beitrag zur theoretischen analyse des fremdenverkehrsangebote' (Contribution to the theoretical analysis of tourism supply). *Jahrbuch für Fremdenverkehr*, 2(1)

Just, R. (1907) *Die Gemeinde Arose, ihr Wirtschaftsleben vor und seit dem Fremdenverkehr* (The community of Arose: Its economic life before and since tourism). Zürich

Kaspar, C. (1994) *Management im Tourismus* (Management in tourism). Bern: Verlag Paul Haupt

Kirstges, T. (1994) *Management von Tourismusunternehmen* (Management of tourism enterprises). Munich: Verlag Oldenbourg

Kotler, P., Bowen, J. and Makens, J. (1996) *Marketing for hospitality and tourism*. New York: Prentice Hall

Krapf, K. (1953) *Die touristische Konsum: Ein Beitrag zur Lehre von der Kosumption* (Tourism consumption: A contribution to the study of consumption)

—— (1957) 'Last hören aus alter Zeit' (Let's hark back to the old days). *Jahrbuch für Fremdenverkehr*

—— (1962) 'Le tourisme, facteur de l'economie moderne' (Tourism: A factor in the modern economy). *Revue de Tourisme, 3*

Krieger, W. (1933) *Werbtechnik im Fremdenverkehr* (Advertising techniques in tourism). Wien

Krippendorf, J. (1971) *Marketing et tourisme* (Marketing and tourism). Bern: Herbert Lang and Cie AG

—— (1986) *Die Ferienmenschen: Für ein neues Verständnis von Freizeut und Reisen* (People on vacation: Towards a new understanding of leisure and travel). Munich: Deutscher Taschenbuch Verlag

Laws, E. (1995) *Tourist destination management: Issues, analysis, and politics*. London: Routledge

Lawson, F. and Baud-Bovy, M. (1977) *Tourism and recreation development: A handbook of physical planning*. London: The Architectural Press Ltd

Leo, J. P. (1988) *Tourism and development in the third world*. London: Routledge

Lerch, P. B. and Levy, D. E. (1990) 'A solid foundation: Predicting success in Barbados' tourist industry'. *Human Organization*, 49(4), 355–63.

Levy, D. E. and Lerch, P. B (1991) 'Tourism as a factor in development. Implications for gender and work in Barbados'. *Gender and Society* 5(1), 67–85.

Lickorish, L. J. and Kershaw, A. G. (1958) *The travel trade*. London: Practical Press

Lundberg, D. E., Stavenga, M. H. and Krishnamoorthy, M. (1995) *Tourism economics*. New York: John Wiley and Sons.

MacCannell, D. (1976) *The tourist: A new theory of the leisure class*. New York: Schocken Books

McDonnell, I., Allen, J. and O'Toole, W. (1999) *Festival and special event management*. Milton, Queensland: John Wiley and Sons

McIntosh, R. (1972) *Tourism: Principles, practices, philosophies*. Columbus, OH: Grid Inc.

—— and Goeldner, C. (1972) *Tourism: Principles, practices, philosophies*. New York: John Wiley and Sons

Marković, S. and Marković, Z. (1972) *Ekonomika turizma* (Tourism economics). Zagreb: Školska knjiga

Medlik, S. (1991) *Managing tourism*. Oxford: Butterworth-Heinemann

Michel, F. (1998) *Tourisme, touristes, sociétés* (Tourism, tourists, societies). Strasbourg, Austria: Harmatan

Middleton, V. T. C. (1979) 'Tourism marketing: Product implications'. *International Tourism Quarterly*, 2

—— and Clarke, J. (2000) *Marketing in travel and tourism*. Oxford, England: Heinemann

Mihalič, T. (2002) 'Tourism and economic development issues'. In R. Sharpley and D. Telfer (eds), *Tourism and development: Concepts and issues*. Clevedon: Channel View Publications, pp. 81–111

Mill, R. C. (1995) *Resorts: Management and operation*. New York: John Wiley and Sons

—— (2008) *Resorts: Management and operation* (2nd edn). New York: John Wiley and Sons

Miller, D. B. and Branson, J. (1989) 'Pollution in Paradise: Hinduism and the subordination of women in Bali', in P. Alexander (ed.) *Creating Indonesian Cultures*. Sydney: Oceania, pp. 91–112

Monk, J. and Alexander, C. S. (1986) 'Free port fallout: gender, employment and migration on Margarita Island'. *Annals of Tourism Research*, 13, 393–13

Morgan, M. (1996) *Marketing for leisure and tourism*. Harlow: Pearson Education

Morgenroth, W. (1927) 'Fremdenverkehr' (Tourism). *Handwörterbuch der Staatswissenschaften*, Vol. 4.

Morrison, A., Rimmington, M. and Williams, C. (1999) *Entrepreneurship in the Hospitality, Tourism and Leisure Industries*. Englewood Cliffs, NJ: Prentice-Hall.

Moutinho, L. (2000) *Strategic Management in Tourism*. Wallingford: CABI International

Müller, H. and Flügel, M. (1999) *Tourismus und Ökologie: Wechselwirkungen und Handlungsfelder* (Tourism and ecology: Interdependencies and domains of action). Munich: Oldenbourg Verlag

Müller, W. K. (1908) *Das Hotelwesen und der Fremdenverkehr in der Schweiz* (The hotel sector and tourism in Switzerland). Jena

Mundt, J. W. (1993) *Reiseveranstaltung* (Organised travel). Munich: Oldenbourg Verlag

Nabel, E. (1983) *Tourism and Culture: A Comparative Perspective*. New Orleans, LA: The University of New Orleans, School of Hotel, Restaurant and Tourism Administration

Naisbitt, J. (1994) *Global paradox*. New York: Avon Books

Nelson-Jones, J. and Stewart, P. (1993) *Practical guide to package holiday law and contracts* (3rd edn). London: Fourmat

Niceforo, A. (1923) *Il movimento dei forestieri in Italia* (Tourism movement of foreigners in Italy). Roma

Norval, A. J. (1936) *The tourist industry: A national and international survey*. London: Pitman and Sons

Ntanyungu, E. and N'Duhirahe, F. (1981) *Tourisme et dépendance: Le Cas de l'Afrique noire*, 4th edn. Itiner aires: notes et travaux no. 6. Geneva : Institut universitaire d'études du développement

Ogilvie, F. W. (1933) *The tourist movement: An economic study*. London: P. S. King and Son

O'Grady, R. (1981) *Third world stopover: The tourism debate*. Singapore: Christian Conference of Asia

Opaschowski, H. W. (1996) *Tourismus: Eine systematische Einführung* (Tourism: A systematic introduction). Opladen: Leske + Budrich

Oppermann, M. and Chon, K. (1997) *Tourism in developing countries*. London: International Thompson Business Press

Pack, A. C. and Sinclair, M. T. (1995) 'Regional concentration and dispersal of tourism demand in the UK'. *Regional Studies*, 29(6), 570–76

Page, S. (1995) *Urban tourism*. London: Routledge

Paloscia, F. (1965) *Economia del Turismo* (The economics of tourism). Roma: Edizioni Le Opere

Patin, V. (1997) *Tourisme et patrimoine* (Tourism and heritage). Paris: La documentation francaise

Pearce, P. L. (1982) *The social psychology of tourist behaviour*. Oxford, England: Pergamon

Pedrotta, F. (1939) *L'industria turistico-alberghiera del Canton Ticino* (The hotel and tourism industry in cantone Ticino). Bellinzona

Phipps, D. (1991) *The management of aviation security*. London: Pitman

Pizam, A. and Mansfield, Y. (1995) *Tourism, crime and international security issues*. London: John Wiley and Sons

—— (1999) *Consumer behaviour in travel and tourism*. London: John Wiley and Sons

Pompl, W. (1998) *Touristik Management 1 and 2* (Tourism management 1and 2). Berlin: Heidelberg

—— and Lieb, M. (2002) *Internationales Tourismus-Management* (International tourism management). Munich: Verlag Franz Vahlen

Powers, T. (1992) *Introduction to management in the hospitality industry* (4th edn). New York: John Wiley and Sons

Prentice, R. (1993) *Tourism and heritage attractions*. London: Routledge

Reason, J. (1974) 'Man in Motion: The Psychology of Travel'. *Journal of Travel Research*, July 1975, 14:1, 27

Ritchie, B. and Crouch, G. (2003) *The competitive destination*. Wallingford: CABI Publishing

Ritchie, J. R. and Goeldner, C. R. (1994) *Travel, tourism and hospitality research: A handbook for managers and researchers*. New York: John Wiley and Sons

Robinson, M., Evans, E. and Callaghan, P. (1994) *Tourism and culture: Image, identity and marketing*. Newcastle: University of Northumbria

Robinson, M., Long, P., Sharpley, R. and Swarbrooke, J. (2000) *Tourism and heritage relationships: Global, national and local perspectives*. Newcastle: University of Northumbria

Ryan, C. and Page, S. (eds) (2000) *Tourism management: Towards the new millennium*. Amsterdam: Pergamon

Schwarz, J.-J. (1976) 'Dynamique du tourisme et marketing' (Dynamics of tourism and marketing). Unpublished doctoral dissertation, Université de droit, d'économie et des sciences d'Aix-Marseille, France

Sessa, A. (1983) *Elements of tourism economics*. Roma: Catal

Shackley, M. (2001) *Managing sacred sites*. London: Continuum

Sharpley, R. and Sharpley, J. (1997) *Rural tourism: An introduction*. London: International Thompson Business Press

Sinclair, T. and Stabler, M. (1997) *The economics of tourism*. London: Routledge

Singh, T. V., Theuns, H. L. and Go, F. M. (eds) (1989) *Towards appropriate tourism: The case of developing countries*. European University Studies, Series X, Tourism, Vol. BD(11). Frankfurt: Peter Lang

Smith, M. and Duffy, R. (2003) *The ethics of tourism development*. London: Routledge

Smith, M. K. (2003) *Issues in cultural tourism studies*. London: Routledge

Smith, V. L. (ed.) (1977) *Hosts and guests: The anthropology of tourism*. Philadelphia, PA: University of Pennsylvania Press

—— and Eadington, W. (eds) (1992) *Tourism Alternatives: Potentials and Problems in the Development of Tourism*. Philadelphia, PA: University of Pennsylvania Press and International Academy for the Study of Tourism

Sönmez, S. F., Backman, S. J. and Allen, L. R. (1994) *Managing tourism crises*. Clemson, SC: Clemson University

Stoye, J. W. (1952) *English travellers abroad, 1604–1667: their influence in English society and politics*. London: Cape.

Stradner, J. (1890) 'Die Förderung des Fremdenverkehrs' (The promotion of tourism). *Kulturbilder aus der Steiermark*. Graz

Stringer, B. (1912) *Sulla bilanza dei pagamenti fra Italia e l'estero* (About the balance of payments between Italy and abroad) Roma

Stutts, A. T. (1990) *The travel safety handbook*. New York: Van Nostrand Reinhold

Tabacchi, G. (1934) *Turismo ed Economia* (Tourism and economics). Roma

Teare, R. and Olsen, M. (1992) *International hospitality management*. London: John Wiley and Sons.

Thoms, W. (1952) 'Die Arten und der Character des Fremdenverkehrsbetriebs' (Types and nature of the tourism enterprise). *In Handbuch für Fremdenverkehrsbetriebes*. Giessen

Timothy, D. J. (2001) *Tourism and Political Boundaries*. Oxfordshire: Taylor & Francis Ltd.

Titzhoff, P. W. (1964) 'Fremdenverkehrstheorie zur Zeit der Dreissigjahringen Kriegs 1630: Der Merkantilist Thomas Mun würdigt die ökonomische Bedeutung des grenzüberschreitenden Reiseverkehrs' (Tourism theory during the times of the Thirty Years War: The mercantilist Thomas Mun recognises the importance of cross-border travel). *Der Fremdenverkehr*, 7

Troisi, M. (1940a) *Nozione economica di Turismo* (The notion of tourism economics). Bari

—— (1940b) *Prime line di una teoria della rendita turistica* (A first attempt of a theory on tourism revenue). Bari

Turco, D. M., Riley, R. S. and Swart, K. (2002) *Sport Tourism*. Morgantown, WV: Fitness Information Technology

Turner, L. (1976) 'The international division of leisure: Tourism and the third world'. *World Development*, 4(3), 253–60

—— and Ash, J. (1975) *The Golden Hordes: International Tourism and the Pleasure Periphery*. London: Constable

Turner, V. and Turner, E. (1978) *Image and pilgrimage in Christian culture: Anthropological perspectives*. Oxford: Blackwell

Vanhove, N. (2005) *The economics of tourism destinations*. Oxford: Elsevier Butterworth-Heinemann

Vargniol, G. (1975) *La planification du tourisme dans les pays en voie de développement: l'example de la Côte-d'Ivoire* (Tourism planning in developing countries: The example of Ivory Coast). Aix-en-Provence: CHET

Vielhaber, A. and Aderhold, P. (1981) *Tourismus in Entwicklungsländer* (Tourism in developing countries). Bonn

Vukonić, B. (1995) *Tourism and religion*. London: Pergamon Press

Wahab, S. E., Crampon, L. J. and Rothfield, L. M. (1976) *Tourism marketing: A destination-oriented programme for the marketing of international tourism*. London: Tourism International Press

Walterspiel, G. (1956) 'Grundlagen der Betriebswirtschaftslehre des Fremdenverkehrsbetriebs' (II) (Fundamentals of microeconomics of tourism enterprises). *Jahrbuch für Fremdenverkehr*, 5(1)

Weaver, D. and Lawton, L. (2000) *Tourism management*. Milton, Queensland: John Wiley and Sons

Wilkinson, P.F. and Pratiwi, W. (1995) 'Gender and tourism in an Indonesian village'. *Annals of Tourism Research* 22(2), 238–99

Witt, S. F. and Martin, C. A. (1989) 'Demand forecasting in tourism recreation'. In C. P. Cooper (ed.), *Progress in tourism recreation and hospitality management*, Vol. 1. London: Belhaven Press, pp. 4–32

Witt, S. and Moutinho, L. (1989) *Tourism marketing and management handbook*. New York: Prentice Hall

Wood, R. E. (1979) 'Tourism and underdevelopment in Southeast Asia'. *Journal of Contemporary Asia*, 9(3), 274–87

Zollinger, W. (1916) *Fremdenverkehr und Zalungsbilanz* (Tourism and balance of payments). Jena

2

Modern mass tourism in China

Some theoretical issues

Julio Aramberri and Yanjun Xie

The quickly awakening dragon

Modern tourism is a recent occurrence in Chinese social life. Even though there is an old tradition of domestic travel within the country, even though great numbers of people moved around during the turmoil created by the Cultural Revolution, mass travel for leisure and vacational purposes started just a few years ago (Richter, 1983; Zhang Qiu et al., 1999).

It was only with the "open door" policies initiated in the late 1970s and in the 1980s that tourism started to grow exponentially (Sofield and Li, 1998). Inbound tourism, both by Chinese living outside the borders of the PRC (the "compatriot" category in China National Tourist Authority's (CNTA) statistics), and by foreigners replaced the formerly tiny domain of travel and hospitality business limited to political, trade and professional purposes (Zhang, 1997). Domestic tourism has grown since then by leaps and bounds at the same time as the Chinese GDP increased 13.7 times between 1978 and 1999 and per capita GDP passed from RMB 379 to RMB 6,705 – nearly 18 times more – in the same period (Zhang Qiu et al., 2003). In 2003 China's GDP reached US$1.4 trillion and per capita GDP went up to US$1,100 (World Bank, 2005).

In spite of such vigorous growth, tourism has only recently been taken up as an academic subject by Chinese scholars and institutions of higher learning (Zhang, 2003b). It should not therefore come as a surprise that theoretical reflection on the many dimensions of tourism in China still finds itself at a burgeoning state (Xiao, 2000). Outside the Chinese academia, the attention paid to China's tourism has not matched its real weight either. A search of the archives of *Annals of Tourism Research* and *Tourism Management*, two of the most influential academic journals for travel and tourism, showed that during the past 30 years their combined articles dealing with China totaled 59, including many short items (Aramberri and Xie, 2003b).

In the past, most academic discussions of China's tourism "have occurred among researchers and writers outside of China, while the opinions and findings of Chinese academics have been hardly heard in the outside world" (Zhang, 2003b, pp. 67–8). For a while, the agenda for tourism research on China was mostly set by foreigners or Chinese scholars working outside the mainland. However, one can see quick changes in the landscape as tourism and travel start to be seen as serious subjects for study and research inside the PRC. A look at the roster of contributors in the two collections on tourism in China edited by Alan Lew and his colleagues (Lew and Yu, 1995; Lew et al., 2003) tells volumes about this trend. The newest book counts a majority of Chinese contributors, even though many of them are active in Western universities. This development is bound to grow in the very near future, as more and more Chinese universities churn out increasing numbers of Master's and PhDs (Du, 2003).

For the time being, however, there are remarkable differences between academic literature written in Chinese and in English, both in the issues studied and in the way they are handled. Most Chinese contributions focus on trend description, while those in English probe deeper into the meaning and impacts of tourism development. With a familiar distinction, one could say that literature in Chinese remains within the advocacy platform or positivist approach, while literature in English looks at China's tourism through a cautionary lens (Jafari, 2001). For the time being, quantitative analysis reigns supreme in China (with well-known exceptions such as Wang, 2000), whereas the debate outside the PRC focuses rather on cultural issues, such as national identities, ethnicity and the relation between tourism and modernity. This chapter will attempt a different approach. Starting with a discussion of the most salient trends in present-day Chinese tourism, it will maintain that they pose some theoretical questions that mainstream Western research usually responds to in the wrong way.

In fact, tourism development in China, if one wants to understand it fully, needs reconceptualization in the light of the ongoing discussion on economic development, especially under the label of globalization (Bhagwati, 2004; Easterly, 2001; Friedman, 2005; North, 1981; Sen, 1999; Stiglitz, 2002). Literature on our own field of tourism (see Part 3) often gives the impression that tourism development might be an autonomous field free of a more general anchorage. Close inspection, though, reveals that this powerful illusion often blurs discussion.

Our task in the following pages will therefore be threefold, to:

*   recall the main historical data of tourism development in China;
*   discuss how they cannot be comfortably reconciled with the main explanatory hypotheses provided by current research on the development of tourism and its underlying general or theoretical assumptions; and
*   propose a different hypothesis to account for the data.

The authors do not claim to have all the answers to the questions raised; they are persuaded, however, that current research will be better served if we change the framework of our enquiries. This makes it mandatory to develop an explanation that will include some general theories of economics and social history.

A truly great leap forward

The detailed description of the bare bones of China's tourism to which so many Chinese scholars have devoted their research efforts has been rewarded with reasonable success. Its main structural aspects are now much better known than they were just a few years ago (Oudiette, 1990). We now consider a short review of its main traits at the inbound, outbound and domestic macro-levels.

Inbound tourism

For the past quarter century, inbound tourism to China has grown at a spectacular rate (Gormsen, 1995a). Figure 2.1 graphically shows the steep ascent between 1990 and 2002. Though the

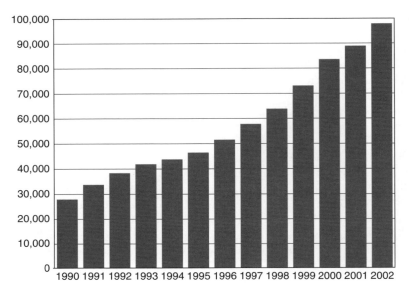

Figure 2.1 China's inbound tourism market 1990–2002 ('000 arrivals)
Source: The Yearbook of China Tourism Statistics (CNTA 2005b)

SARS outbreak in 2003 brought about a decline in the number of foreign visitors, 2004 recovered growth in a spectacular way. The total number of foreign arrivals reached 109 million, growing 19 per cent over 2003. In this way, China has become the fifth ranking tourist destination in the world.

However, the majority of those visitors did not stay overnight in China. In 2004 only 41.8 million did – 37.7 percent of the total. This is possibly accounted for by the fact that proper foreign arrivals are far fewer than those from Hong Kong and Macao. In spite of being seen by the PRC as constituent parts of its nation, those generating markets are not counted as domestic tourists, but as foreign arrivals.

Nearly 85 percent of those 109 million arrivals were Chinese residents in Hong Kong, Macao or Taiwan (Table 2.1). The rest (nearly 17 million in 2004) came from nonChinese markets. A majority (63.4 percent in 2004) originated in Asian nations (Zhang, 2003a). Long-haul visitors have increased from every major source country in the world (CNTA, 2005b).

No matter their ethnic origin, foreign visitors exhibit some similar characteristics: males outnumber females two to one; they are middle-aged and elderly adults; and they concentrate in

Table 2.1 Inbound tourism to China (arrivals in thousands)

	2002	*2003*	*2004*
Total Arrivals	97,908	91,162	109,038
Hong Kong, Macau, Taiwan	84,469	79,759	92,106
Foreigners	13,439	11,403	16,932

Source: CNTA, 2005b; Tourism Forum, 2005

major cities (Beijing, Shanghai, Xi'an and Guilin), although repeaters increasingly travel to medium-sized and interior cities (Shen, 2003).

Overseas visitors create a sizeable flow of foreign currency. In 2000, international receipts reached US$16.2 billion, growing by a factor of 61 since 1978. Four years later, they reached US$25.4 billion with a 57 percent growth. Altogether since the 1978 new economic policies international receipts have seen a nearly 100-fold increase (CNTA, 2005b). The World Travel and Tourism Council (WTTC) estimates that direct and indirect tourist exports in China reached US$34.2 billion in 2002. This amounts to 7.1 percent of all Chinese exports. One does not need to look much further to understand the importance of tourism for the economic policies of the Chinese government (Tisdell and Wen, 1991).

Outbound tourism

A growing section of the Chinese population has the means to travel abroad. However, the number of outbound Chinese travelers does not exactly reflect this fact. Until now foreign travel has been subject to a high degree of administrative intervention that limits the number of countries that can be visited and the amount of money that can be spent abroad, thus holding back its expansion.

However, the outbound market has grown significantly together with the increasing liberalization in travel. From 2000 to 2002 the number of Chinese traveling abroad went from 10 million to 15.7 million (CNTA, 2005a; Tourism Forum, 2005). In 2004 it reached 19 million (Xinghua, 2004; WTTC, 2005). It is expected that by 2020 China will be the fourth largest outbound generating country in the world (Zhang Qiu and Heung, 2001; Zhang Qiu et al., 2003).

Lew (2000) thought it probable that China would soon become a *growth engine* for the whole south and south-east Asian region, a concept that is not just a linguistic utterance, but has the potential to become a theoretical construct apt to be employed in many different contexts.

Domestic tourism

As in most countries, domestic tourism plays a key role in China (Gormsen, 1995b). Table 2.2 synthesizes its development from 1994 to 2000. Except for the 2003 decrease that marked the effects of the SARS crisis, each year has shown considerable growth over the year before. In total, the growth index for domestic tourism in 2004 reached 210 (1994 = 100) with a mean annual increase of 10 percent since the base year.

In their more than 1.1 billion trips, Chinese domestic tourists spent RMB471.1 billion (about 56.8 billion US dollars) revenue, 4.6 times that of 11 years ago (Xinghua, 2005). Rising disposable income due to the quick pace of economic growth plus the introduction of the five-day week and the Golden Weeks have been among the major causes of this impressive expansion (Aramberri and Xie, 2003a; McKahnn, 2001).

The purpose for domestic travel falls into three main categories (Figure 2.2). Although it is difficult to obtain a clear-cut idea, it is possible to suggest that modern mass travel is taking the upper hand, as showed by the great importance of sightseeing and vacationing when they are put together. VFR (visiting friends and relatives) would be closer to older, deferential types of travel, although not completely so. This type of travel also largely reflects the speed of the urbanization process taking place in China. Families in rural areas often receive visits from siblings that migrated to the towns in search of better economic opportunities.

Table 2.2 Domestic tourism in China

Year	Travelers (mn. persons)			Domestic tourism expenditure (bill. Rmb ¥)			Average expenditure per capita		
	Total	Including		Total	Including		Total	Including	
		Travelers from Cities and Towns	Travelers from Rural areas		Travelers from Cities and Towns	Travelers from Rural areas		Travelers from Cities and Towns	Travelers from Rural areas
1994	524.0	204.5	319.4	102.4	84.8	17.5	195.3	414.7	54.9
1995	629.0	245.7	383.3	137.6	114.0	23.6	218.7	464.0	61.5
1996	639.5	256.2	383.3	163.8	136.8	27.0	256.2	534.1	70.5
1997	644.0	259.0	385.0	211.3	155.2	56.1	328.1	599.8	145.7
1998	695.0	250.0	445.0	239.1	155.1	87.6	345.0	607.0	197.0
1999	719.0	284.0	435.0	283.2	174.8	108.4	394.0	614.8	249.5
2000	744.4	329.0	415.0	317.6	223.5	94.0	426.6	678.6	226.6
2001	784.0	374.0	409.0	352.2	265.2	87.1	449.5	708.3	212.7
2002	878.0	385.0	483.0	387.8	284.8	103.0	441.8	739.7	209.1
2003	870.0	351.0	519.0	344.2	240.4	103.8	395.7	684.9	200.0
2004	1102.0	459.0	643.0	471.1	335.9	135.2	427.5	731.8	210.2
2005	1212.0	496.0	716.0	528.6	365.6	163.0	436.1	737.1	227.6

Source: CNTA, 2005a

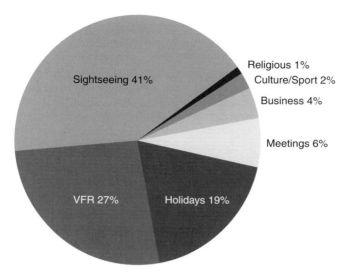

Figure 2.2 Domestic tourism by residents of China by purpose, 2001
Source: The Yearbook of China Tourism Statistics

Conclusion

- Such rapid growth on all counts has not happened without imbalances. A general overview thereof may be found in the special report devoted to tourism in China by Tourism Forum (2005).
- More specifically, government-led investment has bet heavily on the construction of luxury hotels, leaving a gap in affordable accommodation for international and domestic middle income tourists; vocational training lags behind the needs of the new customers (Yu, 2003)
- Travel agencies have engaged in price wars that created much uncertainty as to their financial health; travel guides lack the necessary qualifications in languages and formal education (Wei, 2003; Zhang, 1991).
- The transportation network seems unable to cope with the quick growth in demand (Mak, 2003)
- Serious marketing both in international and domestic markets still has a long way to go (Jeffrey and Xie, 1995; Wang and Ap, 2003).
- Lack of ecological safeguards in many sensitive areas is a big concern (Chu, 1994; Lindberg et al., 2003).

As usual, quick economic and social changes, even in planned economies, proceed in many disorderly, sometimes contradictory ways. However, drawbacks and shortcomings should not push us to lose track of the ball. They happen because the general landscape is changing quite quickly, not the other way around. The blueprint we have just drafted not only takes the observer on a dizzying rollercoaster ride; it also challenges some notions that underlie most of current academic research. First and foremost, it defies the idea that tourism development (and development *tout court*) can happen out of the framework of the global capitalist economy. It seems about time that mainstream research should acknowledge the need to look for a different explanation of tourism development, no matter how painful to its main tenets this may be.

Julio Aramberri and Yanjun Xie

After all, accounting for facts should be the central interest of academic research. That is where we now have to turn our gaze.

A truly great cultural revolution

If you don't have the money, honey, chances are that you will not be traveling. Accordingly, if rapidly increasing numbers of Chinese embark in tourist activities (outbound and domestic), they must have the money – 'disposable income' in academic jargon – to do so. This should come as no surprise when you consider the economic path followed by China since 1979 (Figure 2.3).

> Since 1998, per capital disposable income of urban households and net income of rural households have increased steadily, at respective annual rates of 7.38 per cent and 3.16 per cent. This has boosted domestic consumption.
>
> *(He, 2002, p. 8)*

A sizable part of tourism research has great difficulties grappling with this. Conventional wisdom in tourism research holds some truths self-evident, for example:

- that tourism behavior consists of the interaction between two groups of people, usually known as hosts and guests, locals and visitors, tourers and tourees (van den Berghe, 1994);
- that hosts, locals, and tourees are members of traditional communities usually designated as developing, the South (Crick, 1989, 1995; Graburn, 1989, 2001), or Paradise;
- that guests, visitors, and tourers usually come to those communities from affluent societies, industrialized countries, the North (Dann, 1996a, 1996b);
- that their mutual intercourse is characterized by income inequality, social distance, cultural dissonance, imperialism (MacCannell, 1999, 2001; Nash, 1996), Western hegemony (Appadurai, 1996).

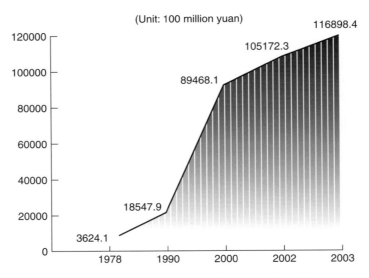

Figure 2.3 Progression of gross domestic product under economic reform
Source: China Internet Information Center, 2005.

This is the theoretical swamp of tourism-as-dependency that limits our capacity to see beyond the horizon. Although it cannot easily be anchored in facts, this misleading hypothesis weighs heavily on most researchers. Even when it is partially faulted in the details, there are few doubts about its general validity (Sofield, 2003). Such a sanguine approach contrasts with the common aspersions meted out to alternative explanations of development like the modernization hypothesis, customarily charged with maintaining that "there [will] be global convergence towards western capitalism" (ibid., p. 41). However, over the past 60 years global convergence towards capitalism (Western and not) has been the most important world trend. Few policy makers still believe that there are credible alternatives to it.

Current mainstream preconceptions that hark back to the dependency template in tourism research should accordingly be taken with a pinch of salt. As shown by the complex system of traditional Indian travel (Singh, 2004), there are millions of not so affluent travelers in that country, as is conceivably the case in many other developing societies as well. If, additionally, we highlight the impressive expansion of modern domestic tourism, it is difficult to avoid the conclusion that our scholarly intuitions need to be reinvented. Tourism is not only the preserve of affluent travelers from developed countries, but also includes increasing numbers in many developing societies. As noted, China is a case in point.

These trends do not fit the dependency template. When it comes to mundane concerns, such as the evolution of the global economy, dependency theories have a dismal predictive record. They were mostly formulated during the 1970s and early 1980s, when the 1950s' economic boom of the central capitalist countries had come to a relative standstill reviving expectations of its systemic demise. As faithful Marxists, dependency theorists customarily announced the final crisis of capitalism every few hours. Late capitalism, neo-imperialism, or post-colonialism was a system in crisis, probably a terminal one. Capitalist development had become a theoretical oxymoron. Dependency theorists saw it as a closed structure where the unevenness between core and periphery was irreversible and growing fast. Baran (1968), for one, explained that Japan's economic success since the Meiji era had been the only possible exception. The country's lack of coveted natural resources kept the imperial powers at bay. Left to itself, Japan was able to grow, but no other country in the periphery would be given a similar chance.

By the time of Baran's prophecy, however, South Korea was already on its way to become a second exception, quickly relayed by Taiwan, Singapore, Hong Kong and Thailand. Lately, China (followed by India) is treading in the same footsteps. The Chinese economy is now the sixth largest in the world with a GDP of US$1.4 trillion (Economist, 2011) and, according to some forecasts, it will surpass the US as world producer number one by mid-century. The present US debate on the outsourcing of jobs to China and India clearly attests to this changed state of affairs, showing at the same time that globalization works in more complicated ways than forecast by friend or foe.

Increased growth also accounts for changing social structures. Scholars as well as travelers to China will notice that massive social changes are taking place. Above all, a tidal wave of migration from the countryside has flooded the cities, which in turn grow exponentially. Migrants aim at participation in the expanding affluence, as urbanites often take the best part of the newly created riches. At present, China's urban population accounts for 31 percent of the total, but it is expected to rise to 60 percent within the next 20 years (Li, 2001).

Together with urbanization, consumption standards have risen, mostly in big towns.

> Consumers in China today are spending their money on housing, transportation, telecommunications, medical and health care, culture, education and entertainment, leisure and tourism. This is remarkable in that not so long ago basic subsistence was a major concern

of many citizens. As expenses for food, clothing and basic necessities dropped, the Engel coefficient (the proportion of food expenses to total consumer spending) of urban residents decreased from 57.5 percent in 1978 to 37.1 percent in 2002; and that of rural residents dropped from 67.7 percent to 45.6 percent.

(People's Daily, 2005, p. 1)

For the urbanites a good part of that growing income is spent in tourism. Domestic tourism expenditures in China have reached 14 percent of disposable income in urban households (Gu and Liu, 2004).

Urbanization, new consumption patterns and middle-class expansion usually go hand in hand. What are the dimensions of the Chinese middle classes? A local study put them at 19 percent of the population in 2001 – around 250 million (Lu, 2002). They are mostly defined in terms of assets, with a range of RMB 150,000–300,000 (US$18,137–36,275) being at its core. Similar figures have been quoted by BNP Paribas-Peregrine and the Chinese National Bureau of Statistics (Xin, 2004).

Chinese middle classes are made up of leading state and public sector cadres; high and mid-level managers in large and medium-sized enterprises; private entrepreneurs; highly qualified professional, scientific and technical workers; some clerical personnel; and some self-employed. Their growth is seen by the CASS report (Lu, 2002) as evidence that Chinese society is increasingly shaping as an olive, unlike the former pyramidal structure of farmers, workers and intellectuals. The study forecasts that the middle classes will account for 40 percent of the population by 2020.

The CASS report (Lu, 2002) has met some degree of skepticism rooted above all in a discussion of its economics. In 2002 Chinese mean disposable income per person reached RMB 4,520 (US$525) with RMB 8,500 (US$1,050) per city dweller. The top 20 percent of the urbanites (around 100 million people) make an average RMB 15,380 (US$1,900). All of them, therefore, are far from the US$5,000 threshold considered the take-off point for discretionary spending and middle-class lifestyles (Economist, 2011). Others stress the persistent levels of extreme poverty in the country and the low living standards of the peasantry as a whole. Another reason for skepticism is the uneven economic development between coastal, urban eastern China and the backward western part of the country (see an adaptation of this argument to tourism development in Wang, 2004).

However, this array of different criticisms may overreach. Dollar comparisons reflect wide swings in purchasing power, as shown by the Big Mac Index created by *The Economist*, and the persistence of poverty should not obscure the fact that it happens against a background of increasing social differentiation that makes it less perceivable. Indeed it is accompanied by a rise in inequality. Gu and Liu (2004) have highlighted that in China the Gini coefficient has seen a tenfold increase between 1991 and 2000. But, for many Chinese, it is a welcome sign of the passing away of the previous era where equality meant generalized want.

There is a theoretical puzzle here. On one hand, since 1950, China has claimed to have broken free from the chain of capitalist development. Even today, China defines herself as a non capitalist society with a planned economy. On the other, the capitalist sector (also known as market social economy) has increasing economic clout. How can we account for this turn of events?

One possible line of explanation (Oakes, 1995, 1998) harks back once again to dependency. In this view, two main versions of modernity compete to steer China's economy. In the first, expressed during the years of Maoist rule, modernity was to be reached as an alternative to the Western model within the national framework of state socialism. The second, the "open door" policies of the post-Mao era, has brought a new form of modernity that may be defined as the modernism of underdevelopment. Oakes does not specify much about the features of this latter strategy, but he points to Hong Kong and Taiwan as the development models preferred by Asian transnational capitalism. Both competing versions of modernity, in his view, provide false roadmaps, and both coincide in promoting China through an equally essentialist strategy. The Maoist path stressed the uniqueness of socialist China, while the second narrative uses a fantasized notion of Chinese tradition as the core for a flexible accumulation of capital. Ever since its inclusion in China's seventh Five Year Plan (1985–90), tourism development has become so central a part of the second strategy that, if we believe Oakes, Chinese theme parks have become the metaphor through which the country is invited to represent itself. Taking his cue from tourist development in a rural and impoverished area of Guizhou he portends that the tourism industry is appropriating some villages to turn them into life-size theme parks to convey "a landscape of 'calming certainty' that legitimizes both the state's and capital's narratives of Chinese modernity" (Oakes, 1998, p. 57).

It is difficult to accept this view. It lionizes some economically minor facts such as the expansion of theme parks in China into a key component of macro socio-economic strategies. Additionally, it does not suggest what stuff non-essentialist development strategies are made of, let alone how they might be implemented. The real issue, however, lies at a deeper level. In today's China there are no two general narratives or strategies vying to steer her development. What we have seen since 1978 is nothing less than the complete discredit and rejection of one of them. Maoist economics based on modernization – through a proletarian revolution with a rural engine; country vs. towns; the peasant-soldier as role model; banning profit; nonstop shake-ups of the state apparatus; and other wishful thinking – have lost the credibility they once held. The experiences of the Great Leap Forward and the Great Proletarian Cultural Revolution led the country up a blind alley, turning its economy into a shambles. Deng and his successors came to the realization that, no matter what the dependency theorists might claim, even a country as great as China could not live with its back to the global (capitalist) economy. The "open door" policies drew the necessary consequences.

The new road may be essentialist, but it is not yet possible to determine. At any rate, until now it has delivered a relative degree of material well-being unknown in China since the T'ang dynasty, when the country was far ahead of the rest of the world.

A different look

Perhaps there is another way to look at the puzzle. Capitalism may not be as transient a system as some people expected and still expect it to be. Some French critics may have it right when they speak somewhat despairingly of the domination of the *pensée unique*, another name for the emergence of global capitalism. Far from being in its final stages, it seems that, at least for the foreseeable future, capitalism will be as much of a permanent fact (Desai, 2002) as the Neolithic agricultural revolution has been for centuries. You may or may not like it, but it will not go away.

It is perhaps not easy to see things this way after all the fog created by modern socialist revolutions. Although this is not the place to discuss them in detail, it looks more and more that instead of skipping capitalism they simply delayed its full expansion to later embrace it in an accelerated way. This has been the process in the former Soviet Union, in China, in Vietnam. Gramsci once spoke of the October Revolution as a revolution against *Das Kapital*. He was not far off the mark. While Marx had no doubts that the dissolution of capitalism would start when and where it would have reached its most complete development, modern socialist revolutions happened in traditional, agrarian societies where capitalism was at a bourgeoning state.

It has been suggested (Skocpol, 1979) that, in spite of the socialist labels their leading elites pinned on themselves, those revolutions followed different ways to the accumulation of capital. The notion had already been circulated at the dawn of the Russian revolution by some Bolsheviks (Bukharin and Preobrazhenskii, 1966; Preobrazhenskii, 1965). With different jargon their thesis may be expressed in the following way: what Marx called primitive capitalist accumulation was not bound to follow the British and American template. Under different historical circumstances, the initial push for the transition of agrarian societies to capitalism might adopt unexpected turns. Where there was not a fully fledged entrepreneurial class to generate the big investments needed and to create the new institutional framework, other social agents would take its place. Bismarckian Germany and Meiji Japan opened the way with their model of a mixed economy with heavy participation by their public bureaucracies and their armies (Skocpol, 1994). Revolutionary Russia and China both had to improvise on the ruins of the old social order; collectivist institutions under the leadership of their communist parties were charged with the task of paving the way to primitive accumulation and successfully forced the peasantry to foot the bill for industrialization. Once this goal was achieved, both societies faced a typically capitalist problem – the gap between productive potential and consumption or how to grow further when consumers have very limited purchasing power. A similar quandary was solved with a turn to consumer-led economy in the US (aka Fordism) at the turn of the twentieth century. When in the 1980s collectivism had clearly run its course in Russia and in China, new formulas had to be found to continue expansion, formulas which were different in each country; we will not focus on how their command economies were dismantled. Our aim is just to stop at highlighting the inner logic of the impressive growth of consumption (including tourist consumption and development) in China that explains the process in a better way than dependency theories can.

One final issue has to be addressed. Critics of mass societies and mass consumption underline that these have been unable to make inequality disappear, and they show that it grows everywhere global capitalism holds sway. To some extent this is a truism, like criticizing the Pope for believing in God. Under capitalism, as Desai (2002, p. 297) translates from Adam Smith, "inequality is the spur to the growth of productivity," productivity the spur to growing disposable income, and disposable income the spur to, among other things, an increase of tourism.

Whether this should be seen as good or bad is an open question that we do not try to address. In our view, the really intriguing problem is *how*, and above all, *why* consumer-led capitalism, for all its undeniable inequalities, is seen as a legitimate way of producing and distributing needed goods and services for increasing millions of people.

Some Foucauldian researchers point to normalization and panopticon-like surveillance as the key for this ample social consensus in post-revolutionary societies (Foucault, 1995; Haugaard, 2002; Ransom, 1997). We disagree. In our view two reasons are considerably more central. The first has to do with the experiences of the recent past. No primitive accumulation proceeds smoothly; the rule is exactly the opposite. Once it is over, few people want to go back to the previous revolutionary excitement and its revolutionary exactions.

The second has to do with an old fact well know to sociologists – relative deprivation (Blau, 1986; Riskin et al., 2001; Tilly, 1996). Most Chinese consumers may not have yet the disposable income to buy as many big ticket items as Europeans or Americans or more affluent Chinese do. However, their consumption has definitely increased relative to that of the older generation. Great numbers experience better living conditions. Supermarkets, domestic labor saving devices, affordable and fashionable clothing, air-conditioners, better transportation systems, and, for many, new cars and new homes have become part of everyday life. Vacations are also spreading fast.

What about those lagging behind? For the time being they seem to think that a more comfortable life can also be their lot. This is not a tangible reward. In fact, many will not make it. Relative deprivation, however, works in many ways. It may be a powerful source of revolt, as usually happens when a majority of people feel that the roads to personal and collective improvement are blocked. But it can also act as a prod for social cohesion. When you see that your neighbors prosper, you readily feel that something similar may happen in your case. Equality in the past often meant abysmal poverty for all; today relative inequality opens the way to upward mobility. What might prevent you from sharing in the bounty if you or your siblings happen to obtain the skills demanded by the new economy?

Mass tourism plays a modest though no less important part in the legitimation of consumer-led capitalism. The billion plus domestic and outbound Chinese travelers in 2004 and 2005 do not seem to have many qualms about the system that made their trips possible. Perhaps one day their attitudes, expectations and reasons will be understood by the academic community in a non-judgmental way. On our side, we are convinced it is about time to start doing so.

References

Appadurai, A. (1996) *Modernity at large: Cultural dimensions of globalization*. Minneapolis, MN: University of Minnesota Press

Aramberri, J. and Xie, Y. (2003a) 'Off the beaten theoretical track: Domestic tourism in China'. *Tourism Recreation Research*, 28(1), 2

—— (2003b) 'Zhongguo Lvyou Yanjiu de Duowei Shiye: Dui Guonei yu Guowai Xiangguang Wenxian de Pingshu' (Multi-vision on Chinese tourism research: Comment on the domestic and foreign relevant literature). *Tourism Tribune*, 6, 14–20

Baran, P. A. (1968) *The political economy of growth* (2nd edn). New York: Monthly Review Press

Bhagwati, J. N. (2004) *In defense of globalization*. New York: Oxford University Press

Blau, P. M. (1986) *Exchange and power in social life*. New York: J. Wiley

Bukharin, N. I. and Preobrazhenskii, E. A. (1966) *The ABC of communism: A popular explanation of the program of the Communist Party of Russia*. Ann Arbor, MI: The University of Michigan Press

China Internet Information Center (2005) Overview. Retrieved on 15 November 2011, from http://www.china.org.cn/english/features/china2004/107000.htm

Chu, Y. (1994) 'Evaluation of sightseeing areas in China'. *Annals of Tourism Research*, 21(4), 837–39.

CNTA (2005a) 'Facts and figures: Outbound tourism'. China National Tourist Authority. Retrieved 20 November 2011, from http://en.cnta.gov.cn/html/2008-11/2008-11-9-21-40-54934.html

—— (2005b) 'China Inbound Travel Statistics for 2004'. China National Tourist Authority. Retrieved on 20 November 2011, from http://www.cnta.gov.cn/html/2008-6/2008-6-2-21-28-45-89.html; http://www.cnta.gov.cn/html/2008-6/2008-6-2-21-28-44-72.html; http://www.cnta.gov.cn/html/2008-6/2008-6-2-21-28-43-61.html

Crick, M. (1989) 'Representations of international tourism in the social sciences: Sun, sex, sights, savings and servility'. *Annual Review of Anthropology*, 18, 307–44

—— (1995) 'The anthropologist as tourist: An identity in question'. In M. F. Lanfant, J. B. Allcock and E. M. Bruner (eds) *International tourism: Identity and change*. London: Sage Publications, pp. 205–23

Dann, G. M. S. (1996a) 'Tourists' images of a destination: An alternative analysis'. *Journal of Travel and Tourism Marketing*, 5(1/2), 41–55

—— (1996b) 'The people of tourist brochures'. In T. Selwyn (ed.) *The tourist image: Myths and myth making in tourism*. Chichester: John Wiley and Sons, pp. 61–82

Desai, M. (2002) *Marx's revenge: The resurgence of capitalism and the death of statist socialism*. London: Verso

Du, J. (2003) 'Reforms and development of higher tourism education in China'. *Journal of Teaching in Travel and Tourism*, 3(1), 103–13

Easterly, W. R. (2001) *The elusive quest for growth: Economists' adventures and misadventures in the tropics*. Cambridge, MA: The MIT Press

Economist (2011) 'Currency comparisons, to go'. *The Economist*. Retrieved 5 December 2011, from http://www.economist.com/blogs/dailychart/2011/07/big-mac-index

Foucault, M. (1995) *Discipline and punish: The birth of the prison* (2nd edn). New York: Vintage Books

Friedman, B. M. (2005) *The moral consequences of economic growth*. New York: Knopf

Gormsen, E. (1995a) 'International tourism in China: Its organization and socio-economic impact'. In A. A. Lew and L. Yu (eds) *Tourism in China: Geographic, political, and economic perspectives*. Boulder, CO: Westview Press, pp. 63–88

—— (1995b) 'Travel behavior and the impacts of domestic tourism in China'. In A. A. Lew and L. Yu (eds) *Tourism in China: Geographic, political, and economic perspectives*. Boulder, CO: Westview Press, pp. 131–40

Graburn, N. H. H. (1989) 'Tourism: The sacred journey'. In V. L. Smith (ed.) *Hosts and guests: The anthropology of tourism* (2nd edn). Philadelphia: University of Pennsylvania Press, pp. 21–36

—— (2001) 'Secular ritual: A general theory of tourism'. In V. L. Smith and M. Brent (eds) *Hosts and guests revisited: Tourism issues of the 21st century*. New York: Cognizant Communication Co., pp. 42–50

Gu, H. and Liu, D. (2004) 'The relationship between resident income and domestic tourism in China'. *Tourism Recreation Research*, 29(2), 25–33.

Haugaard, M. (2002) *Power: A reader*. Manchester: Manchester University Press

He, G. (2002) 'China's economic restructuring and banking reform'. Yomiuri International Economic Society (eds) *Proceedings of the 11th Symposium by IIMA: Emerging China and the Asian economy in the coming decade*, pp. 6–14. Retrieved 15 November 2011, from http://www.iima.or.jp/pdf/paper12e.pdf

Jafari, J. (2001) 'The scientification of tourism'. In V. L. Smith and M. Brent (eds) *Hosts and guests revisited: Tourism issues of the 21st century*. New York: Cognizant Communication Co., pp. 28–41

Jeffrey, D. and Xie, Y. (1995) 'The UK market for tourism in China'. *Annals of Tourism Research*, 22(4), 857–76

Lew, A. A. (2000) 'China: A growth engine for Asian tourism'. In C. M. Hall and S. Page (eds) *Tourism in South and Southeast Asia: Issues and cases*. Oxford: Butterworth-Heinemann, pp. 268–85

Lew, A. A. and Yu, L. (eds) (1995) *Tourism in China: Geographic, political, and economic perspectives*. Boulder, CO: Westview Press

Lew, A. A., Yu, L., Ap, J. and Zhang, G. (eds) (2003) *Tourism in China*. New York: Haworth Hospitality Press

Li, H. (2001) 'China's urbanization rate to reach 60% in 20 years'. *People's Daily Online*, 17 May. Retrieved 11 November 2011, from http://english.peopledaily.com.cn/english/200105/17/eng20010517_70205.html

Lindberg, K., Tisdell, C. and Xue, D. (2003) 'Ecotourism in China's nature reserves'. In A. A. Lew, L. Yu, J. Ap and G. Zhang (eds) *Tourism in China*. New York: Haworth Hospitality Press, pp. 103–28

Lu, X. (2002) *Dangdai Zhongguo Shehui Jieceng Yanjiu Baogao* (A Report on the Study of Contemporary China's Social Strata). Beijing: Shehui Kexue Wenxian Chubanshe (Social Sciences Literature Press)

MacCannell, D. (1999) *The tourist: A new theory of the leisure class* (3rd edn). Berkeley, CA: University of California Press

—— (2001) 'The commodification of culture'. In V. L. Smith and M. Brent (eds) *Hosts and guests revisited: Tourism issues of the 21st century*. New York: Cognizant Communication Co., pp. 380–90

McKahnn, C. F. (2001) 'The good, the bad and the ugly: Observations and reflections on tourism development in Lijiang, China'. In C. B. Tan, S. C. H. Cheung and Y. Hui (eds) *Tourism, anthropology and China: In memory of Professor Wang Zhusheng*. Bangkok: White Lotus Press, pp. 147–66

Mak, B. (2003) 'China's tourist transportation: Air, land and water'. In A. A. Lew, L. Yu, J. Ap and G. Zhang (eds) *Tourism in China*. New York: Haworth Hospitality Press, pp. 165–94

Nash, D. (1996) *Anthropology of tourism*. Kidlington: Pergamon

North, D. C. (1981) *Structure and change in economic history*. New York: Norton

Oakes, T. (1998) *Tourism and modernity in China*. New York: Routledge

Oakes, T. S. (1995) 'Tourism in Guizhou: The legacy of internal colonialism'. In A. A. Lew and L. Yu (eds) *Tourism in China: Geographic, political, and economic perspectives*. Boulder, CO: Westview Press, pp. 203–22

Oudiette, V. (1990) 'International tourism in China'. *Annals of Tourism Research*, 17(1), 123–32

People's Daily (2005) 'Consumption'. *People's Daily*. Retrieved 15 November 2011, from http://english.people.com.cn/data/China_in_brief/Lifestyle/Consumption.html

Preobrazhenskii, E. (1965)[1928] *The new economics*, trans. B. Pearce. Oxford: Clarendon Press.

Ransom, J. S. (1997) *Foucault's discipline: The politics of subjectivity*. Durham, NC: Duke University Press

Richter, L. K. (1983) 'Political implications of Chinese tourism policy'. *Annals of Tourism Research*, 10(3), 395–413

Riskin, C., Zhao, R. and Li, S. (eds) (2001) *China's retreat from equality: Income distribution and economic transition*. Armonk, NY: M. E. Sharpe

Sen, A. K. (1999) *Development as freedom*. New York: Oxford University Press

Shen, X. (2003) 'Short- and long-haul international tourists to China'. In A. A. Lew, L. Yu, J. Ap and G. Zhang (eds) *Tourism in China*. New York: Haworth Hospitality Press, pp. 237–62

Singh, S. (2004) 'India's domestic tourism: Chaos/crisis/challenge?'. *Tourism Recreation Research*, 29(2), 35–46

Skocpol, T. (1979) *States and social revolutions: A comparative analysis of France, Russia, and China*. Cambridge: Cambridge University Press

—— (1994) *Social revolutions in the modern world*. Cambridge: Cambridge University Press.

Sofield, T. H. B. (2003) *Empowerment for sustainable tourism development*. Amsterdam: Pergamon

Sofield, T. H. B. and Li, F. M. S. (1998) 'Tourism development and cultural policies in China'. *Annals of Tourism Research*, 25(2), 362–92

Stiglitz, J. E. (2002) *Globalization and its discontents*. New York: W. W. Norton

Tilly, C. (ed.) (1996) *Citizenship, identity and social history*. Cambridge: Cambridge University Press

Tisdell, C. and Wen, J. (1991) 'Foreign tourism as an element in PR China's economic development strategy'. *Tourism Management*, 12(1), 55–67

Tourism Forum (2005) 'The impact of travel and tourism on jobs and the economy: China and China Hong Kong SAR'. Retrieved 21 November 2011, from http://www.tourismforum.scb.se/papers/PapersSelected/TSA/Paper1WTTC/China_Hong_Kong.pdf

van den Berghe, P. L. (1994) *The quest for the other: Ethnic tourism in San Cristobal, Mexico*. Seattle, WA: University of Washington Press

Wang, N. (2000) *Tourism and modernity: A sociological analysis*. New York: Pergamon

—— (2004) 'The rise of touristic consumerism in urban China'. *Tourism Recreation Research*, 29(2), 47–58

Wang, S. and Ap, J. (2003) 'Tourism marketing in the People's Republic of China'. In A. A. Lew, L. Yu, J. Ap and G. Zhang (eds) *Tourism in China*. New York: Haworth Hospitality Press, pp. 217–36

Wei, Q. (2003) 'Travel agencies in China at the turn of the millennium'. In A. A. Lew, L. Yu, J. Ap and G. Zhang (eds) *Tourism in China*. New York: Haworth Hospitality Press, pp. 143–64

World Bank (2005) 'China at a glance'. World Bank. Retrieved 20 November 2011, from http://devdata.worldbank.org/AAG/chn_aag.pdf

WTTC (World Trade and Tourism Council) (2005) 'Competition monitor: Human tourism: International tourist departures'. Retrieved 24 April 2005, from http://wttc.org/2004tsa/frameset2a.htm

Xiao, H. (2000) 'China's tourism education into the 21st century'. *Annals of Tourism Research*, 27(4), 1052–5.

Xin, Z. (2004) 'Dissecting China's "Middle Class"'. *China Daily*, 27 October. Retrieved 5 December 2011, from http://www.chinadaily.com.cn/english/doc/200410/27/content_386060.htm

Xinghua (2004) *Chinese outbound travel soars 63.7%*. Xinghua News Agency, 17 September. Retrieved 11 November 2011, from http://www.china.org.cn/english/2004/Sep/107371.htm

—— (2005) *Chinese domestic tourism income quadruples in ten years*. Xinghua News Agency, 18 April. Retrieved 15 April 2011, from http://www.china.org.cn/english/travel/126130.htm

Yu, L. (2003) 'Critical issues in China's hotel industry'. In A. A. Lew, L. Yu, J. Ap and G. Zhang (eds) *Tourism in China*. New York: Haworth Hospitality Press, pp. 129–42

Zhang Qiu, H. and Heung, V. C. S. (2001) 'The emergence of the mainland Chinese outbound travel market and its implications for tourism marketing'. *Journal of Vacation Marketing*, 8(1), 7–12

Zhang Qiu, H., Chong, K. and Ap, J. (1999) 'An analysis of tourism policy development in modern China'. *Tourism Management*, 20(4), 471–85

Zhang Qiu, H., Jenkins, C. L. and Qu, H. (2003) 'Mainland Chinese outbound travel to Hong Kong and its implications'. In A. A. Lew, L. Yu, J. Ap and G. Zhang (eds) *Tourism in China*. New York: Haworth Hospitality Press, pp. 277–96

Zhang, G. (2003a) 'China's tourism since 1978: Policies, experiences and lessons learned'. In A. A. Lew, L. Yu, J. Ap and G. Zhang (eds) *Tourism in China*. New York: Haworth Hospitality Press, pp. 13–34

—— (2003b) 'Tourism research in China'. In A. A. Lew, L. Yu, J. Ap and G. Zhang (eds) *Tourism in China*. New York: Haworth Hospitality Press, pp. 67–82

Zhang, L. (1991) 'China's travel agency industry'. *Tourism Management*, 12(4), 360–62

Zhang, W. (1997) 'China's domestic tourism: Impetus, development and trends'. *Tourism Management*, 18(8), 565–71

3

Remodelling the language of tourism*

From monologue to dialogue and trialogue

Graham M. S. Dann

Introduction: changes that have occurred within tourism and the societies from which it is generated

When *The Language of Tourism* first appeared in the mid-1990s (Dann, 1996) much of the West, whence the majority of international tourism originated, was still arguably under the political influence of a prevailing modernist ideology. Whether Republican or Democrat, Conservative or Labour, Christian Democrat or Communist, many of these tourism-generating societies were rationally organised along managerial lines. Targets were typically set for health, education, the economy, and so on, to the extent that almost every facet of human existence became centralised under the overarching power of the state or, in the case of the European Union, the super-state. In spite of the lip service rhetoric of a 'me too' individualism associated with Thatcherism and Reaganomics, and a few cosmetic changes in partisan thinking, such a top-down monological situation in some respects continues today.

Tourism, too, tended to be structured in a similar modernist fashion. Following its initial emergence in the wake of the supreme rationalist project of the Industrial Revolution, it became a logical escape valve for workers who were transported to selected destinations in trains travelling in straight lines as the shortest distance between two points. It was thus no coincidence to find Thomas Cook appearing at this juncture providing all inclusive excursion tours for the proletariat. Nor was it surprising to discover that his underpinning modernist ideology continued as a logo-centric legacy (Wang, 2000) for over a century in the package tour, holiday camp and Club Méditerranée under the pretext of the greater democratisation of tourism. Block booking, charter flights, standardised all-inclusive resorts, McDonaldization (Ritzer, 1993) and Disneyfication (Fjellman, 1992) were the order of the day, and their orders were in turn issued by tour operators and their uniformed holiday representatives.

Under such a dictatorial system, mass tourism proliferated, and with it came its own form of monological communication (Dann, 2001a). Here there was a unilateral, unidirectional conveying of messages from a usually anonymous transmitter, thought to possess a monopoly on

---

* A fuller, more recent version of this chapter is due to appear as a paper in a special issue of the Journal *Pasos*. Reciprocal editorial permissions have been granted.

truth, to a correspondingly faceless and homogeneous public, through a variety of publicity vehicles at every stage of the vacation experience (pre-trip, on-trip and post-trip). There was precious little turn taking or turn signalling (as would be evident in a discussion or telephone conversation, for example), hardly any feedback, and scant interaction between sender and receiver. It was thus an asymmetrical process in which a persuader provided selective information for viewers or listeners cast in the passive mode of persons with enviable wants (rather than needs). It was a euphoric, ideologically laden, cliché ridden text (Dann, 2001b), whose prophetic utterances became tautologically fulfilled. Just as touristic interactions could be considered as associations of distrust between those with wealth encountering those with knowledge (van den Berghe, 1994), once a third player entered the scene – the tourism industry – both power and affluence became concentrated in its hands. It was presumably for this reason that Hollinshead and Jamal (2001, p. 64) spoke of tourism as bolstering 'restrictive, monological and heavily capitalised worldviews which tend[ed] to help concretise pseudo-colonialist, urban-industrial and pungently North-Atlantic/Judaeo-Christian certitudes upon alterity'.

Whatever the medium, written, auditory, visual or a combination of them, the same monological quality was in evidence. Depending on the channel, one party wrote, spoke or performed; the other read, listened or observed.

In those days, many a church was (and many still are) architecturally designed for one-way communication, where the passive congregation was obliged to heed the infallible words of the preacher issuing downwards from the pulpit without any real possibility of interruption or disagreement. So, too, were the *ex cathedra* pronouncements of tourism imparted from on high without fear of challenge, safe in the knowledge that there was a negligible chance of the addressee answering back.

However, there are many signs on the horizon that such a monological situation has begun to change, if indeed it has not partially occurred already. The modernist project, while still mainly the preserve of politicians, has given way to a post-modern ethos that rejects authoritarianism and distinctions based on hierarchies of class, gender and age. In this topsy-turvy, de-differentiated world where previous verticality is replaced by horizontal egalitarianism, the proverbial man-in-the-street is at last able to have his say. In the UK, for example, the television consumer programme *Watchdog* has been running for over 30 years (BBC, 2005a), and elsewhere on the network there are now, more than ever, in programmes such as *Points of View* and *Newswatch*, greater opportunities for on-air viewer feedback to television news and other programmes, with simultaneous responses from BBC producers (BBC, 2005b).

Within the past 15 years or so the Internet, too, has become a key location for the voice of consumers to be heard. Companies, in turn, have the opportunity of responding to dissatisfied clients, and the latter can provide additional feedback as to how their complaints have been addressed. All this verbal to-ing and fro-ing is moreover conducted in the public domain, so that those similarly afflicted can join in with accounts of their own related experiences.

As regards tourism and how it is handled by television can be gauged from the previously mentioned *Watchdog* programme (BBC, 2005a). Here issues are often taken up on behalf of vacationers and those responsible (e.g. tour operators, airlines) are confronted on a live show as to the non-fulfilment of their promises. Typically, matters such as the inadequate pitch of plane seats, the misrepresentation of a hotel by a brochure, unanticipated construction work at a resort, food poisoning, are highlighted. Often these vignettes of disappointment are accompanied by video coverage of the alleged service failures with voiceovers by the aggrieved parties. TV holiday shows, too, incorporate some of this *schadenfreude* material into their popular transmissions, again using video footage supplied by the customer. Indeed, tourists are positively encouraged to take camcorders and cameras with them on their trips (sometimes the equipment is supplied by the television station), if only to provide photographic evidence of their disenchantment.

In relation to the Internet, there are now several avenues for word-of-mouth to assume the electronic features of Word-of-Web (or perhaps, more appropriately, word-of-mouse). Here the voice of satisfaction (word-of-wish) can be registered, as also that of dissatisfaction (word-of-whinge). The channels for such communication are also quite varied, ranging from e-guidebooks (e.g. the chat-rooms provided by the likes of Lonely Planet, n.d., and Rough Guides, n.d.) to general (e.g. Planet Feedback, n.d.) or specific (e.g. Holiday Travel Watch, n.d., Holiday Complaints, n.d.) complaint sites that implicitly or explicitly include holidays in their list of grudges. There are additionally plenty of online locations that feature travel diaries or travel 'blogs' (a subset of frequently updated accounts, e.g. business blogs, political blogs) wherein individuals with similar interests communicate with one another. In this instance, the 'travel(bl)og' is a sort of amateur, interpersonal e-travelogue (using such sites as My Trip Journal, n.d., Travel Pod, n.d., and IgoUgo, n.d.), which, like its print media counterpart, can promote or demote. Since all these interactive channels provide collective evidence of greater democratisation of the language of tourism, surely the time is right for providing updated models that incorporate the change from one-way to two-way and three-way communication between the tourist industry, the tourist and the touree (a term for local inhabitants coined by van den Berghe, 1994).

At this point, it should also be mentioned that, just as such a framework can help fill a theoretical void, so too can it establish an agenda for future empirical investigations. Indeed, it can act as a storehouse for recent growing evidence that supports the contention that the adequate responses of businesses (including travel companies) to customer grievances can achieve higher levels of satisfaction than if there were no complaint in the first place. It can also encourage recent contributions (e.g. Lee and Hu, 2004; Schoefer and Ennew, 2004; Shea et al., 2004), to domains where there is otherwise little research and extend related inquiries to areas where even less attention has been paid. Here one thinks of the vast amounts of unanalysed emails and text messages that tourists send to one another or which they transmit to potential tourists in the form of friends and relatives.

Remodelling the language of tourism

In order to become aware of these opportunities for exploring dialogue and trialogue in 'the language of tourism', as also to establish their theoretical underpinning, it is necessary to provide a series of three models that encapsulates the transition from monologue to more open forms of communication.

Model 1: the language of tourism as monologue

It can be seen from Table 3.1 that there are nine instances of monological communication. They are predicated on three types of participant speaking to themselves and each other singly and without response or significant feedback. Hence the direction of such messages is top-down from sender (arranged horizontally) to addressee (positioned vertically). Examples of each type of discourse contained in the nine possible cells are intended as illustrations that are neither exhaustive nor comprehensive. A brief cell-by-cell commentary follows, one that describes the various situations. The limitations of each implicitly suggest the potential for change.

Cell 1 is where the industry talks to itself. An instance of this type of discourse is in-house training. Here the emphasis is on information and how facts are passed down from management

Table 3.1 The language of tourism as monologue

Addressee	Sender		
	Industry	Tourists	Tourees
INDUSTRY	(1) In-house training sessions; Standardised tourism degree programmes	(2) Complaints; Guest questionnaires; Servqual inquiries	(3) Local print media; Local radio and television
TOURISTS	(4) Traditional media of the language of tourism: e.g., brochures, guidebooks, travelogues	(5) Lectures; Slide shows	(6) Unofficial notices; Graffiti
TOUREES	(7) A priori surveys	(8) Orders	(9) Instructions

gurus having the necessary knowledge and experience to novices lacking such essential require-ments. Teaching and research programmes standardised by the likes of the World Tourism Organisation and designed for tourism students at the graduate and undergraduate levels would also fall into this category.

An example of the industry addressing tourees in a similar monological fashion (cell 7) is the a priori survey. Here a checklist of industry identified, close-ended questions is imposed on respondents without giving them the opportunity to reply in their own open-ended, self-defined terms to issues that they, rather than the researchers, consider to be important.

However, it is cell 4 (where the industry speaks to tourists) that comprises the most familiar and frequent occurrences of monologue. Here the traditional media of 'the language of tourism' are employed (i.e. print, audio and visual media, either singly or in combination) without any feedback from the targeted audience. Brochures, for example, direct verbal and pictorial mes-sages to potential tourists – images that are predominantly supply-driven and featuring the pull factor attributes of destinations selected by tour operators. Such one-way communication, which can also be found in advertisements, travelogues, videos, etc., is facilitated by other allied properties of 'the language of tourism' – tautology, euphoria, sender anonymity and the assump-tion of receiver homogeneity (Dann, 1996). All such monologue forms part and parcel of the modernist project.

An example of tourist-industry monological communication (cell 2) lies in the domain of non-publicised complaints where visitors vent their feelings orally upon tourism personnel working in various sectors of the industry ranging from transportation to entertainment and hospitality, without allowing significant response to remedy the situation. Replies to hotel guest questionnaires where there is no industry feedback to the visitor represent the written analogue to this type of unilateral communication, as are the responses to those perceived service quality ("servqual") inquiries (Weiermair and Fuchs, 1999) that purport to measure differences between visitor expectation and reality without doing anything to remedy the resulting dissatisfaction. Here, even though the initiative has been taken by the industry, attention focuses on the unheeded discourse of the consumer.

Monological tourist-to-tourist messages (cell 5) are more in evidence when the addressee is a potential tourist, ready to be persuaded by the authoritative discourse of the sender. Persons who attend the lectures of returning travellers (in the tradition of those Victorian audiences who listened in silence to the exploits of imperial explorers sponsored by prestigious scientific societ-ies) illustrate the situation, as do their contemporary equivalents who attend the uninterrupted slideshows of their unchallenged, though knowledgeable and experienced, friends and relatives, thereby allowing the latter to gain status points at the expense of the former. Of course, these types of communication may not be entirely monological, particularly where their imaginative speakers encourage debate. However, if they are structured more formally in the framework of a question and answer session, the direction of communication is still vertical from sender to addressee without much opportunity for the latter to participate.

Cell 8, tourist–touree monologue, is typified by tourists issuing orders to members of the host population. Here such asymmetrical communication depends on an assumed role of super-ordination in the tourist and a corresponding imputed role of sub-ordination in the touree, which together indicate expected compliance from the latter. Where the host also forms part of the tourism industry, this type of communication is of the cell 2 variety (see Mayo and Jarvis, 1981 for an example of a belligerent hotel guest shouting commands at a bar tender). Only where it extends to residents more generally is it of the cell 8 variety.

Turning to touree-initiated monologue, cell 3 comprises those cases where members of the visited community address the industry. Typical media for such communication are the local press and radio call-in programmes, particularly where spokespersons for the host society are well educated and articulate.

Cell 6 relates to touree–tourist monologue. An example of such communication is the unofficial notice. This is a written and sometimes illustrated message that does not emanate from the industry (cf. Dann, 2003), but rather from members of the host community. Like tourism notices (cell 4), however, it can range from a simple request, for example, 'please do not park in front of these gates' to a more threatening order, the main difference being that the implied sanction lacks authority. Graffiti also constitute an instance of touree–tourist monologue (see Atkinson, 1988, for examples of related xenophobic bumper stickers), where typically a message denotes extremely unwelcome attitudes to visitors (e.g. 'Yankees go home!'). Yet of this rarely studied unobtrusive measure, it is difficult to think of any cases where tourists have answered back (Kilroy, 1983) by inscribing their own 'writings on the wall' as similarly insulting counter-messages. Hence the monological nature of the communication.

Finally, cell 9 relates to touree–touree monologue. Here an example is the unidirectional instructions that residents leave for one another as they go about their daily lives. Like the unofficial notices of cell 6, these messages do not have the official backing of the industry.

Model 2: the language of tourism as dialogue

Here it is evident that the major difference between dialogue and monologue is that the three key players of the industry, tourist and touree, instead of being considered separately and solely as either senders or addressees, are now regarded as combining both roles, if not simultaneously, then at least consecutively. As a result, and because it is not always possible to identify the initiator of the communication, it means that in Model 2 three of the former nine cells from model 1 are reiterated, i.e., cells 2, 3 and 6 respectively repeat information contained in cells 4, 7 and 8. For that reason, illustrative examples and commentary are correspondingly reduced (see Table 3.2).

First there are the instances of internal dialogue – the industry, tourists and tourees communicating as both sender and addressee among themselves. In cell 1, where message and response are limited to the industry, increased egalitarianism can lead to conversations among equals, as in the brainstorming associated with advertising campaigns, the designing of logos, branding exercises and discussions of the results of customer surveys. True, there has been relatively little academic research of such dialogue (apart from occasional mentions in such texts

Table 3.2 The language of tourism as dialogue

Sender and addressee	Sender and addressee		
	Industry	Tourist	Touree
INDUSTRY	(1) Advertising/Brain storming; In-house discussion of analysed data	(2) As (4)	(3) As (7)
TOURIST	(4) Telephone, letter, Internet feedback sites; Online guidebook forums; Communication with holiday reps; TV consumer programmes	(5) Conversations; Word-of-Web confessions;	(6) As (8)
TOUREE	(7) Focus groups; Local print media; Local radio and TV with responses; *A posteriori* survey	(8) Home-stays; Tribal TV; Jungle tours; Marginal people, e.g., beach boys	(9) Children's essays; Children's drawings

as Morgan and Pritchard, 2000), but missed opportunities do not render the topic any less important.

When it comes, in cell 5, to tourists talking to fellow tourists (e.g. e-mails, blogs, word-of-mouth), it is important to acknowledge that the sort of dialogue that takes place between equals can occur in any of the following stages of a holiday:

- Pre-trip: potential tourists consult actual tourists who have already experienced a given destination.
- On-trip: actual tourists communicate with fellow travellers; actual tourists speak to friends and relatives back home, e.g. by sending postcards. The recipients, in turn, can become potential or actual tourists, or, in cases where the messages are indicative of dissatisfaction, may be dissuaded from travelling to a particular place.
- Post-trip: actual tourists give accounts of their experiences to friends and relatives (cf. on-trip above).

There is thus a constant dialogue across three timeframes, a process that is as iterative and circular as the phenomenon of tourism itself. To the channels of communication previously identified from cells 2 and 4, can be added *inter alia* the contents of conversations (word-of-mouth). A sub-set of the latter comprises 'overheards', picked up by 'systematic lurking' (Dann et al., 1988, p. 28) and often on location. There are also confessions (Roe, 1998), more intimate one-to-one conversations that are often conducted between strangers (e.g. in an airport, on a plane). Here reciprocal anonymity, and occasionally common fear of flying or mutual love of alcohol, often encourage the uninhibited sharing of secrets, thereby possibly contributing to greater discourse validity than if the two parties were merely responding to researcher-driven items on a questionnaire.

Cell 9, where tourees communicate among themselves, has received a certain amount of attention from scholars, especially in academic research into tourism's impact on destination communities. However, the focus tends to be behavioural rather than sociolinguistic. Rarer examples of the latter are Crick's (1989) study of schoolchildren's descriptions of tourist hippies in Kandy, Sri Lanka, and Gamradt's (1995) investigation of Jamaican students' drawings of visitors to the island. Interestingly, both inquiries deal with young people, who can be considered more likely to provide responses of greater validity than their supposedly more sophisticated elders. 'Out of the mouths of babes…'

Second, there are instances of external dialogue:

- Industry–tourist/tourist–industry: cells 2 and 4,
- Industry–touree/touree–industry: cells 3 and 7,
- Tourist–touree/touree–tourist: cells 6 and 8.

As far as industry–tourist–industry dialogue is concerned, instead of content/semiotic analyses of the top-down monological discourse of such media as brochures and NTO catalogues, attention can now centre on the dialogical responses that the industry offers to the complaints of tourists. Such replies can be by letter, phone or electronic communication. Since the first two channels are not normally accessible to the public (except respectively via letters to the editors of newspapers or radio/television call-in programmes), it is mainly through the Internet that such dialogue is in greatest evidence.

Verbal feedback by tourists to holiday tour representatives also allows an operator to identify instances of service failure with a view to correcting them. The previously mentioned TV consumer programmes also provide sectors of the tourism industry with the opportunity to respond to areas of tourist dissatisfaction in a live setting. However, there is an added risk here, in that the victim's case is often mediated by the programme presenter who is typically a journalist eloquently putting forward that side of the argument with the additional hope of a newsworthy story.

Once tourist–industry communication is electronic, the addressee becomes even more exposed, since the Internet has potentially a far wider audience than a national or regional television station. Yet those firms which do deal adequately with tourist complaints often witness increases in customer satisfaction, retention and loyalty (Tyrrell and Woods, 2004). Typically, bottom-up e-communication puts tourists in touch with operators, airlines, hotels, etc., via third party sites whose drop-down menus contain such options as compliment, complaint and comment. Depending on the sector, each of these components has a series of sub-aspects that can accommodate most grievances and areas of satisfaction. Thus Planet Feedback (n.d.), for instance, after identifying the relevant company (e.g. Hilton hotels), allows selection from frequently encountered topics (e.g. check-in, checkout, food service, front desk, housekeeping). While this sort of feedback is commendable, however, the agenda is still a priori and not as dialogical as if it had been set by the customer (a posteriori). Some tourist board websites also provide potential opportunities for tourists to communicate with the industry, as do online guidebooks. The latter are highly sophisticated and thoroughly democratic. Lonely Planet (n.d.), for example (now available in English, French, Spanish and Italian), allows travellers to communicate via e-mails, letters and travel blogs. Its interactive Thorn Tree Forum is open to discussions of experiences, and the rating of accommodation and restaurants, etc., whose assessments can provide current appraisals long before the appearance of the next published edition of the printed guide bringing information that may well be out of date. Indeed, these various types of communication are now so comprehensive that they are presently classified by country and region. Potential travellers who have yet to visit a given destination can also post queries and receive answers from others who have recently been there or are actually *in situ* (e.g. news about the latest Maoist attacks in Nepal). As a matter of fact, these voices of experience may have greater accuracy than such alternative official sources as the Foreign and Commonwealth

Office (UK) or State Department (USA). Rough Guides (n.d.), with similar offerings, even have a chat room discussing the merits and disadvantages of its own publications when compared with rival guidebooks (an electronic debate that lasted from 24 January 2002 to 30 April 2004 but which was still available online on 25 October 2004).

Industry–touree dialogue is found in cells 7 and 3. Now, where the monological accent was previously on imposing industry-led concerns on host communities, there is currently additional scope for listening to the voices of destination residents. Here, instead of the old stimulus–response quantitative surveys, grounded theory qualitative issues can be tackled via an a posteriori approach that can be accommodated via ethnographic research and focus groups. One area that is particularly appropriate for this type of treatment is the self-imagery that destination people would like to project of themselves, their aspirations, goals and quality of life.

Turning to touree-initiated dialogue, here the emphasis is also on destination people communicating with the industry. Usually the relative powerlessness of these residents means that they only do so indirectly, for instance in local newspapers through letters to the editor, or via local radio call-in programmes. The authorities often reply to these voices of dissent in the same media (in the latter case they are typically asked to do so by the programme's moderator in order to achieve 'balance'). Here the industry lets the aggrieved tourees know how fortunate they are in deriving the economic benefits of tourism in exchange for relatively lower social and cultural costs. Dann's (2004a) analysis of Barbadians' adverse reactions to their patronising portrayal in the American TV soap opera *The Bold and the Beautiful* is an instance of this comparatively rare genre. In this example, locals rightly object to their being allocated roles of primitive extras, as little more than pre-modern natives running around in grass skirts, living in rickety shacks and drawing water from a standpipe. However, and as they vociferously point out in one of the island's newspapers, the truth of the matter is that they have a far higher literacy rate than their US audience and are quite au fait with the latest technology. This type of communication, therefore, is a method of de-othering or self-image projection, what Hollinshead (1993) would call 'dis-identification'.

Tourist–touree dialogue (cells 8 and 6) is less frequently encountered since it is typically associated with the sharing of accommodation or some other host–tourist experience (e.g. dining) that previously, under a regime of mass tourism, was only undertaken with fellow tourists. Going under the name of 'alternative tourism' (or one of its many forms), more so perhaps when home-stays are organised by the tourism industry (e.g. agri-tourism), here the emphasis is rather on direct tourist–host interaction. An interesting televised variant of such dialogue can be found in those quasi-anthropological programmes where intrepid, present-day explorers live with remote indigenes and share their broadcast experiences with a home-based audience. Such was the case of a six-part series put out by the British Broadcasting Corporation (BBC, 2005c) under the suitable caption 'Tribe'. The most recent of these episodes saw Bruce Parry engaging with the Sanema people of Venezuela and other programmes witnessed him undergoing dangerous initiation rites and partaking of strange food. Where this type of offering differs from other reality TV shows, such as *I'm a Celebrity: Get Me Out of Here* and *Big Brother*, is that the latter, focusing on pain suffered among equals, deliberately exclude locals.

Then there are those situations where tourees take the initiative in communicating with tourists. At the community level, they are exemplified by such 'fair trade' practices as visitors shopping for souvenirs in Patan's Jawalakhel Handicraft Centre, thereby helping elderly and poor emigré Tibetans in Nepal (McConnachie and Reed, 2002). They are likewise evident in Kathmandu's Ladybird Gift Shop retailing dolls and paper products in support of an organisation for girls at risk (McConnachie and Reed). Touree–tourist communication is also illustrated by locally organised jungle tours in Chiang Mai, Thailand (Cohen, 1989). Here the asymmetry of the discourse between tourists and indigenes has been analysed by Cohen and Cooper (1986). At the one-to-one individual level, host–guest dialogue is epitomised by tourist–beach boy encounters in Barbados, an interesting example of negotiated role reversal and corresponding imputation of motive (Karch and Dann, 1981). Like other instances of sex tourism also falling into this category, in beach boy tourism there is a dialogical trade-off between wealth (tourists) and knowledge (tourees) (van den Berghe, 1994). However, such communication is far from symmetrical, and is ultimately based on First World–Third World disparate power relationships (Karch and Dann).

Model 3: the language of tourism as trialogue

Finally, there is trialogue where three types of communication are envisaged according to the initiator of the discourse, but ultimately rely on self-reflexivity combined with the responses of the other two parties taken together. In some instances the direction of the dependency is reversed. Hence the switching of roles of sender and addressee. Whatever the situation, however, it manages to unite internal and external communication into a three-way process. Hence a change in numeration from the previous two models (see Table 3.3).

The first case of trialogue is industry driven, the result of internal debate (needs identification) and joint dialogue with tourists and tourees. An example (Cells 1 and 2) is a 'meet the people' initiative. Jamaica, being one of the first places to introduce such a programme successfully, saw the Tourist Board (industry) persuading locals that it would be to their benefit to share their common interests with visitors. Tourists were similarly encouraged to interact with Jamaicans on an equal footing and soon 'meet the people' became a regular feature of tours highlighted in overseas brochures (e.g. The Travel Collection, 2005). The experiment was also conducted (some would say 'begun') on cruise-ships where families from forthcoming Jamaican ports-of-call joined the cruise prior to the passengers' arrival, thereby familiarising them with what lay in store for them. There was also the hope that, as a result of this one-day 'taster experience', cruise ship excursionists would at a later date return to the island in the role of long-stay visitors.

An instance of tourist-initiated trialogue (cells 3 and 4) is that variant known as 'volunteer tourism' (Wearing, 2002). Here worthwhile Third World projects are identified and persons are encouraged to participate in them by paying their own way and helping disadvantaged others. Although most of these undertakings are non-touristic in nature (often they are environmentally oriented), and all are located in developing countries, the act of joining in with local people as equals in a shared effort to improve their lives as well as those of the volunteers

Table 3.3 The language of tourism as trialogue

Sender and addressee	Sender and addressee		
	Industry	Tourist	Touree
INDUSTRY	(1)	(3) Volunteer tourism	(5) Grass route tours; Tsunami; Community informatics
TOURIST	(2) Meet the people	(4)	(5) Grass route tours; Tsunami; Community informatics
TOUREE	(2) Meet the People	(3) Volunteer tourism	(6)

can be considered touristic. For that reason, such 'alternative tourism' is beneficial to the industry, particularly with the realisation that it tends to involve the more affluent type of patron.

Finally, there is touree-driven trialogue (cells 5 and 6) in which destination people send messages to the industry and tourists. Often they require assistance if their voices are to be fully heard and translated into action, as in the case of Grass Route Tours (2002) into the townships of Cape Town, for instance. Another example of such trialogue was the Boxing Day tsunami of 2004, a disaster in which thousands of south-east Asians perished, leaving the survivors to address the outside world (principally in English, the language of the BBC and CNN). Much of the devastated area had once been dedicated to tourism, which would take considerable time and funding to recover. However, and just as significantly by association, many of the coastal zones that had not been affected by the floods were similarly adversely and inaccurately portrayed as those that had been ruined. In order to remedy the situation it was essential that factually accurate appraisals should be transmitted – ones that involved all players.

A final instance of this type of trialogue is community informatics, a form of self-representation over the Internet, as for instance in developing the Maori Heritage Trail (Kiwitrails) with its own portal. The community level contact is accessed by a procedure known as 'Web raising', the community 'working together to create a collective asset' (Milne et al., 2005, p. 109) by sharing its skills with local businesses and thereby learning about each other. However, there are problems in such opening up to public gaze, including that of over-authenticity (e.g. showing the gory details of hunting, using the site as a place for religious conversion and inevitably allowing it to be overtaken by advertising, as in the case of Baffin island; Milne, 2006).

Conclusion

Although it can be a hazardous exercise to predict future trends in tourism and parallel developments in theory and method, a general attempt in this direction has already been undertaken in relation to Toffleresque, Simmelian and open-ended versions of reality (Dann, 1999). More specific examples provided here follow the latter approach in relation to one recent paradigm – that of tourism as language.

However, while several scenarios of likely change have been outlined, along with their implicit potential in research, it should be evident that not every possibility has been envisaged by the three models. Nor has it been spelt out, other than by passing references to modifications in the surrounding social ethos, how the transition is effected from monologue to dialogue and trialogue. Given limitations of space, that must constitute an area for further inquiry.

For the moment, though, if one takes an instance of traditional monological communication from the industry as sender to the tourist as addressee (Table 3.1, cell 4), the package tour brochure – which still exists on account of its high conversion rate – does it mean that this type of print medium will continue in its present format when there have been alterations in other parallel media (e.g. the interactive nature of Web-based guidebooks, the movement from travelogue to travelblog)? In other words, why should there not be a respondent-friendly, interactive brochure that allows potential tourists to take virtual tours of resorts, listen to what previous visitors have to say about a given place and even perhaps include the voices of the destination people as to how they relish having outsiders in their midst? It is this last area where the least progress has been made, but it is surely one where, if the foregoing trends to dialogue and trialogue develop as outlined, one can expect the greatest upheaval.

That said, it should be remembered that it is also possible that some of the old monological ways of tourism promotion may continue to be perpetuated. Whereas a few enlightened sectors of the industry now see the advantages of adequately and publicly responding to their customers, there are still several die-hards who prefer to abstain. In fact, and at best, it is estimated that only 15 per cent of tourism companies apologise for their mistakes over the Internet, a rate that drops to just 1 per cent in the case of the worst offenders (Tyrrell and Woods, 2004). American Airlines, US Airways and Southwest, for example, apparently do not see the need to reply to complaints at all, justifying their myopic position in terms of unnecessary expense (ibid.).

Thus there are two possible scenarios of the future development of 'the language of tourism', one denying change, the other promoting it. The former is pessimistic, signifying even more control by the industry over those who gaze – tourists (Urry, 1990) – and those who make a spectacle of themselves – tourees (van den Berghe, 1994). The latter is optimistic, meaning greater liberation for the visitor and the visited as they free themselves via resident–responsive tourism from the shackles of monological publicity to greater dialogical and trialogical employment of self-imagery.

Ontologically, these two positions are respectively rooted in the perennial tension between one and many. Epistemologically they are grounded in the a priori innate ideas of Plato or in the a posteriori, sensory-derived concepts of Aristotle (Dann, 2004b). This chapter, if nothing else, should act as a constant reminder that the meanings structuring tourism as a facet of contemporary existence represent an ongoing struggle between these two dichotomous worldviews. However, they can only be fully revealed by stripping off the manifest content of messages of 'the language of tourism' and by exposing their latent layers of connotation and the ideologies that underpin them.

References

Atkinson, G. (1988) *I hate tourists guidebook*. London: The Britons Against Tourism Association/Grafton Books

BBC (2005a) *Watchdog* (BBC TV programme, 11 January). N. Campbell, J. Bradbury and P. Heiney, Presenters. London: BBC

—— (2005b) Points of view. Retrieved 31 October 2011, from http:www.bbc.co.uk/programmes/b006mysv

—— (2005c) *Tribe* (BBC2 TV programme, January–February). B. Parry, Presenter. London: BBC

van den Berghe, P. L. (1994) *The quest for the other: Ethnic tourism in San Cristóbal, Mexico*. Seattle, WA: University of Washington Press

Cohen, E. (1989) 'Primitive and remote: Hill tribe trekking in Thailand'. *Annals of Tourism Research*, 16(1), 30–61

Cohen, E. and Cooper, R. L. (1986) 'Language and tourism'. *Annals of Tourism Research*, 13(4), 533–63.

Crick, M. (1989) 'The hippy in Sri Lanka: A symbolic analysis of the imagery of schoolchildren in Kandy'. *Criticism, Heresy and Interpretation*, 3, 37–54

Dann, G. M. S. (1996) *The language of tourism: A sociolinguistic perspective*. Wallingford: CAB International

—— (1999) 'Theoretical issues for tourism's future development: Identifying the agenda'. In D. G. Pearce and R. W. Butler (eds) *Contemporary Issues in Tourism Development*. London: Routledge, pp. 13–30

—— (2001a) 'The language of tourism as monologue'. Paper presented at the colloquium Worldscape, 21 August: The communicative power of tourism, University of Liège, Belgium

—— (2001b) 'The self-admitted use of cliché in the language of tourism'. *Tourism Culture and Communication*, 3(1), 1–14

—— (2003) 'Noticing notices: Tourism to order'. *Annals of Tourism Research*, 30(2), 465–84

—— (2004a) '(Mis)Representing the other in the language of tourism'. *Journal of Eastern Caribbean Studies*, 29(2), 76–94

—— (2004b) 'What Aristotle might have asked the future Alexander the Great on Mytilini: Is there anything new in tourism theory?'. Proceedings of the symposium on Understanding tourism: theoretical advances, May, Mytilini, Greece

——, Nash, D. and Pearce, P. (1988) 'Methodology in tourism research'. *Annals of Tourism Research*, 15(1), 1–28

Fjellman, S. M. (1992) *Vinyl leaves: Walt Disney World and America*. Boulder, CO: Westview Press

Gamradt, J. (1995) 'Jamaican children's representations of tourism'. *Annals of Tourism Research*, 22(4), 735–62

Grass Route Tours (2002) *Grass route tours* (brochure). Cape Town: Grass Route Tours

Holiday Complaints (n.d.) Holiday complaints website, available at http://www.holidaycomplaints.com (accessed 15 January 2012)

Holiday Travel Watch (n.d.) Holiday travel watch website, available at http://www.holidaytravelwatch. net (accessed 15 January 2012)

Hollinshead, K. (1993) 'The truth about Texas'. Unpublished doctoral dissertation, Texas A and M University, Texas

Hollinshead, K. and Jamal, T. B. (2001) 'Delving into discourse: Excavating the inbuilt power-logic(s) of tourism'. *Tourism Analysis,* 6(1), 63–74

IgoUgo (n.d.) IgoUgo website, available at http://www.Igougo.com (accessed 15 January 2012)

Karch, C. A. and Dann, G. H. S. (1981) 'Close encounters of the Third World'. *Human Relations*, 34(4), 249–68

Kilroy, M. R. (ed.) (1983) *Graffiti: The empire writes back* (No. 4). London: Corgi Books

Lee, C. C. and Hu, C. (2004) 'Analyzing hotel customers' e-complaints from an Internet complaint forum'. *Journal of Travel and Tourism Marketing*, 17(2/3), 167–81

Lonely Planet (n.d.) Lonely Planet website, available at http://www.lonelyplanet.com (accessed 15 January 2012)

Mayo, E. J. and Jarvis, L. P. (1981) *The psychology of leisure travel: Effective marketing and selling of travel services.* Boston, MA: CBI

McConnachie, J. and Reed, D. (2002) *The rough guide to Nepal.* London: Rough Guides Publications

Milne, S. (2006) 'Baffin Island, Nunavut, Canada'. In G. Baldacchino (ed.) *Extreme tourism: Lessons from the world's cold water islands* (pp. 88–99). Oxford: Elsevier

Milne, S., Mason, D., Speidel, U. and West-Newman, T. (2005) 'Tourism and community informatics: The case of Kiwitrails'. *Tourism Culture and Communication,* 5(2), 127–37

Morgan, N. and Pritchard, A. (2000) *Advertising in tourism and leisure.* Oxford: Butterworth-Heinemann

My Trip Journal (n.d.) My Trip Journal website, available at http://www.mytripjournal.com (accessed 15 January 2012)

Planet Feedback (n.d.) Planet Feedback website available at http://www.planetfeedback.com (accessed 15 January 2012)

Ritzer, G. (1993) *The McDonaldization of society.* Newbury Park, CA: Pine Forge Press

Roe, N. (1998) 'The mile-high confessional'. *Sunday Telegraph* (Review), 8 November, p. 31

Rough Guides (n.d.) Rough Guides website, available at http://www.roughguides.com (accessed 15 January 2012)

Schoefer, K. and Ennew, C. (2004) 'Customer evaluations of tour operators' responses to their complaints'. *Journal of Travel and Tourism Marketing*, 17(1), 83–92

Shea, L., Enghagen, L. and Khullar, A. (2004) 'Internet diffusion of an e-complaint: A content analysis of unsolicited responses'. *Journal of Travel and Tourism Marketing*, 17(2/3), 145–65

Travel Collection (2005) 'O island in the sun'. *Sunday Telegraph Magazine*, 23 January, p. 52

Travel Pod (n.d.) Travel Pod website, available at http://www.travelpod.com (accessed 15 January 2012)

Tyrrell, B. and Woods, R. (2004) 'E-complaints: Lessons to be learned from the service recovery literature'. *Journal of Travel and Tourism Marketing*, 17(2/3), 183–90

Urry, J. (1990) *The tourist gaze: Leisure and travel in contemporary societies.* London: Sage Publications

Wang, N. (2000) *Tourism and modernity: A sociological analysis.* Oxford: Pergamon

Wearing, S. (2002) 'Re-centering the self in volunteer tourism'. In G. M. S. Dann (ed.) *The tourist as a metaphor of the social world.* Wallingford: CAB International Publications, pp. 237–62

Weiermair, K. and Fuchs, M. (1999) 'Measuring tourist judgment on service quality'. *Annals of Tourism Research*, 26(4), 1004–21

4

Researching tourism distribution

Douglas G. Pearce

The importance of developing effective tourism distribution systems has been increasingly recognized in recent years, both in the tourism literature and by the tourism industry. As with other emerging areas of research, the literature on tourism distribution is at present rather fragmented and studies are partial in scope, providing researchers with considerable opportunities and challenges to develop this field further. This paper reports on a major five-year publicly funded project entitled 'Innovation in New Zealand tourism through improved distribution channels' that seeks to address many of these challenges and discusses some of the broader issues that have arisen. Begun in 2002, the project seeks to examine systematically different types of distribution channels, to identify the factors that influence the behaviour and motivations of all channel members, to assess the extent to which different channel structures, practices and relationships influence yield, and to recommend best channel management practices for different markets, regions and forms of tourism (Pearce, 2003).

After the origins of the project are outlined the research design and methodology are discussed, emphasizing a variety of issues associated with large-scale projects. The diverse literatures to which different aspects of distribution channels might be linked are then presented before the general patterns emerging from the results obtained to date are summarized and avenues for future research on tourism distribution are indicated.

Origins

Three sets of inter-related factors gave rise to this project and to the approach adopted: an academic interest in tourism distribution, industry applications and funding regime considerations.

Firstly, the benefits of an integrated approach to the analysis of interdependent channel members was highlighted in a study of New Zealand outbound travel to Samoa (Pearce, 2002a). In particular, that study identified the scope for distribution channels to constitute 'a potentially powerful unifying force by bringing together markets and destinations and by stressing inter-sectoral linkages' (Pearce, 2002b, p. 15). That potential lies in the role which distribution plays in providing 'the link between the producers of tourism services and their customers' (Gartner and Bachri, 1994, p. 164), in serving as the bridge between supply and demand (del Alcázar Martínez, 2002). Such a bridge is especially important given the fragmented nature of much tourism research, where the emphasis is frequently on only one part of a dichotomy (supply or demand, production or consumption, origins or destinations) and where tourism industry related research is notably bereft of unifying concepts and theories (Pearce, 2004).

This broader integrative role of distribution research complements the increased recognition of this part of the marketing mix in its own right, as evidenced by a growing literature on the topic (del Alcázar Martínez, 2002; Buhalis and Laws, 2001; O'Connor, 1999) and by a more explicit acknowledgement of its competitive importance. In this latter regard, Kotler et al. (1996, p. 451) assert that 'a well-managed distribution system can make the difference between a market share leader and a company struggling for survival' while Buhalis (2000, p. 111) argues distribution is 'one of the few remaining sources of real competitive advantage'.

In New Zealand the need for research of an applied nature was underlined in the New Zealand Tourism Strategy 2010. Recommendation 21 of that strategy highlighted the need to 'develop a tourism distribution channel strategy so New Zealand operators have an increased level of influence in the distribution channel' in order to achieve the goal of marketing and managing a world-class visitor experience (Tourism Strategy Group, 2001, p. 41). This requires an increased understanding of the structure and functioning of existing channels. While there may be a good appreciation of the issues by the national tourism marketing body and by some of the larger companies, this understanding is not always found across the industry. This was borne out in the early stages of the research when one of the more established heritage managers interviewed commented with regard to distribution channels: 'Probably the biggest minus is trying to work it all out...I just feel it should not have to be that complicated' (Pearce and Tan, 2004, p. 235).

Much of the complication in the case of New Zealand lies in the distinctive nature of tourism in that country where much international tourism is characterized by circuit travel, involving multiple arrangements and transactions across different sectors in several destinations, commonly in both the North and South Islands. Moreover, a large degree of independent travel occurs amongst both domestic and international visitors (Pearce and Schott, 2005; Stuart et al., 2005). These factors combine to generate a different set of distribution issues than those involving packaged, resort-based travel, the focus of much of the distribution channel research in Europe and elsewhere (del Alcázar Martínez, 2002; Buhalis and Laws, 2001). As a result, applied research in New Zealand has the potential to contribute to a more general understanding of tourism distribution through the different research questions that arise there.

Finally, the nature and scale of the research have been influenced and made possible by the prevailing research-funding regime. The Foundation for Research Science and Technology, which administers the Public Good Science Fund, has encouraged large-scale, multi-year project applications, emphasizing the public good nature of the outputs and end-user uptake of results. This regime has both enabled a larger, more comprehensive approach to the analysis of distribution channels and contributed to the academic and applied nature of the research. In terms of scale, the project analyses the full range of channel members, involves primary data collection in selected locations throughout New Zealand and in five overseas markets, is being undertaken by a team consisting of 1.6 FTE (full-time equivalent) staff, three Master's students and short-term research assistants, and has a budget of $320,000 p.a. over five years. The project is also characterized by the goals of disseminating results to diverse audiences and has a significant human capacity development component through the incorporation of young researchers.

Research design and methodology

The scale of the project has enabled a comprehensive, systematic, multi-stage approach to be adopted. This approach seeks firstly to establish a detailed analytical framework for systematically identifying different types of distribution systems and classifying all members in the channel. Particular emphasis here is being given to identifying different types of channel structure, taking a whole systems approach that incorporates all channel members. This is an ambitious undertaking and contrasts with much of the earlier empirical work that often involved a two-stage or business-to-business approach rather than an analysis of entire distribution channels. The need for a more holistic approach is inherent in Kotler et al.'s (1996, p. 483) definition of a distribution channel as: 'A set of interdependent organizations involved in the process of making a product or service available for use or consumption by the consumer or business user.' The notion of 'a set of interdependent organizations' underlines the need to examine the structure of the entire set of organizations and channel members (including the consumers) and to analyse the nature of the interdependency manifested in the relationships between them. Similarly, Bitner and Booms (1982, p. 40) argued: 'Each intermediary has the power to influence when, where and how people travel.' Again, the implication is that a full understanding of the distribution channels for any destination, market or product will only result from a more systematic and comprehensive approach that takes account of the role and behaviour of each of the channel members.

Secondly, the project seeks to identify the factors that influence the behaviour and motivations of the channel members which determine the nature and strength of the relationships between them and which lead to cooperation or conflict in the channel. The importance of this behavioural component was stressed by Bitner and Booms (1982, p. 40), who noted: 'While structural factors give clues to how the system operates, motivational and behavioural factors provide more complex explanations for why intermediaries do what they do, what influences their decisions, and how they interact with customers and suppliers.' In this project, this search for understanding what factors influence behaviour is being extended beyond the intermediaries to include all channel members, including providers and consumers. This point was well made in the seminal work by Wahab, et al. (1976), who recognized that different channel members have different interests.

Thirdly, an attempt is being made to assess the extent to which different channel structures, practices and relationships impact on tourism growth and influence yield for different channel members and to evaluate the cost effectiveness of different forms of distribution systems. Given that tourism businesses are faced with selecting a single or multiple channels from a range of distribution structures, systematically being able to evaluate the options available becomes a crucial part of an effective distribution strategy. To date, few tools for doing this are available.

Finally, recommendations will be made on best channel management practices for different markets, regions and forms of tourism and guidelines for these disseminated to a wide range of end users.

In order to allow different types of structure and behaviour to be examined while at the same time keeping the project manageable, this multi-stage design is being applied to selected destinations, markets, intermediaries, sectors and forms of tourism.

From an analytical point of view a destination perspective holds much potential for developing typologies (Pearce and Tan, 2002). In particular, adopting a sub-national destination perspective highlights the need to move beyond the analysis of only a single set of suppliers in order to examine channel structures associated with all sectors (e.g. attractions, accommodation, transport) and players (e.g. large and small businesses) and to investigate the ways in which these come together. A destination perspective also provides scope for the analysis of the interplay of the promotion and distribution of individual products and services versus the destination as a whole and for the examination of the role of destination characteristics in the formation of channel structures. Examples of three contrasting types of destination have been chosen to extend the range of possible channel structures and to examine differences in the impact of destination characteristics:

- Wellington, a major urban centre and gateway;
- Rotorua, a major resort destination;
- Southland, a peripheral region.

In the same way that different channel structures and behavioural factors were expected to vary across destinations, it was assumed that differences would occur from market to market. Accordingly, and following discussions with industry representatives, a selection of international markets was chosen taking into account factors such as the size and maturity of the markets, distance from the destination and cultural factors. These are:

- Australia, a mature, short-haul market and New Zealand's largest source of international visitors (622,252 arrivals in the year ended August, 2002);
- the United Kingdom, a major long-haul market experiencing dynamic growth (228,692);
- the United States of America, an important medium haul market (194,302);
- Japan, the largest and most established Asian market and one with distinctive structural characteristics (150,292);
- India, an emerging Asian market (15,717).

Distribution to the domestic market is being studied by including New Zealand visitors in destination-based surveys in Wellington and Rotorua and by focusing on supplier practices to reach the New Zealand market in the destination case studies.

In addition to the intermediaries located in the above markets – for example wholesalers, direct sellers and retail travel agencies in the United Kingdom – New Zealand-based intermediaries are also being interviewed. These are primarily inbound tour operators, travel management companies and professional conference organizers.

Research is being concentrated on five main sectors: accommodation, attractions, transport, conferences and events. In the first of these two sectors the focus is on a range of providers in the focal destinations. Thus a selection of accommodation providers has been included in Wellington, Rotorua and Southland, ranging from large chain hotels to small independent bed and breakfast establishments. Likewise, a range of different types of attractions is being studied, with a particular emphasis on heritage and cultural attractions (Pearce and Tan, 2004). Conferences and events in Wellington were added to the project following the initial stages of the destination-based studies that revealed specific channels for these sectors characterized by quite intense activity of a short-term duration (Smith, 2004). In addition, a more specific examination of distribution channels for adventure tourism, a significant and growing sector in New Zealand, is being carried out, drawing on examples from Queenstown. A nationwide perspective has been adopted in the case of the transport sector whose role is essentially to link different places in a range of networks or circuits, an important consideration given the itinerant nature of much international tourism in New Zealand.

Particular attention is being paid throughout the project to identifying differences in the distribution channels for independent and packaged travel. The latter has attracted the most attention in the international literature to date, given the emphasis there on travel to mass resort destinations. Packages are also a dominant form of travel from some major markets to New Zealand but independent travel is also very significant, not only for domestic tourists but also for some key overseas markets such as Australia and the United Kingdom. As most tourist businesses in New Zealand depend on a mix of independent and packaged clients, understanding any differences in distribution to these major segments was deemed at the outset as likely to be very important. This has since proved to be the case (Pearce and Tan, 2004). While the emphasis throughout is predominantly on leisure travel, special attention has also been given to corporate travel as more businesses are making special arrangements to manage their company travel (Garnham, 2005).

Comparative analysis

Comparative analysis is another key feature of the overall research design. Systematically comparing distribution structures across the selected cases enables general characteristics to be distinguished from features specific to any one destination, market, sector or form of tourism (Pearce, 1993). Similarly, systematic comparison also allows for the transfer of experience between them and will facilitate the formulation of subsequent recommendations on best channel management practices. A major methodological challenge here is to collect and analyse data that not only allows examination of the structure and functioning of particular destinations, markets, sectors and forms of tourism but also enables comparison within and between these different dimensions. This has involved the use of multiple data collection methods and an integration of the different parts of the project.

In the first two phases of the project three main methods were used to collect and analyse the necessary information: in-depth structured interviews, surveys and the analysis of tour operator catalogues, websites and other documentary information. In-depth structured interviews constitute the main means of data collection from the suppliers and intermediaries. The interviews were structured around a checklist of questions which focus on the nature of each business, the markets targeted, the distribution channels used or, in the case of the intermediaries, their role in the distribution of New Zealand product, strategies followed, factors influencing these, relationships established and partnerships developed. This core of common questions provided the basis for comparability across the different cases and respondents but the format followed also allowed issues relating to particular businesses, destinations, markets or channel members to be explored. Key themes were followed throughout the various components of the project that will subsequently facilitate integration of the different facets. For example, the suppliers were asked to identify what factors influence their choice of distribution channels and the selection of channel partners that they work with. Subsequently, the various intermediaries – inbound operators, wholesalers, direct sellers, retail agents – were asked about their choice of suppliers and other distribution partners.

Similar issues have been explored in the visitor surveys that complement the in-depth interviews of suppliers and intermediaries. Some 1,000 visitors each in Rotorua and Wellington were surveyed on an intercept basis at selected sites in the two destinations during January 2003 (Pearce and Schott, 2005). The surveys focused on the visitors' information search and buying behaviour with reference to how they travelled to the destination, the accommodation used and the activities undertaken. This enables the demand data to be compared systematically with the supply-side information in terms of the major themes of the project.

Further triangulation comes from an analysis of operator and wholesaler catalogues and from the websites of suppliers and intermediaries. The catalogues provide a reasonably concrete and comprehensive picture of the products and properties being offered in different destinations to the different markets, whether to groups or on an FIT basis (Pearce and Tan, 2006; Pearce et al., 2004). Similarly, the websites of the intermediaries constitute a basis for comparing the extent and coverage of product in the focal regions while those of the suppliers provide insights into how this channel is being used, for example as a means of providing information and/or enabling transactions (Tan and Pearce, 2004).

Table 4.1, representing the analytical framework for the visitor surveys in Wellington and Rotorua (Pearce and Schott, 2005), shows one way in which this comparative approach is being applied. The analysis follows the presumed sequence of distribution activities from the visitors' perspective – information search, booking and purchase – for domestic and international visitors in the two destinations and across the three key sectors of accommodation, transport and attractions.

In other parts of the project a first level of analysis has occurred on a case-by-case basis, with papers being produced, for example, on distribution channels in Wellington (Pearce et al., 2004), Southland (Stuart et al., 2005) and Rotorua (Pearce and Tan, 2006) and theses being completed on distribution to the Indian and Japanese markets (Sharda, 2005; Taniguchi, 2005). The Wellington case study brings together the perspectives of the suppliers, intermediaries and visitors; that on Southland emphasizes sub-regional, sectoral and market segment differences within a peripheral region; and in the case of Rotorua the distribution mix for attractions is analysed in detail (Pearce and Tan, 2006). The Indian case study examines the characteristics of distribution in an emerging market; that on Japan stresses the more industrialized, integrated nature of distribution channels in that market. These case studies provide the scope to explore the different dimensions of distribution in depth; later, through the common core focus the channel structures and behaviour will be systematically compared across the destinations, markets and forms of tourism, with some provisional similarities and differences being highlighted below.

Sequencing the different facets of the overall project has required careful consideration. Beginning with the destination case studies has proved to be a useful point of departure, enabling

Table 4.1 An analytical framework for examining the visitors' perspective on tourism distribution channels

Distribution Function (multiple channels)	Sector	Destination			
		Rotorua		Wellington	
		Market		Market	
		International	Domestic	International	Domestic
Information Search	Transport Accommodation Attractions				
Booking	Transport Accommodation Attractions				
Payment	Transport Accommodation				

issues to be identified and the methodology to be refined before tackling the more logistically demanding and resource-heavy market studies. Moreover, with these logistical and methodological points in mind, work began in each case on the nearest destination and market, respectively Wellington and Australia, before those further afield were undertaken. Originally it had been proposed to complete the structural analysis before examining the behavioural aspects of the different suppliers and intermediaries. In the event, these were undertaken conjointly within the same set of interviews as, in addition to significantly reducing travel costs, setting up appointments for a single interview with the targeted respondents proved sufficiently challenging without attempting a second.

With these first two stages completed and a clearer picture of channel structure and behaviour having been established, attention is being focused on a small number of representative cases in order to tackle aspects of yield in a more targeted fashion and with much more informed knowledge of the multiple channels in use. This will involve a twofold approach. Firstly, visitors to individual attractions are being surveyed to establish the relative importance of the channels that they have used; the survey will be informed by earlier research on the visitors' perspective carried out at the destination level (Pearce and Schott, 2005). Secondly, the cost effectiveness of the different channels being used by the providers in question is being analysed adapting techniques applied in the accommodation sector (Middleton and Clarke, 2001) but giving emphasis to the comparative analysis of returns from the multiple channels used. This phase is proving demanding due to the commercially sensitive nature of much of the data required and to difficulties relating to accessing information costs and revenue at the level of distinct distribution channels. Although challenging, this phase has been facilitated by the relationships established during the early phases of the project and by the feedback of provisional results to respondents, demonstrating that information useful to the industry can be generated and confidentiality has been respected.

Linking to the literatures

As the project has progressed, the breadth of studies to which research on distribution channels might be linked has become increasingly wide-ranging. This issue is not of course specific to tourism distribution (Pearce, 2004) but the range of literatures to which such research might profitably be linked is a function both of the scale of this project and the integrative and multi-faceted nature of distribution channels. The tourism distribution literature, drawn together in recent books (del Alcázar Martínez, 2002; Buhalis and Laws, 2001; O'Connor, 1999), formed the core on which the initial phases of the project were based but as work has progressed on particular topics these have also been progressively cast in other more specific and hitherto largely non-convergent literatures in order to bring more understanding to the issues at hand. This process is depicted in Figure 4.1, where the core tourism distribution literature is intersected by more specific literatures relating to the case study contexts (e.g. urban tourism, tourism in peripheral areas), types of market, forms of tourism and particular fields of study (e.g. tourist behaviour, tourism and ICT, or information and communication technology). At present the emphasis is on the linkages between the core and the subsets in the outer ring, rather than between the outer literatures, though integration may occur here in the latter phases of the project as the different facets are brought together.

Linking the literatures in this fashion is enabling the distribution channels research to be advanced in a variety of ways. Consideration of the destination case studies in the context of these other literatures is proving a useful means of 'breaking out of the case' (Dann, 1999), of seeing the distribution issues in Wellington or Southland not just in terms of those places

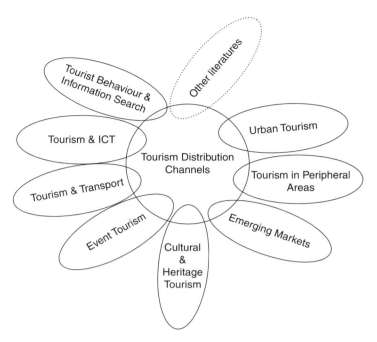

Figure 4.1 Tourism distribution channels and inter-related literatures

but respectively of cities and peripheral regions more generally (Pearce et al., 2004; Stuart et al., 2005). In this way it is hoped to develop a more generalized understanding of tourism distribution systems as well as to contribute to the literatures on urban tourism and peripheral regions, both of which have essentially neglected distribution issues to date. Distribution channels, for example, constitute a fundamental link between cores and peripheries and as such might usefully be added to the structural relationship approach to the study of peripheral regions (Stuart et al., 2005). Likewise, the analysis of distribution to the Indian market has been set not only in the context of emerging and mature tourism markets (Casarin, 2001; King and Choi, 1999) but also of emerging markets more generally (e.g. Arnold and Quelch, 1998). This has enabled the structures and behaviours found in the Indian market to be interpreted in a wider context, with the case demonstrating a number of similarities with broader aspects of emerging markets such as channel fragmentation, multilayering and a lack of stability (Sharda and Pearce, 2005).

In terms of visitor behaviour, the tourism distribution literature is hugely asymmetrical, emphasizing the role of other channel members, the providers and intermediaries, rather than the consumers (Pearce and Schott, 2005). Reference to the tourist behaviour literature shows the emphasis there is primarily on information search rather than on the other two main components of distribution, booking and purchase. By situating the analysis of the visitors' use of distribution channels in these two literatures the research gap that this part of the project is attempting to fill can be demonstrated clearly and, to a limited extent, the results can be interpreted by reference to this earlier work.

Emerging patterns

While a full synthesis of the results must necessarily await completion of other aspects of the project, patterns are starting to emerge from the results that have been reported to date. Some commonalities can be identified but the general picture developing is that a differentiated approach must be taken to formulating effective distribution strategies, a differentiation that takes into account not only key market segments but also sectoral differences and contextual factors associated with particular types of destination and market. Moreover, describing channel structures is not enough; more emphasis must be given to behavioural factors in order to understand why channel members behave as they do and why they use particular channels or change these. In this respect, taking a whole systems approach provides greater insights and understanding, counterbalancing the increased methodological challenges and heavier resources needed.

The results from various parts of the study, for instance, highlight the different distribution issues and channel structures relating to packaged travel, especially that involving series tours, and independent or semi-independent travel. This reflects to a large degree the characteristics and needs of both consumers and suppliers. The Southland study showed distribution channels for businesses serving the group, special interest and semi-independent segments are generally more multilayered, make greater use of inbound tour operators (IBOs), wholesalers and retail travel agents, and have their products pre-purchased in the market, generally either as part of a group or a personalized package (Stuart et al., 2005). Businesses catering to independent travellers, on the other hand, tend to have a greater proportion of direct sales and employ a mix of en route and at destination strategies involving information and sales through other intermediaries, especially information centres and formal or informal networks of other providers. Similar patterns are found in Wellington but the urban tourism product appears less subject to the 'bundling' function typical of the distribution of mass tourism packages to resorts (Pearce et al., 2004). The analysis of the visitor surveys shows independent travellers are generally making a series of decisions about the purchase of individual products, often using multiple channels to collect all their information and make their different transactions (Pearce and Schott, 2005). While some of these results are not unexpected, the project is revealing the need to pay greater attention to distribution to various types of traveller, for the emphasis on packaged travel that has dominated much of the European literature (Casarin, 2001) tells only part of the overall story.

The scale and diversity of the project are also revealing important sectoral differences, drawing particular attention to issues associated with the distribution of attractions, a sector that has been subject to much less research than accommodation or transport but one whose distribution strategies are crucial to successful destination development. The visitor surveys, for example, show that independent travellers use different information sources to find out about transport, accommodation and attractions. Booking and advance purchase are far less common in this latter sector than in the other two (Pearce and Schott, 2005). Likewise, transport and attractions businesses tend to use the Internet differently as a distribution tool: with the former, online transactions have become commonplace; with the latter, the Internet is still used predominantly for information dissemination (Tan and Pearce, 2004). The detailed empirical examination of attractions in Rotorua has revealed a greater diversity in the distribution mix of attractions than is hinted at in the meagre textbook references, the proportion of direct sales ranging from 95 per cent to 20 per cent (Pearce and Tan, 2006). Factors influencing the overall distribution mix include the segments targeted, the characteristics of the attractions and the perceived advantages and disadvantages of different channels with respect to yield, control and seasonality. At the same time, some similarities are to be found between small accommodation providers and attractions operators, with both often being more reliant on direct sales and 'at destination' distribution than large hotels or major carriers (Pearce et al., 2004; Stuart et al., 2005).

The value of taking a whole systems approach, looking at distribution issues across all channel members, has also been confirmed by the additional insights being provided, by the differences being revealed at different channel layers and by the greater ability to cross-check behaviours of various channel members. In the case of the Indian market, for example, the fragmentation of the distribution channels, the heavy dependence on New Zealand-based inbound operators and the relative paucity of direct sales can be explained in terms of the characteristics of the market and of the varying needs and interests of the Indian intermediaries and suppliers (Sharda and Pearce, 2005). Lacking destination knowledge and travel experience, and faced with the complications that circuit travel in larger groups brings, many Indian travellers at present seek the ease and security of a high level of packaging carried out by the Indian intermediaries and the New Zealand IBOs. In turn, the small volume of Indian travellers to New Zealand and associated price issues explain the Indian intermediaries' and the New Zealand suppliers' dependence on the IBOs.

Differences are also found in the use of the Internet across the channel members: providers, especially in the transport sector, use it mainly for sales, whereas intermediaries are increasingly taking advantage of the medium for communication and for marketing, for example using e-shots (Tan and Pearce, 2004). Visitors use the Internet for booking transport more than they do accommodation, in part because online systems are less well adapted at present to immediately confirm rooms compared to seats (Pearce and Schott, 2005).

In the Wellington case study, bringing together the views of the suppliers, intermediaries and visitors has shown a certain amount of congruence in the practices, needs and interests of the different channel members. The visitor survey results, for example, confirm the importance of at destination distribution amongst the small accommodation and attractions providers but the study also raises the question of where responsibility lies for stimulating demand for travel to the city in the first place (Pearce et al., 2004). This integrated approach also showed how guidebooks, the most important source of information used by visitors to find out what there is to see and do in Wellington is also a channel over which the attractions providers have limited or no control while the interviews with intermediaries identified factors leading to the limited inclusion of Wellington in series tour itineraries.

Further synthesis along these lines is now being undertaken before aspects of yield are examined and the best management practice guidelines are drawn up. While many aspects of distribution will have been covered when the project is complete, considerable scope exists for many of the topics to be taken further and for the generality of the findings to be tested in other contexts. For example, the intermediaries' dominance over distribution to peripheral regions appears to be far less critical in Southland where many of the businesses have some choice in who they target and which channels they use (Stuart et al., 2005) compared to the mass, packaged resort-based 'sun, and sea' tourism described by Buhalis (1999) in the Aegean. Clearly, all peripheral regions are not the same and similar work in other regions is needed to develop a more comprehensive picture of distribution issues there. Likewise with cultural tourism: parallel research in Catalonia has revealed many similarities with the New Zealand situation, particularly in terms of the prominence of direct sales to independent travellers, but differences do arise with group visitation due to contextual factors (Pearce, 2005). Group visitation to cultural attractions in Catalonia is dominated by excursionists from the coast, a feature which contrasts markedly with the far greater role of series tours in New Zealand where visits to cultural attractions are often part of a broader country-wide circuit and differing net rates may be offered depending on the volume of business generated by various operators (Pearce and Tan, 2004). Other aspects of distribution arising out of this study could now be developed elsewhere. The exploratory work on empirically measuring the distribution mix of attractions, for example, could be usefully extended to other sectors, while parallel research on other destination–market pairs would enable a better appreciation of distribution and market maturity. In these ways, it is hoped that the project will not only assist with developing more competitive distribution strategies in New Zealand but also, through the methodology developed and examples provided, it will make a contribution to an enhanced understanding of tourism distribution in general.

References

del Alcázar Martínez, B. (2002) *Los Canales de Distribución en el Sector Turístico* (Distribution channels in the tourism sector). Madrid: ESIC Editorial

Arnold, D. J. and Quelch, J. A. (1998) 'New strategies in emerging markets'. *MIT Sloan Management Review*, 40(1), 7–20

Bitner, M. J. and Booms, B. H. (1982) 'Trends in travel and tourism marketing: The changing structure of distribution channels'. *Journal of Travel Research*, 20(4), 39–44

Buhalis, D. (1999) 'Tourism on the Greek Islands: Issues of peripherality, competitiveness and development'. *International Journal of Tourism Research*, 1(5), 341–58

—— (2000) 'Marketing the competitive destination of the future'. *Tourism Management*, 21(1), 97–116

Buhalis, D. and Laws, E. (eds) (2001) *Tourism distribution channels: Practices, issues and transformations*. London: Continuum

Casarin, F. (2001) 'Tourism distribution channels in Europe: A comparative study'. In D. Buhalis and E. Laws (eds) *Tourism distribution channels: Practices, issues and transformations*. London: Continuum, pp. 137–50

Dann, G. M. S. (1999) 'Theoretical issues for tourism's future development: Identifying the agenda'. In D. G. Pearce and R. W. Butler (eds), *Contemporary issues in tourism development*. London: Routledge, pp. 13–30

Garnham, R. (2005) 'Corporate travel agents: Channels of distribution – An evaluation'. Paper presented at the CAUTHE Conference February 2005: Sharing tourism knowledge, Alice Springs, Australia

Gartner, W. C. and Bachri, T. (1994) 'Tour operators' role in the tourism distribution system: An Indonesian case study'. *Journal of International Consumer Marketing*, 6(3/4), 161–79

King, B. and Choi, H. J. (1999) 'Travel industry structure in fast growing but immature outbound markets: The case of Korea to Australia travel'. *International Journal of Tourism Research*, 1(2), 111–22

Kotler, P., Bowen, J. and Makens, J. C. (1996) *Marketing for hospitality and tourism*. Upper Saddle River, NJ: Prentice Hall

Middleton, V. T. C. and Clarke, J. (2001) *Marketing in travel and tourism* (3rd edn). Oxford: Butterworth-Heinemann

O'Connor, P. (1999) *Electronic information distribution in tourism and hospitality*. Wallingford: CABI Publishing

Pearce, D. G. (1993) 'Comparative studies in tourism research'. In D. G. Pearce and R. W. Butler (eds), *Tourism Research: Critiques and challenges*. London: Routledge, pp. 20–35

—— (2002a) 'New Zealand holiday travel to Samoa: A distribution channels approach'. *Journal of Travel Research*, 41(2), 197–205

—— (2002b) 'Current and future directions in tourism research'. *Japanese Journal of Tourism Research*, 1(1), 9–20

—— (2003) 'Tourism distribution channels: A systematic integrated approach'. In E. Ortega, L. González and E. Pérez del Campo (eds), *Best paper proceedings of 6th International Forum on the Sciences, Techniques and Art Applied to Marketing*. Madrid: Universidad Complutense de Madrid, pp. 345–63

—— (2004) 'Advancing tourism research: Issues and responses'. In K. A. Smith and C. Schott (eds), *Proceedings of the New Zealand Tourism and Hospitality Conference 2004*. Wellington, NZ: Victoria University of Wellington, pp. 1–10

—— (2005) 'Distribution channels for cultural tourism in Catalonia, Spain'. *Current Issues in Tourism*, 8(5), 424–45.

Pearce, D. G. and Schott, C. (2005) 'Tourism distribution channels: The visitors' perspective'. *Journal of Travel Research*, 44(1), 50–63

Pearce, D. G. and Tan, R. (2002) 'Tourism distribution channels: A destination perspective'. In W. G. Croy (ed.), *Proceedings of the 5th New Zealand Tourism and Hospitality Research Conference.* Rotorua, New Zealand: Waiariki Institute of Technology, pp. 242–50

—— (2004) 'Distribution channels for heritage and cultural tourism in New Zealand'. *Asia Pacific Journal of Tourism Research*, 9(3), 225–37

—— (2006) 'The distribution mix for tourism attractions in Rotorua, New Zealand'. *Journal of Travel Research*, 44(3), 250–58

Pearce, D. G., Tan, R. and Schott, C. (2004) 'Tourism distribution channels in Wellington, New Zealand'. *International Journal of Tourism Research*, 6(6), 397–410

Sharda, S. (2005) 'The structure and behaviour of distribution channels linking destination New Zealand to an emerging market: A case of the Indian outbound travel industry'. Unpublished Master's thesis, Victoria University of Wellington, New Zealand

Sharda, S. and Pearce, D. G. (2005) 'Distribution in emerging tourism markets: The case of Indian travel to New Zealand'. In S. J. Suh and Y. H. Hwang (eds), *Asia Pacific Tourism Association 11th Conference Proceedings: New Tourism for Asia Pacific.* Pusan, South Korea: Dong-A University, pp. 595–605

Smith, K. (2004) '"There is only one opportunity to get it right": Challenges of surveying event visitors'. In K. A. Smith and C. Schott (eds), *Proceedings of the New Zealand Tourism and Hospitality Conference 2004.* Wellington, NZ: Victoria University of Wellington, pp. 386–97

Stuart, P., Pearce, D. G. and Weaver, A. (2005) 'Tourism distribution channels in peripheral regions: The case of Southland, New Zealand'. *Tourism Geographies*, 7(3), 235–56

Tan, R. and Pearce, D. G. (2004) 'Providers' and intermediaries' use of the Internet in tourism distribution'. In K. A. Smith and C. Schott (eds), *New Zealand Tourism and Hospitality Research Conference 2004.* Wellington, NZ: Victoria University of Wellington, pp. 424–32

Taniguchi, M. (2005) 'The structure and function of the tourism distribution channels between Japan and New Zealand'. Unpublished Master's thesis, Victoria University of Wellington, New Zealand

Tourism Strategy Group (2001) *New Zealand tourism strategy 2010.* Wellington, NZ: Tourism Strategy Group

Wahab, S., Crampon, L. J. and Rothfield, L. M. (1976) *Tourism marketing: A destination-oriented programme for the marketing of international tourism.* London: Tourism International Press

5

Impediments to international tourism

An exploration of issues in five APEC economies

Stephen L. J. Smith

Introduction

Tourism historically is one of the fastest growing economic sectors, but its growth cannot be taken for granted. Events such as terrorist attacks, the outbreak of SARS, and the Indian Ocean tsunami can quickly cause a tourism recession in affected destinations. The impacts of these recessions rapidly ripple throughout an economy, affecting businesses and their employees in tourism and non-tourism industries. However, tourism is affected not just by dramatic events but by day-to-day, systemic impediments to its growth. Many such impediments may be taken for granted because they have either emerged slowly in response to non-tourism issues or were implemented years ago without due consideration for their impact on tourism. Nonetheless, their effects on the ability of tourism enterprises to compete and grow as well as on their effects on the ability of private individuals to travel internationally should not be ignored.

Tourism often is a favoured economic development strategy because of its ability to quickly stimulate income and employment growth, foreign exchange earnings, and government revenues through fees and taxes (UNCTAD, 1998). Tourism not only generates jobs at a higher rate than most other sectors, it is an important source of jobs for new workers and those with minimal skills. The multiplier effect (indirect and induced economic effects) tends to be greater than that of many other sectors. Tourism diversifies economies and stabilizes against fluctuations in other exports, especially manufacturing. On the other hand, the benefits of tourism can be reduced through leakage created by the need to import services or goods, international marketing costs, interest payments on foreign loans, and the payment of franchise or management fees to foreign companies. Leakage is a particular problem for small and developing economies, although it exists in every economy that is open to international trade. Fortunately, leakage tends to decrease over time as an economy develops and domestic sources of goods and services increase. National governments sometimes impose restrictions on the outflow of capital or profit to multinational corporations as a way of reducing leakages as well.

Tourism is highly dependent on infrastructure, not just utilities on which every industry depends, but also virtually all modes of transportation and communication. The sector is strongly influenced by a wide range of government services, from border-crossing formalities to the provision of information. Although tourism is dominated by small and medium-sized enterprises and is supposed to be based on the personal contact implicit in hospitality, the Internet and e-commerce are profoundly reshaping the delivery of tourism information and services.

Tourism is particularly susceptible to external threats. For example, the war in Iraq depressed demand for some international travel, and the rising cost of fuel pushed a number of international air carriers, especially in North America, to the brink of bankruptcy. SARS dramatically affected tourism in a number of nations, particularly Singapore, China, Taiwan, and Canada. The Canadian Tourism Commission (CTC) estimated that SARS resulted in a loss of 662,000 room-nights in April 2003 alone, representing a loss of CA$92 million (CBC News, 2003). The CTC further estimated that SARS and the war in Iraq cost the global airline industry US$5 billion and 6.5 million jobs. More recently, a study by Oxford Economic Forecasting suggested that the impact of the December 2004 tsunami is expected to approach US$3 billion in 2005 and cost around 250,000 jobs (WTTC 2005).

A factor contributing to this vulnerability is that tourism depends on both consumers (private households) and businesses. Thus, anything that affects spending patterns of either source may have a significant impact on tourism demand. Consumers are sensitive to reports of crime, social unrest, and war as well as health or environmental hazards, such as earthquakes and volcanic eruptions. Even weather conditions can significantly affect demand, from typhoons to snow droughts. When conditions in one destination divert visitors, visitors tend to shift to another destination rather than cease travelling.

Business tourism demand is closely linked to the health of the economy in the originating country. Research in Canada, for example, has found that overall tourism demand follows economic cycles but magnifies them by about 40 per cent. In other words, when the economy grows by 1.0 per cent, tourism demand grows by about 1.4 per cent; similarly, when the economy shrinks by 1.0 per cent, tourism demand falls by 1.4 per cent (Wilton, 1998).

In brief, the growth of international tourism depends on healthy economies in origin and destination markets, political stability, freedom from disasters, and the existence of globally efficient logistics supporting transportation, telecommunications, financial flows, accommodation, food services, and other tourism-related services. Government policies, including those governing border crossings, foreign direct investment, access to foreign workers, and the movement of capital, are also key elements in the growth of tourism.

However, impediments and barriers exist in every country that restricts the potential of individuals to travel and the ability of tourism-related businesses to succeed. Working to reduce impediments, where possible, is a goal of the Asia-Pacific Economic Co-operation (APEC). This paper identifies and examines examples of such impediments in five economies.

APEC and tourism

APEC is a multilateral forum, established in 1989, and composed of 21 member economies (the term 'member economy' is used instead of 'nation' because of the inclusion of Chinese Taipei, Hong Kong, and the People's Republic of China in the APEC membership) with borders on the Pacific Ocean. Its member economies are Australia; Brunei Darussalam; Canada; Chile; Chinese Taipei; Hong Kong, China; Indonesia; Japan; Republic of Korea; Malaysia; Mexico; New Zealand; Papua New Guinea; People's Republic of China; Peru; Republic of the Philippines; Russian Federation; Singapore; Thailand; United States of America; and Viet Nam. APEC works to facilitate economic growth, co-operation, trade, and investment in the Asia-Pacific region through non-binding commitments, dialogue, and mutual respect for the views of all participants. It differs from the World Trade Organization and other multilateral trade organizations in that no treaty obligations are required of its participants. Decisions made within APEC are reached by consensus and commitments are undertaken on a voluntary basis.

A key initiative of APEC is the 'Bogor Declaration', which calls for free and open trade and investment in the Asia-Pacific region by 2010 for industrialized economies and 2020 for developing economies. Specifically, the Declaration calls for efforts 'to continue to reduce barriers to trade and investment to enable goods, services, and capital to flow freely among our economies' (APEC, 1994, p. 5). Much of the work on the Bogor Declaration has been assigned to a series of working groups within APEC. One of these, the Tourism Working Group (TWG), has been charged with working to formulate strategies that will improve tourism movements and investment in the Asia-Pacific region. To do so requires an understanding of the nature of current impediments to tourism movements and investments in individual member economies (APEC, n.d.).

In 2000, the APEC Tourism Ministers' meeting in Seoul, Korea, adopted the APEC Tourism Charter that includes four goals of key deliverables for the tourism sector. Table 5.1 summarizes the four goals as well as the key strategies to be pursued in fulfilling each goal.

The first two of these goals directly address the challenge of removing or reducing impediments, and thus the focus of this research was guided by these two goals.

Each member economy of APEC is expected to develop an individual action plan to identify steps for reducing and for removing specific impediments to tourism. The majority of economies have developed such plans, although the level of detail is sometimes quite limited. Moreover, progress in implementing the action plan generally tends to be slow and sporadic because most initiatives require co-ordination among two or more government agencies, adequate financial resources, and possible partnerships with a highly fragmented tourism sector. This project, aimed at identifying impediments in five economies, was seen as an effort to invigorate progress on reducing impediments.

Methods

A 1996 study on tourism impediments (Dain Simpson Associates, 2003) examined impediments in six member economies and resulted in the compilation of a summary matrix of impediments to tourism in co-operation with the Tourism Authority of Thailand on behalf of the TWG. In 2003, the TWG subsequently decided to extend the analysis by examining five more economies and by updating the tourism impediments matrix. A call for volunteer economies was issued to members, with the desire to have a diverse set of economies participating. Five members offered their co-operation: Canada, Chile, Indonesia, Peru, and Philippines.

These participating economies represent a mix of economies although all are market-driven to varying degrees. The relative importance of international tourism in each varies, with the spectrum ranging from Chile as an economy in which international tourism is a relatively new and minor part of the economy, to Canada in which international tourism is well-established and constitutes a significant contributor to Canada's GDP. Moreover, they represent different geographic regions within APEC: North America, South America, and Southeast Asia. It should be noted that although these members are diverse in terms of the importance of tourism, the size of their economy, and the nature of their tourism attractions, they are not intended to be a representative sample of all APEC member economies. Rather, they were selected as case studies because of the willingness of representatives of the tourism ministries in each government to participate in the project.

Table 5.1 APEC tourism goals and associated strategies

Goal	Strategy
1. Removal of impediments to tourism business and investment	• Promote and facilitate productive investment in tourism and associated sectors • Remove regulatory impediments to tourism business and investment • Encourage liberalization of trade in services related to tourism under GATS
2. Increase the mobility of visitors and the demand for tourism products in the APEC region	• Facilitate seamless travel for visitors • Enhance visitor experiences • Promote inter- and intra-regional marketing opportunities and co-operation • Enhance the safety and security of visitors • Encourage non-discriminatory approaches to the provision of visitor facilities and services
3. Sustainably manage tourism outcomes and impacts	• Demonstrate an appreciation and understanding of our natural environment and seek to protect that environment • Foster ecologically sustainable development opportunities across the tourism sector, particularly for small and medium-sized enterprises, employment, and provide for open and sustainable tourism markets • Protect the social integrity of host communities with particular attention to the implications of gender in the management and development of tourism • Recognize, respect, and preserve local and indigenous cultures, and the local and natural cultural heritage • Enhance capability-building in the management and development of tourism
4. Enhance recognition and understanding of tourism as a vehicle for economic and social development	• Harmonize methodologies for key tourism statistical collections, consistent with activities of other international tourism organizations • Facilitate the exchange of information between economies on tourism • Promote the comprehensive analysis of the role of tourism in member economies in promoting sustainable growth • Expand the collective knowledge base of tourism issues to identify emerging issues and assist in the implementation of the APEC Tourism Charter

Adapted from Asia-Pacific Economic Cooperation (n.d.)

The project proceeded through a series of steps:

- Reviewing an inventory of impediments previously compiled by the Tourism Authority of Thailand.
- Contacting officials in the tourism ministries in the five member economies to request detailed information on their perceptions of tourism impediments.
- Interviewing, in person, key government and industry representatives.
- Conducting workshops with industry representatives to identify and discuss impediments from their personal perspectives and experiences.
- Summarizing findings from the above steps and having them reviewed by representatives from the respective tourism ministries to correct any factual errors.

- Developing specific recommendations for individual action plans, in consultation with representatives from each member economy, on steps to reducing or removing the impediments. (It should be noted, though, this aspect of the project is not described in this paper due to space limitations.)
- Developing general recommendations for collective action by APEC members to reduce impediments.

The nature of impediments

The 1996 report on tourism impediments defined tourism impediments as:

> Any factor, real or perceived, such as a regulation, capacity constraint, policy, or operating practice that limits the growth of tourism to or within the APEC Region.
>
> *(Dain Simpson Associates, 2003)*

These include constraints that limit the freedom of the individual to travel to or from economies within the region, or that affect their decision to travel to economies in the region.

They also include those factors that limit the operation, promotion, establishment, or development of tourism-related businesses within the APEC region. These include constraints such as infrastructure capacity, regulatory environments, the financial system, the labour market, the marketing and promotion network, and the introduction of technology (Dain Simpson Associates, 2003).

While this definition and the associated examples provided a useful starting point, the definition needed to be refined for this project. Specifically, the definition potentially includes conditions that industry might perceive as impediments but that reflect legitimate government policy priorities, such as environmental restriction on development in sensitive environments. Thus, the definition was operationally modified to focus on factors that governments might be able to and wish to address through policy or regulatory initiatives, including actions aimed at improving potential visitors' perceptions of safety and security.

Findings

Despite the differences in the details of the social, political, and economic environments of the five member economies, the impediments identified reflect a relatively small number of themes. The following section summarizes these themes. More detailed information on the impediments in each of the five economies can be found in Table 5.2.

Tourism-related policies and regulations

Many impediments and issues cited in Table 5.2 reflect national policy decisions that usually are taken in a context broader than just tourism itself. Nonetheless, these decisions can have a substantial impact on a nation's tourism sector, either in terms of the ability of visitors to enter or leave the country, or of tourism-related businesses to succeed. These include:

- Visa policies are often implemented on a 'reciprocal' basis, in which one government adjusts its visa policies to match those of another government. While some visa requirements have eased in recent years (Indonesia, for example, now makes it possible to apply for and obtain a visa upon arrival at Jakarta's Soekarno-Hatta Airport), tighter regulations

Table 5.2 Summary of impediments to tourism in five APEC member economies

CANADA	
Impediments to individual travel	
Impediment	Comments
1. **Visa requirements**	• All visitors to Canada require a visa, except those from 58 countries and administrative jurisdiction that have been granted exemptions.
2. **Limitations on travel abroad**	• No restrictions.
3. **Foreign exchange (inbound)**	• No restrictions, except cash or equivalent over C$10,000 must be declared.
4. **Foreign exchange (outbound)**	• No restrictions, except cash or equivalent over C$10,000 must be declared.
5. **Customs or barrier controls**	• Visitors entering from the US may expect lengthy delays due to security concerns. • Some restrictions on import of foodstuffs and plants. • Local officers have significant discretion in enforcing regulations.
6. **Departure taxes**	• Many airports impose airport improvement fees; these vary by airport.
7. **Other fees and charges**	• Federal government imposes a C$12 air security charge to all airline tickets sold in Canada. • C$40 fee for air traffic control.
Impediments to the operation of tourism-related businesses	
Impediment	Comments
8. **Business licences and approvals**	• Environmental planning and development laws and regulations at three levels of government (local, provincial, and national); these are not specific to tourism. • Tour operators (including wholesalers, retailers and consolidators), hotels and travel agents are licensed under provincial legislation. • Provinces and territories set residency and citizenship requirements for owners of corporations. • Food service establishments are subject to local inspection and approval regarding sanitation. • Most businesses (not just tourism) are also subject to local fire regulations and inspections.
9. **Import policies**	• Non-discriminatory.
10. **Foreign investment (business)**	• Investment Review is generally required for acquisitions of interests by WTO investors in Canadian businesses with total assets exceeding a threshold set every year; exceptions exist for certain sectors. • Special requirements exist for acquisitions of a cultural business. Investment in Canadian airlines is limited to no more than 25 per cent of assets of the airline. • Direct acquisition of a business involved in providing transportation services with assets of C$5 million or more must be approved by Transport Canada. • Indirect acquisition of transport businesses with assets of $50 million or more or with assets between C$5 million and C$50 million that represent 50 per cent of the total international transaction must be approved.

Continued

Table 5.2 Continued

	• The acquisition of transport businesses working in a federally regulated area with annual gross sales in excess of C$10 million must obtain approval from National Transportation Agency.
	• Investments must demonstrate 'net benefit' to Canadian economy.
11. **Foreign investment (property)**	• Some provincial regulations restrict purchase of farmland or shore frontage by non-residents, or give priority to provincial residents in the acquisition or leasing of public lands.
	• Some provinces impose additional land transfer taxes on foreign purchasers.
12. **Taxes and charges**	• In general, taxed at rates similar to other Canadian industries. Tourism refund scheme allows refunds on GST. Foreign owners face differential land transfer taxes.
13. **Foreign exchange controls**	• No restrictions.
14. **Repatriation of profits or capital**	• No restrictions, but subject to withholding tax on interest and dividends.
15. **Employment**	• Temporary residence for the purpose of employment is subject to approval by the Department of Human Resources and Skills Development Canada. Decision on approval of work permit is based, in part, on whether qualified Canadians are available to perform job. Temporary residence visa is also required. Intra-company transferees working as managers or executives or with specialized knowledge and citizens of Chile, Mexico or US do not need work permits.
	• Restrictions on posting foreign tour leaders in Canada.
16. **Import of promotional materials**	• No restrictions.
17. **Other**	• Proposed regulatory changes to on-duty and driving hours for motorcoach drivers coming into Canada will deter tour operators from developing Canadian itineraries for the US market.
	• Rising insurance rates are limiting to ability of tourism businesses to create new competitive experiences for the international market. Some businesses are operating with reduced insurance coverage, which exposes them to potential bankruptcy in the case of a major claim.
	• Airline restructuring has led to reduced air capacity between Canada and some offshore markets as well as difficulties for international passengers to easily book affordable air transportation between gateway cities and other destinations.

CHILE

Impediments to individual travel

Impediment	Comments
1. **Visa requirements**	• Visas are required for citizens of Guyana, Haiti, Dominica, Cuba, Kuwait, Egypt, Saudi Arabia, United Arab Emirates, most African nations and most Eastern European nations.
	• Citizens of Australia, Canada, Mexico, and the US are charged an 'administration fee' equal to the cost of visa applications by Chilean citizens in those nations.

Table 5.2 Continued

2. **Limitations on travel abroad**	• No restrictions.
3. **Foreign exchange (inbound)**	• No restrictions.
4. **Foreign exchange (outbound)**	• No restrictions.
5. **Customs or barrier controls**	• Import of some goods prohibited for bio-security reasons.
6. **Departure taxes**	• US$26 at airports, added to price of ticket.

Impediments to the operation of tourist-related businesses

Impediment	Comments
7. **Business licences and approvals**	• Municipal patent required for all businesses. • Some environmental regulations affecting developments in agricultural and rural areas and near national parks. • Lengthy delays and high rejection rates for proposed concessionaire activities in national parks. • Rigid legislation governing hours of work, including tourism businesses.
8. **Import policies**	• Non-discriminatory. Tariffs generally low or non-existent.
9. **Foreign investment (business)**	• No restrictions.
10. **Foreign investment (property)**	• No foreign ownership of land within specified limits of the frontier and coast. • Land on Easter Island (Isla de Pasqua) may be owned only by indigenous population.
11. **Taxes and charges**	• Foreign visitors are charged higher fees than Chilean citizens in national parks.
12. **Foreign exchange controls**	• No restrictions.
13. **Repatriation of profits or capital**	• No restrictions on repatriation of profits. • Capital repatriation allowed after one year.
14. **Employment**	• 85 per cent of employees of professional service firms must be Chilean. • 85 per cent of all other firms with 25 or more employees must be Chilean. • Foreign employees must have work visa and valid contract.
15. **Import of promotional materials**	• No restrictions.
16. **Other**	• Multiple public sector agencies are involved in tourism planning, development and marketing, with no central co-ordination. SERNATUR lacks authority to ensure co-ordination and to reduce overlap and inefficiencies among multiple national government tourism initiatives. • Budget and staffing levels for SERNATUR are insufficient to exploit significant marketing opportunities or to meet rising policy and planning demands, including co-ordination of strategic product development. Inadequate research on economic contributions of tourism, effectiveness of marketing campaigns and basic market research.

Continued

Table 5.2 Continued

	• The level of awareness of Chile in potential key international markets is low to nil; the country lacks a strong brand image. • Many national parks are effectively closed to tourism due to concern over environmental impacts. Eco-tourism development is weak and unco-ordinated, and not a priority for the National Forestry Corporation (CONAF). • There is a general lack of awareness of the importance of tourism in government, industry and the general public. Chile does not view itself as a destination country, nor place emphasis on providing good quality tourism services at a competitive price. • The quality of human resources in tourism, especially but not exclusively tour guides, is poor.

INDONESIA

Impediments to individual travel

Impediment	Comments
1. Visa requirements	• Reduction in number of countries offered visa exemptions reflecting both heightened concerns for security as well as the imposition of visa requirements on Indonesian visitors to other countries (reciprocal treatment). • Allowable stays for most visitors cut from 60 days to 30 days. • Staffing shortages limit locations where foreign residents can apply for visas; a particular concern in China, where applicants must go through Beijing Embassy only.
2. Limitations on travel abroad	• No formal restrictions, but pre-payment of income tax required: Rp 100,000 for departure from seaport, Rp 250,000 for land crossings, and Rp 1,000,000 by air.
3. Foreign exchange (inbound)	• No restrictions, but amounts over Rp 5,000,000 per person must be declared.
4. Foreign exchange (outbound)	• Persons carrying over Rp.10,000,000 must have Letter of Permission from Central Bank.
5. Customs or barrier controls	• Imports of more than 200 cigarettes, 50 cigars or 100 grams of tobacco, and more than one litre of alcoholic beverages require payment of duties. • Some import quarantine restrictions on plant and animal products.
6. Departure taxes	• A passenger airport services fee of Rp 100,000 is levied by the airport authority for international travellers and from Rp 9,000 to 20,000 for travellers on domestic routes.

Impediments to the operation of tourist-related businesses

Impediment	Comments
7. Business licences and approvals	• All corporations offering tourism services must be licensed by local government. Approval process is lengthy. • Activities seen as against morals, religion, security and public order, such as casinos, are prohibited.

Table 5.2 Continued

8. Import policies	• Some limitations on importation of capital goods and other goods locally available; subject to 10 per cent VAT, 10 per cent duties and possibly luxury tax up to 75 per cent.
9. Foreign investment (business)	• Foreign direct investment may be made up to 100 per cent foreign ownership in hotels and resorts in selected regions (Eastern part of Indonesia, Kalimantan, Bengkulu, Jambi and Sulawesi). The number of tour operators and travel agencies in Jakarta and Bali is limited to 30. FDI must be divested to Indonesian interests within 15 years of commencement of commercial operation.
10. Foreign investment (property)	• Indonesia does not recognize the concept of freehold land right, although certain rights to use land are recognized.
11. Taxes and charges	• 10 per cent VAT on imports, manufactured goods and most services. • 10 per cent to 75 per cent sales tax on luxury goods.
12. Foreign exchange controls	• Amounts over Rp 5,000,000 being brought in must be declared. Amounts over Rp 10,000,000 being removed must have Letter of Permission from Central Bank.

13. Repatriation of profit or capital	• Payments of dividends, interests, royalties and technical & management fees for services performed in Indonesia to Indonesian and non-Indonesian residents are subject to with-holding tax:
	  – Payment to Indonesian residents (except for technical and management services @ 6 per cent) is 15 per cent.
	  – Payment to non-Indonesian residents is 20 per cent.

14. Employment	• Employment of foreign operational directors, managers, experts and specialized workers is permitted only if Indonesians are not available or qualified to fill these positions or jobs. • An expatriate wishing to take up or continue employment in Indonesia must possess a work permit. Expatriates who hold the post of director must also possess work permits. • FDI joint venture companies must either provide approved training or pay US$100/month/foreign employee to Department of Manpower to support training programmes. • Every foreign expert or expatriate who has worked in Indonesia for 5 years must leave Indonesia and re-apply from outside the country to extend his or her stay beyond 5 years.
15. Import of promotional materials	• Duty is charged on brochures, leaflets, catalogues and promotional materials worth more than US$1,000. • Importation of samples and models is limited to three pieces for display only and must be re-exported; no motor vehicles are permitted.
16. Other	• Media stories and some nations' travel advisories exaggerate the degree of risk associated with travel in Indonesia. • Foreign investors appear still to be uncertain about long-term political stability. • Limited internal domestic air connections. • Poor quality service in some sectors (such as taxis) and a lack of skilled labour in many industries.

Continued

Table 5.2 Continued

PERU	
Impediments to individual travellers	
Impediment	Comments
1. **Visa requirements**	• No visa required for citizens of Western Europe, Asia, South or North America, Australia, New Zealand and South Africa. • Citizens from China, North Korea, Iraq, India, Cuba, Sri Lanka are required to apply for visas. • The visa costs US$14 for personal visitors and US$31 for business visitors – good for 90 days and renewable for up to 90 days. • Tour groups can receive their visas from the Consulates of Peru abroad (processing time: 10–15 days), while individual travellers have to apply for their visas from the Ministry of Interior. • Diplomatic passport holders can obtain their visas from the Ministry of Foreign Affairs.
2. **Limitations on travel abroad**	• No limitations, except for the passport processing fee of US$15 plus US$40 tax intended to protect children in Peru.
3. **Foreign exchange (inbound)**	• No limitations, except cash or equivalent over US$10,000 must be declared.
4. **Foreign exchange (outbound)**	• No limitations.
5. **Customs or barrier controls**	• Border controls and checks imposed to restrict exports of flora and fauna; Restrictions on exports of cultural artifacts more than 50 years old. • The National Institute of Natural Resources under the Ministry of Agriculture also imposes some restrictions on imports of agricultural products (such as seeds, vegetables and fruits) that may be brought to Peru by individual travellers.
6. **Departure taxes**	• US$28.24 for international travellers for airport use and infrastructure. • Additional US$15 charged for international travellers and US$3.50 for domestic travellers.
Impediments to the operation of tourism-related businesses	
Impediment	Comments
7. **Business licences and approvals**	• Foreign investment approval can be obtained at the national level, but business licences are issued at the local level. It usually takes about 1–2 months to complete the approval and licensing process. It may take longer if archaeological sites are involved, in order to protect the sites.
8. **Import policies**	• 10–15 per cent tariffs plus 19 per cent sales tax on imported products; 30–40 per cent excise tax on liquor and cigarettes. • Customs officials have limited English and lack of knowledge about duty-free goods from Ecuador and other Andean member countries.
9. **Foreign investment (business)**	• No particular restrictions on foreign investment, except for 40 per cent ownership for foreigners in TV, newspapers and other cultural products. • For LAN Peru, foreigners can invest up to 49 per cent at the beginning; after six months, the foreign share can increase up to 70 per cent. • Foreigners are allowed to live in Peru if they bring a minimum of US$25,000 and create at least five jobs for Peruvians. • No casinos in hotels under 4-stars or restaurants under 5-forks.

Table 5.2 Continued

10. Foreign investment (property)	• Foreigners are not allowed to buy property less than 50 kilometres from the border for security reasons. • Some restrictions also apply to agricultural land for conservation purposes. • Land occupied by indigenous people is protected – foreigners are allowed to lease or rent the land only.
11. Taxes and charges	• 19 per cent taxes on air tickets and train tickets. • VAT free for foreigners for hotels/lodging. • High airport landing fee.
12. Foreign exchange controls	• No restrictions
13. Repatriation of profits or capital	• No restrictions, but subject to financial transaction tax which stands at 0.1 per cent in 2004. The rate may drop to 0.08 per cent in 2005, then to 0.06 per cent in 2006.
14. Employment	• Up to 20 per cent foreign workers can be brought in and employed in any business establishments, including tourism-related businesses.
15. Import of promotional materials	• No restrictions on tourism promotional materials, but they are subject to import duties unless exempted.
16. Other impediments	• Safety and security concerns of travellers in Peru. • Lack of stability of financial capacities of airlines in Peru. • Environmental protection of tourism resources is weak. • Lack of English-language skills among immigration and customs officials, National Agriculture Sanitary Services Employees and other tourism front-line workers

PHILIPPINES

Impediments to individual travel

Impediment	Comments
1. Visa requirements	• Visas are generally not required to enter the Philippines for up to 21 days. Multiple entry visas permitting longer stays are available but are among the most expensive in the ASEAN region.
2. Limitations on travel abroad	• No restrictions. Filipinos going abroad must present documents, including passport, visa and work contracts/permits for examination to determine authenticity.
3. Foreign exchange (inbound)	• No restrictions. Foreign travellers may bring in any amount of foreign currency. However, amount exceeding US$10,000 must be declared.
4. Foreign exchange (outbound)	• For residents, written declaration of the funds' source and purpose of use is required to bring out foreign currency more than $10,000 or its equivalent. • Non-residents may purchase foreign exchange from commercial banks only with proof they have previously sold the same amount to a bank for pesos. • At airports or other ports of exit, departing non-residents may reconvert unspent pesos of up to a maximum of US$200 without proof of previous sale of foreign exchange to banks.

Continued

Table 5.2 Continued

	• No person may bring in or out of the country Philippine banknotes, coins or checks exceeding PhP 10,000 without authorization by the Bangko Sentral ng Pilipinas (Central Bank of the Philippines).
	• Foreign exchange may be freely purchased outside the banking system.
5. Customs or barrier controls	• No more than two cartons of cigarettes or two tins of pipe tobacco and up to one litre of alcohol may be brought in.
	• Some import quarantine restrictions on plant and animal products.
	• Removal of antiques or national treasures must be approved by National Museum.
6. Departure taxes	• Terminal fee of PhP 550.
	• Travel tax of PhP 1,620 for Filipinos travelling abroad.

Impediments to the operation of tourist-related businesses

Impediment	Comments
7. Business licences and approvals	• No discriminatory licensing for tourism businesses, but there is a lack of standards in procedures.
	• Licensing typically involves multiple approvals and can take up to six months.
8. Import policies	• Many tourism business operators still need information on liberalization.
	• Some high tariffs and customs approvals still exist on products used in tourism such as beef, wine, motorcoaches.
9. Foreign investment (business)	• Foreigners may not invest in small retail businesses (capitalization under US$2.5 million).
	• Foreigners can invest up to 100 per cent in most tourism activities except for transportation, which is limited to 40 per cent.
	• Investment Priority Plan sets annual guidelines for investments.
	• With the passage of the *Foreign Investment Act* (RA 7042 as amended by RA 8179), foreign nationals are now allowed to invest up to 100 per cent equity participation in new or existing economic activities including restaurant operations that are incidental to the hotel business. Foreign equity participation of up to 40 per cent is allowed in the operation and management of utilities (including land, air and water transport).
	• Foreign equity participation is allowed up to 40 per cent of total equity in domestic market enterprises with paid-in equity capital of less than US$200,000. No limit is set for investment in domestic market enterprises with paid-in equity capital over US$200,000.
	• Foreign equity participation is also allowed up to 40 per cent of total equity in domestic market enterprises involved in advanced technology or employing at least 50 direct employees, with paid-in equity capital of less than the equivalent of US$100,000.
	• Foreign equity participation is allowed up to 40 per cent of total equity for ownership of private land and condominiums, as well as the exploration, development and use of natural resources, subject to the provisions of the Philippine Constitution.

Table 5.2 Continued

10. Foreign investment (property)	• Foreigners investing in the Philippines can now lease private lands up to 75 years based on RA 7652 (*Investors Lease Act*). Lease agreements may be entered into with Filipino landowners. Lease period is 50 years renewable once for another 25 years. For tourism projects, the lease is limited to projects with an investment over US$5 million, 70 per cent of which must be infused in the project within 3 years of signing the lease contract.
11. Taxes and charges	• Hotels and restaurants are charged higher electricity rates than other industries. • Local sales taxes are highly variable and sometimes seen as arbitrary by tourism businesses. • Airlines pay customs immigration quarantine charges. • Airlines also add fuel surcharges and 'war risk insurance'; rates vary by airline.
12. Foreign exchange controls	• No restrictions, but amounts over US$10,000 must be declared.
13. Repatriation of profit or capital	• Removal of amounts over US$10,000 acquired as a bank loan must have Letter of Permission from Central Bank. Not required if money is part of personal assets. No more than PhP 5,000 may be removed from the country. • Foreign investments duly registered are entitled to privileges of full and immediate capital repatriation and remittance of dividends and interest. • No restriction to purchase foreign exchange to fund the repatriation provided such foreign exchange is purchased outside the banking system or is obtained from own personal funds. However, registration with the Bangko Sentral ng Pilipinas is required if foreign exchange to repay the repatriation is purchased from a bank.
14. Employment	• Employment of foreign nationals in hotels, resorts, and restaurants must be approved by Department of Labour and Employment.
15. Import of promotional materials	• None, if material is brought in as personal luggage; duty charged if sent as air cargo. • Promotional videos and CDs are charged duty and are subject to screening by Optical Media Board for offensive content.
16. Other impediments	• Terrorist attacks in recent years have led to a lingering perception of risk in visits to the Philippines in some key international markets. • Land reform has resulted in parcels of land of sizes that are not attractive to potential investors. • Bank service charges and holding periods on deposits are seen as excessive by tourism businesses. • Continuity of policies due to political changes.

imposed by the US have resulted in many member economies increasing their requirements for US citizens. Further, Canada has modified its list of nations whose citizens must have visas to enter Canada to conform to the list of the US.

• The nature of the national tourism organization (e.g. whether it is a ministry, a sub-ministry, or an arm's-length organization) and the degree to which it has power to influence tourism policy, planning, and development initiatives among various ministries and departments often have substantial impact of the competitiveness of a member economy's tourism sector. Both government and industry representatives in all of the economies examined felt that the political weight of their national tourism organization did not adequately reflect the importance of tourism in the economy. For example, SERNATUR (Chile's national tourism organization) is mandated to provide strategic direction for tourism policy, product development, international promotions, and tourism research, whereas it has no power to co-ordinate the activities of the various government organizations that actually influence or implement these initiatives. Further, its budget and staffing are inadequate for the expectations placed upon the organization by government and industry.

- Regulations governing the temporary employment of foreign nationals in tourism jobs restrict access to the hiring of temporary foreign workers in most economies. For example, Indonesia permits the employment of foreign operational directors, managers, and other specialized workers only if the company can demonstrate there are no qualified Indonesians to fill the post. Further, any firm in Indonesia employing foreign nationals must pay US$100 per month per foreign employee into a fund to support training of Indonesian workers. Peru, in contrast, has a relatively more liberal labour environment, permitting up to 20 per cent of an enterprise's employees to be foreign workers.

- Limits on foreign investment in or ownership of tourism businesses and land constrain access to capital for growth in the tourism sector. Indonesia, for example, does not recognize the concept of freehold land by private individuals. The Philippines does not permit foreigners to own land. Canada has restrictions on foreign investment in transportation companies as well as on ownership of what are deemed to be 'cultural businesses'.

- Policies and regulations governing airline service to and within an economy constrain the potential for growth in travel between various pairs of economies, and sometimes air capacity within an economy. None of the economies examined permit cabotage; access to gates at gateway airports are generally more restrictive for foreign air carriers than for domestic. Concerns were heard about excessive gate or landing fees in some situations such as Canada's Pearson Airport (Toronto) and at Peru's Jorge Chavez Airport (Lima). Industry representatives in every economy expressed frustrations with perceived inadequacies in internal transportation linkages between gateway airports and secondary destinations around the country. Peru also cited serious financial concerns for its national air carrier, LAN Peru. Airline deregulation and restructuring in Canada has significantly affected the quality of air service in that country.

Safety and security issues

International travel, especially by air, has changed profoundly in most nations since September 2001. Beyond the impact on visa policies, concerns over terrorism have led to new emphases:

- Passenger identification and information systems, including machine-readable passports. Citizens of member economies that do not yet have this technology, such as Filipinos, often experience delays when entering another country. Tighter screening procedures, especially at land borders, can result in significant delays crossing borders. This issue is a particular source of complaint at the Canada–US border.

- Most member economies are careful about screening for bio-security hazards by restricting the importation of many food and animal products and soil. Further, there are attempts at tighter controls to protect the removal of products derived from endangered species. Each of the five economies abides by the Convention on International Trade in Endangered Species. The protection of endangered species was cited as a special concern in Indonesia and Philippines because of their tropical rain forests and high incidence of endangered species. Various restrictions on both visitors and businesses, and inspections of arriving and departing passengers, were seen as justifiable 'impediments' on tourism movement and development by governments in each economy and by most industry representatives (although some questioned whether certain restrictions on development were leading to an 'over-kill' in specific situations).

- The risk of crime and terrorist attacks is rising in the consciousness of many international visitors. Awareness of the potential of crime is spread through word of mouth and media, as well as travel advisories. Such advisories address not only the risk of injury from terrorism but also the risk of theft, muggings, kidnappings, rape, and murder. Risks vary significantly by economy, although it is present in every economy examined. Some cities, such as Lima in Peru, have especially high crime rates. The risk of terrorist attacks against visitors is of special concern in certain parts of Indonesia and Philippines.

Administrative practices

Individuals in every one of the member economies examined referred to problems associated with administrative procedures, including:

- Business representatives in several member economies reported excessive delays in obtaining approvals for business or development applications. For example, Indonesian business leaders claimed that the average time for approval of proposals for a new business initiative was over 300 days. Further, many proposals, especially those involving land developments, require approvals from multiple agencies, which further increases the time before a business could be started or expanded. Bank holding periods on business deposits and service charges are described as excessive by tourism businesses in the Philippines.

- Industry representatives in Canada and Chile reported problems associated with labour regulations. New regulations governing the hours professional drivers (both truck drivers and motorcoach drivers) can be on duty have significantly increased the costs of tour operations and even resulted in the cancellation of some tours from the US into Canada because tour operators were not willing to work under the new restrictive regulations. Limits on hours of work in Chile have caused problems for tourism operators, such as receptive guides or restaurants, when they need to stay open late at night to handle delayed inbound international flights.

- Residents in some member economies experience extended delays in obtaining visas or the need to travel to a distant city to apply for a visa. For example, citizens of the Philippines and Indonesia were reported as experiencing unwarranted delays in applying for visas from the US. Efforts can be seen in some countries to address how they handle visas for their inbound visitors. Indonesia now issues visas upon arrival in the Jakarta Soekarno-Hatta Airport; Chile does not require visas for visitors from a number of nations but charges an entry fee to citizens from a given country equal to the cost of a Chilean citizen applying for a visa to that country. For example, the US charges Chileans US$100 to apply for a visa; Chile has reciprocated, not by requiring a visa from Americans coming to the country, but charging them US$100 as they exit their aircraft.

- Many government officials, especially customs and immigration officers at borders, are free to interpret some policies, often adopting very narrow interpretations of the policy. This was cited as a special irritant at the US–Canada border, where the level of questioning (and the degree of politeness) varies across agents and allegedly by the origin of the visitor. Decisions about the admissibility of visitors or whether a potential visitor is subjected to a secondary (more in-depth) interview are reportedly made on grounds that sometimes appear capricious.
- There are reports of corruption among officials who award contracts or approve business proposals. This was, in particular, the subject of several complaints and media reports in Indonesia during the time of the project.

Infrastructure

Representatives in each of the five economies expressed frustrations about existing levels or quality of infrastructure required to support tourism. While investments are being made in each economy, governmental financial constraints or competing demands for scarce resources mean that improvements are still needed to enhance tourism growth and ensure the sustainable development of tourism in areas such as:

- Airports – including air navigation, runways, baggage handling, and passenger waiting and reception areas in terminals. Peru, in particular, cited the need to improve the internal arrivals hall for inbound passengers; improved ground transportation linkages between the gateway airports in Vancouver, Toronto, and Montreal and their downtowns were identified as a need in Canada.
- Border-crossing facilities – particularly increasing security systems, but also increasing the capacity to handle high flows. Capacity constraints are a special problem in Canada with its long border with the US.
- Highways and bridges – to cope with congestion as well as physical deterioration; every member economy cited needed improvements in this area. Roads outside the Philippine capital of Manila, for example, need substantial upgrading.
- Ferries and ports – improving capacity, upgrading or replacing out-dated or deteriorating facilities; improving inter-island ferry service was cited in both the Philippines and Indonesia. Improving port security against possible terrorist attacks is seen as a need in Canada.
- Water and sanitation systems – expanding capacity, and replacing aging pipes and sewers. This is an ongoing need in many parts of the economies examined.
- Urban streets and sidewalks – repairing deteriorating surfaces; for example, the sidewalks of parts of downtown Jakarta are very uneven, with curbs as high as 50 cm. Traffic congestion arising from private automobiles is an issue in the major cities of every one of the economies examined.
- Air pollution – investments to reduce emissions associated with power generation and the development of technology and regulations to reduce emissions from motor vehicles. This is, for example, a need in Santiago, Chile, and the larger cities of Indonesia as well as across much of Indonesia during times of fires set in the region to clear fields.

Environment and culture

A healthy environment and respect for local cultures are essential for a sustainable tourism industry. A number of policy and regulatory restrictions related to environmental and cultural protection were identified. Some of these are defensible in terms of scientifically demonstrable environmental impacts; others reflect national political agenda and sensitivities. The application of some regulations, particularly related to approvals for business developments and start-ups or licensing, was sometimes challenged as 'over-kill'. Some of the perceived impediments related to the environment and culture include the following:

- Ownership of land, especially access to shorelines, agricultural lands, and borderlands, is a sensitive issue. Certain Canadian provinces have restrictions on ownership of agricultural land or shore frontage by foreigners; some provinces also give priority to provincial residents in the acquisition or leasing of public lands. The Philippines prohibits any ownership of land by non-citizens. Indonesia does not recognize the right to freehold land by individuals although certain rights to use land are recognized. Chile has relatively few land ownership restrictions except for land adjacent to frontiers and the coast, and the restriction that land on Easter Island may be owned only by the indigenous population. Peru also restricts foreign ownership of land near borders on the ground of national security. It also prohibits the acquisition of land occupied by indigenous populations, although such land can be leased. Some of these regulations clearly act as a deterrent to tourism development. While some restrictions can be justified on the grounds of environmental protection or even national security, prohibiting ownership of land by foreigners may be based solely on political grounds even though such policies deter foreign direct investment that would promote tourism growth and job-creation.
- Over-regulation or slow decision-making processes sometimes needlessly frustrates tourism investment and development. Lengthy approval times for business start-up applications were especially cited in Indonesia. Chile has extensive environmental regulations to protect its land base, especially agricultural and environmentally sensitive areas. While there is strong support for environmental protection in Chile, questions were raised about whether some restrictions in certain areas could be eased or, at least, the approval process accelerated. Conversely, Chile's strong free market environment sometimes works against government regulations and certification in the context of, for example, eco-tour operators. Some representatives of the tourism industry felt that greater regulation over the quality of tourism services would actually benefit the industry and ensure higher quality services, and protect scrupulous operators from the fall-out of operators who delivered sub-standard tourism services.
- While member economies refer to sustainable tourism development in their plans and policies, and acknowledge the importance of enhancing the sense of community and of protecting and nurturing their cultural communities, there generally are no monitoring mechanisms or research initiatives to assess whether policies achieve their intended results. Without the ability to show that a particular policy or regulation actually achieves a desired goal, it is difficult to assess whether the policy or regulation represents a reasonable restriction on tourism planning and development or, instead, is an unnecessary bit of 'red tape'.

Taxes

Taxes are unavoidable if a government is to provide social services. However, tourism is increasingly targeted for disproportionate taxation. Part of the reason is that visitors have no political voice in the country they visit, so levying stiff taxes on them is politically expedient. Visitors may be used as the sole source of funding for non-tourism initiatives that a government wishes to pursue but appears to feel lacks sufficient political support to pay for through general revenues. An example of this is the US$40 fee charged to Peruvian passport applicants to support child protection programmes. Other taxation issues include the following:

- Travellers are routinely charged airport fees that may or may not be used to improve airport facilities. They are often charged an additional tax to help pay for security equipment or personnel that are used to protect the general public, not just the travelling public. Fuel surcharges, air navigation charges, and other air-related taxes are increasingly common. While these may represent only a small portion of long-haul, full-fare air ticket costs, they can represent a significant portion of the cost of short-haul airfares. For example, the various air-related taxes in Canada can double the cost of a domestic discount air ticket.
- Excise taxes on alcohol and fuel are common across the member economies. These taxes are charged to all consumers but affect visitors disproportionately because alcohol and gasoline typically represent a higher percentage of visitor spending, rather than resident spending.
- Retail sales taxes and VAT/GST are common among the member economies. Visitors are sometimes exempted from VAT/GST as in Canada or are able to obtain partial rebates, but other member economies, such as Chile and Indonesia, do not yet extend this possibility to international visitors.
- Taxes are sometimes levied on citizens of a country as a condition for their ability to travel internationally. The Philippines government charges a tax of PhP1,620 on citizens seeking to travel internationally. The Indonesian government requires a partial pre-payment of income tax of citizens travelling internationally.

Travel advisories and the media

Each of the member economies studied has been hurt by travel advisories or, more precisely, sensationalistic media stories arising out of these advisories. For example, the outbreak of SARS in Toronto, Canada, which was limited to health care workers in less than a dozen hospitals and clinics, led to dramatic losses in tourism businesses across the city and a drop in travel even to Canadian destinations thousands of kilometres from Toronto. The 2002 bombing in Bali caused an immediate collapse of tourism on the Indonesian island. Ironically, advisories in the US and Canada warned their citizens against travelling to Bali even though there were no travel advisories issued against travel to New York in the wake of the terrorist attack on 11 September 2001, which killed many more people than the attack in Bali. Travel advisories issued by several Western governments warn potential visitors of the risk of theft and violent crime in some sections of Lima, Peru.

In each case, the precipitating event represented a risk but the magnitude of that risk has not always been accurately reported in the media. Generally, the governments of the participating member economies have responded by ensuring the media receive accurate information rather than by attempting to refute the stories directly or to control the stories published (which would be impossible in most cases). Governments of each member economy strive to find the right balance between acknowledging risks to visitors and conveying accurate information about the level of risk. However, ensuring a balanced story and accurate facts are communicated to the public is difficult in an age dominated by headlines, video clips, and Internet blogging that can present distorted, sensationalistic images and stories.

Political status of tourism

The political context of tourism in the five member economies varies significantly. Within the governmental organization, responsibility for tourism is assigned to a range of structures, from a department whose sole mandate is tourism (such as the Philippine Department of Tourism), through departments/ministries where tourism is but one of multiple responsibilities (such as the Peruvian Vice Ministerio de Turismo), to arm's-length agencies (such as the Canadian Tourism Commission). However, in all cases, tourism is seen as having a low political stature and suffering from a high degree of fragmentation. In other words, while many governments pay lip service to the importance of tourism, it does not, in the practice of many national governments, carry political weight commensurate with its economic importance.

Part of this is due to the fact that tourism-related activities and enterprises are spread among many different ministries or departments and industries, with the result that there is no single voice or champion promoting the needs of tourism to government. In particular, tourism is subject to policy priorities and administrative actions by agencies that do not view themselves involved in tourism and yet have a profound impact on the health of the tourism sector in their economy. For example, ministries responsible for issuing visas set policies and implement regulations typically without consultation with the tourism industries who will be serving the needs of visitors who have received those visas. More fundamentally, tourism offices in government often are not consulted about proposed changes in visa regulations. Policy decisions are often made about transportation services in transport ministries without consultation with interested tourism agencies. As one official with Transport Canada put it when approached for an appointment, 'I'm willing to talk with you but I don't know that I have anything worth saying to you. I'm in transportation, not tourism.'

Recommendations for further research

This study identified a range of impediments to the growth of tourism as an internationally traded service – impediments that restrain either the growth of businesses or the ability of individuals to travel internationally (either into or out of an APEC member economy). While some of these impediments may be found in all five economies, strategies to reduce the impediments have to be specific to the circumstance in each economy. These strategies must reflect social and cultural values, the nature and structure of the tourism sector in each economy, and the political environment in which tourism operates. Specific recommendations to address certain impediments in the five member economies were developed from the review of impediments, discussions with public and private sector representatives, and a review of the contents of their individual action plans. These are not presented here due to page limitations. However, a number of broad initiatives were identified that can help create both information as well as a mind-set that promotes awareness of the need for reducing impediments to tourism. These recommendations are identified as initiatives to be pursued under APEC TWG's Collective Action Plan.

Develop performance measures to assess progress towards Goal 3 of APEC's Tourism Charter

Goal 3 (see Table 5.1) is to sustainably manage tourism outcomes and impacts. There is little debate about the desirability of sustainability as a broad principle. However, deciding what the term means in practice and, especially, how to track whether specific policies and practices are contributing to the attainment of this goal requires more work. There is, in particular, a need to develop performance measures that operationally indicate whether policies and practices implemented by a member economy are leading towards a more sustainable tourism sector. These measures must not only be meaningful, reliable, and relevant to the circumstances specific to each economy, they should also – as far as possible – be based on common concepts, metrics, and methodologies. Commonality among the measurement methodologies will allow for more informed tracking and comparisons of progress made in different economies.

Measure tourism's contribution to government revenues

One of the most powerful arguments for removing impediments to the growth of tourism is the lost potential for the economic benefits that can be obtained from wise tourism development and marketing decisions. The contributions to GDP and job-creation are fairly well known and the basic methods for tracking these contributions are well established, most visibly through the recommended methodological framework of the tourism Satellite Account. Unfortunately, the contribution of tourism to government revenues is neither well understood nor systematically and reliably measured.

These contributions take the form of direct taxes (such as business property taxes and income taxes), indirect taxes (such as sales taxes or value-added taxes), government fees (such as charges for business permits, visas, passports, airport security fees, hunting and fishing licenses), admissions to government attractions (such as museums and historic buildings), and duties charged on items imported by private individuals or by businesses in the context of tourism activity. Information collected during the five case studies suggests that tourism is disproportionately taxed compared to many other business sectors. In other words, the percentage of government revenues generated by tourism activity tends to be higher than the percentage of GDP created by tourism. More information – supported by credible and standardized measurement tools, ideally in the context of a module in a Tourism Satellite Account (TSA) – are needed to identify the tax burden on tourism.

Develop initiatives to promote cultural tourism

Tourism leaders in each of the five economies studied identified tourism based on their distinctive culture and heritage as key to sustainable tourism development. Cultural tourism, in this context, is not limited to so-called 'high culture' of theatrical productions, dance, concerts, museums, galleries, and historic sites, although these are important components. Rather, cultural tourism should be broadly conceptualized to encompass tourism that focuses on experiencing aspects of social life in each member economy that makes each economy distinct. This includes cuisine, language, history, archaeology, indigenous peoples, and even ordinary aspects of life that visitors will immediately recognize or categorize as the 'other' (other than their own culture). 'Packaging' of cultural experiences through inventories of market-ready tourism products, quality control, and the development of delivery or distribution channels to make the experiences available to visitors will be essential.

At the same time, potential social impacts of developing, marketing, and delivery of cultural tourism experiences will need to be identified in order to minimize potential negative effects of the commoditization of culture. This work will involve consultation with both tourism service providers as well as local communities, especially any indigenous populations involved, to ensure the appropriate development of cultural tourism products. Special consideration should be given, where appropriate, to the involvement of the local community in the development and promotion of cultural tourism products and the creation of strategies to permit local communities to share in the benefits derived from the promotion of their culture.

Examine the implications of trade liberalization for tourism statistics

Tourism is arguably the most liberalized sector of international trade. The number of commitments made under the General Agreement on Trade in Services (GATS) to open borders to tourism far exceed the number of commitments made for any other sector. This reflects the fact that many nations look to tourism as a strategy to rapidly increase their share of international trade. Tourism offers significant economic benefits that often are achievable with manageable environmental and social impacts, and relatively modest capital investments compared to other industries such as mining and oil and gas extraction. However, the nature of tourism as an area of economic development is often poorly understood by economic policy analysts in national governments. As a result, expectations and potentials associated with tourism often are not integrated with national economic policies and plans.

A prerequisite for ensuring more recognition of tourism in the formation of national policies and priorities is the development of credible statistics on tourism. Moreover, these statistics should be as consistent as possible across different national and international economic statistical systems. Unfortunately, definitions of tourism and related concepts still show significant variations among these systems. The TSA provides a conceptually coherent and logical structure for measurement of tourism as an economic activity that is consistent with the System of National Accounts. However, the World Trade Organization, which manages GATS, has a very different conceptualization of tourism (e.g. the WTO excludes air transportation services from its list of tourism industries). The International Monetary Fund's guidelines for calculating balance of payments in an economy are based on a number of concepts that are not consistent with those of TSAs. For example, the balance of payments methodology does not recognize the concept of travellers (much less, visitors). Work needs to continue to reconcile, to the degree possible, tourism statistical concepts among these various international conventions.

Examine alternative tourism industry–government networking structures

The fragmentation of the tourism sector (accommodations, food and beverage services, attractions, travel trade, convention services, and so on) was cited in every economy examined. Two related problems associated with such fragmentation is the lack of a coherent voice by which tourism industries can speak to government on issues of importance, and the lack of a visible, effective political constituency for tourism that could press for more favourable policy and taxation treatment of tourism enterprises by governments. While no single 'best practice' was observed in the five economies studied, case studies of alternative forms of industry associations and industry–government relations might be examined to identify models or strategies that offer hope for improved communications. Case studies of approaches in member economies that were tried but failed to promote greater co-operation could also be useful. Examples of failure can sometimes be as or even more instructive than successful examples.

Develop case studies of effective media relations during times of crisis

As noted previously, the mass media are drawn to stories involving disasters, whether natural or human-made. Although potentially less sweeping in their immediate impacts, crime and outbreaks of disease also garner media attention, especially if some of the victims are tourists.

Destinations need to be able to deal honestly and effectively with media scrutiny of unfortunate events – addressing the effects, magnitude, and implications of events without contributing to hyperbole or inadvertently feeding hysteria. Unfortunately (or fortunately, depending on one's perspective), many destinations now have experience in communicating bad news to the media and helping to manage the public's understanding of the actual levels of risk as well as recovery efforts. A few examples include the murder of two Canadian tourists in Cancun (2006), Hurricane Katrina along the US Gulf Coast (2005), Hurricanes Emily and Wilma in Cancun (2005), bombing on the London Underground and buses (2005), attacks on tourists in Sharm al-Shaikh (2005), the Indian Ocean tsunami (2004), warnings by ETA that it would once again target tourists to Spain (2004), SARS (multiple member economies, 2003), bombing in Spain (2003), bombings in Bali (2005, 2002). Many more examples can be easily cited – but the point is that many destinations have had to learn to communicate the effects, aftermath, and recovery of crises that have hit them. A series of case studies of the lessons learned – what worked, what did not – in destinations that have dealt with 'bad news' stories can provide valuable assistance to destinations that have yet to deal with crises, or for destinations that will need to deal with them again.

Examine tourism impediments in other economies

The consultative process employed in the review of impediments in this study and the previous one provided valuable information for the participating APEC member economies. The fact-finding and consultative processes facilitated the valuable exchange of information among public and private sector participants. In several cases, the discussions identified impediments (often in the form of administrative practices) that representatives from participating economies acknowledged should receive prompt attention.

Many of the findings provide important insights and information related to Goal 1 of the APEC Tourism Charter (to remove impediments to tourism businesses and investment) and partially to Goal 2 (increase the mobility of visitors and demand for tourism commodities in the APEC region). The examination of impediments to tourism growth provides information that is useful for a wide range of other APEC TWG initiatives. The next stage of work should involve a mix of developing, transitional, and developed economies in APEC. These might include China, the US, Viet Nam, Russia, and Hong Kong. The rationale for suggesting these members is described below.

The issue of the Approved Destination Status granted by China which facilitates the ability of resident Chinese citizens to travel to destinations that have received approval was raised frequently in the workshops held in the five case study economies, and was described as an issue of which a number of agencies would like to have a better understanding. Also, as China is expected to become one of the top destinations in the world in terms of revenues as well as person-visits and an important origin market for other nations, a better understanding of the impediments and potentials of Chinese inbound and outbound tourism is warranted.

Russia, with its social and economic structures continuing to go through dramatic transitions, would be another useful case study. Inbound tourism is not a significant aspect of the Russian economy but the degree to which this is due to impediments under the control of the Russian government (such as visa restrictions or barriers to investment in tourism businesses), weak product development, limited tourism marketing, or other factors merit closer examination.

The United States, as the world's current largest inbound tourism market (in terms of revenues earned) and the largest outbound market (in terms of both person-trips and expenditures), represents a contrasting case to both Russia and China. Its lack of government involvement in tourism development raises questions about whether this 'neglect' represents a source of impediments or, instead, allows tourism businesses to be more responsive to the market. Increasing security concerns, tighter controls at US gateways, and more rigorous border-crossing formalities are certainly impediments. The degree to which tighter regulations constrain international tourism, and whether the full extent of these regulations is justified on the grounds of security, merit examination.

Viet Nam, an economy in a transitional stage but one in which tourism is rapidly emerging as an important export, would also be a useful case study. This economy is exploring a range of tourism development options, including eco-tourism, cultural tourism, and adventure tourism. Opportunities and challenges to the development of various forms of tourism, virtually *de novo*, could offer useful insights into the creation of a new tourism sector in an economy. Finally, as a free market economy, Hong Kong also presents an interesting case study possibility due to its unique relationship with China. Hong Kong's tourism industry is well developed with continual investment in new attractions and infrastructure, but with tight land restrictions. Other impediments may exist that could merit examination.

In conclusion, the potential of tourism to achieve the economic objectives expected of it by policymakers, tourism entrepreneurs, investors, and residents depends on work to reduce or remove impediments to the growth of tourism wherever possible. On the other hand, reducing the potential of negative economic, environmental, and social impacts requires the informed implementation of policies, regulations, and practices that may constrain tourism growth. An objective assessment of existing impediments, including any rationale for their existence, is fundamental to growth of tourism as an internationally traded service.

Acknowledgements

This study would not have been possible without the assistance of the APEC Programme Director, Benyamin Carnadi, and the Project Overseer, Walailak Noypayak, and her team members. The committed support of the officers representing the member economies is gratefully acknowledged. These dedicated professionals helped us organize meetings, contacted workshop participants, handled innumerable logistical details, and provided escorts and translation services, and invaluable, candid insights into the nature of impediments in their respective economies. Without their unflagging patience and assistance, this project could not have succeeded at the level of individual economies. We wish to acknowledge, in particular and in alphabetical order by member economy: Irenka Farmilo (Canada); Monica Anderson and Jaime Toha (Chile); Yulia (Indonesia); Eduardo Sevilla (Peru); and Rolando Canizal and Alex Mactuno (Philippines).

References

APEC (1994) 'APEC economic leaders' declaration of common resolve'. Asia-Pacific Economic Cooperation, Bogor, Indonesia, 15 November. Retrieved 23 October 2011, from http://www.apec. org/Meeting-Papers/Leaders-Declarations/1994/1994_aelm.aspx

—— (n.d.) 'Tourism working group: Asia-Pacific Economic Cooperation'. Retrieved 25 November 2011, from http://apec.org/Groups/SOM-Steering-Committee-on-Economic-and-Technical-Cooperation/Working-Groups/Tourism.aspx

CBC News (2003) 'The Economic Impact of SARS', 8 July. Retrieved 15 January 2012 from http://www.cbc.ca/news/background/sars/economicimpact.html

Dain Simpson Associates (2003) *Impediments to tourism: Phase I*. Woollahra, Australia: Dain Simpson Associates

Stephen L. J. Smith

UNCTAD (1998) *International trade in tourism-related services: Issues and options for developing countries*. Publication no. TD/B/COM.1/EM.6/2. Geneva, Switzerland: UN Conference on Trade and Development

Wilton, D. (1998) *Recent developments in tourism as revealed by the National Tourism Indicators*, Research Report 1998–1. Ottawa: Canadian Tourism Commission

WTTC (2005) 'Global travel and tourism poised for continued growth in 2005 tsunami impact on travel and tourism is significant but limited'. World Travel and Tourism Council, 8 April. Retrieved 24 November 2011, from http://www.caribbeannewsdigital.com/en/noticia/global-travel-and-tourism-poised-continued-growth-2005

Part II

Implications for destination management

6

Assessing the impact of forecast combination on tourism demand forecasting accuracy

Haiyan Song, Kevin K. F. Wong, Stephen F. Witt

Introduction

In the past decades, both causal and noncausal modeling techniques have been extensively applied in tourism demand forecasting (Song, Wong, and Chon, 2003). Noncausal modeling techniques which mainly feature time series modeling approaches typically forecast future tourism demand based on historic trends. Exponential smoothing and the Box–Jenkins procedure have been frequently used in these past studies. Causal modeling techniques often resort to econometric methods to forecast tourism demand taking into consideration the factors which purportedly influence demand changes in the model specification. A number of published empirical papers reveal that noncausal models are often superior to causal models in forecasting tourism demand (Chan et al., 1999; Dharmaratne, 1995; Kulendran and King, 1997; Kulendran and Witt, 2001; Turner et al., 1995; Witt et al., 1994; Witt et al., 2003; Witt and Witt, 1992). On the other hand, there exist in the literature many studies which provide evidence that econometric models are superior to time series models in forecasting tourism demand (Crouch et al., 1992; Hiemstra and Wong, 2002; Kim and Song, 1998; Song et al., 2000; Song and Witt, 2000; Song, Witt, and Jensen, 2003; Song, Wong, and Chon, 2003).

Depending on the forecasting horizon, data frequency, and origin-destination types, tourism demand forecasting accuracy may be different (Witt and Song, 2001). This raises the fundamental research question whether an alternative approach of using appropriately designed combination techniques instead of individual forecasts would generate better forecasts. Would a combination of the forecasts generated by individual techniques be more accurate? A large body of literature has been published in the general forecasting area on combination techniques with accompanying empirical results (Clemen, 1989), both empirical studies and simulation, which provide evidence that combining multiple forecasts often leads to better forecast accuracy than a single forecast.

At the most basic level, an intuitive combination method that can be used is that of a simple average of the single series forecasts that assigns each forecast equal weight without taking the historical performance of the individual forecasts into consideration. Extending this idea, other combination methods which rely on the weights based on the historical performance of the individual forecasts have also been developed. Dickinson (1973, 1975) developed the minimum-variance combining forecast model. Granger and Ramanathan (1984) suggested that the minimum-variance method can be extended to a regression-based method. They suggested an approach which viewed every single forecast as an independent variable and the actual value as the dependent variable, so that an ordinary least squares estimation can be carried out. Estimated coefficients can then be used as forecast weights. Furthermore, the restriction on having combined weights necessarily summing to one could be relaxed to obtain a better fit and forecasting performance. Subsequent studies in the related literature tended to apply regression-based combination forecasts, for example Mills and Stephenson (1987), Holden and Peel (1986), and Crane and Crotty (1967). More sophisticated and complex combination methods have been employed in empirical studies such as Diebold and Pauly (1987) and Granger and Ramanathan (1984), both of which featured an advanced time-varying parameter forecast combination method to estimate the coefficients in the combined regression. Figlewski (1983) and Chan et al. (1999) successfully used a principal component forecast combination method to forecast macroeconomic growth. A discussion of Bayesian issues relating to forecast combination is found in Min and Zellner (1993). These past studies point to the increasing importance and relevance of combining forecasts in mainstream forecasting methodological approaches.

An interesting issue raised in using forecast combination is what researchers call "forecast encompassing." Granger and Newbold (1973) argued that, if forecast 2 does not contain more useful information than that presented in forecast 1, then the latter may be said to be conditionally efficient relative to forecast 2. This would mean that forecast 1 encompasses forecast 2 based on the argument presented in Chong and Hendry (1986). The null hypothesis that forecast 1 encompasses forecast 2 can be tested based on an OLS regression using the residual series of each individual forecast. Necessary assumptions which have to be imposed would be that the forecast errors have a zero mean and are normally distributed. Harvey et al. (1998) also suggested more robust encompassing test methods for the case of nonnormality in the forecast errors. It is noteworthy that encompassing tests are largely applied in the empirical studies (e.g. Ericsson and Marquez, 1993; Fair and Shiller, 1990; Fang, 2003; Holden and Thompson, 1997).

In the present study, one time series modeling approach (integrated seasonal autoregressive moving average, ARIMA) and three modern econometric approaches – autoregressive distributed lag model (ADLM), error correction model (ECM), and vector autoregressive (VAR) model – are applied to forecast international tourist flows to Hong Kong. Two combination methods are then used to combine the individual forecasts. Based on an evaluation of the forecasting accuracy among the single forecasts and the combination forecasts, an attempt is made to determine whether the forecast combination techniques could improve the forecast performance. Finally, a forecast encompassing test is conducted to gain insights into the circumstances in which combination forecasts are likely to outperform each single forecast and other cases where they are not.

Economic factors and data

This study focuses on the forecasts of Hong Kong tourism demand by residents from the top ten origin countries/regions, which are obtained by averaging the annual tourist arrivals to Hong Kong for the period from 2002 to 2004 using data from *Visitor Arrival Statistics* published by Hong Kong Tourism Board (2006). These are: mainland China (9.18 million), Taiwan (2.12 million), Japan (1.13 million), USA (0.91 million), Macau (0.49 million), South Korea (0.45 million), Singapore (0.39 million), UK (0.36 million), Australia (0.34 million), and Philippines (0.30 million).

Hong Kong tourism demand is measured by tourist arrivals from the ten considered origin countries/regions to Hong Kong. A study by Song, Wong, and Chon (2003) revealed that, based on strong economic considerations, the important factors that influence demand for travel to Hong Kong include own price, substitute prices and consumers' income. This serves as a useful guide for selection of relevant economic factors in the specification of the current model.

The own price variable P_{it} can be defined by the relative CPI between Hong Kong and each origin country/region. The exchange rate between the origin and Hong Kong is used to adjust the relative price (see Song, Wong, and Chon, 2003). It is defined as follows:

$$P_{it} = \frac{CPI_{HK} / EX_{HK}}{CPI_i / EX_i} \tag{1}$$

where CPI_{HK} and CPI_i are the consumer price indexes of Hong Kong and origin country/region i, respectively, and EX_{HK} is the exchange rate.

Substitute price is another important factor influencing tourism demand. In this study, six countries/regions are considered to be the most important substitute destinations for Hong Kong: China, Taiwan, Singapore, Thailand, Korea and Malaysia. In instances where mainland China is used in the study as an origin country, Taiwan is excluded from the substitute travel destinations of Hong Kong as (up until recently) it is not possible for tourists from China to travel to Taiwan because of political reasons. The substitute destinations were selected on the basis that they share similar characteristics to Hong Kong in terms of location (eastern Asia) and likely reasons for visiting such as shopping, cuisine, nightlife and visiting temples and historical building sites. The substitute price variable P_{st} (see Song, Wong, and Chon, 2003) is given as:

$$P_{it}^s = \sum_{j=1}^{6} \frac{CPI_J}{EX_J} w_{ij} \tag{2}$$

where $j = 1, 2, \ldots, 6$ denotes the six substitute destinations mentioned above, and w_j is the share of the tourists traveling to the jth substitute country/region among all the tourists to these six countries/regions, which can be calculated from $w_{ij} = \dfrac{TA_{ij}}{\sum_{j=1}^{6} TA_{ij}}$ in which TA_{ij} is the tourist arrivals from country/region i to the substitute destination j. Since the number of tourists arriving at these destinations tends to change as time passes on, w_{ij} is not a certain value but variable at every point in time.

Consumers' income is measured by the index of real GDP of these ten origin countries/regions (see Song, Wong, and Chon, 2003).

Dummy variables are included in the demand models to capture the impacts of "one-off" events. Previous studies examining Hong Kong inbound tourism suggest that the handover of Hong Kong to China in 1997 and the "9/11" incident in 2001 are the most likely factors to have impacted Hong Kong tourism demand. For quarterly data, seasonal dummies are also considered:

$$Seasonal_1 = \begin{cases} 1 & quarter1 \\ 0 & otherwise \end{cases}$$

$$Seasonal_2 = \begin{cases} 1 & quarter2 \\ 0 & otherwise \end{cases} \tag{3}$$

$$\text{Seasonal}_3 = \begin{cases} 1 & quarter3 \\ 0 & otherwise \end{cases}$$

Quarterly data 1984(1)–2004(2) are used in this investigation. The sample for 1984(1)–1999(2) is used for estimation and 1999(3)–2004(2) for *ex post* forecasting. Most of the data relating to tourist arrivals in Hong Kong is extracted from *Visitor Arrivals Statistics* monthly published by the Hong Kong Tourism Board. The tourist arrivals data from ten origin countries/regions to the six substitute destinations are from the *Tourism Statistical Yearbook* published by the UN World Tourism Organization (UNWTO, 2005). Exchange rate and GDP data are from the International Financial Statistics Online Service website of the International Monetary Fund (IMF, 2005). GDP data of Japan, USA and Australia has been seasonally adjusted by these countries respectively. All GDP data are transformed to the index form of 2000 = 100 based on constant prices. Taiwan's exchange rate data is from Taiwan's central bank website and its CPI and GDP data are from Taiwan Statistics Bureau's (2005) website. Macau CPI and GDP data are from Macau Statistics Bureau. However, the latter's quarterly GDP data are available only from 1998(1)–2004(2). The quarterly data for 1984(1)–1997(4) are estimated based on the annual GDP data for the period 1984–97. China's CPI data for 1984(1)–1986(4) and its GDP data for 1984(1)–1998(4) are extracted from Zhang and Okawa (1997).

All variables are transformed to logarithmic form, as Witt and Witt (1995) have shown that most previous empirical studies suggest a log–log linear function can best explain the relationship between tourism demand and its determinants.

Methodology

In this study, one time series modeling method (seasonal ARIMA) and three econometric methods (ADLM, ECM, and VAR) are considered in the empirical analysis of the data.

Seasonal ARIMA

Box and Jenkins (1976) suggested that seasonal autoregressive (SAR) and seasonal moving average (SMA) models may be very useful for modeling monthly or quarterly data. The seasonal ARIMA model in this study is specified based on the standard Box–Jenkins method. Since quarterly data are used, this method is appropriate for fitting the models for the ten origin countries/regions. Dummy variables are not included in these models; as mentioned earlier the noncausal forecasts are generated based on the historic trends of the time series themselves.

Autoregressive distributed lag model (ADLM)

The ADLM specified below follows from the general-to-specific modeling approach. Firstly, a general ADLM for each country/region is specified:

$$Q_{it} = \sum_{n=1}^{8} Q_{i,t-n} + \sum_{n=0}^{8} Y_{i,t-n} + \sum_{n=0}^{8} P_{i,t-n} + \sum_{n=0}^{8} P^{s}{}_{i,i-n} + Dummies \qquad (4)$$

where Q_{it} denotes the tourist arrivals from origin country/region i, and Y_{it} denotes the GDP index of country/region i. P_{it} and P_{it}^{s} are the own price and substitute prices respectively. *Dummies* include "one-off" events and seasonal dummies; n is the lag length of the independent variables.

Eight lags (covering two years) are considered here as many past empirical studies indicate that the influence of these variables usually takes effect for no more than two years. Insignificant variables including dummy variables are removed from Equation (4) one by one starting from the least significant one, which has the lowest t-statistic. The filtering out of the insignificant variables is continued until all the independent variables are significant. All variables included in the final ADLM are statistically significant.

Error correction model (ECM)

The Engle and Granger (1987) two-stage approach is employed to establish the error correction model (ECM). Firstly, a seasonal integration test is performed on each variable to detect seasonal unit roots in the time series. Discussion of the seasonal unit roots test may be found in Dickey et al. (1984), Engle et al. (1989), Hylleberg et al. (1990) and Engle et al. (1993).

In this study we use the test for seasonal unit roots test developed by Hylleberg et al. (1990) (HEGY) to examine the integration properties (seasonal and non-seasonal) of the quarterly series used in this study. To illustrate this test, let Y_t represent the time series under consideration. Then the test can be written in the following forms:

$$Z_{1,t} = (1 + L + L^2 + L^3)Y_t$$

$$Z_{2,t} = -(1 - L + L^2 - L^3)Y_t \qquad (5)$$

$$Z_{3,t} = -(1 - L^2)Y_t$$

where L is a lag operator. These three equations may be further written as

$$\Delta_4 Y_t = (1 - L^4)Y_t = \pi_1 z_{1,t-1} + \pi_2 z_{2,t-1} + \pi_3 z_{3,t-2} + \pi_4 z_{3,t-1} + \varepsilon_t \qquad (6)$$

Equation (6) can be further modified to include (i) a constant, (ii) a constant and seasonal dummies, (iii) a constant and a time trend, (iv) a constant, a time trend and seasonal dummies. Therefore, for each series, five models are estimated.

Hylleberg et al. (1990) generated the critical values for quarterly seasonal unit root tests by Monte Carlo simulation and these critical values are the one-tailed t statistic test for $\pi_1 = 0$ and $\pi_2 = 0$ and F statistic test for $\pi_3 = \pi_4 = 0$. If the null $\pi_1 = 0$ cannot be rejected this suggests that the series Y_t has a non-seasonal unit root at frequency 0. If the null $\pi_2 = 0$ cannot be rejected, this would mean that the series Y_t has an annual seasonal unit root at frequency ½. Accepting the null $\pi_3 = \pi_4 = 0$ suggests that the series Y_t has a biannual unit root at frequency ¼ (¾). Since this method was developed by Hylleberg et al. (1990), it is often referred to as the HEGY test.

In this study the lagged values of $\Delta_4 Y_t$ are added to Equation (6) to whiten the residuals without affecting the distribution of the t statistic under the null (Zhang and Okawa, 1997). The HEGY test shows that the price variables (both P_{it} and P_{it}^s) of each country/region only have non-seasonal unit roots (integrated at zero frequency). Tourist arrivals variables Q_{it} for China, Taiwan, Japan, and Australia have non-seasonal unit roots while the same variable for Macau, USA, Singapore, and the Philippines have both non-seasonal and annual seasonal unit roots (integrated at the frequency 0 and ½). The series of tourist arrivals from the UK, however, has one non-seasonal unit root and two seasonal unit roots at frequency ½ and ¼ (¾). For the GDP variable Y_{it}, a non-seasonal unit root is found in the Japan, USA, Singapore, and Australia series;

a non-seasonal unit root and one biannual seasonal unit root are found in the Taiwan series; and a non-seasonal unit root and two seasonal unit roots are identified in the China, Macau, Korea, UK, and Philippines series.

The seasonal filter $(1 + L)$ can be used to eliminate the seasonal unit root at annual frequency while $(1 + L^2)$ removes the biannual seasonal roots. In addition, $(1 + L + L^2 + L^3)$ takes out both the annual and biannual seasonal unit roots. As a result of applying all these filters, the series are integrated at the same frequency 0. Following this, a general two step ECM may be specified.

VAR model

The vector autoregressive (VAR) modeling method is a system estimation technique which treats all the variables as endogenous. Witt et al. (2003) and Witt et al. (2004) showed in their empirical studies that the VAR model generated relatively accurate medium- and long-term forecasts of tourism demand. In this study, all the explanatory variables are considered as endogenous. Only the items such as a constant, a time trend and dummies are treated as exogenous. An important question to address is how the lag length p of the VAR model is determined. If the lag length is too short, the model will not be able to capture the properties of the true data-generating process while, if the lag length is too long, the degrees of freedom would run out very quickly in the model estimation. In this study, the Aikake Information Criterion (AIC) and Schwarz Bayesian Criterion (SBC) (explained in Song and Witt, 2000) are used to determine the lag lengths of the VAR model. Based on AIC and SBC, the lag lengths of the variables were found to be in the range between two and five for these ten countries/regions under consideration.

Forecasting error

Different statistics are available to measure the errors of forecasts. Witt and Witt (1992) demonstrated that the MAPE (Mean Absolute Percentage Error) is a suitable measure for evaluating the forecasting performance of tourism demand models. This measure does not depend on the magnitudes of the demand variables being predicted, and hence is suitable for comparing the forecasting accuracy among different models as well as among different tourism origin countries/regions. MAPE is denoted as:

$$MAPE = \frac{\sum_{t=1}^{n} \frac{|e_t|}{Y_t}}{n} \tag{7}$$

where e_t is the forecast errors series, Y_t is the actual value of the studied variable, and n is the length of the forecasting horizon. In our study 20 one-step-ahead forecasts are obtained. The MAPEs for the ten countries/regions are presented in Table 6.1.

From Table 6.1, we note that the ADL model exhibits the highest degree of modeling accuracy for three origins (China, Singapore, and UK); the ARIMA model performs best for another three origins (Taiwan, Macau, and Philippines); the ECM is ranked the best for two origin countries (Japan and Korea); and the VAR model is the best for another two origins (USA and Australia). There is no a single forecast method which can always perform well for all origin countries/regions. This result is consistent with the findings at Witt and Song (2001), who demonstrate that the forecast accuracy of each model varies with the origin–destination pair and no single forecasting method can generate the best forecast in all situations.

Table 6.1 Forecasting performance as measured by MAPE

	China	Taiwan	Japan	USA	Macau
ADL	7.93	13.31	13.67	13.26	21.55
ARIMA	11.34	13.61	17.58	19.40	9.81
ECM	10.72	14.69	12.14	14.48	25.92
VAR	9.23	17.18	12.63	8.52	14.26
	Korea	Singapore	UK	Australia	Philippines
ADL	13.87	17.43	10.86	10.02	14.35
ARIMA	15.27	20.57	17.73	15.49	15.60
ECM	13.03	18.89	11.93	13.31	17.60
VAR	11.99	13.58	12.64	9.99	17.41

Combination methods and empirical results

Two forecasting combination methods are used in this study for the forecasting performance evaluation: the simple average method, which gives each forecast value the same weight; and a weighted average method in which the weights are decided based on the past errors associated with the individual forecasting techniques.

The simple average combination is straightforward in combining the forecasts. In practice this method has been frequently used in the literature. Makridakis and Winkler (1983) showed that the simple average of forecasts generated by different models tends to outperform the single forecasts on average. This method gives each forecast the same weight and it can be written as:

$$w_i = \frac{1}{n} \tag{8}$$

where w_i is the weight assigned to model i and n is the number of forecasting models.

Clemen (1989) suggested that the variance–covariance methods of forecast combination tend to generate more accurate forecasts than those generated by individual models. In this method past errors of each original forecast are used to determine the weights in forming the combined forecasts. The basic idea of this method is illustrated here using a pair of forecasts. Let f_{1t} and f_{2t} be two unbiased forecasts of y_t, the composite forecast f_a can then be defined as

$$f_a = (1 - \lambda) f_{1t} + \lambda f_{2t} \tag{9}$$

where $0 \leq \lambda \leq 1$. Let

$$e_{it} = y_t - f_{it} \tag{10}$$

where $i = 1,2,c$. Because of the assumption that the forecasts f_{1t} and f_{2t} are unbiased, e_{it} has zero mean. From Equation (9) and (10) we can obtain:

$$e_a = (1 - \lambda) e_{1t} + \lambda e_{2t} \tag{11}$$

with a variance of $\sigma_c^2 = (1 - \lambda)^2 \sigma_1^2 + \lambda^2 \sigma_2^2 + 2\lambda(1 - \lambda)\sigma_{12}$, where σ_1^2 and σ_2^2 are the variances of the forecasting errors from the two models and σ_{12} is their covariance. σ_2^c is minimized by setting the weight λ equal to

$$\lambda = \frac{\sigma_1^2 - \sigma_{12}}{\sigma_1^2 + \sigma_2^2 - 2\sigma_{12}} \tag{12}$$

The weight in Equation (12) is constrained to range between zero and one. In contrast to the simple average method, this method can assign higher weights to better forecasts and lower weights to poor ones. In practice, because σ_1^2 and σ_2^2 are unknown and the expected values of σ_1 and σ_2 would be equal to zero when the forecasts of the two models are unbiased, we could use the following alternative to calculate the weight:

$$\lambda = \frac{\sum_{t=1}^{T} e_{1t}^2 - \sum_{t=1}^{T} e_{1t} e_{2t}}{\sum_{t=1}^{T} e_{1t}^2 + \sum_{t=1}^{T} e_{2t}^2 - 2\sum_{t=1}^{T} e_{1t} e_{2t}} \tag{13}$$

A more straightforward method of calculating the weight was suggested by Bates and Granger (1969):

$$\lambda = \frac{\sum_{t=1}^{T} e_{1t}^2}{\sum_{t=1}^{T} e_{1t}^2 + \sum_{t=1}^{T} e_{2t}^2} \tag{14}$$

Equation (14) ignores the covariance between e_{1t} and e_{2t}. Some published empirical studies showed that in some cases the mean squared error obtained from Equation (14) is much smaller than that obtained by Equation (13) (see for example, Newbold and Granger, 1974; Winkler and Makridakis, 1983). According to Clements and Hendry (2002), this is perhaps due to the fact that these studies calculated the weights based on a relatively small number of observations. Extension to multiple forecasts cases is straightforward. If there are n individual forecasts to be combined, the weight of the nth single forecast can be expressed as:

$$\lambda_i = \frac{1}{\sum_{t=1}^{T} e_{it}^2} \bigg/ \sum_{i=1}^{n} \frac{1}{\sum_{t=1}^{T} e_{it}^2} \tag{15}$$

Tables 6.2–3 show the accuracy of combining forecasts measured by MAPE in the period 1999(3) to 2004(2). Table 6.2 presents the results of the simple average method while Table 6.3 shows the results obtained from Equations (14) and (15). In the latter combination method the weights are generated from the past performance of the single forecasts, the weights generated from the previous 18 forecast observations are assigned to the 19th forecast, and this window continuously moves until the combination series from 1999(3) to 2004(2) is generated. For example, the forecast errors from 1999(4) to 2004(1) are used to form the weights for every single forecast for 2004(2); the forecast errors from 1999(3) to 2003(4) are used to form the weights for the single forecasts for 2004(1).

In Tables 6.2–3, asterisks are used to denote the fact that the combined forecast accuracy is better than the accuracy of the forecasts generated by each of the individual component models. The results show that all combined forecasts outperform the poorest individual forecast among all combined single forecasts while only just over 50 percent of combined forecasts outperform the corresponding best individual forecast. Furthermore, there is little difference in relative combination forecast versus individual forecast accuracy for the two forecast combination techniques.

That combined forecasts are not always more accurate than the component individual forecasts may be due to the fact that a particular model contains the information of the other models

Table 6.2 MAPE of the single forecasts and the combined forecasts (simple average)

	China	Taiwan	Japan	USA	Macau
ADL	7.93	13.31	13.67	13.26	21.55
ARIMA	11.34	13.61	17.58	19.40	9.81
ECM	10.72	14.69	12.14	14.48	25.92
VAR	9.23	17.18	12.63	8.52	14.26
ADL-ARIMA	8.13	8.56*	13.83	12.20*	12.99
ADL-ECM	8.24	11.67*	11.97*	12.42*	22.00
ADL-VAR	8.49	13.65	12.91	10.51	17.43
ARIMA-ECM	10.61*	12.56*	13.46	14.26*	12.84
ARIMA-VAR	9.00*	11.81*	13.87	12.34	8.18*
ECM-VAR	9.16*	11.95*	11.85*	11.19	19.44
ADL-ARIMA-ECM	8.45	10.42*	12.55	11.99*	14.40
ADL-ARIMA-VAR	8.11	9.69*	12.83	10.48	11.52
ADL-ECM-VAR	8.37	12.08*	12.15	10.97	19.03
ARIMA-ECM-VAR	9.23*	11.71*	12.68	11.59	12.37
ADL-ARIMA-ECM-VAR	8.33	9.78*	12.15	10.96	13.83
	Korea	Singapore	UK	Australia	Philippines
ADL	13.87	17.43	10.86	10.02	14.35
ARIMA	15.27	20.57	17.73	15.49	15.60
ECM	13.03	18.89	11.93	13.31	17.60
VAR	11.99	13.58	12.64	9.99	17.41
ADL-ARIMA	13.00*	12.37*	12.55	12.44	12.77*
ADL-ECM	13.06	16.23*	10.10*	11.34	15.13
ADL-VAR	12.53	14.22	11.51	9.50*	14.75
ARIMA-ECM	12.01*	16.02*	14.40	10.89*	14.09*
ARIMA-VAR	12.24	13.89	12.97	12.72	14.67*
ECM-VAR	11.94*	15.17	10.75*	11.31	14.66*
ADL-ARIMA-ECM	11.84*	14.10*	12.09	10.35	13.69*
ADL-ARIMA-VAR	11.80*	11.83*	10.99	11.45	13.83*
ADL-ECM-VAR	12.25	14.55	10.79*	10.54	14.36
ARIMA-ECM-VAR	11.19*	14.05	12.28	10.51	13.39*
ADL-ARIMA-ECM-VAR	11.14*	13.41*	11.12	10.00	13.47*

Note: The forecasts for 2003Q2 were excluded from the calculation of the MAPEs as this observation is likely to be an extreme outlier on account of SARS.

Table 6.3 MAPE of the single forecasts and the combined forecasts (weighted average)

	China	Taiwan	Japan	USA	Macau
ADL	7.93	13.31	13.67	13.26	21.55
ARIMA	11.34	13.61	17.58	19.40	9.81
ECM	10.72	14.69	12.14	14.48	25.92
VAR	9.23	17.18	12.63	8.52	14.26
ADL-ARIMA	8.10	8.96*	14.11	12.43*	11.72
ADL-ECM	8.43	11.63*	11.88*	12.66*	22.59
ADL-VAR	8.52	12.57*	12.88	10.32	16.90
ARIMA-ECM	10.69*	12.64*	13.54	14.19*	10.17
ARIMA-VAR	9.16*	11.03*	13.92	11.68	8.69*

(Continued)

Table 6.3 Continued

	China	Taiwan	Japan	USA	Macau
ECM-VAR	9.39	11.49*	11.90*	11.06	17.91
ADL-ARIMA-ECM	8.55	10.51*	12.82	12.21*	11.96
ADL-ARIMA-VAR	8.22	9.24*	12.98	10.42	10.58
ADL-ECM-VAR	8.62	11.74*	12.15	10.98	18.24
ARIMA-ECM-VAR	9.55	11.17*	12.79	11.42	9.59*
ADL-ARIMA-ECM-VAR	8.49	9.49*	12.36	10.98	11.02

	Korea	Singapore	UK	Australia	Philippines
ADL	13.87	17.43	10.86	10.02	14.35
ARIMA	15.27	20.57	17.73	15.49	15.60
ECM	13.03	18.89	11.93	13.31	17.60
VAR	11.99	13.58	12.64	9.99	17.41
ADL-ARIMA	13.90	12.67*	12.22	12.32	13.19*
ADL-ECM	13.31	16.20*	10.05*	11.52	15.34
ADL-VAR	12.53	14.70	11.40	9.62*	14.54
ARIMA-ECM	12.11*	15.80*	14.25	10.97*	14.27*
ARIMA-VAR	12.51	13.27*	12.80	12.45	14.65*
ECM-VAR	12.17	14.92	10.45*	11.54	14.91*
ADL-ARIMA-ECM	12.56*	14.32*	11.84	10.50	14.02*
ADL-ARIMA-VAR	12.25	12.27*	10.77*	11.38	13.82*
ADL-ECM-VAR	12.42	14.67	10.56*	10.76	14.61
ARIMA-ECM-VAR	11.47*	14.05	12.03	10.69	13.57*
ADL-ARIMA-ECM-VAR	11.74*	13.60	10.85*	10.22	13.74*

Note: The forecasts for 2003Q2 were excluded from the calculation of the MAPEs as this observation is likely to be an extreme outliers on account of SARS.

under consideration, and hence their combination may not necessarily improve forecasting accuracy. This can be tested by utilizing the encompassing test described in the subsequent section.

Encompassing test and forecasting performance

Consider the case where two forecasting models are involved; if one forecasting model includes some useful information that is not considered in the second model, we would say that the forecasts generated by the first model encompass the forecasts generated by the second model. In this case, the forecast accuracy of the combined forecasts usually is not as good as the better performing model. This can be demonstrated by replacing e_a in Equation (11) with ε_t, the error of the combined forecast:

$$e_{1t} = \lambda(e_{1t} - e_{2t}) + \varepsilon_t \tag{16}$$

Granger and Newbold (1973, 1986) suggested that one could examine whether the forecasts generated by Model 2 contain more useful information than the forecasts obtained from Model 1 through estimating Equation (16). The encompassing test refers to the t statistic for $\lambda = 0$ with the alternative $\lambda > 0$. Granger and Newbold (1973) defined that forecasts generated by Model 1 are "conditionally efficient" to those obtained by Model 2 if the null hypothesis cannot be rejected. However, later literature (Chong and Hendry, 1986) defined this conditional forecasting efficiency as forecast 1 encompasses forecast 2.

Multiple forecasts combination cases are discussed in Harvey and Newbold (2000). Consider the multiple forecast combination:

$$f_a = (1 - \lambda_1 - \lambda_2 - \ldots - \lambda_{K-1}) f_{1t} + \lambda_1 f_{2t} + \lambda_2 f_{3t} + \ldots + \lambda_{K-1} f_{Kt} \tag{17}$$

Similar to the case where two sets of forecasts are combined, Equation (17) can be rewritten as:

$$e_{1t} = \lambda(e_{1t} - e_{2t}) + \lambda_2(e_{1t} - e_{3t}) + \ldots + \lambda_{K-1}(e_{1t} - e_{Kt}) + \varepsilon_t \tag{18}$$

The null hypothesis that forecast 1 encompasses forecast $2, \ldots, K$ is: $H_0 : \lambda_1 = \lambda_2 = \ldots = \lambda_{K-1} = 0$ against the alternative that $H_0 : \lambda_1, \lambda_2, \ldots, \lambda_{K-1}$ are not jointly equal to zero. Since the null $\lambda_1 = \lambda_2 = \ldots = \lambda_{K-1} = 0$ is multi-dimensional, the F statistic should be used as the forecast encompassing test.

Three possible scenarios could occur:

1. If the encompassing tests show that forecast 1 encompasses forecast 2 but not vice versa, this would suggest that forecast 2 does not contain any useful information that is not present in the forecast 1, hence, the combined forecasts of Model 1 and 2 would generally not be as accurate as that of Model 1.
2. If the two forecasts do not encompass each other, the combination of the forecasts should outperform each of the individual models.
3. If the encompassing test shows that forecast 1 encompasses forecast 2 and vice versa, that is the two forecasts contain almost the same information, then the results would be uncertain. These situations can be extended to multiple forecasting combinations.

Table 6.4 presents the encompassing test results. The t statistic is applied to two forecasts cases while the F statistic is used in multiple forecasts combinations. The asterisks denote that the null hypothesis $\lambda = 0$ (or $\lambda_1 = \lambda_2 = \ldots = \lambda_{K-1} = 0$) cannot be rejected at the 10 percent

Table 6.4 Encompassing test results

Null hypothesis	China		Taiwan	
	t-Value	Probability	t-Value	Probability
ADL encompasses ARIMA	−0.61	0.01	0.39	0.01
ARIMA encompasses ADL	1.61	0.00	0.61	0.00
ADL encompasses ECM	−0.40	0.07	0.41	0.10*
ECM encompasses ADL	1.40	0.00	0.59	0.02
ADL encompasses VAR	−1.01	0.00	0.43	0.08
VAR encompasses ADL	2.01	0.00	0.57	0.03
ARIMA encompasses ECM	0.50	0.29*	0.72	0.03
ECM encompasses ARIMA	0.50	0.28*	0.28	0.37*
ARIMA encompasses VAR	1.62	0.01	0.60	0.00
VAR encompasses ARIMA	−0.62	0.29*	0.40	0.03
ECM encompasses VAR	0.89	0.02	0.52	0.01
VAR encompasses ECM	0.11	0.75*	0.48	0.02

(Continued)

Table 6.4 Continued

	F-statistic	Probability	F-statistic	Probability
ADL encompasses ARIMA, ECM	4.22	0.03	4.96	0.02
ARIMA encompasses ADL, ECM	28.84	0.00	10.86	0.00
ECM encompasses ADL, ARIMA	28.88	0.00	7.15	0.01
ADL encompasses ARIMA, VAR	5.86	0.01	4.47	0.03
ARIMA encompasses ADL, VAR	33.67	0.00	10.16	0.00
VAR encompasses ADL, ARIMA	22.36	0.00	5.91	0.01
ADL encompasses ECM, VAR	6.57	0.01	2.72	0.09
ECM encompasses ADL, VAR	35.82	0.00	4.55	0.03
VAR encompasses ADL, ECM	23.90	0.00	3.96	0.04
ARIMA encompasses ECM, VAR	4.74	0.02	6.97	0.01
ECM encompasses ARIMA, VAR	4.75	0.02	4.01	0.04
VAR encompasses ARIMA, ECM	1.19	0.33*	3.45	0.06
ADL encompasses ARIMA, ECM & VAR	4.12	0.02	3.19	0.05
ARIMA encompasses ADL, ECM & VAR	22.44	0.00	6.93	0.00
ECM encompasses ADL, ARIMA & VAR	22.47	0.00	4.58	0.02
VAR encompasses ADL, ARIMA & ECM	15.00	0.00	4.14	0.02

	Japan		USA	
Null hypothesis	t-Value	Probability	t-Value	Probability
ADL encompasses ARIMA	0.12	0.65*	0.30	0.01
ARIMA encompasses ADL	0.88	0.00	0.70	0.00
ADL encompasses ECM	0.78	0.03	0.35	0.05
ECM encompasses ADL	0.22	0.51*	0.65	0.00
ADL encompasses VAR	1.28	0.14*	1.25	0.00
VAR encompasses ADL	−0.28	0.74*	−0.25	0.25*
ARIMA encompasses ECM	1.11	0.00	0.91	0.00
ECM encompasses ARIMA	−0.11	0.67*	0.09	0.76*
ARIMA encompasses VAR	1.03	0.00	1.02	0.00
VAR encompasses ARIMA	−0.03	0.90*	−0.02	0.86*
ECM encompasses VAR	0.32	0.43*	1.03	0.00
VAR encompasses ECM	0.68	0.10*	−0.03	0.81*

	F-statistic	Probability	F-statistic	Probability
ADL encompasses ARIMA, ECM	2.76	0.09	3.85	0.04
ARIMA encompasses ADL, ECM	10.33	0.00	20.34	0.00
ECM encompasses ADL, ARIMA	0.39	0.69*	9.86	0.00
ADL encompasses ARIMA, VAR	1.13	0.35*	18.16	0.00
ARIMA encompasses ADL, VAR	7.60	0.00	53.74	0.00
VAR encompasses ADL, ARIMA	0.07	0.93*	1.33	0.29*
ADL encompasses ECM, VAR	2.67	0.10*	16.56	0.00
ECM encompasses ADL, VAR	0.31	0.73*	28.75	0.00
VAR encompasses ADL, ECM	1.44	0.26*	0.74	0.49*
ARIMA encompasses ECM, VAR	10.70	0.00	45.50	0.00
ECM encompasses ARIMA, VAR	0.56	0.58*	25.87	0.00
VAR encompasses ARIMA, ECM	1.72	0.21*	0.03	0.97*
ADL encompasses ARIMA, ECM & VAR	1.90	0.17*	11.93	0.00
ARIMA encompasses ADL, ECM & VAR	6.75	0.00	34.96	0.00
ECM encompasses ADL, ARIMA & VAR	0.37	0.78*	20.32	0.00
VAR encompasses ADL, ARIMA & ECM	1.10	0.38*	1.03	0.41*

Table 6.4 Continued

Null hypothesis	Macau		Korea	
	t-Value	Probability	t-Value	Probability
ADL encompasses ARIMA	0.77	0.00	0.31	0.02
ARIMA encompasses ADL	0.23	0.04	0.69	0.00
ADL encompasses ECM	−0.02	0.94*	0.81	0.15*
ECM encompasses ADL	1.02	0.00	0.19	0.73*
ADL encompasses VAR	1.16	0.00	0.88	0.01
VAR encompasses ADL	−0.16	0.53*	0.12	0.72*
ARIMA encompasses ECM	0.22	0.00	0.73	0.00
ECM encompasses ARIMA	0.78	0.00	0.27	0.05
ARIMA encompasses VAR	0.44	0.00	0.79	0.00
VAR encompasses ARIMA	0.56	0.00	0.21	0.12*
ECM encompasses VAR	1.54	0.00	0.74	0.03
VAR encompasses ECM	−0.54	0.00	0.26	0.42*

	F-statistic	Probability	F-statistic	Probability
ADL encompasses ARIMA, ECM	39.87	0.00	3.43	0.06
ARIMA encompasses ADL, ECM	7.04	0.01	14.98	0.00
ECM encompasses ADL, ARIMA	84.30	0.00	2.19	0.14*
ADL encompasses ARIMA, VAR	112.72	0.00	5.32	0.02
ARIMA encompasses ADL, VAR	30.44	0.00	18.70	0.00
VAR encompasses ADL, ARIMA	46.98	0.00	1.35	0.29*
ADL encompasses ECM, VAR	25.15	0.00	4.02	0.04
ECM encompasses ADL, VAR	56.06	0.00	2.72	0.09
VAR encompasses ADL, ECM	6.90	0.01	0.43	0.66*
ARIMA encompasses ECM, VAR	19.80	0.00	19.15	0.00
ECM encompasses ARIMA, VAR	160.54	0.00	4.09	0.04
VAR encompasses ARIMA, ECM	31.82	0.00	1.52	0.25*
ADL encompasses ARIMA, ECM & VAR	73.21	0.00	3.49	0.04
ARIMA encompasses ADL, ECM & VAR	19.89	0.00	12.04	0.00
ECM encompasses ADL, ARIMA & VAR	145.36	0.00	2.58	0.09
VAR encompasses ADL, ARIMA & ECM	30.61	0.00	0.96	0.44*

Null hypothesis	Singapore		UK	
	t-Value	Probability	t-Value	Probability
ADL encompasses ARIMA	0.40	0.00	0.21	0.06
ARIMA encompasses ADL	0.60	0.00	0.79	0.00
ADL encompasses ECM	0.26	0.20*	0.18	0.56*
ECM encompasses ADL	0.74	0.00	0.82	0.01
ADL encompasses VAR	0.99	0.00	−0.03	0.95*
VAR encompasses ADL	0.01	0.96*	1.03	0.04
ARIMA encompasses ECM	0.51	0.01	0.88	0.00
ECM encompasses ARIMA	0.49	0.01	0.12	0.46*
ARIMA encompasses VAR	0.73	0.00	0.78	0.00
VAR encompasses ARIMA	0.27	0.01	0.22	0.09
ECM encompasses VAR	0.97	0.00	0.55	0.03
VAR encompasses ECM	0.03	0.88*	0.45	0.06

(Continued)

Table 6.4 Continued

	F-statistic	Probability	F-statistic	Probability
ADL encompasses ARIMA, ECM	11.81	0.00	2.19	0.14*
ARIMA encompasses ADL, ECM	25.34	0.00	28.12	0.00
ECM encompasses ADL, ARIMA	24.33	0.00	6.20	0.01
ADL encompasses ARIMA, VAR	13.95	0.00	2.03	0.16*
ARIMA encompasses ADL, VAR	28.92	0.00	27.59	0.00
VAR encompasses ADL, ARIMA	4.49	0.03	4.82	0.02
ADL encompasses ECM, VAR	6.21	0.01	0.19	0.83*
ECM encompasses ADL, VAR	15.29	0.00	3.44	0.06
VAR encompasses ADL, ECM	0.01	0.99*	2.48	0.11*
ARIMA encompasses ECM, VAR	29.05	0.00	20.84	0.00
ECM encompasses ARIMA, VAR	27.93	0.00	3.28	0.06
VAR encompasses ARIMA, ECM	4.54	0.03	2.33	0.13*
ADL encompasses ARIMA, ECM & VAR	10.29	0.00	2.72	0.08
ARIMA encompasses ADL, ECM & VAR	20.70	0.00	22.27	0.00
ECM encompasses ADL, ARIMA & VAR	19.92	0.00	5.74	0.01
VAR encompasses ADL, ARIMA & ECM	3.70	0.03	4.85	0.01

	Australia		Philippines	
Null hypothesis	t-Value	Probability	t-Value	Probability
ADL encompasses ARIMA	−0.05	0.75*	0.17	0.47*
ARIMA encompasses ADL	1.05	0.00	0.83	0.00
ADL encompasses ECM	0.04	0.79*	0.17	0.50*
ECM encompasses ADL	0.96	0.00	0.83	0.00
ADL encompasses VAR	0.33	0.17*	−0.15	0.69*
VAR encompasses ADL	0.67	0.01	1.15	0.01
ARIMA encompasses ECM	0.56	0.00	0.55	0.01
ECM encompasses ARIMA	0.44	0.00	0.45	0.04
ARIMA encompasses VAR	1.09	0.00	0.60	0.07
VAR encompasses ARIMA	−0.09	0.66*	0.40	0.22*
ECM encompasses VAR	0.78	0.00	0.50	0.04
VAR encompasses ECM	0.22	0.16*	0.50	0.04

	F-statistic	Probability	F-statistic	Probability
ADL encompasses ARIMA, ECM	0.06	0.95*	0.43	0.66*
ARIMA encompasses ADL, ECM	22.28	0.00	6.90	0.01
ECM encompasses ADL, ARIMA	15.58	0.00	5.45	0.01
ADL encompasses ARIMA, VAR	1.61	0.23*	0.69	0.51*
ARIMA encompasses ADL, VAR	27.85	0.00	7.35	0.01
VAR encompasses ADL, ARIMA	4.64	0.02	5.76	0.01
ADL encompasses ECM, VAR	0.97	0.40*	0.28	0.76*
ECM encompasses ADL, VAR	18.14	0.00	5.22	0.02
VAR encompasses ADL, ECM	3.81	0.04	5.13	0.02
ARIMA encompasses ECM, VAR	17.78	0.00	4.09	0.04
ECM encompasses ARIMA, VAR	12.06	0.00	2.90	0.08
VAR encompasses ARIMA, ECM	1.00	0.39*	2.83	0.09
ADL encompasses ARIMA, ECM & VAR	1.12	0.37*	0.50	0.69*
ARIMA encompasses ADL, ECM & VAR	17.88	0.00	4.73	0.02
ECM encompasses ADL, ARIMA & VAR	12.83	0.00	3.78	0.03
VAR encompasses ADL, ARIMA & ECM	3.06	0.06	3.72	0.03

significance level. Comparing the encompassing test results with the forecasting combination results in Tables 6.2–3, we can see that in more than 65 percent of cases among all combination forecasts, the encompassing tests confirm the forecasting combination results in that where a particular model encompasses the other model(s) included in the combination it would not be expected that combining forecasts would result in greater accuracy. But there are still some cases where the encompassing tests are not coincident with the combination results. In the China and Macau models the encompassing tests show that most combination forecasts should perform better than the best single forecast but the combining results in Tables 6.2–3 do not generate similar results. One possible reason is that some regressed residuals series have one unit root which will make the regression unstable. Another possible reason is that if the forecasting errors are not normally distributed, the F test tends to be less robust (Harvey and Newbold, 2000). Moreover, the ordinary least squares (OLS) method is sensitive to outliers, which may lead to inconclusive results. In addition, the possibility of type I error is controlled in the OLS estimation but not type II error. As a result, type II error may occur and reduce the reliability of the regression results when the hypothesis cannot be rejected at the normal significance level.

Conclusion

The objective was to examine whether tourism demand forecasting accuracy can be improved by combining the forecasts generated by various techniques, rather than just focus on the forecasts generated by individual techniques. In this study a seasonal ARIMA and three econometric methods (ADLM, ECM, and VAR) are used to forecast international tourist flows to Hong Kong. Forecasting accuracy is measured by MAPE.

Previous research in tourism forecasting has shown that no single forecasting technique is superior to others in all situations, as the relative performance of forecasting models tends to vary across origin–destination pairs. The empirical results from this study support previous findings as it is found that the performance of each forecasting model varies for different origins and there is no single technique which can perform best in all situations.

A forecasting combination exercise is conducted using two relatively simple forecast combination techniques to see whether the combined forecasts improve forecasting accuracy over the individual models. The empirical results show that forecast combination only improves forecasting performance in the tourism context in just over 50 percent of cases compared with the most accurate individual forecast. This result departs from many past studies in the general forecasting literature (Clemen, 1989), which conclude that forecasting combination generally improves forecasting performance over the individual component models. However, the theory underlying encompassing tests suggests that only if competing models do not encompass each other is it likely that forecast combination will improve forecasting performance over the individual models, and this is broadly supported by the empirical findings from this study and is also consistent with previous studies in the general forecasting literature. Therefore, it is recommended that forecasting combination should always be carried out in conjunction with the encompassing analysis. The two forecast combination techniques yield similar results in terms of their performance relative to individual forecasting techniques.

This study breaks new ground in tourism forecasting research by examining the impact of forecast combination on tourism forecasting accuracy using sophisticated econometric models, though it is only a preliminary attempt with two simple combination methods. The authors will extend this research in the future by employing more complex forecast combination methodologies and examining different forecasting horizons.

Haiyan Song, Kevin Wong, Stephen Witt

References

Bates, J. M. and Granger, C. W. J. (1969) 'The combination of forecasts'. *Operational Research Quarterly*, 20(4), 451–68

Box, G. E. P. and Jenkins, G. M. (1976) *Time series analysis: Forecasting and control* (Rev. edn). San Francisco, CA: Holden-Day

Chan, Y. L., Stock, J. H. and Watson, M. W. (1999) 'A dynamic factor model framework for forecast combination'. *Spanish Economic Review*, 1(2), 91–121

Chong, Y. Y. and Hendry, D. F. (1986) 'Econometric evaluation of linear macro-economic models'. *Review of Economic Studies*, 53(175), 671–90

Clemen, R. T. (1989) 'Combining forecasts: A review and annotated bibliography'. *International Journal of Forecasting*, 5(4), 559–83

Clements, M. P. and Hendry, D. F. (ed.) (2002) *A comparison to economic forecasting*. Malden, MA: Blackwell Publishers

Crane, D. B. and Crotty, J. R. (1967) 'A two-stage forecasting model: Exponential smoothing and multiple regression'. *Management Science*, 13(8), B-501-B-507

Crouch, G. I., Schultz, L. and Valerio, P. (1992) 'Marketing international tourism to Australia: A regression analysis'. *Tourism Management*, 13(2), 196–208

Dharmaratne, G. S. (1995) 'Forecasting tourist arrivals in Barbados'. *Annals of Tourism Research*, 22(4), 804–18

Dickey, D. A., Hasza, D. P. and Fuller, W. A. (1984) 'Testing for unit roots in seasonal time series'. *Journal of the American Statistical Association*, 79(386), 355–67

Dickinson, J. P. (1973) 'Some statistical results on the combination of forecasts'. *Operational Research Quarterly*, 24(2), 253–60

—— (1975) 'Some comments on the combination of forecasts'. *Operational Research Quarterly*, 26(1, Pt. 2), 205–10

Diebold, F. X. and Pauly, P. (1987) 'Structural change and the combination of forecasts'. *Journal of Forecasting*, 6(1), 21–40

Engle, R. F. and Granger, C. W. J. (1987) 'Co-integration and error correction: Representation, estimation and testing'. *Econometrica*, 55(2), 251–76

Engle, R. F., Granger, C. W. J. and Hallman, J. J. (1989) 'Merging short- and long-run forecasts: An application of seasonal cointegration to monthly electricity sales forecasting'. *Journal of Econometrics*, 40(1), 45–62

Engle, R. F., Granger, C. W. J., Hylleberg, S. and Lee, H. S. (1993) 'The Japanese consumption function'. *Journal of Econometrics*, 55(1/2), 275–98

Ericsson, N. R. and Marquez, J. (1993) 'Encompassing the forecasts of US trade balance models'. *Review of Economics and Statistics*, 75(1), 19–31

Fair, R. C. and Shiller, R. J. (1990) 'Comparing information in forecasts form econometric models'. *American Economic Review*, 80(3), 375–89

Fang, Y. (2003) 'Forecasting combination and encompassing tests'. *International Journal of Forecasting*, 19(1), 87–94

Figlewski, S. (1983) 'Optimal price forecasting using survey data'. *Review of Economics and Statistics*, 65(1), 13–21

Granger, C. W. J. and Newbold, P. (1973) 'Some comments on the evaluation of economic forecasts'. *Applied Economics*, 5(1), 35–47

—— (1986) *Forecasting economic time series* (2nd edn). Orlando, FL: Academic Press

Granger, C. W. J. and Ramanathan, R. (1984) 'Improved methods of combining forecasts'. *Journal of Forecasting*, 3(2), 197–204

Harvey, D. and Newbold P. (2000) 'Tests for multiple forecast encompassing'. *Journal of Applied Econometrics*, 15(5), 471–82

Harvey, D. I., Leybourne, S. J. and Newbold, P. (1998) 'Tests for forecast encompassing'. *Journal of Business and Economic Statistics*, 16(2), 254–59

Hiemstra, S. and Wong, K. K. F. (2002) 'Factors affecting demand for tourism in Hong Kong'. *Journal of Travel and Tourism Marketing*, 13(1/2), 43–62

Holden, K. and Peel, D. A. (1986) 'An empirical investigation of combinations of economic forecasts'. *Journal of Forecasting*, 5(4), 229–43

Holden, K. and Thompson, J. (1997) 'Combining forecasts, encompassing and the properties of UK macroeconomic forecasts'. *Applied Economics,* 29(11), 1447–58

Hong Kong Tourism Board (2006) 'Visitor Arrival Statistics', Hong Kong, available at http://www. tourism.gov.hk/english/statistics/statistics_research.html

Hylleberg, S., Engle, R. F., Granger, C. W. J. and Yoo, B. S. (1990) 'Seasonal integration and cointegration'. *Journal of Econometrics,* 44(1/2), 215–38

IMF (2005) *International Financial Statistics,* available at http://www.imf.org/external/data.htm (accessed June 2005)

Kim, S. and Song, H. (1998) 'Analysis of tourism demand in South Korea: A cointegration and error correction approach'. *Tourism Analysis,* 3(1), 25–41

Kulendran, N. and King, M. L. (1997) 'Forecasting international quarterly tourist flows using error-correction and time-series models'. *International Journal of Forecasting,* 13(3), 319–27

Kulendran, N. and Witt, S. F. (2001) 'Cointegration versus least squares regression'. *Annals of Tourism Research,* 28(2), 291–311

Makridakis, S. and Winkler, R. L. (1983) 'Averages of forecasts: Some empirical results'. *Management Science,* 29(9), 987–96

Mills, T. C. and Stephenson, M. J. (1987) 'A time series forecasting system for the UK money supply'. *Economic Modelling,* 4(3), 355–69

Min, C. K. and Zellner, A. (1993) 'Bayesian and non-Bayesian methods for combining models and forecasts with applications to forecasting international growth rates'. *Journal of Econometrics,* 56(1/2), 89–118

Newbold, P. and Granger, C. W. J. (1974) 'Experience with forecasting univariate time series and the combination of forecasts'. *Journal of the Royal Statistical Society. Series A (General),* 137(2), 131–65

Song, H. and Witt, S. F. (2000) *Tourism demand modelling and forecasting: Modern econometric approaches.* Amsterdam: Pergamon

Song, H., Romilly, P. and Liu, X. (2000) 'An empirical study of outbound tourism demand in the UK'. *Applied Economics,* 32(5), 611–24

Song, H., Witt, S. F. and Jensen, T. C. (2003) 'Tourism forecasting: Accuracy of alternative econometric models'. *International Journal of Forecasting,* 19(1), 123–41

Song, H., Wong, K. K. F. and Chon, K. K. S. (2003) 'Modelling and forecasting the demand for Hong Kong tourism'. *International Journal of Hospitality Management,* 22(4), 435–51

Taiwan Statistics Bureau (2005) *Statistical Yearbook,* available at http://www.stat.gov.tw (accessed June 2005)

Turner, L. W., Kulendran, N. and Pergat, V. (1995) 'Forecasting New Zealand tourism demand with disaggregated data'. *Tourism Economics,* 1(1), 51–69

UNWTO (2005) Compendium of Tourism Statistics, available at www.unwto.org (accessed June 2005)

Winkler, R. L. and Makridakis, S. (1983) 'The combination of forecasts'. *Journal of the Royal Statistical Society. Series A (General),* 146(2), 150–57

Witt, C. A., Witt, S. F. and Wilson, N. (1994) 'Forecasting international tourist flows'. *Annals of Tourism Research,* 21(3), 612–28

Witt, S. and Song, H. (2001) 'Forecasting future tourism flows'. In A. Lockwood and S. Medlik (eds) *Tourism and hospitality in the 21st century.* Oxford: Butterworth-Heinemann, pp. 106–18

Witt, S. F. and Witt, C. A. (1992) *Modelling and forecasting demand in tourism.* London: Academic Press

—— (1995) 'Forecasting tourism demand: A review of empirical research'. *International Journal of Forecasting,* 11(3), 447–75

Witt, S. F., Song, H. and Louvieris, P. (2003) 'Statistical testing in forecasting model selection'. *Journal of Travel Research,* 42(2), 151–58

Witt, S. F., Song, H. and Wanhill, S. (2004) 'Forecasting tourism-generated employment: The case of Denmark'. *Tourism Economics,* 10(2), 167–76

Zhang, X. T. and Okawa, T. (1997) *'Cointegration and error correction: Theory and application with Mathematica.* Osaka City: Seseragi Publishing Co.

7

Comparative tourism shocks

Lindsay W. Turner, Chau Jo Vu, Stephen F. Witt

Introduction

Tourist arrivals have been a growing trended series over a long period of time with occasional shocks to arrivals first noticed with the Gulf Oil crisis of 1973. However, more recently these shocks have both widened in their variety of causes and increased in their frequency. This increasing diversity and frequency has drawn significant notice by several authors including Ennew (2003) and Wilks and Moore (2004) on tourism shocks and their impacts in general; Prideaux (1999), UNWTO (1998), Bromby (1999) and Roubini (1999) on the Asian financial crisis; Blake et al. (2001) and Scottish Government (2003) on the impact of foot and mouth disease on tourism in the UK; Blake and Sinclair (2002), ILO (2001) and Brewbaker (2002) on the impact of the 9/11 (11 September 2001) events; Aly and Strazicich (2000) and Pizam and Smith (2000) on terrorism impacts; Travel and Tourism in Hong Kong (Hong Kong Tourism Board, 2004), ATEC (2003) and Canada Tourism (2003) on SARS. Some of the literature tends to focus more upon the recovery process and whether there is a new trend to growth after the shock.

Objective

The degree of impact upon arrivals series has been significant enough to interfere with short-term forecasting and potentially medium-term arrival numbers depending upon recovery rates. Since most industry forecasting is short to medium term now, particularly as a result of the increasing uncertainty, but also because of shorter planning and investment cycles in western countries, there is an increasing need to have greater insight into the nature of shocks to tourist arrivals series. One starting point is to realise that the shocks can be generally categorised into types (see Table 7.1) and from this it is not difficult to hypothesise that different types of shock will have different strengths of impact on tourist arrivals. Wilks and Moore (2004) divide shocks into natural and manmade categories, but this simple dichotomy is not very detailed in regard to the wide range of manmade groupings. Another categorisation is to divide on the basis of impact in regard to direct or direct/indirect impact or duration. Indirect shocks are described to include the Asian financial crisis and the UK foot and mouth disease outbreak. However, the

Table 7.1 Types of tourism shock

Type of Shock	Public Start Month
Air Disasters	
Korean Air Guam	Aug-97
* Singapore Airlines Chinese Taipei	Oct-00
Financial Crisis	
* Asian Crisis	Jul-97
Health Scare	
* SARS	Apr-03
UK/Foot and Mouth Disease	Apr-01
Natural Disaster	
* Guam Cyclone Paka	Dec-97
* Guam Cyclone Pongsona	Dec-02
Chinese Taipei earthquake	Sep-99
Tsunami	Dec-04
UK Heatwave	Jun-03
Political/War	
Afghanistan	Oct-01
China (Tiananmen Square)	Jun-89
Fiji Coup 1	Sep-87
* Coup 2	May-00
Iraq Invasion	Mar-03
Kosovo Conflict	Oct-98
* Nepal Civil Conflict	Jun-01
Persian Gulf War/Iraq	Jan-91
Sri Lanka Civil War	1983-2004
Terrorist Attack	
* Bali	Oct-02
Egypt/Luxor	Nov-97
Japan Sarin Attack	Mar-95
Kenya Bombing	Nov-02
Philippines Hostage taking 1	Apr-00
Hostage taking 2	May-01
* World Trade Centre	Sep-01
Yemen Attack on Cole	Sep-01

Note: * Shock selected for analysis. All start dates are not necessarily the first month the shock began but are the first month the shock became generally publicised.

distinction is really quite unclear in that, seen from the point of view of tourist arrivals impact, neither of these shocks are indirect. Moreover, in regard to duration this is arguably less important than strength, and the two measures (strength and duration) are not the same.

Not all impacts will be negative and cause a reduction in arrivals in all destinations because tourists will substitute destinations on price and likely safety. Consequently, a shock in one destination may cause a decline in tourist arrivals that is then substituted to some degree by growth at another destination. It is not necessarily the case that substitution will be of like kind such as tropical island to alternative tropical island; the substitution could also take the form of a replacement holiday of a different type such as mountain trekking to sea diving/snorkelling. Consequently, unique destinations are also substitutable. There is also likely to be a geographic spread factor associated with shocks both in terms of the extent of destination market downturn, and also in regard to substitution. It is likely that the spread of substituted arrivals will be difficult to measure.

The objective of this research is to attempt to assess whether different shocks can be meaningfully categorised according to their impact, and, if so, whether this knowledge could be used to assess the impact of future shocks of particular types.

Data

Data has been collected on a monthly arrivals basis for 34 countries and regional states over the period 1995–2003 (see Table 7.2). The Chinese Special Administrative Regions and the US regions of Hawaii and Guam have been treated as autonomous regions for the purpose of this study. Not all areas selected have series extending back to 1997, as there is variability between the countries on data availability. The countries/regions selected include all the destinations in Asia-Pacific and North America where data could be obtained. The choice of this world regional area is primarily because these are the regions where most shocks have occurred since 1997. The choice of shocks (see Table 7.1) also relates to the availability and extent of data and the intention to sample from each shock type. For example, the UK foot and mouth disease outbreak was not in the region selected. Data for China is unavailable prior to 1995. The Sri Lankan civil war was longitudinal and difficult to date for specific shock times. The data are supplied by the Pacific Asia Travel Association.

Monthly data has been used in order to be able to measure the depth and extent of shocks. Monthly arrivals are the lowest level of available tourist arrivals data. The data is measured as total arrivals. It would potentially be relevant to divide arrivals by the type of travel at least between holiday, business and VFR groups. It would be reasonable to hypothesise that the greater shock impact would fall on holiday travel in most cases and least on business travel with VFR falling somewhere between. However, data disaggregated by travel type and also monthly is not widely available, and the list of countries where this data can be obtained is relatively small in number.

Table 7.2 Time frame available monthly (from January of year shown) to December 2003

Country	From	Country	From	Country	From
Australia	1996	Indonesia	1995	Pakistan	1995
Cambodia	1995	India	1995	Palau	1996
Canada	1997	Japan	1995	Papua NG	1998
Chile	1998	South Korea	1995	Philippines	1996
China	1997	Laos	1998	Samoa	1997
Chinese Taipei	1997	Macau SAR	1995	Singapore	1995
Cook Is.	1996	Malaysia	1996	Sri Lanka	1995
Fiji	1996	Maldives	1995	Thailand	1995
Guam	1995	Myanmar	1997	USA	1996
Hawaii	1995	Nepal	1995	Vanuatu	1997
Hong Kong SAR	1995	New Caledonia	1998	Vietnam	1995
		New Zealand	1996		

There would also be relevance in measuring flows by country of origin as opposed to total flows. However, again this becomes restrictively difficult. The number of destination flow changes becomes too large to adequately analyse. This is the reason that positive shocks also tend to be difficult to measure. Positive shocks are increasing tourist arrivals substituted away from destinations suffering negative shocks. These substitutions tend to be divided across numerous potential substitute destinations, so that individual positive shocks tend to be smaller than the larger, more geographically concentrated, negative shocks.

Analysis

Not all the shocks are relevant to the 34 destinations under study, and some are beyond the time frame available for analysis. It is also difficult to distinguish some shocks occurring simultaneously such as the 2003 Iraq invasion and SARS.

The time-series for each destination has been examined for the period immediately following each of the relevant crises, with the objective of determining the greatest percentage decrease/ increase and the length in months of the decline/increase. This process involves calculating the percentage change in arrivals between each month and the average percentage change for each month. A decrease/increase is measured as the difference between the average change for the given month (measured over all years) and the percentage change at the time of the shock for the given month. This assumes that the change is a result of the shock, and, while this is to be expected close to the shock destination, it may become less certain further away, or in destinations where there is less relationship in the travel profile (source markets) between destinations.

The extent of the shock is measured by the time (in months) taken for the rate of growth to equal or exceed the average rate of growth for each month after the shock start, or in the case of an increase, the time in months taken for the rate of growth to drop back to the average rate of growth. These comparisons cannot be meaningfully translated into a total tourist arrival loss number, because the return to growth, while signalling the end of the shock, is a rate of growth from a lower/higher base number than would probably be the case if no shock had occurred; that is, the base number that would have been present without the shock remains unknown. Consequently, all that is determined is the percentage decrease/increase against the expected average and the duration in months of the shock.

These calculations most likely tend to underestimate the severity of the shock, because they measure against an expected average and that average evens out growth over several years including the shock year. Nevertheless, the expected average provides a stable benchmark for comparison that permits measurement of relative shock extent and duration well, and provides for a basis of comparison between shocks.

In most cases the change is a decrease but there are also some increases. Increases are not as well measured as decreases this way, because travel substitution mostly involves a spread across several destinations and is less universal across all markets, ideally requiring measurement at an individual origin/destination level, rather than total arrivals basis.

Table 7.3 displays the average and standard deviation results of the analysis for both maximum strength of impact and the duration in months of each shock. The statistics for average impact are divided between the positive and negative impacts. In some cases there were no beneficiary destinations from the shock, namely the airline crash, the Asian financial crisis and 9/11.

The political shock in Nepal yielded the highest average positive shock of 23 per cent, followed by cyclone Pongsona in Guam at 14 per cent. The negative results yielded higher

Table 7.3 Summary statistics for the depth and length of shocks (per cent)

Type of Shock	Average Positive Strength	Average Negative Strength	Overall Average	Overall Std.	Average Length	Std
Air Disasters						
Singapore Airlines CTaipei	0.00	−3.25	−3.25	2.12	1.57	3.28
Financial Crisis						
Asian Crisis	0.00	−17.53	−17.53	19.81	2.36	7.75
Health Scare						
SARS	12.00	−25.40	−23.07	17.12	2.69	12.79
Natural Disaster						
Guam Cyclone Paka	4.25	−13.00	0.57	6.35	1.67	3.12
Cyclone Pongsona	13.60	−46.00	2.75	21.61	1.13	2.69
Political/War						
Fiji Coup 2	9.00	−33.00	−2.18	25.72	2.40	6.52
Nepal Civil Conflict	23.00	−14.69	−11.20	17.00	2.64	8.72
Terrorist Attack						
Bali	6.83	−6.82	−3.13	7.15	1.83	8.11
World Trade Centre	0.00	−11.32	−11.32	8.82	2.58	13.73

averages, with the localised impact of cyclone Pongsona the highest average of −46 per cent. The average impact of the second political coup in Fiji and SARS were also high at −33 per cent and −25 per cent respectively. In terms of the overall averages, including both the positive and negative impacts, the cyclones in Guam yielded higher positive shocks than negative shocks. However, this was not the case for the other shocks which overall were negative, the highest being SARS at −23 per cent followed by the Asian financial crisis at −18 per cent, while perhaps surprisingly Nepal and 9/11 were roughly equal at −11 per cent.

In terms of duration, SARS, Nepal and 9/11 were the longest at 3 months and cyclone Pongsona shortest at one month.

The highest variation in terms of strength across the study area was Fiji's second coup, followed by Cyclone Pongsona. The highest variation in terms of duration was 9/11 and then SARS.

It is possible to look more closely at the geographic spread of the shocks. For this purpose the grid in Figure 7.1 has been created to show the relative locations of each of the capital cities for each of the sample countries.

The relative grid allows for the calculation of the mean centre for each shock and the standard distance deviation for the shocks calculated as weighted means of distance and co-ordinate standard deviations from the weighted means. Figure 7.1 displays these summary measures.

The average strength of the impact of all shocks clusters to the centre of the geographic region of study, as does the average duration of shock. That is, the impact of the shocks in terms of average strength and duration focus geographically to the centre, and tend to spread across the whole region. The degree of spread is better measured relatively by the standard distance deviation. In effect this is the radius of a circle based upon the mean centre. The larger the radius the greater the relative spread of the shock.

The Asian financial crisis and SARS demonstrate the largest geographic dispersion across the region of study in terms of strength of impact as shown by the standard distance deviations

(5.01 and 5.13). SARS and 9/11 have the widest dispersion across the region in terms of duration of shock as shown in Figure 7.2 by the standard distance deviations (1.00 and 1.01). The lowest effect in terms of shock impact is the airline disaster (2.29) and the lowest impact in terms of duration are the Guam cyclones (0.80 and 0.79).

Implications

It is clear that SARS as a health scare had the greatest shock impact in terms of both strength and duration of the shock. Overall the Asian financial crisis was second, particularly in regard to

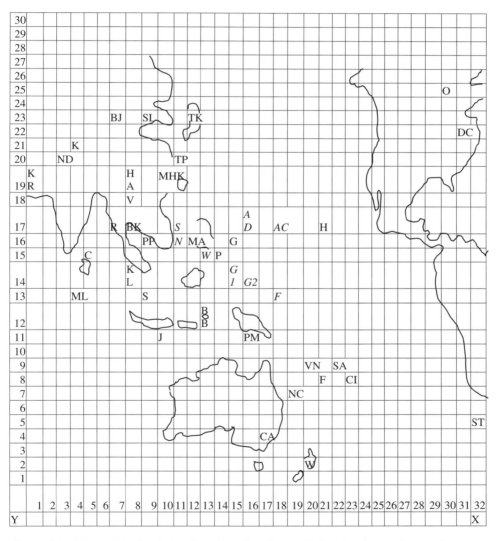

Figure 7.1 Map grid of relative locations for the capital cities for each sample country strength

Key

Country	Capital	Code		Event	WMeanCX	WMeanCY	StdDistDev
Australia	Canberra	CA					
Cambodia	Phnom Penh	PP					
Canada	Ottawa	O					
Chile	Santiago	ST		Strength			
China	Beijing	BJ					
CTaipei	Taipei	TP			WMeanCX	WMeanCY	StdDistDev
Cook Islands	Avarua	CI	AD	Airline Disaster	16.50	16.64	2.29
Fiji	Suva	F	AC	Asian Crisis	18.36	16.98	5.01
Guam	Agana	G	S	SARS	10.78	16.76	5.13
Hawaii	Honolulu	H	G1	Guam 1	15.17	14.24	2.71
Hong Kong	Hong Kong	HK	G2	Guam 2	15.58	14.09	4.47
Indonesia	Jakarta	J	F	Fiji 2	18.05	12.71	4.05
India	New Delhi	ND	N	Nepal	10.73	15.57	4.69
Japan	Tokyo	TK	B	Bali	12.90	14.01	3.28
Korea	Seoul	SL	W	WTC	13.42	14.81	4.24
Laos	Vientiane	V					
Macau	Macau	M					
Malaysia	Kuala Lumpur	KL					
Maldives	Male	ML					
Myanmar	Rangoon	R		Length			
Nepal	Katmandu	K					
New Caledonia	Noumea	NC			WMeanCX	WMeanCY	StdDistDev
New Zealand	Wellington	W	AD	Airline Disaster	15.79	20.21	0.89
Pakistan	Karachi	KR	C	Asian Crisis	12.38	15.98	0.90
Palau	Koror	P	S	SARS	12.09	15.45	1.00
Papua New Guinea	Port Moresby	PM	G	Guam 1	13.97	14.89	0.80
Philippines	Manilla	MA	G	Guam 2	13.56	15.25	0.79
Samoa	Apia	SA	F	Fiji 2	14.81	14.19	0.93
Singapore	Singapore	S	N	Nepal	12.61	14.65	0.95
Sri Lanka	Colombo	C	B	Bali	13.47	14.81	0.91
Thailand	Bangkok	BK	W	WTC	13.18	15.84	1.01
USA	WashingtonDC	DC					
Vanuatu	Vila	VN	Note: Guam 1 and 2 occur at the same grid location G.				
Vietnam	Hanoi	HA					

Note: WmeanCX – Weighted mean coordinate for x axis
WmeanCY – Weighted mean coordinate for y axis

Figure 7.1   Continued

severity of the shock. Furthermore, the political crisis in Nepal had a surprisingly strong impact although this was counterbalanced by strong positive substitution. In the case of natural disasters as represented by the Guam cyclones, the localised shock was very high, but strongly counterbalanced by strong substitution to alternative destinations; this was also true for the political impact of the coup in Fiji.

The 9/11 events were not as significant in this study region as SARS, the Asian financial crisis or Nepal, although the impact was virtually as strong as Nepal, and unlike Nepal not counterbalanced by any positive substitution.

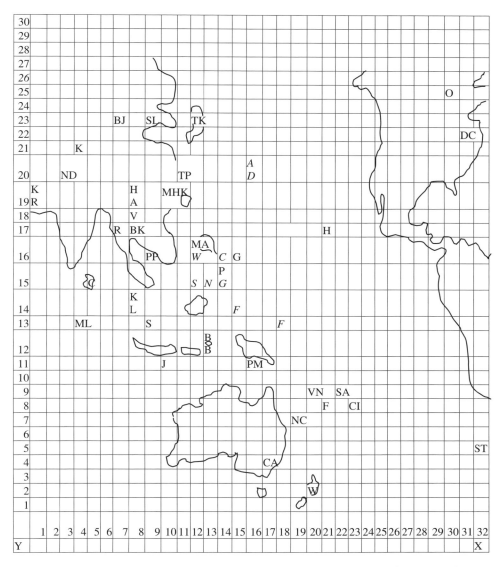

Figure 7.2 Map grid of relative locations for the capital cities for each sample country duration

There is a significant difference between different political crises (Fiji and Nepal) and differ-ent terror attacks (Bali and 9/11). Although this may be expected (because the media focus on 9/11 and Nepal and the spectacular nature of the shocks far exceeded Bali and Fiji) the strength of the difference is large in the order of 8–9 per cent, and the lesser shocks (Fiji and Bali) are more in the order of the impact of the airline disaster overall.

Geographically, the shock strength and length tended to concentrate in the centre of the study region, indicating the overall impacts were not geographically different. However, the spread of the shocks geographically were different with SARS and the Asian financial crisis displaying the widest geographic impact in terms of strength, and SARS and 9/11 the widest impact in terms of length of shock. On the other hand the airline disaster had the least impact in strength across the region and the natural disasters the least impact in terms of duration across the region.

Conclusion

There are limitations in the data available for this analysis and consequently there must be some hesitation in deriving concrete conclusions from the results. Moreover the wide potential variety of shock types (as evidenced by the 2004 tsunami) must give cause for concern on basing forecasted impacts on such a limited sample. However, there are some inferences evident in this analysis. It appears that natural disasters have the strongest likelihood of generating positive travel substitution that may alleviate the overall tourist arrivals downturn; this also appears to be evident in localised political crises and terrorist attacks. On the other hand, it would seem that crises such as airline crashes and financial crises will be less likely to generate positive substitution, along with major geographically widespread shocks such as 9/11 and SARS.

SARS was the most significant shock studied in this data set and had the greatest strength of impact and duration. However, SARS also had a unique characteristic not evident with the other examples of shock. SARS had the month of maximum impact at different times in different countries, extending from March to June 2003. All the other shocks had the maximum impact in the month immediately after the date of occurrence. SARS rolled out across the study region over time as its media coverage extended to report on ever increasing incidents. In fact only a little over 8,000 cases were reported (far fewer than previous flu epidemics) and the death toll was relatively low. What set SARS apart as a high impact shock was the mass media interest and extended sensationalism over several months.

Although the assessment of the impact of the tsunami according to the above should be less because it is a natural disaster (being characterised by more substitution) a lesson was also learned from SARS: not to allow the media to expand the tourism downturn unnecessarily. Organisations such as PATA and the NTO in Thailand were very quick to argue that the best help people could offer was to return as soon as possible as tourists, to spend money in the local economies. Information on the exact extent of the disaster was made available quickly and accurately. Interviews and media stories were co-ordinated and released to counter each potentially sensational claim of travel downturns. This risk management approach may well be very effective with other shocks as they variously occur.

Consequently, while the evidence suggests that a health scare could be the most significant potential shock type, there may be ways by which industry can control unnecessary loss of business. However, if the health scare is genuinely significant then this type of shock has the greatest potential for high impact in terms of both strength and duration.

Localised shocks such as airline disasters, political turmoil and cyclones can be extremely severe in the local centres of shock, but are less likely to cause widespread travel downturns.

Different types of shock are evidenced to have different potential impacts. In the future the travel industry must be most concerned about a health scare, and if it is genuine prepare for a huge impact based on maximum downturns ranging close to 50 per cent and lasting several months. Financial crises and political turmoil are also highly dangerous to arrivals, and, although political crises can lead to positive substitution to some extent, they have the potential for high impact shocks of significant duration. Equally a 9/11-style attack would be severe and long in its impact if it is sensational in nature. Whereas more localised terror attacks may be severe for only the immediate destination. Natural disasters are characterised by high impact and high substitution, making their impact less overall.

References

Aly, H. Y. and Strazicich, M. C. (2000) *Terrorism and tourism: Is the impact permanent or transitory? Time series evidence from some MENA countries*. Columbus, OH: Ohio State University, Department of Economics

ATEC (2003) 'SARS tourism downturn exceeds terrorism impacts'. Australian Tourism Export Council. Retrieved 3 November 2011, from http://www.atec.net.au/MediaReleaseSARS_Tourim_Downturn_ Exceeds_Terrorism Impacts.htm

Blake, A. and Sinclair, M. T. (2002) 'Tourism crisis management: Responding to September 11'. Discussion Paper No. 2002/7, DeHaan Institute, Nottingham University

Blake, A., Sinclair, M. T. and Sugiyarto, G. (2001) 'The economy-wide effects of foot and mouth disease in the UK economy'. Cristel DeHaan Tourism and Travel Institute, Nottingham Business School. Retrieved 3 November 2011, from http://www.notingham.ac.uk/ttri

Brewbaker, P. H. (2002) 'Hawaii economic trends'. Retrieved 3 November 2011, from http://www.hawaii.edu/hivandaids/Hawaii/Hawaii_Trends,_January_2003.pdf

Bromby, R. (1999) 'South Korea leads race for recovery'. *The Australian*, 15 September

Canada Tourism (2003) '2003: A bad year for tourism'. Retrieved 3 November 2011, from http://www41.statcan.ca/2007/4007/ceb4007_002-eng.htm

Ennew, C. (2003) 'Understanding the economic impact of tourism'. Som Nath Chib Memorial Lecture, 14 February 2003, DeHaan Institute, Nottingham University

Hong Kong Tourism (2004) 'Hong Kong tourist arrivals down 6.2 percent in 2003, hit by SARS'. Retrieved 3 November 2011, from http://ehotelier.com/hospitality-news/item.php?id=A1110_ 0_11_0_M

ILO (2001) *The social impact on the hotel and tourism sector of events subsequent to 11 September 2001*. Geneva: International Labour Office

Pizam, A. and Smith, G. (2000) 'Tourism and terrorism: A quantitative analysis of major terrorist acts and their impact on tourism destinations'. *Tourism Economics*, 6(2), 123–28

Prideaux, B. (1999) 'Tourism perspectives of the Asian financial crisis: Lessons for the future'. *Current Issues in Tourism*, 2(4), 279–93

Roubini, N. (1999) 'What caused Asia's economic currency crisis and its global contagion?'. Retrieved 3 November 2011, from http://www.stern.nyu.edu/~nroubini/asia/AsiaHomepage.html

Scottish Government (2003) *Economic impact of the 2001 foot and mouth disease outbreak in Scotland: Final report*. Scottish Parliament. Retrieved 3 November 2011, from http://www.scotland.gov.uk/library5/ agri/eifm-04.asp

UNWTO (1998) *Asian financial crisis and its impact on tourism*. Madrid: UN World Tourism Organization

Wilks, J. and Moore, S. (2004) *Tourism risk management for the Asia-Pacific region: An authoritative guide for managing crises and disasters*. Gold Coast MC, Queensland: Cooperative Research Centre for Sustainable Tourism

8

Why the public should pay for tourism marketing

A public economics perspective

Egon Smeral

Introduction

As the political climate changes and discussion of liberalisation intensifies, the involvement of the government in tourism policy – and especially in tourism marketing at the national level – has increasingly come to be called into question and challenged. As a political mega-trend of the twenty-first century, the pull-out of the government is seen in the context of the liberal economic doctrine as an all-purpose means of increasing economic performance, even when the government pulls out of its responsibilities in the production of public goods. In light of these tendencies, the effort will be made here to determine whether public involvement in tourism marketing – practically understood as the provision of financial support for activities related to tourism marketing – can be justified within the framework of liberal economic policy, and whether it is economically efficient. To compensate for the relative scarcity of literature on this topic, this paper relies primarily on the use of public economics tools. Organisational questions such as the legal form taken by national tourism organisations (NTOs) or the position occupied by public marketing departments in the relevant administrative hierarchies are not dealt with here.

Justification of public involvement in tourism marketing

General

Whether as company-oriented incentive systems or via involvement in tourism marketing, public support is an intervention in market mechanisms. For this reason, public involvement in market economies needs to be carefully justified. Economic theory offers several convincing approaches to such a justification for the public promotion of tourism. Some of the more important approaches are rooted in welfare economics.

In welfare economics analysis begins with the premise that Pareto-optimal allocation of resources prevails, assuming there is perfect competition (see Figure 8.1). In other words, it is not possible to improve one person's position by changing the allocation without making another person's position worse. In a Pareto-optimal situation, public support makes no sense

---

(1) Endowment of resources are taken as a given.
(2) Constancy of both production technology and the product range.
(3) Constancy of preferences over time; preferences are taken as a given.
(4) Formal freedom of choice between alternatives (freedom in production, investment, choice of profession, consumption).
(5) Homogeneity of preferences (no personal or spatial preferences; no preferences for certain goods or services).
(6) Atomistic market structure (many small suppliers and demanders with relatively small market shares).
(7) Complete market transparency (all market actors have complete and free information about the quality and prices of goods).
(8) Unlimited mobility of all factors of production and all goods, especially free entry and exit from the market.
(9) Unlimited divisibility of all factors of production and all goods.
(10) Infinite reaction speed (no time needed for adjustment processes).
(11) No involuntary exchange relationships (absence of technological external effects).

Figure 8.1   The assumptions made by the model of perfect competition

economically because it would reduce public welfare in general; that is, it is not possible to improve things for one person without making them worse for another. However, if a situation occurs where it is not possible to reach Pareto-efficient resource allocation, then there is a 'market failure.' The existence of market failures and also of market distortions justify public intervention in terms of improving market results (Bieger, 2000; Choy, 1993; Kerr et al., 2001; Pike, 2004; Smeral, 1998).

For economic theories characteristics, the perspective outlined here has an essential implication for economic and social policy which can be described as the liberal approach: as long as there are no well-founded counterarguments, individual, self-interested actions increase public welfare. This follows from the idea that self-interested actors will enter voluntarily into an exchange relationship only if it results in their benefit. Since it is generally assumed that individuals' self-interested exchange relationships contribute to increases in overall economic welfare, the liberal doctrine points to the need for justifying any public interventions. This justification could lie in the market exchange relationship between two parties having a positive or negative effect on the welfare of a third party, or in that 'market failure' exists.

It must be said here that no criterion exists to precisely identify where market failure begins and ends. It will always be necessary to make a value judgment on the extent to which a market is working, or whether sufficient market failure exists to call for public intervention.

Economic thinking allows us to name four causes for market failure:

- external effects;
- indivisibilities;
- information deficits; and
- lack of adjustment and flexibility.

These four causes represent contradictions to the important suppositions made by the model of perfect competition. The theory of market failure is thus a systematic analysis of what happens when reality diverges from the assumptions of perfect competition.

In particular, external effects and information deficits play an important role in justifying public involvement in tourism marketing. Joseph Stiglitz recognised and discussed the importance of information asymmetries; in 2001 he received the Nobel Prize in Economics for his extraordinary work (Stiglitz, 2000).

In the context of liberal economic policy, what is also of decisive importance for the justification under discussion is the existence of relatively high transaction costs (e.g. due to a high fragmented supply) and companies often being too small (Müller and Scheurer, 2001). High transaction costs make cooperative efforts and destination development difficult; the reduction of these costs should be one of the main goals of modern tourism policy.

Considerations of transaction costs are not actually part of traditional approaches to the theory of market failure, yet just as external effects do, their existence justifies public intervention.

Where market failure exists, it is by no means automatically guaranteed that the state or any bureaucratic system commissioned by it will in fact be able to improve market results, as there is always the possibility of state and/or bureaucratic failures.

In the end, whether public intervention makes sense or not should be judged by considering whether the net welfare level is higher once the accompanying intervention costs have been taken into account, or whether it is higher when the imperfect market is left to itself.

External effects

In tourism, it is especially the technological externalities which play a role. Such technological externalities exist when there is a physical connection between the production and utility functions of some actors that is not (or not fully) reflected in the relevant market relationships. The result is that the private costs and benefits (i.e. the payment flows experienced by the individual producers or consumers) diverge from the resulting overall social costs and benefits. The difference between these cost and benefit categories (e.g. social benefits minus private benefits, or social costs minus private costs) define the size of the technological external effects (benefits or costs). Where there are technological external effects, market prices are distorted reflections of the actual relations of scarcity because external benefits or costs are not considered.

For public tourism policy, technological externalities come into play because organisations without existing market relations engage in publicly funded marketing activities such as image building and brand management and in so doing generate benefits and income for a wide variety of businesses, for example hotels, restaurants, trading concerns, personal service providers, banks, insurance companies, legal and business service providers, agriculture and forestry, construction, and the food industry (Pearce, 1992). The overall economic benefit is thus significantly greater than individual benefits and income flows; for cost reasons – consider such examples as an image campaign in a foreign country – this overall benefit could not be realised by means of individual initiatives. This particular form of 'market failure', the existence of positive external effects, offers justification for public intervention (Nowotny, 1996). Publicly funded promotion measures are consistent with liberal economic policy only when they can be understood as 'compensation' for triggering positive external effects, or increases in overall economic welfare and/or improvements in market results. Based on individual interests, these positive external effects would not be possible or would be too small.

The scientific discussion takes it as a given that the market fails in allocating so-called 'public goods'. Public goods must be produced by the government because the market fails to provide them. Accordingly, socially desirable goods that the market provides without any special intervention are called 'private goods'.

In general, a good is called a 'public good' when it is not feasible to exclude anyone (at a justifiable cost) from its benefits. In the case of external benefits, non-excludability means that someone who does not pay for consuming the good is nevertheless not barred from consumption (this is the classic free-rider problem). Positive externalities thus come to the fore when no property rights exist – or when there is no way to enforce property rights without unjustifiable cost – so that a public producer cannot disallow actors such as certain hotels or linked industries from consuming the good in question for free. This may be the case with advertising effects, for example (Coase, 1960).

Three reasons can be suggested to explain why the exclusion principle cannot be applied:

*   Exclusion would mean relatively high transaction costs and is thus not economically justifiable. It might even reach the point where exclusion costs are greater than lost benefits.
*   The waiver may be politically motivated (tourism marketing measures are often understood to be indirect subsidies for low-income regions such as mountain or border areas).
*   Technical conditions preclude excludability.

The first two are relevant for tourism, since there are only a few exceptional (and often extreme) situations in which the technical conditions for excludability are not given, for example where the public good in question is police security or national defence.

'Image' is a good example of how difficult and costly it can be to enforce the exclusion principle in cases of external benefit. How would one even begin to go about explaining to a group of hotel guests which of their local hosts had contributed to what extent to their destination's 'image'? And what ostensible reason could a guest have to take advantage of only those local supplies whose sponsors had voluntarily contributed to building the destination's image? Of course, it would be possible to offer premiums to guests who frequent only the businesses of the contributors, but administration costs coupled with the cost of compensating for quality and preference differences would make a loss of any such venture. A further difficulty would be presented by a whole row of businesses such as restaurants, trading concerns, banks, insurance companies, tax advisers and construction firms that benefit only partially from image campaigns.

Because tourism providers who contribute nothing to image building are free-riders who enjoy the benefits of this public good, a situation which results in positive externalities, attempts to finance image building via voluntary contributions would most likely lead to overall under-financing of the undertaking.

If excludability cannot be enforced because of technological externalities (whether for economic or political reasons), it stands to reason that government corrects the market failure and takes steps to provide the good in question, covering the associated costs with public funds. In this context, one speaks of the provision of public goods. The provider can be the government itself or a public service provider (here, an NTO) commissioned by the government. Determining the extent of the public good to be provided and ensuring that it reaches its intended target group can present problems. Theoretically, the optimal amount of a (public) good with externalities is given when the totals of the marginal individual willingness to pay and the marginal costs of providing the public good are equal to one another. Conceivably, a survey or a poll might be taken among the relevant actors in order to determine their willingness to pay, so that the public good could be publicly funded in that amount. However, it must be expected that the relevant actors will act strategically, so that attempts to acquire undistorted information must be made in a very careful manner. Potential free-riders will tend to disguise their true willingness to pay by naming a low value or even total disinterest; the lower the collective willingness to pay is calculated to be, the lower each individual's contribution to public funding via taxes would be. On the other hand, if such a survey or poll is taken among actors who feel certain that their preference for the public good will have no effect on their personal tax burden, they will tend to exaggerate their willingness to pay; by naming disproportionately high amounts, potential free-riders would be able to increase their benefit levels.

Further, public goods have the property of non-rival consumption. This means that the consumption of a public good by an additional consumer leads to no or only negligible marginal cost. One example of this is the benefit accruing to each additional tourism provider as a result of image campaigns and brand management measures.

Public goods characteristically also cannot be rejected. For example, hotel owners who attempted to do this would have to ask each of their guests whether it was publicly funded advertising which had led to their choice of destination; if the answer were yes and the hotel owner had not paid the financial contribution, then the guest would have to be turned away.

Information deficits

General

Information deficits on the part of market actors can impair a market's functioning so that market failure occurs. It is important to differentiate here between lack of knowledge and uncertainty.

Lack of knowledge occurs when market actors simply possess insufficient information, whereby it is possible in principle to close such a knowledge gap. Uncertainty, on the other hand, has to do with future developments, thus representing an information deficit which cannot be remedied, because not even the best forecast made with maximum effort can provide absolute certainty.

Lack of information plays a role in market relationships where market actors on one side are better informed than market actors on the other side. This is described as an asymmetrical distribution of information. In tourism, it is above all the lack of knowledge about the quality of the goods and services being offered that plays a role. Lack of knowledge about benefits is another form of information deficit.

Adverse selection at the expense of the consumer

The consequences of information asymmetries that exist at the buyer's expense can be described as in the following.

One can safely assume that there exist differing quality levels among tourist products. If tourists are able to gain exact knowledge of the quality being offered to them, they can adjust their willingness to pay. In other words, a tourist would be willing to pay a higher price for higher quality and a lower price for relatively low quality. Typically, however, a tourist can assess the true and final quality only after conclusion of the contract because there is an information gap between the contractual agreement and the actual quality of a tourism product. In order to minimise risk, tourists would adjust their willingness to pay to their expectation of what the average quality will be. However, which level of quality an individual tourist will actually encounter is a matter of fortune, be it good or ill.

If tourists adjust their willingness to pay to average quality expectations, then suppliers who offer above-average quality and thus have above-average costs will have relatively low profits or even losses. Even where providers are interested in selling high quality, tourists' information-deficit-induced behaviour forces providers to offer lower-quality goods. If tourists then realise that the average quality is falling, the prices they are prepared to pay will also fall. This leads to reductions in high-quality tourist offerings, so that prices continue to fall, a process which in the worst case continues until only the lowest possible quality is offered and the tourism markets for high quality collapse completely. Low quality pushes high quality out of the market and the resulting prices are accordingly low. This process can be described as 'adverse selection' and leads to tourism market failures. Consequently, government intervention aimed at eliminating information deficits is justified.

Adverse selection at the expense of the buyer is often to be encountered in the case of goods with experience quality as well as in the case of confidence goods.

The quality of experience goods can be judged only after they have been purchased and consumed. Examples include the quality of the meals and other services in a vacation hotel. Confidence goods' lack of quality can be judged only after one has consumed a certain amount of them. In many cases, tourists can never judge the quality of goods consumed (e.g. water quality or food quality).

It is evident that by fulfilling the mandate to disseminate information, public tourism policy can make a significant contribution to bridging the information gap; whether it is by means of media campaigns, events, the electronic presentation of the different tourism products or other activities, public tourism policy can improve market results.

Adverse selection at the expense of the supplier

Adverse selection can also present itself as a problem for tourism providers when they cannot estimate the demand for their services exactly enough. For example, tourists cause considerable costs if they have especially high expectations and/or many special wishes. If providers do not have the market knowledge necessary to assess tourists' expectations *ex ante*, they will calculate their prices so that they will not take a loss on average. However, since this price will be relatively high for more unassuming guests, these guests will forgo the offer. At the same time, there will be more guests with higher expectations who find the offer to be relatively cheap. The result is that prices rise, discouraging even more of the guests who expect less. Tourists with more modest expectations would indeed book vacations but the prices are too high because the providers are not able to accurately assess *ex ante* the cost risks posed by different customer groups. In other words, market results suffer from an information gap between supply and demand and market failure occurs. In offering market-specific knowledge, in making recommendations for services to be provided and in making the results of market research available, public tourism policy can contribute to bridging or even closing the information gap and thus improving market results.

Lack of knowledge about benefits

Where information is lacking, the benefits of certain goods may be systematically falsely appraised so that there comes to be too much or too little demand for them. This is an example of lack of knowledge about benefits.

Lack of knowledge about benefits differs from lack of knowledge about quality in that benefit estimates are wrong even when there is complete certainty about the offer's quality. The further the benefit of a good lies in the future, the more difficult it generally is to assess it. A typical tourism example is a vacation taken as a health care measure (preventive wellness vacation). The prevailing assumption is that potential health vacationers underestimate the benefits of preventive wellness vacations and – at least in their younger years – consume too few of them. Further examples are vacations and journeys made for educational purposes. In all these cases, organisations that implement national tourism policies raise the informational level and improve overall market results.

Uncertainty

Market failure also occurs where businesses experience entrepreneurial insecurity. This is assumed to be the case especially because – in the overall economic context – businesses are too risk-averse and thus invest too little in research. Overly careful practices can diminish market results and exaggerated caution can lead to market failure. In that it offers research results, forecasts and future scenarios, public tourism policy can help to reduce entrepreneurial insecurity and thus to improve market results.

Transaction costs

Transactions costs that arise from initiating, negotiating, handling, controlling and adjusting contracts can negatively influence market results. Where the government does not take action to correct the situation, transaction costs – for example from asserting property rights, from transferring services between businesses, from identifying appropriate transaction partners or from internalising external effects – act as a transaction barrier and prevent the achievement of a Pareto-efficient market situation (Keller, 1999; Williamson, 1975). In other words, transaction costs that are too high lead to supply shortfalls, a situation which should be remedied by government action in the interest of general welfare (Palmer and Bejou, 1995; Pechlaner and Weiermair, 1999). Public tourism policy seeks to reduce transaction costs by assisting in and promoting the development of cooperative efforts and destinations, in order to make tourism supplies possible where high transaction costs would otherwise preclude it. In the context of liberal economic policy, public tourism policy is justified because it is a case of government's exercising influence to reduce businesses' external costs and thus positively influence market results.

Overall economic efficiency of public involvement in tourism marketing

General

On the basis of the theory of market failure and the existence of cost-related transaction barriers, only the necessary reasons for government involvement can be described. In order for economic policy to lead to increased overall economic welfare, additional cost–benefit analyses must be made to ensure that the sufficient conditions for government involvement exist. Public measures are advantageous where the expected benefit (i.e. the positive effect for overall welfare) is greater than the cost involved; ideally, and in the event that they are known, the benefits resulting from the best possible alternative should be taken as the measure of this cost.

Since there is a lack of comprehensive quantitative information on the economic consequences of public measures, these theoretical efforts come to grief in terms of their practical application, as is commonly the case. Recognising these deficits, we must rely on indicators, suppositions, secondary material and estimates.

Effects of tourism marketing

Firstly, the impact of tourism marketing must be assessed, to which end relevant research results can be referenced.

Crouch presents a meta-analysis of some 80 studies that focused primarily on tourism demand (Crouch, 1995). Among other factors, the effects of NTO marketing budgets on the development of tourism demand were discussed by these studies. A central result of Crouch's international study was that tourism demand from abroad shows an average elasticity somewhere between 0.2 and 0.3 in relation to NTO marketing budgets. Although these figures seem to be inflated, obviously because of the difficulties inherent in properly isolating all the effects that impact on tourism demand, they do clearly demonstrate that tourism marketing has a considerable and measurable impact.

Tourism's effects on value added, employment and growth

Tourism marketing is overall economic efficient because of its large value added and employment effects. It is safe to assume that if promotional measures are taken which have similar impacts on the various components of the final demand such as private consumption, investments and visible exports, then tourism as another component of the final demand will trigger conspicuously above-average value added effects. Here, input–output analysis presents unambiguous results.

The results shown to us by input–output analysis are those of the cumulative processes set into motion by tourism demand.

In 2000 in Austria, every €1,000 of tourism demand from abroad led to €820 in value added (see Table 8.1). The hotel and restaurant sector profited most, followed by retail trade, the food processing industries, and the transportation sector.

The input–output table for 2000 represents no special information on tourism demand from Austrian residents, but experience with previous analyses and other studies allow us to assume that there are no significant differences between the consumption structures of residents and foreign visitors or between the relevant value added multipliers.

Along with public consumption, tourism has the highest value-added effect in relation to demand increases resulting from measures of economic policy (see Table 8.1, 'foreign visitors' consumption', 'government') (Smeral, 1995). All other value-added effects in the areas of investment or export are significantly lower.

International comparison of tourism's value-added effects are quite difficult because of varying concepts; nevertheless it is safe to say that due to developed nations' generally low import quotas of tourism demand, as a matter of principle the value-added effects in most of these countries will also be above average.

Tourism results not only in high value-added effects; in the Austrian national economy – as in many other national economies – it has also become a highly significant economic factor. Tourism-related production provides the sole livelihood and means of subsistence for entire

Table 8.1 Value added multipliers per unit of overall demand: input–output table for the year 2000

Sector	Value added multiplier
Residents' Consumption	0.73
Foreign Visitors' Consumption	0.82
Government	0.89
Building Investments	0.79
Equipment Investments	0.35
Exports	0.67

population segments. In other words, public involvement in tourism marketing contributes to ensuring these people's livelihoods, especially those in SMEs in rural areas. It should be mentioned here that promotion and strengthening of structures with a location-based, quasi-monopolistic position (e.g. winter sport, or cultural assets such as music or city ambience) should be preferred to measures concentrating on sectors that are not differentiated enough and have to move to countries with, for example, lower costs, taxes.

Tourism's significance for the national economy and its overall economic contribution to value added is an important indicator for economic policy (OECD, 2000; UNWTO, 2001). The results of the Tourism Satellite Accounts (TSA) can be used to determine this crucial indicator (Laimer and Smeral, 2004; Smeral, 2005): using the TSA concept it was calculated for Austria that direct tourism-related value-added effects accounted for 6.6 per cent of GDP in 2004. A proper overall comparison should, however, also consider the indirect effects exclusive of the business trips of residents. After correcting the TSA results accordingly, it was calculated for Austria that direct and indirect value-added effects accounted for some 9 per cent of GDP in 2004; tourism generated a sales volume of €28.24 billion.

Because of data inavailabilities and the limited implementation of TSA concepts, it is difficult to carry out theoretically correct comparisons of economic significance, so that we must rely on the use of indicators. A relatively strong indicator is the share of tourism exports in GDP. Table 8.2 shows that, while the EU-25 average is approximately 2 per cent, countries such as Austria, Italy, Spain and the 10 new EU countries, as well as non-EU member Switzerland, all show above-average shares in GDP.

Even though the Table 8.2 shows the overall economic importance of tourism only on the basis of the direct effects of tourism exports and thus greatly underestimates it (in general by some 100–150 per cent),[1] the important place that tourism has in the economy is nevertheless very clear. Correct consideration of business trips remains a conceptual problem but influences the overall results only minimally.

Table 8.2 Share of tourism exports in GDP

Country	%
EU-15	2.07
Austria	5.50
Germany	0.96
France	2.11
Italy	2.13
Spain	4.97
Great Britain	1.27
10 new EU-members	3.51
EU-25	2.14
Switzerland	2.90
USA	0.76
Japan	0.09
Russia	1.04
Brasil	0.50
India	0.59
China	1.23
Total	1.22

Source: UNWTO, 200

Table 8.3 Employment multipliers per €100,000 of overall demand, input–output table for the year 2000

Sector	Employment multipliers
Residents' consumption	1.3
Foreign visitors consumption	1.9
Government	1.8
Building investments	1.4
Equipment investments	0.6
Exports	1.0

It should also be considered that tourism is one of the fastest growing areas of demand around the world, so that marketing measures will tend to have greater impact here than in other areas (Costa, 1997; Pike, 2004; Smeral, 2003a, 2003b). Since 1980 the industrialised[2] countries' income from international tourism (real tourism exports) have grown by 4 per cent per year. Compared to the overall economic expansion rate in industrialised nations of some 2½ per cent per year (1980–2004), the above-average growth of tourism becomes quite apparent.

The employment multipliers resulting from tourism demand are the highest in the entire economy (Pike, 2004; Smeral, 1995), due in part to tourism's relatively low import quota (see Table 8.3). It is also due to relatively low labour productivity/relatively high labour intensity in hotels and restaurants, which is in turn mostly due to the specific production conditions, the scarcity of opportunities for technical rationalisation and the structural under-utilisation resulting from seasonal fluctuations in demand.

In Austria, the employment multiplier of foreign tourism demand was 1.9 per €100,000; calculating in the price and productivity increases that took place between 2000 and 2004, the employment multiplier is estimated to decrease by around 10–15 per cent.

In fact, tourism's employment effect presents the strongest argument for promoting tourism. Tourism is a driving force in the creation of jobs, especially for young people, and a significant source of employment in most industrialised and developing countries.

It should also be emphasised that in most industrialised nations the number of employees in hotels and restaurants relative to total employment numbers grew on average in the 1990s – in contrast to overall trends in industrial employment (see Table 8.4).

Table 8.4 Development of employees in the hotel and restaurant industry in selected countries

	Australia	Austria	Belgium	Denmark	Finland	Germany	Italy	Mexico	Netherlands	Poland
	As a percentage of total employment									
1980	.	4.62	1.64	2.15	3.08	2.08	2.15	.	2.55	.
1985	3.38	4.94	2.05	2.27	3.02	2.41	2.34	.	2.81	.
1990	4.35	5.48	2.36	2.42	3.21	2.64	2.59	3.81	3.00	.
1991	4.67	5.54	2.36	2.48	3.07	2.71	2.64	4.09	3.00	.
1992	4.69	5.73	2.41	2.50	2.99	2.88	2.67	4.21	3.13	1.06
1993	4.69	5.92	2.60	2.54	2.90	3.03	2.85	4.25	3.27	1.15
1994	4.94	6.01	2.78	2.61	2.90	3.08	2.98	4.40	3.49	1.35
1995	4.81	6.03	2.82	2.71	2.93	3.15	3.06	4.46	3.67	1.37
1996	4.96	6.04	2.89	2.77	2.98	3.27	3.11	4.20	3.56	1.41
1997	5.03	6.06	2.95	2.77	2.98	3.41	3.09	4.08	3.56	1.43
1998	4.99	6.05	2.98	2.80	2.99	3.56	3.08	4.53	3.52	1.51

(*Continued*)

Table 8.4 Continued

	Australia	Austria	Belgium	Denmark	Finland	Germany	Italy	Mexico	Netherlands	Poland
	As a percentage of total employment									
1999	5.10	6.16	2.92	2.84	3.02	3.76	3.26	4.42	3.53	1.48
2000	5.36	6.16	2.82	2.87	3.04	3.88	3.47	4.43	3.66	1.54
2001	5.26	6.17	2.85	2.85	3.05	3.97	3.70	4.83	3.71	1.60
2002	.	6.29	2.87	2.87	3.05	4.07	3.68	.	3.66	1.56
2003	.	6.46	.	.	.	.	3.84	.	.	.

Source: OECD, 2000

Conclusion

The analysis has shown that the conditions calling for both necessary and sufficient conditions are fulfilled, thus in the context of liberal economic policy, public funding of tourism marketing is justified, provided that government and bureaucracy failures can be precluded.

In formulating this justification, the occurrence of market failures – in particular, external effects and information asymmetries – and the existence of relatively high transaction costs play an important role.

NTOs' marketing activities such as image building and brand management generate positive external effects (i.e. benefits and income) for numerous businesses (hotels, restaurants, retail trade, personal service providers, banks, insurance companies, legal and business service providers, agriculture and forestry, construction, the food industry, etc.). This justifies public funding of such marketing activities, because it can be understood as a payment for generating external effects.

Information deficits describe situations in which one market participant is better informed than the other side (e.g. customer – supplier). In tourism, it is mostly the lack of information about quality that plays a role.

Lack of information about quality exists when tourists demanding a good such as the activities offered at a destination cannot adequately assess that good's quality. Here, the seller is better informed than the buyer and the information is distributed asymmetrically. Lack of information about quality can also come into play where tourists are (naturally) better informed about their quality expectations than their potential hosts are. Regardless of who is affected by a lack of information, competition could lead to situations in which the market for good quality will break down. Closing the information gap is therefore an important goal of public tourism policy, particularly because public intervention would improve market results.

Transaction costs might be a serious obstacle for the achievement of a Pareto-efficient market situation. Too high transaction costs could lead to supply shortfalls. Public tourism policy should focus reducing transaction costs by promoting the development of integrated destinations, in order to increase and/or improve tourism supplies.

Market failures and the existence of transaction costs describe only the necessary conditions for government involvement. For increasing the overall economic welfare, additional cost–benefit analyses must be made. In this context, the facts can be presented:

- The literature offers significant evidence of NTOs' economic impact via tourism marketing. International studies demonstrate that foreign tourism demand shows positive elasticities in relation to NTO marketing budgets.
- Tourism marketing is overall economic efficient because of its large value-added effects. Tourism related expenditures will trigger above-average value-added effects.

- Tourism-related production provides the source of the subsistence for entire population segments, especially those in SMEs in rural areas. Promotion of structures with a location-based, quasi-monopolistic position should preferred to measures concentrating on sectors that are cost and price sensitive and have to move to low cost/tax countries.
- There is also evidence that tourism is one of the fastest growing demand activities, so that public involvement will tend to have a higher effect here than in other sectors.
- The employment effects resulting from tourism expenditures are the highest in the economy. Tourism production is labour intensive and thus an important job generator.

Notes

1 Domestic tourism as well as the indirect effects are not considered.
2 Here the following definition is used: EU-15, Iceland, Norway, Switzerland, Turkey, Canada, USA, Mexico, Japan, Australia and New Zealand.

References

Bieger, T. (2000) 'Perspektiven der Tourismuspolitik in traditionellen alpinen Tourismusländern: Welche Aufgaben hat der Staat noch?'. *Tourismus Jahrbuch*, 4(1), 113–36

Choy, D. J. L. (1993) 'Alternative roles of national tourism organizations'. *Tourism Management*, 14(5), 357–65

Coase, R. H. (1960) 'The problem of social costs'. *Journal of Law and Economics*, 3(2), 1–44

Costa, D. L. (1997, June) *Less of a luxury: The rise of recreation since 1888* (Working Paper 6054). Cambridge, MA: National Bureau of Economic Research

Crouch, G. I. (1995) 'A meta-analysis of tourism demand'. *Annals of Tourism Research*, 22(1), 103–18

Keller, P. (1999) 'Zukunftsorientierte Tourismuspolitik – Synthese des 49: AIEST-Kongresses'. *Tourist Review*, 54(3), 13–17

Kerr, B., Barron, G. and Wood, R. C. (2001) 'Politics, policy and regional tourism administration: A case examination of Scottish area tourist board funding'. *Tourism Management*, 22(6), 649–57

Laimer, P. and Smeral, E. (2004) *Ein Tourismus-Satellitenkonto für Österreich: Methodik, Ergebnisse und Prognosen für die Jahre 2000–2005*. Vienna: WIFO

Müller, H. and Scheurer, R. (2001) *Tourismuspolitisches Leitbild des Kantons Bern*. Bern: Amt für wirtschaftliche Entwicklung (KAWE)

Nowotny, E. (1996) *Der öffentliche Sektor* (3rd edn). Berlin: Springer

OECD (2000) 'Measuring the role of tourism in OECD economies: The OECD manual on Tourism Satellite Accounts and Employment'. Paris: Organisation for Economic Co-operation and Development

Palmer, A. and Bejou, D. (1995) 'Tourism destination marketing alliances'. *Annals of Tourism Research*, 22(3), 616–29

Pearce, D. G. (1992) *Tourist organizations*. New York: Wiley

Pechlaner, H. and Weiermair, K. (eds) (1999) *Destinations-management: Führung und Vermarktung von touristischen Zielgebieten*. Vienna: Linde-Verlag

Pike, S. (2004) *Destination marketing organisations*. Amsterdam: Elsevier

Smeral, E. (1995) 'The economic impact of tourism in Austria'. *The Tourist Review*, 51(3), 18–22

—— (1998) 'The impact of globalization on small and medium enterprises: New challenges for tourism policies in European countries'. *Tourism Management*, 19(4), 371–80

—— (2003a) 'A structural view of tourism growth'. *Tourism Economics*, 9(1), 77–93

—— (2003b) *Die Zukunft des internationalen Tourismus: Visionen für das 21. Jahrhundert*. Vienna: Linde-Verlag

—— (2005) 'The economic impact of tourism: Beyond satellite accounts'. *Tourism Analysis*, 10(1), 55–64

Stiglitz, J. E. (2000) *Economics of the public sector* (3rd edn). New York: W. W. Norton

Williamson, O. E. (1975) *Markets and hierarchies: Analysis and antitrust implications: A study in the economics of internal organization*. New York: Free Press

UNWTO (2001) *Tourism Satellite Account: Recommended methodological framework*. Madrid: UN World Tourism Organization

9

The role of individuals in the development and popularization of tourist destinations

Richard Butler, Roslyn Russell

Introduction

This chapter discusses the role of individuals in the development of and visits to tourist destinations. It is argued that tourism has been and probably always will be highly dependent on individuals, often entrepreneurs in a variety of forms, for its development and subsequent change in a region over time. Indeed, it might be argued that the reason for tourist destinations having undergone or currently undergoing declines in their popularity is due, at least in part, because of the absence of such individuals and their involvement. To be attractive to tourists tends to require both a willingness and an ability to change to meet differences in public taste and preferences for vacation destinations, or constant positive publicity to maintain the perception that the destination is still an appropriate place to visit for a holiday. The history of the development of many tourist destinations has shown that the role of key individuals in these tasks is often of critical importance. There is a clear and strong relationship between the creation of a destination and an appropriate image, and the maintenance of a positive image that continues to attract tourists over time. This chapter argues that it is possible to recognize three distinct forms of individual agents of change and influence in the context of tourism:

- innovators;
- promoters;
- re-enforcers.

The first, and possibly the second, of the three categories of agents of change could also be regarded as 'entrepreneurs' in the generally understood meaning of the term (Russell, 2006), and, while such individuals may be primarily responsible for the initial development and popularity of destinations, it is argued here that it is the continued presence of 're-enforcers' over time which often ensures the continuing popularity of destinations and enables them to avoid decline. The paper illustrates this argument by examining the case of Scotland and its appeal as a tourist destination over the past two hundred years, and illustrates the role of these three types of key individual in the development of tourism in this destination.

Agents of change

Entrepreneurship, from the earliest times, has been a major factor in the development of tourism, and yet, unlike other industries, it has not received the attention it deserves (Russell and Faulkner, 1999; Shaw and Williams, 1998). Individuals such as Thomas Cook and Walt Disney shaped modern tourism through their efforts and their ideals, and provided dramatic and lasting examples of the major differences individuals can make to a region and to an economic sector such as tourism. While individuals such as Disney have had impacts on tourism at every scale, the influence of entrepreneurs can play a major role in destination development at the regional and local level. Their intervention can be critical to the development and competitive advantage of destinations as McKercher (1999, p. 427) notes 'Indeed, the defining moment in most tourism destinations can be attributed to the actions of rogues who actualised its tourism potential.'

Weaver and Oppermann (2000) suggest that there are four types of agent of change or trigger to tourism development in a destination, and that they can be placed in a four cell matrix (Figure 9.1), relating to whether they are intentional or unintentional, and internal to the destination or external. In many cases, innovators and promoters are often external to a destination, and their efforts at development and stimulation of tourism are most often intentional. In the case of re-enforcers, it is less clear if they are more commonly external, and, in some cases at least, their efforts may be unintentional as far as tourism development in a location is concerned.

In the context of innovation in tourism in a destination, the work of Schumpeter is highly relevant. Schumpeter's (1950) seminal contribution of innovation brought a new element to the existing theory of entrepreneurship. From that time, researchers in entrepreneurship have regularly included concepts such as creativity, innovation and change as core ingredients of the entrepreneurial process. Schumpeter's notion of the 'creative entrepreneur' saw innovation as the 'creative response' to change (Hartwell and Lane, 1991), and also as the act of 'combining productive factors'. Schumpeter proposed five categories of innovation:

- production of new goods;
- devising new methods of production;
- creating new markets;
- discovering new sources of supplies;
- creating new types of organization (Cauthorn, 1989).

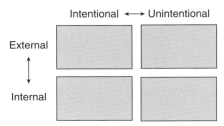

Figure 9.1   Four cell matrix
Source: After Weaver & Oppermann, 2000

Tourism researchers surely cannot avoid noticing the striking similarities between the above processes and core elements of tourism development – producing new tourism products such as theme parks, introducing new methods of providing tourist services such as the Internet and budget air travel, creating niche markets such as ecotourism, increasing new sources of supply by developing new destinations, and developing new types of tourist organization often through the use of IT. Despite these similarities, as noted earlier, tourism research seems to have adopted the same attitude to entrepreneurship as economics, and hence has suffered similar consequences in terms of not paying adequate attention to the role of such individuals in the pattern and process of tourism destination development.

Wright (1951, p. 134) noted that:

> I believe that in every generation of every culture there will be found at the least a few people who speculate about possibilities of doing things – both technologically and socially and who are not content to rest at mere speculation...

The challenge for destinations is to create the right mix of conditions that ensures continued successful operation and competitiveness. Wright also encapsulates very well the actions of entrepreneurs in tourist destinations – they speculate, they act on speculation and they create, as well as sometimes destroying and removing.

An entrepreneur was generally seen firstly as someone who sees a business opportunity and gathers together the resources to realize it. However, over time, the literature has developed a deeper profile of an entrepreneur to include concepts that describe more clearly not only entrepreneurial behaviour and process but also goals and objectives. Schumpeter (1950, p. 83) described an entrepreneur as someone who 'destroys the equilibrium with a perennial gale of creative destruction'. This implies the individual has a role in creating conditions and thus a greater involvement in bringing about change to create opportunities, rather than merely waiting in the wings for an opportunity to present itself. Kuratko and Hodgetts (1998, p. 5) describe an entrepreneur as 'the aggressive catalyst for change' in the world of business. This can be seen clearly in the actions of tourism individual entrepreneurs such as Beau Nash in Bath in eighteenth-century England, and Thomas Cook on the international scale.

It has been argued that, in addition to seemingly ideal economic and political conditions for entrepreneurial activity, a supportive culture must be present in order to 'cultivate the mind and character of the potential entrepreneur' (Mueller and Thomas, 2001, p. 52). For much of its medieval history Scotland was not noted for entrepreneurship, and indeed, remained stubbornly feudal in arrangements and outlook into the eighteenth century. When the environment did change, innovation and invention flourished on a scale not seen before. Scotland experienced the philosophical and scientific movement known as the Scottish Enlightenment and, in the early nineteenth century, there was tremendous support for the writings of native Scots such as Ferguson, Burns and Sir Walter Scott. Scott's deliberate efforts to restore Scotland's image through his literary abilities was both timely and strongly supported, and devastatingly effective as far as tourism was concerned, as noted below and elsewhere (Butler, 1998; Gold and Gold, 1995). Scotland in the late eighteenth century was experiencing the turbulence of military occupation, major changes and improvements in transportation related to military needs, changes in perceptions (of the area from a *terra horribilis* to a romantic playground), and changes in the perceived value of resources (land for sheep rather than cattle production) provided fertile ground for tourism development in the nineteenth century.

It is generally accepted that it is the visitors' image of a destination that is often more important in shaping their decision to visit a specific location than the real attractions of that location (Blank, 1989). Beerli and Martín (2004) have argued that a strong positive and recognizable image is a major factor in influencing potential visitor behaviour and increasing the probability of visitation to a destination. In this chapter the focus is not upon the elements which compose the image (Hunt, 1975), nor the way in which the image is involved in the destination choice (Gartner, 1993), but more on the way in which an image is created and then maintained. The importance of a favourable image is one of the key points noted by Pike (2002) in his comprehensive review of image research, and one of the common problems that destinations often face is being tied to an image which has ceased to be attractive. In this case the destination becomes, as Espelt and Benito (2005) note, the 'prisoner' of its own image and it may be extremely difficult to cultivate and maintain a new and attractive image. A destination is extremely fortunate if it can maintain an attractive image as the area discussed in this chapter has for over a century and a half. It is argued that the maintenance of that attractive image in this case is because of the regular positive *re-enforcement* by a highly visible segment of society, namely the British royal family.

Types of entrepreneur

Russell (2006) has suggested that there are at least five types of entrepreneur: phase–changing, organic, serendipitous, grand–scale and revitalizing. Their presence and their type to a large extent are formed by the function of the macro and micro environmental conditions present at the time of the activity, the individual attributes of the entrepreneurs and the particular time or stage of tourism development. In the Scottish Highlands, several of these forms have clearly been present.

Phase-changing entrepreneurship

The phases in this case refer to stages in the development cycle of a destination (Butler, 1980). In the case of the study area, there was minimal visitation (although what there was consisted of a privileged elite) for what might be considered as pure tourism. Most of the travellers came for enlightenment and education or out of intellectual curiosity. After the impact of Scott, true (pleasure) tourism can be said to have begun in the Highlands, making him (Scott) a possible example of a phase-changing entrepreneur, as, by the time he finished, the area was certainly in the exploration stage, if not moving into involvement.

Organic entrepreneurship

Christaller (1964), one of the earliest pioneers in research on destination development, focused on the emergence of a destination whose magnet was artistic activity rather than simply climate or scenery. Early 'painters' or explorers discover the untouched destinations and then it becomes a 'colony', word spreads and poets, other artists and gourmets follow (ibid.). The 'discovery' of the destination by more tourists opens it up to early entrepreneurial activity. More accommodation is needed, shops, transport and other supporting enterprises develop to capitalize on the tourism activity. This can be seen in Scotland, in terms of the prior visits of writers, artists and others, requiring the development of services and facilities before the appearance of conventional tourists.

Grand-scale entrepreneurs

The most dramatic variations come about when the actions of entrepreneurs are planned and purposeful and they introduce elaborate grand development schemes to the region. These entrepreneurs often bring instant change to the destination, attract bigger or different markets and provide an immediate trigger for the destination to enter a new development phase. To date this form has not appeared in the Scottish Highlands, although the development of winter sports in several areas of Scotland in the 1960s suggests the presence of at least some small-scale entrepreneurs.

Serendipitous entrepreneurs

Thomas Cook is an obvious example of a serendipitous entrepreneur, and his influence was certainly felt in the Scottish Highlands. While Cook's activities were not specific to one specific destination, his innovations opened up many previously inaccessible destinations to tourists, kick-starting their development. Cook, by exploiting new technology, the steam engine in particular, made travel available to the masses. He describes the moment the idea came to him as a 'revelation'. His entrepreneurial activity was the culmination of good timing, new technology and a perceived need in an unrelated industry. Upon his death, the following was a tribute that encapsulated his achievements very well:

> The late Mr Thomas Cook…was a typical middle-class nineteenth-century Englishman. Starting from very small beginnings, he had the good luck and the insight to discover a new want, and to provide for it. He saw that the great new invention of the railway might be made, by the help of a new organization, to provide large numbers of people with pleasanter, cheaper, and more varied holidays than they had ever been able to enjoy before.
> *(Pudney et al., 1953, p. 19)*

Cook introduced the package holiday to Scotland in the mid-nineteenth century, using boats before the railway network was complete, and incorporated transport to, within and from the area with accommodation, guiding services and the provision of entertainment.

Revitalizing entrepreneurs

The revitalizing effect on destinations is not a new phenomenon. A historical account of Bath (Connely, 1955), one of the earliest organized tourist destinations, portrays the activities of Beau Nash and the impact he had on revitalizing Bath as a resort spa town. In the early 1700s, Bath was experiencing severe seasonality and a downturn in market type, so Nash, an entrepreneurial rogue, set about updating everything in the town from the lodgings to the entertainment. He was perhaps, a promoter, an innovator *and* a re-enforcer. Rebirthing a destination locked into stagnation is not for the faint-hearted and something that has rarely been done very effectively in the long term.

These five categories are certainly not intended to be exhaustive but to illustrate that entrepreneurship has a significant role to play in developing tourism in a region and will often be manifested in a variety of ways. The categories are also broad generalizations as each instance of entrepreneurial activity is a function of the individual characteristics and traits of the entrepreneur, the environmental conditions – macro and micro – under which it occurs, and the particular stage of the destination. Certainly several of these types of individual have been present and active in the area under discussion in the two centuries that it has been a tourism destination.

The role of personalities and royalty in tourism: the Scottish Highlands as a tourist destination

It would appear to be generally accepted that tourism destinations benefit from being seen to be popular with iconic figures of the time, particularly those that have a high media profile. While today it may be television soap, film and music 'personalities' who exert the greatest influence on the travel preferences of many, in earlier times the visitation to an area by royalty was seen as a great boon to that location's appeal to other visitors. Spas in Europe in particular eagerly sought the prefix 'Royal', for example Royal Leamington Spa, as this signified not only acceptance and approval by the highest family in the land, but generally that the monarch of the day had actually visited the location, a fact of greater significance because visitors to spas in the eighteenth and nineteenth centuries tended to be those from the 'upper classes' who were keen to be seen with or in the same location as royalty. The success of Bath in particular is well recorded (Connely, 1955) and the visitations to that spa by the Prince Regent was of particular significance in its rising back to pre-eminence amongst British spas in the eighteenth century. Similarly, Brighton, also popularized by the Prince Regent, culminating in his construction of the Royal Pavilion, the ultimate summer cottage, had far greater success as a summer holiday resort than its rather limited physical attributes would have suggested (Gilbert, 1954).

Both Bath and Brighton, however, are fairly close to London, and have had relatively good communications since Roman times, and thus ease of access, appropriate physical attributes and particularly the social connections and organization of those centres, made them somewhat logical choices by members of the royal family for their leisure. Both centres, as well as Harrogate, Leamington, Tunbridge Wells and Buxton, all similarly, if less frequently, visited by royalty and the aristocracy, experienced booms in development and construction of splendid architecture. The Royal Crescent at Bath and the various gardens and squares in Brighton, along with related spa features and ornate piers respectively, are tangible reminders to this day of the significance of royal tourism in the development of these tourist destinations. Such developments were not confined to Great Britain; throughout the continent of Europe places such as Le Touquet, Opatija and Monte Carlo all experienced royal patronage and subsequent extensive development of impressive tourist facilities, and gained a reputation and appeal that has lasted in some cases for more than two centuries. In the light of the argument presented in this chapter, however, it is important to note that in all cases, the spas and resorts had already begun to attract visitors because of the initial efforts of promoters and innovators before they were visited and received patronage from royal 're-enforcers'.

For the past one hundred and fifty years the British royal family has travelled to their summer residence, Balmoral Castle, in 'Royal Deeside' in north-eastern Scotland. This pattern of visitation followed summer tours of the Highlands of Scotland by Queen Victoria and Prince Albert, and became a permanent feature of the Victorian age after the Royal family acquired, demolished and rebuilt the castle at Balmoral in the early 1850s (Brown, 1955). The attraction of Scotland as a holiday location for the British royal family has continued ever since. The late Queen Elizabeth the Queen Mother (herself a Scot) purchased the Castle of Mey in Caithness for holiday purposes, and her grandson, HRH the Prince of Wales spent his second honeymoon on the Balmoral estate. What it is that the royals find attractive about Scotland is not explicit; it may be the standard appeal of impressive scenery, the abundance of sporting and physical exercise opportunities and the cultural heritage, or the absence of much of the pressures of life in the capital and the media coverage which goes on there. Whatever the true reasons, the attractions of Scotland remain strong and ongoing to many present members of the royal family.

The development of Scotland as a holiday destination for the royal family is somewhat surprising, given the distance from London to the Highlands, and the fact that Anglo-German monarchs had been strongly opposed in much of Scotland a few decades earlier. The Jacobite rebellions of the eighteenth century came close to toppling the house of Hanover (Prebble, 1961) and resulted in military occupation and harsh prescriptions on dress and other aspects of life. The later removal of people from extensive areas for sheep farming (Prebble, 1963), and to a lesser extent for the expansion of deer hunting areas (deer forests) (Orr, 1982), further aggravated discontent within the area. The remarkable change in perception of the area noted earlier that occurred over a 25-year period, from 1800 to 1825, owes its occurrence almost entirely to one person.

Sir Walter Scott as a serendipitous entrepreneur and promoter

In 1822 a tartan-clad George IV visited Edinburgh (Prebble, 1988), and was greeted and entertained by hundreds of highland clansmen, descendants of those who died at Culloden. This visit was arranged and stage managed by the novelist and poet Sir Walter Scott. Scott was the major author of his period, his works were read widely, not only in Britain, but also in Europe and North America. His work fitted perfectly with, and was a key part of, the Romantic revolution in literature and art. Popular artists such as W.M. Turner (Butler, 1985), who visited Scotland on six occasions (Irwin and Wilton, 1982), illustrated his books and visited with him, and such was his popularity that the imagery he evoked attracted large numbers of English visitors to Scotland from the early 1820s onwards. Scott's works (e.g. *Rob Roy* and *The Lady of the Lake*) portrayed an image of the noble Highland savage, and were set against a spectacular scenic background. Considerable numbers of English (and other) readers were beginning to visit Scotland to see the settings of his works before the monarch arrived in 1822. The creation of Scotland as a tourist destination was clearly the work of Scott. 'He effectively wrote the script for the promotion of Scottish tourism through the nineteenth and twentieth centuries' (Gold and Gold, 1995, p. 195). In creating this romantic image of the country and its rural inhabitants, he was building on a fictitious image of the Highlands first established by another promoter of the Highlands: Macpherson (1765). In the 1760s, Macpherson had created the Ossian legends, supposedly authentic remnants of Gaelic sagas, and their popularity was widespread, with their fans including Napoleon. These tales, coupled with early scientific descriptions of features of the Scottish landscape meant that the area had been visited throughout the second half of the eighteenth century by a range of scientists (including presidents of the Royal Society), musicians such as Mendlessohn, artists such as Turner and virtually all English poets and authors of note from Johnson and Boswell on, all filling the role of re-enforcers to the efforts of the promoters such as Macpherson and Scott.

At the same time, the potential of the area for fishing and hunting was becoming well established in England. Many Highland estates were confiscated from their previously rebellious Jacobite-supporting clan chiefs after the failure of the last rebellion in 1745. Some of these were purchased by absentee southern landlords, and the previous antipathy towards accepting money for hospitality and shooting and fishing disappeared. It became clear that money could be made from renting the hunting and fishing, and in some cases the ancestral homes to the affluent aristocracy. By the end of the eighteenth century, the renting of Highland estates was becoming increasingly common. The Duke of Bedford is credited with initiating 'the fashionable invasion of English sportsmen' (O'Dell and Walton, 1962, p. 332) with his visit to the Highlands in 1818. Before the end of the century over 200 deer forests (covering some three and a half million acres) were managed specifically for sport in northern Scotland (ibid.).

Although no monarch was to visit Scotland for another two decades after George IV (who did not venture out of Edinburgh on his short visit), Scotland as a tourist destination had become established in aristocratic minds. When Victoria and Albert first visited in 1842 the idea of a summer holiday in Scotland was well established in affluent circles. That such a pattern has remained for a century and a half nevertheless reflects the influence of Victoria, for she was of major significance in re-enforcing the idea of a Scottish summer holiday firmly in the minds of many of the aristocracy and subsequently others who wished to follow in the established fashion of the day.

The environment for tourism development in the Highlands

Of considerable importance to the development of tourism in the Highlands of Scotland was the fact that the opportunities which this region offered in terms of recreation and tourism in the late eighteenth and nineteenth centuries matched very well the passions and tastes of the aristocracy. Armitage (1977) notes that fishing was already popular as a sporting pastime in the fifteenth century, while the hunting of deer had been an aristocratic privilege for a thousand years. Victoria clearly did not dislike hunting and fishing, and engaged in the latter as well as accompanying Prince Albert on deer stalking expeditions (Duff, 1980). Albert was an enthusiastic shot who engaged in deer stalking during the Royal couple's first visit to the Highlands in 1842, when they were hosted at Taymouth Castle by Lord Breadalbane. That visit, stage managed by her host, appears to have been highly influential. Eden (1979, p. 33) notes the way that Victoria described the visit: 'the whole setting [at Taymouth] was as if some great chieftain of feudal times was receiving his sovereign'. The imagery in the description of this visit and the reference to the 'great chieftain of feudal times' reflect clearly the imagery contained in the writings of Macpherson and Scott in their descriptions of imaginary gatherings of Highlands lords and obviously impressed the then young queen.

The desire to acquire a permanent base in the Highlands came about following further visits to Scotland by Victoria and Albert. In 1847 they sailed to Scotland and visited various Highland properties, including Ardverikie (between Fort William and Speyside), now better known as the location for the television series *Monarch of the Glen*, the title of which, according to Hill (1973), is a pun on the famous painting of a red deer by Landseer, Victoria's favourite artist. Victoria's impressions of Scotland remained favourable, despite the 'most dreadful' weather. Balmoral was visited in 1848 and the privacy it offered compared to life in London probably reflect the current royal family's feelings as well as Victoria's, when she noted 'All seemed to breathe freedom and peace, and to make one forget the world and its sad turmoils' (Eden, 1979, p. 34). The existing structure was demolished as it was deemed unsuitable and too small. A larger house was begun in 1853 to a design by Prince Albert. It was decorated in a number of tartans, including a new Balmoral tartan designed by Albert. This relatively insignificant act began what is now known as 'Balmorality' and 'tartanry', features which were to play a major role in re-enforcing the image of Scotland and its tourist industry (Gold and Gold, 1995; Urquhart, 1994). Eden (1979, p. 34) notes that 'The seal was finally set on the popularity and fashion of the Scottish holiday, with all its concomitant sports and pastimes.'

Cumulative influences: royalty as re-enforcers

The fact that the Queen and her Consort returned to Scotland for a summer holiday on a regular basis does not in itself explain the continued international popularity of Scotland as a holiday destination either to the current royal family or to thousands of less distinguished visitors. The explanation is more complex. Scotland was kept in many people's consciousness during Victoria's reign through much, sometimes unrelated, re-enforcement. Those factors already noted, namely, the writings of Scott, the art of Turner and Landseer, the poetry of the Romantics and other giants of Victorian literature all worked together to create and maintain a romantic and artistic image of the Scottish Highlands. Also, the military endeavours of Scottish regiments in the British Army, from the Napoleonic Wars onwards, confirmed the image of the Highland Scot as a brave and loyal warrior. The Scottish Enlightenment made Edinburgh a well-known city of letters, and the contributions of inventors such as James Watt played major roles in the Industrial Revolution, keeping Scotland's name in the minds of the public. During her reign, the frequent and often lengthy visits of Victoria to the Highlands, along with the somewhat less desirable publicity about John Brown, her Scottish servant, all continued to reinforce the idea that a Scottish holiday was a fashionable thing to undertake.

Other innovations also assisted this region to develop as a tourist destination. If one had money and contacts, it was possible to get to Edinburgh by stage coach from London in 60 hours at the beginning of the nineteenth century, but few could afford such rapid travel. However, the development of the railways and steam-powered travel made Scotland a viable potential holiday destination to large numbers of people, as had happened in many other locations. Tourist traffic provided a key component in making several routes in the difficult terrain and thinly populated areas of Scotland more economic, although not until late in the nineteenth century. Of crucial importance too, is the contribution of Thomas Cook (Swinglehurst, 1974), as Cook perceived the great potential of the Highlands for tourism, and the development of his tours brought many middle-class visitors to northern and western Scotland. His organizational and logistic expertise in creating touring circuits and bringing together transport, accommodation and guiding services laid the foundation for the current tourism industry there (Butler, 1985; Cook, 1861).

Cook was well aware of the influence of Victoria on public taste in the nineteenth century, and 'Queen's Views' and the places that Victoria wrote about in her journals (Duff, 1980) featured greatly in his package tours. The Queen's visits to Balmoral were of key importance in providing re-enforcement of the image developed by Scott, by keeping the Highlands in the public eye. These occurred every summer when the Queen and her family, and periodically the Prime Minister of the day, stayed at Balmoral. These positive images were strengthened by those of the tartan-clad highlanders offering gracious hospitality to visitors from the royal family down.

Reinforcement of image in the twenty-first century

Throughout the latter half of the nineteenth century, Victoria and Albert visited Balmoral regularly. After Albert died, the Queen retreated more frequently to Balmoral and her other non-London residences both to grieve and to escape the life and pressures of the capital. Balmoral, in particular, represented an escape from routine in a location that was relatively inaccessible to the media, politicians and others because of its distance from London. While today a considerable number of tourists visit 'Royal Deeside' as it is known in publicity material, the opportunity to see the royal family at other than staged events is no greater than it was in

Victoria's time. Members of the royal family attend religious services at Crathes Church at the estate gates on Sundays, and the Braemar Highland Gathering in early September, but the castle itself and much of the estate is almost invisible to the casual tourist to the area.

Over the past half century, however, some significant changes have taken place at Balmoral. As with Buckingham Palace, a small part of the estate is now open to the public when the royal family is not in residence. The estate has become a tourist facility, reflecting its widespread public appeal and the fact that in recent years at the Queen's insistence, the royal estates have made significant efforts to earn income and reduce the expense on the national budget. Balmoral Estate now has a restaurant as well as a shop which sells estate-produced goods. There are also self-catering cottages available for hire, pony trekking and off-road vehicle tours offered within the grounds, and the estate hosts a half-marathon race annually. All events and public access to the estate are held only when no member of the royal family is in residence. Around 75,000 visitors, over half from overseas, visit the estate each year (Balmoral Castle, n.d.), and over 180,000 walkers take advantage of the freedom of access to open land that exists in Scotland to use the paths and trails on the estate. There are some 120 miles of footpaths and roads which can be used by the public and to handle this aspect of public access a Ranger Service has existed for over 30 years on the estate.

Fishing for salmon has always been one of the major tourist attractions of the Scottish Highlands, and the River Dee is one of the premier salmon fishing rivers in Scotland. The surrounding hills are ideal habitat for red deer and red grouse, and hunting and fishing are major attributes of most of the estates on Deeside and a major factor of considerable value. Deeside, partly because of its physical attributes, therefore, and undoubtedly partly because of its royal connections, became and has remained a somewhat exclusive amenity area with a rich clientele in terms of landowners and those renting sporting estates. The 'average' tourists also visit in considerable numbers, undoubtedly partly to witness the holiday locations of royalty and the affluent classes, but also for sightseeing in an extremely beautiful part of the country. 'Royal Deeside' is one of the major attractions on coach tour itineraries to Scotland. The area has a number of large hotels capable of providing sufficient accommodation at a good standard for today's escorted coach tour market, and good road access, while rail and air access exists at Aberdeen.

The Braemar Gathering, as the Highland games held in that village are known, was established (in 1832) before Victoria and Albert visited the area, but received royal approval and were first attended by Victoria in 1848. It is now a well-established tradition that the reigning monarch is Patron of the Gathering, and the fact that by members of the royal family regularly attending when the Gathering opens on the first Saturday in September, the event has become one of the highlights of the royal calendar. Their patronage of this event ensures a large attendance at the Gathering of tourists and locals and is no small factor in extending the main tourist season in Deeside into September, significantly later than that for the rest of the Scottish Highlands.

The appeal of the Scottish Highlands as a location for second homes has not waned over the decades since Victoria first visited the area. A newspaper article on property prices in Scotland noted that 'The destination of choice for wealthy incomers to Scotland has remained the same since Queen Victoria blazed a trail to the Highlands 150 years ago' (Gordon, 2004, p. 3). A significant number of celebrities have purchased expensive and extensive properties in the Highlands for both leisure and retirement, while others visit for holidays and even marriage (e.g. Madonna). The traditional Victorian outdoor pursuits of deer stalking, grouse shooting and salmon fishing are engaged in only by landowners and the most affluent visitors to Deeside. The vast majority of 'normal' tourists engage only in sightseeing and more passive activities, and what attracts them is the same image that attracted Victoria a century and a half ago. This image consists of impressive mountain scenery, historic buildings, tartan-clad locals and heather-covered hills – in other words, the Romantic image of Scotland created by Sir Walter Scott that is still portrayed on shortbread tins and souvenirs.

This image has often been criticized (Gold and Gold, 1995) as being an artificial and inauthentic creation, and more recently Visit Scotland and the Scottish Executive have decided to promote a more modern image of Scotland, both for tourism and for the country as a whole. However, the Deeside tourism agency (and other organizations in Scotland) continue to promote their attractions in the traditional manner, especially by adorning brochures and other information sources with tartan and images such as castles, bagpipes and mountains. A survey of visitors for the now-defunct Scottish Tourist Board (1993) showed that the vast majority of those surveyed suggested that the image of Scotland should include tartan, the phenomenon which lies at the heart of the traditional and officially abandoned image. The royal family itself is at the heart of the traditional image of Britain and a major tourist attraction, especially to overseas visitors. When visiting Balmoral, most members wear tartan, and the males wear the kilt. The message sent out to watchers is clearly that a holiday in the Highlands of Scotland, and playing the role of a Highland Scot, is a highly acceptable and attractive vacation.

Conclusions and implications: the role of entrepreneurs and re-enforcers in tourism destination development

While the general area of Deeside is extremely attractive, with high-quality outdoor activity opportunities and a considerable number of heritage properties, so too are many other glens in the Highlands of Scotland. There can be little doubt that the greater visibility and attraction of Deeside to tourists lies in its early and continued promotion, gained from its royal connections and the seasonal royal presence. George IV attracted large crowds during his visit to Edinburgh in 1822, but went nowhere else in Scotland. Victoria's many arrivals in Scotland were witnessed by smaller but perhaps even more enthusiastic numbers of people. The precise beginning of general tourist visitation to Deeside is hard to determine. The older hotels in Braemar and Ballater date from the mid-nineteenth century, but their initial purpose was to cater for visiting sportsmen rather than royal watchers. The cost of accommodation in Deeside has always been higher than the average for other rural areas of Scotland (Butler, 1973), and in the first half of the twentieth century this would probably have deterred casual individual tourists from visiting in large numbers. It would not, of course, have been a deterrent to affluent sportsmen. Popularization of Deeside by the average tourist in relatively large numbers began after the Second World War in the form of the coach and car-borne tourism, following road and transport improvements. Additional attractions began to be made available as a regular wider tourist trade developed. The acquisition of historic properties such as Craigievar Castle by the National Trust for Scotland and the opening of Balmoral itself to tourists also increased the attractiveness of the area to visitors. The development of ski facilities at Glenshee and briefly at Mar Lodge in the 1960s also increased tourist numbers to the area and widened general awareness of Deeside in the tourism market.

It is unusual for a destination to remain attractive to the same market for a century and a half. To do so normally requires either continual rejuvenation and modification of the attractions of the destination (often by way of the efforts of new entrepreneurs), and/or continued promotion and marketing. In the case of Deeside, the essential attributes have not changed significantly since Victoria's first visit in 1848, except for the continued annual presence of the royal family since then. There have been no significant entrepreneurial innovations or interventions in Deeside that have retained or increased tourist numbers in the last century. The railway has ceased to run up Deeside, and there have been only minor developments in terms of tourist infrastructure (the ill-fated ski developments at Mar Lodge lasted only a few years and the Glenshee Ski Centre attracts very few summer visitors and has been threatened with bankruptcy because of warmer winters and poor snow conditions). Clearly other factors have proved positive features in maintaining the popularity of Deeside with tourists. The media coverage of the royal family's annual arrival and presence at Balmoral and their visits to Crathes and Braemar has been of crucial importance in keeping Deeside in the public view and the minds of potential tourists, and re-enforcing the image of this area as a tourist destination. Other factors that have re-enforced public awareness include the publication of water colour paintings by HRH the Prince of Wales (including several done at Balmoral) and his children's story, *The Old Man of Lochnagar* (the name of a mountain on the Balmoral estate). The Deeside decision to continue to market the 'old' even if at best only a partially authentic image of Scotland would appear to be appropriate, certainly as long as the royal 're-enforcers' continue to play their part.

Bibliography

Armitage, J. (1977) *Man at play: Nine centuries of pleasure making*. London: Frederick Warne

Balmoral Castle (n.d.) 'Welcome to Balmoral'. Retrieved 31 October 2011 from httw://www.balmoral castle.com

Beerli, A. and Martín, J. D. (2004) 'Factors influencing destination image'. *Annals of Tourism Research*, 31(3), 657–81

Blank, U. (1989) *The community tourism industry imperative: The necessity, the opportunities, its potential*. State College, PA: Venture Publishing

Brown, I. J. C. (1955) *Balmoral, the history of a home*. London: Collins

Butler, R. W. (1973) 'Tourism in the Highlands and Islands of Scotland'. Unpublished doctoral dissertation, University of Glasgow

—— (1980) 'The concept of a tourist area cycle of evolution: Implications for management of resources'. *Canadian Geographer*, 24(1), 5–12

—— (1985) 'Evolution of tourism in the Scottish Highlands'. *Annals of Tourism Research*, 12(3), 371–91

—— (1998) 'Tartan mythology: The traditional tourist image of Scotland'. In G. Ringer (ed.) *Destinations: Cultural landscapes of tourism*. London: Routledge, pp. 121–39

Cauthorn, R. C. (1989) *Contributions to a theory of entrepreneurship*. New York: Garland Publishing

Christaller, W. (1964) 'Some considerations of tourism location in Europe: The peripheral regions-under-developed countries-recreation areas'. *Papers in Regional Science*, 12(1), 95–105

Connely, W. (1955) *Beau Nash: Monarch of Bath and Tunbridge Wells*. London: Werner Laurie

Cook, T. (1861) *Cook's Scottish tourist official directory*. London: Thomas Cook

Duff, D. (1980) *Queen Victoria's Highland journals*. Exeter: Webb and Bower

Eden, R. (1979) *Going to the moors*. London: John Murray

Espelt, N. G. and Benito, J. A. D. (2005) 'The social construction of the image of Girona: A methodological approach'. *Tourism Management*, 26(5), 777–85

Gartner, W. C. (1993) 'Image formation process'. *Journal of Travel and Tourism Marketing*, 2(2/3), 191–216

Gilbert, E. W. (1954) *Brighton: Old Ocean's bauble*. London: Methuen

Gold, J. R. and Gold, M. M. (1995) *Imagining Scotland: Tradition, representation and promotion in Scottish tourism since 1750*. Aldershot: Scolar Press

Gordon, G. (2004) 'Millionaire property hunters find paradise in Scotland'. *Sunday Times – Ecosse*, 24 October, p. 3

Hartwell, M. and Lane, J. (1991) *Champions of enterprise: Australian entrepreneurship 1788–1990*. Double Bay, NSW: Focus Books

Hill, I. B. (1973) *Landseer: An illustrated life of Sir Edwin Landseer, 1802–1873*. Aylesbury: Shire Publication

Hunt, J. D. (1975) 'Image as a factor in tourism development'. *Journal of Travel Research*, 13(3), 1–7

Irwin, F. and Wilton, A. (1982) *Turner in Scotland*. Aberdeen: Aberdeen Art Gallery

Kuratko, D. F. and Hodgetts, R. M. (1998) *Entrepreneurship: A contemporary approach* (4th edn). New York: The Dryden Press

McKercher, B. (1999) 'A chaos approach to tourism'. *Tourism Management*, 20(4), 425–34

Macpherson, J. (1765) *The works of Ossian, the Son of Fingal*, translated from the Gaelic language by James Macpherson. Edinburgh: Edinburgh University Press

Mueller, S. L. and Thomas, A. S. (2001) 'Culture and entrepreneurial potential: A nine country study of locus of control and innovativeness'. *Journal of Business Venturing*, 16(1), 51–75

O'Dell, A. C. and Walton, K. (1962) *The Highlands and Islands of Scotland*. London: T. Nelson and Sons

Orr, W. (1982) *Deer forests, landlords and crofters: The Western Highlands in Victorian and Edwardian times*. Edinburgh: John Donald

Pike, S. (2002) 'Destination image analysis: A review of 142 papers from 1973 to 2000'. *Tourism Management*, 23(5), 541–49

Prebble, J. (1961) *Culloden*. New York: Atheneum

—— (1963) *The highland clearances*. London: Secker and Warburg

—— (1988) *The king's jaunt: George IV in Scotland, August, 1822*. London: Collins

Pudney, J., Cook, T. and Cook, J. M. (1953) *The Thomas Cook story*. London: Michael Joseph

Russell, R. (2006) 'The contribution of entrepreneurship theory to the TALC Model'. In R. W. Butler (ed.), *The tourism area life cycle: Conceptual and theoretical issues* (Vol. 2). Clevedon: Channel View Publications, pp. 105–23

—— and Faulkner, B. (1999) 'Movers and shakers: Chaos makers in tourism development'. *Tourism Management*, 20(4), 411–23

Schumpeter, J. A. (1950) *Capitalism, socialism and democracy*. New York: Harper-Collins

Scottish Tourist Board (1993) 'Survey of visitor attitudes'. Unpublished report, Scottish Tourist Board, Edinburgh

Shaw, G. and Williams, A. M. (1998) 'Entrepreneurship, small business culture and tourism development'. In D. Ioannides and K. G. Debbage (eds) *The economic geography of the tourist industry: A supply-side analysis*. London: Routledge, pp. 235–55

Swinglehurst, E. (1974) *The romantic journey: The story of Thomas Cook and Victorian travel*. New York: Harper and Row

Urquhart, B. (ed.) (1994) *Tartans*. London: The Apple Press

Weaver, D. A. and Oppermann, M. (2000) *Tourism management*. Brisbane: John Wiley

Wright, D. M. (1951) 'Schumpeter's political philosophy'. In S. E. Harris (ed.), *Schumpeter: Social scientist*. Cambridge, MA: Harvard Press, pp. 152–57

10

Home away from home

A research agenda for examining the resort community second home industry in Colorado

Patrick T. Long, Richard R. Perdue, Linda Venturoni

Introduction

Over the past two decades, sustainable development has become a core concept of tourism planning (Weaver, 2008; Smith, 2001). Stakeholder analysis, particularly of host community residents, has become an integral element of resort planning (Perdue, 2003), with the goal of improving local quality of life and economic opportunity. Numerous studies of host community residents have been conducted, focusing on perceptions of tourism's impacts, support for tourism development, and attitudes toward tourism growth management (i.e. Andereck and Vogt, 2000; Korça, 1998; McGehee and Andereck, 2004; Perdue et al., 1990). These studies have consistently identified the effects of tourism development on the cost and availability of real estate as one of the primary impacts of tourism in resort communities (Perdue et al., 1999).

In many resort communities, much of the housing stock is purchased by tourists as second homes both for use during vacations and as an investment. This demand for second homes affects both the character and price of the housing stock. First, particularly in major resort destinations, second homes tend to be large, amenity-rich developments that are naturally much more expensive than the traditional local housing stock (Hall and Müller, 2004a, 2004b). Second, due to the common scarcity of developable land in resort communities, the available housing stock is limited. Second home demand adds to that scarcity, thereby further increasing prices (Cho et al., 2003). Because of these prices, second home demand can lead to a process of gentrification, wherein lower-income full-time residents are unable to purchase homes in the resort community leading to a process of "class colonization" (Phillips, 1993).

A substantial body of research exists examining the distribution of second homes, ownership trends, and impacts of second home development (most notably, Coppock, 1977a; Hall and Müller, 2004b). While this existing research provides an excellent general description of the second home phenomena and its impacts, much of it is not directly applicable to the high-end, luxury second home industry that characterizes most Colorado ski resort communities (Perdue, 2004). Three primary limitations exist in applying the existing second home research to Colorado ski resort communities. First, as with most products, great variance exists within the concept of second homes, ranging from small cabins in remote settings to elaborate trophy homes in gated resort communities (Curry, 2003; Egan, 2000). The existing research has not segmented the second home market and examined differences by product type. Rather, the predominant focus is on describing the "average" second home, the "average" second home owner and overall trends in the marketplace (e.g. Timothy, 2004).

Second, due to the availability of data, much of the second home research has been conducted in Canada and Europe, particularly Great Britain and the Scandinavian countries (e.g. Coppock, 1977a, or Hall and Müller, 2004a). While this research is clearly important and insightful, differences in land ownership and real property tax laws limit its applicability to Colorado resort communities.

Third, as with much of the existing second home research, this research program is motivated by the need for information to guide government policy concerning second home development (Gill, 2000; Gill and Williams, 1994). The existing research clearly indicates that second home development potentially has substantial economic and social impacts on local communities (Müller et al., 2004) and that those impacts vary by community (Coppock, 1977b). It is essential to examine the unique characteristics of Colorado ski resort communities and to understand the implications of those unique characteristics to both second home development and the associated policies.

Thus, the goals of this research program are to develop an inventory of second homes in selected Colorado counties, to examine the economic and social impacts of second home development, and to forecast future development patterns. The purposes of this paper are:

- to provide preliminary data on the size and characteristics of the vacation/second home industry in the Northwest Council of Governments Region of Colorado;
- to examine these results within the context of the existing second home research, and
- to articulate a research agenda examining this industry from the economic, social policy, and business strategy perspectives.

The following sections will provide further background into some unique characteristics of the selected Colorado ski resort communities, describe the preliminary research methodology, and present and discuss the resulting data within the context of the existing research. The paper concludes with our proposed research agenda.

Characteristics of the study region

This research was conducted within four counties of the Northwest Council of Governments Region of Colorado. These four counties include a number of the world's premier ski resorts. Specifically, the study region included Summit County (Keystone, Breckenridge, and Copper Mountain ski resorts), Eagle County (Vail and Beaver Creek), Grand County (Winter Park), and Pitkin County (Aspen and Snowmass). Collectively, these areas hosted approximately 8 million skier days during the 2003/4 season (Colorado Ski Country USA, 2004). With a combined population of less than 100,000 people, this region experienced over 7,000 property transactions in 2003 alone with an aggregate value exceeding $3.8 billion (Blevins, 2004; US Census Bureau, 2005). Jackson County was not included in the study as it is primarily a rural, agricultural county and has little second home development.

Between 1990 and 2000, the study region was the fastest growing region within Colorado with an overall 73 percent population growth. The region's Hispanic population during the same time period experienced 268 percent growth. Regarding the available labor force and projected job growth, although annual skier visits have remained somewhat constant at about

Table 10.1 Study region land ownership

County	Total area (sq. miles)	State land (%)	Federal land (%)	Private land (%)
Eagle	1,688	1	78	21
Grand	1850	5	68	27
Pitkin	970	0	83	17
Summit	608	0	78	22

8 million, job growth has outpaced available workers (CSDO, 2003). In 1999 in Summit County, with annual skier days averaging about 3.5 million over the past few years, there was a shortage of over 4,000 workers. In Eagle County, there was a labor force shortage of 9,797 workers in 1997, a shortage that is expected to grow substantially (estimated to be 20,000 or more) by 2020 potentially increasing the number of workers either needing affordable local housing or being required to commute to their place of employment.

Three unique characteristics of this region and the associated ski resorts have dramatically influenced second home development. First, in most Colorado ski resort communities, the developable land is extremely limited. Much of the land (up to 80 percent in some counties) is owned by federal, state, or local governments and, consequently, unavailable for development (Table 10.1). Further, of the developable land, much cannot be developed due to steepness of slopes, classification as wetlands, and lack of access. If fact, a critical environmental impact issue is the growing tendency to develop these marginal lands, due to scarcity of better, more developable land.

Second, the ownership of Colorado ski resorts has fundamentally changed over the past few decades. An industry historically characterized by independent, privately owned, entrepreneurial companies has transformed into a consolidated, publicly owned, corporate industry. The emergence of Vail Resorts, Inc. (NYSE: MTN) and Intrawest, Inc (NYSE: IDR) has dramatically altered business practices in many Colorado ski resort communities. Vail Resorts, Inc. owns and manages Vail, Beaver Creek, Keystone, and Breckenridge ski resorts in the study region.

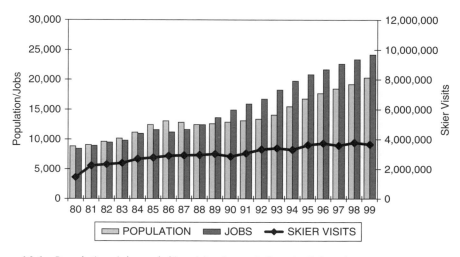

Figure 10.1 Population, jobs and skier visits: Summit County Colorado

Intrawest, Inc. owns Copper Mountain Resort, is a development partner in Keystone Resort, and has recently entered into management agreements to redevelop the Winter Park and Snowmass Resorts, all within the study region. The transition to public ownership, with its focus on shareholder value and quarterly profits, has greatly accelerated real estate development at these resorts (Clifford, 2002). As the speed of development increases, the associated impacts are magnified (Perdue et al., 1999).

Third, Colorado ski resorts are increasingly competing for share in a stagnant market. A primary tactic in this competition has been product improvements in the form of terrain expansions and lift capacity improvements, both of which are very expensive. Replacing a standard double chairlift with a high speed detachable quad lift is at least $6–8 million dollars per mile. A gondola lift costs in the range of $10–12 million. Even when excluding the highly variable litigation costs of gaining the development permits, the costs of terrain expansion are equally impressive; the Blue Sky Basin expansion at Vail Resorts is estimated to have cost $18 million. Further, today's destination skier also expects a complete range of restaurant facilities on the mountains, other winter recreation facilities such as sledding and ice skating, and other amenities, such as warming huts and business centers. The Two Elk Restaurant complex on Vail Mountain is a $12 million facility. Over the last decade, more than $1 billion has been invested in mountain expansions and improvements at existing Colorado ski resorts (Lipsher, 2002). As part of its agreement to manage Winter Park Resort for the City of Denver, Intrawest has agreed to invest $50 million in mountain improvements over the next decade. Much of this expansion is being financed by real estate development and management, further accelerating the level of second home development. In exchange for its Winter Park mountain investments, Intrawest was given development rights to 140 acres at the base of the mountain and is planning between 1,000 and 1,500 new condominiums along with approximately 50,000 sq ft of commercial space.

Study components and early results

Typology of second homes

The first, and not insignificant, challenge of examining second homes in resort regions is developing a viable database that identifies second homes. This is traditionally done on the basis of the owner's primary place of residence. To determine the profile of second homes for the study region, county assessor databases from the four counties were collected and assembled into a GIS database of over 64,000 property records. The database reflected 2000–2001 housing ownership information. These records were recoded to reflect common fields including type of unit (e.g. single family home, condominium), value of unit, square footage and year built. Because there is no indicator within County Assessor records for whether a home is being used as a second home or local residence, a code was added to indicate the current usage of the housing unit based on where the property tax assessment notice was being sent. Out-of-county addresses were marked as "second home." Using this method it was determined that 60 percent of the homes in the four-county study area are second homes. This ranged from a low of 49 percent in Eagle County to a high of 67 percent in Summit County.

Analysis of property values in the study area showed the average price of a single family house in June 2003 in Eagle County to be $785,000 whereas for a multifamily unit (duplex, triplex) the average was $443,000. In Summit County the average for single family housing was $486,000, for multifamily, $255,000. These high-end housing costs and related issues were prominently noted in a July 2004, *Denver Post* newspaper article entitled "Resort sales on a record pace" (Blevins, 2004). The writer indicated that the second home real estate market was being bolstered by "strengthening stock market, baby boomers boasting more discretionary income, lower interest rates luring locals out of the rental pool and climbing prices" and noted that "High-end buyers are driving the surge, especially in Aspen and Pitkin County." He also noted that "New homes are becoming more rare. New land becomes unavailable. Space gets tighter and values soar."

The standard US home market value in 2004 was roughly $100,000; in Pitkin County it was in excess of $1 million; in Eagle County the average exceeded $550,000. The percentage increase in home market values in 1998–2004 for the standard US city was about 18 percent; for Grand County it was over 60 percent and for Eagle County it was in excess of 75 percent.

Further analysis of housing cost data showed that as the value of second home property increased, so did the percentage of second home ownership. For example, 74 percent of those properties valued in excess of $5 million were owned by second home owners whereas only 57 percent of those properties valued in the $100,000 to $200,000 price range were determined to be second homes. Additionally, a large percentage of the study area's housing stock with the highest square footage was owned by second home owners: 67 percent of the homes of 7,000 sq. ft. or more were identified as second homes as were 59 percent of those with 4,000–4,999 sq. ft., 64 percent of those with 5–5,999 sq. ft. and 64 percent of those with 6–6,999 sq. ft. The most common types of second home were condominiums (72 percent) and single family homes (48 percent).

These findings illustrate a number of critical questions for future research. First and foremost, it is important to establish the trend lines in these data. Presuming the levels of growth observed by the popular media and through casual observation, the implications for ownership, size, and amenity characteristics of resort real estate are important both for resort developers and public policy organizations. Second, what are the policy implications of this gentrification process? Third, where will the resort employees live and how will they commute to and from the resort workplace? Colorado Highway 82 between Glenwood Springs and Aspen is rapidly becoming an urban highway with daily commuter traffic issues.

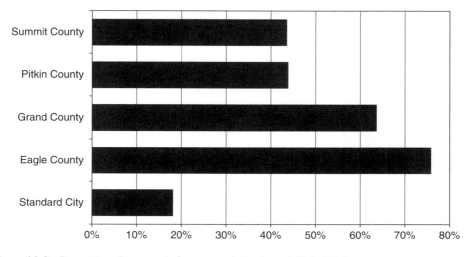

Figure 10.2   Percentage increase in home market values: 1998–2004

Survey of second homeowners and residents

In order to learn about utilization, shopping patterns and behaviors of second homeowners it was necessary to seek information directly from the homeowners. It was also important to determine the similarities and differences of attitudes and opinions of both permanent residents and second home owners for future planning. A questionnaire was sent to a stratified random sample of all homeowners (n = number of homeowners = 64,000, 60 percent of which had been determined to be second homes) in the four-county study area in April 2003; of the 4,300 questionnaires mailed, 1,346 were returned for an overall useable response rate of 32 percent. Some 41 percent of the respondents indicated this was their permanent residence while 56 percent indicated it was their second home used for personal or rental use.

Demographic characteristics

The demographic questions asked in the questionnaire provided for a comparison of second home owners in the region with those described in the National Study of Second Homeowners published in *American Demographics* (Francese, 2003). This national study identified 55–64 as the age cohort most likely to purchase second homes and forecasted great growth in the second home industry nationally as baby boomers (1946–64) are just beginning to enter this age cohort. It was reported that second home owners nationally tend to be high-income, high-asset, highly educated, middle age or older couples, with children nearing adulthood or children no longer living at home. This study confirmed all of these characteristics but showed much higher income levels and even a greater likelihood to be in the 55–64 age bracket than the national study. Median household income reported in the four-county study area for second home owners was $208,330; for residents, $74,416.

Social indicators

The questionnaire asked second home owners to indicate the reasons why they purchased a second home in the study area. Allowing for multiple responses, second home owners indicated most frequently that it was due to the availability of recreational amenities (83 percent) followed by the proximity to ski resorts (73 percent) and the scenery and surroundings (72 percent). Some 49 percent indicated they had purchased their second home for the investment potential; 14 percent of second homes were being used as full-time rentals and 32 percent as part-time rentals; while 50 percent of usage was by owner, family, and friends. Second home owners were more likely to shop locally (0–10 miles), while local residents indicated they were more likely to shop in the "Extended Region" (30+ miles) including the Front Range (Denver, Colorado) area.

Both second home owners and local residents indicated similar recreational interests with 79 percent of residents and 82 percent of non-residents indicating their favorite activity as being walking and jogging. Popular among both groups was downhill skiing (72 percent resident, 79 percent non-resident), hiking (79 percent resident, 75 percent non-resident) and mountain biking (52 percent resident, 45 percent non-resident). When asked to assess the quality of the recreation offerings, 90 percent of the second home owners indicated strong approval of the quality of the recreation opportunities (83 percent of residents indicated the same), 86 percent (73 percent for residents) indicated strong approval for the quality of the parks, trails and open space, with public safety (66 percent) and the appearance of the community (63 percent) being third and fourth in terms of the assessment of quality by second home purchasers.

High on the list of natural resource amenities for second home purchasers were the scenic/ visual qualities of the study area (95 percent), the quality of the air (95 percent), the quality of the water (95 percent), the recreational opportunities (91 percent), and the parks and trails systems (91 percent). These values were almost identical to those expressed by the residents with 90 percent of residents indicating the importance of the scenic/visual qualities, 91 percent indicating the air and water quality, 79 percent indicating the recreational opportunities and 78 percent indicating the importance of the parks and trails system.

Economic indicators

Of importance when projecting the economic impact of second home owners is the pattern of use. The full time household equivalency (FTHE)[1] for a single family residence was 29 percent of annual usage and for a condominium, 23 percent. There was no significant difference found in usage either by income level or value of residence. Respondents indicated 41 percent level of use for December–March, 12 percent for April–June, 32 percent for July–August, and 14 percent for September–November.

Of importance in policy development and planning is an understanding of the current and projected future use of second home properties. Some 50 percent of the responding second home owners indicated their housing unit was currently used by "owner, friends and family", 32 percent that it was used as a part-time rental while 14 percent indicated their unit was part of the full-time rental pool. About 21 percent indicated their unit was used only by the owner.

Regarding future use of second home properties, 47 percent indicated they intended to "increase personal use of their property", while 44 percent suggested they would "maintain their current level of use." Regarding increasing the usage by friends and family, 28 percent indicated yes, while 11 percent indicated they intended to retire to the area and use the property as a permanent residence. Some 17 percent indicated they were likely to use the residence in the future as a part-time rental unit while 7 percent indicated they intended to use the residence as a full-time rental property. This finding would suggest that there will be fewer opportunities in the future for local residents and workers to rent such property within the local community.

Economic base analysis

In order to answer the questions related to jobs generated by second homes it was necessary to identify the economic drivers for the study area and so an economic base analysis (Figure 10.3)

Figure 10.3 Economic base analysis

was conducted (Lloyd Levy Consulting, 2004). This analysis identified that second homes, winter visitors, summer visitors, resident income,[2] and other drivers[3] were the basic drivers that were generating both basic and secondary jobs. This economic analysis addressed three questions:

1   How big is the economic base of each county?
2   What share of the economic base is due to second homes or other drivers?
3   What is the total effect of second homes and other economic drivers, as measured by the basic and secondary jobs they generate?

> Total spending associated with the economic drivers of the four-county region, including Eagle, Grand, Pitkin and Summit Counties, was estimated to be more than $5.3 billion in 2002. Across the region, second home construction and spending was estimated to be the largest driver, supporting about 31,600 jobs or 38 percent of all jobs. Winter tourism, including skiing, supported about 22,300 jobs, or 27 percent of total jobs, and resident spending of non-local income supported about 13,300 jobs, or 16 percent of total jobs.
>
> *(Lloyd Levy Consulting, 2004, p. 14)*

Also, this economic analysis projected that across the region construction of housing units 3,000 sq. ft. and larger supports 2,461 direct basic jobs while the construction of housing units less than 3,000 sq. ft. supports 1,612 direct basic jobs. The analysis also projected that spending by second home owners of units less than 3,000 sq. ft. supports 12,796 direct basic jobs while spending by second home owners of units 3,000 sq. ft. or greater accounts for 4,354 direct basic jobs (ibid.).

Summary and future research agenda

There are a number of findings from this study that are important for understanding the implications of second home development in the region and for future planning and policy development for the study area. First, the extent to which second homes dominate the housing market limiting the housing stock available to local workers. Second, the uniqueness of this specific study due to the degree of wealth that is being invested in second homes exemplified by both their size and value making it virtually impossible for local residents to afford their purchase. Third, the documentation of shopping and recreational patterns which is driving related amenity development. Fourth, the determination of the degree to which the second home economy serves as an economic driver for the region and the dramatic impact future second home development will have on job creation. And, fifth, the establishment of a methodology that can be used to systematically track this development into the future.

It is important to note that local residents and second home owners both hold similar "values" regarding community amenities; they also indicated similar recreational interests. Both groups indicate they visit or live in the region primarily because of these qualities not because of the potential economic gain of property ownership. Thus, both groups have good reason to protect the area's resources and the highly rated quality of life the region currently provides. Both groups should be keenly interested in policies and actions that maintain the area's economic and social well-being.

The "classic" second home owner in this region will, in each of the respective counties, have a median household income of: Eagle, $301,408; Grand, $105,660; Pitkin, $277,500; and Summit, $148,750. Their second home usage would be approximately 90 days per year.

They will not show up in population counts, do not vote locally and do not participate in the local workforce. They are predominantly aged 55–64 and may own a 3rd or 4th home.

The "affordable" local resident will, in each of the respective counties, have a median household income of: Eagle, $62,682; Grand, $47,756; Pitkin, $59,375; and Summit, $56,587. Their home usage will be approximately 330–60 days per year and they live in subsidized housing or houses bought while prices were still affordable. They show up in population counts, vote locally and participate in the local workforce. They may have lived in the area for a long time and are predominantly aged 30–75+.

The workers in the four-county study area employed in the second home basic industry and their families require housing and a wide range of private and public community services. The workers providing these services, in turn, have the same needs. Typically, in a second home resort community there is initial development and maturation of a traditional tourism industry. However, over time, second homes become a large and often dominant part of the physical, economic, and social landscape. Their development creates a demand for workers above that of the traditional tourist industry, especially in housing construction but also in their maintenance, operation, and use. As the number of second homes increase, the demand for workers to support the second home industry increases as well. Knowledge of the effects of this industry is essential to resort community planning including understanding and anticipating the secondary or "multiplier" effects. To not understand the effects can lead to shortages and to major conflicts among the users of the various resources of the area.

Second homes take up large amounts of land in Colorado mountain resort areas where developable land is already in short supply. As a result, the value of second homes and the surrounding land rise above that normally paid for worker housing. As their numbers increase, and the land available for development decreases, a dilemma is created. Second homes have generated the need for more workers, but the rise in property values and subsequent housing costs have made it difficult for the workers to live within a reasonable distance of their place of work.

Traditionally, residential homes and their neighborhoods have provided workers with a decent home and adequate community services. However, second homes are different in that they are not just residences, but an industry creating a demand for workers. Second homes drive up property values, including residential housing for workers. Because of this, it becomes especially important for elected officials and community planners to understand and estimate the secondary effects of second homes in tourist-based economies. With this information, policies can be developed by local governments to protect the natural amenities and provide for the social needs of citizens with each new development and to influence the growth in the economic drivers themselves. To ignore this information concerning second homes within the study region and beyond, casts social and economic fate to the wind.

There are clearly many additional questions that this second home research has raised. The foremost is addressing specifically how this information can be effectively transmitted to community planners and public policymakers for its effective use in growth management and community planning. Follow-up studies for this region will certainly include the addition of other counties to the study area and reanalysis of the property records to include an assessment of the conversion of units that remove them from the local rental pool. Economic changes related to the trend of second homeowners retiring to the area will be analyzed and the survey and economic analysis used to measure changing trends will be updated. The economic drivers will be reassessed and projections of job creation and shortages reanalyzed. All of this information will continually be analyzed for planning and policy implications for the region and discussion will be held at all levels to ensure broad citizen engagement in decisions about the future of the region.

Notes

1 Full time household equivalency (FTHE) was a measure created by the NWCOG Steering Committee to describe the extent to which a housing unit was occupied on a full-time basis by its owner.
2 Resident income includes retiree income, transfer payments, dividends, interest and rent.
3 This includes mining, manufacturing, agriculture and Interstate I-70 thru-traffic expenditures.

References

Andereck, K. L. and Vogt, C. A. (2000) 'The relationships between resident's attitudes toward tourism and tourism development options'. *Journal of Travel Research*, 39(1), 27–36
Blevins, J. (2004) 'Resort sales on a record pace: Colo. real estate deals may surpass 5.7 billion high in 2000'. *Denver Post*, 4 July, p. K-08
Cho, S.-H., Newman, P. K. and Wear, D. N. (2003) 'Impacts of second home development on housing prices in the Southern Appalachian Highlands'. *Review of Urban and Regional Development Studies*, 15(3), 208–25
Clifford, H. (2002) *Downhill slide: Why the corporate ski industry is bad for skiing, ski towns and the environment.* San Francisco, CA: Sierra Club Books
Colorado Ski Country USA (2004) *Season report 2003–2004.* Denver, CO: Colorado Ski Country USA
Coppock, J. T. (ed.) (1977a) *Second homes: Curse or blessing?* Oxford: Pergamon Press
—— (1977b) 'Issues and conflict'. In J. T. Coppock (ed.) *Second homes: Curse or blessing?* Oxford: Pergamon Press, pp. 195–215
CSDO (2003) *Ski county employment estimates.* Denver, CO: Colorado Department of Local Affairs, State Demographer Office
Curry, P. (2003) 'Second to none'. *Builder*, 26(12), 218–26
Egan, N. (2000) 'Scaling up'. *Urban Land*, August, pp. 94–101
Francese, P. (2003) 'Top trends for 2003'. *American Demographics*, 24(11), 6
Gill, A. (2000) 'From growth machine to growth management: The dynamics of resort development in Whistler, British Columbia'. *Environment and Planning A*, 32, 1083–1103
—— and Williams, P. (1994) 'Managing growth in mountain tourism communities'. *Tourism Management*, 15(3), 212–20
Hall, C. M. and Müller, D. K. (eds) (2004a) *Tourism, mobility and second homes: Between elite landscape and common ground.* Clevedon: Channel View Publications
Hall, C. M. and Müller, D. K. (2004b) 'Introduction: Second homes, curse or blessing? Revisited'. In C. M. Hall and D. K. Müller (eds) *Tourism, mobility and second homes: Between elite landscape and common ground.* Clevedon: Channel View Publications, pp. 3–14
Korça, P. (1998) 'Resident perceptions of tourism in a resort town'. *Leisure Sciences*, 20(3), 193–212
Lipsher, S. (2002) 'Breckenridge, Colo.: Ski resort unveils expansion'. *Denver Post*, 11 September. Retrieved 1 November 2011 from http://www.libraryo.com/article.aspx?num=91368027
Lloyd Levy Consulting (2004) *Job generation in the Colorado Mountain Resort economy: Second homes and other economic drivers in Eagle, Grand, Pitkin and Summit Counties executive summary.* Denver, CO: Levy, Hammer, Siler, George Associates
McGehee, N. G. and Andereck, K. L. (2004) 'Factors predicting rural residents' support for tourism'. *Journal of Travel Research*, 43(2), 131–40
Müller, D. K., Hall, C. M. and Keen, D. (2004) 'Second home tourism impact, planning and management'. In C. M. Hall and D. K. Müller (eds) *Tourism, mobility and second homes: Between elite landscape and common ground.* Clevedon: Channel View Publications, pp. 15–32
Perdue, R. R. (2003) 'Stakeholder analysis in Colorado ski resort communities'. *Tourism Analysis*, 8(2), 233–36
—— (2004) 'Sustainable tourism and stakeholder groups: A case study of Colorado ski resort communities'. In G. I. Crouch, R. R. Perdue, H. J. P. Timmermans and M. Uysal (eds) *Consumer psychology of tourism, hospitality and leisure* (Vol. 3). Cambridge, MA: CABI Publishing, pp. 253–64
——, Long, P. T. and Allen, L. R. (1990) 'Resident support for tourism development'. *Annals of Tourism Research*, 17(4), 586–99
——, Long, P. T. and Kang, Y. S. (1999) 'Boomtown tourism and resident quality of life: The marketing of gaming to host community residents'. *Journal of Business Research*, 44(3), 165–77

Phillips, M. (1993) 'Rural gentrification and the processes of class colonisation'. *Journal of Rural Studies,* 9(2), 123–40

Smith, V. L. (2001) 'Sustainability'. In V. L. Smith and M. Brent (eds) *Hosts and guests revisited: Tourism issues of the 21st Century.* New York: Cognizant Communications, pp. 187–200

Timothy, D. J. (2004) 'Recreational second homes in the United States: Development issues and contemporary patterns'. In C. M. Hall and D. K. Müller (eds), *Tourism, mobility and second homes: Between elite landscape and common ground.* Clevedon: Channel View Publications, pp. 133–48

US Census Bureau (2005) 'State and country quick facts: Summit County, Colorado'. Retrieved 1 November 2011 from http://quickfacts.census.gov/qfd/states/08/08117.html

Weaver, D. (2008) *Sustainable Tourism: Theory and Practice.* Oxford: Elsevier, pp. 1–17

Part III
Planning for tourism development

11

Planning sponsored tourism research

An investigation about its structure and trend

Honggang Xu, Jigang Bao, Botao Su

Introduction

Academic planners refer to professors and researchers in universities and relevant research institutes who take part in the practice of tourism planning. Compared with developed countries, academic planners in China play a bigger role in the promotion of the development of the tourism industry, tourism research and tourism education. For example, the first regional tourism plan was initiated by a group of academic geographers when they were engaged in the national land survey and use planning in the 1980s (Fan and Hu, 2003). According to the National Tourism Bureau in 1998, among all the first registered tourism organizations, 69 percent were from universities, 21 percent from social research institutes and 10 percent from science research institutes. These academics are also the main force in the theoretical development of tourism research in China, and at the same time educators of tourism students.

For a long time, the triple roles (i.e. as researcher, planner, and teacher) of academic planners have been reinforcing each other, and indeed serving as an ideal model of linking academic institutions to industries. However, after 20 years of rapid development of tourism planning in China, the shortcomings of the triple-role model of the academic planner have gradually presented themselves, mainly in the academic field. Some researchers commented that studies done by the academic planners are more like a plan or a report rather than a profound scientific research. These studies are normally composed of two parts: a description of a practical problem and the solutions. Most of them do not follow the rigorous process of scientific enquiry. As a result, the researches may help in solving the real world problem but contribute little academically (Bao and Zhang, 2004). Others argue that this is the research paradigm that fits well with the development stage of the tourism industry and has provided foundations for the future research. Overall, with the development of tourism and tourism research, the triple-role model of the tourism planner cannot be sustained and will be replaced by a new paradigm.

This chapter first reveals the background of the emergence of academic planners and the characteristics of tourism plans undertaken by these planners based on a literature review. By applying a qualitative system enquiry method, the study attempts to build a model to understand the structures which determine the changes of the research paradigms. The final discussion is about the problems of the new paradigm.

Background of academic-dominated tourism planning

Demand for tourism plans

Since 1978 when the reform and the open-door policy was initiated, China's tourism industry has become the most promising and fastest growing sector of China's tertiary industry. According to statistics from National Tourism and Travel Administration, there were 108 million international tourists in 2004, a growth of 18 percent and 10 percent compared with the numbers for 2003 and 2002 respectively. The total inbound tourism income was US$25 billion, a growth of 43.7 percent and 22.6 percent compared with 2003 and 2002 respectively. The number of domestic tourists reached 930 million, with total revenue of RMB400 billion, a growth of 5.9 percent and 3.1 percent compared with 2003. There were 28 million outbound tourists, a growth of 38.5 percent and 68.7 percent compared with 2003 and 2002 respectively.

Observing the economic opportunities brought along with tourism development, governments at all levels are eager to use tourism as an economic booster. Tourism industry is given a high priority on the governments' agenda; 25 provincial governments nationwide make tourism industry their pillar industry, leading industry, or key industry (Wei, 2002). Tourism plans as a tool to manage and promote tourism development have been institutionalized.

As a result, demand for tourism plans as the first step to tourism development is rising. Regional tourism plans are required for the local governments to integrate tourism into regional development, budget resources, and reserve land accordingly. Strategic and conceptual plans of resort areas and attractions are screened for potential tourism projects and used as tools to attract investments. Site plans are needed for the approval of construction projects. In summary, the need for tourism plans has been growing rapidly.

Shortage of tourism planner professionals

Along with the boom of the tourism planning industry, there is a great need of tourism planning professionals. Traditionally professionals most relevant to tourism planning are urban planners who have been engaged in recreational planning as part of urban plans. However, since traditional recreational planning is mainly for welfare purposes, the planners are strong on physical design, but weak in socio-economic analysis. As a result the traditional recreational planner cannot really meet the goal of promoting economic development through tourism. In addition, urban planners and architects look down on tourism and recreational planning because tourism is considered to lack scientific foundations. The entry of foreign experts and consulting companies into the Chinese planning market has been constrained because of the lack of accessibility, lack of understanding of the local situation and high costs. That's why the first contract between the Sichuang Government and WTO on provincial tourism planning attracted a lot of attention. In the market for tourism planning, there is a shortage of professional planners.

Chances for geographers to play a major role in the tourism plan market

Although there is a shortage of tourism planning professionals, the trust between clients and the tourism planners still plays an important role in reaching business agreements. Because the history of tourism planning is short and there is a lack of standard procedures to control and evaluate the quality of the tourism plans, it is technically difficult to set details of a tourism plan in the contracts. Even after the National Tourism and Travel Administration issued "General Guidelines of Tourism Plan" and "Management Guidelines of Tourism Development Plans," this problem remains the same because these guidelines cannot really solve the uncertainties in signing contracts because of a lack of details and considerations about the diversification of tourism development, although they have great implications for the promotion of the overall quality of tourism planning (Zhai, 2001). During the planning period and the post-planning period, there are always requests to the professionals from the clients to change and adjust the plans. Therefore, trust-building and cooperation are very important cultural factors for clients to choose planners. University professors tend to be more reliable than business firms, especially in regional tourism development where local government is the client.

As a result, academics whose specialties are closely related to tourism and planning have the opportunity to fill the gap in the tourism planning market. Geographers, who have gained experiences in regional development planning, are more likely to identify the potentials for tourism development within the region, and they have become the first tourism planners. Of course, academics from many different backgrounds, such as economists, architects and other related areas, have also gradually begun to show their interest in this area as the demand for tourism planning has risen dramatically.

Observed patterns of tourism plans undertaken by academics

Accumulation of tourism planning theories and cases

Although tourism planning began in the 1950s in Hawaii and was widely carried out in France and the UK in the 1960s (Wu, 2000), the theories and models of tourism planning obtained internationally were not accessible to Chinese tourism planners at the initial stage. Soon after the development of tourism plans, it was not practicable to directly transfer the theories and methodologies in urban planning, sector industrial planning or land use planning to tourism planning. The academics had to explore and develop new theories and methodologies to formulate plans and to solve particular tourism problems based on their experience and knowledge.

Through a short review of the process of tourism planning models, learning by doing can be easily perceived. In the early 1980s, when tourism planning was initiated in China, planners' efforts were concentrated on identifying the potential tourist attractions, categorizing them and revealing the importance of tourism development to government officials and entrepreneurs. During this period, one of the greatest achievements of tourism research was the formulation of technical indicators to appraise tourism resources by the Geography Institute of the Chinese Academy (Fan and Hu, 2003). With the development of tourism, planners realized the importance of market analysis in tourism plans. Therefore, some of the market theories and methodologies were applied into these tourism plans. Research on tourists' behavior and market segmentation were also carried out with significant achievements. Liu (2001) pointed out that traditional tourism planning dominated by the market-oriented planning models has been broken and will gradually be replaced by tourism recreational planning, landscape, and environmental design.

Along with rapid tourism development, intangible problems have accumulated and been gradually perceived by the stakeholders. It is clear that the economic, social, and environmental implications of tourism development must be examined to sustain tourism development. Thus, economic analysis based on the input–output models was also carried out to identify the significance of the tourism economy in regional development. Community tourism and industrial aspects of tourism were also the focus of tourism research in this period. In this process, the special model of community participation in tourism development is proposed. It has been found that in China it is more important to share the importance of the benefits with the local community than fully participating in the tourism process.

As a result, compared with the tourism planning done by foreign professional tourism planners, Chinese tourism plans tend to address more issues which are unique to the locals. The identification and solution of problems in tourism plans are usually based on scientific enquires. Research-oriented plans are the characteristics at this stage.

However, since the tourism plans are done by academics, some of the tourism plans are more academic than practical. The clients commented that some of the plans were "well structured but not operational," and "some of the plans seems like scraps cited from text books, and therefore are not practical" (Peng, 2000; Wei et al., 2001, p. 13).

Growth of tourism geography

Due to the active participation of geographers in tourism planning, they have received more financial support for their research projects. As a result, tourism geography has boomed as a new discipline. Bao et al. (2003) conducted a statistical analysis of all the articles published in these journals (see Table 11.1) from 1978 to 2003 according to their subjects. Tourism geographers, who had a low profile in academic society, began to flourish, while tourism departments originating from management school and economics schools were not able to experience the same development.

Planning sponsored funds for the research

Despite the increasing importance of tourism in the national economy and the rising status of the tourism research in the academic society, the present funds of tourism research from the Chinese government is minimal. Researchers seeking funding for tourism studies find themselves to be marginalized. For example, the geography department of the National Science Foundation in China is the only official department which funds tourism related research. However, Song and Leng (2004), of the National Scientific Foundation, summarized the funded projects on human geography for over the period of 12 years (Table 11.2) and it could be seen that tourism research received limited grants.

Table 11.1 Tourism geography literature in 10 geographical journals, 1978–2003

Journal	1978–1989	1990–1998	1999–2003	Total	Proportion
Acta Geographica Sinica		14	7	21	2.11%
Geographical Science	2	10	21	33	3.32%
Geographical Research	1	11	11	23	2.31%
Economic Geography	22	62	135	219	22.03%
Human Geography	8	83	137	228	22.94%
Tropical Geography	13	42	52	107	10.76%
Geography & Territorial Research	16	79	45	140	14.08%
Arial Research & Development	7	74	80	161	16.20%
Journal of Natural Resources		7	13	20	2.01%
Arid Land Geography	5	10	27	42	4.23%
Total	84	392	528	994	100%

Table 11.2 Statistical analysis of free application projects on human geography supported by National Natural Science Foundation of China in 1991–2003

Year	Population Geography	Economic Geography	Urban Geography	Political Geography	Culture Geography	Historical Geography	Tourism Geography	Social Geography	Regional Geography	Total
1991	1	3	5		1		1		1	12
1992		2	1		1		2		5	11
1993		3	4		1				3	11
1994	1	4	5				2		4	16
1995	1	4	2		1	1	2		2	13
1996		4	2				2		5	13
1997		3	6	1		1			5	16
1998		5	3	1		1	1	2	2	15
1999	1	5	3	1		1			5	16
2000		6	6			2			2	16
2001		4	10		1		1		4	20
2002		7	8		2	2	2		5	26
2003		10	7		1		1		2	21
Total	4	60	62	3	8	8	14	2	45	206

Source: Song and Leng, 2004

Unlike other agencies such as the Construction Ministry and the National Land Research Ministry, which are important funding sources for the research projects within their sectors, the China Travel and Tourism Administration does not fund tourism research. Therefore, tourism researchers have difficulties competing with academics in other disciplines in terms of research funding.

The enterprises of the Chinese tourism industry are relatively small and lack the financial power and incentives to fund tourism research. Although some consulting services on management are indeed contracted to academics, due to the time, cost constraints and information security, the researchers cannot fully conduct independent research. Therefore, financial resources and the opportunities to get access to data in tourism planning projects enable academic research activities, including academic conferences, PhD dissertations etc.

Dominance of tourism planning and development of postgraduate studies

Planning-oriented research has great impacts on the growth of graduate studies. Among the tourism-related courses, development-oriented courses (e.g. tourism courses from the perspectives of geography, culture, ecology, planning, and MICE) and managerial curriculums (e.g. tourism courses from the perspectives of statistics, accounting, law, marketing, tour guiding and services) are two major components of the tourism curricula in tourism schools or departments in China. According to Yuan et al. (2005), of the total courses offered by the schools of tourism, there are about 111 development-oriented courses and 180 managerial courses. The percentage of development-oriented courses in the tourism curricula indicates that the importance of these courses is widely recognized, although there are fewer of these courses compared with managerial courses.

Wu and Li (2005) further pointed out that among all the tourism-related colleges and universities, 38 of them (65.5 percent) are tourism development-oriented. Furthermore, 12 of the development-oriented schools specialize in tourism planning and design, tantamount to the number of schools which specialize in tourism management (see Table 11.3).

Triple role of research-planning-teaching

In summary, academics in geography and other related areas have opportunities to participate in tourism development. Many academics have become active tourism planners and tourism

Table 11.3 Number of schools entitled to grant Masters' degrees for tourism management and their academic backgrounds

Academic background	Number of tourism schools	Academic background	Number of tourism schools
Geography (pls. Management and History)	22	Chinese	2
Economics (pls. International Business)	15	Architecture	1
History (pls. Economics and Management)	8	Transportation	1
Geology	4	Forestry	1
Food Science and Engineering	3	Sociology	1
Foreign Languages	3	Gardening	1
Agriculture	2		

Source: Materials offered on the official websites of relevant schools (Wu and Li, 2005)

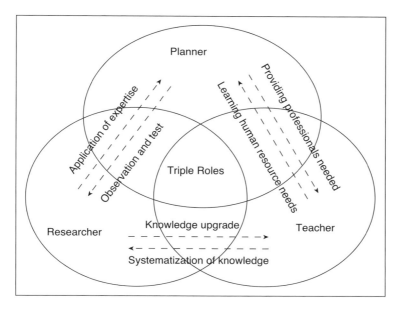

Figure 11.1   The triple role model of the academic planner

industry entrepreneurs, while they remain educators and researchers, as in Figure 11.1. This model benefits both the tourism industry and the tourism research.

First, this model facilitates tourism research in China. By formulating tourism planning for the industry, the researcher is going through the experiential learning process, a model described by Kolb (Kolb, 1984; Kolb et al., 1979). Kolb (1984) perceives experiential learning as a four-stage cycle: observing, thinking, practicing and cognizing.

In order for planning to be effective, academic planners have to observe the tourism phenomena closely, to obtain the statistical data, and conduct interviews with stakeholders, etc. Problems can then be identified and underlying structures built. Based on the model, trends are predicted and plans formulated accordingly. During this process, theories are also formulated, tested, and then improved. In the meantime, these new findings are taught to tourism students.

This triple-role model can help to transfer knowledge and bring innovation to the tourism industry. Tourism is regarded as an industry which is weak in innovation. The Chinese tourism industry is especially weak in innovation because it is dominated by small tourist enterprises lacking in capital and motivation to innovate. Thus universities and research institutions serve as some of the main sources of knowledge and technical support for the industry.

Students can learn to understand the real world problems and become familiar with the tourism industry by working in tourism planning projects supervised by their mentors. Meanwhile, they can also contribute new ideas in critical issues.

A system dynamics model

In order to understand the observed patterns and predict the future behavior, a qualitative system dynamics method, a methodology for studying and managing complex feedback systems, such as one finds in business and other social systems (Sterman, 2000), is applied to explore the underlying structure.

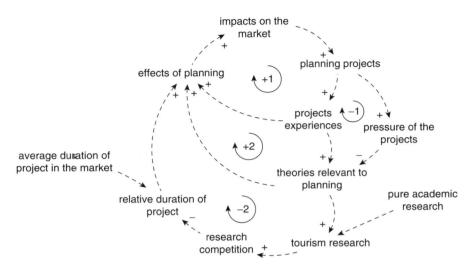

Figure 11.2 Planning sponsored tourism research

The model is composed of two basic structures: positive feedback and negative feedback (see Figure 11.2). The positive feedback loops are those which lead to growth, such as the increasing importance of the industrial funding and the dominance of tourism geography in the academic world. It can be seen that research and practice are reinforcing each other. Along with the rapid development of the tourism industry, many practical problems arise. The tourism industry provides funds which attract tourism academics into the market and help to solve practical problems. The industry thus relies more on them and turns to these academics when new problems arise (see positive loop "+1").

Part of the funds obtained from the industry is used in relevant academic research. So academic progress is made and new knowledge is gained. Equipped with new knowledge, academic planners become more competent in solving real world problems for the industry (see positive loop "+2").

The second basic structure is negative feedback loops that are generated during this process. These negative feedbacks create constraints on further development of the researcher–professional–teacher model. First, as tourism planners, the researchers are under pressure to ensure economic benefits, even financial benefits, within a short period of time. Sometimes solutions are given without scientific reasoning. These practices have impacted on tourism research. As a result, academic papers also tend to be policy- and solution-oriented. The issues which are not directly linked to perceived immediate economic benefits, such as the impacts of tourism development, planning theories, tourism behavior analysis and spatial analysis of tourists flows, have been neglected to some extent (Bao and Zhang, 2004; Wu, 2000).

Zhu and Liu (2004) made a comparison of the main research themes between two prestigious journals, *Tourism Tribune* of China and *Annals of Tourism Research* in the USA (Table 11.4) through the analysis of the key words. The result shows that "tourist behavior and market," "tourism impacts," and "theories and methodologies" received much more attention in tourism research overseas, while domestic tourism research are more policy-oriented, focusing on "tourist resources and planning" and "economics and management of tourism." Social and environmental problems associated with tourism development, such as the distribution of

Table 11.4 Comparison of topics of tourism literature between *Tourism Tribune* and *Annals of Tourism Research,* 2004

Content Journals	Literature Review	Tourism Destination	Tourist Resources and Planning	Tourist Behavior and Market	Tourism Impact	Theory and Method	Economics of Tourism and Management	Total
Tourism Tribune	17	46	65	39	35	53	97	352
Proportion (%)	5	13	18	11	10	15	28	100
Annals of Tourism Research	3	22	18	47	49	43	27	209
Proportion (%)	1	10	8	22	24	21	14	100

Source: Zhu and Liu, 2004

tourist revenue, conflicts between hosts and tourists, and deterioration of natural environment, are overlooked to a certain degree in domestic tourism research.

Methodologies used in tourism development and planning papers were limited to the traditional qualitative and descriptive methods (Bao and Zhang, 2004; Zhang and Lu, 2004). Overall, compared with the growth of the tourism planning activities, quality research in tourism has lagged behind.

Meanwhile, some academic planners who are occupied by planning activities inevitably spend less time teaching and have their students take part in the planning process as apprentices, without giving them systematic training. Therefore the quality of the education of tourism students is uncertain.

Challenges faced by planning sponsored research in the new era

Changes of tourism plans from demand side

With the acceleration of tourism development and globalization, competition among tourism destinations has become more and more intensive. The performance of local government in China is basically evaluated by the number of tourists. The expectations of short-term benefits of the tourism plan are high. Tourism plans are requested to be operational, focusing on the short-term marketing plan, projects portfolios for attracting investments, and destination branding. In some places, the clients prefer an event plan rather than a tourism master plan because an event brings conspicuous effects in a short time. As a result, academic planners who are experts in developing master development plans in a systematic and sustainable way have begun to lose competitive advantage.

Growth of tourism planners

As discussed above, there has been an increase in the number of graduates majoring in tourism planning or related subjects. Despite the fact that tourism education in China suffers from many problems, such as poorly designed curriculums, lack of qualified teachers and low popularity of tourism faculties, it is clear that the trend is for more qualified graduates who will take part in and make contributions to tourism planning in China (Huang, 2001).

Apart from the graduates, an increasing number of international consulting companies have begun to think seriously of moving into the Chinese tourism planning market, after China's entry into the WTO and the opening of its planning market. With the rapid growth of tourism and accumulated experience, the domestic clients also find it feasible and desirable to contract tourism plans with foreign companies in order to be more competitive to attract investment (especially foreign investment) and make their attractions known to more people. Professionals from urban planning institutes also enter and increase the supply of tourism planners. All these factors are raising the level of tourism professionals to a high level.

Pressure for academic planners to focus on academic research

Tourism research and knowledge, like tourism development, are also accumulating rapidly. Apart from studies by tourism geographers, academics from other disciplines, for instance, anthropology and history, are attracted to tourism research and most of their studies focus on academic, not practical problems. What is more, international tourism studies and knowledge have become accessible to Chinese academics. The standards and criteria to evaluate academic research are moving toward international practice. By analyzing the citations of two journals, *Tourism Tribute*, a tourism journal, and *Economic Geography*, a non-tourism journal, respectively, it can be seen that citations began in 1993 and the number of citations for each paper continues to increase, reflecting the tendency for domestic researchers to follow the international academic standards (Zhang, 2002). The problem–solution paper is hardly acceptable. Academics are now under pressure to withdraw from consulting services to do academic research.

These external factors strengthen the negative feedbacks and reduce the cohesion of the triple role. The gradual withdrawal of academic planners from the planning market is illustrated in Figure 11.3.

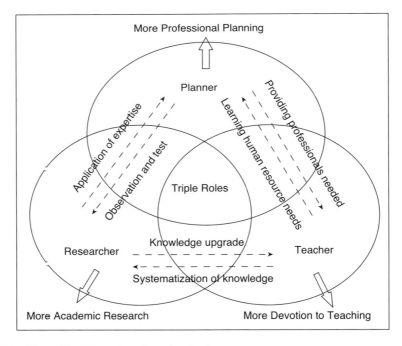

Figure 11.3 The split of the roles of academic planners

Conclusion and discussion

Researchers across the globe in applied sciences such as tourism are facing the same problem: it is necessary for them to ideally play the role of researcher, teacher, and practitioner in order to fully comprehend the problems they intend to deal with, to turn scientific ideas into drivers of industrial innovation, and to pass valuable knowledge down to the next generation. But, in reality, it's difficult to find a balance between these roles.

Although it seems that Chinese academics are gradually turning from the consultation-oriented role to the research-oriented role, the new paradigm also is problematic. In the short run, industries and policymakers will lose access to cutting-edge research and knowledge. In the long run, in the face of strong international competition of tourism destinations and the stresses on tourism resources, the sustainability of tourism development is uncertain. Academic research will also lose ground.

The shift of the paradigm also reflects the stress of globalization on the direction of Chinese tourism research and the local rationality of a triple-role model. Within the tourism world, academics must compete globally and therefore must follow international standards. For the competitiveness of the industry, a strong linkage between industry and academics is necessary. Maybe a shared vision and understanding in the academic world on the rationality of the existing triple-role model should be reached, and then a controlled changing paradigm will facilitate both the academic and the industrial world.

References

Bao, J. G. and Zhang, X. M. (2004) 'Tourism geography in China (1978–2003): A review and retrospect'. *Acta Geographica Sinica*, 59(S1), 132–8

Bao, J. G., Wu, B. H. and Lu, L. (2003) 'Research: Principles, methods, geography in China: 1978–98'. In J. G. Bao (ed.) *Tourism development practices*. Beijing: Science Press, pp. 47–62

Fan, Y. Z. and Hu, Q. P. (2003) 'On the developing course and research progress of China's tourism planning'. *Tourism Tribune*, 18(6), 25–30

Huang, S. S. (2001) 'Problems and solutions on tourism higher education development in China'. *Journal of Guilin Institute of Tourism*, 12(2), 66–9

Kolb, D. A. (1984) *Experiential learning: Experience as the source of learning and development*. Englewood Cliffs, NJ: Prentice Hall

——, Rubin, I. M. and McIntyre, J. M. (1979) 'Learning problem solving'. In D. A. Kolb, I. M. Rubin and J. M. McIntyre (eds) *Organizational psychology: An experiential approach* (3rd edn). Englewood Cliffs, NJ: Prentice Hall, pp. 27–54

Liu, B. Y. (2001) 'Trilism of tourism planning: The characterizing, positioning, forming and orienting of Chinese modern tourism planning'. *Tourism Tribune*, 16(5), 55–8

Peng, D. C. (2000) 'On the present state, problems and countermeasures of the tourism planning work in China'. *Tourism Tribune*, 15(3), 40–45.

Song, C. Q. and Leng, S. Y. (2004) 'Features of recent human geography researches granted by National Natural Science Foundation of China'. *ACTA Geographica Sinica*, 59(S1), 8–10

Sterman, J. D. (2000) *Business dynamics: Systems thinking and modeling for a complex world*. Boston: Irwin/McGraw-Hill

Wei, X. A. (2002) *New treatise for tourism industry development*. Beijing: China Tourism Publisher

Wei, X. A. et al. (2001) 'What kind of tourism planning China needs?'. *Tourism Tribune*, 16(2), 9–15

Wu, B. H. and Li, X. X. (2005) 'A research on higher tourism education in China'. *Tourism Tribune*, 20(S1), 9–15

Wu, R. W. (2000) 'History and future of tourism planning'. *Rural Eco-Environment*, 16(1), 38–40

Yuan, S. Q., Meng, T. X., Miao, F., Zheng, L. X., He, F. F. and Gao, Y. (2005) 'A study on the development of tourism education in institutions of higher learning'. *Tourism Science*, 19(6), 72–5

Zhai, F. D. (2001) 'Problems in tourism planning in present China'. *Journal of Social Science of Hunan Normal University*, 30(6), 71–5

Zhang, H. M. and Lu, L. (2004) 'An initial analysis of tourism research methods in China'. *Tourism Tribune*, 19(3), 77–81

Zhang, J. F. (2002) 'Analysing and pondering over the domestic literature of tourism'. *Journal of Huaqiao University (Philosophy and Social Sciences)*, *2002*(1), 52–8

Zhu, H. and Liu, Y. H. (2004) 'Viewing the difference and trend of Chinese and foreign tourism researches by comparing the articles published on Tourism Tribune and Annals of Tourism Research'. *Tourism Tribune*, 19(4), 92–5

12

Perspectives on tourism planning in China

Yang Wang, Geoffrey Wall

The nature of planning

It is necessary to start with a definition. The term 'tourism planning', often seen in literature, has not been frequently defined. Even though Gunn (1988) and C. M. Hall (2000a) have defined planning, and Inskeep (1991) has listed eight elements of tourism planning, these authors did not define the term explicitly in their books on tourism planning. In the limited number of works that include a definition, tourism planning has been defined in various ways. Some definitions have a predominantly economic focus and refer to tourism planning as the provision of guidance for the use of tourism assets and the development of tourism in a marketable way (e.g. Lickorish and Jenkins, 1997). Some have emphasized the scope of tourism planning, such as the definition of Evans (2000, p. 308) which was modified from that of Page (1995), as 'a process considering social, economic and environmental issues in a spatial context in terms of development, conservation and land use.' Sometimes tourism planning has been defined from mixed perspectives. For example, Wahab and Pigram (1997, p. 279) indicated that the term referred to a process that leads development to be 'adaptive to the needs of the tourists, responsive to the needs of local communities, and socio-economically, culturally and environmentally sound.' Timothy (1999, p. 371) defined it in a way that is more suitable for application to destination areas and their residents: 'Tourism planning is viewed as a way of maximizing the benefits of tourism to an area and mitigating problems that might occur as a result of development.' However, Wall (1996, p. 41) has suggested that planning is a political process that 'empowers some and disadvantages others,' and that maximizing benefits and minimizing costs cannot happen at the same time. Timothy's definition is somewhat ambiguous on this point. In this paper, the definitions of Murphy (1985) and Getz (1987) have been combined so that tourism planning is regarded as being concerned with anticipating and regulating changes in the tourism system and integrating it with broader-scale development. It is a process which seeks to optimize the potential contribution of tourism to human welfare and environmental quality.

Evolution of Western tourism planning

The origin and evolution of tourism planning are closely linked with the history of both planning and tourism. Modern planning arose at the turn of the nineteenth century in the West

(Campbell and Fainstein, 1996). In the Second World War, it was established as a profession and the rational comprehensive planning model (RCP) became a theoretical foundation of planning (Klosterman, 1996). In the 1960s and 1970s, a host of problems, such as slum clearance, urban sprawl and inadequate housing, stimulated the initial demand for public participation in planning (P. G. Hall 1980; Lanfant and Graburn, 1992; Taylor, 1998). The emergence of the 'participation era' (Grant, 1989) or the 'return to the local' (Lanfant and Graburn, 1992) ultimately established public participation as one of the most important components in the Western planning process. A host of different approaches to planning emerged, including incremental planning (Lindblom, 1959), advocacy planning (Davidoff, 1965), transactive planning (Davidoff, 1975), integrated planning (Conyers and Hills, 1984), strategic planning (J. L. Kaufman and Jacobs, 1987), and collaboration planning (Healey, 1992). Each of these approaches, to varying degrees, encourages planners to create a more meaningful role for the public in planning processes and decision making.

Burns (1999) and Costa (2001) have reported a somewhat similar path in the evolution of tourism planning. In the post-war period and into the 1960s, increased disposable income and technological progress such as in aircraft design and expanding car ownership stimulated the growth of mass tourism. Tourism master planning in the mode of rational comprehensive planning emerged at the end of this period. It was aimed at promoting tourism at almost all costs and usually lacked a critical analysis of the tourism sector. With the continual growth of mass tourism, master planning approached its apex in the 1970s but there was commonly a lack of political will in shaping development to the destination's own needs (Burns, 1999). Many tourism destinations formulated their master plans (e.g. Israel's 1976 tourism master plan and Jordan's 1981–85 tourism development plan: see Travis, 2011) during this period. In the 1980s, a decade after their urban planning counterparts, alternative tourism planning approaches were developed associated with the growing awareness of negative socio-cultural and environmental impacts at destinations, and the emerging demands for more than 'four S's' tourism (sea, sand, sun, sex) among experienced tourists (Burns, 1999; Costa, 2001). The major tourism planning approaches have been summarized in Table 12.1 to facilitate synthesis and comparison.

The emphasis on tourism master planning has declined in most developing countries and been replaced by an emphasis on product development and marketing. In contrast, as Haywood (1988) and Wall (1996) have pointed out, comprehensive tourism planning is still widespread in less-developed countries. The national tourism development plan in Fiji in 1973 is one example (Inskeep, 1991). In this case, the planning team (including UNDP and World Bank experts) examined the physical environment and recommended various physical aspects of beach tourism development in Fiji. Although the district governments were carefully consulted, obvious public participation did not happen in the Fiji case, partly because the master plan was constructed at the national level. A different case of comprehensive tourism planning occurred in Alberta, Canada (Gunn, 1988). The planning task was to prepare a master plan that would include a comprehensive review of tourism in Alberta to understand its history, marketing, world position and identify future potential. During the planning process in 1984, there was significant involvement of the private sector through surveys, and this helped to establish a more intimate affiliation between the public and the private sectors.

More recently, the community approach to tourism planning has received much emphasis. This reflects a change in scale from national and provincial/state plans to a more local focus. Three sub-approaches, as shown in Table 12.1, can be identified. Although the three terms are sometimes used interchangeably (as in Jamal and Getz, 1995), they are separated here according to the way that they have been used by specific authors. First, a *collaborative* approach was used in formulating the Hope Valley Visitor Management Plan in Britain (Bramwell and Sharman, 1999).

Table 12.1 Tourism planning approaches

Approaches	Definition/Utilization	Roots	Principles	Main Steps/Tools	The Role of Participation	References
Comprehensive	Conventional goal is to stimulate growth. Reformed approach is to plan the fragmented but interrelated components in the tourism system and to link the tourism sector with larger scale development.	Rational Comprehensive Planning (RCP) and/or principles of participation.	Conventional RCP or Reformative Comprehensive Planning ("the third way of planning"): mainly follow the conventional RCP's steps to explore the situation in a comprehensively participatory way.	Preparation; Set goal; Survey and data analysis; Synthesize and select from alternatives; Plan formulation; Implementation; Evaluation and monitoring.	Goal setting is undertaken in a consultative way with clients (i.e. tourism authorities, project developers, community members, etc.); In the reformed approach, the ideas and concerns of local people, NGOs, and entrepreneurs will be carefully examined in the planning process.	Baud-Bovy, 1982; Burns, 2004; Costa, 2001; Getz, 1986; Inskeep, 1991; Jenkins, 1980; Tosun and Jenkins, 1998
Community (Collaborative planning; Community-based planning and Stakeholder-based planning)	A process of joint decision making among key stakeholders in tourism to resolve problems and/or to manage issues relating to planning and development.	Transactive (Participatory) Planning; Advocacy Planning; Collaborative Planning.	Public participation is the main component of this approach; Participation should start at the beginning of the planning stage to permit broadly-based planning goals and objectives. Ideally, two-way communication and positive participation of various stakeholders should be encouraged.	Different planning methods are adopted based on the situation; common techniques include group setting inquiry; round table discussion, community consulting meetings, in-depth interviews, etc.	A community approach is relevant to participation in its principles and its techniques (planning tools). It is mainly participatory in nature and, theoretically, share decision making and planning processes with whoever is affected by or interested in the decision or plan; thus, it is fundamentally inclusive. However, practicability is sometimes limited because of political, social, cultural and economic constraints.	P. A. B. Clarke, 1996; de Araujo and Bramwell, 2000; Fischer and Forester, 1993; Haywood, 1988; Healey, 1998; Jamal and Getz, 1995; Kumar and Paddison, 2000; Manning, 1999; Mitchell and Reid, 2001; Murphy, 1985; Reed, 1997; Sautter and Leisen, 1999

(Continued)

173

Table 12.1 Continued

Approaches	Definition/Utilization	Roots	Principles	Main Steps/Tools	The Role of Participation	References
Integrated	To respond to different sets of values and objectives and the need for interconnectedness. Often adopted when preparing background information for further detail plan formulation or policymaking.	Integrated Planning: planning of a specific project requires inputs from different sectors.	External integration: implies integration of the tourism sector into the macro system (regional/national development or international market). Internal integration: encompasses various components of tourism (e.g. transportation, accommodation), balances demand and supply, and links the public and private sectors.	Identify the key issue(s) or goals; share experiences and exchange ideas, provide strategies or recommendations collectively. Discussions are mainly taken in a workshop setting, such as stakeholder meetings.	Participation is often limited within government scope but includes various sectors; or between the public and private sectors to facilitate partnership.	Conyers and Hills, 1984; Gauteng Tourism Authority, 2003; Inskeep, 1991; Marcouiller, 1997; Tosun and Jenkins, 1998; TTD, 1996
Strategic	A continual, iterative process that creates a feasible match between internal needs and resources and external environmental conditions.	Originated from private sector; strategic planning (SWOT analysis).	Two scales. At a site scale, oriented to an organization/site's mandate or needs, such as conservation, environmental protection, impact minimization. At a regional scale it provides generalized regional information and guidelines either to foster tourism growth or to recommend management.	Environment scan; Select key issues; Set goals/vision; External and internal environmental analyses; Develop strategies; Develop implementation plan; Monitor, update and start another scan.	Key issues are identified by the client organization. Coordination with local policies and political structure is important. Community participation in collecting information is necessary in this planning approach.	Alipour, 1996; Baidal, 2004; Baker, 1992; Fletcher and Cooper, 1996; Gunn, 1988; J. L. Kaufman and Jacobs, 1987; Mill and Morrison, 1985; Seasons, 1989; TTD, 1999

Approach	Description	Concept/Planning	Process	Assessment	References
Alternative	A continuous research and feedback process that is adaptable and able to respond to rapidly changing environments, generating small changes in steps.	Concept of alternative development; Incremental Planning.	Starts by deciding on 'alternative' tourism development. Planning is then undertaken to determine various aspects of the sector, such as small-scale, locally-owned accommodations, 'Authentic' cultural and natural attractions, year-round market, minimal imports. Public participation in planning and impact analysis.	Theoretically, it is an approach with great possibilities to facilitate the well-being of people because it calls for small-scale, locally-controlled development. Community participation is a main principle. However, these cannot be guaranteed and, sometimes, alternative development is decided top-down as a complementary part of mass tourism.	Busby and Rendle, 2000; Chowdhry, 1990; J. Clarke, Denman, Hickman, and Slovak, 2001; Getz, 1986; Gunn, 1994; Lanfant and Graburn, 1992; Lindblom, 1959; Richter, 1989; Telfer, 2002; Weaver, 1995; Wilkinson, 1989
Sustainable Development	This approach proposes to carry out development to fulfil present human needs in such a way that future generations will not be 'worse off'.	Sustainable development (more like a concept than a planning approach)	As a concept, sustainability has become one of the most used words in tourism planning, mainly from environmental (conservation) and community (sharing benefits and mitigating negative impacts) perspectives. However, very few cases display the procedures of this approach and little evidence exists to show how this 'approach' is being used in practice.	The concept strongly relates to community participation in planning and development since the successful implementation of the concept depends on the full support of the people in the domain. However, the practicability of the concept is questioned, especially among communities living on the margin of basic needs: it may not be realistic to expect them to consider future generations' welfare when they currently lack basic needs.	Baidal, 2004; Chambers, 1987; Hardy, Beeton, and Pearson, 2002; Joppe, 1996; Pigram, 1992; Timothy, 2002; Tosun and Jenkins, 1998; WCED, 1987

The planning process, including a series of collective discussions, involved many stakeholder groups and adopted various participatory techniques. Partially as a result of the process that was adopted, residents broadly supported the plan. An often-cited successful community-based tourism planning case was that in Waikiki, Hawaii. Sheldon and Abenoja (2001) have commented on the extensive efforts, such as the large number of long-term resident attitude studies that were directed towards involving local residents in planning. Successful round-table stakeholder-based tourism planning was undertaken in several sub-regions in British Columbia (Murphy, 1988). Stakeholder workshops brought various stakeholders in the tourism industry (mainly community NGOs and business groups) together to discuss their own expected futures. According to Murphy, a synergistic partnership was established which helped to balance gains in development with other community aspirations.

An *integrated* planning approach was adopted by the Republic of South Africa as a means to unite sectors, geographic areas and private organizations in a way that would promote sustainable tourism (Gauteng Tourism Authority, 2003). The planning task was undertaken with the assistance of, and under the consultation of, the British Department of International Development. Economic, social and environmental guidelines were formulated to direct future tourism policy making.

A *strategic* planning approach was used by Fletcher and Cooper (1996) in Hungary. The main goals that were identified by local tourism authorities were to reduce the pressure of tourism on Budapest by widening the regional distribution of tourists and spreading out the economic benefits. Following an environmental review, Szolnok County was chosen for emphasis. Tourism attractions and facilities were 'discovered' and likely problems were identified during a community survey that was conducted with local NGOs. Goals were then identified as the development or redevelopment of facilities and attractions to meet development needs, while mitigating the risks of social and environmental damage. Short-, medium- and long-term action strategies were then formulated. They relied upon a close relationship between tourism authorities and local organizations, especially local entrepreneurs, for their implementation.

Alternative tourism planning approaches include various emphases, such as ecotourism planning and green, rural, and agricultural tourism planning. An example of such alternative tourism planning is seen in the development of ecotourism in Montserrat (Weaver, 1995). After government departments (Tourism, Agriculture, Trade and Environment) agreed to promote ecotourism, detailed studies were carried out and plans were formulated by external agencies (UNDP) together with local NGOs. In another example, the Korean government decided to promote rural tourism as they were impressed by the successful experience of Japan (Hong et al., 2003). Aiming at both economic returns and raising cultural awareness among urban and rural people, environmentally friendly, small-scale development projects with special events were organized by the Korean government together with resident groups.

Sustainable development has been identified as yet another tourism planning approach by Tosun and Jenkins (1998), C. M. Hall (2000a) and Baidal (2004). However, the practical application of this approach remains in doubt for it is not easy to find examples of its adoption (but see Martopo and Mitchell, 1995). As shown in Table 12.1, sustainability has often been treated as a concept or a goal in tourism planning, rather than an approach to undertaking planning.

A recurring theme within the above approaches/concepts, as summarized in Table 12.1, is the advocacy of participation in decision-making and planning processes. Obviously, it is an important concept and the origin and the definition of participation in planning needs clarification. Participation in tourism planning has been suggested as a way to promote sustainability, to balance economic and social development, to integrate destination planning, to ensure that a 'sense of place' is maintained, to foster a better understanding of complex situations, to develop a common value base, and to increase recognition of interdependence among destination stakeholders (Bahaire and Elliott-White, 1999; Bramwell and Lane, 1993; Gill, 1997; C. M. Hall, 2000b; Jamal and Getz, 1997; Timothy, 1998; Wall, 1997).

This discussion has provided a brief overview of the evolution of tourism planning and the labels that have been assigned to different approaches. A common underpinning theme that has emerged in the developed world is increased attention to participation in planning (see Haywood, 1988; Inskeep, 1991; Keogh, 1990; Murphy, 1985, 1988; Simmons, 1994). Tosun (2000) argued that this has occurred since the 1960s because of the increased needs of governments to respond to community actions. Participation, which is now one of the most important concepts in Western planning, has been defined in various ways: as a process of redistributing power that enables those who hitherto were excluded to control the decision-making process (Arai, 1996; M. Kaufman, 1997; Willis, 1995); as collaborative influence and control over decisions by stakeholders (World Bank, 1996); and as one goal of social change and a method of bringing about change (M. Kaufman, 1997). Researchers, however, have also pointed out that, in some cases, participation results from a top-down decision that is directed or permitted by clients of the planning process with (or without) the intention of sharing the power (Cuthbertson, 1983; Roy, 1998). Thus, participation in this situation is defined as activities undertaken by a planning or management agency to provide the opportunity for local communities to influence decisions regarding developments which will affect their lives (Arai, 1996). Based on the above definitions and the characteristics of the tourism planning approaches that were discussed earlier, participation is defined here as a political process that enables people to take control over the development initiatives, decisions and resources that affect them.

In summary, as a principle of Western planning, participation refers mainly to the process of involving various stakeholders in decision making. In tourism it has been viewed as being a means of improving planning and making development more acceptable. For example, according to advocates of a community approach to planning, participation of the community in negotiating distribution issues (means) leads to a more reasonable distribution of local gains from tourism (ends) (Haywood, 1988; Keogh, 1990; Murphy, 1983, 1985, 1988, 1992; Tosun and Jenkins, 1996). However, participation in the West is not merely a *means*; as a sign of democracy, it is also an *end* in itself (M. Kaufman, 1997). Furthermore, Western researchers discuss participation not merely as sharing in decision making; rather they also discuss participation in terms of sharing in the benefits, such as the discussions of Long and Wall (1996) of cruises and homestays, and Timothy (1999) about street businesses in Indonesia. Benefit-sharing has often been seen as being an outcome of good planning and development, usually involving participation in decision making, or as an item in evaluating tourism impacts.

Objectives and evidence

The purpose of this communication is to examine the evolution of tourism planning in China and, against the background to tourism planning that has been presented above, to comment upon the possible relevance of Western planning models to China. The evidence upon which this communication is based is varied.

First, a review of relevant literature, both Western and Chinese, was undertaken, the former being partially reported above. Second, the authors' varied backgrounds and experiences have been drawn on to inform our discussion. The first author is a graduate in construction management from Tongji University in Shanghai and she completed a Master's degree in Planning at the University of Waterloo. Her thesis research was concerned with the displacement of a

Li minority community in Hainan by the development of a tourism resort. She is building upon this in her doctoral research to examine ways in which similar communities might become more involved in and obtain greater benefits from the tourism developments that are occurring around them.

The second author has been involved in a variety of activities related to tourism, environment and development in China for some 10 years and, prior to that, participated in a number of large planning and development endeavours elsewhere in Asia. In particular, he has directed a five-year project in Hainan on coastal zone management with the overall objective of enhancing the capabilities of the provincial government in Hainan to manage the growing pressures on its coast. One of these pressures is tourism. He directed the Ecoplan China project that has the goal of enhancing the local capacity to undertake environmental planning and management in Hainan as well as elsewhere in China. Both projects have been funded by the Canadian International Agency and are large multi-year initiatives with a variety of partners from universities, government and the private sector, both in Canada and China. He has also been involved in the development of a biodiversity strategy for Inner Mongolia (essentially nature reserve planning and management) as well as tourism plans for Jiangsu, Henan, Hunan and Dalian and a number of other more specific related activities.

Tourism planning and development in China

Few planning cases in China follow the Western style of planning; however, 'few' does not mean 'none'. Several planning cases in China, although not primarily in the field of tourism, can be identified that have used approaches that are similar to those that have been described above. For example, stakeholder-based strategic tourism planning was undertaken in Leshan, China (W. Zhang, 2003). Funded by the United Nations, the project, incorporating various stakeholder groups (government, local business, residents, etc.) through focus groups, surveys and household interviews, identified a series of strategies to protect a World Heritage Site. Another illustration is an IDRC-funded (International Development Research Centre, Canada) agricultural planning project conducted in Yunnan and Guizhou Provinces (Vernooy et al., 2003). As part of the planning process, the rural people were actively involved in identifying their present situation and their urgent needs to improve household livelihoods, and in formulating action plans to address these needs. A further example is an integrated planning project about managing coastal zones in Xiamen, led by UNDP, IMO and GEF (Lau, 2003). In this project, various levels and sectors of government, participating together in workshops, identified problems and management issues, desirable outcomes and designed implementation plans. Thus, public participation in planning along Western lines is possible in China, particularly if it is facilitated by international agencies. Yet, in the literature, the only non-externally assisted planning project in China adopting a similar approach was a community-based land-use planning case in Shanghai, the wealthiest and most modern municipality in the country. There, various urban districts, streets, offices and business associations participated in deciding upon the new land regulations (G. R. Zhang, 2003).

The long-term effects of these various planning initiatives and approaches are hard to determine. As Pretty (1995) argued, the local people often are unable to maintain participation practices once the flow of external incentives stops. Thus, as some researchers have suggested, perhaps it is true that locally established planning practices may last longer when compared with the borrowed approaches, because the latter may not meet local planning needs (Alipour, 1996; de Kadt, 1979; Tosun and Jenkins, 1998). To further explore this question, it is necessary to examine local planning practices in China.

Urban planning in China dates back to the imperial era, when grand capital cities were constructed in accordance with the feudal ideology of social order and hierarchy (Yeh and Wu, 1999). However, it was not until 1989 that the enactment of the City Planning Act established a comprehensive urban planning system in China, to prepare 'rational' city plans to meet the needs of developing socialist modernization (T. Zhang, 2002). Comprehensive planning in China, emphasizing the formulation of land-use plan documents, with different levels of detail and functions, in a top-down process (ranging from urban system plans to detail construction plans), is different from Western rational planning. Comprehensive planning in China attempts to manipulate regional spatial development, and there are no concrete measures to link the planning 'structures' with resource allocation, socio-economic policies or the enforcement of development control (Yeh and Wu, 1999).

With stronger emphasis on economic development and severe competition between municipalities to attract external investment, pressure to speed up development, and an urgent need to have enhanced 'performance', government officials have had to accept gradually that investors and developers are influential groups in planning and development processes in China. This trend is accelerated because planning institutions are gradually becoming more independent of the government and because the services provided by planners are now more and more user-oriented (T. Zhang, 2002). Furthermore, the prevalent closed-door plan-making process (i.e. no public consultation) and the lack of effective monitoring often give politicians and even planners an excuse to bypass planning controls in order to cater for the interests of developers (Yeh and Wu, 1999). In order to reduce domination of development by the minority and to help promote a 'cleaner' government, a greater awareness is now emerging of the need to promote popular participation and monitoring within the planning process. However, to date, these are merely ideas in China (T. Zhang, 2002). T. Zhang's interviews with Chinese planners clearly showed that they had more interest in sharing power with the top than with the bottom. In the words of Yeh and Wu (1999, p. 236):

> In the top-down plan making process, there is inadequate public participation. This does not mean that public participation is explicitly prohibited. But, due to the extremely immobilized local politics, the channel for public participation does not exist and public participation has no real meaning in the context where negotiations mainly take place among government agencies or between government and private investors.

More specifically with respect to tourism, according to the China National Tourism Administration, tourism planning in China is a process of establishing development goals according to the history and present situation of the tourism industry and the requirement of the market, and coordinating and managing the main factors of the tourism sector in order to achieve the goals. As interpreted by Bao and Chu (1999), planning for tourism zones should take into account the carrying capacity, tourists' behaviours and demands, and the economic, social and environmental situations of the locality. However, as Wall (1995) has argued, comprehensive tourism plans in many less-developed countries, focusing mainly on physical planning and the formal employment sectors, are formulated primarily to satisfy the aspirations of higher-level administrations and to attract investors. China is one such place.

Stages of tourism development in China have been summarized in Table 12.2. As show in this Table, tourism planning started in the 1980s. It was developed without theoretical support or unified standards; the planners made plans that reflected their disciplinary backgrounds (Bao and Chu, 1999). The speciality of urban planning, emphasizing construction of infrastructure, had the biggest influence on tourism planning before the mid-1990s (Bao, 2000). The plans

Table 12.2 Stages of tourism development in China

	1949–1977	1978–1985	1986–1991	1992–2001	2002–present
Goal and Objectives	Promoting Socialism and expanding political influence.	Accumulating foreign exchange.	National economic growth.	Market Economy under Socialism and regional development.	Poverty reduction and regional development.
Main Events	National level organization (CBTT) was first set up to control tourism in 70s while was unable to separate government and business/enterprise functions.	Set up local tourism bureaus. Separated government functions (CNTA) with business ones. Introducing tourism planning and education.	End business monopoly and the planned economy. The profit-earning organizations become economic independent. Strengthened the management and regulation in the industry. Promoted domestic tourism.	National government took the regulation role and continually decentralized planning, marketing, promotion and pricing roles to local government. Tax allowance to foreign investment in resorts. Encouraged outbound tourism.	Call for 'people-centred' development. The role of tourism in poverty reduction has gained increasing recognition in the academic cycle and among some insightful officials.
Planning and Participation in Planning	Did not exist.	Planning was first issued at national level in 1983 (CNTA).	Planning purely emphasized economic aspects; had no theoretically support or unified standards, mainly based on urban planning and emphasized facility construction. Local government could issue tourism plans for the areas.	Planning works to balance market supply and demand and emphasize growth, employment, foreign exchange, and regional development. Luxury resort development gave the chance for investors to have a voice in planning for the resort.	An emerging awareness of environmental protection. Human issue is continually ignored in planning. Completely silent on the distribution issue. Planning is an expert task. Community planning and management remain largely unknown.

Development and Participation in Development	Tourism facilities and services were funded and operated by central government.	Local government established local tourism bureaus and they were allowed to operate tourism-related businesses. Foreign investment in hotels was allowed. Collectives could invest in and operate hotels and other tourism projects. Jobs in tourism were assigned to individuals by the state.	Tourism-related training and education and relaxing control opened the opportunity of self-chosen employment in tourism for ordinary citizens. However, tourism, for most Chinese, served as little more than employment.	Resort tourism and large-scale construction provides the opportunity for foreigners, wealthy Chinese and adventurers to rapidly benefit from the industry. Large-scale development further plundered the opportunity for normal people equitably sharing the benefits. Some small-scale businesses operated by local Chinese emerged in some relatively developed tourism destinations.	Continuing resort tourism. However, a gradually growing awareness about poverty elimination in poor rural regions through encouraging the people's participation in tourism development, which may generate the opportunity for broader scale of participation.
Problems	Non-profit, poor service quality and infrastructure.	Lack of planning. The rapid decentralization, which led to a lack of coordination and central-control, resulted in disorder tourism and keen competition among regions.	Lacked of tourism planning expertise and trained staff. Unbalanced investment and poor service quality. Lacked of popular participation in benefit-generation activities.	Unbalanced regional development and ownership. Luxurious resorts were built everywhere. Underestimation of the importance of locally-owned small enterprises for improving people's lives in most of the destinations.	Training provided by employers limits possibilities other than on-job training. Isolated tourism planning focuses merely on tourism sector, which limits its spillover effects on other related trades and on enlarging the distribution of benefits among people.
References	Ritchter, 1983, 1989; Sofield and Li, 1998; G. R. Zhang, 2003a; H. Q. Zhang, Chong and Ap, 1999	Choy and Gee, 1983; Choy, Dong, and Wen, 1986; Gao and Zhang, 1983; Uysal, Wei, and Reid, 1986; G. R. Zhang, 2003a; H. Q. Zhang et al., 1999	He, 1992; Lindberg, Tisdell, and Xue, 2003; Liu and Wall, 2005; Sun, 1989; Tisdell and Wen, 1991; G. R. Zhang, 2003a; H. Q. Zhang et al.,1999	Bao and Chu, 1999; Gang and Kruse, 2003; Yu, Ap, Zhang, and Lew, 2003; G. R. Zhang, 2003a; G. R. Zhang and Lew, 2003; H. Q. Zhang et al.,1999	Gang and Kruse, 2003; HDDR, 2003; Lindberg et al., 2003; Liu and Wall, 2005; G. R. Zhang, 2003a

concentrated on attractions, hotels, water and electricity supplies, and roads and transportation (Cai, 1999).

As the problems of such tourism developments were increasingly recognized, especially issues associated with rapid growth (which is still the dominant emphasis), discussion about market supply and demand and the main components of the tourism sector, such as transportation, accommodation tours, entertainment and shopping, increased (Bao and Chu, 1999). Under the influence of the catchword 'sustainability', tourism planning at the turn of century also began to focus on the use and protection of natural resources (Bao, 2000). However, as shown in Table 12.2, no obvious intent to share planning and decision-making powers more broadly can be perceived. Moreover, the planning approach that has been adopted is essentially silent on the negative social impacts of tourism and on distribution issues and, as a result, is limited in its capacity to improve people's lives (HDDR, 2003). When investment is emphasized in development, more equal benefit-sharing is usually overlooked: those who have resources to input have a greater chance of participating in the development and enjoying its fruits. One section of the population that, among others, has been left behind by this type of planning and development is the rural population in poor regions.

Rural communities in China

More than 800 million people live in the rural areas of China. They account for over 65 per cent of the total population of the country. Although China has experienced great progress in people's quality of life, development over the past 20 years has led to unbalanced conditions between urban and rural areas (and between east and west), and the plight of rural areas in poor provinces is too serious to ignore (Han, 2004). Following Deng's policy whereby 'a part of the population will become rich first through development', the senior government officials decided to encourage large-scale, rapid development with the main purpose of stimulating growth. Because many rural areas in poor regions were remote and lacking in basic infrastructure and development opportunities, and because poor people in rural areas lacked tangible resources, such as capital, these people were typically left behind when fast growth occurred in the cities of the eastern seaboard. Studies in 1999 showed that the growth elasticity of income of the lowest quintile of the Chinese population was only 0.308, suggesting that the poor did not benefit even half as much from growth as the richer segments of society (Gang and Kruse, 2003). Within this section of the population, 42 million remained in absolute poverty in 1999 and another 350 million were labelled as poor. Most of these people live in rural areas where limited natural resources set considerable constraints on employment in agriculture (Q. L. Chen, 2002).

Poor rural people are often excluded from the planning process. They do not have a *Danwei* (collective workplace) to which to report their concerns, and they live far away from the large urban areas, the places where the decisions are made. This also suggests that rural people should be viewed in the context of their 'community'. Rural people spend most of their time in their community territory. The existence of strong family and community networks is a central facet of life for them (M. Kaufman, 1997). In the context of tourism, the communities of concern are the aggregations of local people living in and around tourism zones (Joppe, 1996). In terms of administration, the community is the lowest level of the administrative hierarchy in China – the village.

Although some outside academics, in recommending a sharing in planning of decision making, assume that poor people prioritize alleviation of their powerlessness, such a priority is not usually articulated by the latter. Vernooy et al. (2003) reported that the poor rural people in

Yunnan and Guizhou Provinces in China demanded diversification of their means of livelihood and improvement in their economic situation. The findings have been similar in other parts of the poor regions of China and in other less-developed countries. When landless people in Bangladesh were asked about their priorities, the answers clearly referred to activities which would generate more income (Chambers, 1983). In Zambia, the poor prioritized health, education, money and food (Chambers, 1995). It is widely agreed that poor people will probably want livelihood items such as food, clothing, shelter, work, health, education and water supply more than other higher-order satisfactions (Chambers, 1983, 1986; Doyal and Gough, 1991; Friedmann, 1992; Ghai and Alfthan, 1980; Lara and Molina, 1997). Seldom is the desire to participate in decision making articulated and, indeed, some studies even show that powerless people may feel that they should not be involved in the planning process (Timothy, 1999; Wilkes, 2000).

Another explanation for this phenomenon is that power may not be part of people's culture (Boniface, 1999) and participation may take different forms, reflecting the social, cultural and political attributes of different localities; it may not always follow the Western paradigm of participating in the planning process (Tosun, 2000; Wall, 1995). However, the difficult question remains of how people's basic needs are to be met if a local planning approach cannot undertake the task. Can the Western power-sharing model of participation be followed even though local people may not perceive such participation as an urgent need?

Participation: can it improve poor people's lives?

In answering this question, it is necessary to examine carefully the practicability of rural community participation in planning processes in China. There are a number of difficulties in encouraging and enabling disadvantaged groups to participate in planning and decision-making processes (PDM) (Din, 1998; Timothy, 1999; Tosun, 2000). Table 12.3 summarizes the obstacles preventing the practice of PDM in a top-down political environment, such as in China. These obstacles restrict the utility of PDM being adopted as an initial means of improving people's lives, especially in circumstances where development is rapid and on a large scale as is commonly the case in China. In such circumstances, imposition of PDM is likely to remain little more than an academic exercise.

Table 12.3 The obstacles of practising PDM among rural poor communities in a top-down political environment

Perspective	Obstacles	References
Government	Power centralization and the powerful may be reluctant to relinquish or dilute their power. PDM may be decided from the 'top' to confirm political support or control implementation. Fragmented and complicated government structure. Distance from local communities, both geographically and psychologically. The reluctance to slow down the development speed or accept alternative development. The reluctance to cooperate with groups lacking development resources (such as capital).	Bahaire and Elliott-White, 1999; Butler, 1993; Chambers, 1977, 1983; Clegg and Hardy, 1996; de Kadt, 1992; Elander, 1997; Garcia, 1983; Green, 1979; Haywood, 1988; Jamal and Getz, 2000; Lindberg et al., 2003; P. Long, 2000; Ornelas, 1997; Timothy, 2002; Timothy and White, 1999; Tosun, 2000

(Continued)

Table 12.3 Continued

Perspective	Obstacles	References
Private Sector	Dominant-subordinate relationship exists in PDM because some participants (e.g. business groups) are better organized, educated, informed and with greater skills and resources. Investment power ensures their interests and a certain level of decision-making power which they may not want to share with others. In an immature business environment, business groups may prefer large-scale development so that they can influence decision making and expect a rapid return on invested capital. In an immature business environment, business groups may not be spontaneously sensitive to ecological or local issues. They may merely prefer to see their privileges continue.	Brett, 1987; de Kadt, 1992; Elliott, 1983; Freudenburg, 1983; C. M. Hall and Jenkins, 1995; Reed, 1997; Reich, 1985; Tyler and Dinan, 2001; Wall, 1996; Wanhill, 1997
Planning Experts	The reluctance to share the power with the bottom. Hard to convince various interests. Hard to find common ground among diverse interests in organizing PDM. Hard to blend the ideas of citizens and experts in proceeding with PDM. Hard to involve the least effective participants who lack resources in advocating PDM. Revolutionizing the political structure in a country to decentralize administration goes beyond the control of the planners.	Chambers, 1993; D. R. Hall, 2000; Pigram, 1993; Reed, 1997; Yeh and Wu, 1999
Community/ Policy Takers	Psychologically reluctant to participate because they want to make ends meet and some benefits occur at present. Also PDM may not be part of their culture. Lack of information, education and resources to act. Lack of local associations and mutual-aid business network to solidify the struggle for greater power.	Boniface, 1999; Chambers, 1983, 1986, 1995; Din, 1998; Doyal and Gough, 1991; Friedmann, 1992; Ghai and Alfthan, 1980; Maslow, 1943; Pei, 1998; Reed, 2000; Timothy, 1999; Tosun, 2000; Wall, 1995

This point can be further demonstrated through the failure of the village self-management movement (SM) in China. SM attempts to provide the rural population with the opportunity to participate in the decision-making process within the village territory. However, few successful experiences have been discovered after 20 years of the SM. Yang (2003) found that the movement was sustained in only 10 per cent of the original villages and most of the villages abandoned the programme without saying so openly. The reasons for the lack of success were varied: no tangible support, such as funding, was offered by the programme and little more than lip-service was paid to the concept of 'decentralizing decision-making power' (G. L. Chen and Chun, 2004). Yang indicated that widespread poverty among the participants and a lack of education and awareness of democratic processes were other reasons for the failure of SM. He also suggested that the programme, at least at the initial stage, should be subsistence-related. Finally, the leaders of the villages have often been co-opted by the elite groups, especially the traditional leaders in minority groups (Yang, 2003). Bribery in village elections has been common (G. L. Chen and Chun, 2004). If the village leaders do not truly represent the people, the programme rapidly becomes meaningless.

This discussion further confirms that PDM in China may need to take a different form than is usually advocated in the West. Broader, more inclusive approaches need to be considered in order to understand and advance community participation in China. This is not a reason for questioning the fundamental utility of PDM, but rather that patience and a grounded approach are needed in practical initiatives. According to Timothy (1999), community participation in tourism development can be viewed from another perspective: participation in benefit sharing (PBS). PBS reflects an interest in finding forms of development through which benefits actually reach the majority of the population (C. M. Hall, 1994; M. Kaufman, 1997; Simmons, 1994), along with a moral requirement that a large number of people should not be systematically excluded from the benefits of development nor should they become the unwitting victims of other people's progress (Friedmann, 1992). PBS is defined here as a process or activity through which people participate in opportunities to acquire material wealth, such as in economic activities, and in opportunities to develop human capital, such as in education, training, awareness–generation, social communication and network enhancement.

PBS, especially PBS for the poor, can contribute to development by enhancing the genera-tion of resources, making people more productive, mobilizing local knowledge and increasing the development potential of an area (Chambers, 1983; Friedmann, 1992; M. Kaufman, 1997; Prud'homme, 1995; Reed, 2000). PBS can provide opportunities for people to help themselves instead of being helped once in a while by others through such means as subsidies (Chambers, 1987; Prud'homme, 1995; Rein, 1976). In tourism, PBS may help to sustain local cultures, craft skills and common properties, if people see these as being in their interest (Garrod and Fyall, 1998; D. R. Hall, 2000). Case studies also show that the opportunities resulting from PBS in tourism may result in subsequent investments in health, education and other social facilities (de Araujo and Bramwell, 2000) and may improve local people's technical, communi-cation and business skills (Bao, 2000; Bao and Chu, 1999; Gang and Kruse, 2003; Lindberg et al., 2003).

As important, PBS is practical to implement because sharing the benefits of development has long been one of the most important concepts in administrative policies in China. This can be documented with quotations from the books of many of the dynasties from as far back as the eighth century BC. After the establishment of the People's Republic of China, the Maoist approach of development was characterized by egalitarian income distribution (Kiminami, 1999). Deng Xiao Ping and Jiang Ze Min advocated that a part of the people will become rich first through development. The fourth generation of Chinese leaders called for 'people-centred' development in which the main task is to meet the needs of people, especially those of the rural poor. In other words, PBS should face few political constraints in its pro-motion. Furthermore, as shown in Table 12.4, PBS provides incentives for both decision makers and the rural people themselves to accept the concept in development. In addition, activities undertaken to share the benefits of tourism development may also benefit the tourism industry.

Successful examples of tourism-led poverty reduction that have occurred in some relatively developed rural tourism destinations in China also support the practicality of PBS in terms of both economy and literacy (Bao, 2000; Bao and Chu, 1999; Doorne et al., 2003; Gang and Kruse, 2003; Swain, 1989; Toops, 1993). Such successes, especially in previously very backward ethnic minority communities, offer hope that this can also occur in other rural places in China.

Table 12.4 Impetus and incentives for practising PBS among rural poor communities in a top-down political environment

Perspectives	Impetus and Incentives	References
Government	Poverty reduction through economic and social development is high on government agenda. PBS of the rural poor allows them to be more productive and self-reliant which contribute to the whole society. PBS is consistent with the new development direction in China – 'people-centred' development. PBS helps to relax the existing hazard of urban-rural spillover effects of development.	de Kadt, 1979; ESCAP, 2000; Friedmann, 1992; HDDR, 2003; Richter, 1989; Timothy, 2002
Tourism Industry	PES helps to diversify the tourist product and enrich the tourists' experiences. Opportunities of PBS can enhance local hospitality. PES helps to balance the costs, impacts and benefits of tourism development.	de Kadt, 1979; Manning, 1999; Murphy, 1985; Simmons, 1994; Wall, 1997; Wilson, 1979
Rural Communities	Rural people normally have the desire for material wealth and social improvement. PBS informs a better understanding about the procedures of participation because it relates to villagers' daily life and can germinate from their own traditional and local knowledge. PBS provides the opportunities for the rural poor to get involved in tourism employment which is often accorded a relatively high status and remuneration compared with traditional options. PBS lets tourism-related small businesses, which are small in scale at the beginning, to avoid attracting the attention of outsiders to plunder the opportunities. PBS helps the rural people to acquire new skills, knowledge and experiences which make them gradually stronger through building social capital. PBS helps in the establishment of the local cooperative organizations and other mutual help social networks and enhances local awareness about participation and tourism development. PBS helps rural people to demonstrate their knowledge, creativity and intelligence, changing the negative impression of the rural poor among other stakeholder groups. This may eventually open the door of PDM to villagers.	Burns, 1999; Cukier, 2002; Echtner, 1995; D. R. Hall, 2000; Long and Wall, 1995; Timothy, 1999; Valk, 1990; Walker, Mitchell, and Wismer, 2001

From this discussion, it is necessary to redefine participation to include the PBS perspective and to take the Chinese situation into consideration. Thus, participation can mean involvement in any organized activity in the development process, either to share in the benefits or to be involved in the planning or decision–making processes. PBS in development activities, based on the above definition and discussion is not only a means of gaining more financial resources, but also a process contributing to the increase of knowledge, information, a sense of self-confidence and a strengthening of social relationships.

Can PBS work as an initial intervention for encouraging the participation of rural people in tourism development to improve their lives? Some Western studies suggest that it can but this idea seems not to get the attention that it deserves in the planning field. Arai (1996) argued that empowering people economically and socially can have a great impact on the political dimensions of empowerment. Farrell (1992) and Boniface (1999) have pointed out that, through a strengthened economic position and enhanced awareness and skills, people will spontaneously and confidently demand improved access to decision making. Ghai (1989) argued that provision of economic benefits to members plays an important role in participatory initiatives: people need motivation and incentives that relate to their needs in order to generate action. As summarized in Friedmann's (1992, p. 34) words, 'giving full voice to the disempowered population tends to follow a certain sequence', and the acquisition of financial and human resources may be an initial requirement for effective participation in politics. At the same time, when people get some control, such as when they are provided with the power to influence parts of the planning process, a product that is more closely related to their needs may be developed (Ghai and Alfthan, 1980). The people may become more developmentally independent (Farrell, 1992). This independence will be accompanied by a wish to be in a position to supply a much greater proportion of the required goods, resources, services and management talent which will, in turn, reinforce the PBS process.

In summary, it is suggested that PBS and PDM constitute one interrelated process through which rural people will be progressively empowered (World Bank, 1996). The separation of PBS and PDM in the above discussion is employed merely for convenience and to facilitate presentation. PBS should be initiated first to break some of the local political, social, cultural and economic constraints on participation and so that opportunities for PDM will be generated thereby. PDM will reinforce the success of PBS in the long run.

The participatory spiral

Participation in development, especially among disempowered populations, should be planned in stages in a top–down political situation. In the process of development, land may be expropriated and residents may be displaced. This displacement only worsens residents' situation, and they do not share in the benefits of development. In this case, the local communities become the 'impactees' of development. This chain of events has occurred throughout the world (Philp and Mercer, 1999; Roville, 1988; Trask 2000; Wayakone et al., 1998). Once this problem is acknowledged and the public sector and/or the communities themselves have the desire to change the situation, the poor may firstly be introduced into the development process as 'beneficiaries' – recipients of services, resources, training, information and development interventions (World Bank, 1996). As the capacity of the poor is strengthened and their voices begin to be heard, they become 'clients' who are capable of demanding and paying for goods and services provided by government and the private development sectors (ibid.). Active participation in decision-making and planning processes can then be initiated among the previously poor people (Rein, 1976). Although the voices of such people at this stage may not yet have an influence equal to those who have more power politically (Abers, 1998), they have essentially become partners in development, and not merely another resource or problem that must be dealt with (Farrell, 1992). With investment power, these people may have the confidence and resources to ask to be better 'heard' in initiating development activities. When these people further strengthen their capacity, they may ultimately become 'owners' and managers of the development activities. Previously poor people will then have obtained the highest level of participation (Boniface, 1999; World Bank, 1996). It is not the authors' intention to suggest that the villagers will eventually own the hotels. Rather, if means can be found to facilitate movement up the spiral, 'ownership' will occur in the sense that local people will have greater control over the decisions that impinge upon their lives and will benefit substantially from the developments that occur on their territory. However, local communities, especially the majority of the rural poor, rarely act spontaneously (Din, 1998; Friedmann, 1992) because they lack innovative leadership, adequate financial, material, and technical means, and training (ESCAP, 2000). They may be unable to take advantage of the opportunities and resources that are available at the beginning stage of the development process. Just as pupils require a teacher, the poor need outsiders to take initiatives in this regard and to work with them (Abers, 1998). Therefore, as part of the process, the progress of participation involves consultation or collaboration with diverse individuals and groups outside of the disempowered communities (Ristock and Pennell, 1996). However, empowerment is not a process of treating the poor as 'objects' or 'target groups'; genuine and lasting participation must be a process undertaken for oneself (Friedmann, 1992; Lather, 1991). Based on the above discussion, the participatory spiral model is formulated in Figure 12.1.

This model demonstrates that encouraging rural community participation should start with PBS and proceed to PDM in development. Local people initially have no share of the tourism-generated benefits, then progress through participation in benefit-generation activities to gain resources, knowledge, information, confidence, etc., to the control of the development initiatives and to being in charge of the planning and decision-making processes. Increased effort, along with achievements and progress in economic, social and political dimensions, which reinforce each other, moves the community through the participatory levels in the model. The role of the rural community in the development process may switch from the initial role of impactee, to beneficiary, to client and ultimately to owner. Moreover, the model adopts the concepts of 'outsiders' entry phase' and 'withdrawal phase' to show that outside help is necessary at first. Then, outside influence is gradually reduced and eventually withdrawn when the local people are capable of carrying on alone. This model also accords with the notion that human needs

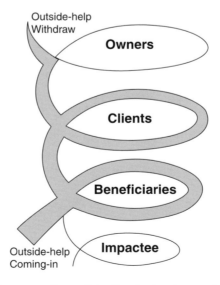

Figure 12.1 Spiral of rural community participation in development

evolve in sequence; human needs are presented not in a static manner, but as changing over time in line with the growth of the economy and the aspirations of people (Doyal and Gough, 1991; Ghai, 1980; M. Kaufman, 1997; Taylor, 1998).

A variety of research questions emerges from this discussion of tourism planning and participation, in combination with the current status of tourism development in China. With respect to tourism planning, one might ask:

- What is the most appropriate approach to tourism planning in China?
- Can the focus of the prevailing planning approach in China be switched from an emphasis on physical and economic perspectives to a concern about residents' needs?
- Should the planning approach in China adopt or incorporate Western planning approaches and, if so, how?

With respect to tourism development, one might ask:

- How can the concept of rural community participation be fused into the planning approach(es) in China?
- How might PDM be effective to a different extent under different circumstances?

Secondly, relating to tourism development:

- Can PBS work as an initial means for improving people's lives, leading later to PDM?
- Can local people protect their own interests or do they need outside help? How might PBS be initiated and who by?
- Will PBS among local people ensure a better distribution of benefits?
- What are the forms that PBS might take in a tourism destination?
- How might different forms of PBS be effective under different circumstances?
- And finally, relating to participation, how do PBS and PDM interrelate and advance each other?
- How do levels, scales and types of tourism development affect community participation?
- How do different forms of community participation contribute to development at community and regional levels and, more specifically, to the tourism industry?

These questions constitute some of the key topics that are being addressed in studies in Hainan based on two primary research approaches:

- analysis of the contents of tourism plans to ascertain the place of local residents in the tourism plans, what roles have they played and are expected to play in the development process, and whether their interests have even been considered; and
- engagement with local communities using participatory research methods.

Conclusions

Shared planning and decision making among various stakeholder groups is a major concept in the prevailing Western approaches to tourism planning (C. M. Hall, 2000a), although the extent of participation, the influences of the participants and the groups involved are variable. Moreover, shared decision making and planning have been viewed as being a means to pursue a more equitable tourism development and to balance the distribution of tourism-led benefits among various stakeholder groups. However, participation is an issue that extends beyond the techniques that are available to planners to facilitate public input; it reflects power relationships, cultural and democratic values, structures of public governance, and institutional arrangements at a destination. In the West, some of these determinant factors may be at least partially conducive to the creation of an environment in which shared planning and decision-making processes can be implemented.

In contrast, the current tourism planning approach in China is heavily focused on economic dimensions and it tends to be isolated from broader development perspectives. It emphasizes tourism market supply and demand and focuses almost entirely on designing and promoting the main components of tourism such as attractions, accommodation, transportation and tours. The planning emphasis, in the terminology of Burns (1999) is 'tourism first', a perspective that concentrates on developing tourism: locating suitable sites for the development of resorts, hotels and other tourist attractions to fulfil the tourists' demands. Although an awareness of sustainability is growing, and tourism planning in China has begun to incorporate the ideas of protecting natural resources and using them carefully, such planning remains silent on distributional issues and on the use of tourism as a means of social development. Moreover, community participation in the planning process continues to be largely unknown in China. As shown in Table 12.3, the external environment is not conducive to the implementation of a Western-style participatory planning process.

In spite of this situation, with the deteriorating situations of rural poverty in some poor regions of China and increasing polarization between urban and rural areas generally, there is a growing demand for poverty reduction through tourism development. As many insightful people in China have pointed out, failing to involve the rural poor in a more productive development process will not only hamper further economic and social development in China, but will also call into question the stability of the society (Q. L. Chen, 2002; Dong, 2002; HDDR, 2003; Xiao, 2001). Therefore, there is an urgent need to incorporate people into the development process to improve their lives and secure their futures. This is in the interest of the people themselves as well as the broader collective.

However, the Western style of shared planning and decision making is not viable as an initial means to facilitate the participation of rural communities in China where tradition prescribes a top-down political process. An approach is needed that is grounded in practical initiatives. Participation in tourism development to share in its benefits (PBS) is practical in China because it faces fewer obstacles from political, social, cultural and economic perspectives when compared with the practice of shared decision making (PDM), particularly at this stage. Based partly on World Bank proposals, a participatory spiral model has been proposed that suggests that PBS should precede PDM, particularly among the rural poor in a top-down planning context. As shown in the spiral model, people start with having no share of the tourism-generated benefits, then progress through participation in benefit-generation activities to eventually assume greater control over development initiatives and to take charge of the planning and decision-making processes. Because poor people rarely act spontaneously, it is necessary that they obtain some outside support along the way. Planners mitigate the 'unavoidable side-effects' of tourism and other forms of development that often accrue unfairly to poor people 'in the way' of 'progress' by doing their best to facilitate their sharing in the benefits of tourism development to the best of their abilities. We are currently exploring, through case studies in Hainan, how community participation might be facilitated in what is currently a top-down political and planning environment, and how PBS and PDM can be initiated and may evolve in such settings. As intermediaries in this process, we will gather and report the situations, desires, concerns and efforts of local community members in places that are in the early stages of tourism development and transfer this information to government officials. Through this indirect communication process, it is hoped that improved policies, plans and planning processes will result, that local benefits will be enhanced, and a greater level of local involvement in tourism development may gradually emerge.

Bibliography

Abers, R. (1998) 'From clientelism to cooperation: Local government, participatory policy and civic organizing in Porto Alegre, Brazil'. *Politics and Society*, 26(4), 511–38

Alipour, H. (1996) 'Tourism development within planning paradigms: The case of Turkey'. *Tourism Management*, 17(5), 367–77

Arai, S. M. (1996) 'Benefits of citizen participation in a healthy communities initiative: Linking community development and empowerment'. *Journal of Applied Recreation Research*, 21(1), 25–44

de Araujo, L. M. and Bramwell, B. (2000) 'Stakeholder assessment and collaborative tourism planning: The case of Brazil's Costa Dourada Project'. In B. Bramwell and B. Lane (eds) *Tourism collaboration and partnerships: Politics, practice and sustainability*. Clevedon: Channel View Publications, pp. 272–94

Bahaire, T. and Elliott-White, M. (1999) 'Community participation in tourism planning and development in the historic city of York, England'. *Current Issues of Tourism, 2*(2/3), 243–76

Baidal, J. A. I. (2004) 'Tourism planning in Spain: Evolution and perspectives'. *Annals of Tourism Research*, 31(2), 313–33

Bao, J. G. (2000) *The investigation of tourism development*. Beijing: Science Press

Bao, J. G. and Chu, Y. F. (1999) *Tourism geography* (Rev. edn). Beijing: Higher Education Press

Boniface, P. (1999) 'Tourism and cultures: Consensus in the making?'. In M. Robinson and P. Boniface (eds) *Tourism and cultural conflicts*. Oxford: CABI Publishing, pp. 287–306

Bramwell, B. and Lane, B. (1993) 'Sustainable tourism: An evolving global approach'. *Journal of Sustainable Tourism*, 1(1), 1–5

Bramwell, B. and Sharman, A. (1999) 'Collaboration in local tourism policymaking'. *Annals of Tourism Research*, 26(2), 392–415

Burns, P. (1999) 'Paradoxes in planning: Tourism elitism or brutalism?'. *Annals of Tourism Research*, 26(2), 329–48

Cai, S. K. (1999) *Self-reflection after Hainan's ten-year development'*. Hong Kong: Sanlian Bookstore (Hong Kong) Ltd

Campbell, S. and Fainstein, S. S. (1996) 'Introduction: The structure and debates of planning theory'. In S. Campbell and S. S. Fainstein (eds) *Readings in planning theory*. Cambridge, MA: Blackwell Publishers, pp. 1–18

Chambers, R. (1983) *Rural development: Putting the last first*. New York: Longman

—— (1986) *Sustainable livelihood thinking: An approach to poverty, environment and development*. London: The International Institute for Environment and Development

—— (1987) *Sustainable rural livelihoods: A strategy for people, environment and development: An overview for ONLY ONE EARTH, Conference on Sustainable Development*. London: The International Institute for Environment and Development

—— (1995) *Poverty and livelihoods: Whose reality counts?* (Discussion Paper No. 347). Brighton: Institute of Development Studies, University of Sussex

Chen, Q. L. (2002) *The discussion of Chinese peasants' diathesis*. Beijing: Contemporary World Publishing Company

Chen, G. L. and Chun, T. (2004) *The investigation of rural Chinese*. Beijing: The People's Literature Publishing

Conyers, D. and Hills, P. J. (1984) *An introduction to development planning in the Third World*. New York: John Wiley and Sons

Costa, C. (2001) 'An emerging tourism planning paradigm? A comparative analysis between town and tourism planning'. *International Journal of Tourism Research*, 3(6), 425–41

Cuthbertson, I. D. (1983) 'Evaluating public participation: An approach for government practitioners'. In G. A. Daneke, M. W. Garcia and J. D. Priscoli (eds) *Public involvement and social impact assessment*, Boulder, CO: Westview Press, pp. 101–9

Davidoff, P. (1965) 'Advocacy and pluralism in planning'. *Journal of the American Institute of Planners*, 31(4), 331–8

—— (1975) 'Working towards redistributive justice'. *Journal of the American Institute of Planners,* 41(5), 317–18

Din, K. H. (1998) 'Tourism development: Still in search of a more equitable mode of local involvement'. In C. Cooper and S. Wanhill (eds) *Tourism development: Environmental and community issues.* New York: John Wiley and Sons, pp. 153–62

Dong, H. (2002) *The investigation of Hainan national farms.* Hainan: The People's Government of Hainan Province

Doorne, S., Ateljevic, I. and Bai, Z. (2003) 'Representing identities through tourism: Encounters of ethnic minorities in Dali, Yunnan Province, People's Republic of China'. *International Journal of Tourism Research,* 5(1), 1–11

Doyal, L. and Gough, I. (1991) *A theory of human need.* Basingstoke: Macmillan

ESCAP (2000) *The empowerment of the rural poor through decentralization in poverty alleviation actions.* Bangkok: Economic and Social Commission for Asia and the Pacific

Evans, G. (2000) Planning for urban tourism: A critique of borough development plans and tourism policy in London'. *International Journal of Tourism Research,* 2(5), 307–26

Farrell, B. (1992) 'Tourism as an element in sustainable development: Hana, Maui'. In V. L. Smith and W. R. Eadington (eds) *Tourism alternatives: Potentials and problems in the development of tourism.* Philadelphia, PA: University of Pennsylvania Press, pp. 115–32

Fletcher, J. and Cooper, C. (1996) 'Tourism strategy planning: Szolnok County, Hungary'. *Annals of Tourism Research,* 23(1), 181–200

Friedmann, J. (1992) *Empowerment: The politics of alternative development.* Cambridge, MA: Blackwell

Gang, X. and Kruse, C. (2003) 'Economic impact of tourism in China'. In A. A. Lew, L. Yu, J. Ap and G. Zhang (eds) *Tourism in China.* New York: Haworth Hospitality Press, pp. 83–102

Garrod, B. and Fyall, A. (1998) 'Beyond the rhetoric of sustainable tourism?'. *Tourism Management,* 19(3), 199–212

Gauteng Tourism Authority (2003) 'Responsible tourism planning framework'. Retrieved 15 November 2011, from http://fama2.us.es:8080/turismo/turismonet1/economia%20del%20turismo/turismo%20 responsable/responsible%20tourism%20report.pdf

Getz, D. (1986) 'Models in tourism planning: Towards integration of theory and practice'. *Tourism Management,* 7(1), 21–32

—— (1987) 'Tourism planning and research: Traditions, models and futures'. Paper presented at the Australian Travel Research Workshop, Bunbury, Western Australia, November

Ghai, D. P. (1980) 'What is the basic needs approach to development all about?'. In D. P. Ghai, A. R. Khan, E. L. H. Lee and T. Alfthan (eds) *The basic-needs approach to development: Some issues regarding concepts and methodology.* Geneva, Switzerland: International Labor Office, pp. 1–18

—— (1989) 'Participatory development: Some perspectives from grassroots experiences'. *Journal of Development Planning,* 19, 215–46

Ghai, D. P. and Alfthan, T. (1980) 'What is the basic needs approach to development all about?'. In D. P. Ghai, A. R. Khan, E. L. H. Lee and T. Alfthan (eds) *The basic-needs approach to development: Some issues regarding concepts and methodology.* Geneva, Switzerland: International Labor Office, pp. 19–59

Gill, A. M. (1997) 'Competition and the resort community: Towards an understanding of residents' needs'. In P. E. Murphy (ed.) *Quality management in urban tourism.* New York: John Wiley and Sons, pp. 55–66

Grant, J. (1989) 'From "human values" to "human resources": Planners' perceptions of public role and public interest'. *Plan Canada,* 29, 11–18

Gunn, C. A. (1988) *Tourism planning* (2nd edn). New York: Taylor and Francis

Hall, C. M. (1994) *Tourism and politics: Policy, power and place.* New York: John Wiley and Sons

—— (2000a) *Tourism planning: Policies, processes and relationships.* Harlow: Prentice Hall

—— (2000b) 'Rethinking collaboration and partnership: A public policy perspective'. In B. Bramwell and B. Lane (eds) *Tourism collaboration and partnerships: Politics, practice and sustainability.* Clevedon: Channel View Publications, pp. 143–58

Hall, D. R. (2000) 'Tourism as sustainable development? The Albanian experience of "transition"'. *International Journal of Tourism Research,* 2(1), 31–46

Hall, P. G. (1980) *Great planning disasters.* London: Weidenfeld and Nicolson

Han, J. (2004) *China: From the urban-rural dual to harmonious development.* Beijing: People's Publishing House

Haywood, K. M. (1988) 'Responsible and responsive tourism planning in the community'. *Tourism Management,* 9(2), 105–18

HDDR (2003) *Centering the people in the development: Establish and practice the scientific development.* Hainan: Department of Reformation and Development of Hainan Province

Healey, P. (1992) 'Planning through debate: The communicative turn in planning theory'. *Town Planning Review,* 63(2), 143–62

Hong, S.-K., Kim, S.-I. and Kim, J.-H. (2003) 'Implications of potential green tourism development'. *Annals of Tourism Research,* 30(2), 323–41

Inskeep, E. (1991) *Tourism planning: An integrated and sustainable development approach.* New York: Van Nostrand Reinhold

Jamal, T. B. and Getz, D. (1995) 'Collaboration theory and community tourism planning'. *Annals of Tourism Research,* 22(1), 186–204

—— (1997) '"Visioning" for sustainable tourism development: Community-based collaborations'. In P. E. Murphy (ed.) *Quality management in urban tourism.* New York: John Wiley and Sons, pp. 199–220

Joppe, M. (1996) 'Sustainable community tourism development revisited'. *Tourism Management,* 17(7), 475–79

de Kadt, E. J. (1979) *Tourism: Passport to development? Perspectives on the social and cultural effects of tourism in developing countries.* New York: Oxford University Press

Kaufman, J. L. and Jacobs, H. M. (1987) 'A public planning perspective on strategic planning'. *Journal of the American Planning Association,* 53(1), 23–33

Kaufman, M. (1997) 'Community power, grassroots democracy and the transformation of social life'. In M. Kaufman and H. D. Alfonso (eds) *Community power and grassroots democracy: The transformation of social life.* London: Zed Books, pp. 1–26

Keogh, B. (1990) 'Public participation in community tourism planning'. *Annals of Tourism Research,* 17(3), 449–65

Kiminami, L. (1999) *The basic analysis on poverty problem in China* (FASID-IDIRI Occasional Paper Series). Tokyo: Foundation for Advanced Studies in International Development, International Development Research Institute

Klosterman, R. E. (1996) 'Arguments for and against planning'. In S. Campbell and S. S. Fainstein (eds) *Readings in planning theory.* Cambridge, MA: Blackwell Publishers, pp. 150–68

Lanfant, M.-F. and Graburn, N. H. H. (1992) 'International tourism reconsidered: The principle of the alternative'. In V. L. Smith and W. R. Eadington (eds) *Tourism alternatives: Potentials and problems in the development of tourism.* Philadelphia: University of Pennsylvania Press, pp. 88–112

Lara, S. and Molina, E. (1997) 'Participation and popular democracy in the committees for the struggle for housing in Costa Rica'. In M. Kaufman and H. D. Alfonso (eds) *Community power and grassroots democracy: The transformation of social life,* London: Zed Books, pp. 27–54

Lather, P. A. (1991) *Getting smart: Feminist research and pedagogy with/in the postmodern.* New York: Routledge

Lau, M. (2003) 'Coastal zone management in the People's Republic of China: An assessment of structural impacts on decision making processes' (Working Paper No. FNU-28). Retrieved 15 November 2011, from Research Unit Sustainability and Global Change, University of Hamburg: http://econpapers. repec.org/paper/sgcwpaper/40.htm

Lickorish, L. J. and Jenkins, C. L. (1997) *An introduction to tourism.* Oxford: Butterworth-Heinemann

Lindberg, K., Tisdell, C. and Xue, D. (2003) 'Ecotourism in China's nature reserves'. In A. A. Lew, L. Yu, J. Ap and G. Zhang (eds) *Tourism in China,* New York: Haworth Hospitality Press, pp. 103–25

Lindblom, C. E. (1959) 'The science of "muddling through"'. *Public Administration Review,* 19(2), 79–88

Long, V. and Wall, G. (1996) 'Successful tourism in Nusa Lembongan, Indonesia?'. *Tourism Management,* 17(1), 43–50

Martopo, S. and Mitchell, B. (Eds.) (1995) *Bali: Balancing environment, economy and culture* (Department of Geography Publication Series No. 44). Waterloo, Canada: University of Waterloo

Murphy, P. E. (1983) 'Tourism as a community industry: An ecological model of tourism development'. *Tourism Management,* 4(3), 180–93

—— (1985) *Tourism: A community approach.* New York: Methuen

—— (1988) 'Community driven tourism planning'. *Tourism Management,* 9(2), 96–104

—— (1992) 'Data gathering for community-oriented tourism planning: Case study of Vancouver Island, British Columbia'. *Leisure Studies,* 11(1), 65–79

Page, S. (1995) *Urban tourism.* London: Routledge

Philp, J. and Mercer, D. (1999) 'Commodification of Buddhism in contemporary Burma'. *Annals of Tourism Research*, 26(1), 21–54

Pretty, J. (1995) 'The many interpretations of participation'. *Focus*, 16(1), 4–5

Prud'homme, R. (1995) 'The dangers of decentralization'. *World Bank Research Observer*, 10(2), 201–20

Reed, M. G. (2000) 'Collaborative tourism planning as adaptive experiments in emergent tourism settings'. In B. Bramwell and B. Lane (eds) *Tourism collaboration and partnerships: Politics, practice and sustainability.* Clevedon: Channel View Publications, pp. 247–71

Rein, M. (1976) *Social science and public policy.* Harmondsworth: Penguin

Richter, L. K. (1983) 'Political implications of Chinese tourism policy'. *Annals of Tourism Research*, 10(3), 395–413

Ristock, J. L. and Pennell, J. (1996) *Community research as empowerment: Feminist links, postmodern interruptions.* Toronto, Canada: Oxford University Press

Roville, G. (1988) 'Ethnic minorities and the development of tourism in the valleys of North Pakistan'. In P. Rossel (ed.) *Tourism: Manufacturing the exotic.* Copenhagen: International Work Group for Indigenous Affairs, pp. 147–76

Roy, J. (1998) *Mechanisms for public participation in economic decision-making.* September. Ottawa: Task Force on the Future of the Canadian Financial Services Sector

Sheldon, P. J. and Abenoja, T. (2001) 'Resident attitudes in a mature destination: The case of Waikiki'. *Tourism Management*, 22(5), 435–43

Simmons, D. G. (1994) 'Community participation in tourism planning'. *Tourism Management*. 15(2), 98–108

Sofield, T. H. B. and Li, F. M. S. (1998) 'Tourism development and cultural policies in China'. *Annals of Tourism Research*, 25(2), 362–92

Swain, M. B. (1989) 'Developing ethnic tourism in Yunnan: Shilin Sani'. *Tourism Recreation Research*, 14(1), 33–39

Taylor, N. (1998) 'Mistaken interests and the discourse model of planning'. *Journal of the American Planning Association*, 64(1), 64–75

Timothy, D. J. (1998) 'Cooperative tourism planning in a developing destination'. *Journal of Sustainable Tourism*, 6(1), 52–68

—— (1999) 'Participatory planning: A view of tourism in Indonesia'. *Annals of Tourism Research*, 26(2), 371–91

Tisdell, C. and Wen, J. (1991) 'Foreign tourism as an element in PR China's economic development strategy'. *Tourism Management*, 12(1), 55–67

Toops, S. (1993) 'Xinjiang's handicraft industry'. *Annals of Tourism Research*, 20(1), 88–106

Tosun, C. (2000) 'Limits to community participation in the tourism development process in developing countries'. *Tourism Management*, 21(6), 613–33

Tosun, C. and Jenkins, C. L. (1996) 'Regional planning approaches to tourism development: The case of Turkey'. *Tourism Management*, 17(7), 519–31

—— (1998) 'The evolution of tourism planning in Third-World Countries: A critique'. *Progress in Tourism and Hospitality Research*, 4(2), 101–14

Trask, H.-K. (2000) 'Native social capital: The case of Hawaiian sovereignty and Ka Lahui Hawaii'. *Policy Sciences*, 33(3/4), 375–85

Travis, A. S. (ed.) (2011) *Planning for Tourism, Leisure and Sustainability: International Case Studies.* Wallingford: CABI

Vernooy, R., Sun, Q. and Xu, J. C. (2003) *Voices for change: Participatory monitoring and evaluation in China.* Ottawa, Canada: International Development Research Centre

Wahab, S. and Pigram, J. J. (1997) 'Tourism and sustainability: Policy considerations'. In S. Wahab and J. J. Pigram (eds) *Tourism development and growth: The challenge of sustainability.* London: Routledge, pp. 277–90

Wall, G. (1995) 'People outside the plans'. In W. Nuryanti (ed.) *Tourism and culture: Global civilization in change?* Yogyakarta, Indonesia: Gadjah Mada University Press, pp. 130–37

—— (1996) 'One name, two destinations: Planned and unplanned coastal resorts in Indonesia'. In L. C. Harrison and W. Husbands (eds) *Practicing responsible tourism: International case studies in tourism planning, policy and development.* New York: John Wiley and Sons, pp. 41–57

—— (1997) 'Linking heritage and tourism in an Asian City: The case of Yogyakarta, Indonesia'. In P. E. Murphy (ed.) *Quality management in urban tourism.* New York: John Wiley and Sons, pp. 139–48

Wall, G. and Long, V. (1996) 'Balinese homestays: An indigenous response to tourism opportunities'. In R. Butler and T. Hinch (eds) *Tourism and indigenous peoples*. London: International Thomson Business Press, pp. 27–48

Wayakone, S., Shuib, A. and Mansor, W. W. (1998) 'Residents' attitude towards tourism development in Dong Hua Sao Protected Area, Laos'. *Malaysian Journal of Agricultural Economics*, 12, 16–32

Weaver, D. B. (1995) 'Alternative tourism in Montserrat'. *Tourism Management*, 16(8), 593–604

Wilkes, A. (2000) 'The functions of participation in a village-based health pre-payment scheme: What can participation actually do?'. *IDS Bulletin*, 31(1), 31–6

Willis, K. (1995) 'Imposed structures and contested meanings: Policies and politics of public participation'. *Australian Journal of Social Issues*, 30(2), 211–27

World Bank (1996) *The World Bank participation sourcebook*. Washington, DC: World Bank

Xiao, Y. (2001) 'How difficult to be a peasant in this modern society?'. In CEAR (China Economy Annual Report) (ed.) *Resuscitation: The problems of Chinese peasants*. Lanchow: Lanchow University Press, pp. 117–20

Yang, Y. C. (2003) *Investigating the problems of self-management in Chinese villages*. Shanghai: Fu Dan University Press

Yeh, A. G. and Wu, F. (1999) 'The transformation of the urban planning system in China from a centrally planned to transitional economy'. *Progress in Planning*, 51(3), 167–252

Zhang, G. R. (2003) 'Tourism research in China'. In A. A. Lew, L. Yu, J. Ap and G. Zhang (eds) *Tourism in China*. New York: Haworth Hospitality Press, pp. 67–82

Zhang, T. (2002) 'Challenges facing Chinese planners in transitional China'. *Journal of Planning Education and Research*, 22(1), 64–76

Zhang, W. (2003) 'Measuring stakeholder preparedness for tourism planning in Leshan, China' (UMP-Asia Occasional Paper No. 57). Retrieved 15 November 2011, from http://fama2.us.es:8080/turismo/turismonet1/economia%20del%20turismo/turismo%20zonal/lejano%20oriente/measuring%20stakeholder%20tourism%20planning%20in%20China.pdf

13

Nurturing "social license to operate" through corporate–civil society relationships in tourism destinations

Peter W. Williams, Alison M. Gill, Julia Marcoux, Na Xu

Introduction

Globalization has resulted in the emergence of large tourism corporations whose influence on the destinations in which they operate have been referred to as "the corporatization of place" (Rothman, 1998). Paradoxically, as the commercial power and market reach of these large tourism corporations have expanded, so has the mix of local authorities and non-government organizations (NGOs) that have emerged to contest or modify their actions (Norcliffe, 2001). This has led to calls for more collaborative approaches to engagement by corporations and destination stakeholders. The way in which these relationships unfold may be central to establishing not only the corporation's social license to operate (Cunningham et al., 2003), but also the overall destination's sense of place (Williams and Gill, 2004).

This chapter provides a framework for understanding relationships between tourism corporations and their destination stakeholders. While a rapidly growing literature exists on stakeholder aspects of strategic planning and business management (Hillman and Keim, 2001; Prahalad and Hamel, 1990; Svendsen, 1998), as well as tourism-related collaborative planning (de Araujo and Bramwell, 1999; Getz and Timur, 2005; Jamal and Getz, 1995; Williams, Penrose, and Hawkes, 1998), there has been little attempt to understand how interactions between corporations and local institutions are implemented and how they evolve in tourism destinations (Flagestad and Hope, 2001). Similarly little has been published concerning how these interactions occur in the context of corporate–civil society stakeholder relationships. Consequently, this paper uses the framework to describe evolving corporate–civil society relationships in the tourism resort destination of Whistler, British Columbia, Canada. The findings provide insights into how such stakeholder interactions affect corporate social license to operate, as well as destination sense of place.

Corporate–community stakeholder framework

The paper's framework for examining corporate–community stakeholder relationships (Gill and Williams, 2006) is built on several theories discussed in the strategic management literature.

In particular, it includes elements of stakeholder theory (Svendsen, 1998), the resource-based view of the firm (Wernerfelt, 1984), corporate social responsibility (Carroll, 1999), corporate environmentalism (Berry and Rondinelli, 1998), and social license to operate (Cunningham et al., 2003). Elements of these paradigms pertinent to the paper's overriding corporate–community stakeholder framework are briefly described in the context of mountain tourism destination management.

Stakeholder theory

Svendsen et al. (2002, p. 1) contend that

> [in] a rapidly globalizing, knowledge-based economy, sources of value creation in business are shifting from tangible assets such as land and equipment, to intangibles such as intellectual and human capital.

Primary stakeholders include shareholders and investors, employees, resource suppliers, customers, community residents, as well as groups speaking for the natural environment (Hillman and Keim, 2001). Clarkson (1995, p. 106) identifies public stakeholder groups as being those "governments and communities that provide infrastructures and markets, whose laws and regulations must be obeyed, and to whom taxes and other obligations may be due". A seminal principle of stakeholder theory relevant to this research is that a corporation is given the social license to operate by virtue of its social contract with external stakeholders (Robson and Robson, 1996). Effective management of these relationships "can constitute intangible, socially complex resources that may enhance firms' abilities to out-perform competitors in terms of long-term value creation" (Hillman and Keim, 2001, p. 127).

Resource-based view of firm

The competitiveness of firms is derived from their distinct tangible and intangible assets (Wernerfelt, 1984). When these resources are unique and/or cannot be replicated by competitors, they produce competitive advantages (Barney, 1991). Priority access to raw materials such as labour, energy, and land are examples of tangible resources that may provide competitive advantage. Examples of intangible resources that can contribute to a firm's competitiveness include its favorable reputation with consumers, responsive corporate culture, and goodwill with suppliers and customers. Acquiring on-going access to such resources may involve considerable investments of human capital in developing positive relationships with external stakeholders. Such engagements can build value with stakeholders (Hart, 1995; Jamal and Getz, 1995) who may be the gatekeepers to resources that firms need (Svendsen et al., 2002). They can also help reduce corporate risks by: introducing more effective management strategies; reducing the chances of adverse public relations; and reinforcing the firm's social license to operate in the marketplace (Harrison and St. John, 1996).

Corporate environmentalism and social responsibility

Corporate environmentalism emphasizes the importance of responding to consumer and political pressures for proactive environmental protection. Competitive advantage is gained by pursuing management strategies which avert the costs of conflict, decrease the need for government regulation and intrusion, and improve the economic efficiency of production processes

(Banerjee, 200_; Delmas and Terlaak, 2001; Gibson and Peck, 2001; Lyon, 2003; Parker, 2002). Successful corporate environmentalism initiatives focus on building greater communication and understanding between the firm and its internal and external stakeholders.

Corporate social responsibility (CSR) concepts and practices extend from corporate environmentalism models (Banerjee, 1998). They emphasize solving and preventing environmental and social problems through collaborations that benefit both businesses and stakeholders (Cragg, 1996). Proponents of CSR believe that such practices facilitate greater cross-fertilization of thinking which leads to more creative and actionable management strategies (Hart, 1995).

Social license to operate

Traditionally, corporations viewed compliance with existing regulatory requirements as their sole legal and social responsibility (Cunningham et al., 2003). Adherence with existing environment, social, and labor requirements was primarily done to avoid liability penalties or to meet moral and social obligations (Wright, 1998). The prevailing philosophy was that going beyond compliance should occur only in situations of "self interest" (Porter and van der Linde, 1995). However, growing regulatory regimes and increasingly litigious civil societies in some jurisdictions have led corporations to consider their social obligations as extending beyond solely meeting legal requirements (Evans, 2001). Corporate leaders consider acquiring approval to function in accordance with community expectations as their social license to operate. While the levels of corporate performance expected by these community stakeholders may extend well beyond minimal legal requirements and be economically challenging, they represent yet another factor in shaping decisions concerning the strategic positioning of some businesses. While there is limited consensus on what social license to operate entails in practice, there is growing recognition of its importance as a corporate strategy. A series of damaging encounters between large corporations and civil society (e.g. Connor and Atkinson, 1996; Moore, 2001; Neale, 1997; van Yoder, 2001), caused by private sector misreading of the terms of their social license to operate, has stimulated a growing corporate interest in establishing stronger relationships with grass roots community stakeholders. As corporations learn more about the influence of civil society organizations as "community gatekeepers", so has the concept of social license to operate grown in relevance to these businesses. The concept may have particular relevance to corporations operating in tourism destinations where many functions critical to the visitor's experience are affected by stakeholders external to individual corporations (Flagestad and Hope, 2001; Murphy and Murphy, 2004).

In a "Western" tourism destination management context, this means that corporations may be granted a social license to operate by different stakeholders (e.g. regulators, employees, customers, investors, suppliers, or local communities), and that each of these parties can revoke the organization's privileges to operate at any time. Indeed it is not unusual for stakeholder relations with such corporations to ebb and flow as the destination evolves through its various stages of development.

Corporate–tourism destination stakeholder model

Based upon the preceding concepts and an understanding of tourism destination management strategies, a conceptual model of corporate–tourism destination stakeholder relationships is presented in Figure 13.1. In this model, corporation and community entities have networks of stakeholders that operate within the context of a destination characterized by the area's unique economic, political/regulatory, socio-cultural, and biophysical environments. The primary

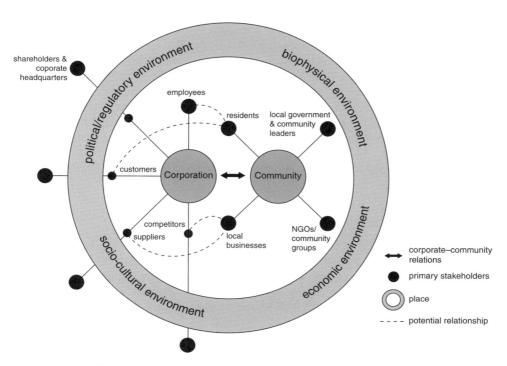

Figure 13.1   A place-based model of corporate–community relationships

corporate stakeholders include customers, employees, suppliers, competitors, and shareholders. With the exception of employees, the majority of these stakeholders are primarily located outside the community, although this concentration will vary with each situation. The community's primary stakeholders are local government and community leaders, residents, local businesses, NGOs, and other community groups. While Figure 13.1 simplifies the complexities of the various interactions between these stakeholder groups, the model suggests (dashed lines) some possible linkages between the various actors. For example, employees are in many instances residents. Other residents may be customers or even shareholders. Local businesses may function as suppliers or competitors.

The model presents a generic situation. There are a number of distinct features that characterize North American mountain resort destinations, including:

- recreation activities occurring mainly on public lands where there is generally a rigorous set of environmental regulations that must be met in the development and operation of such areas (Todd and Williams, 1996);
- a significant proportion of the area's "residents" being second-home owners who do not live permanently in the community (Williams and Gill, 2004);
- a high proportion of employees not being community residents because they are forced to commute to work due to unaffordable housing costs in the destination area (Moore et al., 2006); and
- a high degree of interdependency existing between the corporation and the community due to ongoing tourism destination commoditization processes.

While the corporation represents the main economic driver upon which the community depends, it is also dependent on the community. The community not only provides the regulatory approvals for its development plans, but also helps to maintain the high quality environment and hospitality levels needed to satisfy the company's customers. The ability of the corporation to meet these requirements is dependent to a large degree on how well it establishes a social license to operate with relevant stakeholders in the community. Key destination stakeholders that can act as gatekeepers in providing a social license to operate include civil society groups such as environmental non-government organizations (ENGOs). To a large degree, the relative amounts and types of power distributed amongst these destination stakeholders determine the character of engagement between corporate and community groups as well as the nature of environmental management decisions taken.

Evolving corporate–civil society relationships in Whistler, BC

The following case study illustrates the ways in which a large resort development and management corporation has engaged with ENGOs and other local stakeholders to ensure the continuance of its social license to operate on environmental management matters. It is based on research involving key informant interviews with a purposive sample of 27 interviewees comprised of community members (9), ENGO representatives (14), and personnel from Intrawest corporation's Whistler–Blackcomb (W–B) operations (4) in Whistler, British Columbia (Marcoux, 2004; Xu, 2004). These key informants were selected based on their availability, research subject matter experience, and functional position within the key stakeholder groups (e.g. leaders, managers, and participants in environmental activities in their respective organizations).

A review of stakeholder, resource-based view of the firm, corporate social responsibility, and social license to operate literature guided the development of the standardized survey instruments used to collect the primary data for the study. In these questionnaires a combination of standardized semantic differential, Likert scale, and open-ended questions were used. The semantic differential and Likert scale questions solicited overall opinions on key issues. Accompanying open-ended questions enabled respondents to elaborate on more specific aspects of their responses to those same questions. In addition, customized questions more specific to each stakeholder group (e.g. W–B, ENGO, and broader community representatives) were employed to probe other key dimensions of the relationship between W–B and the Association of Whistler Area Residents for the Environment (AWARE). Themes explored in the questionnaires related to priority environmental goals and objectives of the participating organizations, critical criteria, and motivators for establishing stakeholder relationships, engagement processes, and lessons learned from stakeholder involvement (e.g. perceived benefits and challenges associated with engagement).

Informants were personally interviewed by members of the research team during the summer (August) and the winter (December) of 2003. Interviews were tape-recorded and transcribed. Upon completion of this process, the interviewees were asked to review their individual transcripts for accuracy and offer further elaboration on commentary they had provided. Using their edited responses as a base, overriding similarities and differences in stakeholder responses were identified on a question by question basis. For the purposes of this research paper, only the responses of ENGO and W–B interviewees were used to inform the findings presented. In combination, their responses provide insights into the evolving role and impact that stakeholder relationships play in shaping both corporate and ENGO environmental activities in Whistler.

Case study context

Whistler is widely recognized as one of the most frequented ski destinations in the world. Two massive ski mountains, as well as thousands of hectares of pristine backcountry, challenging alpine terrain, massive glaciers, and crystal clear lakes provide the physical backdrop for the destination's pedestrian village and related community activities. About 80 percent of the destination's 10,000 permanent residents are employed servicing the town, small businesses, and Intrawest, the largest corporation in the community. In the 1999–2000 ski season, Intrawest's Whistler-Blackcomb (W-B) ski operation generated more than two million skier visits, making it the most heavily used ski area in North America (Intrawest, 2003). These visitors provided the impetus for employing about 13,800 people in Whistler and 30,000 people in the region (RMOW, 2002).

W-B was indisputably the main economic producer in Whistler, responsible for generating the lion's share of the destination's business. By virtue of its influence on the drivers of employment, prices, growth, and material standards of living in the destination, it was also capable of using tremendous "allocative" power (Ashworth and Dietvorst, 1995; Flagestad and Hope, 2001) to leverage political decisions in its favour. This power is particularly strong in tourism places which are focused on using economic performance to measure community well-being.

Intrawest's evolving corporate environmentalism

At the time of this study Intrawest's development portfolio included 14 mountain resort operations in a variety of destinations across the globe. Its flagship resort development was located in Whistler and operated by a locally based W-B management team. The W-B group had long recognized that the success of its operations was dependent upon an ability to sustain the area's natural environment. To this end, one of W-B's key objectives was to "continue to improve our commitment to sustainability and environmental excellence" (Intrawest, 2003). Its level of commitment and approach to environmental management evolved over time.

Prior to 1992, Intrawest's W-B management activities focused more on conducting due diligence practices that ensured the safety of mountain guests and staff than on addressing environmental issues. However, an unanticipated on-mountain oil spill in 1992 alerted the company to the importance of having a sound environmental management system in place – one that acknowledged that "regulatory compliance was not sufficient" (W-B respondent #1) to prevent accidents capable of creating significant environmental damage. In response to the incident, they immediately committed W-B to addressing the spill's effects and putting standards in place which would ensure that such an environmental disaster would not happen again. In addition, they provided community stakeholders with timely and transparent reports on the incident's impacts as well as the mitigating actions they were taking. Not only did the spill provide an early lesson to W-B concerning the need for a comprehensive environmental approach to its business operations, but it also offered them an insight concerning the importance of maintaining a strong social license to operate with key stakeholders in the community.

In response to the oil spill incident, W-B created its first comprehensive environmental management system (EMS) to guide its mountain operations in 1994 (Todd and Williams, 1996). Over the years, this EMS gradually evolved to a point where it incorporated many of the principles and guidelines for sustainability as outlined by the National Ski Area Association's *Sustainable Slopes Charter* (NSAA, 2000) and *The Natural Step Framework* – an environmental management framework that helps organizations and communities understand and move towards sustainability (Nattrass and Altamore 2003). These principles guided W–B in its planning, design, construction, operation, internal education, and outreach activities.

Linkages with community stakeholders were continually nurtured especially with respect to new planning, education, and outreach programs. For instance, W–B was initially involved as an "early adopter" of the Natural Step Framework, and the subsequent development of *Whistler 2020: Moving Toward A Sustainable Future*, the destination's comprehensive sustainability plan (RMOW, 2004). It also collaborated with several community and non-government organizations to implement specific parts of the destination's 'Whistler: It's Our Nature' program (Nattrass and Altamore, 2003). This initiative was operated by a local ENGO and supported local businesses, households, and other organizations in adopting more sustainable practices.

Associated with their activities, W–B had an environmental vision, created to guide current practices with respect to environmental matters. The stated vision was:

> To contribute to the goal of sustainability by developing, through its environmental management system, the highest level of environmental stewardship in the North American mountain resort industry. (W–B respondent #1)

Because of W–B's immediate proximity to the resort destination, many of the company's environmental strategies not only influenced the organization's internal stakeholders, but also affected surrounding community groups and activities. Simultaneously, the ultimate effectiveness of many of W–B's strategies depended on the support of local stakeholders. Specific initiatives that required community stakeholder engagement and support included programs linked to fish and wildlife management, bear and marmot habitat preservation, glacier protection, water and energy conservation, environmental education, and social event sponsorship. W–B won several environmental awards and much community recognition for its leadership role in nurturing strong corporate–community relations with respect to citizenship and environmental stewardship.

Stakeholder management

W–B defined stakeholders as "those individuals or groups who live or work in the municipality of Whistler and who affect, or are affected by, our mountain operation activities" (W–B respondent #2). They included Whistler residents, businesses, local government institutions, tourism marketing organizations, and non-governmental agencies. Two overarching groups comprised W–B's primary environmental stakeholders. They were:

- institutional and regulatory stakeholders such as the Resort Municipality of Whistler and Tourism Whistler that provided much of the formal regulatory and infrastructural guidance required by W–B; and,
- non-governmental environmental and community organizations such as the AWARE, Whistler Area Naturalists, and Whistler Fisheries Stewardship Group that offered much of the informal moral suasion, credibility, and support needed to acquire and retain a social license to operate in the destination.

To illustrate W–B's stakeholder management approach, this paper describes the corporation's engagement philosophies and methods related to AWARE.

Evolving corporate engagement with AWARE

AWARE was originally formed in 1987 to pressure local government to enact a recycling program. Its success in this venture evolved into grander responsibilities associated with being a leading community advocate on numerous other environmental issues. These included a very controversial proposed golf course development which it said would significantly damage the ecological integrity of the area. Although the development project eventually went ahead, AWARE gained a large degree of community credibility and local government legitimacy based on the way it conducted itself during this process (Xu, 2004).

AWARE played a significant role in shaping the destination's informal response to a variety of environmental management issues. Depending on the organization's collective capacities, as well as the specific issue being addressed, AWARE fulfilled a variety of functions. These reflect typical ENGO roles identified in the literature (Burns, 1999; Jamal, 1999; Lama, 2000) and included:

- creating public awareness of emerging environmental issues related to proposed development activities;
- exerting political pressure on local and regional governments, as well as corporations to ensure that development occurs in an environmentally responsible manner;
- identifying risks and assessing environmental impacts associated with existing and proposed developments;
- initiating, planning, carrying out, and monitoring the effects of environmental enhancement projects; and,
- protecting local values from being captured by powerful business operations.

AWARE's ability to achieve its objectives was based largely on its credibility and legitimacy as an environmental champion. As a non-producer community group, it had only a small fraction of the allocative power (Ashworth and Dietvorst, 1995) possessed by W–B and other destination producers. However, in contrast it carried a substantial level of "authoritative" power. Growing concern in Whistler about sustainability issues helped to position it as a source of credible knowledge and as the leading "environmental watchdog" for local residents. Consequently, its approval was frequently sought by both government and developers in matters related to activities that impact on the destination's environment.

Drivers of corporate–ENGO engagement

Several potential drivers motivate the establishment of corporate–ENGO relationships (Elkington and Fennell, 1998). From a business perspective, a company may enter into such partnerships in order to build a brand image which increases its credibility with markets and strategically important stakeholders (Bendell, 2000). Specifically, such involvement can influence public opinions concerning corporate environmental and social performance (Svendsen, 1998). Moreover, by working with ENGOs, a company can use "outside" perspectives to improve its approach to "inside" practices (Harrison and St. John, 1996). ENGOs can be a valuable source of new ideas and critical thinking. Inviting them to participate in business planning processes either as advisers or board members can increase the effectiveness of corporate initiatives (Rondinelli and Berry, 2000). Furthermore, financial and natural resource savings as well as eco-efficiencies can be achieved through partnerships with environmental groups due to their expertise and ability to mobilize volunteers (D. E. Murphy and Bendell, 1997). Partnering with environmental groups can generate good publicity and result in less protest or government intervention in corporate practices (Harrison and St. John, 1996).

Other drivers contribute to increasing the willingness of ENGOs to collaborate with businesses. These include growing recognition that:

- the achievement of sustainable development agendas requires the active participation of business stakeholders in addressing environmental matters scare tactics for getting public attention are unsustainable in the longer term;
- constructive collaborative approaches rather than radical actions focusing on generating antagonism often result in more sustainable results;
- the perceived and actual declining regulatory role and capacity of governments to address environmental issues requires NGOs to seek environmental solutions and resources with/from private sector partners; and,
- increasing awareness of corporate social responsibility has led business leaders to be increasingly willing to listen to and seek collaborations with ENGOs in environmental planning and management activities (Elkington and Fennell, 1998; D. E. Murphy and Bendell, 1997).

The extent and type of engagement between W-B and its environmental counterparts varied depending upon the perceived power and legitimacy of the stakeholder as well as the urgency of the issue being addressed. In the mid-1980s W-B tended to act in isolation of the community. "The company had their own design panel, their own set of rules and could do things that other people couldn't" (W-B respondent #3). As the power and legitimacy of some of the more established ENGOs in Whistler grew, so did W-B's interest in working with them. This was especially apparent with the largest and highest profile of Whistler's ENGOs: AWARE. Because of AWARE's informal position as the community's "environmental watchdog", W-B paid particular attention to it on environmental issues. This interest in engagement increased as the company's developmental activities grew.

While there were points of antagonism between AWARE and W-B in previous years, over time the relationship shifted from being primarily adversarial to more collaborative and solution seeking in character. While some critics perceived AWARE's agenda as being co-opted by W-B's priorities, proponents of the relationship believed that it brought together resources and talents that could "galvanize and connect the community around initiatives that can make the destination a more desirable place to live and visit" (ENGO respondent #1). Other AWARE respondents also felt that such an approach increased the efficiency and effectiveness with which decisions and actions concerning environmental management could be made.

Overall, W-B informants claimed that the most important benefits of establishing and nurturing stakeholder relationships with AWARE (and other similar organizations) were linked to: enhancing the image and credibility of the company with respect to its environmental activities; and, subsequently increasing the efficiency with which it obtained formal approvals to proceed with proposed development and management activities (Table 13.1). Conversely, AWARE stakeholders claimed that the most important advantages obtained from their engagement with W-B included: increasing their ability to "leverage" the resources needed to address environmental problems; and, being able to address solvable issues in a non-bureaucratic and pragmatic fashion.

Engagement strategies

Accurately identifying stakeholders and creating the circumstances suited to effective dialogue with them are keys to successful engagement (Cragg, 1996). Specific strategies needed for effective

Table 13.1 Top perceived drivers of W-B–ENGO stakeholder relationships

Perceived Importance of Drivers of W-B's Engagement with AWARE	*Perceived Importance of Drivers of AWARE's Engagement with W-B*
• Desire for enhanced credibility with government, community and market (High) • Need for increased efficiency in obtaining development approvals (High) • Desire to "head off" negative public confrontations (High) • Interest in cross-fertilization of ideas (Medium) • Interest in educating key stakeholders about rationale and strategies for environmental activities (Medium)	• Desire for greater leverage in addressing "solvable" problems (High) • Search for less bureaucratic and action-oriented solutions (High) • Need for more resources (e.g. funding, technical and management expertise) (Medium) • Desire to build a problem-solving as opposed to antagonistic community culture (Medium) • Interest in cross-fertilization of ideas (Medium)

and imaginative engagement include: establishing trust, encouraging inclusiveness, ensuring responsiveness, and demonstrating commitment.

While some companies formalized strategies for engaging stakeholders, W-B provided little formal clarity in this regard. Their philosophy was based on an understanding that:

- overall engagement makes "good business sense";
- when "issues are solved collaboratively, decisions are improved upon and trust is built";
- early engagement is more economically efficient "as you get it right the first time" and do not have the costs associated with changing plans or designs to accommodate stakeholder interests at a later time. (W-B respondents 2003)

They operationalized this philosophy, by incorporating various ingredients of effective stakeholder engagement into their actions on a situational basis.

Trust

Trust is needed for engagement strategies to be effective. It is most often nurtured and maintained by open interaction and transparency between the engaged groups. Trust is risked when the engaged parties fail to be transparent about how issues are being handled and/or not forthcoming about sharing information relevant to the problem. Transparency can be characterized by honesty, integrity, and openness. It is one of the key indicators of a good relationship between a corporation and its stakeholders.

Transparency

Managers at W-B believed that transparency was a "key factor for gaining community support" (W-B respondent #2). For instance, a senior W-B executive met regularly with other leaders of the community in a group called One Whistler. This senior level group meetings addressed strategic and more pervasive destination development and management issues that required the operational attention of community stakeholders. Issues and proposed actions created by W-B and other organizations that appeared contradictory to the values of the resort community were addressed in an open and transparent fashion. This kept W-B and its community leaders (including AWARE) abreast of emerging issues and concerns early on so that mutually beneficial solutions could be created prior to controversial events happening.

Inclusiveness

Inclusiveness refers to the level of involvement that organizations give their stakeholders in decisions that affect them or that they can affect. For W–B, inclusion did not necessarily imply direct stakeholder participation in the making of its decisions. However, it did infer that the perspectives of all those with a stake in the decision's outcome would be included in the process of arriving at the selected course of action.

Establishing inclusive relationships with Whistler's growing list of community stakeholder groups was increasingly challenging. W–B used a networking approach to determine who was included in the engagement process. In this approach they identified which groups were related directly to the issue as well as those who are indirectly impacted via other exchanges, communications and actions. For instance, AWARE had relationships with its members, and these individuals have interactions with other constituencies such as their families, retailers, financial institutions, who may have been engaged in other relationships with W–B. The approach de-emphasized the centrality of W–B in addressing environmental matters alone, and encouraged communication, support, and actions with stakeholders from the broader community. This is particularly important in destination communities where the entanglements amongst individuals who are involved in many different community organizations can be significant.

By understanding the interrelationships and communication patterns that existed within and between destination stakeholder organizations, W–B strategically selected those alliances which created the greatest leverage for its activities. Its pragmatic approach to determining whom and how specific stakeholders were included is situational in character. Depending on the issue, the level and type of inclusion ranged from formally engaging a wide range of stakeholders in public forums, meetings, and workshops to total immersion of some specific interest groups in targeted activities of the company. While approaches varied with the intent of the engagement, W–B suggested that the more they place stakeholders in the reality and context of the management problem, the greater the probability that stakeholders would create solutions that met with corporate and community approval. They suggested that such approval (i.e. social license to operate) made implementation of potential options more feasible.

Responsiveness

Responding to stakeholder issues in a proactive, timely, and appropriate manner built trust and credibility for W–B. In order to "win the hearts and souls of the community we must demonstrate an interest in community issues and 'walk the talk'" (W–B respondent #4). For instance, by being pro-active and responsive to the community's overriding comprehensive sustainability initiative, W–B was able to secure a valuable social license to operate from many of the destination's most influential environmental stakeholders. This "social capital" was invaluable in helping the organization negotiate approval for a range of other development initiatives in the community.

Commitment

The success of any relationship depends upon the level of commitment of all participants. Having common or complementary goals provides the basis for commitment. Once these goals have been established, participants are more apt to move toward the achievement of these milestones in a collaborative manner. While stakeholders may have asymmetrical motivations, goals, and organizational capacities behind engagement, commitment to making the process work increases when the purpose of the interaction is attractive to both. This is more apt to occur if the parties share certain cultural values and fundamentally respect each other's legitimacy and integrity.

For W–B and AWARE, the common goals were environmental conservation and the economic success of the resort. The nature of the ski industry demanded that W–B capitalize on the natural environment within which it operated. At the same time, W–B recognized that protecting the quality of the region's environment was a value held by AWARE and other community stakeholders. "It is the glue that brings W–B together with many of its stakeholders"(AWARE respondent #1). Despite missteps along the way, W–B's environmental initiatives became a means of bringing the company and AWARE together on a variety of planning fronts. AWARE stakeholders agreed that W–B was astute and possessed good business sense when it came to involving the community in decisions that affected them. "They intuitively understand the need to protect the environment" (AWARE respondent #2).

Situational applications

An example of W–B's situational application of the preceding ingredients of effective stakeholder engagement was demonstrated with respect to a ski area expansion project proposed by the company in the Piccolo-Flute backcountry area of Whistler Mountain. When initially announced by W–B, the development created considerable controversy amongst local stakeholders who were emotionally attached to the site. Locals felt that this pristine terrain should remain relatively inaccessible to visitors. In response to initial concerns, W–B invited local advocacy groups (including AWARE) to discuss the intent and potential options for utilizing the area in a sustainable fashion. Despite W–B being within its legal rights to develop this area, an excursion and on-site workshop activities were organized by W–B to develop clear channels of communication concerning the intent of the project, as well as to identify key issues of conflict that had to be addressed before any social license to operate would be approved. Based on considerable front-end dialogue, local stakeholders identified and supported more favorable non-mechanized backcountry development options that protected the pristine character of the area.

A key to the success of this initiative was a desire on the part of W–B to engage AWARE and other parties in a two-way dialogue about the project. This exchange could only occur if both parties were willing to participate, and had the organizational capacity to engage in such a discourse. W–B had in place personnel with the social and technical skills needed to guide a proactive dialogue. Similarly, AWARE's membership included people with capable communication and negotiation talents.

W–B's transparency in sharing its intent for the area, its inclusiveness of AWARE and other stakeholders with the capacity and willingness to participate in the dialogue, its responsiveness to their concerns, and its commitment to reinforcing shared environmental and socio-cultural values in the area helped it achieve commercial goals and reinforced its social license to operate within the destination community.

Perceived benefits of stakeholder engagement

While stakeholder engagements between W–B and AWARE varied in type and intensity over the years, participants in these relationships identified a range of perceived benefits emanating from the interactions. Those benefits contributing to W–B's social license to operate in Whistler are summarized in Table 13.2. Overall, both W–B and ENGO respondents agreed that such engagements had been most effective at:

- improving environmental decision making by bringing into plan a broader range of development options than might have normally been considered;
- enhancing credibility, trust, and commitment amongst community and company stake-holders with respect to the probable outcomes of selected development activities;
- building a common vision and goals between the company and the community through the development of shared environmental values;
- strengthening the company's "triple bottom line" by reducing the costs of liability and risk containment associated with development projects; and,
- increasing the reputation and visibility of the destination with key internal and external stakeholders.

Discussion

This chapter described the overriding motivations, strategies, and benefits associated with W–B's stakeholder engagement initiatives with ENGOs in Whistler. While there were challenges

Table 13.2 Perceived benefits of W–B–ENGO stakeholder engagement

Potential benefits of stakeholder engagement	Estimated level of perceived benefit amongst W-B respondents*	Estimated level of perceived benefit amongst ENGO respondents*
Improved environmental decision making		
• Generation of more innovative alternatives	Moderate	High
• Consideration of greater range of potential effects	High	High
• Creation of "win–win" solutions	High	Moderate
Improved community trust and commitment		
• Quicker response to planning approval requests	Moderate	Moderate
• Increased community awareness with respect to potential outcomes	High	High
• Increased credibility and support for outcomes (social licence to operate)	High	High
Common vision and goal		
• Increased opportunities for shared environmental values	High	High
• Improved knowledge transfer between employees and community stakeholders	Moderate	High
• Enhanced opportunities for synergistic community actions	Moderate	High
Positive contribution to "triple bottom line"		
• Reduced costs of liability and risk containment	High	High
• Reduced costs of gaining development approvals	Moderate	Uncertain
• Reduced employee retainment costs	Moderate	Uncertain
• Strengthened reputation and visibility of destination and company amongst key stakeholder groups	High	High

*Estimates based on qualitative interpretation of overall responses.

associated with these relationships in the past, overall engagement initiatives became less confrontational and more constructive in character. Several factors help to explain this situation. These are discussed in the following paragraphs.

Connection to place

The lion's share of W-B's full-time employees lived and worked in Whistler. Consequently, many of them shared concerns and interests similar to those raised by other community businesses and residents. Whistler's past community visioning processes identified a remarkable level of consensus amongst business and community-based stakeholders concerning local environmental, social, and economic priorities for the destination. As such, it is less likely that W-B's employees would willingly make decisions that were contrary to the commonly held environmental values of the community.

> It's a little different in Whistler, because senior managers live here, so they are part of the community. Resort managers must live in the community, join the social club, and send their children to the local school. Otherwise they are the folks from out of town. (W-B respondent # 2)

Corporate-community stakeholder entanglement

The "web of entanglement" between organizations, businesses, and residents in Whistler was pervasive and complex. Local residents frequently had dual roles within the destination (e.g. working for the company to protect its competitive natural assets, while living a lifestyle built on access to the same environment attributes). This duality offered

> broader perspectives on environmental and social impacts and the consequences of development. It strengthens opportunities to reinforce values and actions of importance in both corporate and community life in a genuine and forceful manner. Additionally, it helps establish levels of trust and respect that carry over into actions in corporate and community spheres. (AWARE respondent #2)

Community trust and respect

At a basic level, personal contact and mutual trust between W-B employees and AWARE stakeholders were critical ingredients in forging successful engagement initiatives. Through such engagements the participants shared different concepts, learned other perspectives, and refined their own viewpoints on appropriate strategies. Such dialogues also provided opportunities to scrutinize the resolve and commitment of their counterparts to achieving commonly defined goals. This led to enhanced personal credibility and respect – something beyond their respective roles as corporate managers or ENGO leaders. While corporations are still driven by "bottom-line" operating mandates, the approaches they used for decision making can potentially lead to better outcomes that have the backing of a social license to operate granted by community stakeholders.

Evolving structures and actions

As competition in the global tourism marketplace continues to increase, so does the need for corporate–community stakeholder partnerships, alliances, and dialogue (KPMG Management

Consulting, 1995). As never before, there is a need to bring together the allocative power of corporations with the authoritative power of community stakeholders in order to compete on the world stage (Scholzman and Tierney, 1986). An emerging outcome of such processes of engagement in Whistler was an evolution in the character and actions of the engaged parties and the institutions they represent. While initial engagements between W-B and its community partners often commenced from divergent points of view, the ensuing dialogues frequently created new relationships and understandings between the engaged groups. This in turn has spawned new realities with respect to how the stakeholder organizations and institutions planned to conduct their respective environmental activities in the future. This reflects the perspectives of Giddens (1986) and Hall (1994) who suggest that the evolution and management of power relations governs the interactions between individuals, organizations, and agencies. This influences the structure of the institutions as well as the policy and programs they implement.

Such interactions reshaped the ways in which W-B and community stakeholders (governmental and non-governmental) led the destination on a path towards greater sustainability. The development of stakeholder connections between what seemed initially to be opposing power bases reflected a growing capacity of producer and non-producer institutions in Whistler, as well as a considerable level of commitment to engaging one another for individual and collective goals.

Appropriate tension

While some proponents of strong W-B–ENGO relationship building believe that such collaborations encourage greater opportunities for improved "on-the-ground" environmental actions, others fear a loss of credibility and power if the ENGOs are perceived to have been co-opted by the corporation. These perspectives are at the heart of a healthy tension that must be managed and nurtured by the collaborating partners. For organizations like AWARE, the management challenge is to select the type of engagement that fosters actions in line with the community's vision and environmental priorities, without its "environmental watchdog" voice being muted by corporate priorities. AWARE's perceived independence and option to engage in more aggressive pressure tactics were invaluable tools and important precursors to meaningful forms of engagement with W-B.

For W-B, the management challenge was to engage with AWARE in ways that respected the organization's independence yet nurtured relationships that will help it retain its "social license to operate". Beyond utilizing AWARE to help identify and address environmental challenges related to the company's operations, W-B required the ENGO's independent and critical approval for its existing and proposed development activities. Consequently, it was as important to nurture and support the independence and vigilance of such "outsider" organizations as it was to directly collaborate with them. In this respect, W-B's social license to operate was dependent on receiving permission from a credible organization that was perceived to have not been co-opted by the corporation. Notwithstanding the value of closer stakeholder relations between AWARE and W-B, the paradox is that there remained a need for a critical and independent voice in Whistler's public arena. Consequently an important management challenge for both W-B and AWARE is not to try to resolve the paradox, but rather to manage it effectively.

Conclusions

This chapter presents a range of characteristics that epitomize the nature of corporate-civil society stakeholder relationships in a specific "Western style" tourism destination. Many of the characteristics identified reinforce motivations, engagement strategies and outcomes reported in the literature. The discussion suggests that over several years that a constructive synergy emerged between W-B and its primary ENGO stakeholders. However, this did not occur without recurring challenges. For instance, since the completion of the research for this chapter's case study, W-B's ownership has changed three times. As it shifted from being the flagship resort in a Canadian-owned Vancouver-based private sector company in 2003, to an internationally owned asset in a large venture capital company (Fortress) in 2008, to its most recent status as a publicly traded Canadian-owned and Whistler-operated company (Whistler Blackcomb) in 2010, its "social license to operate" has evolved. When acquired by the bottom-line focused Fortress organization, W-B's legitimacy as partner in Whistler's journey towards sustainability ebbed significantly. Much uncertainty existed about the share-price driven and shareholder orientation of Fortress and how that foucs would align with Whistler's sustainability priorities. This concern largely evaporated when Fortress was "sold off" to the more locally oriented W-B company. Such shifts point to some interesting vulnerabilities associated with nurturing and retaining social license to operate.

In a corporate context, contextual conditions (e.g. magnitude and scope of the issue, personal and professional risk associated with decision making, changes in organizational leadership) can quickly alter the character of stakeholder engagement. This is the case especially if the level of engagement is built solely around personal considerations. More opportunity for sustained engagement exists if collaborative activities extend well beyond personal connections and issue-dependent arrangements to include more formalized process-oriented relationships.

Similarly, investigations in other jurisdictions where Intrawest operates suggest that the W-B approach to stakeholder engagement was not universally applied (Williams et al., 2007). Indeed, evidence from other geographic locations suggests that a more proactive approach to ENGO stakeholder involvement might have led to better long-term results for the corporation and the communities in which it operated (ibid.). However, more research is needed concerning what approaches to engagement generate the most productive results under varying circumstances.

In an era of growing corporate influence and power, it is probable that corporations such as Intrawest and now W-B will increasingly be compelled to not only conduct their businesses within existing formal regulatory environments established by government, but also operate within the informal social value systems of the destinations in which they locate. As a consequence, the expedience with which they are able to move forward with their own agendas will increasingly be linked to their ability to meet expected legal requirements as well as obtain and maintain their social license to operate.

Only limited research has been conducted to inform tourism corporations and ENGOs concerning those engagement strategies that serve the interests of their shareholders and stakeholders. Specific themes for future research follow.

Communication

Simply engaging stakeholders does not guarantee that successful outcomes will come from such relationships. Communication strategies that strengthen the ability of all parties to effectively transmit their own perspectives, receive the viewpoints of others, and understand how to process and collectively use such information are needed to support such engagements. Communication research should focus on creating effective means for the assessment, measurement, and reporting of stakeholder activities and how they vary in their situational appropriateness.

More research is also needed concerning the character of effective stakeholder dialogue. While considerable practitioner support exists concerning the importance of such discourse, little academic research has addressed methods of actively engaging stakeholders in effective dialogue.

Power

Understanding the role of power and its influence on corporate–community stakeholder relationships is needed. Many tourism destinations experience asymmetrical distributions of power that typically make real stakeholder engagement challenging if not impossible. In the case of Whistler, there was a seemingly more equitable sharing of specific types of power between W-B and its community stakeholders. More research is needed to determine how power and social behavior manifest themselves in varying stakeholder engagement situations.

Networking

In many "Western" tourism destinations, corporations are increasingly being viewed as entities embedded in a complex web of symbiotic relationships with other organizations and institutions. This perspective decentralizes the role of the corporation as the champion of change or action and creates the need for more community-led initiatives. More research is needed to explore how destination stakeholders should best organize their networks in order to achieve specific goals. While corporate- and community-based models of destination management exist, research concerning which networking strategies are most appropriate for engaging stakeholders in activities that lead to social license to operate for destination producer groups is needed.

Transferability

As with most case study research, this chapter's findings are geographically, temporally, and institutionally specific. It is quite probable that its outcomes with respect to specific strategies would vary from place to place. Indeed, research conducted in other settings by the authors suggests that this may be the case. However, there are some underlying principles and perspectives presented which are worthwhile exploring in terms of their presence and significance in other settings. The model presented in the paper offers a lens from which to examine such relationships. Only case study research of this type conducted in a variety of settings will determine the transferability and utility of the engagement approaches uncovered in this chapter.

References

de Araujo, L. M. and Bramwell, B. (1999) 'Stakeholder assessment and collaborative tourism planning: The case of Brazil's Costa Dourada project'. *Journal of Sustainable Tourism*, 7(3/4), 356–78

Ashworth, G. J. and Dietvorst, A. G. J. (eds) (1995) *Tourism and spatial transformations*. Wallingford: CAB International

Banerjee, S. B. (1998) 'Corporate environmentalism: Perspectives from organizational learning'. *Management Learning*, 29(2), 147–64

—— (2001) 'Managerial perceptions of corporate environmentalism: Interpretations from industry and strategic implications for organization'. *Journal of Management Studies*, 38(4), 489–513

Barney, J. (1991) 'Firm resources and sustained competitive advantage'. *Journal of Management*, 17(1), 99–120

Bendell, J. (2000) *Terms for endearment: Business, NGOs and sustainable development*. Sheffield: Greenleaf

Berry, M. A. and Rondinelli, D. A. (1998) 'Proactive corporate environmental management: A new industrial revolution'. *Academy of Management Executives*, 12(2), 38–50

Burns, P. (1999) 'Editor's note: Tourism NGOs'. *Tourism Recreation Research*, 24(2), 3–6

Carroll, A. B. (1999) 'Corporate social responsibility: Evolution of a definitional construct'. *Business and Society*, 38(3), 268–95

Clarkson, M. E. (1995) 'A stakeholder framework for analyzing and evaluating corporate social performance'. *Academy of Management Review*, 20(1), 92–117

Connor, T. and Atkinson, J. (1996) *Sweating for Nike: A report on labour conditions in the sport shoe industry* (Community Aid Briefing Paper No. 16). Seattle, DC: Nike

Cragg, W. (1996) 'Shareholders, stakeholders and the modern corporation'. *Policy Options*, 17, pp. 15–20

Cunningham, N., Kagan, R. A. and Thornton, D. (2003) *Shades of green: Business, regulation and environment*. Stanford, CA: Stanford University Press

Delmas, M. and Terlaak, A. (2001) 'A framework for analyzing environmental voluntary agreements'. *California Management Review*, 43(3), 44–63

Elkington, J. and Fennell, S. (1998) 'Partners for sustainability'. *Greener Management International*, 24, 48–60

Evans, G. (2001) 'Human rights, environmental justice, mining futures'. Retrieved 31 October 2011, from http://www.austlii.educ.au/au/other/HRLRes/2001/14

Flagestad, A. and Hope, C. A. (2001) 'Strategic success in winter sports destinations: A sustainable value creation perspective'. *Tourism Management*, 22(5), 445–61

Getz, D. and Timur, S. (2005) 'Stakeholder involvement in sustainable tourism'. In W. Theobald (ed.) *Global tourism*. New York: Elsevier, pp. 230–47

Gibson, R. and Peck, S. (2001) 'Pushing the revolution: Leading companies are seeking new competitive advantage through eco-efficiency and broader sustainability initiatives'. *Alternatives*, 26(1), 20–29

Giddens, A. (1986) *Central problems in social theory*. London: Macmillan Press

Gill, A. and Williams, P. W. (2006) 'Corporate responsibility and place: The case of Whistler, British Columbia'. In T. Clark, A. Gill and R. Hartmann (eds) *Mountain resort planning and development in an era of globalization*. New York: Cognizant Communication, pp. 26–40

Hall, C. M. (1994) *Tourism and politics: Policy, power and place*. New York: John Wiley and Sons

Harrison, J. S. and St. John, C. H. (1996) 'Managing and partnering with external stakeholders'. *Academy of Management Executive*, 10(2), 46–60

Hart, S. L. (1995) 'A natural-resource-based view of the firm'. *Academy of Management Review*, 20(4), 986–1014

Hillman, A. J. and Keim, G. D. (2001) 'Shareholder value, stakeholder management and social issues: What's the bottom line?'. *Strategic Management Journal*, 22(2), 125–39

Intrawest (2003) 'Play: Intrawest Annual Report 2001'. Retrieved 31 October 2011, from http://highered.mcgraw-hill.com/sites/dl/free/0070891737/75681/Intrawest2001AR1.pdf

Jamal, T. B. (1999) 'The social responsibilities of environmental groups in contested destinations'. *Tourism Recreation Research*, 24(2), 7–17

Jamal, T. B. and Getz, D. (1995) 'Collaboration theory and community tourism planning'. *Annals of Tourism Research*, 22(1), 186–204

KPMG Management Consulting (1995) *Developing business opportunities through partnering: A handbook for Canada's tourism industry*. Ottawa: Industry Canada

Lama, W. B. (2000) 'Community-based tourism for conservation and women's development'. In P. Godde, M. Price and F. M. Zimmermann (eds) *Tourism and development in mountain regions*. New York: CABI International, pp. 221–38

Lyon, T. (2003) '"Green" firms bearing gifts'. *Regulation*, 26(3), 36–40

Marcoux, J. (2004) 'Community stakeholder influence on corporate environmental strategy at Whistler, BC' (Research Paper No. 362). Unpublished Master's thesis, Simon Fraser University, British Columbia

Moore, J. (2001) 'Frankenfood or doubly green revolution: Europe vs America on the GMO debate'. In A. H. Teich, S. D. Nelson and S. J. Lita (eds) *AAAs science and technology yearbook*. Washington, DC: American Association for the Advancement of Science, pp. 173–80

Moore, S., Williams, P. W. and Gill, A. (2006) 'Finding a pad in paradise: Amenity migration's effects on Whistler, British Columbia'. In L. A. G. Moss (ed.) *The amenity migrants: Seeking and sustaining mountains and their cultures*. Wallingford: CABI International, pp. 135–47

Murphy, D. E. and Bendell, J. (1997) *In the company of partners: Business, environmental groups and sustainable development post-Rio.* Bristol: Policy Press

Murphy, P. E. and Murphy, A. E. (2004) *Strategic management for tourism communities: Bridging the gap.* Clevedon: Channel View Publications

Nattrass, B. and Altamore, M. (2003) *Dancing With the Tiger: Learning Sustainability by Natural Step.* Gabriola Island, BC: New Society Publishers

Neale, A. (1997) Organisational learning in contested environments: Lessons from Brent Spar'. *Business Strategy and the Environment,* 6(2), 93–103

Norcliffe, G. (2001) 'Canada in the world'. *Canadian Geographer,* 45(1), 14–30

NSAA (2000) *Sustainable slopes: The environmental charter for ski areas.* Lakewood, CO: National Ski Areas Association

Parker, C. (2002) *The open corporation: Effective self-regulation and democracy.* Cambridge: Cambridge University Press

Porter, M. E. and van der Linde, C. (1995) 'Green and competitive: Ending the stalemate'. *Harvard Business Review,* 73(5), 120–34

Prahalad, C. K. and Hamel, G. (1990) 'The core competence of the corporation'. *Harvard Business Review,* 68(3), 79–91

RMOW (2002) *Whistler 2002, Vol. 1: Charting a course for the future.* Whistler, BC: Resort Municipality of Whistler

—— (2004) *Whistler 2020: Moving toward a sustainable future.* Whistler, BC: Resort Municipality of Whistler

Robson, J. and Robson, I. (1996) 'From shareholders to stakeholders: Critical issues for tourism marketers'. *Tourism Management,* 17(7), 533–40

Rondinelli, D. A. and Berry, M. A. (2000) 'Environmental citizenship in multinational corporations: Social responsibility and sustainable development'. *European Management Journal,* 18(1), 70–84

Rothman, H. K. (1998) *Devil's bargains, tourism in the twentieth-century American West.* Laurence, KS: University Press of Kansas

Scholzman, K. and Tierney, J. (1986) *Organized interests and American democracy.* New York: Harper and Row

Svendsen, A. (1998) *The stakeholder strategy: Profiting from collaborative business relationships.* San Francisco, CA: Berrett-Koehler

Svendsen, A., Boutilier, R., Abbott, R. and Wheeler, D. (2002) *Measuring the business value of stakeholder relationships.* Burnaby, BC: Centre for Innovation in Management, Simon Fraser University

Todd, S. E. and Williams, P. W. (1996) 'From white to green: A proposed environmental management system framework for ski areas'. *Journal of Sustainable Tourism,* 4(3), 147–73

van Yoder, S. (2001) 'Beware of the coming corporate backlash'. *Industry Week,* 250(5), 38–42

Wernerfelt, B. (1984) 'A resource-based view of the firm'. *Strategic Management Journal,* 5(2), 171–80

Williams, P. W. and Gill, A. (2004) 'Addressing carrying capacity issues in tourism destinations through growth management'. In W. Theobald (ed.) *Global tourism.* London: Elsevier, pp. 194–212

Williams, P. W., Gill, A. and Ponsford, I. (2007) 'Corporate social responsibility at tourism destinations: Toward a "social licence to operate"'. *Tourism Review International: An Interdisciplinary Journal,* 11(2), 133–44

Williams, P. W., Penrose, R. and Hawkes, S. (1998) 'Shared decision-making in tourism land use planning'. *Annals of Tourism Research,* 25(4), 860–89

Wright, M. S. (1998) *Factors motivating proactive health and safety management* (Research Report No. 179/1998). London: Health and Safety Executive

Xu, N. (2004) 'The changing nature of corporate-environmental non-governmental organization relationships: A Whistler case study' (Research Paper No. 358). Unpublished Master's thesis, Simon Fraser University, British Columbia

14

A consensus-building approach for optimizing tourism as a sustainable development strategy

The case of the tourism policy forum

Donald E. Hawkins, Sheryl Marie Elliott

You can't manage knowledge, but you can create an environment where knowledge flows easily. For me, it's less important to capture all of the knowledge we have and it's more important to be connected to the people who have the knowledge.

(Parcell, 2005, p. 727)

Introduction

As one of the largest global industries and employers, tourism has a significant role in the economies of developed and developing countries alike. It is increasingly an important development strategy for addressing poverty reduction, economic growth, biodiversity, and conservation, and, specifically, the United Nation's Millennium Development Goals (MDGs) (UN, 2000).[1] According to the World Bank's "World Development Indicators" 2002 report, more than 70 percent of the world's poorest countries rely on tourism as a key economic growth engine (World Bank, 2002). The WTTC reported a 154 percent growth in tourism absolute earnings for the least developed countries (LDCs) during the period 1990 to 2000, and a 74.8 percent growth in international tourist arrivals for those countries during the same period (UNWTO, 2002).

Acknowledging this reality, development assistance projects are increasingly using tourism as a means of fostering sustainable development. However, there is a scarcity of information concerning appropriate engagement levels for development assistance in efforts to enhance tourism revenues for developing economies. For many years tourism and its contribution to the global economy remained ill-defined for the general population, and often not well understood even by those in the industry, including policymakers. In a survey conducted by the World Travel and Tourism Council in 1991, 150 policymakers in 14 countries were asked to rate industries according to their perceived importance to the world economy. Among 13 world industries, tourism was rated near the bottom, as 11th in importance. When the study was repeated the following year, tourism fared somewhat better, rising to number eight in perceived economic importance (WTTC, 1992). There are also difficulties in balancing the public sector role while maintaining a competitive private sector environment, which determines, in part, whether or not benefits from tourism will actually reach the poor host communities who are at the front line of receiving tourists (Milne and Ateljevic, 2001).

Development assistance for tourism has but a short history of 30 to 40 years. In most countries, tourism continues to be an ongoing social, economic and environmental challenge. With nearly 50 bilateral and multilateral donor agencies involved in development assistance for tourism, the logistical challenges of communication and cooperation are significant, due to language differences and differing investment strategies and approaches to tourism development. At the same time, improved information communication technologies (ICT) have emerged in the past two decades, particularly the Internet and the world wide web (WWW), to create greater efficiency in the global sharing of knowledge and knowledge management (KM). However, harnessing ICT and global information inputs requires a systematic KM approach whereby information and knowledge can be equitably communicated and shared, leading to the generation and implementation of policies and strategies for optimizing tourism growth in the developing countries of the world.

This study presents the case of the 2004 UN World Tourism Organization (UNWTO) Tourism Policy Forum, held at George Washington University in Washington, DC, where ICT facilitated the consensus building approach that was used for constructing a knowledge management network among development assistance donors and recipients, for the purpose of improving tourism's contribution to sustainable development goals. The consensus building approach is presented in Figure 14.1.

The consensus building approach was based on assumptions that there is a need for:

- more structured coordination among all development assistance partners working in this arena, particularly at the regional and national levels;
- benchmarking and learning from best practices across regions and sectors concerned with tourism and sustainable development;
- common guidelines and instruments to assist with the implementation and evaluation of projects and programs that use tourism as a tool for sustainable development.

The general assumption of the consensus building approach developed for the Tourism Policy Forum is that sustainable forms of tourism development can best be achieved through the KM process whereby research and intellectual property can help tourism enterprises and destinations achieve new capabilities that assure their long term viability and success. The construct behind KM, which was introduced into business literature in the 1990s, is that individuals should be encouraged to share ideas and knowledge to create value-added products and services (Ruhanen and Cooper, 2004). A KM framework encourages organizations to capitalize on their intellectual assets (e.g. employee skills, or an organization's dynamic capabilities) as opposed to traditional commodity assets and physical goods (e.g. oil, gas, minerals, factories). Nielson (2005, p. 5) suggests that the shift towards KM frameworks occurred in the twentieth century when "we made a transition from a matter-based economy to a knowledge-based economy, where most of a firm's value is embedded in knowledge assets." In defining new applications of knowledge management, Spender (2005, p. 102) contends that

> KM is about identifying as wide a range of knowledge assets as possible—be they forms of knowledge, or knowing, or proficient practice at the individual, group, organizational, cluster, industry, region or national level—and bringing them into our theorizing about maximizing efficiency, profit, or market power.

A Consensus Building Approach for Optimizing Tourism's Potential as a
Sustainable Development Strategy in Developing Countries: The Case of the WTO Tourism Policy Forum

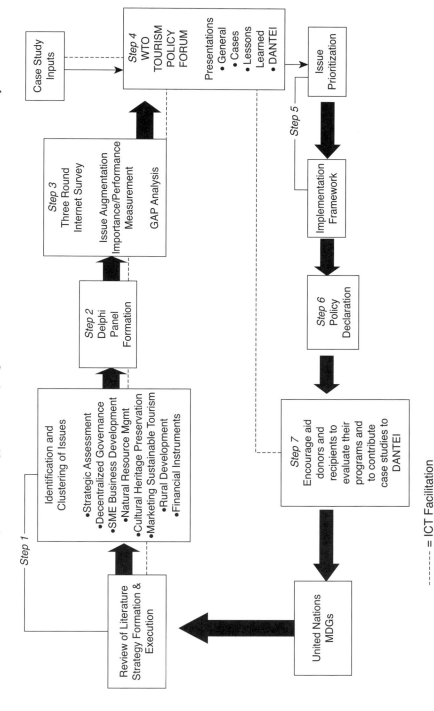

Figure 14.1   Tourism policy forum consensus building approach

Levy (2005, p. 65) describes such KM processes as a "convergence of mental technologies along with network technologies designed to leverage the bench strength of an organization's human capital." The most important development in information communication (IC) network technologies facilitating KM has obviously been the Internet and the world wide web. In most instances of KM approaches, organizations are involved with both explicit and tacit knowledge flows. Nielsen (2005) describes explicit knowledge as knowledge that can be transmitted through symbols and language, whereas tacit knowledge is knowledge that is intuitive.

Ruhanen and Cooper (2004) argue that the tourism sector has largely not benefited from KM approaches due to the fact that the sector is comprised for the most part of small to medium-sized enterprises who do not have the time or interest in research. They also maintain that tourism organizations have not embraced KM because these organizations have been largely service- and product-based. They propose a "knowledge value chain" to assist the sector in capitalizing its intellectual assets. This value chain includes four steps:

1. Determine the strategic need for knowledge.
2. Determine the knowledge gap between the knowledge needed and that available.
3. Narrow the knowledge gap by developing new knowledge.
4. Diffuse and apply available knowledge to stakeholders through commercialization processes.

Frechtling (2004) argues that two more steps are needed:

5. Stakeholder appreciation of knowledge to achieve objectives.
6. Feedback on success in achieving objectives.

Frechtling's research concludes that there is little or no research on knowledge transfer between researchers and "salient stakeholder groups" (private, public, and nonprofit sector tourism organizations). His study concluded that there was little transfer of knowledge between tourism research "generators" and tourism practitioners.

As development agencies are increasingly engaged in sustainable forms of tourism development, due to increased demand from developing countries for tourism-related lending and advice, the need for information, knowledge gathering and sharing is particularly critical. At the same time, literature continues to question the effectiveness of donor aid projects. In examining "History, independence and aid in Lesotho" the Near East Foundation summarized, "The bones of failed aid projects litter Lesotho, just as they do most of sub-Saharan Africa" (Near East Foundation, 1998, p. 14). A regional sub-Saharan scholar, Stephen Gill, suggests that foreign experts and local bureaucracies are the problem. He states that, although these groups may have good plans and intentions, "the crucial element of accountability and feed-back from communities affected by such projects is often lacking" (Gill, 1993, p. 77). He argues that what is needed is a "better balance of aid, local participation, and control...which actually empowers people, institutions or communities to improve their standard of living without creating long-term dependency on donors" (ibid.). In *Ills of Aid*, Reusse (2002) also argues that aid agencies are not accountable and essentially detached from taxpayer scrutiny from the country providing the aid.

Thus, the design of the consensus building approach of the Tourism Policy Forum was to create an environment whereby knowledge can easily flow, whereby donor aid accountability systems and reviews can be integrated, and whereby a system of connections among people who have and need knowledge can be accessed. The objective of such a consensus building approach, incorporating a knowledge management framework, was to assist developing countries in achieving the Millennium Development Goals (MDGs) set forth by the United Nations,

Table 14.1 Knowledge management framework and the consensus building approach of the Tourism Policy Forum

Steps	TPF	Cooper and Ruhanen	Frechtling
Step 1	Research and Review of Literature Strategy Formulation and Identification and Clustering of Issues	Determine the strategic need for knowledge	
Step 2	Delphi Panel Formation		
Step 3	Issue Augmentation (Importance/ Performance Measurement Gap Analysis	Determine the knowledge gap between the knowledge needed and that available	
Step 4	Tourism Policy Forum (Case study inputs, presentations, lessons learned, DANTEI)	Narrow the knowledge gap by	
Step 5	Issue Prioritization Implementation Framework	developing new knowledge	
Step 6	Policy Declaration	Diffuse and apply available knowledge to stakeholders through commercialization processes	Stakeholder applications of knowledge to achieve objectives
Step 7	Future Actions (Encourage aid donors and recipients to evaluate their programs and contribute case studies to DANTEI) United Nations MDGs (poverty reduction, environmental sustainability, global partnership for development)		Feedback on success in achieving objectives

and in particular, goals one, seven and eight: eradicate extreme poverty and hunger; ensure environmental sustainability; and develop a global partnership for development.

The seven–step consensus building approach for the Tourism Policy Forum (see Table 14.1) incorporated the stages of the "knowledge value chain" suggested by Rhuhanan and Cooper (2004) with the additional two suggested by Frechtling (2004). The KM framework was created to facilitate the transformation of knowledge into capabilities and actionable plans.

Methodology and consensus building approach

The consensus building approach utilized established qualitative research methodologies in the seven-step process including content analysis (for the initial clustering of issues), Delphi panel (for prioritizing issues in terms of importance/performance measurement for GAP analysis), and nominal group process (NGP) techniques (for further issue distillation and prioritization, formulation of recommendations, and the development of an implementation framework).

Central to the focus of the Tourism Policy Forum is that there are shortfalls (gaps) across a spectrum of issues, in terms of relative importance, as well as the ability (i.e. performance) of the aid donor or recipient organization to meet the challenge of addressing a particular issue. The consensus building approach used for the Tourism Policy Forum incorporated seven research steps.

Step 1: Review of literature and identification of themes

A review of the current discussions in literature and an examination of development agencies' funding of tourism projects in LDCs was first conducted to identify the primary themes or strategic directions concerned with tourism development. The eight themes that emerged from this review and examination included:

- strategic assessment, planning, and implementation;
- decentralized government and capacity building;
- small and medium-sized enterprise development and competitiveness;
- natural resource and protected area management;
- cultural heritage preservation;
- marketing sustainable tourism products;
- rural development; and
- financial instruments and enabling environments.

Step 2: Expert panel and the Delphi method

The consensus model approach then utilized a research process, the Delphi method, which was first developed by the Rand Corporation in 1963 to predict, through a consensus of experts, what places in the United States might become atomic bomb targets of the Soviets (Dalkey and Helmer, 1963; Helmer, 1966). The Delphi process was later expanded for use in other disciplines, including medical and social science research. The Delphi is a qualitative research method, which involves "structuring a group communication process so that the process is effective in allowing a group of individuals, as a whole, to deal with a complex problem" (Linstone and Turoff, 1975, p. 3). It involves a panel of experts, not a random sample of respondents (population survey). Delphi studies involve iterative rounds, usually incorporating a semantic differential scale, with the group opinion fed back to the panelists in each subsequent round in the form of the range and distribution of the responses (quartile rankings, means, modes, etc.). Panelists are asked to re-evaluate their previous response in iterative rounds, considering the group opinion, and then again respond to the same problem statements or issues as well as new ones suggested by panelists (Moutinho and Witt, 1995). One of the long considered disadvantages of the Delphi is panel member attrition in the iterative survey rounds advance. In recent years, ICT via the Internet has greatly compensated for this drawback and the Delphi method is now used in a diverse range of fields and applications. An Internet search revealed over 745,000 links. The Internet has greatly facilitated a system of instant communication globally, and at a fraction of the cost when compared to older forms of ICT, such as postal mail, telephone, fax, etc.

For management purposes, the panel for this phase of the consensus building approach was set not to exceed 125 participants. In constituting the panel, geographic area and sector of expertise were considered, with members selected to reflect representative units, as shown in Table 14.2.

In the formation of the panel, the objective was not to achieve unit parity, but, in order to assure adequate representation at the geographic and sector level, it was considered essential to establish minimum population thresholds by using the acceptance minima shown in Figure 14.2.

In structuring the panel, thresholds for representation in the study, while imperfect and artificial, were designed to limit any region or sector from dominating the results of the survey. Thresholds were set to ensure that no category represented by the survey population would make up more than twice the average, nor less than half the average as indicated in the above equation. The threshold equation was developed for an earlier study that incorporated the Delphi process for the World Tourism Organization's Tedqual project (UNWTO, 1997).

Table 14.2 Expert panel

Expertise by region	Frequency	Percent
East Asia and the Pacific	13	10.7
Europe and Central Asia	13	10.7
Global	33	27.2
Latin America/Caribbean	21	17.4
Middle East and North Africa	10	8.3
South Asia	10	8.3
Sub-Saharan Africa	21	17.4
Total	**121**	**100**

Expertise by sector		
Development Agency	25	20.7
Education	33	27.3
Government	13	10.7
NGO	15	12.4
Private Sector	35	28.9
Total	**121**	**100**

Step 3: Gap analysis and importance/performance measurement

The design plan for this study included a three-round online consensus building survey of experts utilizing an importance/performance measurement tool to identify issues and issue shortfalls (gaps). Importance/performance analysis was introduced by Martilla and James (1977) as a method for understanding customer satisfaction as a function of both expectations related to salient attributes ("importance") and judgments about their performance ("performance") (Magal and Levenburg, 2005). Importance/performance literature falls into two areas: research that deals with the identification of performance gaps (generally measured as performance minus importance); and research that involves the plotting of mean ratings on importance and performance in a two-dimensional grid (termed the "Action Grid" by Crompton and Duray, 1985) to produce a four-quadrant matrix that identifies areas needing improvement, as well as areas of effective performance (Graf et al., 1992; Skok et al., 2001).

For Sectors

$$M\frac{(TP)}{TS} = .50\frac{(121)}{5} = 12.0 = \mathbf{12}$$

Geographic Area

$$M\frac{(TP)}{TR} = .50\frac{(121)}{6} = 10.0 = \mathbf{10}$$

Sectors	**Geographic Area**
M=Minimum set point (.50)	M=Minimum set point (.50)
TP=Total Number on Panel	TP=Total Number on Panel
TS=Total Number of Sectors	TR=Total Number of Geographic Areas

Figure 14.2 Panel acceptance minima
Source: UNWTO, 1997

The consensus building approach used in the Tourism Policy Forum produced qualitative data, which could then serve as an initial step in identifying issues. Being able to conduct the multiple-round survey online was considered an important feature of this study. The Internet provided an efficient means whereby such a study could involve the participation of individuals throughout the world, be completed within a relatively short period, then tabulate and report the results of each survey round back to the panelists through a website.

In the first round of the survey, panelists were presented with a set of issues organized according to the Tourism Policy Forum's eight strategic themes. Listed below each theme were three issues that emerged from the literature review as the important "need areas" for sustainable development through tourism in developing countries. The panelists were requested to rate the issues according to the importance (of the need area) in fulfilling the promise of tourism's potential as a sustainable development strategy in developing countries. Next, they were asked to rate the issue statement based on the performance capacity of aid donors and developing country recipients to meet the challenge of addressing the identified issues (1 being the lowest performance and 10 the highest performance).

The panelists were also given the opportunity to add any issue or "need area" they would like to bring to the survey panel's attention for judgment in the next round. If panelists did not feel qualified to judge a particular issue, they were instructed simply to select "no opinion." 121 individuals agreed to serve on the Tourism Policy Forum panel. While Delphi surveys typically encounter the problem of participant drop-off in subsequent panel rounds, the opposite occurred in this online application of the Delphi. It appeared that the immediate reporting of each round's results to all participants by email (which directed participants to the next survey round on a website) stimulated interest, resulting in greater participation rates for each survey round. Increased participation with each round also suggests that participants found the online survey efficient and easy to use. In the first survey round, 41 percent of the Delphi panel participants responded.

In the second round, the results were reported back to the panelists. Means were calculated for each issue in terms of the issue's importance, as well as aid donor or aid recipient performance in meeting that issue's challenge. The issues were rated according to the gap, the greatest difference in means (i.e. where importance would be considered highest and performance considered poorest). Panelists' "write-in" issues from the first round were included for consideration in the second survey round. Annex 1 contains a listing of the priority issues identified for each strategic theme. In the second survey round, 50 percent of the Delphi panel participants responded.

In the third round, the three top-rated issues in each theme area, again rated according to the greatest gap, were reported back to the panelists. In this final round, the panelists were asked to make recommendations or suggest solutions for closing the gap for each issue. Participants in the Tourism Policy Forum were also invited to submit recommendations addressing the identified issues. In the third survey round, 94 percent of the Delphi panel participants responded.

Thus, the consensus building approach for the Tourism Policy Forum involved a combination of qualitative assessment techniques including the Delphi panel and iterative rounds of polling, the importance/performance analysis, and the gap measurement methodological stream of the importance/performance analysis.

The 24 issues that panelists were asked to rate in the first round of the survey grew to 67 issues to be rated in the second round. In the third and final round of the survey, the top 25 issues that emerged from panelists' polling were presented for consideration and recommended solutions. From this round, 15 to 20 recommendations per issue were identified and vetted by a committee, who condensed duplicated statements. In the end, there were 10 to 12

Table 14.3 Tourism policy forum objectives

Tourism policy forum objectives
1. Exchange views with bilateral & multilateral donor organizations, as well as representative recipients.
2. Discuss sustainable tourism development policies in relation to the MDGs.
3. Report on WTO general initiatives in relation to sustainable tourism and development and particularly the WTO ST-EP program to bring sustainable tourism development into the service of poverty elimination.
4. Share promising practices for sustainable development and consider lessons learned from exemplary tourism projects supported by donors.
5. Formulate recommendations for utilizing tourism as a sustainable development tool for achieving MDG outcomes.

recommendations per theme area that would be available for live working group discussion and debate when the Tourism Policy Forum convened in Washington, DC, in October 2004. Recommendations generated from the survey became a starting point for the more detailed assessment process that would take place at the Tourism Policy Forum.

Step 4: Tourism Policy Forum

The purpose of the 2004 Tourism Policy Forum was to convene educators, knowledge management experts and other informed professionals, representative government policymakers, and business leaders to focus on the critical policy issues facing global tourism and to offer recommendations for the future. The objectives of the Forum are listed in Table 14.3.

The Forum attracted 200 participants and more than 200 observers from 52 countries, representing tourism ministries, development assistance agencies, UNWTO and other UN organizations, education institutions, NGOs, and private businesses. The three-day Forum program included keynote addresses, panel discussions, the presentation of case studies, and special workgroup sessions. Representatives from the Inter-American Development Bank, the World Bank Group, the United States Agency for International Development (USAID), and UNWTO gave keynote presentations. The Forum also included panel discussions by ministers of tourism from South Africa, Jordan, Nicaragua, Honduras, Lesotho and Andorra, as well as panel discussions of bilateral donors (SNV, GTZ, USAID and CIDA, among others). Case study presentations organized for each of the eight strategic themes produced a set of challenges and lessons learned that later served to stimulate thinking in the concurrent workgroup sessions. During those sessions, participants were asked to prioritize the issues and recommendations, and develop an action plan for implementing the recommendations deemed most important.

Step 5: Issue prioritization, recommendations and implementation framework

The online survey and issue identification process in steps 2 and 3 provided the Tourism Policy Forum participants a platform for discussion within the eight established thematic areas. Specialized working group sessions were conducted during the Forum for formulating concrete recommendations and implementation steps. The first half of each session was dedicated to case study presentations made by five or six experts in the session theme area. The intent of these presentations was to provide ideas and lessons learned for the working group discussions that took place during the second half of the session, with participants divided into three groups corresponding to the three priority issues generated through the consensus building survey. Each working group was presented with 10 to 12 recommendations related to a priority issue generated through the survey, and asked to consider them as written, amend them, adapt them, or add new ones. Each group then voted to determine the two or three most important recommendations, and, finally, the group was asked to develop an implementation framework that covered *what* mechanisms were to be used, *how* they would be accomplished and by *whom*. The group's findings were captured on flip charts and presented to all Forum participants during morning and afternoon plenary sessions.

As an illustration of results generated from this approach, one theme area is presented: decentralized governance and capacity building. Under this theme, the following three issues were identified through the survey process:

- local capacity to plan, monitor and regulate tourism development in the evolving decentralization policies of LDCs;
- adequate budget allocations from central government;
- communication and collaboration between central and local government planning and budgeting cycles.

For one such issue, "Adequate budget allocations from central government," recommendations generated through the survey are listed in Table 14.4 and those added by the working groups at the Tourism Policy Forum are listed in Table 14.5.

Table 14.4 Adequate budget allocations from central government 1

Adequate budget allocations from central government
Recommendations Generated Through Survey Process
(Note: Highest priority recommendations listed in Bold Face)

1 **Link budgets to clear strategies, plans and envisaged outcomes. Benchmarking, evaluation and monitoring should be integral. Central government should be provided with tangible results of the impacts of their investment in tourism. This will help them justify their budget allocations to their constituencies and also provide them with a frame of reference for future budget allocations.**
2 **Build strong economic arguments for government support and government investment in tourism. Tourism satellite accounts, employment data and regional development theory are all important components of this, but also political support requires strong advocacy groups to undertake the lobbying.**
3 Prioritize budgets and focus on areas/aspects of tourism with greatest potential.
4 Encourage collaborative relationships by tourism ministries with other departments (culture, sport, natural resources, agriculture, education).
5 Create new ways for self-sufficiency, such as in-kind & in-cash awards.
6 Make allocations transparent to the public from the bidding process to evaluations.
7 Publish budget information on relevant websites.
8 Implement appropriate cost recovery mechanisms so as to provide the necessary capital to expand, operate, and maintain infrastructure. Promote private sector participation in infrastructure–PPI.
9 Explore partnering with tourism enterprises to extend private sewage and waste and treatment facilities, such as the facilities at larger hotels, to local communities.
10 Increase the awareness of key indicators of the importance of tourism at public and political levels.
11 **Measure the local economic impact of tourism and use results as a tool for strategic planning, budgeting and resource allocations.**

Table 14.5 Adequate budget allocations from central government 2

Adequate budget allocations from central government
Recommendations Added by Working Group
(Note: Highest priority recommendations listed in Bold Face)

12 **Use Government budgets to support local communities, develop structures, build capacity, facilitate partnerships/agreements between stakeholders (PPI's).**

13 Develop budgets that have finance mechanisms and money (various sources).

14 **Build strong economic arguments for government support and government investment in tourism. Tourism satellite accounts, employment data and regional development theory are all important components of this, but also political support requires strong advocacy groups to undertake the lobbying.**

Working groups then developed an implementation framework for each of the prioritized recommendations, as illustrated in Table 14.6.

The complete set of issues, recommendations, and implementation framework results are available in the Tourism Policy Forum section of the DANTEI website (http://www.dantei.org).

Step 6: Policy declaration

The culminating activity of the Forum was the "Washington Declaration on Tourism as a Sustainable Development Strategy." This was based upon reports submitted by reporters at each session to the Declaration Committee Chair, Professor Pauline Sheldon from the University of Hawaii at Manoa. During the Forum, the resolution was drafted to reflect the consensus of the participants on conclusions and recommendations focused on the role of tourism in sustainable development. At the final session, the draft declaration was circulated to the participants and then discussed. Based upon the points raised, the Declaration was revised in final form. It was forwarded to the Secretary General of the UNWTO for consideration and included in the final proceedings of the Tourism Policy Forum, published by UNWTO in early 2005.

Set forth in this document were the following agreed resolutions:

* To build partnerships of equal opportunity and fair representation within destinations, and to strengthen their leadership;

Table 14.6 Adequate budget allocations from central government 3

Build strong economic arguments for government support and government investment in tourism. Tourism satellite accounts, employment data and regional development theory are all important components of this, but also political support requires strong advocacy groups to undertake the lobbying.	
What?	• Measurement of local economic impact of tourism and use results as a tool for strategic planning, budgeting and resource allocations).
	• Private sector support to make the argument.
	• Independent tourism research unit with sub regional levels (national/local).
How?	• Links to various initiatives including role of advocacy, universities, private sector, civil society.
	• Must be self sustaining.
	• Dissemination between ministries and universities (2 way).
Who?	• Local universities with connections to international support /expertise.

- To engender local community awareness of the tourism planning process and its benefits;
- To foster buy-in for the concept of sustainability by all sectors including the sharing of guidelines and good practices;
- To delegate the authority for decision-making to the appropriate community level and build capacity there, and empower local development authorities;
- To encourage and facilitate brand awareness and a collective image for a destination community;
- To recognize the uniqueness of the business perspective as different from that of the public sector and to communicate effectively in business language;
- To develop cross-sectoral demonstration projects that illustrate linkages, inter-relationships and working partnerships;
- To call upon governments, bi-lateral and multi-lateral institutions to facilitate access to capital of all kinds, and to provide guidance, training and support on how to access such funding;
- To develop land-use policies through a participatory process, and to provide policy incentives for private land owners;
- To enhance communication and coordination between agencies including the use of advanced information communication technologies;
- To develop educational programs directed to tourism policy stakeholders including local communities to promote the understanding of cultural/heritage resources, and the need for preservation and social responsibilities;
- To encourage the development of a regional network of researchers, practitioners and donor agencies for sustainable tourism development.

Step 7: Encourage aid donors and recipients to evaluate programs and contribute to DANTEI

Through the consensus building approach it was evident that all of the donor agencies shared the common ground of currently being unable to accurately define their engagement with the tourism sector in terms of financial commitment or knowledge of tourism projects' past successes and failures. There was agreement that an internal auditing of tourism projects by individual agencies would be a useful next step (considering this was being done by the World Bank and USAID already). While some of these issues are internal, indicators of success or failure and best practice could be benchmarked internationally for everyone's benefit.

An analysis of the case studies presented at the Forum showed a total of 60 different and specific challenges and 74 lessons learned in the eight theme areas. The special workgroup sessions produced more than 20 implementation steps (frameworks) for mitigating the issues where there was the greatest gap in the importance and performance index measurement. The consensus building approach brought various stakeholder groups together on a common global stage, all facilitated by advances in ICT, and all committed to working towards a better common future.

One of the specific outcomes of the Tourism Policy Forum process was the establishment of the DANTEI (Development Assistance Network for Tourism Enterprise and Investment) website. At the Forum, UNWTO and George Washington University (GWU), sponsors of the Tourism Policy Forum, demonstrated a web-based platform (www.dantei.org), developed to share information and knowledge about best practices, tools, and guidelines for tourism directed toward sustainable development outcomes.

The website was developed to help potential development assistance recipients (particularly government and civil society) access funding resources, and was also used to support the Tourism Policy Forum by showcasing the presentations and case studies. DANTEI could conceivably expand to provide a platform on which development agencies could share information, and a portal through which they could access capacity building training programs or useful tools and post best practices/lessons learned from project cases.

Accessible information about tourism and sustainable development is currently scattered over 150 websites, development assistance agency databases, and hundreds of books and publications. There is no neutral platform to filter, search for, or add to case studies, best practices, and information on donor-funded tourism projects, their outcomes, benefits, or costs. Existing sites tend to focus on the promotion of specific agendas, for example linking tourism to objectives such as biodiversity conservation, small business development, cultural heritage preservation.

Conclusion

The consensus building approach underpinning the Tourism Policy Forum facilitated the building of knowledge networks – government, private sector, civil society, etc. – to collaborate, not compete, and to leverage strengths and insights. The KM approach incorporated the latest ICT technologies (the Internet, websites, email, list servers, etc.) together with older forms of ICT (conferences, presentations, workgroups, and nominal group process techniques) to bring together disparate groups and interests, in order to find solutions and illuminate common issues. The approach utilized the Internet and recent developments in ICT to coalesce global thinking on the most salient issues and provided a live forum (UNWTO Tourism Policy Forum) to:

- review the identified issues;
- validate and augment recommendations addressing the issues; and
- devise mechanisms that can lead to actionable solutions.

The process focused on the future of tourism as a significant contributor to the fulfilment of the United Nations Millennium Development Goals (MDGs). One outcome of this integrated approach is a searchable interactive database driven website, Development Assistance Network for Tourism Enhancement and Investment (DANTEI), that addresses the tourism-relevant information needs of government, NGO, and university aid recipients as well as researchers, investors, and bilateral or multilateral agencies engaged in the development assistance process.

While much success is deemed to have come about from the consensus building approach, forums in the future must address some of the problems that integrative ICT alone cannot solve. For example, problems still remain as to how to identify the right "experts" to be on the issue identification Delphi panel, how to keep even a higher percentage of "expert" panellists motivated, engaged and responding in all polling rounds, and how to apply the results from such a collaborative research endeavor.

For the most part, though, a KM framework facilitated by ICT has enabled developing countries and donor assistance organizations to take a better look at how tourism can be an effective strategy for sustainable development that will contribute to the realization of MDGs. The consensus building approach presented in this chapter is a step in that direction.

Annex 1

Tourism Policy Forum themes and issues identified through the survey

Decentralized governance and capacity building

Issues

1. Local capacity to plan, monitor and regulate tourism development.
2. Adequate budget allocations from central government.
3. Communication and collaboration between central and local government planning and budgeting cycles.

Rural development

Issues

4. Realistic assessments of opportunities undertaken.
5. Local communities included in rural tourism planning decisions.
6. Linkages with local productive sectors (e.g. agriculture, co-ops, artisans, chambers of commerce) developed.

SME (small and medium-sized enterprises) development and competitiveness

Issues

7. Cooperation and support mechanisms among SMEs (e.g. business councils, shared resources, collective marketing strategies).
8. Entrepreneurship and investment mentoring.
9. Development of diagnostic tools, such as value chain analysis, for defining limiting factors (e.g. quality standards, access to markets and access to finance).

Natural resource and protected area management

Issues

10. Better coordination between agencies responsible for natural resources management and tourism development.
11. Community awareness of the value of natural resources to long-term quality of living.
12. Flexibility in conservation financing and management including participation of private sector, NGOs and communities.
13. Policy incentives for private landowners to contribute to natural resource protection (e.g. conservation easements, conservancies, transfer development rights).

Cultural heritage preservation

Issues

14. Cultural authenticity needs to be viewed as a competitive advantage.

15. Stronger linkages between the private sector and cultural heritage preservation.
16. Creative funding of cultural heritage preservation (e.g, certification programs before accessing public money).

Foreign direct investment and enabling environments

Issues

17. Sharing of profits back to the community or region of production.
18. Strong sustainable tourism policies to guide FDI.
19. Policy reforms more effectively addressed to support tourism development.

Strategic assessment, planning and implementation

Issues

20. Effective public, private and civil society partnerships to enhance the effectiveness of tourism planning and implementation.
21. Available impact research data for decision-making, e.g. environmental impact assessment data, cultural impact assessment data, economic indicators and trends.
22. Strategic planning linked to realistic implementation expectations and actions.

Market access and export development

Issues

23. Provision of market research, realistic targets, and distribution channels for tourism products and services.
24. Technical capacity training for indigenous access to markets.
25. Regional collaboration to create greater marketing clout.

Note

1 On September 8, 2000 the United Nations General Assembly (UNGA) adopted a resolution that set forth the UN's MDGs. In essence these are eight goals that deal with poverty reduction, universal primary education, gender equality, infant mortality reduction, maternal health, disease prevention (particularly HIV), environmental sustainability, and global partnerships for development.

References

Crompton, J. L. and Duray, N. A. (1985) 'An investigation of the relative efficacy of four alternative approaches to importance performance analysis'. *Journal of the Academy of Marketing Science*, 13(4), 69–80

Dalkey, N. and Helmer, O. (1963) 'An experimental application of the Delphi Method for the use of experts'. *Management Science*, 9(3), 529–53

Frechtling, D. C. (2004) 'Assessment of tourism/hospitality journal's role in knowledge transfer: An exploratory study'. *Journal of Travel Research,* 43(2), 100–107

Gill, S. J. (1993) *A short history of Lesotho from the Late Stone Age until the 1993 elections*. Morija, Lesotho: Morija Museum and Archives

Graf, L. A., Hemmasi, M. and Nielsen, W. (1992) 'Importance-satisfaction analysis: A diagnostic tool for organizational change'. *Leadership and Organization Development Journal*, 13(6), 8–12

Helmer, O. (1966) *Social technology*. New York: Basic Books

Levy, J. (2005) 'The fourth revolution'. *T+D*, 59(6), 64–5

Linstone, H. A. and Turoff, M. (1975) *The Delphi Method: Techniques and applications*. Reading, MA: Addison-Wesley Publishing Company

Magal, S. R. and Levenburg, N. M. (2005) 'Using importance-performance analysis to evaluate e-business strategies among small businesses'. Proceedings of the 38th Hawaii International Conference on System Sciences. Retrieved 3 November 2011, from http://csdl.computer.org/comp/proceedings/hicss/2005/2268/07/22680176a.pdf

Martilla, J. A. and James, J. C. (1977) 'Importance-performance analysis'. *Journal of Marketing*, 41(1), 77–9

Milne, S. and Ateljevic, I. (2001) 'Tourism, economic development and the global-local nexus: Theory embracing complexity'. *Tourism Geographies*, 3(4), 369–93

Moutinho, L. and Witt, S. F. (1995) 'Forecasting the tourism environment using a consensus approach'. *Journal of Travel Research*, 33(4), 46–50

Near East Foundation (1998) 'History, independence and aid in Lesotho: Littered with the bones of failed projects'. Near East Foundation, 1 January. Retrieved 3 November 2011, from http://neareast.org/main/news/article_pr.aspx?id = 92

Nielsen, B. B. (2005) 'Strategic knowledge management research: Tracing the co-evolution of strategic management and knowledge management perspectives'. *Competitiveness Review*, 15(1), 1–13

Parcell, G. (2005) '"Learning to fly" in a world of information overload'. *Bulletin of the World Health Organization,* 83(10), 727–9

Reusse, E. (2002) *The ills of aid: An analysis of Third World development policies*. Chicago, IL: Chicago University Press

Ruhanen, L. and Cooper, C. (2004) 'Applying a knowledge management framework to tourism research'. *Tourism Recreation Research*, 29(1), 83–8

Skok, W., Kophamel, A. and Richardson, I. (2001) 'Diagnosing information systems success: Importance-performance maps in the health club industry'. *Information and Management*, 38(7), 409–19

Spender, J. D. (2005) 'Review article: An essay of the state of knowledge management'. *Prometheus*, 23(1), 101–16

UN (2000) *55/2. United Nations Millennium Declaration*. UN, 8 September. Retrieved 6 May 2005, from http://www.un.org/millennium/declaration/ares552e.htm

UNWTO (1997) *An introduction to TEDQUAL: A methodology for quality in tourism education and training*. Madrid: UN World Tourism Organization

—— (2002) *Tourism and poverty alleviation*. Madrid: UN World Tourism Organization

World Bank (2002) *World Development Indicators 2002*. Washington, DC: World Bank

WTTC (1992) *The travel and tourism industry perceptions of economic contribution*. London: World Travel and Tourism Council

15

Exploring social representations of tourism
Analysing drawings of tourism

Gianna Moscardo

Images are a central element of tourism. Tourism marketers spend much time and effort choosing destination images in order to entice potential visitors. Potential visitors spend much time and effort perusing destination images in order to choose a travel destination. Actual visitors spend time and effort finding and/or creating visual images to take home as personal souvenirs or symbols of achievement and status. At a more abstract level, images of tourism are at the core of government policies, business plans and community perceptions. Although the concept of 'image' has been explicitly used in the areas of destination choice and tourism marketing and is recognised in critical analyses of the representations of tourism destinations and their residents, its potential role in other aspects of tourism is less clearly presented and discussed. This chapter will report on an exploratory qualitative analysis of images of tourism based on drawings of tourism completed by advanced tourism management students. More specifically, it will argue that social representations theory offers some useful directions for improving our understanding of the role of images in tourism.

Analysing visual images in tourism

An examination of the tourism literature reveals the existence of two main themes in research on visual depictions or images. The first of these is the critical analysis of images used in postcards, guidebooks, brochures and maps with an emphasis on understanding their role in the social and cultural construction of various tourism representations. Typically this work is conducted within the areas of anthropology, sociology, geography and cultural studies. The second theme can be found in marketing research, often based implicitly on concepts from consumer psychology, into destination attractiveness, choice and evaluation. In this latter theme, the research focuses on individuals and their perceptions of visual images.

Visual images and tourism representations

This first theme in tourism research into visual images is centred on understanding the role that visual images play in the production and reinforcement of representations of tourist places and the people that inhabit them. These analyses are driven by critical analyses derived from semiotics, discursive analysis or some combination of both these approaches (Albers and James, 1988; Hall, 1997; Jenkins, 2003). In this tradition representations are seen as frameworks that combine narratives, concepts, ideologies and shared meanings about a destination or group of people. These shared meanings allow for communication within cultural and social groups (Hall, 1997). Representations direct tourist attention and behaviour, and reflect and reinforce existing power structures and dominant ideologies (Albers and James, 1988; Jenkins, 2003). The role of research is to deconstruct these representations and place them in their social, cultural, political and temporal context (Jenkins, 2003). In this tradition there have been studies of the images of various places and cultural groups as portrayed in postcards (Albers and James, 1988; Markwick, 2001; Mellinger, 1994), destination brochures (Ateljevic and Doorne, 2002; Echtner, 2002; Jenkins, 2003), guidebooks (Bhattacharyya, 1997) and maps (Hanna and Del Casino, 2003). These studies have concentrated their attention on how various ideologies and existing representations are presented in visual materials developed by destination marketers. These representations of destination communities have implications not just for the behaviour of tourists but also for how residents see themselves and how they perceive tourism and its social and cultural impacts (Ashworth, 2003; Moscardo and Pearce, 2003; Walsh et al., 2001).

These studies have all relied upon analyses of visual images selected by the researchers. More recent research has begun to explore the choices of visual images made by the tourists themselves with the use of a technique called visitor employed photography (VEP) (MacKay and Couldwell, 2004). VEP studies examine how tourists use, create and reproduce existing representations in their own travel photography (Jenkins, 2003; Markwell, 1997; Russell and Ankenman, 1996).

This type of research highlights the link between individuals and their social context and the shared negotiations that underpin the process of creating representations (Albers and James, 1988). Jenkins (2003) describes the circle of representation that is often cited in studies of tourist photography. In this circle marketers create destination images, visitors then seek the icons and contents of these images; once found the visitors photograph these icons, recreating the marketing images or representations and completing the circle. Jenkins goes on to argue that it is important not to forget the role that individuals can play in changing and developing these representations. In essence she argues that the circle of representation is more like a spiral where individual tourists anchor layers of additional symbolism based on their experiences to the existing central stereotypes or icons. In a similar fashion Markwick (2001) suggests that representations of destinations change partly as result of changing political and social circumstances at the destination, and partly in response to changes in tourists' expectations and motivations. Although research into tourism representations is primarily focused on the social level of analysis, there is recognition of the importance of a link between individuals and this social context.

Destination marketing research

By way of contrast, the second theme of tourism research based on visual images is almost exclusively concerned with the individual tourists and how they use and interpret visual images to develop their own destination images and make destination choices. In this research area, photographs are often used as the stimuli in studies designed to determine preferences for, and evaluations of, destinations (Fairweather and Swaffield, 2001; MacKay and Couldwell, 2004; MacKay and Fesenmaier, 1997; Naoi et al., 2006). The aim here is to improve the effectiveness of marketing efforts (Day et al., 2002). Although there has been debate over how to define destination images (Pike, 2002), most definitions suggest that these destination images are a type of attitude. In social psychology attitudes can be defined as cognitive representations or frameworks that organise information about a topic and contain an evaluative dimension and directions for behaviour (Olson and Zanna, 1993).

Social representations theory

Several authors have called for a broadening of research approaches to destination images (Kim and Richardson, 2003; Pike, 2002; Selby and Morgan, 1996) and others have suggested that the two traditions of research into visual images could be brought closer together by focusing on the interaction between the individual and social levels of analysis (Jenkins, 2003). One theoretical approach that may be able to achieve this connection between the social and the individual level of analysis of images is social representations theory. Social representations can be defined as

> mental constructs which guide us [and] define reality. The world is organized, understood and mediated through these basic cognitive units. Social representations consist of both concrete images and abstract concepts, organized around figurative nuclei which are a complex of images.
>
> *(based on Moscovici, as cited in Halfacree, 1993, p. 29)*

Social representations share many characteristics with both the concepts of tourism representations and destination images as attitudes. Specifically, social representations provide a framework for understanding and making sense of experiences and guiding behaviour (Fredline and Faulkner, 2000). According to Andriotis and Vaughan (2003, p. 173) social representations are a means for 'constructing and understanding social reality'. Social representations theory also shares common ground with critical analyses of tourism representations through the argument that representations are created through social interaction with the aim of assisting in social communication (Moscovici, 2001).

Two critical features distinguish social representations from the concepts of destination images and tourism representations. The first is that visual imagery is specifically placed as the central component of social representations, and not seen solely as a manifestation of a representation (Philogene and Deaux, 2001). The second feature is that much more detailed attention is given in social representations theory to the link between the individual and the social levels of analysis (ibid.).

Central role of visual imagery

According to Moscovici (2001) two important processes are central to the construction and operation of social representations: anchoring and objectification. Anchoring allows individuals and social groups to make sense of new and unfamiliar concepts by comparing them to existing categories and knowledge. In particular a new situation or concept is compared against existing prototypes or exemplars of a category (De Paolis, 1990). This process is then complemented by the operation of the second process – objectification. Through objectification an abstract and unfamiliar concept is made ordinary, simple and concrete by associating it with a visual image (Moscovici, 2001). In these two processes, then, visual depictions are central to the social representations.

Linking individual and social levels of analysis

A core part of social representations theory is the link between the individual and the social or collective. Social representations are generated from social interaction and then exist in their own right, repeated in media and in further social interactions between group members who share them. In turn social representations are adapted and incorporated into individual cognitive systems to assist in building social identities and to guide individual and group behaviour (Moscovici, 2001). Social groups vary in their cohesion and so Moscovici suggests that there are three levels or types of social representation:

- hegemonic representations that are widely shared and therefore relatively stable. These are most like the tourism representations discussed in previous sections;
- emancipated social representations that may be shared within subgroups but lack widespread acceptance and/or use;
- polemical representations that arise out of conflict between groups and typically represent alternative views or beliefs about a topic.

Social representations have been used in a wide variety of other areas including:

- experiences of consumption (Lunt and Livingstone, 1992);
- definitions of rural space (Halfacree, 1993);
- perceptions of risk (Joffe, 2003);
- ideas of profit (Moliner, 1995);
- attitudes and behaviours in relation to organ donations (Moloney and Walker, 2002);
- beliefs about rule breaking behaviours (Verkuyten et al., 1994);
- resident and tourist perceptions of wild animals (O'Rourke, 2000);
- perceptions and definitions of social class (Mahalingam, 2003);
- sex role stereotypes (Campbell and Muncer, 1994);
- beliefs about ethnic groups (Philogene, 1994);
- public responses to new technologies (Wagner et al., 2002); and
- attitudes towards user pays fees for access to natural settings (Lee and Pearce, 2002).

Using social representations theory in tourism

In tourism, social representations theory has already been used to analyse community attitudes towards and responses to tourism development (Andriotis and Vaughan, 2003; Fredline and Faulkner, 2000; Pearce et al., 1996; Yuksel et al., 1999). There is a link between community perceptions of tourism and the representations of destinations and their residents chosen and promoted by tourism marketers (Pritchard and Morgan, 2001). Figure 15.1 summarises the actual and potential roles of social representations theory in the analysis of how the three main groups of tourism participants make sense of, and respond to, tourism.

The three main groups of participants presented in Figure 15.1 are the tourists, the host communities and the organisations and individuals involved in the marketing and promotion of tourism. The intersection between each of the pairs of these groups creates an area for potential social representations. The intersection between marketers and tourists is where the current marketing research into destination images lies; the intersection between tourists and communities is where the research into tourism representations of destination and hosts is located; and the intersection between communities and marketers offers a new area of focus on social representations of tourism. It is important to distinguish between social representations of tourism and representations of destinations and hosts developed and perpetuated through tourism. Several of the critical analyses of tourism representations refer to Urry's (1990) concept of the 'tourist gaze' on destinations and hosts (Jenkins, 2003; MacKay and Couldwell, 2004). The model set out in

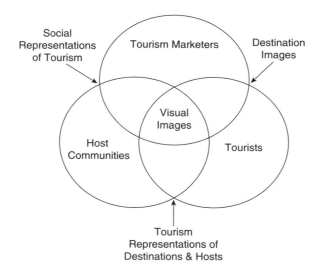

Figure 15.1   A preliminary social representations framework for tourism images

Figure 15.1 suggests that this idea could be extended to include a marketing gaze on tourists and communities, and a community gaze on tourism itself.

Exploring social representations of tourism through an analysis of drawings

The previous discussion can be summarised by highlighting three key points. Firstly, there is widespread agreement that visual images are important in tourism. Secondly, the existing research has focused almost entirely on destination images and photographic images. Thirdly, social representations theory could be a useful guide to understanding the role of visual images in tourism in a broader sense than just destination images. The present study is based on these three points and has involved the use of drawings of tourism as a method for exploring social representations of tourism. The aim of this exploratory study is to demonstrate the method of analysing drawings, and to begin to examine the possible content of social representations of tourism.

Only one tourism-related study could be found that analysed drawings. This study by Gamradt (1995) analysed drawings of tourists made by Jamaican school students. The aim was to provide an avenue for local voices to present their perspectives on tourism and its conse-quences for this destination. Gamradt content-analysed the drawings and found three dominant themes: the presentation of commercial activities as associated with tourism; the use of planes and ships to represent long distance travel; and that students generally saw tourists in a positive light. The present study offers a similar analysis of drawings of tourism made by three groups of university students.

The sample

A total of 80 drawings were completed by three groups of students including 16 Italian students enrolled in an international tourism Master's programme conducted in Italy, 47 Australian students enrolled in a third-year-level tourism policy and planning subject as part of a tourism management degree in a regional Australian university, and 17 students from a variety of different countries participating in a tourism research seminar at the same regional Australian university. This latter group was made up of 12 male and 5 female participants, and included students from China, Africa, India, Singapore, Thailand, Malaysia, Peru, Mexico, the United States and Norway who were enrolled in a variety of post-graduate courses in business and tourism management. All of the students who participated in the tourism research seminar were either on leave from a tourism management position or had held a tourism management position prior to coming to Australia; they had an age range of 25–40. The Italian students, who were evenly split into 8 males and 8 females, were enrolled in a programme with the specific aim of training senior government and private sector managers to contribute to tourism development in the Mediterranean region. Their age range was 25–30 and they had no prior formal education in tourism. The Australians were the youngest group with an age range of 18–22 and made up of 12 male and 35 female students. Students graduating from this Australian course typically find employment in government departments related to tourism, in regional tour operations or in tourism marketing organisations. Overall the sample is one of current and future tourism managers and policy advisers with varying levels of experience with, and education about, tourism.

The method

In each case the participants were asked at the beginning of either the seminar or subject to draw their image of tourism. Those who sought more detail about the task were told to imagine that they had met someone who didn't speak the same language and they had to describe tourism to that person without words. The aim of the exercise was to encourage the participants to think about the assumptions that they made about tourism and to identify the elements that they considered to be important in tourism. According to Potter (1996) social representations are developed from a combination of direct personal experiences, information shared in social interaction, and information from media and other sources such as art and formal education. What distinguishes a social representation from an individual attitude are shared visual images or symbols. Thus we can argue that a social representation exists within a group of people if they as individuals identify a commonly shared visual image. In the present study the aim of the analysis of the drawings was to explore the existence of these shared visual images. In responding to the request to draw an image of tourism, the individual respondents could draw upon any combination of their own experiences as tourists, as hosts, as service personnel, and as destination managers as well as information shared amongst themselves and from the media and other sources. If no social representation existed within this group and each respondent drew an image based only on their own personal experiences as a host or a guest or a manager, then we would expect to find in a group from so many different places, a range of idiosyncratic and widely varying images with little or no commonality.

Content analysing the images

Some authors draw a distinction between content and semiotic analysis (Albers and James, 1988; Jenkins, 2003). According to these authors, in studies of photographs content analysis is concerned with classifying and counting concrete or specific visual elements, while semiotic analysis seeks to identify the underlying messages that are symbolised by the combinations or compositions of these elements. Unlike studies examining photographic images, the drawings in the present study were made up of pictograms or symbols. For example, in the drawings three different symbols were included to represent money: a simple $ sign, drawings of paper notes with a $ in the centre, or a bag with a $ sign on the outside. These were all coded as symbols for cash or money. In essence the elements in the drawings were symbols blurring the distinction between a content and semiotic analysis. Each drawing was examined and the graphic symbols included in the image were listed. This resulted in a simple classification scheme similar to those typically used in content analyses, but of symbols rather than photographic elements. For each drawing the occurrence of a symbol was counted only once regardless of the number of times it was repeated in a drawing. The drawings varied in terms of the number of symbols included, with the Italian group generally including a larger number of elements in their drawings. For the Australian group the range was 2–12 symbols with a mean number of 5.6 symbols per drawing, while for the Italian students the range was 5–14 with a mean of 8.8, and for the International group the range was 1–12 with a mean of 5.5 symbols included in a drawing.

Elements of the drawings of tourism

Once all the drawings had been coded the first step in the analysis was to examine the relative frequency of occurrence of the elements. Table 15.1 provides an overall summary of this step with frequency distributions for all three groups and the total sample. The table has been split into three sections with the first section containing those elements that appear to be relatively common in all three groups, suggesting some core elements of a hegemonic social representation of tourism as essentially consisting of international travel by happy people to sunny, coastal destinations. These were labelled the core elements and were similar to the main themes noted by Gamradt (1995).

Table 15.1 Frequency of occurrence of symbolic elements

Symbolic element	Italian group (n=16)	Australian group (n=47)	International group (n=17)	Total (n=80)
Core elements				
People (typically stick figures)	20	34	10	64
(No expression/smiling)	(12/8)	(18/16)	(5/5)	(35/29)
Forms of long distance travel	14	29	11	54
(Plane/cruise ship)	(8/6)	(16/13)	(6/5)	(30/24)
Beaches	13	31	8	52
(Developed/undeveloped)	(5/8)	(19/12)	(3/5)	(27/25)
Sun	10	19	5	34
Palm trees	8	18	4	30
Group membership elements				
Movement between places	5	7	5	17
Globe/Earth	3	9	4	16
Cars/buses/trains	6	7	3	16
Cash/money	4	10	1	15
Built attractions (museums/churches)	12	1	1	14
High rise buildings (not at a beach)	2	8	4	14
People engaging in watersports	2	6	3	11
Cameras	4	5	2	11

(Continued)

237

Table 15.1 Continued

Symbolic Element	Italian Group (n=16)	Australian group (n=47)	International Group (n=17)	Total (n=80)
Mountains	4	2	4	10
Animals	2	4	4	10
Trees/vegetation (not palm trees)	5	0	4	9
Labelled hotel	1	6	1	8
Beach umbrellas	5	3	0	8
Idiosyncratic elements				
People sunbathing	3	5	0	8
Unhappy people	2	3	2	7
Service staff/local residents	2	2	3	7
Suitcases	2	3	2	7
Tourist icon (Eiffel tower/Coliseum)	3	2	1	6
People holding hands	3	1	1	5
Food/wine	3	2	0	5
Diagram	0	1	4	5
Labelled restaurant/bar	1	3	0	4
Traditional architecture	0	0	4	4
Home	3	1	0	4
International flags/symbols	2	1	1	4
Pollution	2	1	1	4
Heart	2	0	1	3
Labelled shops	0	2	1	3
Brands (Sony/Coke/Fuji)	2	1	0	3
People with a dream bubble	1	0	1	2
Asian tourist	1	0	1	2
Tour guide	1	0	1	2
Tourist information sign	1	1	0	2
Apple	0	0	1	1
Swimming pool	1	0	0	1
Postcard	1	0	0	1
Airport	1	0	0	1
Eyes	0	1	0	1
Guidebook	0	1	0	1

The second section of the table contains elements that were relatively frequent within a group but not necessarily across all three groups of participants. These were labelled the group membership elements. For example, there appeared to be a second set of elements in the images drawn by the Italian students consisting mainly of built attractions and non-coastal settings. In a similar fashion, the Australian students more frequently incorporated symbols of money, the earth, high-rise hotels and beach activities into their images. It is likely that these reflect emancipated social representations of tourism. No clear pattern could be discerned for the International group, which is not surprising given their wide range of cultural backgrounds and levels and types of tourism experience. The third section of the table contains a series of symbolic elements included by only a few of the participants reflecting a range of individual experiences and perceptions. These were labelled the idiosyncratic elements.

The presentation of simple frequencies can obscure important patterns within the data as it gives only minimal information about the co-occurrence of symbols. The second step of the

Table 15.2 Summary of patterns of co-occurrence of symbolic elements in drawings

Inclusion of elements	Italian group (n=16)	Australian group (n=47)	International group (n=17)	Total (n=80)
>74% of all elements were core elements	25%	26%	18%	24%
50–74% of all elements were core elements	31%	47%	41%	42%
25–49% of all elements were core elements	25%	15%	23%	19%
1–24% of all elements were core elements	19%	3%	6%	7%
No core elements included in drawings	0%	9%	12%	7%
No idiosyncratic elements included	0%	44%	47%	34%
1 idiosyncratic element included	31%	38%	18%	32%
>1 idiosyncratic element included	69%	18%	35%	34%

analysis therefore examined the co-occurrence of symbols. The results of a preliminary analysis of the co-occurrence of elements within the three sets is given in Table 15.2. As can be seen from Table 15.2, in each group nearly all of the respondents incorporated at least one core element. Further, for more than 50 per cent of the participants in each group, core elements made up at least half of all the elements included in the drawings. By way of contrast, nearly half of both the Australian (44 per cent) and the International (47 per cent) groups include none of the idiosyncratic elements.

The pattern of results suggest that most drawings were made up of a selection of core symbols, accompanied by some symbols related to the group membership and supplemented by some individual idiosyncratic elements. Further examination of these patterns of co-occurrence of elements suggested the existence of three main social representations. There appear to be two variations of a hegemonic social representation. Both of these used many of the core elements but were characterised by the choice of either undeveloped beaches or developed beaches.

Figure 15.2 contains an example of a drawing based on an undeveloped beach from each of the three groups. The first is from the International group, the second from the Australian group, and the third from the Italian group. As can be seen the image is remarkably similar across all three groups. The first two images are simpler with fewer symbols and this is repeated with an overall pattern of more symbols included in all drawings by the Italian group. Further, the Italian example includes some low-rise buildings on the beach and this was also a pattern repeated across the group with only one beach in the Italian sample that had no built elements. These two patterns are consistent with Moscovici's (2001) processes of anchoring and objectification. Anchoring involves choosing a prototype of something to act as the core of the social representation. In this case the prototype for the social representation of tourism appears to be a beach – either undeveloped or developed. For the Italian group the prototype includes some buildings and it seems likely that this reflects their personal experiences of Mediterranean beaches. This process of anchoring is also evident in the existence of a second common pattern, or emancipated representation, in the Italian drawings that consisted of a set of built attractions such as churches, castles and ruins. Here it seems that the prototype for some Italian students was based on a different exemplar of tourism, common in Europe, based on cultural heritage attractions.

The process of objectification involves the simplification of a concept and in the present study the simplest drawings came from the groups with the most experience of the phenomenon. The two groups with greater experience of tourism tended to have simpler social representations.

Figure 15.3 provides a similar set of examples of drawings, this time based on a developed beach and presented in the same order as in Figure 15.2. Again the three examples share many

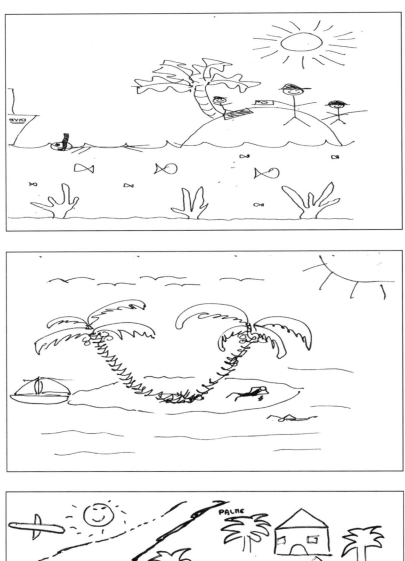

Figure 15.2   Social representations based on an undeveloped beach

Figure 15.3 Social representations based on a developed beach

of the same features despite the differences in drawing style. All three include people, boats, palm trees and high-rise buildings. Again the Italian example is more complex and includes more abstract symbols, such as arrows to indicate movement. Symbols for money can also be seen in two of these examples. High-rise buildings not at a beach and money were particularly common in the Australian drawings and this is an example of how different groups can develop different social representations reflecting their shared experiences and ongoing communication. Students in this group are enrolled in a tourism programme within a business degree and it is possible that this context highlights the economic and business aspects of tourism.

Finally, a third, less common social representation appeared to be based around the central element of a globe or symbol for the Planet Earth. This type of drawing appeared in all three groups, again in a similar format, although less frequently than the developed and undeveloped beach option. Figure 15.4 provides three examples of this globe-based image. It is possible that this is an emerging social representation that may reflect participation in tourism management education with its emphasis on the international and systemic nature of tourism, as it was most common in the Australian group, which had the most experience of tertiary tourism management education.

Moscovici (2001) argues that it is important to search for what is common in people's perceptions in order to understand the core elements of social representations. In the present study the core elements of long-distance transport, sunny beaches and happy people seem to be the anchors for a hegemonic social representation of tourism. These patterns were similar across several different geographic locations for the data collection and across multiple cultural groups included in the study. In addition the themes are similar to those reported by Gamradt (1995) from Jamaican school children's images of tourists and consistent with the findings of a New Zealand study that asked residents to choose from several different definitions of tourists (Lea et al., 1994). In this study it was found that the concept of a tourist was likely to be associated with international and leisure travel.

It is also interesting to note the elements that were included only rarely in the drawings, such as negative environmental impacts, and contact between hosts and guests. It is important to note that some students did recognise more negative aspects of tourism. Figure 15.5, for example, presents an image with the core hegemonic elements of long-distance transport and a developed beach. But this is accompanied by pollution and a somewhat sinister political figure in the foreground. Figure 15.6 provides a gentler image, again with the core hegemonic elements, but this time it is interesting to note that the ship of tourism is named the *Titanic*. Overall, though, it appears that the social representations presented in these drawings were mostly positive images of tourism. More research is needed to determine if these drawings reflect hopes and ambitions or are simply descriptions of tourism.

Some future research directions

The results of the present study suggest that participants' drawings may be a fruitful type of visual depiction for further study of social representations of tourism, destination images and tourism representations of destinations and hosts. The results also suggest that there may exist several social representations of tourism as a phenomenon. While it would be possible to suggest simply that more research into social representations would be useful, it may be more valuable to highlight some specific areas where the study of social representations may be of particular value. To that end three areas have been identified, corresponding to each of the overlaps identified in the framework presented in Figure 15.1.

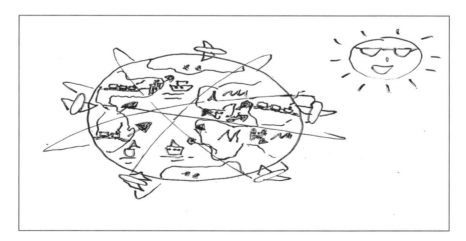

Figure 15.4 Social representations based on a globe

Figure 15.5   A negative representation of tourism (Australian student)

Figure 15.6   An International student drawing of tourism

Community preparedness for tourism

The first area lies within the study of the social representations of tourism held by various destination communities and the social groups within them. Social representations of tourism are important in that they provide a way to share meaning and communicate and they direct attention and behaviour. Put simply, communities, governments and businesses will make decisions about tourism development and control based on the social representations of tourism that they hold. Moscardo's (2005) analysis of case studies of tourism development in rural and peripheral regions highlighted ten main themes that influenced the outcomes of tourism development:

- the culture, history and circumstances of the community;
- the role and effectiveness of formal planning;
- the emergence of tourism leaders and entrepreneurs;
- effective mechanisms for community involvement and ownership;
- coordination of public and private interests;
- the role of government and other agencies;
- community capacity;
- market analysis;
- development of infrastructure; and
- connections to tourism distribution networks.

In addition, Moscardo organises these themes into a three-stage approach to tourism development:

- determining the pre-conditions for tourism;
- establishing the pre-requisites for tourism; and
- finding and using various tools for tourism development.

It is argued here that the first stage is about understanding community preparedness for tourism, and an important aspect of this preparedness is analysing just what communities understand about tourism and its likely consequences. In other words, studies of social representations of tourism may provide some insight in the expectations, fears and hopes of communities who seek, or are subjected to, tourism as a development strategy.

Destination branding

The second research area is essentially related to the overlap in Figure 15.1 labelled destination images, but also connects to the intersection between destination images and tourism representations of destinations. Destination branding has become a major catchphrase in the tourism marketing and promotion literature (Morgan et al., 2003). The central element of destination branding is the creation of a brand personality (Ekinci, 2003). Essentially brand personality refers to the attribution of human personality traits such as sophistication, friendliness, sincerity and confidence to a product or service brand (Aaker, 1997). The argument is that consumers will associate personality characteristics with the brand and with people they believe are typical consumers of the brand. But tourism destinations are more than consumption experiences, they are also places where people live. In the case of tourism destination brands then, three possible sets of associated personalities exist:

- the personality of the destination itself;

- the personality of typical visitors to the destination; and
- the personality of the people who live there.

Although destination branding is an emerging area in tourism research and practice, it does not seem that destination communities have been given much of a role in the development of destination brand personalities. Indeed it is possible that in many destinations residents are unaware of the personality that is being promoted to visitors. Community reactions to destination brand personalities is therefore an area where analysing the social representations that communities hold of themselves and their homes as a tourist destination could be of benefit in suggesting ways communities can retain greater control over tourism processes.

Sources of information for tourists' representations of destinations and hosts

The third area is an extension of the critical analysis of representations of destinations and hosts. In this aspect of tourism, two trends are of note: the rising use of the Internet for tourism promotion and the dissemination of tourism information, and increasing calls for more interpretation of destination and host communities as a component of sustainable tourism. The Internet provides tourists with a wide range of images, both verbal and visual, and arguably tourism marketers have less control than ever over the information that tourists can use to develop their own individual destination images (Money and Crotts, 2003). The Internet incorporates a number of different sources within one. It includes web pages from tour operators and destination marketing organisations, information from government agencies, and testimonials from other travellers. The Internet also offers the potential to communicate with similar others and share travel and destination experiences and it includes visual images, both static and moving, and real-time images, as well as a variety of text in a range of formats. The Internet therefore offers an excellent opportunity to study the development of more complex destination images or social representations.

Finally, there is the area of interpretation or the structured presentation of information about a destination to visitors. Guides, interpretive centres and museums all provide information to visitors about destinations and their residents, and interpretation is often seen as an important element of sustainable tourism (Newsome et al., 2002). Much of the research into interpretation in tourism settings has been focused on understanding the effectiveness of different techniques of interpretation. Only in the world of heritage and museums has attention been focused on the content of interpretation and its contributions to the representations of places and peoples that visitors have (Richter, 1999; Uzzell, 1996). Interpretive products and services therefore offer another area for the exploration of tourism representations and the images that tourists have of destinations.

References

Aaker, J. (1997) 'Dimensions of brand personality'. *Journal of Marketing Research,* 34(3), 347–56

Albers, P. C. and James, W. R. (1988) 'Travel photography: A methodological approach'. *Annals of Tourism Research,* 15(1), 134–58

Andriotis, K. and Vaughan, R. D. (2003) 'Urban residents' attitudes toward tourism development: The case of Crete'. *Journal of Travel Research,* 42(2), 172–85

Ashworth, G. J. (2003) 'Heritage, identity and places: For tourist and host communities'. In S. Singh, D. J. Timothy and R. K. Dowling (eds) *Tourism in destination communities.* Wallingford: CABI Publishing, pp. 79–98

Ateljevic, I. and Doorne, S. (2002) 'Representing New Zealand: Tourism imagery and ideology'. *Annals of Tourism Research,* 29(3), 648–67

Bhattacharyya, D. P. (1997) 'Mediating India: An analysis of a guidebook'. *Annals of Tourism Research,* 24(2), 371–89

Campbell, A. and Muncer, S. (1994) 'Sex differences in aggression: Social representations and social roles'. *British Journal of Social Psychology,* 33(2), 233–40

Day, J., Skidmore, S. and Koller, T. (2002) 'Image selection in destination positioning: A new approach'. *Journal of Vacation Marketing,* 8(2), 177–86

De Paolis, P. (1990) 'Prototypes of the psychologist and professionalisation: Diverging social representations of a developmental process'. In G. Duveen and B. Lloyd (eds) *Social representations and the development of knowledge.* Cambridge: Cambridge University Press, pp. 144–63

Echtner, C. M. (2002) 'The content of Third World tourism marketing: A 4A approach'. *International Journal of Tourism Research,* 4(6), 413–34

Ekinci, Y. (2003) 'From destination image to destination branding: An emerging area of research'. *e-Review of Tourism Research (eRTR),* 1(2), Retrieved 2 November 2011, from http://ertr.tamu.edu/index.php?option=com_content&view=article&id=138:volume-1-issue-2-august-2003-commentaries-1-&catid=100:volume-1-issue-1-4-2003-&Itemid=54

Fairweather, J. R. and Swaffield, S. R. (2001) 'Visitor experiences of Kaikoura, New Zealand: An interpretative study using photographs of landscapes and Q method'. *Tourism Management,* 22(3), 219–28

Fredline, E. and Faulkner, B. (2000) 'Host community reactions: A cluster analysis'. *Annals of Tourism Research,* 27(3), 763–84

Gamradt, J. (1995) 'Jamaican children's representations of tourism'. *Annals of Tourism Research,* 22(4), 735–62

Halfacree, K. H. (1993) 'Locality and social representation: Space, discourse and alternative definitions of the rural'. *Journal of Rural Studies,* 9(1), 23–37

Hall, S. (1997) 'The work of representation'. In S. Hall (ed.) *Representation: Cultural representations and signifying practices.* London: Sage, pp. 13–74

Hanna, S. P. and Del Casino, V. J., Jr. (2003) 'Introduction: Tourism spaces, mapped representations, and the practices of identity'. In S. P. Hanna and V. J. Del Casino Jr. (eds) *Mapping tourism.* Minneapolis, MN: University of Minnesota Press, pp. 1–27

Jenkins, O. H. (2003) 'Photography and travel brochures: The circle of representation'. *Tourism Geographies,* 5(3), 305–28

Joffe, H. (2003) 'Risk: From perception to social representation'. *British Journal of Social Psychology,* 42(1), 55–73

Kim, H. and Richardson, S. L. (2003) 'Motion picture impacts on destination images'. *Annals of Tourism Research,* 30(1), 216–37

Lea, S. E. G., Kemp, S. and Willetts, K. (1994) 'Residents' concepts of tourism'. *Annals of Tourism Research,* 21(2), 406–10

Lee, D. and Pearce, P. L. (2002) 'Community attitudes to the acceptability of user fees in natural settings'. *Tourism and Hospitality Research,* 4(2), 158–74

Lunt, P. K. and Livingstone, S. M. (1992) *Mass consumption and personal identity.* Buckingham: Open University Press

MacKay, K. J. and Couldwell, C. M. (2004) 'Using visitor-employed photography to investigate destination image'. *Journal of Travel Research,* 42(4), 390–96

MacKay, K. J. and Fesenmaier, D. R. (1997) 'Pictorial element of destination in image formation'. *Annals of Tourism Research,* 24(3), 537–65

Mahalingam, R. (2003) 'Essentialism, culture, and power: Representations of social class'. *Journal of Social Issues,* 59(4), 733–50

Markwell, K. (1997) 'Dimensions of photography in a nature-based tour'. *Annals of Tourism Research,* 24(1), 131–55

Markwick, M. (2001) 'Postcards from Malta: Image, consumption, context'. *Annals of Tourism Research,* 28(2), 417–38

Mellinger, W. M. (1994) 'Toward a critical analysis of tourism representations'. *Annals of Tourism Research,* 21(4), 756–79

Moliner, P. (1995) 'A two-dimensional model of social representations'. *European Journal of Social Psychology,* 25(1), 27–40

Moloney, G. and Walker, I. (2002) 'Talking about transplants: Social representations and the dialectical, dilemmatic nature of organ donation and transplantation'. *British Journal of Social Psychology*, 41(2), 299–321

Money, R. B. and Crotts, J. C. (2003) 'The effect of uncertainty avoidance on information search, planning, and purchases of international travel vacations'. *Tourism Management*, 24(2), 191–202

Morgan, N., Pritchard, A. and Piggott, R. (2003) 'Destination branding and the role of stakeholders: The case of New Zealand'. *Journal of Vacation Marketing*, 9(3), 285–99

Moscardo, G. (2005) 'Peripheral tourism development: Challenges, issues and success factors'. *Tourism Recreation Research*, 30(1), 27–43

Moscardo, G. and Pearce, P. L. (2003) 'Presenting destinations: Marketing host communities'. In S. Singh, D. J. Timothy and R. K. Dowling (eds) *Tourism in destination communities*. Wallingford: CABI Publishing, pp. 253–72

Moscovici, S. (2001) 'Why a theory of social representations?'. In K. Deaux and G. Philogene (eds) *Representations*. Oxford: Blackwell, pp. 8–35

Naoi, T., Airey, D., Iijima, S. and Niininen, O. (2006) 'Visitors' evaluations of an historical district: Repertory grid analysis and laddering analysis with photographs'. *Tourism Management*, 27(3), 420–36

Newsome, D., Moore, S. A. and Dowling, R. K. (2002) *Natural area tourism*. Sydney: Channel View Publications

Olson, J. M. and Zanna, M. P. (1993) 'Attitudes and attitude change'. *Annual Review of Psychology*, 44(1), 117–45

O'Rourke, E. (2000) 'The reintroduction and reinterpretation of the wild'. *Journal of Agricultural and Environmental Ethics*, 13(1), 145–65

Pearce, P. L., Moscardo, G. and Ross, G. F. (1996) *Tourism community relationships*. Oxford: Pergamon Press

Philogene, G. (1994) '"African American" as a new social representation'. *Journal for the Theory of Social Behaviour*, 24(2), 89–109

Philogene, G. and Deaux, K. (2001) 'Introduction'. In K. Deaux and G. Philogene (eds) *Representations*. Oxford: Blackwell, pp. 1–7

Pike, S. (2002) 'Destination image analysis: A review of 142 papers from 1973 to 2000'. *Tourism Management*, 23(5), 541–49

Potter, J. (1996) 'Attitudes, social representations and discursive psychology'. In M. Wetherell (ed.) *Identities, groups and social issues*. New York: Sage, pp. 119–73

Pritchard, A. and Morgan, N. J. (2001) 'Culture, identity and tourism representation: Marketing Cymru or Wales?'. *Tourism Management*, 22(2), 167–79

Richter, L. K. (1999) 'The politics of heritage tourism development'. In D. G. Pearce and R. W. Butler (eds) *Contemporary issues in tourism development*. London: Routledge, pp. 108–26

Russell, C. L. and Ankenman, M. J. (1996) 'Orang-utans as photographic collectibles: Ecotourism and the commodification of nature'. *Tourism Recreation Research*, 21(1), 71–8

Selby, M. and Morgan, N. J. (1996) 'Reconstruing place image: A case study of its role in destination market research'. *Tourism Management*, 17(4), 287–94

Urry, J. (1990) *The tourist gaze*. London: Sage

Uzzell, D. (1996) 'The hot interpretation of war and conflict'. In D. L. Uzzell (ed.) *Heritage interpretation volume one*. London: Belhaven Press, pp. 33–47

Verkuyten, M., Rood-Pijpers, E., Elffers, H. and Hessing, D. J. (1994) 'Rules for breaking formal rules: Social representations and everyday rule-governed behavior'. *Journal of Psychology*, 128(5), 485–98

Wagner, W., Kronberger, N. and Seifert, F. (2002) 'Collective symbolic images coping with new technology: Knowledge, images and public discourse'. *British Journal of Social Psychology*, 41(3), 323–54

Walsh, J. A., Jamrozy, U. and Burr, S. W. (2001) 'Sense of place as a component of sustainable tourism marketing'. In S. F. McCool and R. N. Moisey (eds) *Tourism, recreation and sustainability*. Wallingford: CAB International, pp. 195–216

Yuksel, F., Bramwell, B. and Yuksel, A. (1999) 'Stakeholder interviews and tourism planning at Pamukkale, Turkey'. *Tourism Management*, 20(3), 351–60

Part IV

Human capital for tourism development

16

Tourism, migration and human capital

Knowledge and skills at the intersection of flows

Allan M. Williams

Introduction

This paper starts from two propositions relating to tourism–migration relationships and knowledge transfer. First, there has been considerable interest in recent years in ideas relating to 'tourist–migrant' workers, that is, in the complex interrelationships between economic and cultural/tourism motivations, particularly amongst young people. However, this represents only one of the many economic relationships between tourism and migration, two phenomena that often have been studied in isolation (Williams and Hall, 2002). There is a need for a better understanding of how these are entwined in an economy of flows (Hudson, 2004), shaping economic outcomes in the tourism sector. Secondly, there has also been a neglect of the role of labour mobility in knowledge transfer, innovation and competitiveness – and this is particularly notable in an industry such as tourism, where demand and, in part, production, are essentially based on mobility. International tourists seek out experiences and services beyond their usual countries of residence, and the resulting demand for knowledge in the labour force that provides these creates a potentially significant role for migrant workers. This paper brings these themes together, in order to explore the role of migration in the creation and transfer of knowledge and skills in tourism.

The paper is divided into four sections:

* It briefly reviews some salient features of research on labour in tourism production that provide insights into migration and knowledge.
* It reviews some of the generic theories relating to the nature of knowledge and knowledge transfer, and notes that these have largely been absent from research on the tourism sector.
* It considers the specific role of migration in knowledge creation and transfer. In particular, it critiques some of the limiting assumptions of previous research on migration and human capital. Instead, there is a need to identify different types of knowledge, and how these are acquired and transferred by migrants under different conditions.

- It explores some of the ways in which the knowledge, created and transferred by migrants, contributes to tourism production. There is still limited direct research on this topic, but the paper is able to draw on some emerging, if fragmented, insights in diverse research areas. As such the paper seeks to map out an agenda for future research that will bring new perspectives to studies of tourism production, while constructing bridges to different research arenas.

Labour and tourism production

There is still surprisingly little research on the role of labour in the production of tourism services, given the importance of labour costs in most segments of the tourism industry, let alone on labour migration. Some of the key features of this research, in relation to migration and knowledge transfer, are summarised below, drawing on Shaw and Williams (2004).

First, given the importance of labour costs in tourism, and a reputation for paying relatively low wages (especially, in developed economies), there has been considerable interest in how downwards pressures are exerted on these. Riley et al. (2002) provide an exhaustive review of this issue, and identify three main sets of factors, that can be related to migration:

- *Job attributes of attractiveness, acquisition of transferable skills and ease of learning.* These contribute to a large potential labour market, high levels of mobility and the detachment of productivity from skill levels. As a result, managers take a short-term view of employment and training, whilst years of service are also poorly rewarded in the determination of wages. Migration is encouraged by these job attributes, but it also contributes to lower wages.
- *Industrial structure and economic factors.* Fluctuations in tourism demand require employment flexibility in the labour force. Migration usually facilitates flexibility in the destination country. The small scale of most tourism enterprises also means there are only limited opportunities for advancement within firms and weak occupational hierarchies. Therefore, internal labour markets tend to be relatively weak compared to external ones. This means that intra-company labour migration is limited, compared to so-called 'free agent' labour migrants (Kanter, 1995).
- *Psychological issues.* Employees obtain non-material job satisfaction from employment as well as wages, so are more tolerant of low pay. This relates to the complex motivations of tourism–migrant workers, discussed later, where non-material rewards may outweigh material ones.

The research in this area offers mixed implications for understanding the role of knowledge transfer via migration. However, we can conclude that the factors which condition low wages in tourism also facilitate selective types of migration flows and employment opportunities for migrants. As a result, the detachment of skills from productivity, weak internal labour markets and the importance of non-material rewards all contribute to highly selective opportunities for knowledge transfer.

Secondly, tourism employment has distinctive psychological features, notably in respect of work orientation. Goldthorpe et al. (1968) developed the use of the term 'work orientation', emphasising that there are 'holistic' attitudes towards work: both materialistic and non-materialistic. Non-material rewards have several dimensions. Some are related to place association – most tourism jobs are, almost by definition, in attractive locations, which compensates for low material rewards. Other attractions for tourism employees may include the diverse tasks to be undertaken in a flexible environment (in other words, the avoidance of routines), and opportunities for host–guest interactions. Work orientation has particular relevance for the complex relationships between tourism and migration, with migrants being motivated by both material and non-material goals (especially place attraction). This is captured in the work of Uriely (2001), who conceptualises migrant workers in terms of their engagement in tourism, and their tourism and place-oriented motivations. The key consideration then is the ability of firms to capture the knowledge carried by employees with such work orientation.

Thirdly, there is considerable research on labour market flexibility. This has its roots in the work of Atkinson (1984), who differentiated between numerical and functional flexibility: the first implies changes in employment levels in response to demand fluctuations, whilst the second suggests the movement of workers between tasks within firms, in response to spatio-temporal changes in demand within the establishment. Shaw and Williams (1994) extended this conceptualisation to the tourism industry, when they classified the variety of employment 'contracts' in tourism – casualisation, temporary, seasonal, part time, homeworking under contract, etc. – in terms of four axes: regularity of working hours, functional versus numerical flexibility, employment security and availability of material and fringe benefits. Lockwood and Guerrier (1989) have critiqued the Atkinson model in their analysis of major UK hotels. They observed relatively little functional flexibility in hotels and, while there was evidence of numerical flexibility strategies, the wages and benefits of part-time workers were not significantly different to those of 'core' workers. Similarly, Milne and Pohlmann (1998) found that numerical flexibility was common in Montreal hotels. The confirmation of the importance of numerical flexibility reinforces the view that labour market mobility – including migration – is likely to be particularly important in the tourism industry. It is one readily available strategy for increasing or decreasing labour supply in response to the particularities of demand (notably its temporal 'lumpiness'). International migrant workers tend to be seen as disposable in employment strategies that are driven by numerical flexibility, as Nancy Folbre (2001, p. 187) comments:

> The great advantage of temporary immigrants is their compatibility with last-minute methods of inventory control. If you don't need them, you don't order them. If you accidentally get too many, they can be returned.

This poses questions about the effectiveness of knowledge transfer from workers to organisations in the context of such labour market dynamics.

Fourthly, labour market segmentation, drawing on wider divisions in society, offers possibilities for employers to depress labour costs. The segmentation of workers (by race, age, gender, etc.) provides a basis for paying lower wages relative to the value of work to some (usually more weakly organised or vulnerable) social groups. The key to this is the social construction of job content, linked to the system of remuneration. Some jobs are constructed as 'unskilled work', simply because they are undertaken by particular social groups, and this is used to justify paying lower wages, irrespective of the real skill or knowledge content of these jobs. One of the major sources of labour market segmentation is migrant versus non-migrant status. The precise nature of such segmentation depends on national regulatory frameworks. For example, unregistered migrants are more likely to be found in more marginal jobs, whether in the formal or the informal economy. But arguably they also contribute to reducing absolute and relative labour costs, by accepting lower wages and reducing labour shortages, thereby depressing overall wage levels. Clearly labour migration is recognised in the literature on labour market segmentation in tourism, although perhaps less so than, for example, gender segmentation. However, the implications for understanding the use, transfer and acquisition of skills have not really been explored in the tourism industry, even though the social construction of jobs around migrant status has significant implications for the recognition of individuals as knowledgeable workers.

Finally, while labour costs are important, the role of labour can not be reduced to this simple economistic view. As Baldacchino (1997, p. 92) argues, 'workers cannot be forced to work without a modicum of consent on their part; nor do workers agree to sell an exact quantity of labour'. The amount of work done, and how it is done, requires consent and active worker input. This applies particularly to 'front line' service employees who have to respond (perform) to the emotional needs and expectations of clients, as well as the requirements of managers. Therefore, managers may be more concerned with realising satisfying tourist–worker encounters than reducing labour costs, and may seek to increase rather than reduce labour inputs per tourist. Employers who take a long–term view seek to balance the two goals. In other words, as Hudson (2001, p. 109) argues in a broader context, 'in the final analysis…companies are concerned about unit production costs, not nominal wages per se'. And this approach means that employers will be more attentive to the various types of knowledge possessed by workers.

In general, formal and technical skills and training are relatively low in the tourism industry, as Riley et al. (2002) argue, although there are exceptions, such as airline pilots and top chefs. However, the effective performance of many tourism jobs also requires other less formal skills such as personal interaction or self–presentation skills, or close familiarity with and knowledge of the needs and tastes of a regular international client group. This underlines two points. First, these encultured and embodied types of knowledge (discussed later) tend to be embedded in individuals; in many tourist jobs they are not easily codified into knowledge at the organisational level. Once such workers are lost, they will not easily be replaced, so that firms which are focused on quality issues or on unit costs, have to prioritise retaining individuals who possess these forms of knowledge. Secondly, this poses questions about the transferability of many of the forms of knowledge embedded in migrant workers. At first sight, international migrant workers may not possess the culturally specific knowledge required for front of house jobs in tourism. But, if the dominant client groups are international tourists, then the migrant workers may possess highly valorised knowledge.

This brief review serves to underline the argument that, when focusing on individual migrant workers, there are specific conditions in the tourism industry that mediate their economic role. The above discussion focused on downwards pressures on costs, psychological orientation, flexibility, segmentation and the notion of total unit costs. These all mediate the role of workers – including migrants – in knowledge creation and transfer. This is critical because of the emphasis placed on knowledge as the key to competitiveness. Drucker (1993, p. 38) expressed this forcefully when writing that 'Knowledge is the only meaningful resource today. The traditional "factors of production"…have become secondary.' Although this overstates the argument, the need to understand the complexity of knowledge transfers is paramount.

Forms of knowledge and knowledge transfer

There is a vast literature on inter- and intra-firm knowledge transfer, and more generally on knowledge creation (see, e.g., Dierkes et al., 2001, and Easterby-Smith, 2003). However, given the specific focus in this chapter on the relationship between migration and knowledge transfer, we focus on two themes: different forms of knowledge at the level of the individual, and different generic models of knowledge transfer. Consequently, this chapter does not engage with the substantial research on organisational practices and 'organisational knowledge', amongst many other topics. The focus on individual knowledge can be defended on theoretical grounds, related to the role of cognition. For example, Huber (1991) argues that knowledge can only reside at the individual level, although others (e.g. Nelson and Winter, 1982) contend that there are organisational routines that persist independently of individuals (Empson, 2001). Following Lam (2000), in this chapter we take individual knowledge to be *all* the knowledge possessed by an individual that can be applied independently to particular tasks.

A considerable body of theory has grown up around the notion of individual knowledge. Nonaka and Takeuchi (1995), in their seminal work *The Knowledge Creating Company,* argue that knowledge is created through interaction between individuals at various levels within an organisation. And organisations are unable to create knowledge unless this is shared with others. An earlier, and perhaps the best known, starting point is Polanyi's (1966) famous distinction between tacit and codified knowledge. They are of course interdependent, and tacit knowledge is required for effective use of explicit or codified knowledge. Tacit knowledge exists in the background of consciouness, which Poanyi famously expressed as 'we can know more than we can tell'. To some extent it can be transferred via electronic means, such as video conferencing. However, some forms of knowledge are only, or at least more effectively, transferable through the co-presence of individuals. Migration is, of course, one means for bringing about co-presence, and we return to this later in the chapter.

Since Polanyi's pioneering work, there have been a number of attempts to refine the understanding of individual knowledge, and these have been summarised by Venzin et al. (1998):

- Tacit knowledge: a person knows more than he can express in words (Polanyi, 1966).
- Embodied knowledge: results from the experiences of physical presence (e.g. from participating in a particular project) (Nonaka and Takeuchi, 1995).
- Embrained knowledge: depends on cognitive abilities that allow recognition of underlying patterns or reflection on basic assumptions (Blackler, 1995).
- Embedded knowledge: knowledge is embedded in a variety of contextual factors. For example, shared knowledge is generated in different language systems, or organizational cultures (Brown and Duguid, 1991).

Although there are overlaps between these categories, there are also significant differences. The concept of 'embedded knowledge', in particular, poses questions about context and or place, and therefore about the role of mobility versus the situational contingencies (whether place or organisational specific) of knowledge transfer. What types of knowledge can only be held by individuals, and imparted through direct inter-personal relations, and what are the constraints on such transfers? These are key questions in relation to the role of migration in the tourism industry.

Before the last question can be addressed, however, there is a need to consider a second theme: the principal modes by which knowledge transfers are effected between firms. Much of the literature originating from the management literature seems to assume that most knowledge is transferred within (transnational) companies via discrete codified parcels (manuals, databases, reports, etc.) or via intra-company labour mobility of various types (Salt 1988; but also see Mahroum, 2001, on this limiting assumption). However, knowledge transfer also occurs beyond the boundaries of individual firms.

Gertler (2003) identifies three formats for inter-firm knowledge transfer which bring together research strands from management and economic geography: learning regions, communities of association and knowledge enablers.

- *Learning regions:* This literature (Maskell and Malmberg, 1999) starts from the logical premise that tacit knowledge is most effectively shared, face to face, by individuals who share some key features: the same language, shared norms and personal knowledge of each other through previous collaboration or interaction which has facilitated mutual trust. The emphasis on face-to-face contacts, and locally grounded trust, leads to the conclusion that geographical clustering facilitates tacit knowledge transfers. However, Allen (2000, p. 28), amongst others, considers that the importance of geographical clustering, and locally grounded relationships, has been overstated. Instead, he argues that 'the translation of ideas and practices…[is] likely to involve people moving to and through local contexts, to which they bring their own blend of tacit and codified knowledges'. In other words, he implicitly recognises the importance of human mobility.

- *Communities of practice:* This is probably the best known of the literatures in this field. It argues that groups of workers are informally bound together by shared expertise and experience, and over time their collaboration in problem-solving, story telling, etc., facilitates tacit knowledge transfers (Wenger, 1998). Individuals are bound together by shared understandings, developed through effective networking. In this view, organisational and relational proximity are far more important than geographical proximity. Knowledge transfers may occur locally within organisations, or they may be across regional or even national boundaries, within or beyond companies. Brown and Duguid (1991) contend that close-knit communities of practice are usually constituted as face-to-face communities. This does not imply localised proximity, only that there are opportunities for frequent face-to-face contacts (at professional association meetings etc.). The role of migration in this schema is ambiguous.

- *Knowledge enablers:* In this conceptualisation, a key role is played in knowledge transfer by 'knowledge activists'; they are 'boundary spanners', who are critical in disseminating or sharing information (van Krogh et al., 2000). There are micro-communities (small in number, say five to seven individuals) who have worked together in the past, and this facilitates direct, face-to-face interaction, allowing knowledge transfer across boundaries to other work communities. If international borders constitute significant boundaries, then international migrants have significant, and distinctive, potential to act as boundary spanners.

One of the key differences between these theories is the importance they attach to knowledge transfer via geographically localised, as opposed to distanciated, relationships. However, framing the debate in this way creates a false polarisation. Instead, it is more useful to follow Oinas (2000) who, writing about competencies rather than knowledge, emphasises that both local and non-local ties are formative influences, and the balance between them is essentially an empirical not a theoretical question. This raises questions about the precise mechanisms that facilitate either local or distanciated ties and interactions. In the next section, we focus on one such mechanism: migration.

Migration and knowledge transfer

A number of implications follow from the assertion that tacit knowledge can only be effectively transferred amongst individuals who share a common social context. Gertler (2003) argues that tacit knowledge is most effectively acquired experientially, hence spatial distance is an obstacle. The last point is also emphasised by Nonaka et al. (2000, p. 5): 'tacit knowledge is non-transferable without the exchange of key personnel and all the systems that support them'. Migration is one means for effecting an exchange of key personnel, and – as the work of Saxenian (2000) on Silicon Valley demonstrates – a critically important one in many economically dynamic regions. However, given that knowledge is most effectively transferred between those with shared social contexts, there are limits to the extent to which some types of knowledge are transferable between different settings. Hence, the conditions which facilitate knowledge transfer in, say, high-tech regions (e.g. shared understandings of scientific working practices, and knowledge), may not hold in other sectors such as the media or tourism industries.

It is surprising that migration research has paid relatively little attention to the transfer of knowledge per se (but see Williams, 2006). There is, of course, a considerable literature about the transfer of skills (which implicitly includes knowledge), based on the notion of human capital. Due to the difficulties of quantifying many skills and competencies, researchers have mostly focused on qualifications, income and occupational positions, all of which are easier to measure than say social or personal skills.

Similarly, the human capital literature does not address broader issues relating to the different forms of tacit knowledge, as set out above. This was recognised by Li et al. (1996) who called for research on what they termed 'total human capital'. One of the main implications of this approach is that it questions the assumption that skilled workers who take unskilled jobs abroad – perhaps in tourism – constitute human capital brain waste or brain loss. They may not be in jobs which require high-level qualifications, but there may be opportunities to use particular types of knowledge (e.g. of particular national groups of tourists). Similarly, this perspective questions the view that 'unskilled' migrants do not effect knowledge transfers, which is implicit in the way that the human capital and the skills literatures tend to focus on highly skilled workers and managers. Rather, there is a need to question what is understood by knowledge. In reality, unskilled workers may acquire non-occupationally specific competences, such as language or communication skills, which can be valorised, either abroad or through return migration. And they bring new perspective to both the performance of particular tasks, as well as the organisation of work – if they are listened to.

There is therefore a need to examine in more detail how 'total human capital' is constituted. Reich (1992) identifies three types of skill: technical (involving high levels of symbolic manipulation), routine (repetitive work) and social (which facilitate communication and social interaction). Given the emphasis on quantitative indicators, most research has focused on technical and routine skills (as measured in terms of qualifications and occupations), while social skills have been neglected. Evans (2002) provides a more detailed analysis of what he terms 'the competencies' which can be acquired through learning (by all workers), identifying five main types in his 'starfish' model:

- Content related and practical competences (e.g. willingness to carry out a variety of duties);
- Competences related to attitudes and values (e.g. responsibility, or reliability);
- Learning competences (e.g. openness to learning, or perceptiveness);
- Methodological competences (e.g. networking skills or ability to handle multiple tasks); and
- Social and interpersonal competences (e.g. communication skills or awareness of others' viewpoints).

Research on migration has persistently neglected many of these competencies. Even where individual migrants hold what are socially constructed as unskilled jobs, these can provide opportunities to acquire a range of competencies. This reinforces the importance of adopting a more rounded perspective on knowledge and migration. Openness to learning, perceptiveness, networking, communication skills and social awareness are particularly important competences that migrants may acquire in a range of jobs in tourism.

Foreign language competence is one very specific but important form of communication skill that can be acquired by international migrants. Human capital theories have addressed this, not least because it is relatively easily measurable. This has been conceptualised as 'language capital' (Dustmann, 1999). At one level, foreign language skills provide individuals with the communication skills necessary to achieve social recognition whilst working abroad or in particular circumstances after return migration (e.g. securing jobs with foreign-owned companies). But language skills can also be commodified more directly, as a particular form of professional expertise, for example being able to work with foreign language documents, or liaising with foreign clients. The economic value of foreign language skills to migrants, in realising the benefits of investment in education through higher wages, has been empirically verified (e.g. Dustmann, 1994).

Globalisation gives a particular twist to the valorisation of 'language capital', which increasingly need not be country specific. Some languages (notably English) constitute 'the ground floor' of the world hierarchy of languages (van Parijs, 2000). This leads simultaneously to regionalisation and globalisation. Migrants are attracted to particular countries (e.g. the UK, USA, Ireland, Australia, Canada, New Zealand) in order to acquire English language capital. But this opens up global employment prospects, because of the prevalence of English as the language of international business, and of the Internet. This has particular resonance for international tourism in two parallel ways: acquiring or possessing country specific language skills, such as Japanese or Korean, and the value of English as a 'ground-floor language' constituting the everyday 'transaction language' of global tourism.

In one of the few detailed studies of the non-technical competences acquired by migrants, Williams and Balaz (2005) analysed knowledge acquisition and transfer amongst returned migrants to Slovakia from the UK. They interviewed almost 200 return migrants, comparing those who had worked abroad in professional and managerial occupations and those who had migrated as au pairs (live-in domestic helpers, who are also seen partly as engaging in cultural tourism). They found surprising similarities in how different migrants evaluated their experiences. Most au pairs and professional/managerial migrants were strongly positive in their self-evaluation of the impact of migration on their income and status. This was mainly because what they valued most was the acquisition of English language competence, followed by self-confidence, enhanced networking capacity and self-presentation skills. In different ways, these enabled many returned migrants to acquire better-paid or different jobs on their return to Slovakia. In other words, we need to rethink which migrants are involved in knowledge transfer; it is not the preserve of professionals and managers. In this, we agree with Coe and Bunnell (2003, pp. 438–9) that 'we use the term "knowledgeable" migrants/individuals to denote people who embody any form of knowledge...that is of economic value to others, and can enact knowledge transfer by moving across space'. In the next section, we consider the implications of this perspective for understanding the tourism industry.

Rethinking the role of migration in tourism labour

Labour mobility is of course a significant feature of the tourism industry, as recognised by Riley (2004, p. 135):

> The basic components of most mobility studies are movement, motives and effects, and these can be applied at all levels of abstraction in relation to the phenomenon. In this respect the literature uses a range of frameworks that runs from, at the macro-level, trans-national migration through to, at the micro-level, individual job change, whilst taking-in inter-sector, geographic, inter-organisational, and occupational mobility. It is worth noting that tourism employment, somewhat unusually, involves significant mobility in all these categories.

However, research on the role of migration in the production of tourism services has been limited. One of the main lines of investigation has been seeking to understand the high levels of mobility in tourism, and Riley (2004) provides a theoretical approach to this issue. The majority of tourism jobs involve skills that can be acquired relatively quickly through short periods of training or practice. They are part of a secondary labour market, characterised by diverse and accessible job opportunities that, in turn, encourage mobility. But he also argues the need to consider motivations and personality factors, and how these interact with structural factors: 'Indeed the very fact that mobility is possible is part of the attractiveness of the industry in the first place, so structure and motive go hand in hand' (Riley, 2004, p. 137).

Szivas and Riley (1999) also considered mobility in relation to personal orientations to working in tourism. They identified five such orientations:

- Instrumental utility: an easy and convenient industry to earn a living;
- Entrepreneurial outlook: interest in developing a small business with attached life-style;
- Positive orientation: enjoying tourism jobs for their own sake;
- Refugee mentality: flight from problems faced in other sectors; and
- Uncommitted wanderer orientation: travelling more important than the job.

The second to fifth orientations here signal the importance of non-economic motives in tourism-related migration. This needs to be seen in the context of a range of consumption- and production-related tourism–migration links (Williams and Hall, 2002). For many migrants, working in tourism is not necessarily a preferred option, but the outcome of the strong external and weak internal labour markets in this sector compared to other industries. However, for many migrants, there are positive associations of working in tourism, and here we focus on this group. More specifically, this directs attention to Uriely's (2001) useful typology of tourism–migration:

- Travelling professional workers: mainly work-related, and engage in tourism activities as a by-product of travelling.
- Migrant tourism workers: travel in order to make a living, but only amongst tourism places given their pleasure orientation.
- Non-institutionalised working tourists: work while travelling to support their trip.
- Working-holiday tourists: work is part of their tourism experience, e.g. volunteer conservation workers.

The first type are migrants, with dominantly materialistic motives, who work in tourism mainly because of the employment opportunities that are available. The second type, the migrant tourism worker, has mixed economic and tourist motivations. He or she is attracted to a particular tourism destination because of its tourism attractions, and they work in order to support their visit (often seasonally). The attraction may be a specific place (e.g. Paris) or – more generically – a type of tourism destination (e.g. ski resorts). For the third type, the primary motivation is the experience of travelling abroad, and for some this may be a form of adventure tourism, with elements of self-discovery. Work (in any sector) is instrumental in supporting their tourism objectives. Finally, there are those for whom work is part of their tourist experience, notably those working on conservation projects in attractive or challenging locations. There are, then, several forms of tourism–labour migration (in addition to the migrants who work in tourism as a "last" resort), but the implications for knowledge transfer remain poorly understood. The picture is further complicated if a temporal horizon is entered into the analysis to allow for the migration cycle (King, 2002), or cycles of departure and return: migrants may not be listened to as knowledgeable in the tourism industry while working abroad, but they may acquire knowledge which is valued on return to their country of origin (or, indeed, to a third country).

We consider each of Uriely's (2001) first three types of migrants in turn (the last is a relatively minor category of workers), and explore further their economic relationships, especially in terms of knowledge creation and transfer.

Travelling professional workers

This is the group that is most commonly referenced in the general labour migration literature (Beaverstock, 2002). They are a group of managers and professionals who develop their careers through migration. This can be self-organised (the free agents or free movers referred to earlier), or can constitute managed intra-company mobility. Both have implications for knowledge transfer.

In the case of intra-company transnational moves, there are two competing models. Morgan (2001) distinguishes between the multinational and the global company. The multinational company is hierarchical, and communication is focused on the home country HQ. Managers' careers are centred on this, and they will move down to branch plants, for postings, but will always remain focused on the home base. In contrast, the global company has:

> a thick web of communications possibilities, vertically and horizontally. Managers' careers would be varied and would involve movement across different subsidiaries, as well as into head office. Senior management would reflect a wider group of nationalities and experiences than in the multinational enterprise. Learning would be dispersed, often disorganised but usually multi-directional in terms of its effects.
>
> *(Morgan, 2001, p. 22)*

In this case, migration is a key mechanism, indeed an inherent component, of company strategies for the management of knowledge transfer. Classically, it is most likely to be found in those two tourism sectors with the highest levels of transnational ownership: hotels and airlines. Migration may become an essential part of the career development strategies of many managers. Gunz (1998) sees this in terms of managers deliberately accumulating human capital (knowledge) through a sequence of jobs. However, a note of caution is required here, for Ladkin and Riley (1996) contend that the hierarchical, intra-company model of careers is not characteristic of hotel managers. Rather, they argue that inter-organisational mobility not intra-organisational mobility is dominant, that is inter-company not intra-company moves.

The knowledge transfers effected by intra-company mobility are likely to be highly structured, being managed by companies to achieve particular ends such as the dispersion of company practices or organisational contacts, providing opportunities to acquire knowledge of local markets, and to develop social networks. However, the possibility of unforeseen outcomes in knowledge transfer in this context should not be underestimated. In contrast, inter-company moves have less predictable impacts, although they will be structured by the work culture and organisational framework of the destination company.

Migrant tourism workers

Migrant tourism workers travel in order to make a living, but only amongst those places with particular tourism environments. They are typified by ski or surfing instructors who may move seasonally between work locations, but also include more universally transferable types of tourism occupations, such as chefs or receptionists. And non-institutionalised working tourists work while abroad to fund their travels, and include, for example, a large proportion of young tourists on gap years between school, university and permanent work, or who take time out from permanent employment. At first glance, and examining the types of job involved, the knowledge transfers associated with these categories, especially the latter, appear limited. However, if the social skills identified by Reich (1992) are considered, these migrants can be seen to have a far greater role to play in knowledge transfer.

The last argument is exemplified by employer surveys. For example, 'foreign skills' (linguistic and cultural knowledge) are valued by many prospective employers. Dawkins et al. (1995) found that the 'foreign skills' most valued by employers were foreign language proficiency, experience of contacts with foreign people, having lived or worked in a foreign country, specific cultural knowledge, knowledge of foreign business ethics and practice, and formal study of a foreign country. This is broadly confirmed by Aitken and Hall's (2000) findings that in New Zealand the most important 'foreign skills' for tourism firms were specific cultural knowledge (e.g. of the service expected by particular key national market segments), followed by extensive contacts with foreign people and knowledge of foreign business practices and ethics. These skills are likely to be particularly important in nationally segmented niche markets. For example, many Koreans and Japanese are employed in hotels and restaurants in Australia and New Zealand, where there are significant numbers of Korean or Japanese tourists. In terms of types of knowledge, these are classic examples of embodied knowledge (language skills). However, they also include embedded knowledge (e.g. in response to tourists who seek service delivery that is similar to that in their own country). In other words, while such embedded knowledge is necessarily context dependent, because it is shaped by situational factors and shared meanings, these tourism firms seek to create hybrid versions of this knowledge in the tourism destinations.

The importance of migrants' embodied knowledge should not be under-estimated. Crang's (1994) study of waiters in themed restaurants provides one of the most detailed case studies of performance in the hospitality industry. Customers expect certain performances from waiters and waitresses, whilst also actively contributing to these performances. More generally, Crang (1997, p. 147) argues that tourism products are experiential and interactional (involving employees and tourists), whilst 'tourist places are not just imagined places, they are also performed places; and tourism employees are not just actors on a stage, they have to act out that stage'. This means not only that the labour process cannot be predetermined by managers, but also that managers need to attract and retain the staff who have valued embodied knowledge. Migrants represent the mobility of embodied knowledge, which can be critical in those work performances that require culturally specific and linguistic knowledge. The very process of the internationalisation of tourism therefore reinforces the value of international migrant labour, in respect of both embodied and embedded skills. Moreover, many of these skills can be acquired outside of the tourism work place. Therefore, tourism firms potentially can tap into a wide range of migration and return migration flows, all of which transport various types of knowledge.

Conclusions and research agenda

The central argument which emerges in this chapter is that tourism firms are, in effect, located amidst multiple flows of different types of knowledge. Some of these are highly structured, as within firms, while others flow around them more autonomously, as epitomised by 'free mover labour migrants'. Not all of these involve corporeal mobility, let alone migration, and it is important to recognise the importance of communities of association, and learning regions, as alternative channels for tacit knowledge transfer, as well as the more obvious role of codified knowledge in the form of training manuals, websites, etc. In many ways, the tourism industry is no different to any other industry in respect of the role of migration in knowledge transfer.

However, the very nature of international tourism, involving the (international) mobility of demand poses particular needs in respect of embodied, and – almost contradictorily – embedded, knowledge transfers through labour migration. Of course, many of the migrants who work in tourism do so by default or for serendipitous reasons. But the nature of the international tourism experience means there are some highly specific and targeted tourism-related labour flows (Uriely, 2001; Williams and Hall, 2002). Tourism firms do require workers who have embedded knowledge of the country of origin of the tourists, and of particular foreign languages. It is this particular conjunction of the mobility of tourists and (potential) tourism workers that lies at the heart of distinctive knowledge creation and transfer processes in tourism.

Of course, the role of labour migration in respect of knowledge should not be overestimated. In practice, there can be considerable barriers to firms utilising migrants' skills and knowledge. First, there are limits to the extent to which individual migrants can transfer tacit knowledge to other workers. By its very nature, tacit knowledge cannot always be articulated. Secondly, if knowledge is deeply embedded within and inseparable from the practices and activities that people undertake, it cannot exist independently of them, that is, it is context dependent. Hence, while migrant workers may have advantages in terms of dealing with groups of tourists of their own nationality, their knowledge is constrained by the cultural and other specificities of dealing with them in different locales. Thirdly, individuals may be unwilling to share knowledge; knowledge hoarding may manifest itself at the individual level, or at a group level, being influenced by the development of sub-cultures within an organisation (Alvesson and Karreman, 2001). Fourthly, there are issues about the receptiveness of individuals to knowledge transfers from those who can be 'othered', such as migrants: sources of resistance lie in issues of positionality (especially focusing on race and ethnicity), transcultural communication and social identities.

Turning to the future, this chapter points to three significant areas of tourism research. First, there is a need for empirical studies to identify the types of knowledge transfer which can be articulated through migration, and to explore the differences which exist between tourism sub-sectors, organisational types and places. Second, there is a need for ethnographic research, exemplified by detailed case studies of particular firms, that will allow exploration of how migrants engender flows of knowledge within firms, and how these are translated into work and organisational practices, but also how and why they are resisted. And, finally, further work on reconceptualising tourism as constituted of flows of workers, tourists, capital and knowledge will open up new perspectives on competitiveness, innovation and productivity in the sector.

References

Aitken, C. and Hall, C. M. (2000) 'Migrant and foreign skills and their relevance to the tourism industry'. *Tourism Geographies: An International Journal of Place, Space and the Environment*, 2(3), 66–86

Allen, J. (2000) 'Power/economic knowledges: Symbolic and spatial formations'. In J. Bryson, P. W. Daniels, N. Henry and J. Pollard (eds) *Knowledge, space, economy*. London: Routledge, pp. 15–33

Alvesson, M. and Karreman, D. (2001) 'Odd couple: Making sense of the curious concept of knowledge management'. *Journal of Management Studies*, 38(7), 995–1018

Atkinson, J. (1984) *Flexibility, uncertainty and manpower management* (Report no. 89). Brighton: Institute of Manpower Studies, University of Sussex

Baldacchino, G. (1997) *Global tourism and informal labour relations: The small-scale syndrome at work*. London: Mansell

Beaverstock, J. V. (2002) 'Transnational elites in global cities: British expatriates in Singapore's financial district'. *Geoforum*, 33(4), 525–38

Blackler, F. (1995) 'Knowledge, knowledge work and organizations: An overview and interpretation'. *Organization Studies*, 16(6), 1021–46

Brown, J. S. and Duguid, P. (1991) 'Organizational learning and communities-of-practice: Toward a unified view of working, learning, and innovation'. *Organization Science*, 2(1), 40–57

Coe, N. M. and Bunnell, T. G. (2003) '"Spatializing" knowledge communities: Towards a conceptualization of transnational innovation networks'. *Global Networks*, 3(4), 437–56

Crang, P. (1994) 'It's showtime: On the workplace geographies of display in a restaurant in southeast England'. *Society and Space*, 12(6), 675–704

—— (1997) 'Performing the tourist product'. In C. Rojek and J. Urry (eds) *Touring cultures: Transformations of travel and theory*. London: Routledge, pp. 137–54

Dawkins, P., Kemo, S. and Cabalu, H. (1995) *Trade and investment with East Asia in selected service industries: The role of immigrants*. Canberra: Bureau of Immigration and Population

Dierkes, M., Antal, B., Child, J. and Nonaka, I. (2001) *Handbook of organizational learning and knowledge*. Oxford: Oxford University Press

Drucker, P. F. (1993) *Post-socialist society*. London: Butterworth-Heinemann

Dustmann, C. (1994) 'Speaking fluency, writing fluency, and earnings of migrants'. *Journal of Population Economics*, 7(2), 226–36

—— (1999) 'Temporary migration, human capital and language fluency of migrants'. *Scandinavian Journal of Economics*, 101(2), 297–314

Easterby-Smith, M. M. (2003) *The Blackwell handbook of organizational learning and knowledge*. Oxford: Blackwell

Empson, L. (2001) 'Introduction: Knowledge management in professional service firms'. *Human Relations*, 54(7), 811–17

Evans, K. (2002) 'The challenges of "making learning visible": Problems and issues in recognizing tacit skills and key competences'. In K. Evans, P. Hodkinson and L. Unwin (eds), *Working to learn: Transformative learning in the workplace*. London: Kogan Page, pp. 7–28

Folbre, N. (2001) *The invisible heart: Economics and family values*. New York: New Press

Gertler, M. S. (2003) 'Tacit knowledge and the economic geography of context, or the undefinable tacitness of being (there)'. *Journal of Economic Geography*, 3(1), 75–99

Goldthorpe, J. H., Lackwood, D., Bechhofer, F. and Platt, J. (1968) *The affluent worker: Industrial attitudes and behavior*. Cambridge: Cambridge University Press

Gunz, H. (1998) 'Organizational logics of managerial careers'. *Organization Studies*, 9(4), 529–54

Huber, G. (1991) 'Organizational learning: The contributing processes and the literatures'. *Organization Science*, 2(1), 88–115

Hudson, R. (2001) *Producing places*. New York: Guilford Press

—— (2004) 'Conceptualizing economies and their geographies: Spaces, flows and circuits'. *Progress in Human Geography*, 28(4), 447–71

Kanter, R. M. (1995) 'Nice work if you can get it: The software industry as a model for tomorrow's jobs'. *The American Prospect*, 6(23), 52–65

King, R. (2002) 'Towards a new map of European migration'. *International Journal of Population Geography*, 8(2), 89–106

von Krogh, G., Ichijo, K. and Nonaka, I. (2000) *Enabling knowledge creation: How to unlock the mystery of tacit knowledge and release the power of innovation*. New York: Oxford University Press

Ladkin, A. and Riley, M. (1996) 'Mobility and structure in the career paths of UK hotel managers: A labour market hybrid of the bureaucratic model?'. *Tourism Management*, 17(6), 443–52

Lam, A. (2000) 'Tacit knowledge, organizational learning and societal institutions: An integrated framework'. *Organization Studies*, 21(3), 487–513

Li, F. N. L., Findlay, A. M., Jowett, A. J. and Skeldon, R. (1996) 'Migrating to learn and learning to migrate'. *International Journal of Population Geography*, 2(1), 51–67

Lockwood, A. and Guerrier, Y. (1989) 'Flexible working in the hospitality industry: Current strategies and future potential'. *Journal of Contemporary Hospitality Management*, 1(1), 11–16

Mahroum, S. (2001) 'Europe and the immigration of highly skilled labour'. *International Migration*, 39(5), 27–43

Maskell, P. and Malmberg, A. (1999) 'The competitiveness of firms and regions: "Ubiquitification" and the importance of localized learning'. *European Urban and Regional Studies*, 6(1), 9–27

Milne, S. and Pohlmann, C. (1998) 'Continuity and change in the hotel sector: Some evidence from Montreal.' In D. Ioannides and K. G. Debbage (eds) *The economic geography of the tourist industry: A supply-side analysis*. London: Routledge, pp. 180–94

Morgan, G. (2001) 'Transnational communities and business systems'. *Global Networks*, 1(2), 113–30

Nelson, R. and Winter, S. (1982) *An evolutionary theory of economic change*. Cambridge, MA: Harvard University Press

Nonaka, I. and Takeuchi, H. (1995) *The knowledge creating company*. Oxford: Oxford University Press

Nonaka, I., Toyama, R. and Nagata, A. (2000) 'A firm as a knowledge-creating entity: A new perspective on the theory of the firm'. *Industrial and Corporate Change*, 9(1), 1–20

Oinas, P. (2000) 'Distance and learning: Does proximity matter?'. In F. Boekma, K. Morgan, S. Bakkers and B. Rutten (eds) *Knowledge, innovation and economic growth: The theory and practice of learning regions*. Cheltenham: Edward Elgar, pp. 57–69

van Parijs, P. (2000) 'The ground floor of the world: On the socio-economic consequences of linguistic globalization'. *International Political Science Review*, 21(2), 217–33

Polanyi, M. (1966) *The tacit dimension*. London: Routledge Kegan Paul

Reich, R. (1992) *The work of nations: Preparing ourselves for 21st century capitalism*. New York: Vintage Books

Riley, M. (2004) 'Labour mobility and market structure in tourism'. In A. Lew, M. Hall and A. M. Williams (eds) *A companion to tourism*. Oxford: Blackwells, pp. 135–45

Riley, M., Ladkin, A. and Szivas, E. (2002) *Tourism employment: Analysis and planning*. Clevedon: Channel View Publications

Salt, J. (1988) 'Highly skilled international migrants, careers and internal labour markets'. *Geoforum*, 19(4), 387–99

Saxenian, S. (2000) *Silicon Valley's new immigrant entrepreneurs* (Working Paper No. 15). San Diego, CA: The Centre for Comparative Immigration Studies, University of California

Shaw, G. and Williams, A. M. (1994) *Critical issues in tourism: A geographical perspective*. Oxford: Blackwell

—— (2004) *Tourism and tourism spaces*. London: Sage

Szivas, E. and Riley, M. (1999) 'Tourism employment in conditions of economic transition: The case of Hungary'. *Annals of Tourism Research*, 26(4), 747–71

Uriely, N. (2001) '"Travelling workers" and "working tourists": Variations across the interaction between work and tourism'. *International Journal of Tourism Research*, 3(1), 1–8

Venzin, M., von Krogh, G. and Roos, J. (1998) 'Future research into knowledge management'. In G. R. von Krogh, R. Johan and D. Kleine (eds) *Knowing in firms: Understanding, managing and measuring knowledge*. London: Sage, pp. 26–66

Wenger, E. (1998) *Communities of practice: Learning, meaning, and identity*. Cambridge: Cambridge University Press

Williams, A. M. (2006) 'Lost in translation: International migration, learning and knowledge'. *Progress in Human Geography*, 30(5), 588–607

—— and Balaz, V. (2005) 'What human capital, which migrants? Returned skilled migration from Slovakia to the UK'. *International Migration Review*, 39(2), 439–68

—— and Hall, C. M. (2002) 'Tourism, migration, circulation and mobility: The contingencies of time and place'. In M. Hall and A. M. Williams (eds) *Tourism and migration: New relationships between production and consumption*. Dordrecht: Kleuwer, pp. 1–52

17

Reflections on the social construction of skills in hospitality

Preliminary findings from comparative international studies

Tom Baum, Frances Devine, Hanan Kattara, Hai-yan Kong, Wilson Osoro, Rivanda Meira Teixeira, Kong-Yew Wong

Introduction

Work in personal services such as hospitality is widely described as 'low skills' in both the academic literature (Shaw and Williams, 1994; Westwood, 2002; Wood, 1997) and the popular press. This stereotype is challenged in the context of hospitality in the work of a number of writers (Baum, 1996, 2002; Burns, 1997; Nickson et al., 2003) on the basis that this represents a Western-centric and product-focused perception of work and skills. The study reported in this paper seeks to contribute empirically to this debate by reporting preliminary findings from a trans-cultural, international comparison of work, training and skills application in one area of hospitality operations – that of the hotel front office.

The role of skills and skills development through training in the contemporary economy is a matter of considerable academic and political debate. There appears to be an inexorable move towards a redefinition of the economy of many countries in terms of poorly defined skill thresholds so that comparative statements about countries as high- or low-skill economies are paraded without seeming critical analysis of what such assertions actually mean. Public policy in many countries focuses on the development of what are seen as a high–skill employment and business environment (Brown et al., 2001). At the same time, most developed or high–skill economies also depend to a significant extent on an alternative economy based on what are loosely and pejoratively described as 'low-skill' jobs. Little critical analysis has been undertaken with respect to what such descriptors actually mean. 'Low skills' can be seen in terms of the actual technical requirements of the job – this is the most common interpretation – or as an indicator of the value that society places on work in the area in question. The two interpretations may have some overlap but are not necessarily synonymous.

This chapter reports preliminary findings from an empirical exploration of the extent to which our understanding of hospitality skills is socially and culturally constructed. Specifically, the research addresses the underpinning (generic) and job-specific skills that are required in the delivery of hotel front office tasks in hotels of comparable standard across a range of cultures and contexts. In undertaking this, the study will build on a previous pan-European study of hotel front office work (Baum and Odgers, 2001; Odgers and Baum, 2001). Hotel front office has been chosen because, while it is not the 'lowest' of the skills areas in hospitality, it represents an area where external and internal change have impacted greatly in recent years and where there is some evidence of changing skills expectations and technical deskilling among employers and educational providers.

The study comprises an international comparative study of front office work across both developed and developing country contexts, based on both quantitative and qualitative data. The outcomes of this ongoing study include detailed comparison of work, broadly within a common designation, in hotel front office, drawn from fieldwork in a number of locations as part of a study that will encompass approximately 15 locations worldwide upon its completion. The findings of this preliminary report on the research project explore the extent to which the skills expected and delivered are common across 7 selected locations where the study has been completed (Brazil, China, Egypt, Kenya, Kyrgyzstan, Malaysia and Northern Ireland). This forms the basis of tentative conclusions regarding the social and cultural construction of our understanding of skills and work in this area.

Skills and the hospitality sector

The hospitality sector is a case environment for the consideration of skills within the wider services sector. Despite its low status, it is one of the fastest growing sectors in the economy of most countries (developed and developing) and is challenging from a skills perspective in both bouyant and recessionary labour market conditions. Broad estimates suggest that up to 10 per cent of the global workforce are employed in hospitality-related work and, as a consequence, this is a sector that cannot readily be ignored. There is a significant coverage of the changing skills environment within the labour process literature, addressing issues such as deskilling (Elger, 1982), gender (Jenson, 1989), technology substitution (Cavestro, 1989; Coombs, 1985) and the development of skills though apprenticeship training (More, 1982). The focus in much of the literature, however, is on skills within traditional industrial sectors to the relative neglect of services. Consequently, attempts to classify skills (Noon and Blyton, 1995) are limited in their understanding of the nature of service work and the skills required in its delivery (Keep and Mayhew, 1999).

Many aspects of hospitality work have much in common with other areas of service delivery. There is, however, an argument that it is the context and combination of these skills that does generate unique attributes (see e.g. Lashley and Morrison, 2000 on the nature of hospitality; Hochschild, 1983; Morris and Feldman, 1996; Seymour, 2000 and their discussion of emotional labour; and the contribution of Warhurst et al., 2000 in adding the concept of aesthetic labour to the skills bundle in hospitality). Therefore, the debate about skills issues, in the context of hospitality, is informed by wider, generic consideration about skills in the context of changing employment, technology and vocational education, within both developed and developing economies. The major gap in understanding, which this study seeks to address, is the extent to which work which is perceived to be low skilled in the Western, developed context can be described in this way in other contexts because of differing cultural, communications, linguistic and relationship assumptions which underpin such work in developing countries.

Hospitality work in areas such as front office exhibits considerable variety. The traditional research focus on hospitality work concentrates on areas that provide, primarily, food and beverage (Gabriel, 1988; Mars and Nicod, 1984) and, to a lesser extent, accommodation. Coverage of this discussion is well served by reference to Wood (1997), Guerrier and Deery (1998) amongst others. Research in other areas of hospitality work, such as hotel front office, is much more poorly served (Bird et al., 2002; Vallen and Vallen, 2000) and this study draws on a limited range of work in these areas. The 'newer' areas include functions and tasks that exhibit considerable crossover with work that falls outside normal definitions of hospitality in food and drink manufacture: office administration, IT systems management and specialist areas of sports and leisure. Indeed, it is fair to say that, although there is long-standing debate as to whether the hospitality industry is 'unique' (Lashley and Morrison, 2000; Mullins, 1981), there is little doubt that there is little unique about hospitality skills. Most of the skills that are employed within the sector also have relevance and application in other sectors of the economy. Those employed in areas where there is considerable skills overlap with hospitality, such as the areas listed above, may well see themselves in terms of their generic skills area rather than as part of the hospitality labour market.

The characteristics and the organisation of the hospitality industry are subject to ongoing restructuring and evolutionary change. There are major labour market and skills implications of such change as businesses reshape the range of services they offer (Hjalager and Baum, 1998) or respond to fashion and trend imperatives in the consumer marketplace (Warhurst et al., 2000). Vertical diversity in hospitality work is represented by a more traditional classification that ranges from unskilled through semi-skilled and skilled to supervisory and management. This 'traditional' perspective of work and, therefore, skills in hospitality is partly described by Riley (1996) in terms that suggest that the proportionate breakdown of the workforce in hospitality at unskilled and semiskilled levels is 64 per cent of the total with skilled constituting a further 22 per cent of the total. Abdullah's (2005) figures for Malaysia, while not based on directly comparable data, suggest that non-managerial positions break down into unskilled (19 per cent) and skilled/semi-skilled (42 per cent). These figures hint at a major difference in perceptions of skills within the sector between developed and developing economies.

These simplifications mask major business organisational diversity in hospitality, reflecting the size, location and ownership of businesses. The actual job and skills content of work in the sector is predicated upon these factors so that common job titles (e.g. restaurant manager, sous chef) almost certainly mask a very different range of responsibilities, tasks and skills within jobs in different establishments.

The skills profile of hospitality is influenced by the labour market that is available to it, both in direct terms and via educational and training establishments. The weak internal labour market characteristics in themselves impose downward pressures on the skills expectations that employers have of their staff and this, in turn, influences the nature and level of training which the educational system delivers. There is an evident cycle of down-skilling, not so much in response to the actual demands of hospitality or of consumer expectations of what it can deliver, but as a result of the perceptions of potential employees and the expectations that employers have of them.

Hospitality work is widely characterised in both the popular press and in research-based academic sources as dominated by a low-skills profile but Burns (1997) questions the basis for categorising hospitality employment into 'skilled' and 'unskilled' categories, arguing the post-modernist case that this separation is something of a social construct. This construct is rooted in, firstly, manpower planning paradigms for the manufacturing sector and, secondly, in the traditional power of trade unions to control entry into the workplace through lengthy apprenticeships. Burns bases this argument on a useful consideration of the definition of skills in hospitality, noting that:

> the different sectors that comprise hospitality-as-industry take different approaches to their human resources, and that some of these differences...are due to whether or not the

employees have a history of being 'organised' (either in terms of trade unions or staff associations with formalised communication procedures).

(Burns, 1997, p. 240)

This strong internal labour market analysis leads Burns to argue that skills within 'organised' sectors such as airlines and hotel companies with clearly defined staff relationship structures, such as the Sheraton, are recognised and valued. By contrast, catering and fast food 'operate within a business culture where labour is seen in terms of costs which must be kept at the lowest possible level' (Burns, 1997, p. 240) and where skills, therefore, are not valued or developed. Burns' definition of hospitality and hospitality skills seeks to go beyond the purely technical capabilities that those using 'unskilled' or 'low-skills' descriptors assume.

This case is also argued by Poon (1993), who notes that new employees in hospitality:

Must be trained to be loyal, flexible, tolerant, amiable and responsible…at every successful hospitality establishment, it is the employees that stand out…Technology cannot substitute for welcoming employees.

(Poon, 1993, p. 262)

Burns' emphasis on 'emotional demands' as an additional dimension of hospitality and hospitality skills has been developed in the work of Seymour (2000). Her work builds upon the seminal earlier work of Hochschild (1983) who introduced the concept of emotional work within the services economy. Hochschild argues that service employees are required to manage their emotions for the benefit of customers and are, in part, paid to do this. Likewise, Seymour recognises that what she calls 'emotional labour' is a concept of relevance to work in both fast food and traditional areas of service work. She concludes that both areas demand considerable emotional elements in addition to overt technical skills.

Burns rightly argues that the low-skills perspective of hospitality is context-specific and drawn from a Western-centric view of hospitality. He cites the inappropriateness of these assumptions when applied to environments such as the Soloman Islands, Sri Lanka and the Cook Islands. Likewise, Baum (1996) questions the validity of claims that hospitality is a work area of low skills. His argument is based on the cultural assumptions that lie behind employment in Westernised, international hospitality work whereby technical skills are defined in terms of a relatively seamless progression from domestic and consumer life into the hospitality workplace. In the developing world, such assumptions cannot be made as employees join hospitality and hospitality businesses without Western acculturation, without, for example, knowledge of the implements and ingredients of Western cookery. Learning at a technical level, therefore, is considerably more demanding than it might be in Western communities. Social and interpersonal skills also demand considerably more by way of prior learning, whether this pertains to language skills (English is a widespread prerequisite for hospitality and hospitality work in countries such as Thailand) or wider cultural communications. On the basis of this argument, Baum contends that work that may be unskilled in Europe and the USA requires significant investment in terms of education and training elsewhere and cannot, therefore, be universally described as 'low skilled'. This issue is one that is beginning to assume significance in Western Europe as a combination of service sector labour shortages and growing immigration from countries of Eastern Europe and elsewhere means that skills assumptions in hospitality can no longer be taken for granted. The current hospitality labour market in the Republic of Ireland illustrates this situation where service standards are under challenge as the industry recruits staff from a wide range of former eastern bloc countries.

It is also useful, in summary of this section of the debate, to consider hospitality work in the light of the work of Noon and Blyton (1995). Their approach is to consider skills in terms of personal attributes, job requirements and the setting of work. This approach, with a focus on the context of work, both from an individual and organisational point of view, is much more sympathetic to the realities of diversity within hospitality work, as argued above by Burns and Baum. Noon and Blyton appear to accept that what is skilled work in one context may be less so in another, influenced by both the cultural context of the work and also by the availability and application of technology. It is argued, therefore, that a simple labelling of hospitality work as 'unskilled' is both unhelpful and unjustifiable.

Methodology

This chapter reports initial findings from a study that will, eventually, permit comparison between some 15 locations worldwide. The methodology adopted within this study is common to all locations and is based on a self-completed questionnaire which looks at who hotel front office staff are, their backgrounds, training profiles, working experience and perceptions of skills and skills development. In each selected location, 4 star and 5 star hotels were selected (recognising that such star designations do not allow for truly accurate comparison) as those properties most likely to be operating in the international market. In most cases of fieldwork, the focus of the study is on a discrete location within the country, generally a large urban area, although two of the completed studies have a more national focus (China, Kenya). As a result of this approach, the number of participating hotels in each location varies significantly (in Kyrgyzstan, for example, only three properties could be identified that fitted into this classification), while the population in other locations was considerably greater.

The study was undertaken with the assistance of collaborating researchers in most locations. The choice of locations was, to a certain degree, opportunistic in that participation was determined by access to resources and personnel to conduct the study locally. Table 17.1 shows the study locations where the survey has been completed. However, further research is currently being undertaken in order to extend the scope of the study.

In conducting the survey, initial contact was with the general manager of intended sample hotels, seeking permission to conduct the survey locally in her/his property. Once permission was agreed, questionnaires were distributed for completion by all front office staff and collected at an agreed time by the researchers. In addition, where permission was granted, follow-up

Table 17.1 Research locations

Country	Survey conducted	Data analysed
Kyrgyzstan (Bishkek)	X	X
Northern Ireland (Belfast)	X	X
Egypt (Cairo)	X	X
Brazil (Curitiba)	X	X
Kenya (national)	X	X
Malaysia (Kuala Lumpur)	X	X
China (Shandong Province)	X	X

Further locations are being sought to extend the scope of the study.

unstructured discussion on key survey themes was initiated with front office staff in order to probe these in greater depth although information from this aspect of the study is not presented in this paper. Response rates within individual hotels were high, ranging from 60 per cent to 100 per cent of those in the front office team.

Preliminary findings

This chapter reports findings from seven locations: Brazil (Curitiba), China (Beijing, Tianjin, Shanghai, Jinan, Qingdao and Weihai), Egypt (Cairo), Kenya (Nairobi, Mombasa, Safari Lodges), Kyrgyzstan (Bishkek), Malaysia (Kuala Lumpur) and Northern Ireland (Belfast), in order to give a flavour of the outcomes of the wider survey.

Who are the front office employees?

Responses were mainly received from front office staff in all three research locations across a range of levels: management and supervisory staff, senior and junior staff, and trainees. A small number of respondents worked in other front office functions such as portering (Table 17.2).

This finding is in partial agreement with Odgers and Baum (2001), who noted a weakening of traditional workplace hierarchies in front office, with a decline in the position of junior or assistant receptionists. Dependence on more junior positions remains evident in Kyrgyzstan (Table 17.3).

The gender breakdown points to very significant differences between the seven research environments, suggesting variation based on both cultural and economic factors. The female domination of front office work is consistent with Odgers and Baum's (2001) survey of such work across eight Western European countries, but is also an interesting reflection of work in urban Chinese locations. In the former Soviet Republic of Kyrgyzstan, the predominant position of males in front office work is, on the face of it, surprising in that in the past this would have been an area dominated by female workers. However, the findings here point to

Table 17.2 Position of respondents (%)

Position of Respondent	Brazil (n=64)	China (n=276)	Egypt (n=96)	Kenya (n=107)	Kyrgyzstan (n=20)	Malaysia (n=52)	Northern Ireland (n=64)
Department Manager	6	3.3	8	7	10	7	22
Supervisor	5	10.2	14	18	20	20	19
Senior Staff Member	41	15.8	53	26	20	23	23
Junior Staff Member	23	60.9	8	53	50	19	22
Trainee	2	9.8	11	3	0	8	9
Other	23	0	6	0	0	13	5

Table 17.3 Gender of respondents (%)

Gender	Brazil (n=64)	China (n=276)	Egypt (n=96)	Kenya (n=107)	Kyrgyzstan (n=20)	Malaysia (n=52)	Northern Ireland (n=64)
Female	33	64	24	49	30	71	88
Male	67	36	76	51	70	29	12

male encroachment on areas of work which provide relatively well-paid opportunities in international companies. The Kenyan findings show the most balanced workforce in gender terms.

Among front office employees in Malaysia, all respondents were full-time employees, working 48 hours or more per week and a similar picture emerges in China where 99.4 per cent of front office workers were full time. In Northern Ireland, all but five (8 per cent) of the respondents worked full time in the hotel front office, committing 39–49 hours per week to the job. In Kenya, all but one of the sample was in full-time employment. A similar pattern was found in Kyrgyzstan where 3 of the sample (15 per cent) were not full time. In Egypt, however, as many as 33 of the sample (34 per cent) were part-time employees, while in Brazil 33 per cent of employees interviewed were part-timers. Among these were most of the female respondents to the survey. Split shifts, a particularly unpopular model of working, were worked by 7 respondents (11 per cent) in Northern Ireland, by 10 (16 per cent) in Brazil, by 7 (35 per cent) in Kyrgyzstan, by 40 Kenyan respondents (37 per cent) and by 44 in Egypt (46 per cent).

Front office employees and their education

Very different patterns of educational attainment were evident across the seven survey respondents (Table 17.4). The Egyptian and Kyrgyz samples pointed to high levels (half or more) with university-level education, something rather less common in Brazil, China and Northern Ireland, the latter confirming the weakening of higher educational requirements for work of this nature across Western Europe (Odgers and Baum, 2001). The high number of those completing their education at secondary level is noticeable in Brazil but, at the same time, almost 50 per cent of the Brazilian sample had studied front office at some level before entering the industry. Specialist vocational education to diploma level dominates among Kenyan respondents, pointing to the strong role of the main educational provider for the sector in that country, Kenya Utalii College, in meeting the skilled labour market needs of the hospitality sector. A similar pattern is evident in Malaysia where the absence of graduates is particularly noticeable, perhaps reflecting the general demand for higher-level skills within that economy.

Working experience of front office employees

The hotel industry is widely associated with high levels of staff turnover. The findings from all seven survey samples contradict this generalisation and point to relative stability within front office teams, with over 70 per cent of Brazilian, Egyptian, Kenyan and Kyrgyz respondents

Table 17.4 Educational attainment (%)

Educational Level	Brazil (n=64)	China (n=276)	Egypt (n=96)	Kenya (n=107)	Kyrgyzstan (n=20)	Malaysia (n=52)	Northern Ireland (n=64)
Primary	3	0	10	0	5	2	0
Secondary	35	3.9	8	21	20	32	28
Vocational	9	26.1	2	6	5	10	14
Certificate/Diploma	20	48.9	28	71	10	49	33
Bachelor's Degree	27	17.1	48	0	55	7	25
Master's Degree	3	1.1	2	2	5	0	0
Other	3	2.9	2	0	0	0	0

Table 17.5 Duration of work in current hotel (%)

Duration of work	Brazil (n=64)	Egypt (n=96)	Kenya (n=107)	Kyrgyzstan (n=20)	Malaysia (n=52)	Northern Ireland (n=64)
Less than one year	9	10	15	10	27	24
One to two years	15	15	10	20	19	27
Two to four years	26	32	28	55	27	26
More than four years	50	43	47	15	27	23

having worked in their current hotel for over two years. In Malaysia, the comparable figure is 54 per cent while in Northern Ireland, it is 49 per cent (Table 17.5). In China, 75 per cent of the sample are working in their hotel of original employment.

The patterns with respect to the time that front office staff have spent in their current positions are very different, however (Table 17.6). Brazilian, Egyptian and Kenyan staff are significantly more likely to have remained in their current post for two or more years (65+ per cent) than is the case in Malaysia (42 per cent), Kyrgyzstan (40 per cent) or Northern Ireland (19 per cent).

Table 17.6 certainly confirms relative stability within the front office workforce. Egyptian and Kenyan employees are, by a considerable margin, the most likely to seek promotion within their current work area. However, overall, 89 per cent of Egyptian and Kenyan respondents, 85 per cent of those from Kyrgyzstan and Malaysia and 81 per cent of those from Brazil see their future careers within the hotel sector (Table 17.7). By contrast, the comparable figure for China is 32 per cent and for Northern Ireland 39 per cent, potentially representing a significant skills loss to the sector.

Table 17.8, reporting intentions to stay within respondents' present job, indicates a significant degree of uncertainty within four of the sample workforces. Respondents from Egypt and

Table 17.6 Duration of work in current position (%)

Duration of work	Brazil (n=64)	Egypt (n=94)	Kenya (n=107)	Kyrgyzstan (n=20)	Malaysia (n=52)	Northern Ireland (n=64)
Less than one year	6	16	22	20	33	48
One to two years	13	18	10	40	25	33
Two to four years	27	31	43	30	33	11
More than four years	54	35	25	10	9	8

Table 17.7 Next career move (%)

Career Move	Brazil (n=64)	China (n=276)	Egypt (n=96)	Kenya (n=107)	Kyrgyzstan (n=20)	Malaysia (n=52)	Northern Ireland (n=64)
Promotion in my current job	47	53.3	75	75	40	52	38
Move elsewhere in this hotel	29	9.4	3	2	20	13	9
Move to another hotel	5	5.4	11	10	25	15	14
Move out of the hotel sector	14	17.8	11	11	15	15	23
Other	5	14.1	0	2	0	5	16

Table 17.8 Plans to remain in current job (%)

How long do you plan to remain in current job?	Brazil (n=64)	China (n=276)	Egypt (n=96)	Kenya (n=107)	Kyrgyzstan (n=20)	Malaysia (n=52)	Northern Ireland (n=64)
Less than 6 months	7	8.0	14	3	0	8	8
6 months–one year	15	19.4	31	11	10	8	22
Between one and five years	25	30.9	22	41	30	42	17
No plans at this stage	53	41.7	33	45	60	42	53

Table 17.9 Promotion opportunities (%)

Promotion opportunities in my current hotel are	Brazil (n=64)	China (n=276)	Egypt (n=96)	Kenya (n=107)	Kyrgyzstan (n=20)	Malaysia (n=52)	Northern Ireland (n=64)
Excellent	14	8.3	43	32	10	17	11
Satisfactory	35	42.6	54	46	40	47	47
Poor	37	10.1	0	13	30	11	33
Don't Know	14	39.1	3	9	20	25	9

Northern Ireland appear least committed to their current position, while those in emerging tourism destination countries appear most committed to their current employer.

Table 17.9 further points to the positive career perspective of front office employees in Egypt and Kenya, with 97 per cent and 78 per cent respectively believing promotion opportunities to be excellent or satisfactory. Comparable figures for Brazil, China, Kyrgyzstan, Malaysia and Northern Ireland are 49 per cent, 50 per cent, 64 per cent and 68 per cent, reflecting rather greater uncertainty within these working groups.

Perspectives of work in hotel front office

Respondents were asked to respond to statements about working in hotel front office, based on a scale of 1 to 5, where 1 equates to 'Disagree Strongly' and 5 equates to 'Agree strongly' (Table 17.10). The ranking pattern of responses shows major differences, while actual ratings also vary significantly between the seven samples in terms of the range of means generated

Table 17.10 Working in hotel front office

Statement about hotel front office work	Mean and rank response on 5-point scale						
	Brazil	China	Egypt	Kenya	Kyrgyzstan	Malaysia	Northern Ireland
Front office work is a challenging and demanding area of work	3.61 (9)	4.30 (1)	3.80 (7)	4.46 (3)	3.60 (8)	4.11 (2)	4.61 (1)
I enjoy meeting and greeting customers within my job	4.56 (1)	4.19 (2)	4.11 (1)	4.71 (1)	3.35 (11)	4.08 (3)	4.52 (2)

(Continued)

Table 17.10 Cont'd

Statement about hotel front office work	Mean and rank response on 5-point scale						
	Brazil	China	Egypt	Kenya	Kyrgyzstan	Malaysia	Northern Ireland
I enjoy the organisational parts of my job	4.40 (2)	4.16 (3)	4.06 (3)	4.17 (6)	4.10 (3)	3.81 (5)	4.28 (3)
I enjoy the use of technology within my job	3.94 (7)	4.11 (4)	4.11 (1)	4.27 (4)	4.25 (2)	3.71 (6)	4.19 (4)
Front office work is all about personality	4.13 (5)	3.84 (7)	4.00 (6)	3.64 (9)	4.30 (1)	4.13 (1)	4.05 (5)
My area of work is well respected by my family and friends	4.03 (6)	3.77 (8)	4.06 (3)	3.96 (7)	3.85 (6)	3.13 (10)	3.91 (6)
Front office is my preferred field for work and career progression	3.39 (10)	3.74 (9)	3.75 (8)	4.22 (5)	3.90 (4)	3.92 (4)	3.75 (7)
Most work in front office is common sense	4.39 (3)	3.93 (6)	3.59 (9)	3.16 (10)	3.65 (10)	3.67 (8)	3.58 (8)
A specialist course (in hospitality) is useful for front office work	3.72 (8)	3.60 (10)	4.06 (3)	4.51 (2)	3.70 (7)	3.49 (9)	3.48 (9)
I would like the opportunity to work in other areas of the hotel industry	4.14 (4)	3.94 (5)	3.54 (10)	3.83 (8)	3.90 (4)	3.71 (7)	3.37 (10)
I was familiar with most of the tasks in front office before I started work in this area	3.15 (11)	3.38 (11)	3.27 (11)	2.94 (11)	3.60 (8)	2.75 (11)	3.00 (11)

Rank order correlations within the seven sample responses
Spearman's r for:
    Brazil and Egypt = +0.36
    Brazil and China = +0.55
    Brazil and Kenya = +0.15
    Brazil and Kyrgyzstan = −0.08
    Brazil and Malaysia = +0.45
    Brazil and Northern Ireland = +0.34
    China and Egypt = +0.29
    China and Kenya = +0.49
    China and Kyrgyzstan = −0.04
    China and Malaysia = +0.62
    China and Northern Ireland = +0.81
    Egypt and Kenya = +0.69
    Egypt and Kyrgyzstan = +0.03
    Egypt and Malaysia = +0.44
    Egypt and Northern Ireland = +0.57
    Kenya and Kyrgyzstan = −0.06
    Kenya and Malaysia = +0.55
    Kenya and Northern Ireland = +0.63
    Kyrgyzstan and Malaysia = +0.17
    Kyrgyzstan and Northern Ireland = +0.03
    Malaysia and Northern Ireland = +0.72★
★ = Significant at the 5% level

within each survey. What is interesting is the differing levels of correlation between the sample responses. The very close correlation between China and Northern Ireland in this context is particularly noticeable. The Kyrgyz ranking of hotel work attributes appears to show virtually no relationship to those of the other five samples whereas comparison of some of the responses from Brazil, Egypt, Kenya, Malaysia and Northern Ireland show rather greater similarity although not statistically significant at the 5 per cent level.

Importance of specific skills within front office work

Respondents were asked to respond to statements about skills required for work in hotel front office, based on a scale of 1 to 5, where 1 equates to 'Very low importance' and 5 equates to 'Very important' (Table 17.11). Significant variations were found in the mean and ranking of skills by the four samples. Correlations based on the ranking of skills shows relatively close agreement between respondents from across all samples with the exception of Egypt and Kyrgyzstan.

Significance levels point to similarities across pairings that appear to cross cultural, economic and tourism sector differences. For example, perceptions of the relative importance of specific skills is close between Malaysia and Brazil, Kenya and Northern Ireland. The Chinese findings, however, point to similarities in responses to both less- and more-developed environments. The findings, overall, point to some consensus across environments with regard to how front office work is perceived.

Consideration of skills which might be considered of considerable importance to work in hotel front office, that of languages, points to findings which are very consistent with those of Odgers and Baum (2001), who noted that in English speaking countries far fewer front office

Table 17.11 Importance of skills in front office work

Importance of Skills	Mean and rank response on 5 point scale: Brazil	Mean and rank response on 5 point scale: China	Mean and rank response on 5 point scale: Egypt	Mean and rank response on 5 point scale: Kenya	Mean and rank response on 5 point scale: Kyrgyzstan	Mean and rank response on 5 point scale: Malaysia	Mean and rank response on 5 point scale: Northern Ireland
Communication (oral)	4.81 (3)	4.56 (1)	4.18 (10)	4.78 (3)	4.60 (2)	4.62 (1)	4.89 (1)
Customer care	4.87 (1)	4.25 (6)	4.45 (3)	4.84 (1)	4.85 (1)	4.48 (3)	4.88 (2)
Interpersonal skills	4.53 (5)	4.25 (7)	4.45 (3)	4.55 (5)	4.35 (3)	4.55 (2)	4.86 (3)
Team work	4.86 (2)	4.33 (3)	4.62 (1)	4.80 (2)	4.15 (5)	4.35 (4)	4.86 (3)
Use of FO equipment	4.30 (9)	4.29 (5)	4.52 (2)	4.73 (4)	3.65 (10)	3.78 (9)	4.59 (5)
Professional and ethical standards	4.77 (4)	4.43 (2)	4.22 (9)	4.54 (7)	4.15 (5)	3.84 (8)	4.47 (6)
Communication (written)	4.34 (8)	3.92 (12)	4.44 (6)	4.55 (5)	4.35 (3)	4.02 (6)	4.38 (7)
Use of technology	4.49 (7)	4.12 (10)	4.31 (8)	4.34 (9)	3.75 (8)	3.78 (10)	4.27 (8)
Health and safety	3.71 (12)	4.02 (11)	3.97 (13)	4.23 (11)	3.95 (7)	3.60 (11)	4.13 (9)
Leadership qualities	4.52 (6)	4.31 (4)	4.45 (3)	4.33 (10)	3.60 (12)	4.00 (7)	4.08 (10)

(Continued)

Table 17.11 Cont'd

Importance of Skills	Mean and rank response on 5 point scale: Brazil	Mean and rank response on 5 point scale: China	Mean and rank response on 5 point scale: Egypt	Mean and rank response on 5 point scale: Kenya	Mean and rank response on 5 point scale: Kyrgyzstan	Mean and rank response on 5 point scale: Malaysia	Mean and rank response on 5 point scale: Northern Ireland
Marketing	4.05 (11)	4.17 (9)	4.32 (7)	4.41 (8)	3.55 (13)	4.04 (5)	3.72 (11)
Accounting	3.68 (13)	4.18 (8)	4.03 (11)	4.07 (12)	3.65 (10)	3.57 (12)	3.70 (12)
Legal issues	4.29 (10)	3.67 (13)	4.03 (11)	4.03 (13)	3.70 (9)	3.39 (13)	3.69 (13)

Rank order correlations within the seven sample responses
Spearman's r for:
  Brazil and Egypt = +0.40
  Brazil and China = +0.69
  Brazil and Kenya = +0.77*
  Brazil and Kyrgyzstan = +0.58
  Brazil and Malaysia = +0.74*
  Brazil and Northern Ireland = +0.76*
  China and Egypt = +0.29
  China and Kenya = +0.50
  China and Kyrgyzstan = +0.21
  China and Malaysia = +0.53
  China and Northern Ireland = +0.61
  Egypt and Kenya = +0.64
  Egypt and Kyrgyzstan = +0.10
  Egypt and Malaysia = +0.52
  Egypt and Northern Ireland = +0.48
  Kenya and Kyrgyzstan = +0.66
  Kenya and Malaysia = +0.80*
  Kenya and Northern Ireland = +0.92*
  Kyrgyzstan and Malaysia = +0.59
  Kyrgyzstan and Northern Ireland = +0.78*
  Malaysia and Northern Ireland = +0.78*
* = Significant at the 5% level

staff are equipped to communicate with guests who may not wish to communicate in the local language (Table 17.12). In both Egypt and Kyrgyzstan, hotel staff are far more likely to have skills across a range of languages beyond their mother tongue than are their counterparts in Northern Ireland. The findings with respect to Brazil are the most dramatic, with the full sample claiming levels of functional fluency in four languages, including their native Portuguese.

Table 17.12 Fluency in languages (n)

Number of Languages (including mother tongue)	Brazil (n=64)	Egypt (n= 96)	Kenya (n = 107)	Kyrgyzstan (n=20)	Malaysia (n=52)	Northern Ireland (n=64)
1	0	0	0	0	0	44
2	0	77	3	4	20	18
3	0	13	43	7	21	2
4	60	4	44	8	6	0
5 or more	4	2	17	1	5	0

Language skills in Kenya reflect the multilingual culture of that country. A very significant majority of respondents were fluent in three languages, namely their tribal language, Kiswahili and English; a wide range of additional African and European languages were reported in addition. Within the Chinese sample, although some respondents reported limited English, Japanese and Korean skills, overall only a small minority were able to function with languages other than Mandarin and/or their regional dialect.

Conclusions

In this chapter, a flavour of comparative outcomes is presented, with only limited attempts to speculate about the reasons why differences exist within the data sets generated by the four studies. For a variety of reasons, the data here has limitations, not least because of the sample size from one of the studies based as it is on the only international standard hotels in the research location. However, at this point, it is possible to draw a number of tentative inferences from the data analysed:

- Employees bring very different education and training profiles into a largely common (technical) workplace – reflective of economic, labour market but also cultural factors.
- Front office work shows clear gender differences across different cultural contexts.
- Employees bring very different skills profiles into the work area in areas such as languages beyond their mother tongue.
- Variations may reflect employer expectations and demands as well as industry structure factors.
- Employment stability varies greatly according to context – length of service within a particular hotel and in a specific job ranges from short-term to fairly lengthy.
- Career ambitions vary across contexts, from a firm commitment to front office work and the hotel sector in general to rather looser commitment to the work area.
- There is considerable divergence among respondents with regard to the importance of specific aspects of front office work varying across contexts.
- Perceptions of the skills required to undertake such work do not vary as significantly as might have been anticipated.
- Career aspirations and plans are different across contexts.
- Comparison between developed and developing country contexts does not necessarily throw up clear distinctions although there is evidence of a relationship between factors such as job stability, vocational focus, perceived status of front office work and the developing country environment.
- There are variations in notions of job status, perceived position with a skills hierarchy, careers and career opportunities, vocational commitment and skills development in the workplace.
- The findings raise questions with respect to the basis for common skills-development programmes employed by multinational hospitality companies.
- The findings also raise questions with regard to the nature of 'off-the shelf' educational programmes which have historically been used across emerging/developing hospitality destinations, especially those which are donor agency-led (EU, USAid, UNDP, WTO) as these programmes may not reflect the local cultural skills context.

In some respects, these findings may appear to confirm anticipated differences in work and perceptions of work that are the result of a combination of economic, political, cultural and other factors. Further data analysis will enable a clear picture to emerge and permit the extraction of firmer conclusions. These preliminary findings are of considerable importance in that they provide justification for further development of this project along the lines indicated earlier in this chapter. Notwithstanding the apparent attempts of multinational companies and major development agencies that generally assume otherwise, this paper suggests that there is evidence to support the contention that hotel work, specifically in front office, is socially constructed and needs to be viewed from a more context-driven perspective.

References

Abdullah, L. A. (2005) 'The potential of the human resources in the Malaysian hospitality environment: The way ahead in the 21st century'. In *Proceedings of the Third Asia-Pacific CHRIE (APacCHRIE) Conference 2005*. Kuala Lumpur: CHRIE, pp. 777–88

Baum, T. (1996) 'Unskilled work and the hospitality industry: Myth or reality?'. *International Journal of Hospitality Management*, 15(3), 207–9

—— (2002) 'Skills and training for the hospitality sector: A review of issues'. *Journal of Vocational Education and Training*, 54(3), 343–63

Baum, T. and Odgers, P. (2001) 'Benchmarking best practice in hotel front office: The Western European experience'. *Journal of Quality Assurance in Hospitality and Tourism*, 2(3/4), 93–109

Bird, E., Lynch, P. and Ingram, A. (2002) 'Gender and employment flexibility within hotel front office'. *The Service Industries Journal*, 22(3), 99–116

Brown, P., Green, A. and Lauder, H. (2001) *High skills: Globalization, competitiveness and skill formation*. Oxford: Oxford University Press

Burns, P. M. (1997) 'Hard-skills, soft-skills: Undervaluing hospitality's "service with a smile"'. *Progress in Tourism and Hospitality Research*, 3(3), 239–48

Cavestro, W. (1989) 'Automation, new technology and work content'. In S. Wood (ed.) *The transformation of work*. London: Unwin Hyman, pp. 219–34

Coombs, R. (1985) 'Automation, management strategies and the labour process'. In D. Knights, H. Willmott and D. Collinson (eds) *Job redesign: Critical perspectives on the labour process*. Aldershot: Gower, pp. 142–70

Elger, T. (1982) 'Braverman, capital accumulation and deskilling'. In S. Wood (ed.) *The degradation of work? Skilling, deskilling and the labour process*. London: Hutchinson, pp. 23–53

Gabriel, Y. (1988) *Working lives in catering*. London: Routledge

Guerrier, Y. and Deery, M. (1998) 'Research in hospitality human resource management and organizational behaviour'. *International Journal of Hospitality Management*, 17(2), 145–60

Hjalager, A.-M. and Baum, T. (1998) *Upgrading human resources: An analysis of the number, quality and qualifications of employees required in the hospitality sector*. Brussels: Commission of the European Union

Hochschild, A. R. (1983) *The managed heart: Commercialisation of human feeling*. Berkeley, CA: University of California Press

Jenson, J. (1989) 'The talents of women, the skills of men: flexible specialization and women'. In S. Wood (ed.) *The transformation of work? Skill, flexibility and the labour process*. London: Routledge, pp. 141–55

Keep, E. and Mayhew, K. (1999) *Skills task force research paper 6: The leisure sector*. London: DfEE

Lashley, C. and Morrison, A. (eds) (2000) *In search of hospitality*. Oxford: Butterworth-Heinemann

Mars, G. and Nicod, M. (1984) *The world of waiters*. London: Allen and Unwin

More, C. (1982) 'Skill and the survival of apprenticeship'. In S. Wood (ed.) *The degradation of work? Skill, deskilling and the labour process*. London: Hutchinson, pp. 76–93

Morris, J. and Feldman, D. (1996) 'The dimensions, antecedents and consequences of emotional labor'. *Academy of Management Review*, 21, 986–1001

Mullins, L. J. (1981) 'Is hospitality unique?'. *Hospitality*, September, pp. 30–33

Nickson, D., Warhurst, C. and Witz, A. (2003) 'The labour of aesthetics and the aesthetics of organization'. *Organization*, 10(1), 33–54

Noon, M. and Blyton, P. (1995) *The realities of work*. Basingstoke: Macmillan

Odgers, P. and Baum, T. (2001) *Benchmarking of best practice in hotel front office*. Dublin: CERT

Poon, A. (1993) *Hospitality, technology and competitive strategies*. Wallingford: CAB

Riley, M. (1996) *Human resource management in the hospitality and tourism industry* (2nd edn). Oxford: Butterworth-Heinemann

Seymour, D. (2000) 'Emotional labour: A comparison between fast food and traditional service work'. *International Journal of Hospitality Management*, 19(2), 159–71

Shaw, G. and Williams, A. (1994) *Critical issues in hospitality: A geographical perspective*. Oxford: Blackwell

Vallen, G. K. and Vallen, J. J. (2000) *Check in, check out: Front office management* (6th edn). Upper Saddle River, NJ: Prentice Hall

Warhurst, C., Nickson, D., Witz, A. and Cullen, A. M. (2000) 'Aesthetic labour in interactive service work: Some case study evidence from the "New Glasgow"'. *Service Industries Journal*, 20(3), 1–18

Westwood, A. (2002) *Is new work good work?* London: The Work Foundation

Wood, R. C. (1997) *Working in hotels and catering* (2nd edn). London: Routledge

18

Stewardship in family businesses
Implications for sustainable tourism

Donald Getz, Lyn Batchelor

Introduction

Values shape most interpersonal and business dealings, and the operation of a private business rests on the values of owners and their families. Individual and family decisions to invest in or purchase a business, its development, and ultimate disposition or inheritance, affect tourism, communities and destinations in many ways. Sustainable tourism is therefore in large part dependent upon the values held by important actors in the industry.

This chapter explores how values, and especially the concept of stewardship, can impact upon sustainable tourism in economic, environmental and social terms. Indeed, the very notion of 'sustainable tourism', from the perspectives of all three pillars, often rests on a foundation of successful business ventures. This is particularly true if owners operate in ways that oppose or restrict social, environmental and competitive programmes and strategies. It is also valid in terms of positive contributions made by owners and families, such as adapting green operations and taking leadership within communities and the industry.

The study of both tourism entrepreneurship (see e.g. Morrison et al., 1999) and family business in tourism (see Getz and Carlsen, 2005; Getz et al., 2004) are quite new. Researchers have just begun to study important issues affecting the foundation and survival of tourism businesses, and in particular have not examined values and beliefs in any systematic way. Stewardship, described in this chapter as the foundation ethic supporting sustainable businesses, has not been studied within the family business context in its tourism dimensions.

In the first part of this chapter the nature and importance of family business in tourism is outlined. Particular attention is paid to several themes within family business studies that pertain to sustainable development, including the tourist experience, the community, business viability, destination competitiveness and environmental responsibility. Then values in family business are examined, focusing on the concept and implications of stewardship.

A short case study is presented of O'Reilly's Rainforest Guesthouse in Australia, which illustrates many of the themes and issues pertaining to family business studies within tourism and hospitality, and in particular focuses on values and beliefs as they influence a multi-generational business. In the conclusions a conceptual model is illustrated to help shape theoretical advances in this area of study. The model incorporates antecedents to stewardship, a definition of stewardship in family business, and implications for sustainable tourism. Specific research needs and approaches are identified.

Family business studies in tourism

'Family business' has no commonly accepted meaning. Indeed, Sharma et al. (1996) comprehensively reviewed the literature and found 34 definitions. Birley (2001) argued that in some countries the term 'family business' is not used, nor is it understood. At the most basic level a family business can be defined as an enterprise which, in practice, is controlled by members of a single family (Barry, 1975). This definition can encompass businesses that involve only one owner, often called 'sole proprietorship' firms. 'Copreneurial' ownership, where a couple owns and operates the business, is especially common in small tourism and hospitality businesses.

Chua et al. (1999) argued that the theoretical essence of a family business lies in the *vision* of its dominant family members. The vision must be to use the business for the betterment of the family – potentially across more than one generation. Birley (2001, p. 75) also concluded that 'owner/manager attitude is a more productive approach to describing and understanding the family business sector than the more traditional methods of equity or managerial control'. In this approach the vision (or motives and goals) and behaviour of the firm are differentiated from non-family businesses and from businesses in which family involvement makes no difference to its operations or future development.

The exact scale and significance of family businesses remains subject to definitional and measurement problems, so mostly we have estimates. Westhead and Cowling (1998) reported a number of studies which have found that family firms account for over two-thirds of all businesses in Western, developed economies. In Europe, 70 per cent of businesses are family owned or controlled (Lank et al., 1994; Thomassen, 1992). Middleton (2001) noted that in Europe 95 per cent of tourism businesses, generating perhaps one-third of total tourism revenue, are micro-businesses and most of these are family businesses. Although family business is also common in China (Kuhlmann and Dolles, 2002), there is little information available on tourism businesses.

Why is the family business important in tourism studies? The argument advanced in this chapter is that the nature of the tourism experience is potentially shaped by owners and their families, and that the very sustainability of enterprises, communities and destinations is affected by decisions made in accordance with owners' goals and the family vision. These may not be in accordance with the normal business aims of profit, growth or competitiveness.

The tourist experience

Owners and their families can be an important part of the tourism experience, especially when the business brings customers into the family's home or land. When the family becomes part of the attraction it can be said that 'family branding' is occurring, and this could become a powerful competitive advantage. Many tourism and hospitality businesses require a high degree of host–guest contact, often to the point where family and work become blurred. The owner or owner's family members directly provide guests with accommodation, hospitality, entertainment, information and interpretation, food or activities. Contact between hosts and guests is sometimes a motive for establishing the business, but also a potential source of stress through loss of privacy, handling many demands and complaints, and time pressures.

The community

The family is at the heart of many communities. If the family also happens to be in business, its potential contributions to community viability and culture are magnified, and so too are its responsibilities. What happens when family businesses disappear and the families move away? The community at a minimum loses continuity and a degree of stability. And if those departing are not replaced by other families the community loses population – and without children its future. Families, their values and actions are also of concern to communities in terms of leadership in economic development and the environment. Because family-business owners tend to be rooted in their communities, or might want to make a positive contribution to their selected homes, they should be expected to provide leadership.

Business viability

Small family businesses experience a high failure and turnover rate. One of the hallmarks of tourism is highly cyclical demand, creating cash flow problems and affecting overall profitability. Seasonality also affects families, sometimes negatively and also by offering a lull during which pursuit of family and lifestyle goals can dominate. How individuals and families adapt to, or combat, seasonality is of considerable importance within the sustainability context (Getz and Nilsson, 2004).

The theme of 'family vision' is problematic when most owners in this industry do not plan for succession or inheritance, or it is simply not practical for them (Getz and Petersen, 2004). The family vision in these businesses has more to do with personal and copreneurial lifestyles, autonomy-seeking, and realizing a decent economic return on effort. A special case exists when a 'family legacy' of real property or something else of value is at stake.

Destination competitiveness

The profit-maximizing, growth-oriented entrepreneur has been found to be a small minority within family businesses in tourism and hospitality (Getz and Petersen, 2005).

Numerous lifestyle entrepreneurs, content with simply sustaining their small businesses, are unlikely to be innovative or responsive to destination positioning strategies.

Mobilizing the growth-oriented entrepreneur, who exists as a small subset in tourism, should be a priority of economic and destination development agencies, as should the task of identifying latent entrepreneurship among those constrained by limited capital or professional advice.

Environmental responsibility

Tzschentke et al. (2004) conducted an exploratory study of accommodation operators' motivations for adapting environmental practices. Much of the literature on small business suggests the prevalence of a low level of eco-literacy and a shallow environmental ethic in small businesses. In this research 30 Scottish accommodation owner–managers were interviewed, revealing that multiple factors were involved, including cost savings, social concerns, psychological benefits and ethics. 'Environmental stewardship' was revealed in expressions of values that guided environmental actions, including moral obligation and preserving one's own environment. A responsibility towards future generations was at the root of some of the practices being studied.

On the basis of research in rural Western Australian, Carlsen et al. (2001) found some evidence suggesting that family- and owner-operated businesses are positively inclined towards adopting sustainable tourism practices in their businesses. A substantial proportion (42 per cent) of the respondents indicated that an interest in heritage or nature conservation was a motivator in establishing their business, and some groups – in particular tour operators and farm-based accommodation businesses – demonstrated higher levels of interest and support.

Conservation and lifestyle goals are apparently closely related in the rural tourism and hospitality sectors, suggesting that families can be attracted to set up businesses that, from the beginning, will incorporate a sustainable philosophy. Bramwell (1994, p. 5) observed that: 'Increasing prominence is now given to rural communities and individual local residents and businesses and to their role and degree of control in shaping rural tourism in the context of external forces.' The question of who takes responsibility for environmental stewardship is of particular importance in rural areas, as they are frequently subject to strong, controversial and sometimes damaging development pressures. Crucially, the sustainable tourism paradigm, according to Weaver and Fennel (1997, p. 78), 'emphasizes small-scale, locally owned and operated enterprises…which are already integrated into the local economy'.

Values and family businesses

Cowan and Todorovic (2000, p. 4) described three layers of values in the context of business strategy. 'Surface values' are 'openly stated, moral positions and behavioral rules' that are based on religion, law and common sense. They are clearly visible in actions and in statements about what we believe. 'Hidden values' are at the basis of longstanding beliefs, attitudes and traditions within an organization, and they are difficult to change. They might be called 'core values'. Finally, at the base, are invisible 'deep values' which constitute a world view and relate to basic human survival.

Ethical decisions and actions are based on values, according to Cowan and Todorovic (2000, p. 4). They also quoted Ulrich et al. (1999) who, in the book *Results Based Leadership* said 'Leaders who understand their company's and their personal values build lasting results… lacking clear values, rudderless leaders constantly shift from goal to goal.'

Aronoff and Ward (2001, p. 1) discussed psychological benefits linked to values, including pleasure and meaning derived 'from sustaining cross-generational relationships and striving towards mutual goals'. They further stated that values are rooted in 'members' emotional bonds, blood ties and shared history'. In terms of outcomes, they claimed that 'vital synergies' can arise from a commitment to values.

One of the proclaimed benefits of a value system is the ability to adapt, and this can include risk taking where solidarity and commitment support 'appropriate risk taking' (Aronoff and Ward, 2001, p. 8). Forging alliances is facilitated through shared value systems with allies, and by the trust implicit in a family business based on values.

Stewardship

Stewardship can be defined as 'the responsibility for taking good care of resources entrusted to one' (Wikipedia, n.d.), including natural resources and the human and other assets of an organization. It is often associated with the 'land ethic' held by farmers and other owners who believe they do not possess, but merely manage resources. Sometimes the words 'sacred trust' are used to underline the religious dimensions of stewardship.

There is a very strong theological basis to the concept of stewardship, at least in Western cultures, as witnessed in this quote from the National (USA) Catholic Rural Life Conference 1949:

> Ownership of land does not give an absolute right to use or abuse, nor is it devoid of social responsibilities. It is in fact a stewardship. It implies such land tenure and use as to enable the possessor to develop his personality, maintain a decent standard of living for his family and fulfill his social obligations. At the same time, the land steward has a duty to enrich the soil he tils and to hand it down to future generations as a thank offering to God, the Giver, and as a loving inheritance to his children's children
>
> *(NCRLC, 1949, p. 425)*

In this prcnouncement is an admonition to land owners to follow a creed that sounds very much like principles of sustainable development. As well, in the context of family business studies, the church makes it clear that family succession is an integral part of good land steward-ship – although it might be possible to argue that the reference to 'his children's children' is allegorical and really means 'for future generations'.

Turning to the mainstream of family business literature, which consists more of advice to owners than it does research chapters, Aronoff and Ward (2001, p. 32) proclaimed:

> we have found stewardship to be the most important value in families who are successful in passing businesses from one generation to the next. To be a good steward is to take personal responsibility for leaving resources better than they were when they came into your care. Stewardship springs from the ancient idea that the wise management and passing on of property is an honorable role that brings meaning and pride to the steward.

To Aronoff and Ward, the opposite of stewardship is 'proprietorship', making it clear that they believe such an attitude to be selfish and perhaps destructive. However, they also believe that stewardship means continuous growth of the family business, taking risks and hard work. Family values also enter into this argument, as 'Families who believe in stewardship have an opportunity to pass on a more generous, future-oriented perspective. This equips the children of successful, wealthy business families to cope better with inherited wealth and privilege' (Aronoff and Ward, 2001, p. 33).

The concept of 'legacy' is closely related to stewardship. In its simplest, dictionary meaning, a legacy is an inheritance – usually money or property. In the context of a family business, Aronoff and Ward (2001, p. 2) describe the 'living legacy' of 'a dynamic, resilient value system'. Another legacy is that of the learning organization, or an institutional memory and stability that enables effective long-range planning. A shared vision is another form of legacy, resulting in enduring meaning and motivation. 'A legacy of values is often the only goal worthy of all the effort and risk' and 'A legacy of values gives wealth – and life – meaning' and 'spiritual or philosophical legacy' (Aronoff and Ward, 2001, pp. 18, 45) through an 'ethical will' is one way to attempt to pass on values.

Case study of O'Reilly's Rainforest Guesthouse

In this case study the main themes discussed above are brought into focus by examining one successful, multi-generational family business. A profile of the business reveals that family branding is employed strategically by the O'Reillys, and they do make their family part of the guest experience. Through a survey of family members on their values, the research provides direct evidence of family vision and goals, and sheds light on their interpretation of several dimensions of stewardship – including community responsibility, environmentalism and the legacy.

Profile of the business

O'Reilly's Rainforest Guesthouse is an internationally acclaimed ecolodge located a two-hour drive south of Brisbane, capital city of Queensland, Australia, and about 1.5 hours west of the famous Gold Coast resorts. It is surrounded by the Lamington National Park, a World Heritage reserve. The guesthouse lies at 930 metres altitude and is reached by a twisty, narrow, but sealed mountain road. The national park service has a campsite and information centre very close to the guesthouse. Day visitors use a large car park next to the guesthouse, which, in 2000, attracted 22 per cent of their visitors from overseas.

The guesthouse business started in 1926, and the year 2001 marked 75 years of continuous operation. The modern, tourism-award-winning enterprise bears little resemblance to the original bark-clad guesthouse that provided the original shelter for visitors to Lamington National Park. It has been kept under family ownership through three generations (the fourth generation is still too young to be involved), and many family members have worked in the business. The O'Reilly family name is so legendary in Australia that it has become a valuable brand.

O'Reilly's sought and were awarded advanced ecotourism accreditation from the Ecotourism Association of Australia. Although they do not use the term 'ecolodge', it does fit their operation in a number of ways. Perhaps the biggest difference is that the guesthouse has continued to move up-market into the luxury accommodation category.

Capitalization of the family brand is ongoing. Gran O'Reilly's Store, at the guesthouse, includes a bistro, gift shop and other provisions. It is very popular with day-visitors to the park. There is now an O'Reilly's line of clothing, gifts, nature videos and wine from their Canungra Valley Vineyards.

The company is managed by a board of directors which includes two family members from each of two family trusts, and three non-family directors. Family trusts were established to ensure that ownership and control rests permanently with the family, and not with individuals who might sell off their shares. The board makes operational decisions under guidance of the chairperson and executive director (who are non-family). Structured, monthly board meetings are held.

The non-family trustees are vital, both in helping to avoid in-family management problems and in counselling individual family members; they were sought by the family after a process of setting out desirable attributes. Personal relations already existed with the external directors before they were asked to sit on the board. Regular family meetings are held every six months to keep everyone informed and to get their input. Family businesses, according to Shane O'Reilly, tend to take a long-term perspective on everything, whereas traditional company directors often focus on short-term returns.

The O'Reilly's believe in professionalism, to the point of bringing in non-family directors, a general manager and others. Jobs are advertised by the human resources manager and both family and outsiders can apply. A written 'family employment policy' covers this issue. As the business expanded and increased in complexity, family members have had to adapt. If they cannot cope with their responsibilities, family membership is no guarantee of a job. On the other hand, the board of directors will pay for a complete university education for family members wanting to enter the business in a professional capacity.

The family trusts present a dilemma that will have to be resolved. At issue is the means to extract value for family members while maintaining family control. Dissolving the trusts and issuing shares, which could include retention of majority control, might still have a serious cultural impact on the company through dilution of family influence on the board of directors, as well as having major tax implications.

Going completely public could eventually result in the O'Reilly name remaining only as a brand, a commodity to be bought and sold. A number of expansions were contemplated, primarily to increase accommodation for both guests (two-bedroom, spa villas) and staff (self-contained units), and to continue moving up-market. Approval was obtained to construct up to 50 cabins one kilometre from the guesthouse, but the recent improvements took priority. The cabins have been sold off plan (i.e. sold before building began) and construction was begun in 2005. The company was also planning to sell 50 per cent of Canungra Valley Vineyards.

The O'Reilly family survey

Shane O'Reilly, managing director of the company, worked with university researchers in 2003 to construct a survey for all family members, in advance of the planned family retreat. It was agreed that the survey would combine some general questions related to values, attitudes and entrepreneurship with some very pointed questions about the future of the business itself.

There were 26 respondents ranging in age from 13 to 70 years old. Most respondents were in their 30s or very early 40s. There were 14 female and 12 male respondents; 19 respondents were family members, 5 were spouses of a family member, and 2 were partners of family members. Of the family members, 2 respondents were second generation, 13 third generation, and 4 fourth generation (the 13- and 17-year-olds). All of the quotations are from the questionnaires in this survey.

Vision and goals

Almost everyone in the family agreed that the business should be kept growing, and, although there was mostly support for the current strategy of the business, it was not as high. The family is not strong on taking risks, however. It appears that everyone would be comfortable with growth and expansion if the risks were minimal. As the family grows, there is a risk of a split. If those without feel alienated they might oppose risk-taking and lobby for changes in ownership and control.

The business creates a strong sense of family pride, including recognition that the family name is one of the most valuable business assets – as revealed in these two quotes:

> As the business continues to grow I think that it should not just look at future projects before first looking after what it has already achieved, making sure that it is all up to the family standards. From the presentation through to the environment that these be maintained and well managed before moving on to the next project.

> For the business to grow, best be able to retain the O'Reilly family hospitality that it is famous for.

Social and environmental responsibility

The family survey appeared to reaffirm the core values that had sustained the business over 75 years. This family firmly believes that high moral and ethical standards must apply, and that it must make a positive environmental and social contribution. There was also general agreement that each generation must pass on a more successful business. There was no real argument with social and environmental responsibility; no one wanted to harm the natural environment that served as the core attraction of the business.

Maintaining the environmental standards is important to the family, as shown by these quotations:

> The business needs to keep a family orientation as that is what makes us different to our competitors. A long term focus of growth is necessary, with emphasis on minimal environmental impact.

> The main goal I would like for the family business is to be more environmentally aware and focused. As the business has expanded we have lost our obligation to preserve the natural environment, which was the key ideology of the founding generations. Thus despite our lack of current emphasis on eco-tourism and the preservation of the environment I hope that one day our family business will one day become the leaders of the eco-tourism industry and actively work for the preservation of our unique surrounds.

> I would also like to see a greater emphasis placed on our environmental responsibilities. As the guesthouse continues to grow it is in danger of being just another big resort spoiling the beauty of the surrounding National Park. I believe we should be seen to give back to a National Park that entices people to come and stay at our guesthouse. This could be, for example, by making the guesthouse as sustainable as possible or funding/promoting research or rehabilitation work in the Park. We need to be seen as more in touch with our surrounds. I would like to return in some form within the next ten years of hopefully improving people's environmental awareness. Sometimes, I feel some of the family/ management need to be reminded of its importance.

Ownership and control

Two statements explored family views on maintaining ownership and/or control of the business and land. Only 14 of 25 agreed it should be kept in family ownership, while 9 were neutral. There was a real split in responses to the statement 'the land and the business must always be kept under family control, not necessarily ownership', with 9 agreeing, 9 disagreeing, and the rest neutral. Most (17 of 25) did agree that 'it is the responsibility of each generation to pass on a more successful business', with none disagreeing. The following quote from one family member appears to summarize the dilemmas faced when simultaneously attempting to grow the business and preserve its assets for the next generation.

> I feel that, though we need to grow and take risks, we should also look at consolidating what we have already. The guesthouse is about to expand greatly – with cabins – and I fear that we will lose sight of our core business, i.e. the guesthouse and striving to make everyone feel special. If the cabins prove a success, GREAT!, then let's get [undecipherable] to our guests and filling to rooms. I personally want a successful and profitable business to

hand on to the fourth generation. We should consolidate our business and make it the very best it can be, which I believe is the best in the industry.

One respondent recommended two specific mechanisms for keeping everyone committed:

Goals of the business in the next five years: have no debt, and have an internal stock market set up within the business so family members can sell to other family members, as well as having a fourth-generation succession plan in place.

Overall, there were a few clear and unavoidable issues to be resolved. Growth and risk taking were not uniformly supported by the family. There was a fair amount of sentiment expressed for returning to the core business. Some significant differences of opinion existed between those working in the company and those outside it, and in particular with regard to the trusts.

Without doubt, the sharpest dilemma was what to do about the family trusts. Enough family members wanted change to make this a pivotal issue at the retreat. The idea of an internal stock exchange had been discussed enough for it to gain supporters. That would require a fundamental shift in how the family business was structured and how its profits were distributed.

Conclusions

It can be concluded that O'Reilly family members in general believed in stewardship of both the natural environment on which their business depended, and on the preservation of family ownership and control. A number of potential conflicts and dilemmas were also revealed. O'Reilly's has succeeded across three generations, which is longer than most inter-generational family businesses endure. Often disharmony among owners sets in, resulting in sale of the business and loss of family control. In other families, ownership spreads so widely among distant relatives that cliques form and power struggles predominate.

Using the available literature, and incorporating insights gained from the O'Reilly's case study, Table 18.1 has been formulated to suggest research topics and to help advance theory related to stewardship and family businesses. First the model suggests the likely antecedents to stewardship, then presents a working definition of stewardship; thirdly, a number of specific implications are listed for both family business management and sustainable tourism.

Antecedents

The dimensions of stewardship that are of interest here, both an environmental ethic and strong ties to the family business or land, must have their origins in religion (or other philosophical belief systems), or in deep-rooted cultural norms and traditions. There might be unique familial versions of stewardship passed down through generations, but that is conjecture. Circumstances are definitely an important factor, as many of the family businesses studied to date have not had any realistic chance of being passed on to inheritors within the family (Getz and Nilsson, 2004).

Both the presence and absence of stewardship values should be studied. If we assume there is a natural tendency towards holding this set of values, are there specific barriers to its incorporation into family business practices? Are there countervailing value sets that supersede or take the place of stewardship? It might be argued that normal business goals pertaining to profit maximization and normal family survival goals might be viewed as being more important

Table 18.1 Stewardship in family businesses

ANTECEDENTS (The Foundations of Belief in Stewardship)

- Religion and philosophy (a world view encompassing humanity's place in the ecosystem and focusing on personal and family responsibility to nature and others)
- Culture (values linked to particular ethnic, racial or cultural groups)
- Personal experiences and reference sets (work and leisure experiences that shape life interests and preferences, such as a desire to live in rural areas or close to nature; education and self-learning)
- Family traditions (for example, a history of owning land or hotels); Ties to the land (farming and other resource-dependent occupations that might shape beliefs and values)

THE MEANING OF STEWARDSHIP in FAMILY BUSINESSES

- A belief in the owners' personal, or collective family responsibility to preserve and where possible enhance the business, the land (i.e. the family's resource base), and the environment for future generations – and especially for creating and passing on a viable inheritance within the family. Stewardship also entails a belief in one's responsibility to others (i.e. the community) and to perpetuation of the values on which stewardship is based.

IMPLICATIONS for FAMILY BUSINESSES AND SUSTAINABLE TOURISM

A propensity to:

- preserve family ownership and/or control of land and business assets
- employ family members
- achieve succession within the family (inheritance)
- pass on family values and traditions to the next generation
- provide a high level of personal service to visitors; be part of the experience
- engage in responsible tourism (e.g. green operations)
- provide leadership in the community
- form and participation in networks and alliances (within family, community and the industry)
- seek competitive advantages for, and adding value to the family business (in order to leave as much or more than one inherited)
- develop and exploit family branding (based on perceived qualities associated with family businesses)

(at least under some circumstances), or that greed and other forms of self-serving behaviour are more common.

It can be suggested that antecedents for the O'Reillys' sense of stewardship include their Irish Catholic roots, although this was not explicitly questioned. Certainly their pioneering heritage, the creation of family legends and an intimate relationship with nature across several generations, gave rise to close ties to the land.

The meaning of stewardship in family businesses

The survey of the O'Reillys' family values revealed clearly a collective sense of responsibility to the community, environmental protection and preserving a legacy for future generations. Some tension did exist on exactly what shape the legacy might take, but this was more a matter of sorting out possible structures for ownership and control of the business, and some questioning of business strategy. However, without further systematic research there is no way of knowing the extent to which this one family's vision and its stewardship values represents the core or the full range of meanings attached to stewardship in family businesses.

Implications for family business and sustainable tourism

The structure and implications of stewardship within a family business appear not to have been studied explicitly. A land or environmental ethic should translate into positive actions that could be termed 'green' or 'responsible' or 'sustainable' practices. If it covers a responsibility for preserving and enhancing the family assets (land, business or other forms), then it should translate into actions intended to conserve assets, yet Aronoff and Ward (2001) argued that risk taking actually helps define stewardship. Does the desire to preserve family ownership or control of assets take precedence over environmental ethics? In the O'Reilly's case a balance appears to have been found, but the environmental ethic was clearly something that had to be discussed and reaffirmed.

If stewardship encompasses the need for establishing and preserving an intergenerational legacy it should lead to a clear succession plan or an ownership structure (like O'Reilly's) that will pass on the business intact. However, circumstances clearly act against the prospect of succession in many families, so how is this aspect of stewardship channelled or replaced when succession is not possible? Where inheritance does occur, how are family values actually passed on, and if they are not what happens? Is stewardship something that can be rediscovered, or will it lie dormant?

Family branding, network building, seeking allies and partners, and other profit or asset-enhancing strategies might be related to stewardship in the sense that a long-term perspective is implicit in the concept. In fact, the O'Reillys spoke of the ability and need for families to resist short-term goals.

'Clan' economies are a related concern. If family businesses grow large, and especially if they begin to coalesce through the generations and branches of an extended family, a kind of clan economy is formed. The business might be viewed as a guaranteed job or source of dividends for family members, rather than a sacred trust for all to preserve. In any family business there is a constant tension between the prospect of asset stripping to maximize income, and asset growth and conservation to ensure long-term viability.

Clearly family businesses face many internal challenges and some potentially serious value contradictions. In multi-generational cases the families or their leaders must evolve and constantly reinvent ways of dealing with these issues. Aronoff and Ward (2001) recommend explicit discussion of values during regular family forums, and the O'Reilly's case study shows the benefits of using family inputs for gaining a deep understanding of how family members feel about the issues and their vision for the future.

Perhaps the greatest research need, linking family businesses, stewardship and sustainable tourism, is the study of how values translate into action or decisions that impact directly or cumulatively upon the environment, community and destination competitiveness. For example, the O'Reillys' decision to expand their business with new accommodation development must have involved consideration of benefits and risks to the family business, environmental feasibility and impacts, and the level of support within the family. Connecting values and stewardship to business actions remains a difficult but important research challenge in all tourism settings.

Acknowledgements

Special thanks are given to Shane O'Reilly for cooperating fully with the case study, and to the other family members who completed surveys.

References

Aronoff, C. and Ward, J. (2001) *Family business values: How to assure a legacy of continuity and success*. Marietta, GA: Family Enterprise Publishers

Barry, B. (1975) 'The development of organisation structure in the family firm'. *Journal of General Management*, 3(1), 42–60

Birley, S. (2001) 'Owner-manager attitudes to family and business issues: A 16 country study'. *Entrepreneurship: Theory and Practice*, 26(2), 63–76

Bramwell, B. (1994) 'Rural tourism and sustainable rural tourism'. In B. Bramwell and B. Lane (eds) *Rural tourism and sustainable development*. Clevedon: Channel View Publications, pp. 1–6

Carlsen, J., Getz, D. and Ali-Knight, J. (2001) 'Environmental attitudes and practices of family businesses in the rural tourism and hospitality sectors'. *Journal of Sustainable Tourism*, 9(4), 281–97

Chua, J., Chrisman, J. and Sharma, P. (1999) 'Defining the family business by behavior'. *Entrepreneurship: Theory and Practice*, 23(4), 19–37

Cowan, C. and Todorovic, N. (2000) 'Spiral dynamics: The layers of human values in strategy'. *Strategy and Leadership*, 28(1), 4–12

Getz, D. and Carlsen, J. (2005) 'A framework for family business theory and research in tourism and hospitality'. *Annals of Tourism Research*, 32(1), 237–58

Getz, D. and Nilsson, P. A. (2004) 'Responses of family businesses to extreme seasonality in demand: The case of Bornholm, Denmark'. *Tourism Management*, 25(1), 17–30

Getz, D. and Petersen, T. (2004) 'Identifying industry-specific barriers to inheritance in family businesses'. *Family Business Review*, 17(3), 259–76

—— (2005) 'Growth and profit-oriented entrepreneurship among family business owners in the tourism and hospitality industry'. *International Journal of Hospitality Management*, 24(2), 219–42

Getz, D., Carlsen, J. and Morrison, A. (2004) *The family business in tourism and hospitality*. London: CABI

Kuhlmann, T. and Dolles, H. (2002) *Sino-German business relationships during the Age of Economic Reform*. Munich: Iudicium

Lank, A., Owens, R., Martinez, J., Reidel, H., de Visscher, F. and Bruel, M. (1994) 'The state of family business in various countries around the world'. *The Family Business Newsletter*, May, pp. 3–7

Middleton, V. (2001) 'The importance of micro-businesses in European Tourism'. In L. Roberts and D. Hall (eds) *Rural tourism and recreation: Principles to practice*. Wallingford: CABI, pp. 197–201

Morrison, A., Rimmington, M. and Williams, C. (1999) *Entrepreneurship in the hospitality, tourism and leisure industries*. Oxford: Butterworth-Heinemann

NCRLC (1949) 'The moral bases of land tenure' (The National Catholic Rural Life Conference). *American Journal of Economics and Sociology*, 8(4), 425–6

Sharma, P., Chrisman, J. and Chua, J. (1996) *A review and annotated bibliography of family business studies*. Boston, MA: Kluwer

Thomassen, A. (1992) 'European family-owned businesses: Emerging issues for the 1990s'. In R. J. Richards, Jr. (ed.) *The Family Firm Institute 1992 Conference proceedings: Family business at the crossroads*. Boston, MA: Family Firm Institute, pp. 188–204

Tzschentke, N., Kirk, D. and Lynch, P. (2004) 'Reasons for going green in serviced accommodation establishments'. *International Journal of Contemporary Hospitality Management*, 16(2), 116–24

Ulrich, D., Zenger, J. and Smallwood, N. (1999) *Results based leadership*. Boston, MA: Harvard Business School Press

Weaver, D. and Fennel, D. (1997) 'The Saskatchewan vacation farm operator as entrepreneur'. In S. Page and D. Getz (eds) *The business of rural tourism: International perspectives*. London: Thomson International Business Press, pp. 162–87

Westhead, P. and Cowling, M. (1998) 'Family firm research: The need for a methodological rethink'. *Entrepreneurship: Theory and Practice*, 23(1), 31–56

Wikipedia (n.d.) 'Stewardship'. Retrieved 15 November 2012, from http://en.wikipedia.org/wiki/Stewardship

Part V
Emerging forms of tourism

19

Entertainment science and new directions for tourism research

Philip L. Pearce

Introduction

The central aim of this chapter lies in exploring the concept of entertainment as a way of invigorating a number of tourism research areas. The sequence of discussion points commences with a consideration of certain kinds and styles of entertainment. Next, the presentation of a relatively new study area in the academic spectrum, an area potentially entitled entertainment science, will itself be entertained (cf. Bryman, 2004). It will be argued that entertainment science reaches beyond cultural studies of tourism (Baerenholdt et al., 2004; Howard, 2003; Inglis, 2000) and is a particularly adaptable specialism of interest capable of augmenting tourism research. Specific areas for attention in entertainment science will be considered, focussing in turn on the ownership and production of entertainment, the consumption of entertainment and education, training and employment in the world of entertainment. Throughout, the styles of entertainment particularly relevant to tourism settings will be the primary focus of attention. In establishing some new connections and refreshing existing tourism–entertainment analyses, the discussion will culminate in a framework for guiding research themes and agendas. The concluding section of the paper argues that without specifying conceptual frameworks for novel research themes, the identification of an entertainment wedge penetrating the circle of tourism interest will be dissipated, resulting in the kind of non-cumulative, ad hoc and disoriented approach to tourism study which already troubles a number of tourism scholars (Aramberri, 2001; Dann, 1999; Rojek and Urry, 1997).

Entertainment

Entertainment will be considered in this chapter as the commercial or semi-commercial structuring, display and performance of people and resources for focussed consumption. As studied in this context entertainment is provided by an organisation or business and while commercial imperatives may not dominate, covering costs is a ubiquitous consideration in the staging of entertainment. Some examples of tourism-connected entertainment can illustrate the key criteria under review and provide a link to interrelated concepts in contemporary tourism analysis.

Entertainment can be conceived as functioning at three levels:

- a simple augmentative role to a larger product or experience;
- a key component of a product or experience; and
- occupying the totality of the experience and time.

For example, an illustration of the simple augmentative role is provided by the Grand Canyon Railway which transports passengers from Williams, Arizona, to the southern rim of the Grand Canyon. During the two-hour journey costumed western cowboys provide a number of diversions, including an episode of posing as train robbers boarding the train and, in comical style, harassing the passengers. It is a supplementary entertainment to the main role of the company, which is the efficient transport to the environmental attraction of the Grand Canyon itself. Similar minor augmentative roles can be seen in the action of wandering musicians and magicians in theme parks and cities and in the planned sub-routines involving humour and misadventure amongst tourist guides and service personnel. Attention to these kinds of settings and performers is not new in tourism, but together with the next two categories of entertainment, fosters a new realisation that these forms of display and action can constitute their own study area and an analysis of these activities might add insight to tourism's directions.

The second category of entertainment is when the performers and resources engaged in the entertainment represent a key component of the tourism experience and setting. This level encompasses both the Disney-inspired applications of edutainment and the more market-oriented uses of interpretation (Bryman, 2004; Uzzell, 1998). There are hundreds of global examples but many take the form of being within an attraction or environmental setting where the performer or product makes a telling contribution to the total visitor experience. For example, in Hawaii, at the Polynesian Culture Centre, the 30-minute presentation by the Samoan spokesperson in a Samoan staged space blends skilled performance, comedy, audience participation and self-mockery to convey modest cultural insights about Samoan culture. The co-existence of other 'shows' and films at such sites is central to the notion that this unit of entertainment is only a component production piece, but masterful and mindfulness inducing presentations of this sort may be an important key to the success of the total setting (cf. Moscardo and Pearce, 1999).

A third category of entertainment involves the total time being filled by the one entertainment event. Some of these entertainment styles may be relatively passive for the spectators, such as a sedate Viennese classical music performance or cultural dance and display events. Others have a more physical or participatory character. Examples include dance clubs, night clubs and casino-based entertainment evenings. This wider ambit of entertainment leads to links with concerts, circuses, theatre, film and spectator sport. Environmental attractions involving wildlife can sometimes also be structured as a total entertainment experience with the behaviours of the animals constituting the performance and the access provided by the managing organisation representing the spectator infrastructure.

This brief review of tourism-connected entertainment has established some important distinctions and conjunctions among the topics under consideration. The kind of entertainment being described is largely produced and provided by others rather than being performed and created by tourists themselves from their own resources. This distinction partly assists in marking off the tourism connected entertainment from some leisure activities. Further, the tourism-connected entertainment is conceived of as requiring customer or consumer travel and mobility and ensures that home-based entertainment is not under review. Importantly the entertainment being considered is not free or unstructured so that, while sitting in a café in Barcelona watching the passing crowds may be advertised as culturally entertaining, such activities are not being considered in this context.

For tourism academics and analysts the focus of entertainment as defined above is likely to bring to mind a diverse array of recent literature and pre-existing analyses. This suite of links can include the contemporary work of Uriely (2005) on conceptualising the tourist experience, the experience economy of Pine and Gilmour (1999), the production of entertainment and interpretation (Bryman, 2004; MacDonald, 1997; Moscardo, 1999; Ritzer, 1999; Uzzell, 1998) and attempts to elaborate and reposition tourism studies with concepts of mobility, chaoplexity and slow time (Cooper et al., 2005; Farrell and Twining-Ward, 2004; Franklin, 2003; Hall, 2005; Matos, 2004; Woehler, 2004). For other researchers the shadow of older traditions of work may be seen as adumbrating tourism-connected entertainment including ideas about staging (Goffman, 1959), dramaturgical analyses (Harre, 1979), insincerity and authenticity (Boorstin, 1962; MacCannell, 1976) and gaze and hyperreality (Eco, 1986; Rojek, 1993; Urry, 1990).

While several of these connections could be individually pursued, it is possible to do more than gesture at individual links to research work on entertainment. A holistic appraisal of tourism research trends and entertainment studies will be pursued by defining and contextualising entertainment science.

Entertainment science

Entertainment science is the systematic study of the ownership, organisation, delivery and consumption of entertainment opportunities. This nascent study area can be cast as a hybrid form of social science because it seeks in an academic way and using existing research tools to understand the factors which shape entertainment offerings and the consumption and consequences of those offerings (cf. Becher, 1989; Gomm, 2004). It draws on management, psychology and sociology and presents a rich reservoir of examples and cases for consideration by tourism interested scholars. Entertainment science is not yet established as a study field but its beginnings can be detected in business, leisure, psychology and sociology where there are emerging analyses of the syntheses among sports, festivals, theme parks, tourist attractions, shopping centres, media and film (Bryman, 2004; Harris, 2005; Kahneman et al., 1999).

The term 'science' is stressed in this new formulation. One can anticipate an objection to the use of this generic label with the possible claim that it overly stresses quantitative positivist frameworks (cf. Phillimore and Goodson, 2004; Singh, 2004). The term 'science' is being used here in its 'best sense' where it indicates an openness to new ideas and where the itch of ignorance is assuaged by logic, a mastery of the information available and accessible public reporting (Gould, 2004). There is certainly no intention to create a little pocket of positivism (cf. Outhwaite, 2000). Certainly entertainment science can be methodologically eclectic in the way researchers and analysts consider the phenomenon and its tourism connections. The term 'science' is preferred here to that of cultural studies or creative industries which each have their own wider ambit of influence and which are more interpretive, avowedly postmodern and more idiosyncratic in their contribution to systematic information based knowledge (Harris, 2005).

In order to fulfil the promise that entertainment science can provide a new direction or reinvigoration of some areas of tourism study four key issues will be addressed:

• the value of a structured approach to entertainment as a general source of new thinking in tourism, allied to but distinct from other regenerative approaches;

- the ownership and production of entertainment,
- entertainment and the consumer, and
- entertainment employment.

Entertainment science and rethinking tourism

Amongst some scholars, there has been an identifiable level of disappointment in the progress of tourism research. It is easy to find examples of such despair as the points are stressed with unusually frank and vivid phrases. In a previous meeting of the International Academy for the Study of Tourism Dann (1999, p. 14) suggested:

> Instead of there being a desirable cumulative corpus of knowledge that is emic, comparative, contextual and processual what we frequently encounter is a ragged collection of half-baked ideas that constitute largely case confirmed wishful thinking.

Such sentiments are echoed by Meethan (2001, p. 2): 'Tourism, at a general analytical level... remains under-theorised, eclectic and disparate.' A range of other analysts repeat similar views with Aramberri (2001) noting the lack of tourism theory, Franklin and Crang (2001) suggesting that tourism scholars are missing the complex social and cultural processes underpinning tourism's growth, while Rojek and Urry (1997) wonder whether tourism is even useful as a term of social science. The doubts about and the challenges to tourism research are indeed plentiful and they have existed for some time (cf. Crick, 1989; Dann et al., 1988). One significant implication of this unease about tourism study in this chapter lies in considering what kinds of emerging new directions are rising from these deliberations. Importantly, by reviewing these new lines of attack the special contribution of an entertainment science focus in relation to tourism study can then be established.

A number of tourism authors have begun to reconceptualise tourism as a special form of the study of human mobilities in space and access time. Coles et al. (2004), Hall (2005) and Cooper et al. (2005) represent good examples of this direction with the core argument being that tourism study can be usefully connected to powerful mathematical and conceptual models in mobility studies. Such analyses already exist in the broader transport, geography and life path literature. By linking to existing social science traditions the mobilities emphasis has quickly gestated some new tourism research concepts including space–time prisms, mobility biographies and the application of distance decay functions. The focus on people in space and time argues for and identifies significant constraints on travel and tourist behaviour, and there is an incipient link to tourist and leisure experiences which in turn form part of the entertainment science conceptualisation (Crouch, 2005; Lew and Cartier, 2005).

Another important new direction with the potential to reshape tourism thinking lies in expanded yet more fluid and dynamic systems models of tourism functioning. The work of Farrell and Twining-Ward (2004) represents an important statement in the genesis of this reworked systems approach to tourism. Three ideas are blended together in this new tradition to stimulate future tourism study. First, the contribution of sustainability science is advocated as an important ecological and managerial connection for tourism scholars (Holling and Gunderson, 2002). Sustainability considerations are already well represented in tourism study but for Farrell and Twining-Ward this sustainability emphasis needs to be fully linked to an expanded rather than a narrow view of the tourism system. In particular the earlier uses of the term 'systems' in tourism study is seen as too insular and mechanistic. The third force for stimulating tourism research development in this model is the notion, if not the full mathematical application, of chaos complexity theory (cf. Hovinen, 2002; Russell and Faulkner, 1999). Some insights generated by this expanded tourism system model with its sustainability and chaos–complexity components include the view that stable systems may have multiple fluctuating states – perhaps an important insight for tourism seasonality – and that systems are not simple hierarchical models but intermeshed in semi-autonomous parallel levels or panarchies. Additionally the approach also suggests that the study of tourism could usefully employ quasi-experimental appraisals to evaluate the effects of environmental and planning practices in tourism. The continued application of chaos and complexity approaches to tourism is, however, not assured since while the concepts have appeal as broad analogues of tourism processes the mathematical power and data-driven interpretations inherent in the approach are likely to be very difficult to achieve with social sciences and tourism data (Kiel and Elliott, 1996). Nevertheless chaos theory approaches in particular stimulate tourism researchers to connect variables in non-linear ways. For example, chaos complexity-based thinking may achieve some significant conceptual gains in terms of fostering visual models which highlight ceiling, floor and a variety of discontinuous, folded functions as possible underlying mechanisms of tourism processes. Few direct links have been made between chaos complexity approaches and the present interest in entertainment but some connections can be suggested as the two areas of tourism research grow. In particular chaos notions have an interesting applicability to fashion trends and the consumer adoption of new practices. Chaos theory approaches may provide, if not mathematically, then at least by their logic, novel ways for analysts of entertainment to better understand new consumer enthusiasms. In particular chaos approaches may assist ideas such as tipping points and innovation diffusion models (Gladwell, 2000).

Another powerful redirection of tourism research effort lies in providing a stronger focus on experience. This topic, while present throughout the development of tourism studies as a theme of importance (cf. Cohen, 1979; Krippendorf, 1987; Pearce, 1982, 1988; Ryan, 1995, 2002; Urry, 1990), has been reaffirmed by the work of Pine and Gilmour (1999) on the experience economy. The significance of the Pine and Gilmour contribution lies in promoting the study of experience as the heart of a new kind of economic and business style; a style which is set to at least coexist with and at times supersede earlier modes of production such as the direct selling of goods and services. Pine (2004), for example, argues that, by delivering a memorable, enhanced experience to a customer whether in a hairdressing saloon or a theme park, the business entrepreneur creates repeat business with multiple possibilities of selling new or additional products for higher profits. In the experience economy the seller is a stager of experiences rather than a manufacturer or service provider and customers seek personal, notable, multisensory experiences rather than standardised benefits (cf. Franklin, 2003). Importantly for the seller and the provider a more intensive form of social interaction underlies the experience economy.

Numerous connections exist between contemporary tourism writing and Pine and Gilmour's experience economy. Pine (2004) suggested that tourism is a prime exemplar of the experience economy and even a cursory examination of tourism marketing itself, as well as tourism marketing studies, reinforces the central point that destinations are repeatedly represented as sites for visitor experiences (cf. Cooper et al., 2005).

Uriely (2005, p. 209) observes that there are 'ample academic works regarding this subject... spread across several sub-areas of tourism' and has attempted to identify trends in the recent work on experiences. He suggests four contemporary directions. He notes that tourism experiences are now less differentiated from leisure experiences, that tourism experiences are now considered as less stereotypical and more diverse, that research attention has shifted from the nature of the objects or settings seen to the interpretation of those viewing the setting and that there is greater tolerance for multiple ways of analysing tourist experiences. Uriely then cautiously summarises these emphases as a postmodernist view of tourist experiences but carefully notes that future research should not be overly committed to subjectivities and should still pay attention to the kind of visited setting and the form of tourism as major determinants of the subjective experience.

The experience economy thrust which is defining a new direction in tourism research can be seen as the banner of tourism research development to which the entertainment science emphasis is mostly closely tied. And, yet, entertainment science offers something a little more than simply being a part of the experience economy push. Entertainment science brings to the fuller discussion of tourism an explicit set of statements about power, ownership and entrepreneurship. Additionally it reconsiders the concepts of benchmarking, flow and quality in performance appraisals by consumers and offers insights into slow time or rich time experiences. And, importantly in an academic context, it makes analysts pay attention to tourism workers, their education and skills and the daily quality of their work lives. A more detailed justification of these anticipatory claims can be established by considering select facets of entertainment science.

Entertainment: ownership and production

Many tourism businesses in many parts of the world can be classified as small or micro-businesses (Riley et al., 2002). Many of these tourism businesses operate in only one sector, such as accommodation or local transport, although Poon's (1993) analysis of new tourism highlighted some moves towards greater cross-sectoral ownership, influence and integration. Entertainment-related businesses provide much more dramatic examples of integration, not just within tourism sectors but across whole business domains. For example, Rupert Murdoch's empire has investments and ownership not just in the world of print media but in television, film, sports teams and casinos. Richard Branson's Virgin company in its many divisions has influence in music, airlines, banking and travel. The Disney Corporation has involvement with sports teams, theme parks, film and television. Anheuser-Busch has ownership of theme parks and sports teams and still functions as a brewing company (National Vanguard Books, 2004). These shifting patterns of ownership – particularly as applied to theme parks, hotels, film, casinos and sports teams – offer the tourism researcher a new perspective on tourism development, effectively what Foucault calls the 'eye of power' (Foucault, 1980, p. 155). Foucault stresses that the controlled architecture of places embodies key owner-based cultural values supported by a system of surveillance:

> The system of surveillance…involves very little expense. There is no need for arms, physical violence, material constraints. Just a gaze. An inspecting gaze, a gaze which each individual under its own weight will end by interiorising to the point that he is his own overseer, each individual thus exercising this surveillance over and against himself. A superb formula.

The argument that through design and surveillance powerful organisations control the tastes and consumer interests of a somewhat duped public is a core theme in popular culture writing (Harris, 2005). It is perhaps finding its clearest expression in tourism-linked writing in the work of Bryman (2004) on Disneyisation which in turn builds on the work of Ritzer (1993, 1999). The focus on ownership in Ritzer's work on McDonaldisation extends to five production mechanisms and outcomes. These key qualities are:

- an emphasis on efficiency – conceptualising the experience or product in assembly line terms to reduce the labour;

- a calculated approach to component parts of the experience/product;
- predictable standardised products;
- control through technology; and
- minimal compliance with the costs of the approach to the larger society.

These kinds of process, while highly effective and profitable for McDonald's or a casino operation, seem to be at odds with the experience economy emphasis on personal, memorable, socially connected processes. Ritzer's work anticipates this kind of incongruity and suggests that McDonaldisation as an outcome of business philosophy, results in disenchantment – the dislike that people come to feel for coldly rational organisations. Ritzer (1999) advocates a corrective which he terms re-enchantment to overcome the depletion of meaning and social contact which an overly technical calculated and efficient profit drive system can generate. Ritzer's work has numerous critics, many noting that there is a cultural and regional customisation of McDonald's and that customers as skilled consumers recognise what they are getting making them less dissatisfied and more complicit users rather than complaining consumers (Harris, 2005).

This analysis of ownership in relation to consumption and even closer to the present interest in entertainment is extended in the work of Bryman (2004) on Disneyisation. In particular Bryman examines the processes by which the principles of Disney theme parks are influencing, even dominating many sectors of contemporary society. The first of these ownership generated influences is theming which is seen by Bryman (2004, p. 15) as

> The application of a narrative to the institution or object…a veneer of dreaming and symbolism to the objects to which it is applied…that transcends or at the very least is an addition to what they actually are.

Theming is widespread in the very core settings where entertainment is on offer and is visible in amusement parks, restaurants, malls, heritage shopping, museums and shopping outlets. A second principle defining Disneyisation is hybrid consumption, where the guiding ownership principle is to get people to stay longer in settings to purchase more products. The rearrangement of architectural spaces and forms to support these cultural values, as highlighted by Foucault (1975), involves such settings as theme parks, museums, zoos and shopping malls, all now merging into less-distinct entities. The customer and tourist reactions to these hybrid environments will be outlined in the next section. Two further mechanisms – merchandising and performative (or emotional) labour – complete Bryman's portrayal of Disneyisation. The role of merchandising is to label, promote and sell goods which bear images and logos germane to the company's range of consumption experiences. The diversity ranges from conventional souvenirs through to clothing, music and corporate training systems. Performative labour is a further defining element of Disneyisation and links well with the broader treatment of this concept in entertainment science settings.

An analysis of tourism–entertainment ownership can also be studied at a smaller scale. For example, Donlon and Agrusa (2003) report that the French quarter of New Orleans depends in part on adult entertainment clubs for its tourism appeal. Like other businesses capital is invested in this tourism resource in order to generate profit for the owner. The notoriety of the clubs together with the historic associations of New Orleans constitute a tourism resource built on performances, dance and entertainment routines. Donlon and Agrusa's analysis emphasises that this kind of entertainment is strictly business, the clubs are commercial spaces and the entertainers viewed as expedient talent whose sole purpose is to extract money from the visitors' wallets. Donlon and Agrusa (2003, p. 121) report that:

> From 1975 to 2000 venture capital injections (businessmen pouring cash into an apparent opportunity to gain strong profits) updated and up-scaled many such settings, attempting to reposition them in the competitive hospitality marketplace. Investors included publicly traded companies listed on the stock exchange.

From large-scale enterprises to small businesses the entertainment science emphasis in the topic area of ownership and production suggests that tourism research might re-engage with social science work on business management, power and control systems. There are few studies interviewing and researching the eye of power that is the perspectives, philosophies and goals of those who construct tourism environments. How do such significant organisers of the tourism world generate their ideas, what makes them choose the styles and designs to which visitors respond and what views do they hold about the future of entertainment and consumer response? Entertainment science with its multifaceted interests in many kinds of themed settings and the pre-existing work on the principles defining Disneyisation could be a stimulus to this work.

Entertainment and the consumer

In appraising consumer reaction to entertainment simple satisfaction measures are likely to be inadequate. For some time now the realm of satisfaction studies has recognised that direct satisfaction questions work well for instrumental and enabling conditions surrounding tourist and consumer settings but less well for expressive and complex material (Noe, 1999; Schmitt, 1999). The move is from assessing satisfaction to appraising enjoyment and pleasure, and insightful studies frequently incorporate the notion of the skilled specialist versus less familiar naïve users. Uriely's work on the changing treatment of experience in the social science literature is relevant here with the view that there are many types of audiences or consumers and many interpretations of the quality of the entertainment or performance being evaluated. Much work has been conducted in the fields of cultural studies, literature and the humanities under the broad rubric of criticism. Such work defines and refines the sources of pleasure in numerous entertainment offerings. While some of this work is outside of the commercial sphere of entertainment with which this paper is concerned, there are some powerful cross-situational variables worth considering. These factors include reactions to entertainment built around insight, benchmarking, involvement, effort, tension balance and resolution. These evaluations, which have varying applicability to different types of entertainment, can be specified in more detail:

- Insight refers to the participant's capacity to see more meanings than are immediately presented as well as an ability to reinterpret and maximise meaning (cf. Barthes, 1973). It tends to be an intellectual enjoyment of the offering.
- Benchmarking refers to the capacity, cultural capital in some senses, of the participant to appraise the performance or entertainment against other offerings including those drawn from other entertainment sectors (Bourdieu, 1986).
- Involvement and effort refer to the participant's multisensory participation and travel cost in experiencing the entertainment setting (Franklin, 2003). High levels of involvement and

time–space effort tend to be associated with high levels of enjoyment and pleasure (Pine and Gilmour, 1999).

• The concept of tension creation and resolution refer to the actual challenges of spectating with enjoyment and pleasure dependent in part on the resolution of the intellectual and physical tension the entertainment may create.

In modelling these entertainment science variables influencing consumer reaction, they can be seen as meshing into two more generic outcome factors: a sense of flow and subjective or perceived appraisals of quality (cf. Csikszentmihalyi, 1975; Jones et al., 2003; Rojek, 2000). These ideas are expressed in Table 19.1.

The precise measurement of the kinds of variables and factors described in Table 19.1 represents an important methodological challenge for analysts of entertainment science, the experience economy and tourism. Pine (2004) proposes a number of possibilities including notions of sacrifice, defined as the gap between what consumers want and what they will accept, as well as analysing the dramatic structure of entertainment. Further, he notes the importance of willingness to pay as a benchmarking process in comparisons of entertainment offerings. He also suggests the value of the concept of authenticity in this context, a suggestion that tourism researchers are likely to see as limited due to waning enthusiasm for its usefulness and its limitations (cf. Pearce, 2005; Ryan, 2002). For entertainment itself rather than all of the experience economy-linked offerings, the strength and the structure of the narrative or theming have been suggested as important determinants of quality particularly as strong narratives can create insight, meet benchmarking standards and deal well with tension creation and its resolution. For the more physically involved entertainment offerings including the appreciation of dance and music, Csikszentmihalyi and Rojek's (2010) adaptation of flow may be critical with the expressive enabling conditions of benchmarking involvement and effort figuring prominently in evaluating the performance as successful and generating pleasure (cf. Daniel, 1996).

Table 19.1 Entertainment evaluation: the elements defining the consumer reaction

Pre-condition	Expressive Inputs		Integrative Expressive Reactions		Consequences
Satisfaction with instrumental attributes	• insight (cultural capital) • benchmarking (cultural capital and experience) • involvement (multisensory input) • effort (travel or time-space costs) • tension creation (skill (needs and motives) challenge) • resolution (required skill challenge)	→	• Perceived Quality • Flow	⇨	Experiential states of pleasure and enjoyment

One direction for tourism researchers resulting from these considerations lies in the more sophisticated treatment of satisfaction and outcome appraisals to tourism products and services (cf. Kozak, 2002). Both quantitative and qualitative appraisals are called for here as researchers grapple to understand when and how tourism entertainments work and fail for different market segments and audiences.

Entertainment and employment

Three interrelated concepts assist in clarifying some of the special employment issues germane to entertainment science. The three linked concepts are emotional labour, performative labour and aesthetic labour. Emotional labour, which now has a wide currency in the human resources literature, recognises that many service sector jobs require employees to maintain a set of emotional styles for the smooth functioning of their position (Hochschild, 1983). For example, nurses and doctors have to be at least positive and optimistic rather than depressive and neurotic, salespersons have to be approachable and helpful, and contemporary academics have to be enthusiastic in their delivery. Performative labour, which is of even more relevance to entertainment science suggests that more than basic social skills and emotional control are required of the employee since in this instance the actions, style and setting require a theatrical performance delivering rehearsed scripts in well specified roles (Bryman, 2004; Crang, 1997). Aesthetic labour directs attention to the physical appearance of the employee where people have to have the right look or sound, usually linked to body shape and facial features (Bryman, 2004). Where performers are the centre piece of tourism-linked entertainment there are undoubtedly strong aesthetic and performative labour requirements. The notion that this kind of work is stressful and debilitating for employees is not consistent and indeed some research in tourist attractions has found that it is the managerial treatment of employees rather than the performative role which troubles more workers (Law et al., 1995).

Several promising lines of work can be explored in the employment dimensions of entertainment science. Some researchers have begun the search for personality style predispositions, which might assist individuals in working well in performative settings (Lee-Ross, 1999). In Hawaiian resorts Adler and Adler (2003) have observed that fixed pay scales for all categories of resort worker can limit enthusiasm for the job and fail to reward growing performative competence. Further exploration of how entertainment workers are paid can be identified as central to future study (Riley et al., 2002). Job rotation systems are used in some existing tourism theme parks so that employees move repeatedly from role to role thus maintaining a fresh and easier emotional commitment to the person in front of them. The applicability of employee control and empowerment in these settings is a potentially fruitful research and managerial exercise. For the categories of the tourism–entertainment spectrum where the performers are the true stars of the event, an examination of fame, careers and dealing with popular recognition at various levels is also an analytic direction.

There are important possibilities in studying and creating the training and educational opportunities for entertainment employees. The technical skills of remaining enduringly positive even when harassed by unreasonable patrons is already a standard part of the pedagogy of the so called Hamburger and Disney Universities (Crang, 1997; Harris, 2005). The ways in which tourism education can respond to an expanding connection between tourism and entertainment would seem to be numerous. Already many institutions offer courses in festival and events management, sports management and media production. One promise of entertainment science is to foster amongst tourism educators the recognition that many of their graduates will work in areas where entertainment matters, whether it be themed shopping malls, events management or heritage settings, and the inclusion of these areas into tourism degrees might enhance the significance and power of existing programmes.

Frameworks for entertainment science research

One way to engage researchers in new topic areas in tourism lies in providing a set of structures or frameworks to stimulate and shape interest. Dann (1999), for example, suggests there is value in reconceptualising tourism through such useful rubrics and heuristics as concept stretching, reversing conventional wisdom, scope broadening and resolving paradoxes. In a similar vein Pearce (2004) notes that for Asian tourism researchers greater international recognition and incorporation of local work might follow if frameworks concentrating on cultural comparisons, technological impacts and the reactions of minority or muted groups were emphasised. For the organisation of new research efforts in entertainment science, the guiding structure of this research piece can be revisited forming a nine-cell model of research topics. On the one hand studies can be directed at three levels of focus – where entertainment is an occasional or augmentative offering, where it occupies a significant component of a tourism experience and where it is the all inclusive holistic offering. These three levels of analysis can in turn be cross-referenced by the major themes in entertainment science already described – power and ownership, consumer reactions, and employment and training. The resultant nine-cell framework is presented in Table 19.2 and some indicative but certainly not exhaustive research directions are included within each of the specific cells.

The framework outlined in Table 19.2 can be used in a number of ways. In addition to the focus in each cell, an across the rows or down the columns set of research exercises can be suggested. In the cross-row research the consideration of augmentative entertainment practices, their role and use by organisations, public reaction to these structures and employees' views of them could form a number of case studies offering a cumulative inductively derived conceptual account of how these performances assist tourism settings (Eisenhardt, 1989). Similar contrasts could be provided across the other two rows in Table 19.2. The vertical connections could also be explored, with the emphasis on this occasion being an investigation of whether such forms of entertainment grow from the smaller cases to the larger components. Additionally, consumer reaction to these offerings may have their own logics and benchmarks or it could be established, following Table 19.1 reviewed earlier, that a cross-level view of entertainment is the most insightful approach. For the employment and training column the careers of employees in entertainment represent an obvious cross-level link, with further issues of employee satisfaction, stress and training requirements representing investigative possibilities. Some of this work may usefully be done at a descriptive level.

It is, however, also possible to follow more conceptual and theoretical themes through the rows and columns of Table 19.2. Concepts such as gaze, power, surveillance, theming, cultural capital and flow all appeal as organisers of entertainment science study cells. Methodologically the new tolerant eclecticism which characterises much tourism publishing could also be reinforced and extended in entertainment science (Phillimore and Goodson, 2004). Observation and archival analysis can be suggested as important techniques in seeing how performances are enacted and received, but there is a place too for systematic survey work uncovering the multivariate determinants of pleasure and enjoyment.

In a literal sense entertainment is the holding and capturing of the attention of people through the efforts of others. Perhaps entertainment science can hold and capture the attention of tourism researchers as they seek to understand both the commercial and social dimensions of existing and future tourism.

Philip L. Pearce

Table 19.2 A framework for entertainment science research

Themes in entertainment science

		Power and Ownership	Consumer and Audience Response	Employment and Training
	Augmentative part of operation • queues • waiting lines • greeters • public relations • guides	• Choice and theming of performance • Surveillance and control of entertainment • Crowd and scene setting management • Creation and recognition of opportunities for entertainment	• Satisfaction • Mindfulness • Tension creation and reduction • Filled time	• Career entry • Training systems • Personality predispositions • Emotional labour experiences
Level of entertainment operation	Core Component of operation • shows • displays • events • features • attraction rides • exhibits	• Investment in component • Connection to total operation • Profitability • Merchandising • Architecture form and layout	• Enjoyment and pleasure • Cultural capital • Insight • Learning • Flow, quality appraisal • Rich time/slow time	• Career development • Educational needs • Personality predispositions • Skill development • Performance labour experiences
	Totality of entertainment offering • key events • major performances • integrated attractions • sports • special purpose films	• Choice of location, talent, timing • Profitability • Merchandising • Architecture form and layout and control	• Immersion • Enjoyment • Pleasure • Insight • Flow, quality appraisal • Rich time/slow time	• Fame and popularity • Performance maintenance • Aesthetic labour experience

References

Adler, P. and Adler, P. (2003) *Paradise laborers hotel work in the global economy*. Ithaca, NY: Cornell University Press

Aramberri, J. (2001) 'The host should get lost: Paradigms in the tourism theory'. *Annals of Tourism Research*, 28(3), 738–61

Baerenholdt, J., Haldrup, M., Larsen, J. and Urry, J. (2004) *Performing tourist places*. Aldershot: Ashgate

Barthes, R. (1972) *Mythologies*. London: Paladin

Becher, T. (1989) *Academic tribes and territories: Intellectual enquiry and the culture of disciplines*. Milton Keynes: Society for Research into Higher Education and the Open University Press

Boorstin, D. J. (1962) *The image: A guide to pseudo-events in America*. New York: Harper and Row

Bourdieu, P. (1986) *Distinction: A social critique of the judgement of taste*. London: Routledge

Bryman, A. (2004) *The Disneyisation of society*. London: Sage

Cohen, E. (1979) 'Rethinking the sociology of tourism'. *Annals of Tourism Research*, 6(1), 18–35

Coles, T., Duval, D. and Hall, C. M. (2004) 'Tourism, mobility and global communities: New approaches to theorising tourism and tourist spaces'. In W. Theobold (ed.) *Global tourism*. Oxford: Heinemann, pp. 463–81

Cooper, C., Fletcher, J., Fyall, A., Gilbert, D. and Wanhill, S. (2005) *Tourism: Principles and practice* (3rd edn). Harlow: Pearson Education

Crang, P. (1997) 'Performing the tourist product'. In C. Rojek and J. Urry (eds) *Tourism cultures: Transformation of travel and theory*. London: Routledge, pp. 137–54

Crick, M. (1989) 'Representations of international tourism in the social sciences: Sun, sex, sights, savings, and servility'. *Annual Review of Anthropology*, 18, 307–44

Crouch, D. (2005) 'Flirting with space: Tourism geographies as sensuous/expressive practice'. In C. Cartier and A. Lew (eds) *Seductions of place*. London: Routledge, pp. 23–35

Csikszentmihalyi, M. (1975) *Beyond boredom and anxiety*. San Francisco, CA: Jossey Bass

Daniel, Y. P. (1996) 'Tourism dance performances: Authenticity and creativity'. *Annals of Tourism Research*, 23(4), 780–97

Dann, G. (1999) 'Theoretical issues for tourism's future development: Identifying the agenda'. In D. Pearce and R. Butler (eds) *Contemporary issues in tourism development*. London: Routledge, pp. 13–30

Dann, G., Nash, D. and Pearce, P. L. (1988) 'Methodology in tourism research'. *Annals of Tourism Research*, 15(1), 1–28

Donlon, J. G. and Agrusa, J. F. (2003) 'Attraction of the naughty-gentlemen's clubs as a tourism resource: The French Quarter example'. In T. Bauer and B. McKercher (eds) *Sex and tourism*. New York: The Haworth Press, pp. 119–34

Eco, U. (1986) *Travels in hyper reality*. London: Picador

Eisenhardt, K. M. (1989) 'Building theories from case study research'. *Academy of Management Review*, 14(4), 532–50

Farrell, B. and Twining-Ward, L. (2004) 'Reconceptualising tourism'. *Annals of Tourism Research*, 31(2), 274–95

Foucault, M. (1975) *Surveiller et punir: Naissance de la prison*. Paris: Gallimard

—— (1980) *Power/knowledge: Selected interviews and other writings 1972–1977* (trans. C. Gordon). New York: Pantheon

Franklin, A. (2003) *Tourism: An introduction*. London: Sage

Franklin, A. and Crang, M. (2001) 'The trouble with tourism and travel theory'. *Tourist Studies*, 1(1), 5–22

Gladwell, M. (2000) *The tipping point*. London: Abacus

Goffman, E. (1959) *The presentation of self in everyday life*. New York: Doubleday

Gomm, R. (2004) *Social research methodology*. Basingstoke: Palgrove MacMillan

Gould, S. J. (2004) *The hedgehog, the fox and the magister's pox: Mending and minding the misconceived gap between science and the humanities*. London: Vintage

Hall, C. M. (2005) *Tourism: Rethinking the social science of mobility*. Harlow: Pearson Education

Harre, R. (1979) *Social being*. Oxford: Blackwell

Harris, D. (2005) *Key concepts in leisure studies*. London: Sage

Hochschild, A. (1983) *The managed heart: Commercialization of human feeling*. Berkeley, CA: University of California Press

Holling, C. and Gunderson, L. (2002) 'Resilience and adaptive cycles'. In L. Gunderson and C. Holling (eds) *Panarchy: Understanding transformation in human and natural systems*. Washington, DC: Island Press, pp. 25–62

Hovinen, G. R. (2002) 'Revising the destination lifestyle model'. *Annals of Tourism Research*, 29(1), 209–30

Howard, P. (2003) *Heritage management, interpretation identity*. London: Continuum

Inglis, F. (2000) *The delicious history of the holiday*. London: Routledge

Jones, C. D., Hollenhorst, S. J. and Perna, F. (2003) 'An empirical comparison of the four channel flow model and adventure experience paradigm'. *Leisure Sciences*, 25(1), 17–31

Kahneman, D., Diener, E. and Schwarz, N. (eds) (1999) *Well being: The foundations of hedonic psychology*. New York: Sage

Kiel, L. D. and Elliott, E. (eds) (1996) *Chaos theory in the social sciences: Foundations and applications*. Ann Arbor, MI: University of Michigan Press

Kozak, M. (2002) 'Destination benchmarking'. *Annals of Tourism Research*, 29(2), 497–519

Krippendorf, J. (1987) *The holiday makers: Understanding the impact of leisure and travel*. London: William Heinemann

Law, J., Pearce, P. L. and Woods, B. A. (1995) 'Stress and coping in tourist attraction employees'. *Tourism Management*, 16(4), 277–84

Lee-Ross, D. (1999) 'Development of the service pre-disposition instrument'. *Journal of Management Psychology*, 15(2), 148–56

Lew, A. and Cartier, C. (2005) 'Conclusion: Centering tourism geography'. In C. Cartier and A. Lew (eds) *Seductions of place*. London: Routledge, pp. 301–6

MacCannell, D. (1976) *The tourist: A new theory of the leisure class*. New York: Schocken Books

MacDonald, S. (1997) 'A people's story: Heritage, identity and authenticity'. In C. Rojek and J. Urry (eds) *Touring cultures: Transformations of travel and theory*. London: Routledge, pp. 155–75

Matos, R. (2004) 'Can slow tourism bring new life to Alpine regions?'. In K. Weiermair and C. Mathies (eds) *The tourism and leisure industry: Shaping the future*. New York: The Haworth Press, pp. 93–102

Meethan, K. (2001) *Tourism in global society: Place, culture and consumption*. London: Palgrave

Moscardo, G. (1999) *Making visitors mindful: Principles for creating sustainable visitor experiences through effective communication*. Champaign, IL: Sagamore

Moscardo, G. and Pearce, P. L. (1999) 'Understanding ethnic tourists'. *Annals of Tourism Research*, 26(2), 416–34

National Vanguard Books (2004) 'Who rules America?'. Retrieved 3 November 2011, from http://www.natvan.com/leaflets/WRA

Noe, F. (1999) *Tourism service satisfaction*. Champaign, IL: Sagamore

Outhwaite, W. (2000) 'The philosophy of social science'. In B. S. Turner (ed.) *The Blackwell companion to social theory* (2nd edn). Oxford: Blackwell, pp. 47–70

Pearce, P. L. (1982) *The social psychology of tourist behaviour*. Oxford: Pergamon Press

—— (1988) *The Ulysses factor: Evaluating visitors in tourist settings*. New York: Springer Verlag

—— (2004) 'Theoretical innovation in Asia Pacific tourism research'. *Asia Pacific Journal of Tourism Research*, 9(1), 57–70

—— (2005) *Tourist behaviour: Themes and conceptual schemes*. Clevedon: Channel View Publications

Phillimore, J. and Goodson, L. (eds) (2004) *Qualitative research in tourism*. London: Routledge

Pine, B. J., II (2004) 'Tourism and the experience economy'. Paper presented at the Tourism and Travel Research Conference, Montreal, July

—— and Gilmour, J. (1999) *The experience economy*. Boston, MA: Harvard Business School Press

Poon, A. (1993) *Tourism technology and competitive strategies*. Wallingford: CAB International

Riley, M., Ladkin, A. and Szivas, E. (2002) *Tourism employment: Analysis and planning*. Clevedon: Channel View Publications

Ritzer, G. (1993) *The McDonaldization of society: An investigation into the changing character of contemporary social life*. London: Sage

—— (1999) *Enchanting a disenchanted world: Revolutionising the means of consumption*. Thousand Oaks, CA: Pine Forge Press

Rojek, C. (1993) *Ways of escape*. Basingstoke: Macmillan

—— (2000) *Leisure and culture*. Basingstoke: Macmillan

—— (2010) *The Labour of Leisure: The Culture of Free Time*. Thousand Oaks, CA: Sage

—— and Urry, J. (1997) 'Transformations of travel and theory'. In C. Rojek and J. Urry (eds) *Touring cultures: Transformations of travel and theory*. London: Routledge, pp. 1–19

Russell, R. and Faulkner, B. (1999) 'Movers and shakers: Chaos makers in tourism development'. *Tourism Management*, 20(4), 411–423

Ryan, C. (1995) *Researching tourist satisfaction: Issues, concepts, problems*. London: Routledge

—— (ed.) (2002) *The tourist experience* (2nd edn). London: Continuum

Schmitt, B. H. (1999) *Experiential marketing: How to get customers to sense, feel, think, act and relate to your company and brands*. New York: Free Press

Singh, S. (2004) 'Coming full circle: Tourism concepts, knowledge, and approaches'. *Tourism (Zagreb)*, 52(4), 307–16

Uriely, N. (2005) 'The tourist experience: Conceptual developments'. *Annals of Tourism Research*, 32(1), 199–216

Urry, J. (1990) *The tourist gaze: Leisure and travel in contemporary societies*. London: Sage

Uzzell, D. (1998) 'Interpreting our heritage: A theoretical interpretation'. In D. Uzzell and R. Ballantyne (eds) *Contemporary issues in heritage and environmental interpretation: Problems and prospects.* London: The Stationery Office, pp. 77–97

Woehler, K. (2004) 'The rediscovery of slowness, or leisure time as one's own and as self-aggrandizement?'. In K. Weiermair and C. Mathies (eds) *The tourism and leisure industry: Shaping the future.* New York: The Haworth Press, pp. 83–90

20

Major trends in contemporary tourism

Erik Cohen

Introduction

About forty years ago on a visit to the rather remote Tonga islands, I was astonished and dismayed when I noticed, among the locally produced wood carvings offered to visiting cruiser tourists on the beach market of Nuku'alofa (the capital of Tonga) a figure of King Kong. Since there are no monkeys on Tonga, or for that matter on any Pacific island, I perceived the carving as an astonishing and annoying instance of cultural pollution in such a tradition-bound society. However, when I complained about that to a native anthropologist, he just brushed away my objection, claiming that King Kong had become part of Tongan culture, having been introduced to the islands through the motion pictures. At the time I found it hard to accept that response. Today, I am engaged in the study of tourism to the cowboy towns and festivals of the American West – not in the United States, but in Thailand, where the local "cowboy culture" has become an increasingly popular tourist attraction.

The image of the world promoted in modern tourism resembles that of a geographic map, with differently colored patches representing discrete, sharply bounded socio-cultural territories, each with its distinct and overlapping ethnic, linguistic, religious and cultural traits; this image still prevails, though it is increasingly at variance with the process of mutual interpenetration of cultures, reaching ever more remote parts of the world, even before their penetration by tourism.

In the wake of globalization and the accompanying processes of growing mobility of people, goods, capital, information and cultures (Urry, 2000), much of the contemporary, increasingly "postmodern" world is becoming, on the one hand, ever more homogenized (Ritzer, 1993) and, on the other, hybridized (Kapchan and Strong, 1999) and "glocalized" (Raz, 1999; Robertson, 1995). These tendencies precipitate the emergence of new trends in contemporary tourism, to which the paradigms which had been proposed for the analysis of modern tourism are no longer readily applicable. These trends thus pose a challenge to the researcher to develop new analytical tools. In this chapter, I shall outline three of the major trends in contemporary tourism and propose some ideas for the reformulation of the paradigmatic approach to the study of the relationship between tourism and modernity to suit the current, increasingly "postmodern" situation.

In the concluding chapter of my book on contemporary tourism (Cohen, 2004) I argued that it is characterized by two contrasting trends: a postmodern decline of the "quest for otherness" (and hence for genuineness and authenticity) leading to the diminution of the extraordinariness of the tourist experience and to the gradual merger of tourism and leisure; and a resurgent "modern" quest for ever more extreme otherness on Earth and, incipiently, space, leading to the merger of tourism and exploration. The analysis of these trends will be further elaborated here, together with an important third trend: "fantasy" tourism, overlooked in Cohen (2004). As the point of departure of my analysis, I shall use Dean MacCannell's paradigm for the study of modern tourism (MacCannell, 1973, 1976).

Tourism and modernity

In the broadest sense, the aim of tourists, as Nelson Graburn (1977) noticed some time ago, is to experience something "extraordinary" – something different from their everyday experience at home. What that extraordinariness consists of, however, is a contested matter, lying at the heart of a prolonged theoretical controversy regarding the relationship between tourism and modernity (Boorstin, 1964; MacCannell, 1973, 1976; Wang, 2000). That controversy has been constitutive of the development of a theoretical approach to tourism in sociology. MacCannell, the leading early theoretician in the field, proposed a paradigm for the sociological study of tourism, by linking the tourist's quest to some basic features of modern life. Though MacCannell's approach was criticized on theoretical grounds (Wang, 1999) as well as empirical grounds (Selänniemi, 2001), I still believe that the linkage he established is fundamentally sound, though its empirical manifestations were weakened by variations in the underlying factors which MacCannell's totalizing approach did not sufficiently consider (Cohen, 1979a; Edwards, 1996). MacCannell's approach is, hence, still a useful point of departure for the study of tourism in an increasingly "postmodern" world, but has to be reformulated to suit the novel circumstances.

MacCannell regarded tourism basically as a compensatory mechanism, ameliorating the dissatisfactions at the basis of modern life. Modern man is seen as alienated from his spurious, mundane surroundings and society; driven by a quest for "authenticity," missing in his society of origin, he looks for it elsewhere, in other places (and other times) beyond the confines of modernity (MacCannell, 1976). Those places are imagined (and advertised) as still pure and genuine, uncontaminated by the forces of modernity – resembling those differently colored patches on the map; they are believed to be "authentic" in an "objective" (Wang, 2000) sense – i.e. pre-existing the penetration of tourism, integral to local society and environment, and untampered with by the agents of tourism. But tourism is said to have a paradoxical effect; its very penetration into a locality marks it as a "destination" and its sights as "attractions," leading eventually to their transformation. This brings about the emergence of "staged authenticity" in maturing destinations – the covert (mis)representation of by now spurious attractions as if they were genuine. Tourism development in modernity thus engenders covertly staged "tourist settings" devoid of authenticity; in touristically developed situations the modern tourist's serious quest for authenticity is thus thwarted – he or she is unable to penetrate the false "fronts," with which they are presented, into the "back" regions of real local life. Authentic life, even if it still exists in the destination, remains beyond the tourist's grasp.

The basic structure of this paradigm, proposed for the study of tourism in modernity, can be reformulated for the study of tourism in postmodern situations, but such a reformulation necessitates the deconstruction of MacCannell's basic notion of "staged authenticity."

This notion can be interpreted as a pair of "counter-concepts" (Koselleck, 1985; Olsen, 2002), in which "authenticity" is the positive, and "staging" the negative term. The prioritization of authenticity in the discourse on modern tourism has focused critical attention on that term, to the detriment of the analysis of "staging," which on the whole remains a residual term. However, a consideration of the principal modalities of staging and of their referents appears to be a promising point of departure for the reformulation of MacCannell's paradigm to suit postmodern situations.

In an early article (Cohen, 1979b) I drew a distinction between "covert" and "overt" staging of attractions. However, I missed then the theoretical significance of this distinction; while MacCannell recognized the significance of covert staging for modern tourism, I missed that of overt staging for postmodern situations.

Covert staging can be seen, in Erwin Goffman's (1974) terms as a form of unacknowledged or unmarked "fabrication": contrary to the impression tourists are intended to have, the staged attraction is not part of the lived-in-world or everyday reality of the destination, but a separate "frame" insidiously put up for tourist consumption. It is thus a mode of falsification, and as such the only kind of staging of theoretical interest to MacCannell. But this leaves out the many significant modes of overt staging in contemporary tourism: the various marked "frames" which, despite an explicit physical or symbolic indication that they are *not* part of the lived-in-world of the destination, attract large – and increasing – numbers of tourists. A detailed discussion of such modes would bring us off the main line of argument. But a few analytically distinct types ought to be noted. Some overt modes of staging have external referents: they are either metaphors of some (absent or inaccessible) "originals," as is the case with "reproductions" or "simulations" of sites, events or objects; or they are metonyms as in the case of collections (of art objects or specimens in museums, zoos or herbaria, or of the material culture of different ethnic groups in a theme park): they consist of "real" objects, displaced from their "original" setting, brought together and artfully displayed as reminders of nature or culture in other places or times. But – central to the following argument – some other overtly staged attractions have no external referents – they are creations of pure imagination and as such completely self-referential. One of the principal arguments to be made in this article is that in tourism, in an increasingly homogenized, regulated world, overtly staged attractions play an ever more dominant role; and that among such attractions those based on imaginary, self-referential themes are particularly prominent – indeed, sophisticated contemporary technology endows them with such a degree of apparent realism that they become "hyper-real" (Baudrillard, 1988).

That overtly staged attractions are explicitly marked as not constituting part of everyday reality does not necessarily make them naïve or fully transparent entities. Rather, they might be used to convey a variety of hidden messages of a political, cultural or commercial nature, and as such to serve the ulterior purposes or interests of their initiators or owners. This is commonly the case in the artful arrangement of museum collections, as, for example, the manner in which the Tel Aviv Museum of the Jewish Diaspora promotes an implicit Zionist ideological message of exodus, dispersal and redemption (Golden, 1996; Shinhav-Keller, 2000), and – particularly – in the manner theme parks, whose exhibits are under less scientific scrutiny than museums, are constructed. Such a powerful, but hidden political use of theme parks is beautifully illustrated in S. Errington's (1998) study of the Taman Mini theme park outside Jakarta, where the arrangement of the various ethnic groups of Indonesia, represented by their house types, ostensibly reflects President Suharto's state ideology of "Unity in Diversity" – but the layout of the park in fact assigns them a peripheral position, while stressing "the centrality of Javanese overlordship within the national cosmography" (ibid., p. 216). However, such hidden messages inscribed in overtly staged attractions are an altogether different issue than covert staging of authenticity in MacCannell's sense, and belong to the domain of the study of the "political economy of attractions," which, whatever its importance, is not the topic of this article.

Tourism and postmodernity

"Postmodernity" is a complex, in many respects problematic, but important concept. Various authors emphasize different traits of postmodern situations. For present purposes, it suffices to outline those traits which affect – in different ways – the main trends in contemporary tourism.

Postmodernity is often characterized by the breakdown of "master narratives" which have served in the past as the foundations of comprehensive world views, whether those of the great world religions or even of modern rationalism and "scientism," the prioritization of scientific over religious or other interpretations of the world. It thus denies the singleness of truth and admits the existence of multiple versions or truths in the interpretation of phenomena (cf. Cohen, 2007). Fundamental truths and beliefs of modernity are destabilized, and diverse world-views are equalized. There occurs a fragmentation of the modern, supposedly coherent, perception of reality and a concomitant destabilization of personal identities, which become multiple and shifting. The distinction between high and low culture is erased. The various "finite provinces of meaning" (Schutz, 1973), such as play, art, fantasy and drug-inspired hallucination, are not any more clearly distinguished from the "paramount reality," the shared, intersubjective reality of the lived-in world, whose boundaries were supposed to be sharply defined in modernity. Similarly, the boundaries between functionally differentiated domains of modern life, such as work and leisure also become blurred – the postmodern world is "de-differentiated." Consumption, rather than work, increasingly becomes the center of the individual's life and the principal activity defining his or her identity.

Postmodernization is driven, or at least closely associated, with the forces of globalization, which have engendered an unprecedented mobility of people, capital, goods, information and cultures (Urry, 2000). These forces blur the "traditional" boundaries between cultures and lead, on the one hand, to a world-wide cultural homogenization, captured in such terms as "McDonaldization" (Ritzer, 1993) or "Disneyization" (Bryman, 1999) of the world; and, on the other hand, to the mixture of diverse cultural elements, conceptualized in such terms as cultural fusion (Cohen, 2000), hybridization (Kapchan and Strong, 1999), glocalization (Raz, 1999) or transnationalism. Though the exact extent of such processes is contested (Guillén, 2001) and has been empirically little documented, some authors believe that they tend to penetrate the remotest parts of the world, thus adulterating the cultures of isolated tribes and destroying the pristine qualities of virgin islands.

Postmodernity is also conceived by some authors as "the age of simulation," "the generation of models without origin or reality: a hyperreal" (Baudrillard, 1988, p. 167); it is a world of copies without originals, and hence without authenticity. The relationship between the real and the sign, the simulacrum, is said to have become inverted: the simulacrum in the postmodern world determining the real: Disneyland is the "real" America (ibid.). The process may go further: the castle of the Magic Kingdom in Las Vegas is a copy of the castle of the Magic Kingdom in Disneyland – but the latter can be seen as a simulacrum without a referential (or original). Similarly, the Thai cowboy culture is copied from the contemporary American cowboy culture, specifically from Western movies; those movies, in turn, while only tenuously related to the historical American West (Johnson, 1998), constitute its "reality" in popular consciousness, in Thailand as elsewhere.

Ironically, because of the shifting, mobile and unstable nature of contemporary life, "travel" (Rojek and Urry, 1997) became a dominant metaphor to characterize the postmodern situation, though the joint processes of homogenization and cultural hybridization appear to have for many people reduced the very attractiveness of travel for pleasure. Indeed, MacCannell (2001) recently complained about the growing similarity between destinations and asked whether the increasingly homogeneous travel experience will eventually destroy the reason for travel. Leaving aside for the moment the sweeping totalization implicit in such statements, it is important to note that they indicate a crucial difference between the theoretical assumptions underlying the analysis of postmodern as against modern tourism. According to MacCannell's paradigm, the modern tourist, though living in a spurious world, has assumed that authenticity can still be found elsewhere – in other places (and other times) – an assumption upon which the effectiveness of the notion of "staged authenticity" has been based. But, according to theorists of globalization and postmodernity, the expectation that extraordinary and authentic experiences can be obtained anywhere is unwarranted in the contemporary situation. The question hence arises, how do contemporary tourists relate to and respond to this assumedly changed state of affairs?

I suggest that potential tourists may respond to the postmodern view of the world in three distinct ways, each of which gives rise to one of the major trends in contemporary tourism:

1   They may accept that there exist constraints on the availability of authentic and other "extraordinary" experiences in a homogenized, postmodern world, and resign themselves in their travels to the enjoyment of fine distinctions within the domain of the familiar; this leads to the emergence of the "post-tourist" (Ritzer and Liska, 1997).
2   They may accept that there exist constraints on the availability of authentic and other "extraordinary" experiences within the confines of the contemporary world, but search for them in other "finite provinces of meaning;" in the realm of tourism this search will lead them to enjoy the "extraordinary" but simulated experiences offered by technologically sophisticated theme parks and similar enterprises, whose productions of the fantastic, while admittedly "out of this world," attain the character of the "hyper-real" (Baudrillard, 1988; Eco, 1986).
3   They may contest the totalizing claim that authentic and other "extraordinary" experiences are unavailable in the contemporary world, and engage in a quest for them in its expanding margins, which appear to lie outside the influence of the dominant forces in the contemporary world, and of the tourist system – in the as yet relatively inaccessible regions of the Earth and, eventually, in space – a quest which demands inordinate efforts, skills and financial resources.

Each of these responses engenders a distinct trend, with particular consequences for the dynamics of contemporary tourism; we now turn to a discussion of these trends.

The post-tourist's quest for distinction

The sophisticated and reflective postmodern individual, resigned to the progressive homogenization and to the alleged vanishing of genuine originals from this world, surrenders to an often playful enjoyment of surfaces of sites, objects and events (Cohen, 1995; Dunn, 1999; Mitchell, 1998); while the modern, authenticity-seeking tourist, suffers from the "tourist Angst" that he will be taken in by a fake (cf. MacCannell, 1973), the "post-tourist" does not delve into the provenience of enjoyable attractions. In postmodernity, enjoyment and even plain fun and play become socially acceptable motives for travel, replacing the modern quest for the authentic as a primary legitimizing motive for tourism. Post-tourists do not care for genuineness and may prefer the substitute for the real thing, if it is nicer, "prettier" or more comfortable: the swimming pool to the sea, the artificial flower to the real one, the accessible well-made copy to the distant, fading original. They may prefer "kitsch" to "art," even as the boundaries between these cultural domains become increasingly blurred, kitsch becoming ever more artistic, art (ironically) imitating kitsch.

But the most distinctive feature of post-tourists is that, rather than engaging in a futile quest for the strange and exotic, they depart on their trip in search of familiar, but distinctive, experiences which are not available (or not affordable) at home. Theirs is a quest for "distinction" (Bourdieu, 1984) in consumption, in the double sense of satisfying distinct, often sophisticated tastes, as well as of achieving social distinction by demonstrating the possession of cultural capital. Post-tourists engage primarily in cultural tourism, and are eager consumers of the varied products of contemporary culture; they seek distinctive musical, theatrical and similar performances, cultural festivals, exhibitions, fairs, fashions, cuisines, shopping opportunities, nightlife, sports events, and various arts and crafts which are more innovative or more sophisticated, of a higher quality, at a greater variety, of a higher prestige value (or greater affordability) than those available at home. The post-tourist may seek novelty, but within the domain of global, contemporary culture – rather than engage in a quest of the otherness of disappearing "authentic" ethnic or other strange cultures. However, fused or hybridized novel cultural products, such as "fusion cuisines," often thriving on the contrast between incongruent elements incorporated in them (Cohen, 2000), might become increasingly attractive to such tourists. But, on the whole, in this trend of contemporary tourism, "extraordinariness" is at the minimum – and can therefore be appreciated only by individuals with a relatively highly developed sense of distinction. Post-tourism appears therefore to be a class-related phenomenon, characteristic mainly of the upper social classes. However, it is far from restricted to a tiny elite: in the prosperous contemporary West – and increasingly in some non-Western countries – growing numbers of people possess the economic as well as the cultural capital to participate in it.

This trend dovetails with a desire of big metropolitan cities in developed countries – and increasingly also in developing ones – to revitalize their declining centers by creating major new cultural institutions such as museums, opera houses, concert, convention and exhibition halls, or by hosting cultural and commercial events, such as festivals of contemporary music, theater, film or cuisines, and by staging major exhibitions and fairs. These cities compete fiercely to host various commercial, cultural and sportive mega-events. Such projects and events are intended for both locals as well as domestic and foreign tourists; they often serve to place a city on the world tourist map. A striking example of such an effort to revitalize a city by cultural tourism is the erection of the architecturally impressive new Guggenheim Museum in the deteriorating center of the city of Bilbao, in the Basque region of Spain, which virtually overnight turned the city into a major tourist destination (Lacy and Douglass, 2002). Such cultural institutions, being novel, vital and multi-purpose in character, do not fit well the theoretical categories used in the study of modern tourism – they could not be defined as either "authentic" or "staged;" they are "beyond authenticity" (ibid.). Some major cities in the non-Western world, such as Singapore and, more recently, Bangkok, began similarly to strive to establish themselves as centers of contemporary global culture and thus as emergent "world cities" – rather than to present themselves just as exotic destinations featuring colorful ethnic or folkloristic attractions.

The proliferation of novel cultural institutions, integral to the urban ambience, tends to erase the boundary between tourism and ordinary leisure. On the one hand, they serve simultaneously different audiences: the local urban population, domestic, as well as international tourism; they do not constitute segregated "tourist spaces." On the other hand, in an era of ever increasing mobility and falling travel costs, the ordinary action space of members of upper classes grows in scope: it becomes increasingly routine for them to travel relatively long distances just to attend a particular cultural event. It is therefore difficult to say whether they engage in tourism, or whether such lengthy trips are just ordinary leisure excursions, the contemporary counterpart of a visit to the local theater or cinema in earlier times.

The mass tourist's quest for fantasy

Not all contemporary people are resigned, like the post-tourist, to the diminished opportunities for exciting 'extraordinary" experiences in the increasingly globalized and homogenized postmodern world; while forgoing the search for authenticity, in the "objective" sense, in the contemporary reality they may seek "existential authenticity" in other "finite provinces of meaning," and especially in the realm of fantasy, provided by overtly staged displays in a variety of specialized enterprises, and especially by theme parks (Wang, 2000).

I suggest that the quest for "fantasy" is becoming, in a homogenized world, a substitute for the tourist quest for "objective" authenticity, above all among broad contemporary social strata; "fantasy" is capable of provoking a ludic sense of "existential authenticity" in the individual, even though he or she are fully aware of the "unreal" nature of the source of its production. MacCannell's (1973, 1976) argument regarding tourism and modernity can thus be reformulated to suit postmodern circumstances.

It will be remembered that, according to MacCannell, moderns-as-tourists seek compensation for the absence of authenticity in their own spacious world in the "real" life of others – outside the boundaries of modernity. But, as MacCannell himself recently claimed (MacCannell, 2001), there appears to be no "outside" to the contemporary homogenized world – no escape from its incessant sameness. It hence follows that the encompassing homogenization of the contemporary world could only be escaped by stepping outside it – into the realm of other "finite provinces of meaning," and especially that of "fantasy." I argue that "fantasy," which is by definition a sphere of experience "out of this world" comes to play in postmodern situations an analogous role to the authentic "other places," outside the reach of modernity in MacCannell's model. Whereas the quest for authenticity was the typical touristic response to the dissatisfactions of modernity, the quest for the fantastic is the typical response to the postmodern homogenization of the world. But, whereas the modern tourist's quest for authenticity was thwarted by the tourist system's tendency to create covertly staged tourist spaces, the satisfaction of the quest for fantasy is not affected by the overtly staged nature of the attractions which provide experiences of the fantastic.

"Fantasy" may have always been a means of private escape, especially for deprived individuals, and it played a significant role in folklore and the arts of the past. But I believe that fantasy came to entertain an unprecedented leading role in contemporary popular culture in its various manifestations – literature, films, television and video games. Tourism is just another domain in which fantasy became increasingly paramount. Moreover, even as the motifs and contents of fantastic displays aimed at tourists deviated ever more extremely from everyday reality, the increasingly sophisticated technological means of their production came so convincingly to simulate reality that the individual is absorbed and enchanted by them – at the extreme, like in "deep play" (Geertz, 1973), experiencing a sense of "existential authenticity." The exorbitantly fantastic thus acquires, for the individual, the character of the "hyper-real." This, in turn, may have repercussions upon institutional changes in the "real-world," exemplified by such processes as "Disneyization" (Bryman, 1999).

In the domain of tourism, the experience of fantasy is provided, above all, by the big, multi-purpose, technologically highly sophisticated theme parks and similar enterprises, catering to a national or even a worldwide audience. Their prototypes are obviously the Disneylands, which set the trend for similar establishments around the world. Walt Disney himself stressed that "his park was not about 'reality'" (Mintz, 1998, p. 49) and he wanted the visitors to feel that "they are in another world" (King, 1981, p. 121). Disney apparently recognized long ago the growing importance of the structurally induced quest for fantasy in the contemporary world.

The typical concrete form which the experience of the fantastic takes in theme parks is that of simulated imaginary rides, acting synergetically on several senses – sight, sound and bodily feelings. Many of the most sophisticated rides do not refer at all to external "reality"; they are either completely self-referential inventions or reproduce fantastic themes from other realms of popular culture – especially the cinema. Thus one of the recently established theme parks, the huge Universal Studios Japan (USJ), features a number of rides, most of which are based on fantastic themes of Hollywood films, the latest addition being the apparently highly popular Spiderman ride (Nation, 2004).

Other theme parks offer simulated sights and events from the "real" external world. Some of the technologically highly sophisticated simulations may create the illusion of actually experiencing the real thing.

One kind of such theme parks conjures up scenes or events from the past to different degrees of historical accuracy: the prehistoric Australian rain forest (Moscardo and Pearce, 1986), or life in a Viking settlement (simulated in York's Jarvik Centre) (Meethan, 1996) or in Lincoln's New Salem (Bruner, 1994). Another kind of theme park brings together, to varying degrees of sophistication, models of selected landmarks or simulations of distinctive environments from various regions of a country or of the world, as in Shenzhen's "Splendid China Miniature Scenic Spots" (Sofield and Li, 1998), Pattaya's "Mini Siam" and "Mini World" (Cohen, 2001), Jakarta's "Taman Mini" (S. Errington, 1998) or Williamsburg's "Busch Gardens" (Mintz, 1998). Since entertainment rather than factual accuracy is the primary purpose of such theme parks, they may include some more fanciful components; thus, the "Busch Gardens" feature in their simulations of distinctive Old Country European environments, such rides as "The Loch Ness Monster" and "Drachen [dragon] Fire" (Mintz, 1998). Finally, some theme parks offer close simulations of "real" experiences which are for technological, financial or other reasons accessible only to a few, usually highly specialized and trained individuals; thus, the latest Walt Disney World's attraction, the "Mission: Space" ride, seeks so tightly to simulate reality that it uses the same technology as that which served to train the NASA astronauts (Nation, 2003). It is the comprehensiveness of the illusion of "reality" experienced on such rides which sets them apart from other forms of mass entertainment.

Large-scale theme parks stand in a dialectic relationship to the locality in which they are established. It is commonly believed that tourism to a locality is engendered by its ambience, "spirit of place" (Selwyn, 1996) or "placeness;" theme parks, as more or less self-contained entities, could in principle be located anywhere if sufficient space is available; they thus appear to reduce the significance of "placeness" in the tourists' choice of destinations. However, as they mature, such parks eventually tend themselves to become a distinguishing landmark of a locality, and thus to endow it with a particular kind of "placeness" – they became the place where a displaced or placeless, "out of this world" fantastic experience can be enjoyed.

In contrast to the experience of the "post-tourist," in which the "extraordinariness" of the trip is minimized, the "extraordinariness" of the experience of the fantasy-seeking tourist is maximized. Though overtly staged – and, as such, clearly marked off from "reality" – the near totality of the "hyper-real" simulations which sophisticated theme parks offer tends to endow them with a ludic (playful) pseudo-religious quality (Cohen, 1985; Moore, 1980) – a surrogate "Other world" for a disenchanted reality.

Extreme tourism on the expanding margins

Like any totalizing claim, the argument regarding the globalization, homogenization and glocalization of the so-called postmodern world is a contested matter. The question is not whether or not those processes took place but, rather, how comprehensive is their penetration? Do there still remain regions on Earth which are as yet relatively unaffected by the forces of globalization and the accompanying process of expansion of the tourist system, or have those forces reached into the most remote places on the globe, as for example MacCannell (2001) seems to believe. There exists no unequivocal answer to that question. It can be conceded that complete otherness, of the kind Lévi-Strauss was searching for in his early travels, may well have vanished; it may be correct, as MacCannell (1992) has argued, that no genuine "primitives" are left on Earth. Human activity affects, to varying degrees of intensity, the remotest regions of the Earth: the oceans are denuded of fish; the vastness of Antarctica is affected by pollution. Remnants of relatively "untouched" wildlife and luxuriant "pristine" nature are becoming increasingly rarer, as they are progressively penetrated by the forces of development, or "preserved" as valuable tourism assets. Places on the margins of the tourist system, which were at an earlier time accessible to any traveler "off the beaten track," such as wild animal preserves, are being turned into exclusive tourist destinations, access to which is, for reasons of sustainability, increasingly more restricted, and often more costly, thereby provoking problems of touristic equity (Cohen, 2002). But there still remain extensive regions on Earth which are relatively lightly touched by the forces of globalization, and as yet remain (except for some established routes, such as the Sepik river excursions into the rain forests of Papua New Guinea; F. Errington and Gewertz, 1989) outside the reach of the tourist system. However, this system has a well-known expansionist tendency. Many once-remote and relatively inaccessible areas, previously the domain of backpackers and travelers, became selectively incorporated into the tourist system (Westerhausen, 2002). Indeed, the threat that these regions will soon be "spoiled" by the forces of globalization and penetration by the tourist system, is a powerful motivation for enterprising tourists to visit them "before it was too late" (F. Errington and Gewertz, 1989). A kind of tourist is emerging who resists not only the penetrating forces of globalization, but also what appears to be the defeatist attitude of "postmodern" tourists to the possibility of "authentic" experiences of otherness in the "real" world. These are not the contemporary backpackers, most of whom travel on "beaten tracks off the beaten tracks" of more sedate tourism. Rather, these are more sophisticated and persistent individuals who spend a good deal of money and time purchasing the necessary equipment, and training and planning for excursions into the often inhospitable margins of the tourist system. In some respects, they resemble the gentlemen explorers of the past, though they are in quest of experiences, rather than knowledge; they are "extreme" tourists.

The margins of the tourist system can be conceived as consisting of several increasingly more remote and less accessible zones. The first zone consists of some peripheral regions of the inhabitable non-Western world which, for different reasons, as yet remain outside the confines of the tourist system. One such region was, at least until recently, the ex-communist and post-communist world, access to many parts of which was restricted during the period of communist rule. This huge region is now being rapidly opened up for tourism; indeed, China, the most attractive of the post-communist countries for tourism, is rapidly becoming one of the most popular destinations in the world. But several other such regions still remain, for various reasons, such as lack of infrastructure, unhealthy climates and political instability, outside the confines of the tourist system: new states of central Asia, the interiors of Africa and South America, much of the Indian sub-continent. Even in popular Southeast Asia, there are still broad areas of little touristic penetration, though one of the most important among them, the Upper Mekong region, will apparently soon be opened up. Even in the touristically much exploited Pacific, there are still many peripheral islands hardly touched by tourism and only relatively lightly by the forces of globalization.

While this first zone presents only moderate resistance to penetration by the tourist system, the second, more marginal one – the remaining huge, uninhabitable and inhospitable regions of the Earth – will prove much more resistant: the desolate deserts, the high mountain ranges, the polar regions and the deep seas. Admittedly, some relatively small stretches of these vast regions have been opened to tourism: the iconic example is the route to the summit of Mount Everest (Brown, 1996); luxurious and expensive cruises are plying the margins of Antarctica (Reich, 1980; Smith, 2001), and organized "expeditions" into desert areas are offered by specialized tour-agencies. But on the whole most of these regions stay, and will probably remain for the foreseeable future, outside the reach of the tourist system.

Those remote and inhospitable regions are the ones which present a challenge to practitioners of various forms of "extreme" tourism: danger-, thrill- or adventure-seeking individuals, in quest of extraordinary but authentic experiences in both the objective as well as the existential sense of "authenticity" (Wang, 2000). This kind of individual is comparatively rare, since the penetration of such inhospitable areas demands a combination of skills, determination and experience, as well as often considerable financial resources, which are beyond the ability of most members of the traveling public. Such audacious individuals invest great efforts, expose themselves to considerable risks and often go to great expenses for equipment, training and travel arrangements to take extended expeditions into the remaining relatively uncharted parts of the world. The increase in the number of people who desire to take such risks may indicate a growing resistance to the homogenizing forces of globalization, an extreme variant of a stubborn "modern" quest for authenticity in an increasingly postmodern world.

To be sure, some of these individuals are not unaffected by influences of postmodern culture, whether that be consumerism or a tendency to turn their feats into spectacle. Thus, in contrast to most backpackers, "extreme" tourists seem to be keen on state-of-the-art equipment, and are trend-setters in the introduction of new outfits and technical gadgets to the market for less adventurous tourists. Some also turn their feats into spectacle – as in the case of paragliding off the summit of Mt. Everest, recorded by a television crew (Brown, 1996).

Some extreme tourists, in order to increase the thrill and danger of the trip, impose upon themselves substantial constraints as they seek to accomplish feats dangerous in themselves: "free" rock-climbing of high cliffs, solo trekking of deserts or unassisted crossing of polar regions. Such feats are often performed to gain publicity for themselves or for a cause, more as a status-enhancing spectacle than an authentic experience.

However, the remotest marginal zone, and the one most resistant to penetration by the tourist system is not on Earth, but rather in the endless expanses of space beyond it. These are the new and expanding margins of the tourist system.

I have no intention of speculating about the future of space tourism; there are too many imponderables involved. But there appears to exist a widespread enthusiasm about space travel, manifesting itself, among others, in the popularity of simulated space rides and airplane trips to the edge of space, on which weightlessness is experienced (Presse-Agentur, 2004).

Space tourism certainly harbors opportunities for "extraordinary" experiences of a strange reality – indeed, so strange that it may transform the individual, as attested already by the "greening" of the early astronauts (Time Magazine, 1972). In fact, the experience may be so strange and frightening as to scare off, rather than attract, many ordinary people, who might prefer the security of the simulated experience of space to the thrill of the real thing.

At the moment space travel is still the exclusive privilege of a very few, super-rich individuals, who combine their ability to spend tens of millions of dollars with the physique and tenacity to train intensely for a brief journey into space. Though space travel may in the near future become more widely available, it will still remain limited to a relatively small number of adventurous individuals. Even though it appears to be the ultimate adventure, we should note some significant differences between space travel and the various forms of "extreme" adventure tourism on Earth, and pay attention to some of the constraints inherent in this nascent form of tourism.

Space tourists differ from self-reliant earthly adventure travelers in several important ways. Space travel appears to constitute a combination of contrasting traits, unknown in tourism on Earth – a combination of some aspects of the role of adventurer and that of the mass tourist. On the one hand, space tourism as presently perceived, is certainly a risky undertaking, demanding skills, fortitude and endurance – possible to a higher degree that that demanded of most adventure tourists. But, on the other, in sharp contrast, space tourism, at least at the present stage, does not demand, or even permit, any personal initiative or individual "heroic" actions on the trip. Rather, it involves discipline, and, if at all, participation in teamwork, in which the space tourist – not being a specialist – can at most play only a very limited role.

Not unlike the mass tourist, the space tourist travels in an "environmental bubble" of the Earth's environment, and is much more strictly isolated from the hostile surroundings of space than is any mass tourist even from the strangest environments on Earth. The space tourist's experience of space is thus restricted to the visual sense, just like that of the mass tourist traveling in an organized group through a foreign country. However, while for the latter the bodily experiences inherent in the trip may be annoying – crowded or uncomfortable seats, bumping roads, jet lag – for the space tourist, bodily experiences, though not necessarily pleasant, are part of the attraction of the trip: the high pressure of ascent and descent or weightlessness in space, are desired bodily states for which the space tourist trains intensely prior to the trip. The simulation of such experiences appears to be one of the principal attractions of such theme park rides as "Mission: Space."

For the moment, space travel is just that: travel. There is no arrival at a destination in space. The question thus remains: to what extent will the harsh climates and desolate landscapes of the Moon, Mars and the other accessible planets prove attractive enough, beyond their present novelty value, to "ordinary" individuals to undertake lengthy, strenuous, dangerous, uncomfortable and expensive journeys into space so that the tourist system prevalent on Earth will eventually expand to cosmic proportions.

Conclusion

The three major trends in contemporary tourism, discussed in this chapter, present different combinations between the perception of the contemporary world and the touristic attitude toward it:

1   *Distinction tourism* is characteristic of individuals possessing a relatively high degree of cultural capital, sophistication and reflexivity who perceive the contemporary world as thoroughly postmodern and resignedly adjust their touristic attitude to its constraints: they become "post-tourists," pursuing the enjoyment of fine distinctions within the domain of the familiar, rather than seeking some "extraordinary" experiences of authenticity and otherness, which are believed to have vanished from that world. Increasingly integrated into the patterns of the post-tourists' daily life, this form of tourism tends to merge seamlessly with ordinary leisure.

2   *Fantasy tourism* is characteristic of a wide strata of individuals, of a relatively lower degree of cultural capital, who find the attractions available in an increasingly homogenized world insufficiently exciting, and hence prefer the thrill of the "extraordinary" in the realm of fantasy, rather than reality; that thrill is primarily provided by overtly staged simulations offered by theme parks and similar establishments, which take on the character of the "hyper-real" owing to their technological accomplishment. While forgoing the experience of "objective" authenticity, such tourists may achieve a heightened sense of "existential" authenticity from their playful but deep involvement with the simulated displays of the fantastic. The popularity of this kind of tourism fits the growing popularity and importance of fantasy as a pre-eminent theme in contemporary popular culture.

3   *Extreme tourism* is practiced by individuals who contest the claim that there are no authentic experiences to be had in tourism. They seek the excitement, thrill and risk of travel in those remaining regions of the Earth – and, ultimately, in space – which are as yet relatively lightly touched by those processes and by the tourist system. Theirs is a quest for a heightened, synergetic experience of combined "objective" and "existential" authenticity. For personal and financial reasons such tourism is limited to a small number of adventurous individuals, resembling in some respects the gentlemen explorers of earlier times. Though at the outset a "modern" quest for authenticity in an increasingly homogenized world, extreme tourism is nevertheless touched by features of postmodernity, such as consumerism and the tendency to turn impressive feats into spectacle.

The wider implications of these trends for the tourist system and contemporary society in general remain to be explored. Only some of their more obvious consequences have been explored in this chapter.

Distinction tourism tends to encourage the transformation and revitalization of the urban centers of the more developed parts of the world, as they seek to become "world cities," global centers of culture and cultural tourism, attractive to sophisticated "post-tourists."

Fantasy tourism tends to encourage the "touristic transition" (Cohen, 2001) of mature tourist destinations, as they seek to complement or substitute their declining "natural" attractions with a variety of "contrived" attractions, among which theme parks, especially those featuring simulations of high technological sophistication, play a significant role.

Extreme tourism appears to be a trend-setter in the market for outfits and technical gadgets for less adventurous tourists; more significantly it will probably play a crucial role as a precursor of a major future reorientation of tourism – towards space.

Erik Cohen

References

Baudrillard, J. (1988) 'Simulacra and Simulations'. In J. Baudrillard (ed.) *Selected Writings*. Stanford, CA: Stanford University Press, pp. 166–84

Boorstin, D. J. (1964) *The image: a guide to pseudo-events in America*. New York: Harper and Row

Bourdieu, P. (1984) *Distinction: A social critique of the judgement of taste*. London: Routledge

Brown, D. (1996) 'Genuine fakes'. In T. Selwyn (ed.) *The tourist image*. Chichester: John Wiley and Sons, pp. 33–47

Bruner, E. M. (1994) 'Abraham Lincoln as authentic reproduction: A critique of postmodernism'. *American Anthropologist*, 96(2), 397–415

Bryman, A. (1999) 'The Disneyization of society'. *The Sociological Review*, 47(1), 25–47

Cohen, E. (1979a) 'A phenomenology of tourist experiences'. *Sociology*, 13(2), 179–201

—— (1979b) 'Rethinking the sociology of tourism'. *Annals of Tourism Research*, 6(1), 18–35

—— (1985) 'Tourism as play'. *Religion*, 15(3), 291–304

—— (1995) 'Contemporary tourism: Trends and challenges'. In R. Butler and D. Pearce (eds) *Change in tourism*. London: Routledge, pp. 12–29

—— (2000) 'Cultural fusion'. In E. Avrami, R. Mason and M. de la Torre (eds) *Values and heritage conservation*. Los Angeles, CA: The Getty Institute, pp. 44–50

—— (2001) 'Thailand in "touristic transition"'. In P. Teo, T. C. Chang and K. C. Ho (eds) *Interconnected worlds: Tourism in Southeast Asia*. Amsterdam: Pergamon, pp. 155–75

—— (2002) 'Authenticity, equity and sustainability'. *Journal of Sustainable Tourism*, 10(4), 267–76

—— (2004) *Contemporary tourism: Diversity and change*. Amsterdam: Pergamon

—— (2007) 'The "Post-Modernization" of a Mythical Event: Naga Fireballs on the Mekong River', *Tourism, Culture and Communication*, 7(3), pp. 169–181

Dunn, R. (1999) 'Populism, mass culture and the avant garde'. *Theory, Culture and Society*, 8(1), 111–35

Eco, U. (1986) *Travels in hyperreality*. San Diego, CA: Harcourt, Brace and Jovanovich

Edwards, E. (1996) 'Postcards: Greetings from another world'. In T. Selwyn (ed.) *The tourist image*. Chichester: John Wiley and Sons, pp. 197–221

Errington, F. and Gewertz, D. (1989) 'Tourism and anthropology in a postmodern world'. *Oceania*, 60(1), 37–54

Errington, S. (1998) *The death of authentic primitive art and other tales of progress*. Berkeley, CA: University of California Press

Geertz, C. (1973) 'Deep play: Notes on the Balinese cockfight'. In C. Geertz (ed.) *The interpretation of cultures*. New York: Basic Books, pp. 412–53

Goffman, E. (1974) *Frame analysis: An essay on the organization of experience*. New York: Harper and Row

Golden, D. (1996) 'The museum of the Jewish Diaspora tells a story'. In T. Selwyn (ed.) *The tourist image*. Chichester: John Wiley and Sons, pp. 223–50

Graburn, N. H. H. (1977) 'Tourism: The sacred journey'. In V. L. Smith (ed.) *Hosts and guests*. Philadelphia: University of Pennsylvania Press, pp. 17–31

Guillén, M. F. (2001) 'Is globalization civilizing, destructive or feeble? A critique of five key debates in the social science literature'. *Annual Review of Sociology*, 27(1), 235–59

Johnson, M. L. (1998) *New Westerns: The West in contemporary American culture*. Lawrence, KS: University Press of Kansas

Kapchan, D. A. and Strong, P. T. (1999) 'Theorizing the hybrid'. *Journal of American Folklore*, 112(445), 239–53

King, M. J. (1981) 'Disneyland and Walt Disney World: Traditional values in futuristic form'. *Journal of Popular Culture*, 15(1), 116–40

Koselleck, R. (1985) *Futures past: On the semantics of historical time*. Cambridge, MA: MIT Press

Lacy, J. A. and Douglass, W. (2002) 'Beyond authenticity: The meanings and uses of cultural tourism'. *Tourist Studies*, 2(1), 5–21

MacCannell, D. (1973) 'Staged authenticity: Arrangements of social space in tourist settings'. *American Journal of Sociology*, 79(3), 589–603

—— (1976) *The tourist: A new theory of the leisure class*. New York: Schocken

—— (1992) 'Cannibalism today'. In D. MacCannell (ed.) *Empty meeting grounds: The tourist papers*. London: Routledge, pp. 17–73

—— (2001) 'Remarks on the commodification of culture'. In V. L. Smith and M. Brent (eds) *Hosts and guests revisited*. New York: Cognizant Communication Corporation, pp. 380–90

Meethan, K. (1996) 'Consuming (in) the civilized city'. *Annals of Tourism Research*, 23(2), 322–40

Mintz, L. (1998) 'Simulated tourism at Busch Gardens: The old country and Disney's World showcase, Epcot Center'. *Journal of Popular Culture*, 32(3), 47–58

Mitchell, R. D. (1998) 'Learning through play and pleasure travel: Using play literature to enhance research into touristic learning'. *Current Issues in Tourism*, 1(2), 176–88

Moore, A. (1980) 'Walt Disney World: Bounded ritual space and the playful pilgrimage center'. *Anthropological Quarterly*, 53(4), 207–18

Moscardo, G. M. and Pearce, P. L. (1986) 'Historic theme parks: An Australian experience in authenticity'. *Annals of Tourism Research*, 13(3), 467–79

Nation (2003) 'New Disney ride out of this world'. *The Nation* (Bangkok), 11 October, p. 3B

—— (2004) 'Japanese theme park looks to Spider-man as Saviour'. *The Nation* (Bangkok), 22 March

Olsen, K. (2002) 'Authenticity as a concept in tourism research'. *Tourist Studies*, 2(2), 159–82

Presse-Agentur, D. (2004) 'A short flight for man, a milestone for humanity'. *The Nation* (Bangkok), 6 October, p. 10A

Raz, A. E. (1999) 'Glocalization and symbolic interactionism'. *Studies in Symbolic Interaction*, 22, 3–16

Reich, R. J. (1980) 'The development of Antarctic tourism'. *Polar Record*, 20(126), 203–14

Ritzer, G. (1993) *The McDonaldization of society*. Newbury Park, CA: Pine Forge Press

—— and Liska, A. (1997) '"McDonaldization" and "post-tourism"'. In C. Rojek and J. Urry (eds) *Touring cultures: Transformations of travel and theory*. London: Routledge, pp. 96–109

Robertson, R. (1995) 'Glocalization: Time-space and homogeneity-heterogeneity'. In M. Featherstone, S. Lash and R. Robertson (eds) *Global modernities*. London: Sage, pp. 25–44

Rojek, C. and Urry, J. (1997) 'Transformations of travel and theory'. In C. Rojek and J. Urry (eds) *Touring cultures: Transformations of travel and theory*. London: Routledge, pp. 1–19

Schutz, A. (1973) 'On multiple realities'. In A. Schutz (ed.) *Collected papers* (Vol. 1). The Hague: M. Nijhoff, pp. 207–25

Selänniemi, T. (2001) 'Pale skin on playa del anywhere: Finnish tourists in the Liminoid South'. In V. L. Smith and M. Brent (eds) *Hosts and guests revisited*. New York: Cognizant Communication Corporation, pp. 80–92

Selwyn, T. (1996) 'Introduction'. In T. Selwyn (ed.) *The tourist image*. Chichester: John Wiley and Sons, pp. 1–32

Shinhav-Keller, S. (2000) 'Looking back to the future: Representation, memory and identity – The case of the museum of the Jewish Diaspora'. Unpublished doctoral dissertation, Hebrew University of Jerusalem, Israel

Smith, V. L. (2001) 'The nature of tourism'. In V. L. Smith and M. Brent (eds) *Hosts and guests revisited*. New York: Cognizant Communication Corporation, pp. 53–68

Sofield, T. H. B. and Li, F. M. S. (1998) 'Tourism development and cultural policies in China'. *Annals of Tourism Research*, 25(2), 362–92

Time Magazine (1972) 'The greening of the astronauts'. Time Magazine, 11 December. Retrieved 2 November 2011, from http://www.time.com/time/magazine/article/0,9171,878100,00.html

Urry, J. (2000) 'Mobile sociology'. *British Journal of Sociology*, 51(1), 185–203

Wang, N. (1999) 'Rethinking authenticity in tourism experience'. *Annals of Tourism Research*, 26(2), 349–70

—— (2000) *Tourism and modernity: A sociological analysis*. Amsterdam: Pergamon

Westerhausen, K. (2002) *Beyond the beach: An ethnography of modern travellers in Asia*. Bangkok: White Lotus

21

Resort management analysis
Current and future directions

Peter Murphy

Introduction

Resorts have been a feature of travel and tourism for a long time. Their origins can be traced back to Roman times when the concept spread throughout Europe in the wake of their conquering legions. From the simple origins of public baths and restorative mineral springs their typical structure became 'an atrium surrounded by recreational and sporting amenities, restaurants, rooms, and shops' (Mill, 2001, p. 4), a description that still describes many modern resorts.

Since those early days of resort development the popularity of this element of tourism has waxed and waned; but it has survived the changing times by adjusting its early model to suit new tastes and conditions, to become a new force in today's relatively stable and prosperous times. Early on, the original health purpose of resorts was supplemented and eventually overtaken by social and political motivations, as exemplified by the resurrection of the hot springs at Bath, England, which became an important part of the English royal court circuit. This pattern was followed in the 'New World' by the railways, using hot springs resorts in the wilderness national parks to draw the wealthy and privileged westward, as in the case of Canadian Pacific's Banff Springs Hotel in Alberta, Canada. Today similar grand and enticing resort concepts are being developed throughout the hinterlands of Europe, helping to lure the wealthy and influential to new areas of potential economic and social development. An example of this is in the Gulf States, where several major luxury integrated resort complexes have been built or are under construction to provide another face to these Muslim states and to assist them in diversifying their economies. An example of this trend is the US$2.9 billion Emirates Palace in Abu Dhabi, which:

> Although it has fewer than 400 rooms, the hotel features 128 kitchens and pantries, 1002 custom-made Swarovski crystal chandeliers...a layout so sprawling staff will soon be equipped with golf carts to navigate the corridors, 'some of them...over a kilometre long'... room prices range from a modest US$608 a night to US$12,608 (subject to a 20 per cent service charge).
>
> *(Pohl, 2005, p. 12)*

It is not only the wealthy who now enjoy the benefits of resorts, for the growth of industry and commerce has brought such delights within the reach of the masses. They have either followed the past elite to their secluded 'hide-away' resort retreats as exemplified by the development of Brighton around the Prince of Wales's Brighton Pavilion; or they have stimulated the building of their own style of mass resort, as in the case of seaside resorts such as Australia's Gold Coast or gambling resorts such as Las Vegas, and even combining the two interests in Atlantic City. Furthermore, resorts for the working class have been developed in various forms, ranging from camps to chalets and dormitories as exemplified by the Butlins camps and the Roompot parks in The Netherlands.

Despite this track record of successful adjustment and mutation over the centuries the study of this particular phenomenon has generated only a modest level of interest among tourism academics – even in this era of supposed attention to sustainability. Evidence of this situation and possible reasons for it may be found in a tabulation of recent articles linked to resorts in the three leading tourism journals over the past five years.

A review of articles that were related in any way to resorts, either stated or inferred, was compiled from the period 2000 to 2004 (Table 21.1). It revealed a total of 53 references, which consisted of either full articles or short research notes. The journal that had the most extensive coverage of resort-related articles was *Tourism Management*, which recorded 45 percent of the noted articles. This journal's management focus was evident in its emphasis on business- and user-related topics, plus its contribution in all the other identified categories. The *Annals of Tourism Research* was the second major source with 30 percent of the identified articles and these articles revealed its social science perspective, with the highest number of papers relating to the evolutionary model and its concerns with general planning issues. In comparison to the first two, the *Journal of Travel Research* revealed its Business School roots, with the strongest focus on 'business considerations'. The different foci of the three journals along with the extensive range of topics, even when some have been collapsed into a generic format, reveal the extensive nature of resort activities and their impacts which make them relevant to a variety of domains and research questions. As such, there is a broad interface between the issues found in resort domains and those examined in other areas of tourism research; but some feel resorts deserve to

Table 21.1 Resort-related articles in key journals 2000–2004

Journal	Business Considerations*	User Analysis**	Resort Evaluation	Stakeholder Analysis	Carrying Capacity	Planning	Seasonality	Image	Total
Annals of Tourism Research	3	3	4	2	–	3	1	–	16
Journal of Travel Research	8	2	2	–	–	–	1	–	13
Tourism Management	5	6	2	4	4	–	–	1	22
Total	16	11	8	6	4	3	2	1	51

* Business Considerations include – competitiveness, benchmarking, yield management, satisfaction, value, loyalty, and service quality topics.
** User Analysis includes – gambling, skiers, cruise ship passengers, golf and retirees.

be studied in their own right because they are an identifiable subset of the tourism market with their own needs and issues.

Included amongst those who feel resorts should be examined on their own merits are Inskeep, Gee and Mill, each of whom makes a case for paying special attention to resorts due to some distinctive differentiating factors. Inskeep (1991) states that particularly well-designed resorts can become attractions in themselves and he devotes a chapter to 'planning tourist resorts' under the umbrella of community tourism. Within this framework he emphasizes two factors:

- Resorts are a business. They need to start their planning with a market analysis and demand assessment, which should then be matched with a product assessment of how well the proposed area can match expected market demand.
- Community relations need to be considered carefully if there is a resident population living on or near the resort site, because of positive and negative impacts from such a development.

Gee (1996) considers resorts differ from other sorts of tourism destination in that:

- they cater primarily for vacation and pleasure markets;
- the average length of stay is longer and hotel rooms need to be larger and better equipped;
- they must be self-contained because most resorts are isolated;
- the recreational bias of resorts makes them highly seasonal;
- resort management must be 'visible management', that is everyone 'must be infused with the idea of total hospitality, warm relationships, and unstinting round-the-clock service to guests'.

Mill (2001) considers resorts have a combination of elements that make them distinctive. These are:

- the recreation attractions that draw guests to the resort;
- housing, food and beverage services that cater to people at the resort; and
- activities to occupy the guests during their stay.

Within these descriptors of resorts and their management needs certain commonalities can be identified. Resorts are distinctive in that they:

- are established as businesses;
- convert visitors into guests;
- attempt to hold their guests on-site by providing a critical mass of activities;
- attract guests and hold them with superior quality facilities; and
- cosset guests with superior service.

Such descriptions of the resort structure and approach are considered sufficient by some to distinguish resort management from other forms of management within tourism, but how does their situation relate to theoretical developments and what are resorts' current and future management issues and directions? These are questions that this chapter intends to address and answer within the context of this conference.

Resorts and theoretical developments

If one is going to study a phenomenon such as resorts, with a goal to assessing their links to theory and to providing useful management information, one appropriate avenue of research is to use the analytical approach of scientific inquiry (Berry and Marble, 1968; Pojman, 2003). This involves a three-step process:

1 describe and classify the phenomenon – in this case resorts;
2 explain what is happening in terms of a resort's internal business matters and its external relations with the host community;
3 combine the first two steps into an ability to predict future outcomes and behaviour. This last step is the ultimate goal of science and can provide the direction resort communities and individual business operators within them are seeking.

At this point most students of resort management would claim we are at the explanation stage, seeking to understand the internal and external forces that are moulding current resort patterns.

If we apply some of the better known social science and business theories to the scientific enquiry of resorts we can see a productive theoretical and management symbiosis emerging.

Describe and classify

In terms of step one there has been considerable attention paid to describing the wide range of resorts and attempting to define them. Those who have attempted to classify resorts include Pearce (1989), Krippendorf (1987), Ayala (1991), Gee (1996) and Prideaux (2000). Within these varied descriptions of resorts several consistencies emerge that help to distinguish resorts from other forms of tourism. First, there is confirmation of the business focus of resorts in the vast majority of the definitions. Second, the business focus is one that emphasizes capturing and holding guests. Third, an important part of that business process is to satisfy guest expectations with outstanding facilities and service. Fourth, the scale of resorts can vary from an individual establishment to an urban destination.

All of these dimensions can be seen in the current resort development in Dubai, where resorts are being erected to help diversify the local economy and attract more air passengers to use Dubai as a stop-over or destination.

> For Dubai, that day (when the oil runs out) is only about ten years away. It has already developed its economy to the point where oil accounts for just 7 percent of GDP…Dubai has made a series of huge investments…Along the coast are luxury (resort) hotels, the Wild Wadi Water Park, new (artificial) offshore islands (resort complexes)…Already more than 5 million tourists arrive every year, a number that could easily double with the opening of new attractions (such as Burg Al Arab resort hotel and the Ski Dubai indoor ski resort).
>
> *(Economist, 2006, p. 56)*

The principal theoretical contribution to the classification system of step one is Butler's 'Tourism Area Life Cycle' (Butler, 2006). Although this model has been criticized for not being an explanatory theory it has proven to be sufficiently robust as a descriptive theory, accurately portraying the general evolution of a wide variety of resort and tourist destinations around the world. This is because the Tourism Area Life Cycle is based on two explanatory theories, the family life cycle which helps to explain the evolving demand patterns of consumers for tourist destinations and the product life cycle which helps to explain supply side adjustments to evolving markets. These provide the underpinnings to what has proved to be a regular six-point evolutionary process for tourist destinations: exploration, involvement, development, consolidation, stagnation, decline or rejuvenation. As in the case of all social science and management theory there are some exceptions to this pattern, where resorts for example are planned centrally and superimposed on a community, as in the case of Cancun, but the general pattern has occurred so frequently it has become accepted by resort management as an important framework to their decision making. There is a constant referral to keeping 'on top of the wave' of the S curve in the TALC theory.

Explain

To move to step two we need to understand what we have classified in step one, and the TALC theory is a classic example of this necessity. One of the early criticisms of Butler's model was the lack of explanation concerning why destinations moved from stage to stage, and the consequent difficulty in identifying the causes and timing of these significant events within the model (Haywood, 2006). Two theories which can help to explain the TALC's evolutionary curve for resorts are the Family Life Cycle and Product Life Cycle theories, plus the ecological model of community tourism.

The Family Life Cycle reflects the changing socio-economic circumstances that can be expected within a household over the life of its founders (Carter and McGoldrick, 2005):

- Stage 1 is the formation of the household through marriage or some other form of commitment. At this stage the couple is labelled by the marketers as 'Double Income, No Kids' (DINKS), with few major commitments and a strong interest in leisure and recreation.
- Stage 2 is the start of a family and a large house mortgage, so the spending in tourism is reduced and the travel more restricted to domestic markets.
- Stage 3 is child launching, when children begin to leave home, mortgage levels are reduced or non-existent, and adults have more time and money to spend on travel.
- Stage 4 is the early years of retirement and a growing time for travel as individuals now have more discretionary time and money available to them.
- Stage 5 comes with the loss of a spouse or partner, and increasing physical limitations to travel.

While the Family Life Cycle was first mooted in the era of stable nuclear families, many of its socio-economic principles can still be applied to the greater variety of households that exist today. The impact of a home purchase is dramatic on any form of household and still reduces spending in other areas, unless the household is extremely fortunate. The popularity of travel for the young and seniors is still strong, as these groups represent significant market segments for tourism in general and resorts in particular. The seniors market will be used later in this chapter to demonstrate its growing importance to resort development and management.

The Product Life Cycle proposed that most products go through various stages of development and production. Many new products are introduced to the market each year, and most of them are variations on existing themes like a new car model. The important second stage is the trial period for the new product, when opinion leaders try it out and make their personal recommendations. If all goes well the third stage is the adoption phase. It is at this juncture when the public at large decides to follow the recommendations of the opinion leaders and purchases the product in volume. This is the stage at which the product can be classified as a success and the company reaps the rewards of its research, development and marketing costs. The fourth stage is a saturation of the market, meaning in some cases one sale or experience is enough for most people (a movie or bungee jump) or in other cases the purchase satisfies for many years (a house or university degree). Stage five represents a decline in production levels, as the market now depends on replacement or the arrival of new consumers via new household creations or international markets to create demand (like cigarettes).

The parallels between the Product Life Cycle and TALC are obvious and have been acknowledged by Butler. The relevance to resorts as a specific leisure product is particularly germane because few resorts are unique in terms of what they provide, they are simply variations on existing themes such as snow resorts or beach resorts. Thus, when they are introduced into the growing crowded market they need to be noticed and they need to be tried. In this regard many resorts attempt to lure celebrities and events so the opinion leaders will visit and be seen trying out this new product. But the key will be whether the targeted market segments will adopt this new product and make repeat visits or recommendations to others. Even if a resort succeeds in reaching the success of stage four it must prepare against stage five and its forecast of decline. Some resorts prepare for this by reinventing themselves, with new attractions, others decide to age with their clientele and become mature resorts catering primarily for a certain lifestyle. Throughout both the Family Life Cycle and Product Life Cycle resorts will need to balance their offerings and look to the future if they are to be ready for it.

The question of balance and looking to the future are key elements of the ecological model proposed by Murphy (1985) in his community tourism approach. He has demonstrated the link between destination stakeholders and the general principles of ecological equilibrium, emphasizing the need for balance between such forces as economic return, social vitality, environmental sustainability and the general quality of life for tourism and its host communities. In terms of resorts this explains the need for both internal and external management processes and emphasizes the need to work with the local community and environmental setting, in order to achieve the best outcomes for as wide a range of stakeholders as possible.

Predict and forecast

Murphy's ecological model for community tourism is an early attempt to explain the mutual benefits of sustainable development, a theory that has received increased attention as a means to predict future outcomes of current management techniques. Murphy and Price (2005) have identified 15 themes to the modern concept of sustainable development that include social, environmental and political considerations in addition to economic and development concerns, but all these themes reflect an attempt to balance economic goals with social and environmental goals. Sustainable development theories attempt to demonstrate the benefits of a systems approach to tourism development and planning, but they have proved to be difficult to implement and test.

Two techniques that could help in the area of testing and refining the sustainable development theory are stakeholder analysis and triple bottom line auditing. Stakeholder analysis attempts to identify the principal actors and impact groups in any development, and by focusing on their needs and priorities helps to concentrate on potential collaborative strategies (Murphy and Murphy, 2004). The triple bottom line audit is one way to examine how well a development is meeting its economic, social and environmental goals. By offering a simplified audit process and structure Elkington (1999, p. 93) suggests the triple bottom line approach can provide 'new sustainability indicators' that can measure and guide our progress in this direction.

Examples of some of these theories and techniques are being applied within resorts, most notably within the growing number of eco-resorts such as Kingfisher Bay resort on Fraser Island, the largest sand island in the world and a designated World Heritage site. This resort has designed a facility that has minimum impact on the environment and focuses on teaching visitors about that environment and their place within it. Besides the expected guided tours the resort has put 'on show' its waste treatment plant. This reminds visitors they have an inevitable impact, but with careful treatment human waste can become benign, and can even be turned into a recycling revenue source when the resort ships its bags of fertilizer back to the mainland.

To provide the infrastructure and resources to operate as a sustainable business resorts must first succeed in winning customers, and the theory many have found helpful in this regard is Porter's theory on competitive advantage. Porter has written several books on various aspects of this theory over the years (Porter, 1980, 1990, 1998), but the crux of his thinking is that to compete in today's global market a business must differentiate itself and control costs in terms of its selected target markets. For resorts this means selecting a market segment or segments they feel they can satisfy, then to present a product that will be noticeable to that segment in the crowded marketplace; in the process they need to ensure they are offering value for money. This means that a business developed along these lines does not have to be a five star international resort; they can range over a variety of affluence levels and scales to address the varied needs and demands of customers. In practical terms resorts will need to focus on the target markets they can best serve, they will need to draw them to an attractive and healthy setting, and satisfy their expectations in order to convert them into repeat customers or enthusiastic recommenders. What are described as the 'attract–hold–satisfy' elements are discussed in the next section.

Challenges of resort management

All resort operations need to consider their future returns on investment (ROI) if they are ever to recoup the extensive capital investments that are called for and they are to become long-term sustainable businesses. Such considerations of present and future development opportunities will involve both their internal business environment, the external physical and social environment of their host community, and global trends – in short an environmental scanning process (Bourgeois, 1980; Daft et al., 1992). Many resorts have been swept up in the dream of creating something special, some without adequate analysis of their competitive situation and sustainable development options.

An example of the enthusiasm for resort development and its potential contribution can be seen in western Canada. A British Columbia task force into resort development would like to see resort development 'take full advantage of the opportunities provided by the 2010 Olympic and Paralympics Winter Games'. It recommends that in order to achieve this goal a province-wide resort strategy should be created that will provide:

- increased business certainty for resort development within the economic climate;
- increased clarity of access for potential resort developers;
- a more predictable investment environment;
- increased exposure in the international tourism market;

- reduced conflict between previously competing users of Crown Lands; and
- expanded use of existing facilities (Minister of State for Resort Development, 2004).

In this way it is hoped to build upon the current C$9.2 billion spent by resort tourists each year in the province, plus increase the current C$178 million in taxes and 26,000 employed in resorts (Minister of State for Resort Development, 2004). In the process the proponents hope to develop more tourism opportunities for British Columbia's rural regions and to convert more of those resorts into four season operations, which will emulate its star performer – the Whistler/Blackcomb Mountain Four Season Resort.

In Australia a Tourism Task Force (2003, p. 4) report on Australia's resort situation stated 'Despite the growth of domestic and international tourism in the last two decades, resorts in Australia have performed poorly from a profitability and investment perspective.' They reported that Australia's resorts were achieving lower room yields than city hotels or serviced apartments. Their profitability was low, producing only a gross average return of 10–19 percent *before* interest, tax and amortization expenses. For the preceding ten years you could have received a guaranteed 5 percent return risk free from Australia's banks. It comes as no surprise, therefore, that several major Australian resorts have been sold at a loss by their original owners. Such experiences are common around the world, and need to be addressed if resorts are to continue to provide their unique contribution to tourism's options array.

If resorts are to become successful businesses they need to attract a sufficient number of guests throughout the year to provide a satisfactory return on investment and need to use theory to assist them. This will involve an assessment of current conditions and probable future situations. Tables 21.2 and 21.3 represent an attempt to provide a preliminary evaluation matrix to guide such strategic resort management decisions. Since resorts are synonymous with business the matrices have been divided into a demand and supply configuration.

In terms of demand they will need to attract enough visitors throughout the year to make it worth staying open. They should either attract these visitors as pre-booked guests or be able to convert passing through visitors into overnight stays, to provide a sufficient market for its

Table 21.2 Evaluation matrix of current challenges

		SUPPLY		
	Business Considerations	Economic/Business	Social Impacts	Environmental Impacts
D E M A N D	Attract	Differentiate (branding)	Employment generation and/or diversification	Natural attraction with development potential
	Hold	Sufficient mass of activities	Supportive attitude of staff and residents	Special Place – Activities blended successfully into environmental setting
	Satisfy	Quality products and service leading to value	Positive reaction to social interactions with staff and host community	Activities and total experience enhanced by setting

Table 21.3 Evaluation matrix of future challenges

		SUPPLY		
	Business Considerations	Economic/Business	Social Impacts	Environmental Impacts
D E M A N D	Attract	Activities and Products for Seniors	Security	Conservation
	Hold	Commitment Combination leisure and retirement centres	Personalized Duty of Care and Risk Management	Motivation to become involved
	Satisfy	Caring service	Social groupings Multi-functional facilities	Environmental Stewardship

accommodations sector. The resorts need to hold the guest over a few days to give them a chance to experience the full range of recreation and leisure opportunities on display. In the process resorts should increase their yield, as guests sample more of their offerings. The overall goal of resorts is to satisfy their guests and encourage them to either return or become goodwill ambassadors. The first group becomes loyal customers, the second those influential 'word of mouth' contacts.

On the supply side, for resorts to become the economic entities that contribute to the array of tourism products and to their host communities' general welfare, they need to be managed in a sustainable manner. One way to achieve this is to be guided by Elkington's (1999) triple bottom line audit. This retains an emphasis on the economic–business impacts of the resort, incorporating both economic and business principles to produce a development plan that is both profit-oriented and sustainable. That is joined by social impact assessments to ascertain whether the resort development is having beneficial, benign or negative impacts on local people and the host community. Such assessments look for signs of social and cultural change, along with quality of life measures. The third aspect of the audit is an environmental impact assessment of the resort's affect on its physical surroundings. This involves utilization of the carrying capacity concept and adoption of the notion of acceptable levels of change.

The above outlines of a possible demand and supply configuration for resort management can be combined with the identified components of each, to provide an evaluation matrix (Tables 21.2 and 21.3). Within the 3 × 3 matrices have been placed some 'best practice' options for resort management, based on seeking a sustainable development position using the triple bottom line audit approach in association with identified basic demand functions. The propositions in each cell have been proposed as illustrative key and generic objectives. They are not expected to be complete, since we have seen that resorts are complex and varied tourism products. They should, however, guide individual resorts, at all scales, to assess how well they are addressing their various needs in order to attain sustainability. As in all cases where a complex system is being simplified by dividing it up into component parts, to examine and predict outcomes, some of the cells are likely to overlap. That is, the cells should not be interpreted as being mutually exclusive, but rather as different emphases within a continuing holistic appraisal.

Another thing to note is that evaluation and sustainable development involves examining a moving feast. For we know that tourism is an agent of change and that the local socio-cultural setting and physical landscape are bound to be altered over time by a resort's presence. We also know that weather conditions and consumer preferences can and will change over time, with some significant potential impacts on the demand for resort vacations. So it is relevant to extend the matrix into the future and attempt to identify some coming trends, hence the division of the evaluation matrices into a 'current' and 'future' scenario.

Resort management analysis: current challenges

The current emphasis for resort management in terms of attracting guests is one of providing a distinctive product within a positive social and environmental setting. So operating horizontally we can see different, yet related, emphases along the three dimensions of the triple bottom line audit (Table 21.2). In economic and business terms, today's highly competitive global market forces all resorts to stand out by differentiating themselves from their realistic competitors. Many are attempting to do this by applying Porter's (1980) competitive advantage principles and through branding to increase their top of mind awareness amongst consumers. However, branding a product becomes more challenging as its size and complexity grows, so what might work well for a resort hotel or integrated resort complexes will be harder to achieve with large urban resort destinations. As Kotler et al. (1993, p. 32) observe 'few places (cities and states) have managed to create strong brand names and images for the products and services they supply'.

The immediate social impacts of resort development, especially in isolated areas, is their employment opportunities, which can either provide welcome new employment or offer a different form of employment to the local area. These economic outcomes of resort development provide significant social benefits, ranging from improved individual quality of life to more extensive social amenities and services.

Part of the attraction to customers and locals will be the increased emphasis on the quality of the local environment, which should be nurtured and developed using sustainable development principles if it is to provide an attractive setting to whatever activity focus has been adopted by the resort. In some cases the natural environment will be an integral part of the resort's product, in others it will function as a backdrop; but in all cases it must be healthy and attractive in appearance if it is to complement the resort's business objectives.

Once the guests have arrived they must be held and encouraged to use as many of the provided facilities as possible, if the resort is to maximize its yield. To achieve this a resort will need to provide a sufficient 'critical' mass of activities. Critical in the quantity sense that there are enough things to do to hold a guest for a few nights, and in the quality sense of providing logical packages of supporting activities aimed at the same market segments.

Guests should feel welcomed and comfortable in their new setting. An important component to such feelings is the attitude of staff and local residents. If staff are content with the resort's human resource practices, have received sufficient training and instruction, and feel they are being treated fairly, then they are more likely to provide the sort of superior service resorts strive to offer. If local residents are positive about the resort's presence and contribution to the local economy they also are likely to be more welcoming.

Guests will feel they have entered a special place if they see a healthy physical setting and don't see their own waste products. When guests enter a resort they expect to be transported to some wonderful place, as Disney discovered and built on with his 'fantasy land' (Bryman, 1995) and Lapidus incorporated into his renown resort hotel designs, such as the Fountainblue and Eden Rock in Miami Beach (Stern, 1986). Part of this fantasy will be a pleasant landscape, often one that is distinctive from the guests' home environment and one that calls to be photographed. To help maintain the image of these special place landscapes they also need to be protected from the guest, for guests like all travellers pollute and create wear and tear on the environment. It is essential for resorts that are not attached to city water and sewerage systems to provide their own, and to a standard that can leave no doubt about their effectiveness. Consequently, isolated resorts should have clean and tested drinking water systems, backed up so to speak with tertiary or quaternary waste water treatment plants. In addition litter should not be seen, so it should be collected regularly and disposed of in an ecologically friendly manner.

A primary goal of business should be to meet and possibly exceed customer expectations, and thereby satisfy their selected target market. A key ingredient to this will be quality products and service that contribute significantly to the customers' perceived value of their experience. The provision of quality products is mainly an issue of investment, but 'the core product being marketed is a performance' (Berry and Parasuraman, 1991, p. 5), so service quality is required also to achieve a resort's full potential. All of this has to be synchronized and managed in order to reliably satisfy the guest.

Since a performance on the resort stage involves an interaction between customers and staff and/or residents it is vital to ensure a positive technical and social interaction between the concerned parties. This will involve appropriate training and education for both the technical and social components of the performance. Heskett et al. (1997, p. 11) maintain:

> service profit chain thinking maintains that there are direct and strong relationships between profit; growth; customer loyalty; customer satisfaction; the value of goods and services delivered to customers; and employee capability, satisfaction, loyalty, and productivity.

The strongest relationships in this chain have been identified as those between '(1) profit and customer loyalty, (2) employee loyalty and customer loyalty, and (3) employee satisfaction and customer satisfaction' (Heskett et al., 1997, p. 12). Also, 'Each resort and its site are unique, and (its planning and development) must be adapted to the local situation' (Inskeep, 1991, p. 211). In resort experiences the environment will be a vital physical contributor to customer satisfaction and resort profit, so the design and placement of buildings should be integrated into the local setting in such a way as to support and reflect the ambience that first attracted the guest. In this manner the resort experience will be enhanced by the setting, and the need for stewardship of that physical setting will be enhanced by its rising value.

Resort management analysis: future challenges

The future management priorities for resorts will naturally be a continuation of past and present processes, influenced by future conditions. While forecasting future conditions is not an exact science it is possible to extrapolate certain demographic, economic and environmental circumstances into the future, as environmental scanning currently encourages us to do. In addition to these continuations there will always be random events that will shock the system, which will require some form of contingency planning.

Utilizing the concept that demography represents our destiny, this chapter focuses on one factor that is expected to influence resort futures and is susceptible to management influence, namely the growing presence and influence of our seniors. In terms of economic and business concerns it will focus on the ageing populations in Western countries and their increasing interests in health and retirement options. The social impacts will focus on the growing role of security in these troubled times, especially as it relates to seniors. The environmental impacts will be examined with respect to the gradual degradation that is occurring on this planet and seniors growing role in the world's conservation movements (Table 21.3).

To attract guests in the future a natural target segment would be the growing seniors market. We can already see a growing interest in health and wellness in many resort locations, and such interest is not confined to the hot springs resorts. The Daydream Island resort in Australia's Whitsunday Islands has resurrected itself around a wellness theme. What has started will become a major focus as populations age and people seek alternative lifestyles and therapies. In addition to the health facilities guests will be tempted by the light exercise and recreation opportunities provided by many resorts, particularly the golf and swimming pool facilities, and by the healthy menu creations emerging from the various kitchens. Some guests will be so pleased with their pampered body servicing they will be tempted to repeat their visit or even to relocate to the resort. More resorts are accommodating such thoughts with the building of second or retirement homes, which in many cases provide them with the sort of cash flow they need to maintain or enhance the facilities they provide.

On the social impact side the seniors, and other resort visitors, will become more appreciative of resorts' capacity to offer security. At the lower scales of resort hotel and integrated complexes the privately owned and operated facilities can impose whatever level of security they feel is attractive to their guests. This will involve obvious security checks at the main gate and less obvious but still present security within the building or complex. Such procedures will be more difficult to implement in the more open and public space of a resort destination, but an increase in police budgets and defensive land use and landscaping can be expected.

In terms of environmental impacts, future demand will place an emphasis on the attraction of conservation. As seniors leave behind their long-term homes for the relaxation and retirement of a resort they will want to live among beautiful grounds and healthy nature. They are likely to champion the qualities of their new home environment and want to see its flora and fauna protected, as this is the environment they have chosen for their final days.

To hold guests in the future resorts, especially the seniors, will require resorts to become combination leisure and retirement centres. They will need to find ways to separate the boisterous guests from those seeking tranquillity, and to help manage retirement periods that can last thirty or more years. Under those circumstances the guest will pass from a state of active independence to one of dependency on doctors and nursing, and may well need to move to different forms of housing within the resort. Likewise, the associated recreation facilities will need to embrace a wider range of physical abilities. Swimming pools will need ramps and warmer water, and golf courses easier cart access and playing conditions. This leads to a point where the seniors may well need their own facilities if they are to live out their lives in such medical-resort style retirement.

On the social side risk management will evolve beyond the issues of resort security and financial exposure to involve a more personal assessment of long-term guests' risk situation – in other words, a more personalized interpretation of the 'duty of care' concept. This is underway at present, with the growing health assessment and recommendations role of many wellness centres. As some guests become more regular visitors or permanent residents such assessment and advice can be more formalized, in terms of local medical contacts and hospital visits. Duty of care can be directed to new areas such as guests' intellectual, hobby and financial interests.

Environmental matters can be expected to take a role in the guests' education and hobbies area if properly nurtured. Most guests to a resort will have been attracted by its environmental setting, but the seniors will have more time and a stronger motivation to become directly involved. Their strong numbers in National Trust and Audubon societies around the world support their commitment to heritage and the environment. The political knowledge and power of seniors make them a significant lobby for conservation and they are becoming champions for nature enhancement and a greater sense of place.

To satisfy the seniors' market will require a caring service, one that builds on super service, to include watchfulness and companionship in later years. Future seniors can expect to spend longer in retirement than preceding generations, and some resorts will become quasi-rest homes. They will offer the full range of resort facilities for healthy independent retired couples, and more specialized facilities and smaller units to those who become widowed or who encounter poor health. These specialized units will be in quieter areas, often attached to a central socializing area, and have features such as safety bars in the bathroom, emergency call buttons, and 24-hour nursing assistance on call. Such resort facilities are starting to appear along the coast of Queensland, Australia's prime retirement state.

The social impact of such developments for the resort is not expected to be major, if appropriate planning and zoning are undertaken. The seniors' needs are not expected to clash with those of other guests until they seek more solitude and privacy, and then they should find the type of secluded facility as outlined above within the grounds of larger resorts. Their personal social needs should be satisfied to the highest level because the resort setting will provide the type and level of interaction they have voluntarily selected, whilst such a small scale concentration of retirees should make it easier for the surrounding communities to cope with their special needs. It is conceivable that some resort retirement facilities can be utilized by local communities, much the same way as happens currently with some gym, spa and golf club memberships.

In terms of environmental impact the development of resorts with rest home capability or focus are likely to continue with the environmental stewardship referred to earlier. Indeed, one can imagine that as the earth continues to degrade its environment, it will be places like resorts that lead the way in championing local environmental conservation because it is in their own interest. There is a good match between resort environmental approaches and the Winter and Ewers (1989) model of ecological management. 'In the Winter model there are six principles that are considered essential for the long term success of a responsibly managed company' (Callenbach et al., 1993, pp. 14–15). These are quality, creativity, humaneness, profitability, continuity and loyalty, all of which have been addressed in some way in Table 21.3.

Summary

This chapter has attempted to show that resort management is a distinctive part of general tourism management, with its defining focus on a business venture that needs to attract, hold and satisfy its guests within the threefold description of sustainable development. The very use of the term 'guest' over that of consumer or visitor implies that resorts are something special, that they go out of their way to please their customers. Focus on the quality of technical facilities and personal service ensures an emphasis on value, but as in all cases it must be directed at the appropriate and appreciative market segments. The evidence suggests that some resorts in the process of building their spectacular and expensive product have lost sight of making a profit in order to remain sustainable.

In order to assist resort management in developing their triple bottom line sustainability they could adopt a scientific enquiry approach to their strategic decision making. By using existing social science and business theories and techniques resort management could be assisted in achieving the general goal of sustainable development and in their contribution to the overall success of local tourism. Using the theory can assist resort management in clearly identifying, explaining and predicting trends that can be used to prepare for the future, as illustrated in the current and future scenarios used in this chapter.

Current management challenges revolve around the concept of sustainability, based on the profitable conjunction of economic, social and environmental dimensions over an extended period. The period under consideration needs to be extensive because the time line for resorts between conception and opening can extend over several years or decades. While the triple bottom line audit emphasizes the economic viability of an operation, these need to be tempered with social and environmental considerations, each of which can have definite impacts on the bottom line of a resort's finances. Table 21.2 reveals that, with the appropriate market research and business model, it is possible to blend the three dimensions of the triple audit into a sustainable resort business venture.

The future for resorts seems secure since resorts have survived past historical changes, and to some extent we seem to be experiencing a new Roman period, with a dominant world power and relative prosperity and stability. The paper has chosen to bow to the power and destiny of the god of demographics in this new Roman era, with a focus on the growing seniors market and their expected interest in resort-like retirement. Not all retirees will be drawn to resort temptations, but there are sufficient numbers who believe apparently in 'spending their children's inheritance' to make this a significant segment. Table 21.3 reveals seniors and resorts will be well suited, and that in some situations it would be logical for resorts to become multifunctional by providing both tourist and retirement facilities for some guests.

This chapter considers that resorts will continue to evolve and provide a distinctive component to the overall tourism product. They will continue to appeal to both specialized and mass market segments due to their association with luxury and value. However, their association with quality and value may develop a wider appreciation in the future. It is possible that, as they protect and conserve their local environments for their own purposes, they may be creating oases in an increasingly stressed environment that will become an object of government interest and involvement – as we see with today's national parks. Likewise, their commitment to a duty of care philosophy combined with profit may tempt government to seek partnerships in areas of providing health services to the elderly and other groups. The seed for such synergies is already in place in the various social tourism policies of some European governments.

References

Ayala, H. (1991) 'Resort cycle revisited: The retirement connection'. *Annals of Tourism Research*, 18(4), 568–87

Berry, B. J. L. and Marble, D. F. (1968) *Spatial analysis*. Englewood Cliffs, NJ: Prentice-Hall

—— and Parasuraman, A. (1991) *Marketing services: Competing through quality*. New York: Free Press

Bourgeois, L. J., III. (1980) 'Strategy and environment: A conceptual integration'. *Academy of Management Review*, 5(1), 25–39

Bryman, A. (1995) *Disney and his worlds*. London Routledge

Butler, R. W. (ed.) (2006) *The tourism area life cycle*, Vol. 1. Clevedon: Channel View Publications

Callenbach, E., Capra, F., Goldman, L., Lutz, R. and Marburg, S. (1993) *EcoManagement: The Elmwood guide to ecological auditing and sustainable business*. San Francisco, CA: Berrett-Koehler Publishers

Carter, B. and McGoldrick, M. (2005) *The expanded family life cycle: Individual family and social perspectives* (3rd edn). New York: Pearson

Daft, R. L., Fitzgerald, P. A. and Rock, M. E. (1992) *Management*. Toronto: Dryden

Economist (2006) 'Arabian dreams'. *The Economist*, 4 March, pp. 56–9

Elkington, J. (1999) *Cannibals with forks: The triple bottom line of 21st Century business*. Oxford: Capstone Publications

Gee, C. (1996) *Resort development and management* (2nd edn). East Lansing, MI: Educational Institute of the American Hotel and Motel Association

Peter Murphy

Haywood, K. M. (2006) 'Evolution of tourism areas and the tourism industry'. In R. W. Butler (ed.), *The tourism area life cycle* (Vol. 1). Clevedon: Channel View Publications, pp. 51–69

Heskett, J. L., Sasser, W. E., Jr. and Schlesinger, L. A. (1997) *The service profit chain: How leading companies link profit and growth to loyalty, satisfaction, and value*. New York: Free Press

Inskeep, E. (1991) *Tourism planning: An integrated and sustainable development approach*. New York: Van Nostrand Reinhold

Kotler, P., Haider, D. H. and Rein, I. (1993) *Marketing places*. New York: Free Press

Krippendorf, J. (1987) *The holiday makers*. London: Butterworth-Heinemann

Mill, R. C. (2001) *Resorts: Management and operation*. New York: John Wiley and Sons

Minister of State for Resort Development (2004) *Recommendations of the BC Resort Task Force*. Victoria, BC: Author

Murphy, P. E. (1985) *Tourism: A community approach*. London: Methuen

—— and Murphy, A. E. (2004) *Strategic management for tourism communities: Bridging the gaps*. Clevedon: Channel View Publications

—— and Price, G. G. (2005) 'Tourism and sustainable development'. In W. F. Theobold (ed.), *Global tourism* (3rd edn). Burlington, MA: Elsevier Butterworth-Heinemann, pp. 167–93

Pearce, D. G. (1989) *Tourist development* (2nd edn). Harlow: Longman Scientific and Technical

Pohl, O. (2005) 'Lazing in lap of luxury, at $16,375 a night'. *The Age*, 18 March, p. 12

Pojman, L. P. (2003) *The theory of knowledge*. New York: Wadworth

Porter, M. E. (1980) *Competitive strategy*. New York: Free Press

—— (1990) *The competitive advantage of nations*. New York: Free Press

—— (1998) *On competition*. Cambridge, MA: Harvard University Press

Prideaux, B. (2000) 'The resort development spectrum: A new approach to modeling resort development'. *Tourism Management*, 21(3), 225–40

Stern, R. A. M. (1986) *Pride of place: Building the American dream*. Boston: Houghton-Mifflin

Tourism Task Force (2003) *Resorting to profitability: Making tourist resorts work in Australia*. Sydney: Tourism Task Force

Winter, G. and Ewers, H.-J. (1989) *Business and the environment: A Handbook of industrial ecology with 22 checklists for practical use and a concrete example of the integrated system of environmentalist business management*. Hamburg: McGraw-Hill

22

Developments in space tourism
Current and future research

Geoffrey I. Crouch, Timothy Devinney, Jordan J. Louviere

Introduction

The first space tourist, Dennis Tito, paid for a seat on a Russian Soyuz rocket and spent a week at the International Space Station in April 2001. A year later, Mark Shuttleworth repeated this experience. A third space tourist, Lance Bass had been training for a similar space trip scheduled for October 2002 until negotiations between Bass's representatives and the Russian Space Agency broke down (Berger, 2002). The NASA Shuttle Columbia disaster in February 2003 resulted in the cessation of further shuttle flights for a considerable period and the suspension, at the time, of further flights by other would-be orbital space tourists.

Instead, as a result, over the following years attention shifted to sub-orbital space tourism developments. This has focused on the race among over 20 private teams to be the first to successfully launch a fully privately developed, manned spacecraft into space. And in June 2004, a team called Scaled Composites and headed by Burt Rutan with funding from Paul Allen, a Microsoft pioneer, achieved this goal flying their spacecraft known as *SpaceShipOne*. In October 2004 this team went on to win the US$10 million Ansari X-Prize (Dinerman, 2004; Xprize Foundation, n.d.), which was established in the 1990s to encourage commercial space tourism enterprise in the same way that aviation prizes in the early twentieth century stimulated airplane technology and commerce (Economist, 2004a; Taylor, 2004). The Ansari X-Prize required the successful team to privately develop a reusable spacecraft and to fly the craft to a minimum height of 100 kilometres, with a pilot and the equivalent weight of two passengers. To demonstrate the craft's reusability, this had to be repeated within a period of two weeks. Richard Branson was quick to capitalize on the publicity and opportunity by agreeing, immediately after the successful flights, to purchase Scaled Composite's technology in order to commence commercial operations, purportedly in about three years, and to be known as *Virgin Galactic* (Space.com, 2004).

Since then, a new prize, the America's Space Prize, worth US$50 million, has been announced by another commercial space entrepreneur, Mr. Robert Bigelow (David, 2004; Malik, 2004), to stimulate development of a private, commercial spacecraft capable of going much faster and higher into orbit. Bigelow's company, Bigelow Aerospace, plans inflatable orbiting space hotels.

All of this activity has created debate and discussion concerning the most appropriate means of regulating commercial space operations (Antczak, 2004; Berger, 2004; David, 2004, 2005a, 2005b; Miller, 2005; Werner, 2004a, 2004b). Views range from those who argue that safety must be guaranteed through strong regulation, to those who fear such regulation will stifle development. In the meantime, other new teams and ventures have announced their own plans to pursue commercial operation goals (e.g. CNN, 2005; Malik, 2005). The race for private, commercial, sub-orbital ventures has stimulated US lawmakers and the Federal Aviation Administration (FAA) to draft a licensing system that would permit these space flights to take place. It has been reported (Pasztor, 2004) that the FAA and the US Congressional House Science Committee are likely to introduce controls over crew training and standards for the physical condition of passengers, together with requirements for the disclosure of vehicle-safety history, initial banning of flights over international waters and foreign territory, signing of waivers by passengers and insurance. However, the legislation being drafted is aimed at limiting such controls on the basis of 'caveat emptor' or 'buyer beware', so that a space tourism industry is provided with a favourable environment in which to get started – not unlike the pioneering days of the aviation industry.

President Bush, in January 2004, announced a new NASA programme for a return of manned missions to the Moon and possibly on to Mars. His plan also saw the end of formal American government involvement in the ISS, once construction is complete, and the need for new launch technologies to replace the Space Shuttle. Although this plan for NASA made no mention of a role for space tourism, it has been argued that space tourism may in fact be pivotal to the success of future space endeavours. The private sector may eventually gain control of the ISS and the sheer number of potential tourist space flights could mean that vastly more efficient, low-cost launch vehicles eventually emerge out of the competitive and entrepreneurial developments of the private sector rather than government space programmes, driven by economies of scale and learning effects:

> The challenge for future administrations will be to integrate the entrepreneurs and their companies into the space exploration program. If they do so, scientists and private citizens alike will colonize space. If they don't, President Bush's ambitious agenda is likely to have a hard time getting off the launching pad.
>
> *(Dinerman, 2004, p. D6)*

The role the private sector could play in this new vision could be considerable:

> Even space enthusiasts now warn that only private enterprise will truly drive human expansion into space ... What might cause market forces to take up the mission? Tourism and entertainment are both possibilities.... The true space entrepreneurs in America, the people who are building realistic, privately funded spacecraft for tourism, and moon satellites for entertainment, have had no government handouts or incentives. They push on regardless. They are the pioneers most worth applauding.
>
> *(Economist, 2004b, p. 9)*

Marketing research imperatives

In the past year private commercial space tourism has been demonstrated to be technologically feasible. However, what has yet to be demonstrated is the commercial feasibility of 'space tourism' (ST). Although, there is good reason to believe that there is a strong desire on the part of many people – such as Bono and William Shatner – to travel into space, this desire is generally expressed as an abstract latent desire independent of the cost and reality of what a touristic space experience might entail. Unlike many other adventure activities we know little about the characteristics of what will make a 'value for money' experience for those wishing to partake of a flight into near earth, or earth, orbit. Although numbers have been bandied about, few people know what the actual cost of a ticket will be – other than it will be expensive – or what the training might entail, or how it might exclude many people. But how would individuals react to placing their life in someone else's yet-to-be-proven hands? What, for example, would be the reaction to the first death, or near death, experience in a private tourist vehicle?

There is no doubt that some, perhaps many, will convert their desire into action (indeed some already have), but just how many? Space tourism operators need to be concerned with more than addressing just the issues of cost, time and risk to customers. They need also to understand how other design variables will affect customer perceptions and demand. For example, how will the design of the spacecraft itself affect customers? The wide variety of possibilities from rocket planes to parachute ascents to vertical-take-off to capsule return to splash downs to horizontal landings on runways, and so on, will have a multitude of implications on factors such as cost, risk, flight duration, comfort, training needs, viewing configurations, launch and return locations. There is little doubt that few, if any consumers, know or understand these options and their implications. The public also has the choice of options ranging from high-altitude jet fighter flights to zero-g flights to sub-orbital space tourism and orbital space tourism. How will space tourists decide between engaging in any of these activities now and delaying their participation until prices drop, risks improve or better information is available? Commercial space tourism entrepreneurs therefore have very many marketing questions that remain to be answered.

Towards the commercialization of space tourism

The path to commercial success for any new product is long and arduous. Marketers know that for every successful product there are many others that fail along the way. Therefore, difficult and complex decision making is required. However, when the new product being developed is merely a new model of an existing product with an established market history, there is often some good information available on which these decisions can be partly based. But when the product is an entirely 'new-to-world' innovation, much greater risk and uncertainty is involved.

The purpose of marketing research is to enable better decision making throughout the new-product development process and subsequently through the complete life cycle of the product. When one considers the level of investment that will be required to establish a viable commercial space tourism industry, the current embryonic stage of the industry and the degree of 'unknowns' involved, and therefore the financial risks entailed, rigorous and reliable marketing research is imperative.

Market demand and customer behaviour: what do we know so far?

Several studies of public interest in space tourism have been conducted, either by 'independent' academic researchers, government or public organizations, or commercial enterprises wishing to numerically substantiate their hope that space tourism is a viable investment (Crouch, 2001). In the case of this latter group of interested parties, although some of the results are available, these should be interpreted in light of the potential vested interests involved.

The most concerted effort to examine public interest in space tourism in a variety of countries has been carried out by Collins and others who studied public interest in Japan, the US and Canada (Collins, Iwasaki et al., 1994; Collins, Kanayama et al., 1994; Collins, Maita et al., 1996; Stockmans et al., 1995). In their 1993 Japanese study, 3,030 Japanese were asked whether they would like to travel into space: 80 per cent of the respondents under the age of 60 responded positively compared to about 45 per cent of respondents older than 60. On average, females were about 5 percentage points lower than males in their response to this question. About 20 per cent of interested respondents also indicated a preparedness to spend a year's salary or more on an opportunity to travel into space.

Stockmans et al. (1995) also surveyed 1,020 households in a telephone poll across the US and Canada, closely modelled on the earlier Japanese survey. Over all age groups, 62 per cent expressed an interest in travelling to space, with a clear decline as a function of age from 83 per cent for those in their 20s to 27 per cent for those over 60 years of age. Women were again less interested than men by about 10 percentage points on average. There was similarly a clear preference for longer (2 to 3 days or more) rather than shorter trips (a day or less). Of those interested in a trip to space, 2.7 per cent expressed a willingness to pay three years' salary and 10.6 per cent indicated they would pay one years' salary.

O'Neil et al. (1998) reported the results of a joint NASA/STA (Space Transportation Association) study of a sample of 1,500 US families conducted in 1996. They found that 34 per cent of respondents 'would be interested in taking a two-week vacation in the Space Shuttle in the future', and 42 per cent were interested in the concept of space travel aboard a space cruise vessel offering accommodation and entertainment programmes similar to an ocean-going cruise ship. In response to the question 'What would you be willing to pay per person for such an experience?' 7.5 per cent indicated US$100,000 or more.

Another US study, Commercial Space Transportation Study Alliance (CSTS, 1994), involving an alliance of six US Aerospace Corporations, produced three demand curves (low, medium and high probability). The low-probability (or optimistic) scenario yielded estimates of demand varying between 200 passengers and 3 million passengers worldwide annually for ticket prices of US$1 million and US$10,000 respectively. By comparison, the high-probability (or pessimistic) scenario produced a range of 20 to 6,000 passengers annually.

The German market was surveyed by Abitzsch (1996) following the Collins et al. studies to estimate national demand: 43 per cent of Germans expressed an interest in participating in space tourism, a lower proportion than the Japanese (80 per cent) and Americans/Canadians (62 per cent). Abitzsch's estimates for global market demand, derived by consolidating his and the various Collins et al. results, produced more price elastic figures than the CSTS study, ranging from 170 passengers per year at a price level of US$500,000 to 20 million passengers at US$1,000.

Barrett (1999) replicated the Collins' surveys (Collins, Iwasaki, et al., 1994; Collins, Kanayama, et al., 1994; Collins, Maita, et al., 1996; Stockmans et al., 1995) in the United Kingdom on a much smaller sample of only 72 people: 35 per cent of respondents stated an interest in taking a trip into space, and 12 per cent were prepared to pay one year's salary for such a tour.

Another US survey by Roper Starch Worldwide (1999) asked 2,002 Americans to assess interest in, and demand for a six-day trip from the Earth to the Moon and back on a luxurious space cruise ship for the Bigelow Companies. To the question, 'If you had the money, how interested would you be in taking this adventure?' 35 per cent answered 'interested' or 'very interested'.

An unpublished study, by Kelly Space and Technology (n.d.), used Harris Interactive polling services to interview 2,022 respondents in the 'high income sector of the [US] population' to estimate space tourism demand. This survey estimated that the demand for orbital space travel would grow to about 4,000 passengers annually from 2015–25, and 10,000 passengers from 2010–20 for suborbital travel. The methodology used employed a choice-based conjoint analysis (Space Adventures, n.d.).

Futron Corporation (2002), in a study for NASA and conducted by Zogby International, surveyed 450 affluent Americans. The principal findings were that suborbital space travel could reach 15,000 passengers annually by 2021, representing revenues in excess of US$700 million, and that, by the same time, orbital travel was forecast to reach 60 passengers per year, amounting to revenues of US$300 million. Surprisingly, perhaps, half of the respondents indicated that they would be indifferent to travelling in a privately developed suborbital vehicle with a limited flight history versus a government-developed spacecraft. As the other studies have suggested, Futron concluded that 'Orbital travel is a fairly elastic market; there are significant jumps in demand when the price drops to US$5 million and again at US$1 million.'

Recently Crouch and Laing (2004) assessed Australian public interest in space tourism using, for comparative purposes, a survey approach similar to a number of the studies summarized above. The study demonstrated a level of interest in the prospects for public space travel in Australia which is broadly comparable with the results of similar studies conducted in Japan, the US and Canada, the UK and Germany. The findings suggest that, conceptually at least, a majority of respondents would like to travel into space if they could (58 per cent of respondents), but cost, safety and product design factors would have a significant impact on consumer response. Demographic and behavioural characteristics of consumers are also strongly associated with these attitudes and interests. Younger respondents and male respondents were found to be statistically significantly more interested in space tourism. As one might expect, a strong positive association was found between current risk-taking behaviour in recreation and leisure activities and desire to travel into space. Consistent with other survey results, to the question, 'How long would you like to stay in space?', the modal response was two to three days (37 per cent). Although the majority of respondents indicated they would be prepared to pay between one to three month's salary, 12 per cent indicate they would be willing to forego a year's salary or more.

What do we need to know?

The most important need is to be able to obtain a reasonable prediction of the actual demand for space tourism rather than mere interest or desire (as market research studies to date have done). However, this is quite difficult to achieve when an entirely new industry with no market demand, track record or history is available upon which demand estimates can be based or extrapolated. Furthermore, market demand is not some hidden quantity waiting to be discovered or revealed. That is, there are many possible market demands – if you like, there is a probability distribution of demand and this distribution is a function of a wide range of factors, some of which include:

- the price of various space tourism options;
- the risk inherent in these options;
- the competitive dynamics as the industry unfolds between different space tourism ventures and between different forms of space tourism (e.g. zero-g flights, sub-orbital ST, orbital ST); and

- the wide array of attributes which define each space tourism alternative (e.g. duration and level of training required, type of launch and return spacecraft used, national identity of the operator, launch location, duration of the flight).

The challenge of estimating and forecasting the size of the market for space tourism is considerable and faces a number of challenges. With the exception of the two individuals who have travelled into space as tourists to date, there is no history of commercial space tourism that might reliably point to future consumer attitudes and behaviour in this market. Future market research must address the many important variables involved. Situational factors such as economic trends and events, global political developments and conflicts, and changing public attitudes will also shape the context of consumer choice towards space tourism.

Most importantly, however, public attitudes and interest towards space travel and tourism are not measures of actual future demand or choice behaviour. Indeed, past marketing research experience suggests the likelihood that such surveys substantially overestimate market demand, particularly in the short term. Potential space tourism consumers currently know very little about space tourism and the characteristics of space tourism products and experiences that may emerge in the years ahead. This lack of knowledge and information on the part of consumers raises a further caution concerning the conduct and interpretation of market research studies.

How can we find out?

There are, however, behavioural theories and research methodologies which can potentially address these challenges. Discrete choice modelling (DCM) (Louviere et al., 2000) using random utility theory (RUT) (McFadden, 1986), in conjunction with Information Acceleration (IA) (Coltman et al., 2004; Urban et al., 1997) provides a rigorous and reliable means currently available for making progress in answering problems of this nature.

Discrete choice models decompose the total utility of each choice alternative into its component parts. They enable a researcher to estimate how much each attribute – the key differentiator between alternatives – contributes to the decision to choose an alternative. RUT postulates that choices can be decomposed into a systematic and observable/explainable component, and a random and unobservable/unexplainable component. The systematic component represents the decision strategy used by the individual(s) (known as a utility function) and the random component represents all possible unobserved influences on decisions. The approach leads to different probabilistic discrete choice models that represent the underlying process generating the choices. DCM is therefore based on a sound, well-tested behavioural theory that recognizes that preferences (and the choices that reveal them) have both deterministic and random components.

Gathering the data required to enable the DCM of consumer choice in space tourism would entail the design and execution of consumer choice experiments. This approach is ideal in situations where:

- organizations need to estimate demand for new products with new attributes or features;
- explanatory variables have little variability in the marketplace;
- explanatory variables are highly collinear in the marketplace;
- new variables are introduced that now explain choices;
- observational data cannot satisfy model assumptions and/or contain statistical 'nasties' that lurk in real data; and
- observational data are time consuming and expensive to collect.

Where the modelling of future changes, trends or circumstances is required or where new or different choice attributes need to be evaluated for their likely impact, experimental choice modelling is particularly useful. In combination with IA methods, it is possible to model consumer adjustments to very new products or choice features. IA was developed in the early 1990s, using multimedia and information technology to accelerate consumer learning, in recognition of the fact that traditional methods failed to forecast the uptake of new technologies accurately due to a failure to: provide accurate information to potential users about relevant aspects of new technologies/products; simulate learning processes associated with new innovations and their evolutionary paths; and recognize that individuals and organizations make decisions and choices about technologies/products, and that market outcomes depend on these elemental behaviours. The IA approach is also applicable where very new choice environments or product features are of interest. So with these methods one can combine information about possible futures with ways in which consumers choose possible future products conditional on that information. IA is thus a powerful and flexible way to forecast the likely adjustment in response to futures and technologies. Coltman et al. (2004) recently developed significant advances in IA methods and applications that allow for cheaper and more robust estimation of demand where the context in which that demand is arising is unknown.

Pilot-testing the approach

Employing the approach of Coltman et al. (2004) a pilot test was undertaken in April 2005. The pilot examined how the public might react when faced with four potential space tourism alternatives spanning high-altitude jet fighter flights, zero-gravity flights, sub-orbital space tourism, and orbital space tourism. That is, for the purpose of this particular application, the pilot focused on how the attributes of these four alternatives influenced how individuals might choose between the alternatives, with a focus on zero-gravity flights and sub-orbital space tourism. The pilot provides an assessment of the role that the attributes play in influencing choice between, but not within, each of the four types. It would, however, be straight forward to design a similar but different choice experiment that examined choice among alternatives within one of these types of space tourism alternatives, such as sub-orbital space tourism. This would enable an assessment to be made of the relative role that each attribute plays in influencing choice between one sub-orbital space tourism venture and another.

The process

The pilot choice experiment proceeded as follows:

*   A list of important attributes for each of the four types of space tourism was developed with the assistance of several industry advisors, each with various areas of knowledge and expertise. For example, Appendix 1 lists these attributes for the zero-gravity flights and sub-orbital space tourism categories. An attribute is a product feature or characteristic, such as 'price', which is assumed to impact consumer choice.
*   For each attribute, various levels were identified. These levels are the 'values' that each attribute takes within the controlled choice experiment. For example, the sub-orbital attribute, 'price', was manipulated over eight levels as follows: US$10,000; US$40,000; US$70,000; US$100,000; US$130,000; US$160,000; US$190,000; US$220,000. In most cases, levels were indicated narratively. In some cases, however, images were used to illustrate certain levels. For example, the zero-gravity flights attribute, 'Zero-G space per

passenger', was depicted using four different images showing different levels of passenger crowding within the aircraft.

- A large fractional factorial choice experiment was designed to control the manipulation of each of the levels for each attribute forming each of the four alternatives. As the number of attributes across each of the four types of space tourism modelled is large, the factorial combination of all of these attributes is enormous. Thus, a fraction of this full factorial set of all possible combinations must be used such that the main effects of each factor can be isolated. This requires the design of an orthogonal main effects plan (OMEP). This is a sophisticated field and further explanation is beyond the scope of this current paper.

- For the purpose of this pilot, the target population was the Australian general public. The choice experiment was completed by 736 respondents. These respondents were recruited from an online survey panel created by Pure Profile, a commercial provider. This panel is broadly representative of the Australian general population. However, a minimum number of high-income respondents from the panel was predetermined.

- The survey was conducted online. The survey initially explained the research and then provided an overview, using text and pictures, of each of the four types of space tourism. The next section of the survey provided a glossary of all attributes. Each respondent was then asked to evaluate a series of hypothetical scenarios (see below) within which various space tourism options were presented. The final section of the survey included a series of questions concerning leisure and adventure activities undertaken, equipment owned and licenses or certifications held; past travel activity; exceptional activities; military or service training; attitudes toward risk; and demographic questions (gender, age, household income, education, property values and other assets).

Hypothetical choice scenarios

The core element of the survey concerned the evaluation of a series of choice scenarios. There were two sets of these scenarios. The first set focused on zero-gravity flights and respondents were presented with several scenarios, each showing a detailed zero-gravity flight alternative, plus a high-altitude flight and a sub-orbital flight alternative. The second set instead focused on sub-orbital flights; competing alternatives included a zero-gravity flight and an orbital flight. Appendix 2 illustrates an example of a screen display of one scenario from the first set.

Each scenario shows three space tourism options and each option is explained in terms of the key attributes as explained above. The value or level of each attribute in each option is indicated in the scenario as manipulated by the fractional factorial experimental design. The scenarios included hotlinks for each attribute which opened a window with a detailed explanation of the attribute to avoid the need to return to the full glossary.

Each respondent then responded to each scenario by answering three questions (Appendix 2) that indicated which of the three options they preferred most, which they preferred least, and on which, realistically, they would actually spend time and money if they were available in the next 12–24 months.

Overview of preliminary results from the pilot

We briefly describe the preliminary results from the choice experiment that focused on sub-orbital choices. More than 35 variables (called 'attributes') that describe possible future choice options were experimentally manipulated, each varying over 2 to 16 levels as needed to describe future variations. This recognizes that there is not one possible space tourism option, but in reality many millions of possibilities. The objective of the choice experiment is to quantify the effects of the attributes on choices among Zero-G (ZG), Sub-Orbital (SO) and Orbital (OR) choice options. Of course all three options might be unacceptable for whatever reason, and so we also include the option to choose no options.

Our sample consists of predominantly high income and/or high net-worth individuals. By comparison, the 90th percentile for individual weekly disposable income in Australia in 2003 was around A$850, which would be approximately A$1,130 before taxes, or A$59,000 annually. Table 22.1 indicates that about 70 per cent of our sample is above the 90th percentile in annual household income. Thus, our sample is biased towards individuals who have the income or net worth to potentially afford the prices of the services studied.

Table 22.1 Sample income distribution

Income category midpoints	Total	%	Cumulative (%)
<$30,000	101	13.7	13.7
$46,799.50	62	8.4	22.1
$57,199.50	55	7.4	29.5
$70,199.50	66	9.0	38.5
$90,999.00	119	16.2	54.7
$129,999.50	131	17.8	72.5
$181,944.00	102	13.9	86.4
$233,999.50	34	4.6	91.0
>$265,000	66	9.0	100.0
Total	736	100.0	

Table 22.2 shows the average number of choices in the experiment across all scenarios. These averages hide large variations in response to attribute level combinations. For example, SO choices range from nearly 23 per cent at the lowest prices tested to around 9 per cent for the highest prices tested. The table indicates that there were no differences in the choices of the services studied on average by level of household income. We further analysed differences by combining income and assets to create individuals who were above or below the median in

Table 22.2 Choice frequencies and income effects

Choice	Total sample (%)	Sample > $90,000 HH Income (%)
Zero-G	35.7	37.8
Sub-Orbital	14.6	14.0
Orbital	12.1	12.8
None of the options	37.6	35.3
Total	100.0	100.0

income and net worth. An analysis of the response of these two groups to the prices of SO services indicates no differences in the response curves to price. Thus, our sample should be regarded as representative of 10 per cent or less of the Australian population, who should be able to afford to purchase at least some of the services offered if they so choose.

Turning to the results of the choice experiment, not surprisingly price was a significant driver of choices for all options. For Sub-Orbital (SO) options, choices decrease approximately logarithmically, and the rate of decrease is virtually identical for low or high wealth individuals. We also find a logarithmic decrease in choices as a function of the ratio of SO trip price to an individual's total income or assets (see Figures 22.1 and 22.2). The choice models allow us to capture differential substitution effects due to price, such that as the price of SO increases, individuals substitute ZG or OR or None much more than would be expected if they were not substitutes.

Other attributes that are significant drivers of SO choices include the following:

- Country of SO operator has a large effect, with our sample preferring Australia and the USA, and reacting quite negatively to Russia and Japan.
- The joint effect of years of operation and the number of harmful incidents is very interesting, and underscores the important role of safety. That is, if there have been few harmful incidents, choices increase approximately linearly in years of operation. But if there have been harmful incidents, choices decrease approximately linearly in years of operation.
- The type of craft proposed for the trip also drives choices, with a VTO rocket associated with significantly more choices than other types and an HTO rocket plane associated with significantly fewer choices.
- The type of Zero-G floating experience was a significant driver of choices, with individuals preferring to float free compared with being strapped to their seats.
- The amount of launch vehicle training significantly impacts choices, with less-extensive training significantly preferred to more.

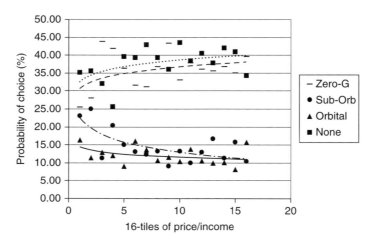

Figure 22.1   Effects of price/income on choice

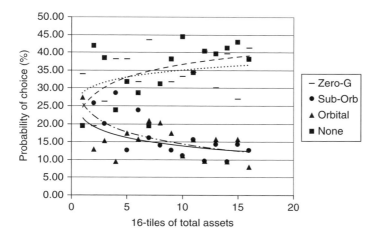

Figure 22.2 Effects of price/assets

- The availability of educational enhancements significantly drives choices, with individuals strongly preferring none, and negatively reacting to a presentation by a space scientist.

There were other minor attribute effects, and some of these may reach statistical significance when we pool the datasets to allow for more extensive and detailed analysis. Of course, potential operations of SO services also need to know who the likely target customers are, and so we also included a number of individual difference variables in our model analyses (also called 'covariates'). A number of these effects are very large, as we note below:

- There is a large gender difference, with females being significantly less likely to choose any of the options than males, and also being much more likely to choose no options.
- There are significant age differences, with the probability of individuals choosing SO decreasing approximately logarithmically with age. Concurrently, the probability of choosing nothing also increases approximately logarithmically with age.
- There are both income and asset effects on choices, with SO choices tending to increase with increases in income or assets; however, the effect is much more dramatic for OR choices than SO choices.
- We also examined a number of measures of risky behaviour, including, for example, the number of relatively high-risk activities an individual engages in, how many risky 'toys' they own. These measures suggest that choices of SO exhibit an inverse-U shaped relationship with these risk measures, but that choices of OR are exponentially related to them.
- Highly educated individuals exhibited significantly less interest in SO than less-well educated individuals.

Conclusions

For good reason, the emerging space tourism industry has, to date, focused primarily on technological considerations. And, no doubt, technological concerns will remain critical for many years to come. But, as more attention turns toward issues of commercialization, it is imperative that sound, state-of-the-art marketing research is carried out to understand better the panoply of consumer behaviour questions the industry must confront. Without the sort of information that good quality marketing research can supply, commercial ventures and investors must be prepared to 'fly blind'.

The major marketing research hurdle facing space tourism concerns the fact that this is a 'new-to-world' product. For all intents and purposes, we have no past consumer behaviour data that might be used to forecast demand or understand consumer perceptions of, and reactions to, product design, development, pricing and promotion decisions. Traditionally, what occurs in markets like this is that bold predictions are made about the first movers, though few if any of them manage to survive as they invariably serve as the experimental test bed on which consumers assess the appropriateness of the new offering (Golder and Tellis, 1993).

What our study shows, however, is that there are tools and techniques available that can be used to help address this hurdle and provide a more direct assessment of possible future scenarios of the demand for space tourism. Random-utility theory-based methods of discrete choice modelling, in conjunction with information acceleration techniques, provide the most applicable approach to this problem. These methods are theoretically sound and very flexible from a practical implementation perspective. In addition, the results are immediately operational in the sense that they can inform not just marketing but design. Hence, it is possible to apply the approach to any marketing research question in space tourism which can be defined in terms of:

- two or more choice options or alternatives; and
- each alternative can be characterized in terms of a set of attributes and levels that establish the product features likely to affect consumer choice behaviour.

The pilot test summarized in this paper provides one example of the type of application toward which this technique can be applied.

Acknowledgements

We wish gratefully to acknowledge the assistance of the following members of the Industry Advisory Group:

Dr. Buzz Aldrin	Sharespace
Derek Webber	Spaceport Associates
Paul Young	Starchaser Industries
Peter Diamandis	Zero-G Corporation and X-Prize Foundation
Eric Anderson	Space Adventures
Patricia Grace-Smith	US Federal Aviation Administration

We also thank Michael McGee and Steve Cook from Future and Simple, Sandra Peter at the Australian Graduate School of Management, and Jennifer Laing at La Trobe University for their valuable assistance.

Appendix 1

Table 22.3 An example of sub-orbital space tourism attributes

Zero-G flights		
	Attributes	Levels
Price	1. Price of Zero-G flight experience	8 levels: From US$1,000 to US$8,000
Operators	2. National identity of operator	8 levels: US/Russia/China/UK/France/Germany/Japan/Australia
	3a. Zero-G flight experience of operator (in years)	8 levels: From 'no experience & no harmful incidents' to '10 years experience & some harmful incidents'
Safety	3b. Safety history of this venture	
	4. Safety history of other Zero-G ventures	4 levels: From 'no incidents of harm' to passengers to '1 loss-of-life accident'
	5. Safety standard of this venture as judged by independent experts	2 levels: meets required standard/significantly exceeds required standard
Duration of experience	6a. Total time in Zero-G	8 levels: From '10 loops – 4 mins.' to '25 loops – 16 mins.'
	6b. Number of Zero-G parabolic loops	
Type of aircraft	7. Aircraft type	2 levels: modified American Boeing 727/modified Russian Ilyushin 76
Location	8. Airport type	2 levels: normal civilian airport/private airport
	9. Proximity of airport for Zero-G departure	4 levels: From 'within a 1 hour drive' to 'requires an international flight'
Amenities	10. Zero-G space per passenger	4 levels: Images showing different levels of crowding/space
	11. Passengers per assisting crew member	4 levels: 6/4/3/2
Activities	12. Opportunity to conduct Zero-G activities/games	2 levels: limited to floating only/several activities available
Training and testing	13. Duration of pre-flight training	4 levels: 2 hours/4 hours/6 hours/1 day
	14. Stringency of physical requirements	4 levels: very low/low/moderate/high
	15. Further educational enhancements	4 levels: none/presentation by space scientist/presentation by little-known NASA astronaut/presentation by well-known NASA astronaut
Legal factors	16. Licensed status of operator	2 levels: has an operating license from the one local authority/has an operating license form the US Federal Aviation Administration (FAA) and several other licensing authorities
	17. Insurance coverage	2 levels: passenger travels at own risk or takes out own insurance coverage/fully covered by operator's insurance policy

SUB-ORBITAL SPACE TOURISM

	Attributes	Levels
Price	1. Price of sub-orbital flight	8 levels: From US$10,000 to US$220,000
Operators	2. National identity of operator	8 levels: US/Russia/China/UK/France/Germany/Japan/Australia
	3a. Sub-orbital experience of operator (in years)	8 (7) levels: From no experience & no fatal accidents to 10 years experience & one fatal accident
Safety	3b. Safety history of this venture	4 levels: From no fatal accidents to > 2 fatal accidents
	4. Safety history of other sub-orbital ventures	
	5. Safety standard of this venture as judged by independent experts	2 levels: Meets required standards/exceeds required standards
Duration and altitude	6. Duration of weightlessness (and maximum altitude)	4 levels: From 3 mins. (110km.) to 10 mins. (150km.)
	7. Total duration of sub-orbital flight	4 levels: From 20 mins. to 90 mins.
Type of craft	8. Launch craft/sub-orbital craft/return craft combination	4 levels: Plane and detachable rocket/vertical rocket launch and parachute capsule return/balloon ascent, detachable rocket and capsule return/rocket plane
Location	9. Launch location type	4 levels: From normal airport to remote, unpopulated site
	10. Launch and return location geography	4 levels: North America/Europe/Asia/Australia
	11. Return location	4 levels: From same as launch location to 100 miles downstream from launch location
Amenities	12. Seating and viewing arrangements	4 levels: From small window shared with another passenger to each passenger gets their own large window
	13. Number of accompanying passengers	4 levels: From 1 to 10
Activities	14. Zero-G floating	2 levels: Strapped to seat, no floating possible/free to float
	15. Opportunity to conduct Zero-G activities/games	2 levels: No, insufficient time and space/yes
Training, testing and preparation	16. Overall duration of the space experience training and flight package	4 levels: From 3 days to 4 weeks
	17. Medical testing	4 levels: From simple to full medical testing

	18. Parachute training required	4 levels: From none to full free-fall training involving 25 jumps
	19. Launch vehicle training	2 levels: Limited training required/extensive training required
	20. Further educational enhancements	4 levels: From none to presentation by well-known NASA astronaut
Legal factors	21. Licensed status of operator	2 levels: From the launch site local authority/From several licensing authorities including the FAA and NASA
	22. Insurance coverage	2 levels: passenger travels at own risk or takes out own insurance coverage/fully covered by operator's insurance policy
	23. Terms for withdrawal by customer	2 levels: flexible payment and withdrawal terms and conditions to inflexible payment and withdrawal terms and conditions with high financial penalties

Appendix 2

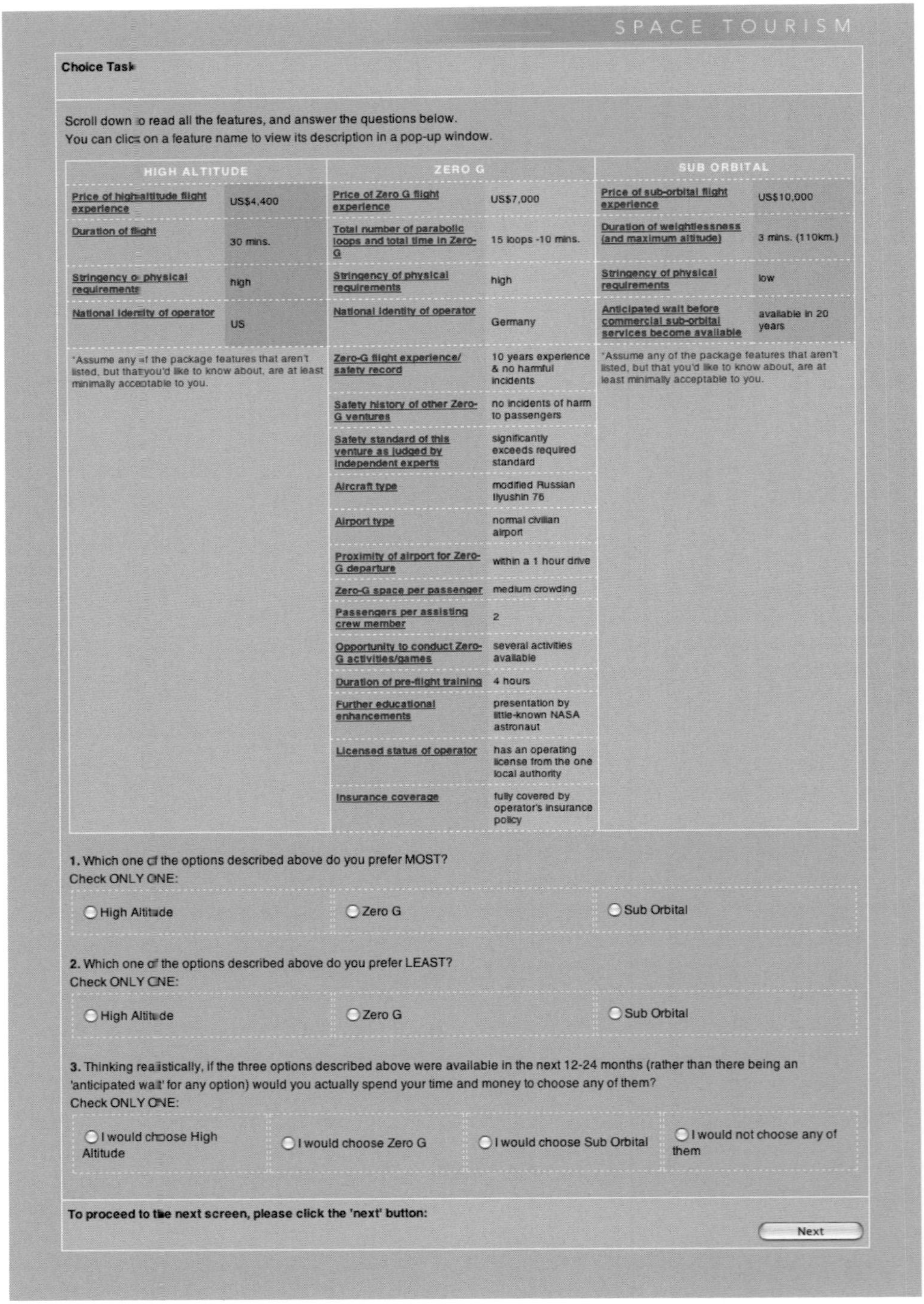

SPACE TOURISM

Choice Task

Scroll down to read all the features, and answer the questions below.
You can click on a feature name to view its description in a pop-up window.

HIGH ALTITUDE		ZERO G		SUB ORBITAL	
Price of high-altitude flight experience	US$4,400	Price of Zero G flight experience	US$7,000	Price of sub-orbital flight experience	US$10,000
Duration of flight	30 mins.	Total number of parabolic loops and total time in Zero-G	15 loops -10 mins.	Duration of weightlessness (and maximum altitude)	3 mins. (110km.)
Stringency of physical requirements	high	Stringency of physical requirements	high	Stringency of physical requirements	low
National identity of operator	US	National identity of operator	Germany	Anticipated wait before commercial sub-orbital services become available	available in 20 years
*Assume any of the package features that aren't listed, but that you'd like to know about, are at least minimally acceptable to you.		Zero-G flight experience/ safety record	10 years experience & no harmful incidents	*Assume any of the package features that aren't listed, but that you'd like to know about, are at least minimally acceptable to you.	
		Safety history of other Zero-G ventures	no incidents of harm to passengers		
		Safety standard of this venture as judged by independent experts	significantly exceeds required standard		
		Aircraft type	modified Russian Ilyushin 76		
		Airport type	normal civilian airport		
		Proximity of airport for Zero-G departure	within a 1 hour drive		
		Zero-G space per passenger	medium crowding		
		Passengers per assisting crew member	2		
		Opportunity to conduct Zero-G activities/games	several activities available		
		Duration of pre-flight training	4 hours		
		Further educational enhancements	presentation by little-known NASA astronaut		
		Licensed status of operator	has an operating license from the one local authority		
		Insurance coverage	fully covered by operator's insurance policy		

1. Which one of the options described above do you prefer MOST?
Check ONLY ONE:

○ High Altitude   ○ Zero G   ○ Sub Orbital

2. Which one of the options described above do you prefer LEAST?
Check ONLY ONE:

○ High Altitude   ○ Zero G   ○ Sub Orbital

3. Thinking realistically, if the three options described above were available in the next 12-24 months (rather than there being an 'anticipated wait' for any option) would you actually spend your time and money to choose any of them?
Check ONLY ONE:

○ I would choose High Altitude   ○ I would choose Zero G   ○ I would choose Sub Orbital   ○ I would not choose any of them

To proceed to the next screen, please click the 'next' button:

[Next]

Figure 22.3 Example of a hypothetical choice scenario

References

Abitzsch, S. (1996) 'Prospects of space tourism'. Paper presented at the 9th European Aerospace Congress: Visions and limits of long-term aerospace developments, Berlin, May

Antczak, J. (2004) 'Space tourism faces safety regulations'. Space.com, 7 October. Retrieved 6 May 2005, from http://www.space.com

Barrett, O. (1999) 'An evaluation of the potential demand for space tourism within the United Kingdom'. Spacefuture.com, March. Retrieved 5 November 2011, from http://www.spacefuture.com/archive/an_evaluation_of_the_potential_demand_for_space_tourism_within_the_united_kingdom.shtml

Berger, B. (2002) 'Russia withdraws lance bass' name from October Soyuz mission'. Space.com, 9 September. Retrieved 10 September 2002 from http://www.space.com

—— (2004) 'House passes private spaceflight bill'. Space.com, 20 November. Retrieved 5 November 2011, from http://www.space.com/news/spaceflight_bill_041120.html

CNN (2005) 'Sweden mines space for tourist dollars'. CNN, 23 March. Retrieved 24 March 2005, from http://edition.cnn.com

Collins, P., Iwasaki, Y., Kanayama, H. and Okazaki, M. (1994) 'Potential demand for passenger travel to orbit: Engineering construction and operations in Space IV'. In *Proceedings of Space '94* (Vol. 1) Albuquerque, NM: American Society of Civil Engineers, pp. 578–86

Collins, P., Kanayama, H., Iwasaki, Y. and Ohnuki, M. (1994) 'Commercial implications of market research on space tourism'. *Journal of Space Technology and Science*, 10(2), 3–11

Collins, P., Maita, M., Stockmans, R. and Kobayahi, S. (1996) 'Recent efforts towards the new space era' (AIAA Paper No. 96–4581) Paper presented at the 7th American Institute of Aeronautics and Astronautics International Spaceplanes and Hypersonics Systems and Technology Conference, Norfolk, VA, November

Coltman, T. R., Devinney, T. M. and Louviere, J. J. (2004) 'Utilizing rich multimedia methods for the elicitation of preferences for radical future technologies'. In *Where science meets practice*. Amsterdam: ESOMAR, pp. 271–88

Crouch, G. I. (2001) 'The market for space tourism'. *Journal of Travel Research*, 40(2), 213–19

Crouch, G. I. and Laing, J. H. (2004) 'Australian public interest in space tourism and a cross-cultural comparison'. *The Journal of Tourism Studies*, 15(2), 26–36

CSTS (1994) 'Commercial space transportation study'. Unpublished manuscript, Commercial Space Transportation Study Alliance, May

David, L. (2004) 'Rules set for $50 million "America's Space Prize"'. Space.com, 8 November. Retrieved 9 November 2004, from http://www.space.com

—— (2005a) 'Doctor's orders: The right stuff for space tourists'. Space.com, 25 March. Retrieved 5 November 2011, from http://space.com/missionlaunches/050325_space_tourism.html

—— (2005b, April 20) 'Rutan: Space tourism will thrive, but regulations already interfering'. Space.com, 20 April. Retrieved 5 November 2011, from http://www.space.com/news/050420_faa_hearing.html

Dinerman, T. (2004) 'Space: The tourist frontier'. *Wall Street Journal*, 22 January, p. D6

Economist (2004a) 'One small step for space tourism'. *The Economist*, 18 December, pp. 127–8

—— (2004b) 'A grand but costly vision'. *The Economist*, 17 January, p. 9

Futron Corporation (2002) 'Space tourism market study: Orbital space travel and destinations with suborbital space travel'. Retrieved 5 March 2003, from http://www.futron.com

Golder, P. N. and Tellis, G. J. (1993) 'Pioneer advantage: Marketing logic or marketing legend?'. *Journal of Marketing Research*, 30(2), 158–62

Kelly Space and Technology (n.d.) 'Space transportation market demand, 2010–2030' (NRA8–27 Final Report). Retrieved 15 June 2005, from http://www.kellyspace.com

Louviere, J. J., Hensher, D. A. and Swait, J. D. (2000) *Stated choice methods: Analysis and application.* Cambridge: Cambridge University Press

McFadden, D. (1986) 'The choice theory approach to marketing research'. *Marketing Science*, 5(4), 275–97

Malik, T. (2004) 'America's Space Prize: Reaching higher than sub-orbit'. Space.com, 6 October. Retrieved 10 October 2004, from http://www.space.com

—— (2005) 'Space tourism group picks Florida launch'. Space.com, 9 March. Retrieved 5 November 2011, from http://www.space.com/missionlaunches/aera_spacetourism_050309.html

Miller, L. (2005) 'Space entrepreneurs worry about fed regulations'. Space.com, 10 February. Retrieved 14 February 2005, from http://www.space.com

O'Neil, D., Bekey, I., Mankins, J., Rogers, T. F. and Stallmer, E. W. (1998) *General public space travel and tourism, Vol. 1: Executive Summary*. Washington, DC: National Aeronautics and Space Administration and the Space Transportation Association

Pasztor, A. (2004) 'Travel's final frontier'. *The Wall Street Journal*, 29 January, pp. D1, D8

Roper Starch Worldwide (1999) 'Spacecruiseship study'. Unpublished manuscript. Roper Starch Worldwide

Space Adventures (n.d.) 'Space tourism market analysis'. Unpublished manuscript. Space Adventures

Space.com (2004) 'Virgin Galactic to offer public space flights'. Space.com, 27 September. Retrieved 28 September 2004, from http://www.space.com

Stockmans, R., Collins, P. and Maita, M. (1995) 'Demand for space tourism in America and Japan, and its implications for future space activities' (Paper No. AAS 95–605). In *Advances in the Astronautical Sciences: Sixth International Space Conference of Pacific-Basin Societies* (Vol. 91). Marina del Rey, CA: American Astronautical Society, pp. 601–10

Taylor, C. (2004) 'The sky's the limit'. *Time*, 29 November, pp. 48–52

Urban, G. L., Hauser, J. R., Qualls, W. J., Weinberg, B. D., Bohlmann, J. D. and Chicos, R. A. (1997) 'Information acceleration: Validation and lessons from the field'. *Journal of Marketing Research*, 34(1), 143–53

Werner, E. (2004a) 'Senate dispute may scuttle space tourism bill'. Space.com, 14 October. Retrieved 10 November 2004, from http://www.space.com

—— (2004b) 'Congress passes space tourism bill'. Space.com, 9 December. Retrieved 10 December 2004, from http://www.space.com

Xprize Foundation (n.d.) 'X Prize Foundation: Revolution through competition'. Retrieved 20 January 2004, from http://www.xprize.com

Part VI
Insights into tourism evolution

23

Global touristscapes in a rainforest

Ecotourism in Sabah, Malaysia

Shinji Yamashita

Introduction

In what the anthropologist Arjun Appadurai has called "global ethnoscapes," the world is engulfed in a global flow of people crossing borders. According to him, "ethnoscapes" means "the landscape of persons who constitute the shifting world in which we live: tourists, immigrants, refugees, exiles, guest workers, and other moving groups and individuals constitute an essential feature of the world and appear to affect the politics of (and between) nations to a hitherto unprecedented degree" (Appadurai, 1997, p. 33). Of these moving groups and individuals in the global ethnoscapes, it is estimated that over 80 percent are tourists.

According to the World Tourism Organization (UNWTO), 980 million tourists traveled across national boundaries in 2011. This figure is expected to amount to be 1.6 billion in 2020.[1] As a part of the global ethnoscapes, this paper discusses "global touristscapes," a term of my invention following Appadurai's terminology, which is adopted to describe the landscape of international tourists, focusing on the State of Sabah, Malaysia. In the expanse of global tourism, Sabah is just a small example, but to understand the dynamics of global touristscapes one must pay attention to local conditions. One can observe the global tourism processes not only in megacities such as New York, London or Tokyo, but also in remote places such as Sabah, which is located at the north-eastern part of the island of Borneo once covered with tropical rainforests.

Sabah is now becoming a new site of international tourism. As the basis of the state economy, Sabah has been strongly dependent on its exports of primary commodities from the agricultural and forestry sectors. However, according to Chuan and Arroyo (1988, p. 2), by 1980 Sabah's commercial forest available for logging was reduced to about 2 million hectares, against 5.3 million hectares in 1972. By 1985 the Forest Department of Sabah estimated the remaining unlogged forest to be 1.5 million hectares. In other words, the reduction of commercial forest from 1972 to 1985 was 3.3 million hectares, which gives an average logging rate of 286,000 hectares per year. The area of the rainforests has thus reduced from 86 percent to 51 percent of the total area of Sabah over the past thirty years. The forestry sector is now thought of as playing a smaller role in the future due to the state government policy of trying to ensure more sustainable management of natural resources (Sabah State Government, 1996, p.12).

In place of forestry, the importance of tourism as a means of regional economic development has been recognized since the mid-1980s. Tan Sri Bernard Dompok, the former Minister of Tourism and Environmental Development[2] states:

> Tourism is now second only to the manufacturing sector in foreign exchange earnings and its economic importance has led to tourism being given greater emphasis; the country intends to make it an industry contributing to the new sources of growth required for socio-economic development.
>
> *(New Sabah Times, 21 May 1998)*

By pursuing this policy, the State Government intends not only to profit from tourism but also to conserve the tropical rain forests in Borneo, the second largest in the world after the Amazon. In this context, ecotourism deserves special attention.

This chapter examines how ecotourism is practiced in Sabah, especially by analyzing the cases of the eastern coast of the state, Sukau on the Kinabatangan river basin, and the islands of Mabul and Sipadan, based on my own field research during the term of my research from 1999 to 2004.[3] My research methodology is ethnographic, based on the qualitative data obtained from formal and informal interviews with the officials of the Sabah State Government, the chairman and marketing manager of STPC (Sabah Tourism Promotion Corporation, currently Sabah Tourism Board), tour operators in Kota Kinabalu, the capital city of Sabah, local eco-lodges and resorts managers, local tour guides, local people in the host villages, and tourists from various countries. I also made participant observation of various ecotour programs in Sabah during the term of my research. In addition, I surveyed statistical data mainly at STPC and newspaper clippings regarding tourism development in the region at IDS (Institute for Development Studies) in Kota Kinabalu.

My ethnographic analysis will reveal an irony in Sabah ecotourism, which arises from its position between tourism development and nature preservation, between tourism and transnational political economy, and between innocent tourists and terrorist politics. However, I will discuss the irony and difficulties inherent in ecotourism which should be confronted and laid bare, because of the claims that it may provide an important resource in facing the challenge of the global environmental crisis in today's world. I would argue that the community-based ecotourism in Sabah's recent homestay program shows a possibility in this direction. In so doing, this chapter will contribute to shedding new light on future directions of tourism and the study of sustainable tourism.

Tourism development in Sabah

Before entering into the theme of ecotourism, it is necessary to give a general picture of tourism development in Sabah. According to the Malaysia Tourism Promotion Board, international tourist arrivals to Malaysia in 2000 totaled 12.8 million. This was an increase of 29 percent compared with the 7.9 million in 1999. But it went down 10.5 million in 2003 due to the SARS (Severe Acute Respiratory Syndrome) epidemic break in Asia, then recovered again, with up to 15.7 million in 2004. Although one could observe up and down of the number of international tourist arrivals due to the political, economic, and epidemiological condition of the world, Malaysia ranked third in Asia (following China and Hong Kong) and seventeenth in the world in terms of international tourist arrivals in 2003. Total revenue from the international tourism sector in 2004, was RM29.7 billion.[4]

Looking at tourist arrivals by nationality for 2004 (Table 23.1), it is characteristic of the Malaysian tourism market that tourists from East and Southeast Asian countries comprised 86 percent of the total arrivals, especially tourists from ASEAN (Association of Southeast Asian Nations) countries who made up 78 percent of the total. Among them 61 percent (9.5 million) came from Singapore, 10 percent (1.5 million) from Thailand, 5 percent (790,000) from Indonesia, and 3 percent (454,000) from Brunei. Therefore, ASEAN, particularly neighboring Singapore, is the major market for Malaysian tourism. For the majority of Singaporeans, Malaysia is a place mainly for shopping, visiting friends or relations, eating out, or just filling up their car tanks with Malaysia's lower priced petrol (EIU, 1990 cited in King, 1993, p.107). In contrast, most of the Indonesians are labor migrants rather than tourists. Regarding the East Asian market, China and Japan are two major countries: 3.5 percent (550,000) came from China

Table 23.1 International tourist arrivals to Malaysia 2004

Country of residence	Arrivals
Singapore	9,520,306
Thailand	1,518,452
Indonesia	789,925
Brunei	453,664
China	550,241
Japan	301,429
Taiwan	190,083
Hong Kong	80,326
South Korea	91,270
India	172,966
West Asia	126,050
Canada	32,822
USA	145,094
Australia	204,053
UK	204,409
Denmark	11,884
Finland	11,308
Norway	9,437
Sweden	25,960
Germany	53,783
Russia	6,627
Italy	20,036
France	32,562
South Africa	16,511
Others	1,134,208
Grand Total	15,703,406

Source: Immigration Department of Malaysia, Kuala Lumpur

and 1.9 percent (301,000) from Japan. Of the Westerners, who occupy only 5 percent of the total arrivals 1.3 percent (204,000) were from United Kingdom, 1.3 percent (204,000) from Australia, and 0.9 percent (145, 000) from the United States.

Of the 15.7 million international tourist arrivals to Malaysia in 2004, only 1.77 million (1.1 percent) visited Sabah and 2.24 million (1.4 percent) visited Sarawak.[5] In other words, Sabah and Sarawak, two states located in Malaysian Borneo, occupy only 2.5 percent of the total international tourists to Malaysia. This is because Sabah and Sarawak are located far from the mainland capital; Sabah and Sarawak do not have international hub airports with direct flights from foreign countries. In this sense Sabah is a "backward" (therefore, new) region of tourism development in Malaysia.

Turning to the Sabah tourism market, visitors to Sabah increased from 520,000 in 1995 to 1.77 million in 2004 (Table 23.2). As for the international tourists, the number increased more than four times from 182,000 in 1995 to 792,000 in 2004. One could say therefore that Sabah tourism grew steadily in spite of negative factors to tourist development such as the Asian economic crisis in 1997, terrorism on 9/11 2001, and the SARS epidemic in 2003.[6]

The Sabah tourism market has several characteristics. First, following the general pattern of tourist arrivals in Malaysia as a whole, Asian tourists play an important role. Looking at the statistics for the year 2004, 82 percent of international visitor arrivals in Sabah are from East and Southeast Asian countries. Neighboring ASEAN countries account for 54 percent of visitors, with 37 percent (290,000) coming from Indonesia. But the latter are not necessarily tourists but labor migrants; the same is the case with Filipinos.[7]

Taiwan accounted for the majority of tourists, with a share of 10 percent (79,000) of the total international visitors. The share of Taiwanese tourists was 27 percent in 2000 but the figure dropped in 2003, presumably due to the SARS epidemic. But Taiwanese people are still the majority of international tourists in Sabah.[8] This may be due to the accessibility from Taiwan. It takes only two or three hours to fly from Taiwan to Sabah. Chinese tourists from Mainland China and Hong Kong have also increased greatly in recent years.

In 2004, 44,000 Japanese visited Sabah, a small proportion of the almost 300,000 who visited Malaysia that year. Most Japanese tourists who visit Sabah come to the famous diving spots of Sipadan and Mabul islands. Westerners, including Europeans, Northern Americans, Australians and New Zealanders, account for about 16 percent of the total, with the British making up the majority, possibly to reflect upon their former colonial connections. Numbers of other European tourists have increased in recent years. The number of Australian tourists has also increased, because they shifted to Sabah after the Bali bombing incident in 2002. Among these visitors, as we will discuss later, it is the Japanese and Western tourists who show the greatest interest in ecotourism.

Ecotourism planned

The status of Sabah tourism at the time of my research was based on the Sabah Tourism Master Plan compiled by the Ministry of Tourism and Environmental Development, the Sabah State Government, which outlined Sabah's tourism development plan from 1995 to 2010. The Master Plan begins with an overview of the Sabah economy, and places tourism within the new economic development of Sabah, which could replace the forestry sector, as mentioned at the beginning of this paper. In this scheme, "ecotourism" or "nature tourism"[9] is considered to hold a strategic position in which Sabah makes use of tourism without destroying its unique "unspoiled nature" (Sabah State Government, 1996, p. 20). Therefore, Dompok, the former Tourism Minster, emphasized: "nature tourism has also been identified

Table 23.2 Visitor arrivals to Sabah 1995–2004

Country of origin	1995	1996	1997	1998	1999	2000	2001	2002	2003	2004
(ASEAN)										
Indonesia	28,357	31,467	32,653	91,188	117,424	116,120	120,332	233,857	208,128	290,147
Philippines	17,052	17,374	33,645	44,819	45,740	45,887	42,133	46,897	53,865	51,383
Brunei	11,603	7,762	6,027	9,978	9,625	32,175	42,782	50,274	55,989	72,946
Singapore	12,488	9,845	6,741	7,759	9,085	12,012	12,033	11,415	14,072	14,847
Thailand	738	726	478	439	390	407	517	585	1,500	1,831
(Asia)										
Hong Kong	9,693	6,642	3,775	8,258	12,658	12,182	14,057	12,002	15,133	15,810
Taiwan	26,245	22,958	27,762	57,303	87,540	111,952	94,769	65,506	49,509	78,675
Japan	16,430	14,249	9,614	10,589	9,062	12,124	13,943	25,569	24,500	44,006
China	1,948	1,853	906	1,639	4,195	5,232	8,387	12,505	25,165	49,959
South Korea						5,830	5,507	14,074	24,539	30,117
(Europe)										
UK and Ireland	16,030	14,314	10,840	9,149	13,410	18,544	19,690	18,263	23,883	27,658
Other European countries	12,841	11,916	7,331	6,585	6,931	10,682	10,952	13,820	26,256	40,618
(Oceania)										
Australia and New Zealand	6,883	5,191	4,319	4,661	4,619	5,762	6,178	6,824	22,514	42,281
(America)										
USA	10,187	7,772	9,357	5,683	5,678	11,010	6,076	6,010	8,131	9,382
Canada	3,070	2,812	2,148	2,177	2,937	3,175	4,641	4,456	9,650	9,938
Others	8,671	7,225	4,109	4,671	6,637	5,844	5,012	6,207	6,878	9,938
International	182,236	162,106	159,705	264,898	335,931	408,938	406,009	528,264	569,712	792,308
Malaysian	333,928	279,931	214,105	158,386	148,060	365,537	512,514	579,092	681,742	980,963
Total	516,164	442,037	373,810	423,284	483,991	774,475	918,523	1,107,356	1,251,454	1,773,271

Source: Sabah Tourism Board

for its potential as a supporting approach to sustainable regulation and utilization of natural resources" (*New Sabah Times*, 21 May 1998).

Sabah also has potential for developing cultural tourism on the basis of the ethnic diversity of its population. According to Susie S. Gonsilou (1994), a study by IDS (Institute for Development Studies) in 1990 listed 69 ethnic groups in Sabah compared with 49 in the peninsula and 29 in Sarawak. There is sufficient diversity in the traditional lifestyles and cultural practices of Sabah to enhance cultural tourism in the state through careful development and promotion. However, at present, one must say that the cultural heritage in Sabah has not yet been fully developed for touristic purposes, although a number of dances, songs and crafts have been widely promoted.

Following the IUCN (World Conservation Union) International Ecotourism Consultancy Program, the Malaysian National Ecotourism Plan, Guidelines for Sabah, compiled by the Sabah State Ministry of Tourism Development, Environment, Science and Technology defined ecotourism as

> environmentally responsible travel and visitation to relatively undisturbed natural areas, in order to enjoy and appreciate nature (and any accompanying cultural features, both past and present), that promotes conservation, has low visitor impact and provides for beneficially active socio-economic involvement of local populations.
>
> *(Ministry of Tourism Development, 1999, p. viii)*

One should then understand ecotourism as a component of "sustainable development" that meets the needs of the present without compromising the ability of future generations to meet their own needs. This kind of tourism has developed since the mid-1980s with growing environmental consciousness in the contemporary world. The key issue is therefore how to solve the conflict between development and conservation. This is particularly the case with Sabah where natural resources are central ingredients in its history of development since the nineteenth century. Ecotourism, then, will provide a strategy for development in which development and conservation are pursued at the same time.

On this point, Tengku Datuk Dr. Zainal Adlin, chairman of STPC (Sabah Tourism Promotion Corporation, currently Sabah Tourism Board), stated the following:

> I think that ecotourism has always been our niche that we want to promote, and so far it is growing steadily and positively. Whatever destination we may have, we are very aware that we cannot go beyond our carrying capacity. We have our ecotourism master plan, not only for Malaysia but also particularly for Sabah. Of course we work within the context of the Sabah Tourism Master Plan. Because of it our ecotourism is going very positively and sustainable. We want to do sustainable tourism.
>
> *(Z. Adlin, personal communication, September 2000)*

In this respect, it is interesting that the governmental department of tourism in Sabah is integrated with sections of tourism and environment. In the keynote address to the seminar on nature tourism as a tool for development and conservation held in 1994, the Minister of Tourism and Environmental Development at that time, Y.B. Encik Tham Nyip Shen, pointed out:

> My ministry places a high priority on the need to consider, in the planning process, the environmental fragility of resources such as forests, water, air, coral reefs and soil. The fact that environmental development is one of the twin responsibilities of my ministry puts the

tourism sector under very close scrutiny in this respect. The general approach to development of nature tourism in the State has been to conserve and enhance our renewable natural resource and also to create awareness among tourists of the importance of conserving the fragile environment.

(Chuan, 1994, p. xii)

Since 1966 the State Government of Sabah has created six state parks, including Kinabalu Park, Tunku Abdul Raman Park, Pulau Tiga Park, Croker Range National Park, Turtle Island Park, and Tawau Hill Park within which touristic activities are strictly controlled, and in which tourist facilities blend with the natural surroundings. Among them, Kinabalu Park is the most popular with Mt. Kinabalu, the highest mountain (4,095 meters) in Southeast Asia, which was designated Malaysia's first World Heritage site by UNESCO in 2000. These state parks are then important foci of ecotourism in Sabah. In addition, there are several wildlife sanctuaries on the east coast such as Sepilok Orangutan Rehabilitation Center, Kinabatangan River Basin, and Danum Valley, as well as on off-Sempurna Islands, such as the islands of Sipandan and Mabul, in which tourists enjoy watching wildlife in the tropical rain forests or diving in the coral seas.

The Visit Sabah 2000 project put an emphasis on promoting ecotourism with the theme, "Malaysian Borneo: the New Millennium Nature Adventure Destination," which focused on tropical forests and seas with unique wild animals and plants such as orangutans, the Rafflesia flowers, pitcher plants (*Nepenthes villosa*). Gordon C. Yapp, the marketing manager of STPC, told me that the primary aim of this event was to create tourism awareness in Sabah. With this awareness, ecotourism may belong to, as Chong (1993, p. 3) stated, "a highly specialized segment of tourism…based on people's interest in nature and conservation and their willingness to travel to pursue this interest." As such, ecotourism is an attempt to pursue quality rather than quantity of tourism.

Ecotourists in Sabah

Ecotourists whom I encountered in Sabah in 1999 and 2000 were mostly Westerners, and sometimes Japanese.[10] Although Taiwanese tourists were numerous in Sabah, their participation in ecotourism was very rare. They were typical mass tourists who used group package tours, while enjoying the deluxe resort hotel, eating delicious food, and shopping.

It is interesting to note that tour operators in Sabah specialize in different kinds of tourist markets, which correspond to different types of tourism commodities, according to ethnic lines such as Europeans, Japanese and Taiwanese. Ecotours are popular especially in the European market, which is usually operated by European-oriented tourist agents. Japanese diving tourists may be included in the category of ecotourists, though they regard themselves as "divers" rather than "ecotourists."[11]

In the tourist market, ecotourism is regarded as a special niche for wealthy tourists who come from the rich countries of the North. Indeed the price of ecotours is generally expensive. For example, in 2000 the Borneo Rain Forest Lodge at Danum Valley cost RM350 (US$92) per night plus the entry permit, and Sipadan Water Village Resorts at Mabul Island cost US$380 for the first night and US$100 per night for the following nights, although food and transportation were included. Mowforth and Munt (1998, p. 131) cited a column on ecotourists which includes a profile of a 58-year-old retired World Bank agricultural economist, described as follows:

Meet a member of the new "whoopie" club – wealthy, healthy, older people. Like many ecotourists, they are from the rich industrialized countries, aged between 44 and 64 years of age, and this growing elitist club has "been there and done that." Not for them the packed beaches of the mass tourist resort...These travelers have exhausted traditional destinations and are now in search of original, preferable pristine destinations. As the gap widens between retirement and death, and an ageing population grows, these rich people are destined to make up the core of the future eco-travelers.

In addition, from his research on the ecotourism in Costa Rica the Japanese anthropologist Mitsuho Ikeda (1996) argues that ecotourism is a cultural product of Western middle-class values and ideology toward the natural environment. Therefore, it is a good example of Pierre Bourdieu's conception of the class distinction of taste, because travel, like knowledge of food, wine, arts and music, may assist in differentiating one's sophisticated self from others who lack such knowledge or appreciation (Bourdieu, 1984; Mowforth and Munt, 1998, p.130).

Seen from this point of view, ecotourism becomes a sort of "ideological framing" as discussed by Dean MacCannell (1992, p. 1). Namely, nature for ecotourism is ideologically framed by contemporary environmentalism within which affluent middle-class tourists search for meaning and value in nature. In this sense ecotourism is clearly a socio-cultural production in which nature becomes a form of "symbolic capital" and is staged as a wonderful paradise for a certain type of tourist.

Ecotourism observed

During my research in 1999 and 2000, I engaged in participant observation of ecotours at several places such as the islands of Mabul and Sipandan, Danum Valley, Sukau on the Kinabatangan river basin, and the Sepilok Orangutan Rehabilitation Center. In 2004 I revisited Sukau, Mabul, and Sipandan to follow-up my research. Based on these field observations, we will now consider the cases of Sukau and the Mabul and Sipandan islands.

Wildlife watching tours at Sukau on the Kinabatangan river basin

Along the Kinabatangan river basin there remain tropical rainforests. These forests function as wildlife sanctuaries. The Sukau Rainforest Lodge is located in the Kinabatangan Basin, 15 minutes by boat from Sukau, which is 135 kilometers from Sandakan. The lodge was opened in 1995 by Borneo Eco Tours Company, which has specialized in ecotourism in Borneo since 1991. The lodge is built on stilts using various local hardwood species and is completely self-sufficient in water and power supply, utilizing rain water and solar energy, following the environmental codes of responsible tourism under the Green Globe program of the World Travel and Tourism Council and the Pacific Area Tourism Association (PATA) Green Leaf Program. The company also emphasizes local community participation in running the lodge.

Albert Teo, the managing director of Borneo Eco Tours Company, explained about his involvement in the ecotourism project:

> I think this is a new market in Sabah. So when we started this in 1991, we were basically a pioneer of ecotourism in the region. The word "ecotourism" was just coined then. I did not know exactly what I was involved in. So our project was like learning. Even today we are still learning. We are trying out new theories, new ideas, new concepts and applying it in our local contexts
>
> *(A. Teo, personal communication, September 2000)*

Tourists who participated in the ecotour program were mostly Europeans, usually older couples, and some were Japanese. They went along the Kinabatangan river in motor canoes and enjoyed watching wildlife such as snakes, lizards, hornbills, orangutans, proboscis monkeys, and occasionally elephants (Figure 23.1). In the guest book of the lodge, many of these tourists recorded their experiences. For example:

> Wonderful to stay two nights here far into the jungle of Borneo. This is an unforgettable experience, really something out of the ordinary. So far away from traffic and pollution this truly is a place for relaxation.

> What a wonderful change from life in New York. We saw more monkey than we could count; lots of birds. We enjoyed our river trips, outdoor dining, and just relaxing. Listening to the sounds of life in the rainforest. Hope we can come back and bring our family.

> I hope this center in the forest is the model for the next Millennium.

The Kinabatangan river basin in this way provides tourists with rich tropical fauna and flora to observe, relaxation far away from metropolitan centers, and a sustainable model for the future.

However, seen from the other side, animals were in fact driven into the remaining forests, because the original forests were cut down for logging and then for the planting of oil palms particularly from the 1960s through the 1980s. Actually, seas of oil palm plantations surround the Kinabatangan river basin forests. Looking at the forests in this way, one cannot help feeling that ecotourism is ironically a final form of exploitation of the Sabah's tropical forest. Or one may say that what tourists do under the name of ecotourism is rooted in what Renato Rosaldo

Figure 23.1 Wildlife watching in an ecotour program at Sukau on the Kinabatangan river basin

(1989, Chapter 3) has called "imperialist nostalgia," in which imperialists are missing something that they had destroyed. A further paradox can be observed in that oil palm products from the "artificial" plantation are sold under the catchy rubric of "natural" goods in Japan and elsewhere in the world.

Moreover, as to the principle of local benefits which the ecotourism enterprise emphasizes, in my research in 2000 some villagers in Sukau complained that the lodges, which they regarded as foreign, hired very few local villagers. For eco-lodge managers it is often difficult to get qualified workers from the local society. And it often happens that some locals receive benefits while others do not. It is not easy to adjust an uneven distribution of economic interests which could bring about tensions and conflicts into the local society.

Diving into the coral seas at the islands of Mabul and Sipadan

On the island of Mabul, which is located thirty minutes by boat from Sempurna, I stayed at the Sipadan Water Village Resort.[12] Built in the Bajau style of *kampung air* ("water village," or houses on piles built in the sea), the resort was opened in 1995 as a Japanese–Malaysian joint venture. Tourists were mostly from Japan.[13] In Japan, diving has created a new category of tourism over the last fifteen years or so; Sipadan has become famous among Japanese divers since the early 1990s. Most of the tourists at the Sipadan Water Village were repeat divers who had visited the island several times. Tourists who came from Chiba, the Metropolitan Tokyo area, commented:

> It is wonderful to stay at the Water Village. In the sea I can see various fishes. I have seen their eyes through the camera in the water. That was a fabulous healing experience.

> Commuting in Tokyo is quite stressful. At home we always put on television without watching. Here there are neither commuting trains nor televisions. I like such a life. That is why I come here repeatedly.

As for employees at the Sipadan Water Village, it is interesting to observe that the majority of workers are Filipinos. Ken Pan, the executive director of the resort, commented:

> Sabah is very close to the Philippines. So we have a lot of Filipinos who migrate over here to look for jobs. The main reason we are employing Filipinos is that they speak English, while local people here cannot do so very well. Hopefully in the future, if they can speak English, of course we will try to employ as much local people as possible. But in the meantime, it is imperative for some staffs like the front office, we have them speak English.
>
> *(K. Pan, personal communication, September 2000)*

So it is Filipinos rather than Malaysians who welcome the visitors at this Malaysian resort.[14] Actually, on the island of Mabul there are Filipino settlements with approximately 2,000 people. The "ethnoscape" of the Sipandan Water Village is therefore quite transnational: established as a Japanese–Malaysian joint venture mainly for international tourists serviced by Filipino migrant workers within a Malaysia–Indonesia–Philippines border zone.

Ken Pan further commented on the fish bombing practiced around this area in the 1970s and 1980s:

> So one of the reasons why we set up the resort here was to help our government to stop fish bombing. To educate the local people by saying that fish bombing

destroys the corals and the future of the region. We are then giving them alternate jobs.

(K. Pan, personal communication, September 2000)

If the fishermen stopped fish bombing because of ecotourism, it could be considered to have had a positive result for the local environment. But I witnessed fish bombing at places not far away. There is also the fact that Sipadan, 30 minutes by boat from Mabul, seems to be going beyond its "carrying capacity." The island is quite environmentally fragile because it is so tiny that it takes only ten minutes to walk round it. Therefore, the state government had to introduce regulations restricting the number of visitors and tourist operators on the island, and banned overnight staying from January 2005.

Furthermore, in April 2000, a shocking incident took place in which an armed Filipino Muslim group led by Abu Sayyaf, said to be related to the terrorist group Al Quaeda, captured 21 people, including 10 Western tourists, on the island of Sipadan and took them hostage to the island of Jolo, in the southern Philippines. In September 2000, the Abu Sayyaf group struck again on another island, Pandanan, and three Malaysian resort workers were kidnapped. These terrorist attacks break the peaceful dream of ecotourism and remind us of another reality of the current world system.

Homestay program: a possibility of community-based ecotourism

As mentioned earlier, ecotourism practiced in Sabah does not necessarily satisfy the local community. This is because the players involved are basically outsiders such as government officials and travel agents based in the capital city. The local people feel that they only offer the place without gaining profits. In this respect, the homestay program may be an interesting device for promoting the profits for local communities.

The homestay program is a program introduced in Sabah in 2002 by the Ministry of Tourism, Environment, Science and Technology. To join the program, the community must meet government requirements on cooking food and hygienic conditions. According to Sabah Homestay Directory 2002, 15 homestays from 10 regions joined the program.

In 2002 and 2004, I visited several homestays which joined this program such as Koposizon Homestay at Papar, Misompuru Homestay at the Rungus community near Kudat, Tambunan Village Homestay at Tambunan, and Miso Walai Homestay at Batu Puteh on the Kinabatangan river basin. In the following, I will concentrate on Batu Puteh Misowalai Homestay program, which was considered to be the most successful case.

Batu Puteh Village is located at the intersection of the Kinabatangan river and the road to Laha Datu, about three hours' drive from Sandakan. It is a village of *Orang Sungai* (the "River People"). *Miso Walai* means "one house" in Sungai language which symbolizes the "spirit of local culture and homeliness that will be shared by all who visited the area."[15] The local newspaper reports: "Homestay creates bond between tourists and host families that tears are shed when it comes to departure" (*The Borneo Post*, 23 November 2003).

In the homestay program, tourists can participate in village life and access nature and the culture of the local community. The website of Miso Walai Homestay mentioned "Do's and Don'ts in the village" about dress and actions so that tourists could share some of the local lifestyle. Activity programs included river cruises, cultural performances, jungle trekking, handicraft making, paddy planting, farming, and wedding ceremonies. The villagers who participate in the homestay program provide rooms and food. In 2002, there were about

40 rooms provided by 21 supporter families. It cost RM40 (US$11 in 2002) per night, which included three meals. If you join the activity programs such as the river cruise or the jungle trekking in the village forest, you pay additional fees.

The organization called MESCOT (Model Ecologically Sustainable Community Tourism) manages the Miso Walai homestay program. About 30 volunteer villagers are involved in this organization. It was established in 1997 for promoting the local tourism development with the financial support of WWF (World Wide Fund for Nature) Malaysia branch, but since 2003 it has become integrated in a newly established organization called "Kooperasi Pelancongan Miso Walai Homestay," or Miso Walai Homestay Tourism Cooperation.

According to Mohd. Hasim Abd. Hamid (personal communication, September 2004), chairman of the organization, they accepted 425 visitors in 2002, and 530 visitors in 2003, some 40–50 visitors per month on average. Homestayers spent two or three nights. The organization received RM73,850 in 2002 and RM110,383 in 2003, which included not only homestay lodgings but also boat services and others. They plan to build an "eco-camp" in the village in the near future.

In general, the homestay programs in Sabah still lack in basic marketing planning skills and therefore many tour operators doubt the homestay products. However, as the case of Miso Walai Homestay shows, it is an interesting attempt to develop community-based ecotourism by the local people themselves for their own benefit.

Conclusion

In my field research in Sabah in 1999–2004, there were two unforgettable scenes of the tourist-scapes. One is a scene at Sukau in September 1999. I was on a boat trip along the Kinabatangan river watching wildlife in the forests. At a certain bend in the river, the oil palm plantation suddenly came into view beyond the thin part of the forest. At that moment I got the feeling of coming out of a dream of the magical tour into the real world. The rainforest reservation area occupies only 5 percent of the total area of Sabah, so ecotourism may be just a symbolic activity to satisfy the ideology of environmentalism. In reality the thin forests that remain along the Kinabatangan river are surrounded by seas of oil palm plantations.

The other scene is a Malaysian Army helicopter at the heliport of the Sipadan Water Village Resort on Mabul island when I revisited in August 2004. With its roaring sound the helicopter was about to take off to scout the "pirate-terrorists" who were haunting this international border zone. As mentioned, terrorist attacks on the tourist resorts have occurred several times since April 2000. This ecotourist paradise is now guarded by the Army to keep the peace.

There are two fundamental problems: economic development and environmental preservation on the one hand, and terrorism and peace on the other. In these problems one could see the microcosm of a contemporary world. It is in this contradictory microcosm that the Sabah Government and tour operators stage ecotourism sometimes by using foreign capital and foreign guest workers. Tourists come from the rich countries of the North. Through their participation in ecotourism, they may contribute to the preservation of Sabah's valuable natural heritage. However, it is they who consumed and destroyed the rainforests in the past. Furthermore, they could be potential targets of terrorist attacks in the politics of terrorism. Global touristscapes in Sabah are thus made up by various players in a complex way.

It is clear that ecotourism is important for Sabah's sustainable development strategy in which a subtle balance between nature and people, and between development and sustainability, must be maintained. However, in reality, as we have seen, irony is the word which characterizes the ecotourism practice and global touristscapes in Sabah. It is urgent, then, to go further so that we could improve the system of "working with", in which the players of ecotourism – government, tourism industry, tourists, local people and outsider analysts[16] – can together contribute to the solution of these complex problems. The community-based ecotourism in the homestay program may indicate a possibility in this direction if it develops successfully.

Notes

1 World Tourism Organization website: http://www.unwto.org.

2 The Ministry changed its name to the Ministry of Tourism Development, Environment, Science and Technology, and then to the current Ministry of Tourism, Culture and Environment.

3 The research was carried out as part of the project "Socio-Cultural Process of Development: Sabah and BIMP-EAGA (Brunei, Indonesia, Malaysia, Philippines – East ASEAN Growth Area)." Organized by Professor Kôji Miyazaki of Research Institute for Languages and Cultures of Asia and Africa, Tokyo University of Foreign Studies, the project was carried out from 1999 to 2004 with the financial support of a grant-in-aid for scientific research by the Japanese Ministry of Education, Culture, Sports, Science and Technology (later by the Japan Society of the Promotion of Science) in cooperation with Institute for Development Studies (IDS), Kota Kinabalu, Sabah, Malaysia. The field research was done during the terms of September–October 1999, September–October 2000, August–September 2001, September–October 2002, March 2004, and August–September 2004. I have already published part of the result of the research in my earlier works in English (Yamashita 2009a: 194–198) and in Japanese (Yamashita 2009b: 97–120).

4 In this chapter I use basically the statistical data at the time when I carried out my research in Sabah, namely the year of 2004. According to later data, international tourist arrivals in Malaysia in 2011 increased to 24.77 million with RM58.3 billion receipt. See Tourism Malaysia website: http://www.tourism.gov.my

5 Source: Sabah Tourism Board and Immigration Department, Sarawak.

6 According to the latest statistical data available now, the number of visitors to Sabah increased to 2.84 million in 2011, which included 846,000 international visitors. See Sabah Tourism Board website: http://www.sabahtourism.com.

7 They may come as tourists and remain as illegal guest workers. In 1997 it was estimated that of Sabah's total population of 2,663,800, about 30 percent (784,100) were non-Malaysian immigrants, including approximately 410,000 illegal immigrants – 290,000 Indonesians and 120,000 Filipinos (Kurus, 1998), and half of them were illegal.

8 In 2011 Taiwanese tourists numbered 52,000. Their share of the international tourist market became smaller in recent years. See http://www.sabahtourism.com/corporate/visitor-arrival-statistics/.

9 In Sabah, terms of "ecotourism" and "nature tourism" are often used interchangeably, though some people prefer "nature tourism" to "ecotourism," saying that "ecotourism" is an ambiguous term without clear definition.

10 Calculating from Sabah Tourism Board statistical figures in 2004, Japanese and Western tourists (from Japan, Australia, New Zealand, Europe, USA. and Canada) had a 22 percent share of Sabah's total international tourism market (see Table 23.2, p 363). As the share of ecotourism in the tourism market in the world is said to be around 10 percent, this is not necessarily small. Albert Teo, the managing director of Borneo Eco Tours Company, explains that there may be no tour operators who deal 100 percent with ecotours; it is a matter of degree, 80 percent or 30 percent for ecotours.

11 Japanese tourist industry is reluctant to adopt the word "ecotourism," saying that in Japan it is regarded as a special tour to the unexploited areas without sufficient marketable demand. So they usually use the term "nature" tourism, though "ecotourism" is becoming popular as well.

12 The resort uses the name of "Sipadan," although it is not located on Sipadan but on Mabul Island, because Sipadan is a well-known diving spot.

13 When I revisited Mabul in August 2004, however, the situation had changed. The numbers of Japanese tourists had decreased and Italian tourists had become more numerous. There were also tourists from Singapore and west Malaysia.

14 When I went back in August 2004, however, I found that the numbers of Filipino workers had decreased, and there were more Malaysian. This was due to the recent change of Sabah's immigration policy, which made it more difficult for employers to hire foreign workers.

15 Miso Wala: Homestay website: http://www.misowalai.com.my/do.html accessed in August 2002. The current website (integrated in MESCOT Initiative) is http://www.misowalaihomestay.com/ (accessed 24 November 2011).

16 The Japanese Society of Ecotourism calls these five players of ecotourism "pentagon of ecotourism" which collaborate together to realize an ideal ecotourism.

References

Appadurai, A. (1997) *Modernity at large: Cultural dimensions of globalization*. London: University of Minneapolis Press

Bourdieu, P. (1984) *Distinction: A social critique of the judgment of taste* (trans. R. Nice). Cambridge, MA: Harvard University Press

Chong, V. T. (1993) 'Ecotourism: Sabah's niche in the worldwide travel and leisure market'. *Berita IDS*, 8(5), 3–5

Chuan, T. T. (ed.) (1994) *Issues and challenges in developing nature tourism in Sabah*. Kota Kinabalu: The Institute of Development Studies

Chuan, T. T. and Arroyo, C. (1988) 'Towards perpetuating Sabah's forest resources'. *Berita IDS*, 3(4), 2–4

Gonsilou, S. S. (1994) 'Incorporating cultural elements in tourism development'. *Berita IDS*, 9(4), 4–9

Ikeda, M. (1996) 'Kosutarika no Eko-tsûrizumu' (Ecotourism in Costa Rica). In S. Yamashita (ed.) *Idô no Minzokushi* (Ethnography of transnational migration). Tokyo: Iwanamishoten, pp. 61–93

King, V. (1993) 'Tourism and culture in Malaysia'. In M. Hitchcock, V. King and M. Parnwell (eds) *Tourism in South-East Asia*. London: Routledge, pp. 99–116

Kurus, B. (1998) 'Migrant labour flows in the East ASEAN'. *Borneo Review*, 9(2), 156–84

MacCannell, D. (1992) *Empty meeting grounds: The tourist papers*. London: Routledge

Ministry of Tourism Development (1999) *Plan ekopelancongan kebangsaan Malaysia: Garis Panduan untuk Negreri Sabah (The Malaysian national ecotourism plan: Guidelines for Sabah)*. Kota Kinabalu: Ministry of Tourism Development, Environment, Science and Technology

Mowforth, M. and Munt, I. (1998) *Tourism and sustainability*. London: Routledge

Rosaldo, R. (1989) *Culture and truth: The remaking of social analysis*. Boston, MA: Beacon Press

Sabah State Government (1996) *Sabah tourism master plan*. Kota Kinabalu: Sabah State Government

Sabah Tourism Board (2005) *Visitor arrivals and international visitor profile statistics: Visitor arrivals January–December 2004*. Kota Kinabalu: Sabah Tourism Board

Yamashita, Shinji (2009a) 'Southeast Asian tourism from a Japanese perspective'. In M. Hitchcock, V. King and M. Parnwell (eds) *Tourism in Southeast Asia: Challenges and new directions*. Copenhagen: Nias Press, pp. 189–205.

—— (2009b) *Kankô jinruigaku no chôsen: 'Atarashii chikyû' no ikikata (Challenges for the anthropology of tourism: Transnational lives on the 'new globe')*. Tokyo: Kodansha, pp. 97–120

24

Tourism in post-socialist countries of south-eastern Europe

Trends and challenges

Anton Gosar

Introduction

The purpose of this chapter is to elaborate on changes that impacted the tourism sector of the so-called 'transitional economies' of south-eastern Europe since the fall of the Berlin Wall. Three factors are to be considered: the political and economic transition from communism/socialism to democracy and market economy; the dramatic developments as the violent disintegration of Yugoslavia impacted on the infrastructure at large; and the change of the European political map due to the European Union's enlargement and creation of new nation states. Several political and military events and economic turning points were linked to the reduction or increase of tourist visits. New national strategies of the states' economic sectors are briefly discussed and elaborated in detail, using the example of the new state of Croatia.

Westerners' attention was focused on the post-socialist transition from around 1990, as communism started to fade away. Ian Jefries' (1993) discussion focused on the generalities of the transition in the post-soviet republics and the former communist countries of east-central Europe; very limited interest was shown for the instable south-eastern Europe, in particular the western Balkans. Williams and Balaz (2001) switched from Jefries' country-by-country general analyses to the discussion of problems of several sectors of the economy – in their case tourism, retailing and consumption. By covering a variety of aspects in human geography, Turnock (2002) on this issue is more complex. Tourism is viewed as a major economic tool to be used in development. Again, the lack of discussion of the progress of the tourism economy in the area of former Yugoslavia is more than evident. The ongoing wars might have been the reason. Instability, violence and wars have made ways in tourism literature much earlier. But, aspects of security and instability related to tourism are recently again in the foreground of public interest (Mansfeld and Pizam, 2005). Vukonić's (1997) book on *Tourism in the Whirlwind of War* was an excellent prelude to this exceptional book. In the next chapter we will follow Vukonić's discussion by empirically analysing the effects of the military confrontation on the territory of former Yugoslavia ('Balkan wars') on tourism in Serbia and Montenegro.

Based on measurements of visitor arrivals, tourism amenities and receipts, south-eastern Europe was and is, as a tourist destination, lagging behind western Mediterranean destinations. With 35 million visitors per year, 110 million bed-nights and 1.6 million tourist beds available, the region could not compare with such giants as France, Spain or Italy. Neighbouring Italy alone registers twice as many visitors, has close to 150 million bed-nights and has more tourist beds to offer than all the nation states of south-eastern Europe together. In 2004, Greece was the leading tourist destination of the region (14 million visitors, 45 million bed-nights), followed by Croatia (8m, 43m), Bulgaria (5m, 7m) and Romania (4m, 8m). Comparing accumulated tourist bed-nights and the nation state population, Croatia is leading (9.5), followed by Greece (4.3) and Slovenia (2.1) (Table 24.1).

With the exception of Greece, countries of the region have, since the Second World War and up to the fall of the Iron Curtain in 1989, experienced communist rule and centrally planned economies, the 'socialist economy'. Despite the named 'prerequisites', the Mediterranean area of Yugoslavia was in the 1980s listed among the five most-visited European destinations. The coasts of the former Yugoslav provinces (republics) Slovenia, Croatia and Montenegro have observed growth similar to Spain's. That progress came to a halt with the disintegration of Yugoslavia. In 1991/2, ethnic violence erupted in Yugoslavia, as several republics declared independence. The subsequent military confrontations minimized and/or hindered international arrivals. What had been one of the world leaders in tourism found its tourist industry struggling. In the aftermath of the confrontations, sovereign nation states Bosnia-Herzegovina, Croatia, Macedonia, Serbia, Montenegro and Slovenia made their entry on the global tourist market. Emerging new countries had to struggle with the destination recognition at first. Croatia in particular managed its promotion well. In 2005 Croatia (again) became the most desired destination of the German tourist market. Bulgaria, Romania and Albania experienced the

Table 24.1 South-eastern Europe: international inbound tourism (in 000s)

Year Country	1968 Visitors	1978 Visitors	1988 Visitors	1992 Visitors	1996 Visitors	2000 Visitors	2004 Visitors	2004 Bed-nights	2004 Tourism Index**
Albania[+]	–	–	–	111	119	317	383	1034	0.32
Bosnia and Herzegovina	170	250	394	1	99	171	153	392	0.11
Bulgaria[+]	1783	4570	7594	1322	2980	2785	5563	7055	0.88
Croatia	2083	3853	5621	1271	2649	5831	7912	42516	9.52
Greece[+]	879	3961	7564	9331	9233	13096	14308	45376	4.27
Macedonia	94	215	221	219	136	224	216	778	0.38
Romania[+]	1451	3685	5142	3798	2834	3274	4793	8010	0.36
Slovenia	678	877	1137	616	832	1090	1484	3833	2.05
Serbia & Montenegro	718	1190	1272	156	301	239	481	1650	0.21
SE Europe	7856	18601	28945	16825	19183	27027	35293	110644	1.66

+ = including one-day visitors
** = Tourists' Bed-nights vs. Population, 2004
Source: Savezni Zavod Za Statistiku (1971), UNWTO (1981, 1991, 1999, 2005b)

effects of the transition from the 'socialist' to market economy simultaneously. Where peace and democracy, together with a market economy, were soon established, current tourist arrivals are already comparable to their best in history. Progress has been made in each of these countries, with Slovenia and Croatia being in the forefront of a successful transition.

South-eastern Europe: geography, economy and politics

South-eastern Europe is one of eight major economic regions of Europe. The size of the region (766,000 sq. km) is comparable to the seven other European regions; population-wise (65 million inhabitants) the area is below European average, with a density of only 85 inhabitants per sq. kilometre (Table 24.2). Geographically the region is the south-easterly periphery of Europe and next to the continent's land bridge to Asia, to the Near and Middle East. The tourist attractions of the area are related predominantly to the Mediterranean climate/geomorphology (the Black Sea, the Aegean Sea, the Adriatic Sea) and the heritage of Western culture (Greece). The abundance of cultural, ethnic and religious wealth in the rough Mediterranean hinterland (with its karstic alpine ridge, and the mineral rich Carpathian/Balkan mountains) are the result of a constant struggle of world powers to control the area. The term 'shatter belt' is used in political circles to identify the troubled past and present of the region. The iconographies of the Orthodox and Catholic Christian religions are enriched by the presence of the only autochthonous Islamic community in Europe: the Bosnians. Two nation states of the area, Greece and Slovenia, are members of the European Union; Croatia is joining in 2013. With regard to economic characteristics, the majority of the countries of south-eastern Europe are not aligned with most demographic and economic indicators of the European Union. The GDP per capita (US$4,000) is on average 5 times lower than the EU average; the GDP per capita of Bosnia-Herzegovina (US$1,310), the least-developed nation state of the area,

Table 24.2 The basic economic geography of south-eastern Europe, 2002

COUNTRY	SIZE/POPULATION (in km²/in 000 inh.)	POPULATION Years: 15–65+ (in %)	GDP (per capita in US$)	CO₂ Emissions (per capita in Tons)
ALBANIA	28.748/3.150	28/7	1.450	0.9
BOSNA-HERZEGOVINA	51.129/4.112	17/10	1.310	4.8
BULGARIA	110.994/7.965	15/16	1.770	5.2
CROATIA	56.542/4.465	16/15	4.540	4.4
GREECE (EU)	131.957/10.631	15/19	11.660	8.5
MACEDONIA	25.713/2.038	22/10	1.710	5.5
ROMANIA	238.391/22.300	17/14	1.870	3.8
SERBIA-MONTENEGRO	102.173/8.160	26/18	1.400	–
SLOVENIA (EU)	20.253/1.964	15/15	10.370	7.3
SE Europe	765.900/64.785	19/14	4.009	5.1
EU – 25	4.000.900/454.800	17/16	21.270	8.5

Source: von Baratta et al. (2005)

is, due to its recent tragic past, 16 times below. On another scale, the population figures for young people in Albania is 4 times larger than those for the older generation, Albania being therewith the most 'reproductive' nation state of Europe. The same country produces almost no CO_2 emissions (0.9 per cent); total CO_2 emissions of the region, another indicator of development, are just two-thirds of the EU average.

The general political and economic setting of south-eastern Europe, where ethnic disputes in its core (Yugoslavia) lasted through the last decade of the twentieth century, and where the transition from communism to democracy has been slow, the 1990s were characterized by the hindrance of traffic, forced migration, limits to the free flow of people and goods and slow economic development, even downfall, in particular in the tourism sector (except in Greece). The examples of Serbia and Montenegro are typical. There, international visits had fallen from above 2 million tourists to just a couple of hundred thousand a year. After democratic and economic reforms in 2002 the arrivals have jumped to a half a million (Table 24.3). All of these processes have had a negative effect – in the short run (1991–5) – on Greek tourism

Table 24.3 Serbia and Montenegro: tourists* and the instability/stability factors**

YEAR	Tourists*	INSTABILITY CAUSES AND RESOLUTIONS IN THE REGION OF WESTERN BALKANS**
1988	2,549.000	Serbian nationalistic agitation for a unified Yugoslavia. Slobodan Milošević gaining power.
1989	2,372.000	The Fall of the Berlin Wall (November 9).
1990	2,093.000	Start of the rebellion of Serbs in the Croatian Krajina Province.
		Yugoslavia – end of communism: free elections in Slovenia and Croatia.
1991	954.000	Declaration of independence by Slovenia and Croatia (June 25th). Subsequent wars.
		The Brioni Agreement (July 7th): Slovenia and Yugoslavia (Serbia & Montenegro) agreed on terms of Slovenian independence.
		Declaration of independence of Macedonia (September 8th). Internationally recognized (Greece) as FYRM – Former Yugoslav Republic of Macedonia,
1992	156.000	Declaration of independence by Bosnia & Herzegovina (January 9th). Subsequent war.
1993	276.000	
1994	247.000	
1995	228.000	The Bosnian Srebrenica massacre – committed by Serbs on Muslims (July 11th).
		Croatia gaining territorial sovereignty by military action (August, 4–21). War in Bosnia-Herzegovina died out.
		The Dayton Peace Treaty (November 21th): Bosnia & Herzegovina established as two-entity nation-state.
1996	301.000	
1997	298.000	Soldiers of the UN initiated ALBA (Dawn) mission arrived in Albania (April 15–August 12) to make ground for free elections and democracy.

Table 24.3 (*Continued*)

YEAR	Tourists*	INSTABILITY CAUSES AND RESOLUTIONS IN THE REGION OF WESTERN BALKANS**
1999	152.000	NATO bombing campaign on Serbia & Montenegro (March–May).
		The Kumanovo Accords (June 10th): Serbia & Montenegro agrees on peace terms for Kosovo Province.
2000	239.000	Democratically elected government of Serbia and Montenegro (October 5th).
2001	367.000	Former president Slobodan Milošević being extradited to the United Nations War Crime Tribunal in The Hague (June 28th).
		Privatization Law (July 1st).
2002	448.000	
2003	481.000	Assassination of Serbian Prime Minister Zoran Djindjic (March 12th).
		Serbia & Montenegro - Croatia: Agreement on borders, border regimes and border crossings (December 10th).
2004	577.000	

* no. of foreign visitors.
** major political and other events which have caused violence, wars and general instability along with major positive developments to stabilize the region.
Source: Savezni Zavod Za Statistiku (1992, 2004), von Baratta et al. (2005)

as well. Greece has experienced since 1996 a constant increase of tourist visits (+6.8 per cent yearly).

Tourism in south-eastern Europe

In the context of the twenty-first century's double-digit world tourism revival, south-eastern Europe reports relatively equally good results. The yearly increase of arrivals by 10.1 per cent, since 2000, is considerable higher than in the rest of Europe where it grew by 4 per cent. This is driven in particular by the comparatively solid performance of Croatia (+22.5 per cent), Slovenia (+8.2 per cent) and Greece (+6.9 per cent). The emerging of 10 new EU members in 2004, as well as the EU's inclusion of Bulgaria and Romania in 2007, determined positive growth rates in all major warm sea destinations of the region (Table 24.3). The yearly improvement of tourism receipts has been, since 2000, particularly high in countries where major events took place, such as Greece (+6.7 per cent), and where the previous incomes of the tourist industry were low: Albania (+21.1 per cent), Romania (+18.1 per cent), Bulgaria (+17.9 per cent) and Serbia Montenegro (+7.4 per cent). The expansion of low-cost airlines has encouraged intra-regional tourism in traditional (Greece) and emerging destinations (Slovenia, Croatia), replacing the charter airlines spectrum of flights, as they still dominate in other transitional countries of the area. The EU enlargement was a factor to consider in 2004, as curious Western tourists have overrun capital cities of new member states. The switch to the euro in 2000 made tourism services in most EU countries (Greece) more expensive. The transitional economies enjoyed the competitive price factor of still being outside the eurozone and remaining emerging economies. The overall tourism development is gaining also due to improved infrastructure and educated human resources (UNWTO, 2005a).

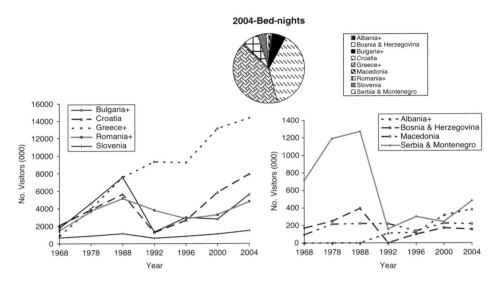

Figure 24.1   South-eastern Europe: bed-nights, 1968–2004

On average, tourism receipts are small in comparison to Western destinations. In 2002 countries of the region reported to UNWTO the following income from tourism (in million US$):

- Albania US$487.0 (11.0 per cent of GNP);
- Bosnia-Herzegovina, US$111.0 (2.1 per cent);
- Bulgaria, US$1,344.0 (9.5 per cent);
- Croatia, US$3,811.0 (18.8 per cent);
- Greece, US$9,741.0 (7.9 per cent);
- FRY Macedonia, US$96.0 (1.9 per cent);
- Romania, US$ 612.0 (1.5 per cent);
- Serbia and Montenegro, US$77.0 (0.7 per cent);
- Slovenia: US$1,083.0 (5.5 per cent).

The income made by the tourist industry is noticeable in summer holiday destinations, such as the Greek Aegean Islands, or in Croatian Istria and Dalmatia– as they make over 25 per cent of the respective provinces' GNP (UNWTO, 2005b).

Western Europe is the tourism generating area of the region, with Germany providing the greatest number of tourists. With the exception of the less-developed tourist destinations of Albania, Bosnia-Herzegovina, Macedonia and Serbia–Montenegro, German-speaking tourists dominate the region. Italians, too, are numerous in particular in Albania, Croatia, Romania, Greece and Slovenia, whereas Austrian and Slovenian citizens continue to visit the northern Adriatic (Croatia). The once numerous Dutch and Scandinavian tourists too are cautiously returning (Jordan, 2000). Croatia tries hard to attract potential visitors on the British and American tourist markets. Greek citizens have recently discovered the attractions of their northern neighbours, Albania (7.9 per cent Greek visitors) and Macedonia (11.1 per cent

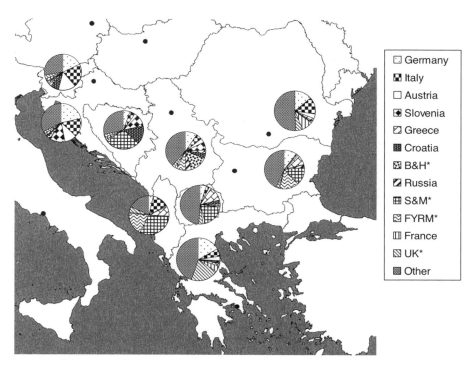

Figure 24.2 South-eastern Europe: tourism generating countries

Greek visitors), whereas Albanians make 7.4 per cent of Greek and Macedonian arrivals in 2002 (Figure 24.2).

Regarding accommodation amenities available, two diverse trends come to the foreground. A reduction of the overall number of beds in hotels, motels and bed-and-breakfast establishments and an increase of higher-quality establishments, as international hotel chains have made investments into strategically important tourist amenities. The decline of the number of tourist amenities was experienced in the first half of the 1990s in particular, as the bed-capacity in hotels and similar establishments was reduced by 24.3 per cent. The most troubled south-eastern Europe tourist destination Bosnia-Herzegovina is in this negative regard ahead (−75.3 per cent; −35,261 beds), but in Croatia too capacities have been reduced by almost two-thirds (−62.3 per cent) and a reduction of 318,000 beds. Romania, Bulgaria, Albania and Macedonia have in general kept their share and number of beds and are now increasing other amenities. The stagnation or reduction of accommodation amenities is not exclusively a result of the lack of regional security and the unstable political situation (in Croatia expelled nationals took refuge in hotels), but also results from the transition from the centrally planned socialist economy to Western market economy. As a typical case one could name Slovenia (where no substantial instability was registered), but the number of beds have been reduced by 15,526 units (31 per cent). Many units, owned previously by hotel enterprises, have turned into privately owned leisure-apartments. Greece, a country with an established democracy and market economy, can be found on the other side of the spectrum. Between 1988 and 2002, Greece increased the size of its tourist accommodation capacity by almost 53 per cent (Figure 24.3).

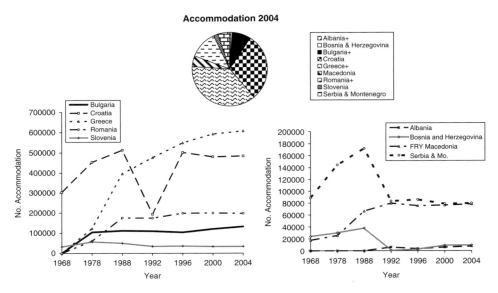

Figure 24.3 South-eastern Europe: accommodation in tourist establishments, 1968–2004

If the overall picture of the transition has to be understood, different nation states' privatization concepts have to be taken into consideration. State-owned leisure establishments (dachas) and social leisure housing units have often switched to individual foreign and domestic elites. The new governments of south-eastern Europe's transitional nation states saw a welcome source of income in the gaming and gambling industry as well. In 2004 all but one country (Albania) had casinos in operation. Leading in the number of casino operators is Croatia (45), followed by Slovenia (18), Romania (15) and Serbia and Montenegro (14). On the lower end of this sector of the tourism industry is Bulgaria (10), Greece (9), Macedonia (7) and Bosnia-Herzegovina (1), whereas Albania is in the process of issuing 5 gambling permits in 2005. Most of the casinos are located in capital cities (Bucharest, Zagreb: 12; Belgrade: 8; Sofia: 6; see Figure 24.1). Some casino enterprises in Greece, Slovenia and Serbia-Montenegro (including Kosovo) have organized online gambling as well. In accordance with the EU directives these activities must be banned from further operation by 2005 ('Casino City, n.d.').

Since a market economy was introduced in the tourism sector of south-eastern Europe, on average a decade and a half ago, countries of the region have gone through a whirlwind of change, the result of the regional instability and the transition itself. Many outcomes of these processes are not finished yet, some have successfully been concluded and the tourism industry in respective countries has been adapted to Western standards. The following transitional problems were recognized:

• The transition vent with diverse pace legally and 'sort of legally' towards its goal, namely towards accommodating single nation state's economy to Western standards. The denationalization and reprivatization processes have in 2005 not come to a conclusion yet. In particular in Bulgaria, Romania and the many new and old nation states of the western Balkans.

- Restructuring of ownership and organization of tourist enterprises is still in progress in all countries of the region, except for Greece. Institutions and enterprises providing services in tourism have grown tremendously. The once single nation state's tourism agency, which managed and controlled the complex tourism sector of the economy, was replaced by numerous spatially and functionally diverse actors. The interaction among them does not function well. A state-wide electronic reservation system, meant to serve individual customers, is years away. Competition is felt in a limited way: as prices, drawn by the market economy, become competitive, the variety of services is missing as all players focus on similar products.

- Private and corporate ownership of amenities in tourism has grown in an anarchic, regionally diverse and unpredictable way. Travel agencies, hotels and other players of the tourism economy show ownership of diverse players on the regional, national and global scale of economies. Along with specialized tourism businesses, banks, insurance agencies and other financial institutions, oil and gas providers, supermarket chains, pharmaceutical firms, publishing houses, trade enterprises etc. own shares in this sector.

- Foreign investors have, with the exception of Slovenia, become a major player. Transnational banks, international hotel chains and travel agencies and other non-local corporations (airlines) own a large number of once state-owned tourist enterprises. Major urban hotel structures, built and maintained during the times of communism, have become, due to their strategic positions, foreign or corporate owned. The once socialist, 'workers-owned' well-fare tourism amenities have become profit-oriented enterprises.

- A real estate and a stock market came into existence. Islands went up for sale, the number and localities of tourist amenities in pristine environments have grown. Elite and middle-class alike purchased, to their wealth alike, suitable Mediterranean leisure amenities.

- New types of tourism amenities and services were invented and/or copied, older amenities have been improved. The western-type leisure forms have become popular (theme-parks, watering places, adrenalin rush activities). Along borders and in major cities, gaming and gambling took place. New health and wellness (tropical image) as well as sport and country clubs (golf) took its form.

- Former national, regional and local tourism strategies have been abandoned, in some states new have been invented. But in several transitional countries of south-eastern Europe no binding rules or strategies are/were in place. Corruption has therefore had, at least for a limited time, a major say in the development of the tourism and catering sector of the economy.

The geographic characteristics of tourism flows show a recent increase of the regional exchange of tourist visits. As this trend is growing, the share of tourists from once heavily participating areas of Europe has been reduced in relative but not absolute terms. A reverse trend has been registered since 2002 in Croatia. Indeed, Germans and other Central Europeans are (slowly) returning to the area, but the once extreme popularity of South-eastern Europe in Britain, Holland and Sweden has generally vanished. Greece must be excluded from this remark. According to WTO data, the following geographic zones of regional and of continental interactions can be identified:

- The 3 regionally interrelated circles: increased tourism exchange between nation states on the territory of former Yugoslavia; within the Danubian and the Alpen–Adria region

(Austria, Italy, Slovakia, Hungary, Romania, Croatia and Slovenia); within the area of the southern Balkans (Bulgaria, Macedonia, Greece and Albania);

- The traditional tourism generating circle of Western Europe: Germany, Netherlands, Great Britain and, recently, France;
- The potential tourism generating countries of North and East-Central Europe: countries: the Czech Republic, Poland, Lithuania, Latvia, Estonia, Russia.

Case study: Croatia – strengthening the image and dealing with new challenges

In the year 1990, Yugoslavia realized 88 million bed-nights, of which 43 million were foreign and 45 million domestic. The republic of Croatia, the Mediterranean province of the multi-ethnic state, achieved 52 million bed-nights (34 million foreign, 18 million domestic). Croatia registered almost 60 per cent of the entire tourist turnover of the country, that is, 79 per cent of foreign and 41 per cent of domestic tourist visits. Up until the 1960s, Croatia's visitors were primarily domestic guests. Domestic tourism was encouraged through social policies of the communistic government and the centrally planned economy of the state (five-year develop-ment programmes), which has had, up until the 1970s, closed or semi-open borders. Yugoslav citizens have realized 40 per cent of arrivals and 47 per cent of bed-nights in the province (republic). Tourists with residency within Croatia made one third of the total (33 per cent of arrivals and 30 per cent of bed-nights). At the beginning of the 1960s foreign tourists joined in at a somewhat lower rate (27 per cent of arrivals and 22 per cent bed-nights). With the unrestricted opening of borders (Yugoslav citizens could freely exit/enter the country), changed foreign policy (Yugoslavia became a founding member of the Unallied Movement) and with the increased economic links to the west (Germany), a turnover regarding visits to the Mediterranean Adriatic coast took place. In the following two decades foreign visitors to Croatia made up to 55 per cent of all visits and close to two-thirds of all bed-nights in Croatian resorts. Out of close to 70 million bed-nights, at the peak of visits in 1988, Yugoslav citizens made around 22 million. Citizens of Yugoslavia, residing outside of Croatia, made close to one-third (31 per cent) of 'domestic bed-nights'. Croatia was the primary tourist destination for residents of Slovenia (42 per cent) and Bosnia-Herzegovina (51 per cent). The Serbs preferred the Montenegrin Adriatic coast (just 24 per cent in Croatia) (Pirjevec, 1985). Compared to traditional patterns of international visitors, the length of stay of domestic guests was a mere two-thirds of theirs. Foreign visitors preferred to stay on average 7.1 days (in 1985), whereas Croats spent an average of 4.9 days at their beloved resorts.

As the Yugoslav political situation deteriorated in the 1990s, international as well as in-state tourism shrunk in terms of numbers and length of stay. Disregarding the worst years (1991–4), as military conflicts flared up near most of Croatian Mediterranean resort towns, except in Istria, the situation regarding visits and bed-nights was less than 10 per cent of the previous decade's peak. In 1995, Dalmatia, being close to battlefields, was visited almost exclusively by Croat nationals (72 per cent). Istria, being well distant, registered 84 per cent and the Kvarner Bay tourist area 68 per cent international visits. As the sovereign Croatian nation state in early August regained control over its territory, tourist arrivals were a mere 25.8 per cent of the previous decade; Croats themselves showed a drop of 37.2 per cent, whereas international visitors were down by 82.2 per cent. The length of stay reduced to just 3.9 days for domestic and to 5.7 days for international visitors (Radnić and Ivandić, 1999). Tourism did not regain strength until early in the new millennium. The post-war economic consolidation became complex as different facets of the transition from 'socialism' to 'capitalism' were added. It is not the intention of this chapter to elaborate on several 'strange' privatization deals and over-takings by domestic/international private and public institutions (Jordan, 2000). In 2004 Croatia's tourism was still about 10 per cent off of its best 'performance' regarding visits and less than 30 per cent of its best 'bed-night' yearly results. But five years later, in 2009, visits and bed-nights had already overrun the peaks of the 1980s (see Figure 24.4).

Tourism in Croatia is predominantly an issue of the Mediterranean regions: about 80 per cent of arrivals and 90 per cent of bed-nights are achieved in the Adriatic coastal resorts. As such, the majority of tourist amenities are of seasonal character (summer). In 2004 55.4 per cent of tourist accommodations (beds) were in concrete structures, around 200,000 in hotels (40.2 per cent); the remaining 400,000 units were on campsites, in boats/marinas, etc. Weather-related visits could therefore increase the accumulated number of tourists and their length of stay per year high enough, or result in a disastrous season. According to UNWTO (2004), in 2002 Croatia had close to 80,000 rooms in hotels, bed-and-breakfast places and apartments. The occupancy rate of these amenities is, regarding its seasonal character, understandably low. At the peak of Croatia's economic performance in the 1980s, the occupancy rate was close to 84 days or three months a year; in 1990, it fell below the 20-day mark; in 2004 it revived and went up to 56 days, close to two months a year. What the Croatian destina-tion management planners need to do urgently is prolong the summer season and modernize the structure of amenities in the tourism sector of the economy. In the period 1995–2005 the Croats did well in promoting nautical tourism by almost doubling moorings in marinas (Table 24.4).

The structure of foreign demand has changed since independence. New markets in east-central Europe have emerged; Western markets have cautiously responded to the new tourist destination by the name 'Croatia'. In the early twenty-first century, tourists from Great Britain, historically an important factor of Croatian tourism, amounted to less than 45 per cent of the pre-independence years, but increasing slowly. Germans have since 2000 increased their presence to about 80 per cent of the pre-war visits. They are again one of the tourism generating coun-tries for Croatia, followed by Italy, Austria, Slovenia and the Czech Republic. In accordance with this ranking, Croatia's tourism has geographically become dependent on short-distance

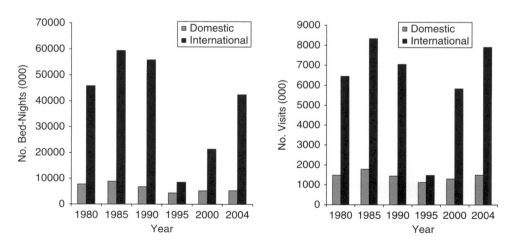

Figure 24.4   Croatia: domestic and international arrivals, 1980–2004

Table 24.4 Croatia: accommodation and selected touristic facilities, 1980–2004

	ACCOMMODATION All tourist-beds*	ACCOMMODATION Tourist-beds in hotels and similar+	PORTS Moorings**	OCCUPANCY RATE
1980	692001	495940	6451	21.7%
1985	820251	561440	7321	22.6%
1990	862680	589333	7227	16.7%
1995	649258	523528	7432	5.6%
2000	759057	479232	12201	14.1%
2004	871178	483069	13763	15.2%

* = including camping places on camping sites, boats on mooring, etc.
\+ = all accommodation facilities – without the inclusion of camping sites
** = number of moorings in nautical ports
Source: Savezni Zavod Za Statistiku (1981, 1986, 1991, 1996, 2005)

regional visits of residents of Bosnia, Slovenia, Austria, Hungary, Italy, Slovakia and Germany (south). They are responsible for 56.8 per cent of all, and 71.2 per cent of international arrivals (Table 24.5). Destine European tourists and, in part, American tourists are missing. Instead of making land based visits (all-inclusive hotel arrangements) they are returning to Croatia as cruise ship passengers for a daylight port/city visit of Dubrovnik, Korčula, Hvar, Split, Zadar and Šibenik.

Analyses of the daily tourist expenditures showed that in 1998 a Croatian as a tourist was, along with the tourist from Slovenia ($30.68) and the Netherlands ($29.29), a 'moderately spending' guest ($29.57). Visitors from post-socialist countries of east-central Europe, such as Hungary, Slovakia, Poland and the Czech Republic, have had lower daily expenditures ($24.21–$26.49). Higher daily expenditure were recorded by guests from Great Britain ($38.30) and Germany ($34.53). But, as elaborated, their return rates to the area are modest. Croatia's Institute of Tourism therefore, in the mid-1990s, in regard to the mid-term destination management policy, made the following suggestions (see Table 24.6):

Table 24.5 Croatia: tourists according to residency, 1980–2004 (in 000s)

	ALL	INTERNATIONAL VISITORS TO CROATIA							
	CROATIA	EX – YU*	AUSTRIA	ITALY	GERMANY	UNITED KINGDOM	HUNGARY	SLOVAKIA	CZECH REPUBLIC
1980	7929	1436	2436	421	420	1595	224	108	–	181**
1985	10125	1739	2780	580	766	1976	429	107	–	332**
1990	8497	1580	2460	547	998	1874	457	117	–	193**
1995	2610	1125	356	247	221	274	25	34	27	119
2000	7137	1305	1048	640	1012	1048	85	250	187	711
2004	9412	1501	1119	741	1232	1580	208	403	176	664

* = area of former Yugoslavia, excluding Croatia – now sovereign nation-states: Bosnia and Herzegovina, Macedonia, Serbia and Montenegro, Slovenia (75%–89% of all Ex-YU visits).
** Czechoslovakia
Source: Savezni Zavod Za Statistiku (1981, 1986, 1991, 1996, 2005)

Table 24.6 Croatia: visits to and bed-nights in major sea-side resort areas*, 1980–2004 (in 000s)

	VISITS						BED-NIGHTS					
	1980	1985	1990	1995	2000	2004	1980	1985	1990	1995	2000	2004
Istrian Peninsula (Poreč)	1697	2320	2251	1391	2080	2276	16223	20974	19726	9510	14285	15515
Kvarner Bay & Islands (Opatija, Crikvenica)	1581	2071	2043	1130	1651	1626	11429	14384	13809	6249	9208	8897
North Dalmatia & Islands (Zadar, Šibenik)	814	987	952	182	868	1153	6825	8305	7727	1142	5300	6017
Central Dalmatia & Islands (Split)	1206	1505	1330	338	895	1049	10378	12571	10630	1850	5494	5920
South Dalmatia (Dubrovnik)	723	890	803	158	469	593	4846	5752	4892	889	2782	3280
% of Croatia tourist visits/bed-nights	75.9	76.8	86.8	82.1	90.1	71.2	92.7	90.9	90.8	91.5	96.5	82.9

* = counties ("županije") with the coastline (Adriatic Sea)
** = Source: Bulić (2001)
Source: Savezni Zavod Za Statistiku (1981, 1986, 1991, 1996, 2005)

- In order to provide for the return of the pre-war demanding Western European market, it is necessary to develop innovative tourism products and to raise the level of quality, according to the existing European standards and trends. Along with the financial means, such actions need time.
- Tourists from geographically close markets should become valuable guests. Accordingly, one has to encourage the domestic tourist demand, which has in the past often been neglected due to its supposedly unprofitable aspect.
- Encouragement of regional and domestic travels should not be limited to maritime, Mediterranean destinations. Domestic demand could speed up the development of urban and rural tourism in the continental part of Croatia as well. This could also help preserve valuable natural and cultural resources. Examples from neighbouring countries and the eastern Mediterranean (Slovenia, Greece) show that the domestic and regional demand is a considerable and stable part of the tourism economy (Mikačić, 1998).

By 2004 many of the goals, set a decade earlier, had already been achieved. The importance of Mediterranean destinations in the Croatian tourism industry had reduced, respectively by 15 and 10 per cent, to just above 71 per cent in arrivals and 83 per cent the bed-night numbers. But the main focus of Croatian tourism has not changed. Overwhelmingly sea, sand and sun tourism prevails. The recent promotional slogan 'Croatia – the Mediterranean as it once was' supports it by neglecting the growing 'Caribbean ambiences' of other Mediterranean destinations and by putting the original and traditional in nature and culture as priority. At the beginning of the twenty-first century this phrase enabled Croatian managers to hide their relatively low-quality tourist services, which have due to instability and the lack of the investment-ready capital not changed much since the 1980s. The situation has slowly changed and amenities have since improved. Additives to 'the tradition' have been more or less accepted, but in a limited amount and just in certain spheres of leisure and recreation. Sporting activities related to sea and coast are the most successful (Fox and Fox, 1998). Along with yachting, underwater discoveries and other warm-seas attractions, tennis facilities have been added, golf-places planned and bicycle paths constructed. The success of Croatian sports (tennis, soccer, water polo, etc.) gratifies such investments on several levels of public and political acceptance.

Due to its geo-strategic position and the general trend in the industry, Croatian tourism has made efforts, along with their neighbours, to develop the gaming and gambling sector of the economy. Large casino operators, such as Casino Austria, have or are planning to have their share in the gaming and gambling operations along the Adriatic. Since Italy is geographically close, and Italians are traditional guests and known by their playing habits, Croatia opened 18 American-style and about 30 smaller gambling establishments. Half of them are located in resorts of the Istrian peninsula, less than one hour from the Italian border. Recently, sustainable development projects are marking the tourism sector of the Croatian economy as well. There are eighty Blue Flags flying on Croatian beaches, marking the extreme quality of coastal waters of Europe (Bošković and Šerović, 2000). The Mediterranean waters in the Adriatic Sea have become less polluted, as less tourists visit and aluminium plants, cement factories and other coastline manufacturers have had to close down due to global economic impacts.

Less visited by tourists are the hinterlands. There, vine-routes are promoted and tourism on farms projected, in Istria in particular, less so in Dalmatia. Resort hinterlands have become most valuable assets for real-estate agents. There, the 'Toscana effect' is hoped for and/or feared of – as it is in the island communities as well. Since 1991, due to a variety of reasons – land-ownership of an 'enemy' (in the Yugoslavian conflict), speculative purchases/ sales (speculative and/or progress envisioned), changes in the master plan of municipalities,

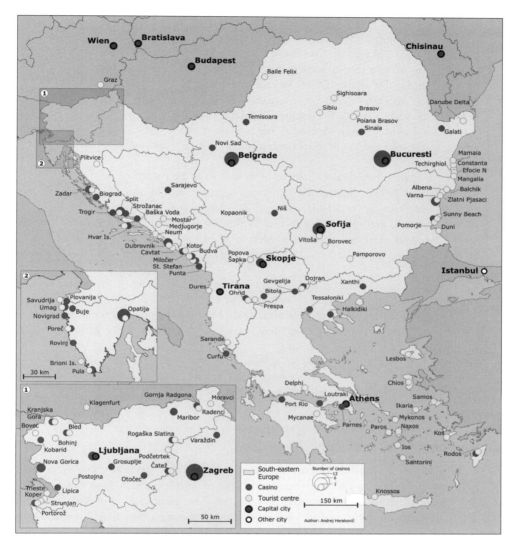

Figure 24.5 Map of south-eastern Europe

interest of the 'new rich' and the world elite, etc. – more than 100,000 properties have been bought by non–residents and foreigners. There is not a clear picture available yet to elaborate on transactions of capital and real estate matters in relation to the tourism sectors. The transition is still in progress (Vrtiprah and Ban, 2000). As a result, the following obvious spatial and functional changes must be mentioned (see Figure 24.5):

- Several international hotel chains, such as Hilton (Dubrovnik), Sol Melia (Umag), Iberostar (Cavtat), Archotels, Intercontinental and Sheraton (Zagreb), Grand Heritage, Hostin, Wrens, have entered Croatia. Foreign investment groups, led by financial institutions such

387

as Montecatini and Hypo Alpen-Adria (Pula, Savudrija), have invested in tourism-related real estate. European travel and tourism corporations, such as OMV, Thompson/TUI (Opatija, Poreč, Crikvenica), have made their way into the tourism sector of the Croatian economy by sharing tourist services with local entrepreneurs and investing into tour-operators, hospitality establishments and accommodations.

- Non-tourist enterprises led by Croatia's development and own profit-making personalities, such as Bernie Ecclestone's 'Formula 1 Racing' (Brioni Is.), and the emigrant Andronico Lukšić's South American ore capital (Poreč's 'Plava laguna' hotels) were among major stakeholders in tourist enterprises in the early days of transition to a market economy.
- An overwhelming benefit for Croatia and its visitors is the construction of the highway-net by several French, Italian and American investors, led by the US Bechtel Group. In 2004, in Dalmatia and Istria, close to 400 kilometres of new four-lane highways have been made available to the public. In the first decade of the twenty-first century several hundred more are under construction or planned. The most important goal is to link Croatia's most southern Dubrovnik tourist and resort area with the European highway net.
- Croatian ports have opened their piers and anchorages to a variety of Mediterranean and American cruise ship companies. Congestion in harbours and limited daytime-only use of the tourist infrastructure in the historical towns by cruise-ship tourists is not in the interests of resort entrepreneurs any more. It was a welcome addition to the traditional resort tourism in the early times of transition.
- German, Irish and British low-cost airlines have included Croatian coastal resorts in their networks, therewith to some extent replacing the previous well-established charter operations of domestic/national and regional airlines.

Conclusion

At the turn of the twenty-first century the tourism industry of the post-socialist countries of south-eastern Europe had to overcome multi-layered hurdles, which have not been felt in other East-Central European countries of transition. The disintegration of Yugoslavia has had disastrous effects on the immediate business environment and on the regional economy as a whole, along with problems related to the transition from a socialist to a market economy and to the rivalry of newly established nation states. Regional political processes, such as EU integration and the increasingly globalized economy, including tourism, have also impacted trends in tourist visits and in the tourist industries' perspectives of the eight regional countries that have been analysed. Detailed analyses of the tourism sector of Croatia have showed diverse ways of recovery, which other regional economies, in particular Slovenia, Bulgaria and Romania, have also set paths to. Promotional slogans, like 'Croatia – the Mediterranean as it once was' and 'Slovenia Invigorates' express the different approaches countries have set to reach this goal. New tourism strategies and regional development master plans have replaced old. Ecologically conscious development is regarded a priority.

The once prosperous tourist destinations of south-eastern Europe, in the mid-1980s among the top European tourist destinations, became at the beginning of the last decade of the twentieth century unrecognizable on the tourist map of the world. At the beginning of the new millennium tourists were still one-third down on visits two decades previously. Several developments in the global arena (terrorism, wars) and domestic situation (investments, privatization) in 2005 elevated international visits almost to the stage they once had. Europe is the tourism-generating area for the region. But the regional preference of the tourism-generating countries has changed: less continental and increased regional exchange of tourists has taken place recently. Three circles of regional interdependence and two weaker circles of west>east/north>south long-distance reliance is registered. The quantity of accommodation facilities has reduced by 9.4 per cent but, with increased numbers of foreign brand name hotel chains entering, have increased their quality. Once unthinkable tourism products, such as gaming and gambling, have strengthened the existing Mediterranean natural and cultural tourist attractions of the area. Increasingly, but slowly, the triple E (education, experience, emotion) and triple A (adventure, attraction, alternative) products are becoming available on the market, somewhere even replacing the popular triple S (sun, sea, sand) type of tourism. Some destinations stick – to a large extent – to the old tradition, like Croatia. The highly praised sustainable development trend in tourism is often a 'paper tiger', as in countries of the region the environmentally most critical stage has for the moment been reduced.

Croatia – regarding tourism the most successful country in transition in south-eastern Europe – shows a well-formed and continued recovery from the direct and broader effects of the 'Balkan wars'. Several tourist enterprises of the world named Croatia the 'Tourist Destination of 2006'! Croatia and Slovenia, the two new sovereign nation states rising out of the ashes of Yugoslavia, in 2005 surpassed the 1980s' mark of tourist arrivals. But the structure of tourist visits is, at present, comparably different. Instead of hosting British, Dutch and Scandinavian tourists, a regional tourism exchange takes place. Up to 75 per cent international visitors reside in countries bordering the named nation states or are residents of the two respective nations themselves. Just southern and eastern regions of Germany 'spoil the picture'. Croatia's intention to reduce the impact of Mediterranean tourism has had a limited success. Still, the traditional maritime orientation prevails (71 per cent in arrivals and 83 per cent in bed-nights) as new nautical and sports-related programmes have been added. Foreign investments in the tourism sector of the economy are in Croatia, as in other south-eastern European tourist destinations, recognizable to a large extend.

Since the statistics are known and major orientation paths already in place what use can be made of them by south-east European countries and their tourist economies? This is the question that must be addressed by all countries and regional players with interest in the future of tourism. There is little doubt that conditions for the growth of tourism on a global and regional scale are increasingly favourable. Most effective in this region would be the strengthening of intra-regional cooperation. At present the promotion of most, if not all, players in the region is aimed at tourism-generating countries of the pre-transition era – Germany, Netherlands, Great Britain, Italy, etc. – ignoring the fact that close to 50 per cent of international visitors come from their neighbourhood, less than 1,000 km away. This has to become a competitive factor in particular if the energy situation and its pricing are to be taken into account. Denial of this fact is partly cultural and partly politically stimulated and must be overcome. In order to compete effectively with European and emerging tourism regions worldwide in addition the tourism industry of south-eastern Europe must:

- become increasingly environmentally conscious, and address this issue in other sectors of the economy as well;
- place greater emphasis on strategic planning issues in order to reduce the harmful environmental and socio-cultural aspects of tourism;

• raise the profile of the industry locally, regionally and nationally; the fragmented nature of the industry needs state involvement, in particular in consumer protection, cooperation between the industry sectors and in sustainable development programmes.

References

Bošković, D. and Šerović, S. (2000) 'Restrukturiranje i prilagođavanje turističke ponude Hrvatske Europskim i svjetskim trendovima' (The restructuring and the adjustment of the tourism supply of Croatia towards European and world trends). *Turizam*, 48(2), 153–66.

Bulić, N. (2001) 'Hrvatski turizam 2000 i prognoza do 2005' (Croatian tourism in the year 2000 and prognosis up to the year 2005). *Turizam*, 49(2) 192–200

Casino City (n.d.) 'Croatia gambling'. Retrieved 12 May 2006, from http://www.casinocity.com/hr/casinos.html

Fisher Weltalmanach (2005). *Zahlen, Daten und Fakten*. Frankfurt: Fischer Verlag

Fox, J. and Fox, R. (1998) 'In search of the lost British tourist'. *Turizam*, 46(4), 203–19

Jefries, I. (1993) *Socialist economies and the transition to the market: A guide*. London: Routledge

Jordan, P. (2000) 'Hrvatski turizam pred izazovima globalizacije' (Croatian tourism and the challenge of globalization). *Turizam*, 48(2), 195–203

Mansfeld, Y. and Pizam, A. (2005) *Tourism, security and safety: from theory to practice*. London: Elsevier Butterworth-Heinemann

Mikačić, V. (1998) 'Turizam Hrvatske: stanje i perspective' (State of Croatian tourism and its perspectives). *Hrvatski geografski glasnik*, 60(1), 17–46

Pirjevec, B. (1985) 'Mogučnosti i granice budučeg razvoja turizma u Jugoslaviji' (Chances and limits of the future development of tourism in Yugoslavia). Unpublished doctoral dissertation, University of Zagreb, Croatia

Radnić, A. and Ivandić, N. (1999) 'War and tourism in Croatia: Consequences and the road to recovery'. *Turizam*, 47(1), 43–54

Savezni Zavod Za Statistiku (1971) *Statistički godišnjak, SFRJ 1970* (Statistical Yearbook of the Socialist Federal Republic of Yugoslavia 1970). Belgrade: Savezni Zavod Za Statistiku

—— (1981) *Statistički godišnjak, SFRJ 1980* (Statistical Yearbook of the Socialist Federal Republic of Yugoslavia 1980). Belgrade: Savezni Zavod Za Statistiku

—— (1986) *Statistički godišnjak, SFRJ 1985* (Statistical Yearbook of the Socialist Federal Republic of Yugoslavia 1985). Belgrade: Savezni Zavod Za Statistiku

—— (1991) *Statistički godišnjak, SFRJ 1990* (Statistical Yearbook of the Socialist Federal Republic of Yugoslavia 1990). Belgrade: Savezni Zavod Za Statistiku

—— (1992) *Statistički godišnjak Jugoslavije, 1980–1991* (Statistical Yearbook of Yugoslavia 1980–1991). Belgrade: Savezni Zavod Za Statistiku

—— (1996) *Statistički godišnjak, SFRJ 1995* (Statistical Yearbook of the Socialist Federal Republic of Yugoslavia 1995). Belgrade: Savezni Zavod Za Statistiku

—— (2004) *Statistički godišnjak Jugoslavije, 1992–2003* (Statistical Yearbook of Yugoslavia 1992–2003). Belgrade: Savezni Zavod Za Statistiku

—— (2005) *Statistički godišnjak, SFRJ 2004* (Statistical Yearbook of the Socialist Federal Republic of Yugoslavia 2004). Belgrade: Savezni Zavod Za Statistiku

Turnock, D. (2002) *The human geography of east-central Europe*. London: Routledge

UNWTO (1981) *Yearbook of tourism statistics 1980*. Madrid: UN World Tourism Organization

—— (1991) *Yearbook of tourism statistics 1990*. Madrid: UN World Tourism Organization

—— (1999) *Yearbook of tourism statistics 1998*. Madrid: UN World Tourism Organization

—— (2003) *Tourism market trends: Europe 2002 edition*. Madrid: UN World Tourism Organization

—— (2004) *Tourism market trends: Europe 2003 edition*. Madrid: UN World Tourism Organization

—— (2005a) *WTO world tourism barometer* (Vol. 3, Issue 1). Madrid: UN World Tourism Organization

—— (2005b) *Compendium of tourism statistics: 2005 Edition (Data 1999–2003)*. Madrid: UN World Tourism Organization

von Barratta, M., Albrecht, B., Baumann, W.-R., Brander, S., Eshenhagen, W., Hartmann, C., et al. (2005) Der Fischer Weltalmanach 2005: Zahlen, Daten, Fakten (The Fischer World almanac 2005: figures, data, facts) Frankfurt am Main: Fischer Taschenbuch Verlag

Vrtiprah, V. and Ban, I. (2000) 'Turizam u Dalmaciji u uvjetima globalizacije' (Tourism in Dalmatia within conditions of globalization). *Turizam*, 48(2), 215–32

Vukonić, B. (1997) *Tourism in the whirlwind of war*. Zagreb: Golden Marketing

Williams, A. H. and Balaz, V. (2001) *Tourism in transition: Economic change in Central Europe* (Tourism, Retailing and Consumption). London: I.B. Tauris

25

Landscape as theme park

Tourist consumption and identity of place in contemporary Japan under conditions of rapid demographic change

Malcolm Cooper, Jeremy S. Eades

Introduction

This chapter is primarily speculative, bringing together a rather disparate group of themes we have been engaged with over the past few years: the results of globalization, the strategies of peripheral regions and communities in the face of demographic decline, processes of tourism and migration, and attempts to keep local cultures going. How these different threads may relate to each other is shown later, but to start with the discussion looks at a series of remarkable population pyramids recently published by the Japanese Government (Figure 25.1; Buckley, 2004), the purpose being to demonstrate that Japan will need large supplies of immigrant labor for the foreseeable future if the economic effects of the *korei shakai* or aging society is to be warded off.

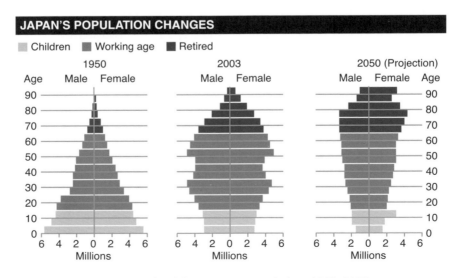

Figure 25.1 The changing profile of the Japanese population, 1950–2050

What these pyramids illustrate dramatically for Japan is something we are all aware of; the rapidly changing life expectation and declining birthrates in developed countries over the past half-century (for a summary of recent work in Japan see Knight and Traphagen, 2003; Traphagen, 2000, p. 11). The tale is well known: during the twentieth century most of the advanced industrial societies moved towards increased life expectancy and decreased fertility – more old people and fewer children. As infant mortality rates dropped and fewer children were needed on the land or were barred from working in the factories and mines, and as the costs of education rose, the response was to have fewer children, and new technologies (contraceptives, safe and legal abortions) helped this desire to reduce costly larger family size. By the late twentieth century, the birthrate in Japan and most of the other industrialized countries had fallen so low that any population growth was due to immigration and people living longer. Japanese women with a life expectation of well over 80 are the longevity champions of the world and men are not far behind, so much so that this pattern has been able to stave off the effects of declining fertility on the total Japanese population size for some time. The impact will probably run out around the end of the first decade of the twenty-first century, with the population peaking at 130 million, after which it will plummet. By 2050 it will be back to Second World War levels, or around 70–80 million, if no new offsetting trend occurs. Less apocalyptically perhaps but in its own way a difficult question for policy response, the percentage of the population over 65, which stood at around 10 percent in 1985 is due to climb to 26 percent in 2025. This will be an increase in actual numbers from 12.5 to 31.5 million; one with considerable implications for the economy and society (Traphagen, 2000).

These changes are well illustrated in the pyramids. The first one shows for 1950 the kind of classic pyramid typical of developing countries, with high fertility, steady mortality (though fewer males in the 40–60 age groups as a result of the Second World War), and few people in the older age groups. The second one shows the impact of the dramatic fertility decline in the post baby-boom period, with the pyramid well on the way to becoming inverted. The middle-aged groups have the largest population, while the population of children is already in steep decline (Knight and Traphagen, 2003). But the projection for 2050 is in many ways the most interesting: the population pyramid has become inverted, with the decline in fertility continuing steadily and with most people surviving into their 80s. Indeed one of the most remarkable features is that the residual category of women above 90 will then be so large that it becomes an extrusion, suggesting that the graph ought to be continued up into the post-100 or even post-110 age groups before it gradually fades away.

In this chapter, a simple question is asked: what will these changes mean for tourism in Japan, apart from the fact that there will be a lot more old people around? Indeed, if the third pyramid is to be believed and the population really will be nearly halved in the next 50 years, the question of whether many of the more peripheral communities in Japan will survive at all needs to be addressed, tourism or no. Perhaps their only future is to become like the ghost villages in Shiga prefecture to the east of Lake Biwa (near Kyoto), or those which Knight (1995, 2003a, 2003b) describes in the Wakayama area of Kansai. Some pointers to the fate of these communities in tourist terms can already be discerned in a series of studies carried out in the past 20 years; what this chapter does is to try and put them together in some kind of model, and then project this forward over the next 50 years to see what will happen to tourism in the Japanese rural periphery.

The title of the chapter refers to the fact that many communities in Japan are already turning their landscapes into quasi if not actual theme parks in order to attract tourists, capital and more residents. Over the next 50 years this process of conversion could become a Darwinian struggle for survival as the body count outside the major cities across the country diminishes.

A large percentage of the 70 million Japanese of the future will be accounted for by the megacities of the heartland – the Tokyo and Osaka regions – and the other regional hubs of over a million inhabitants along the high-speed railway line from Tokyo to Fukuoka. That does not leave much demographic room for the rest of the country, so, as demographic melt-down takes place, we have to ask the question: what are people going to do with all the rural space?

Speculation about these matters is not of course new. It is a commonplace that an aging population needs more expensive care and medical facilities, and that, as society ages, the number of people actually working and paying taxes to support them is gradually reduced, creating a crisis for both the pension and welfare systems. It is also well known that, after the Second World War, Japan urbanized quickly in one of the most dramatic periods of economic growth in history (Johnson, 1982). The European countries got their labor for reconstruction from their colonies and refugees. Refugees figured in the reconstruction of Japan as well, but after that labor for reconstruction came increasingly from rural communities freed of debt to landlords because of the Occupation land reforms (Dower, 1979). Farming became increasingly mecha-nized, with a much reduced demand for labor, and the farmers in the population themselves dwindled and aged, forming now perhaps the most geriatric labor agricultural labor force in Japanese history. In the process, men ran out of potential wives and had to import them from overseas (Hisada, 1992, cited in Yamashita, 2003), or stay bachelors, and members of many rural communities simply voted with their feet. One of the most striking images in Shiga Prefecture near the former imperial capital of Kyoto are the deserted houses with pots and pans in Marie Celeste mode still on the stoves in the kitchens. There are clothes and even children's toys in the chests and drawers elsewhere in the houses, and ceramics and lacquer ware neatly wrapped in newspaper, all of which appeared to stop in 1973. Is this the paradigm of life in the peripheral Japanese community of the future even with tourism?

Globalization, change and regional development in Japan

Economically and socially, what has happened and what will happen in regional Japan is firmly based in the globalization of trade and investment in the post Second World War world (Murphy and Price, 1994; Wahab and Cooper, 2001; Waters, 1995). Globalization involves the exchange of goods, services and people on a global scale and has increasingly affected all national economies and polities in recent years. Japan is no exception, although its experience of all the social and cultural forces of globalization is moderated by an intense feeling (and by resulting policy) of Japanese-ness as expressed in the term *Nihonjinron* (Cooper et al., 2006). This term describes an approach to globalization that is designed to reduce its impact on domes-tic traditions and structures through restricting the take-up of external methods and mores (though not with respect to fast food and theme parks like Disneyland and Universal Studios). In this way immediate shocks to the Japanese polity and society through the experience of globalization and cultural change have been able to be held at arm's length during the past 50 years, except in terms of externally generated economic impact, where for example the nation experienced 10 years of deflation after 1995 while at the same time exports of goods have been rising.

Globalization has impacts on countries and regions in the modern world in the following ways:

- stretched social relations – the development of cultural, economic and political connections across the globe (including infrastructural networks and global markets);

- regionalization – increased interconnection between states that border each other;
- intensification – of economic and policy interactions on a global scale (including regulatory and accreditation of standards organizations); and
- interpenetration – the extent to which apparently distant cultures and societies now come face to face with each other at the local level, creating increased diversity and possible conflicts.

Each of these impacts is readily observable through the medium of tourism as it is perhaps the most ubiquitous industry on a global scale in the twenty-first century (Yamashita, 2003). International and domestic travel is facilitated to, in and from developed countries like Japan by high disposable incomes, political and social stability, geographical proximity, and the development of world trade (and its political and financial as well as physical infrastructures). Equally, tourism as an industry is increasingly favored by policymakers as an instrument of economic development – the high ratio of labor to capital and the rapidity of development compared to other economic sectors make tourism particularly attractive to national policymakers (Sorensen, 2002). In addition, the increasing commodification of culture enables a country or region to capitalize on the images, dreams and expectations of both tourists and local populations (Appadurai, 1995; Bhaba, 1994; Urry, 1990). All these factors are at work in the context of Japan, as will be shown below.

At the national and regional level Getz (1986) has identified four approaches to the use of tourism as a developmental tool. These are:

- boosterism: tourism is good, cultural and natural resources should be exploited for the benefit of tourists, development is defined in business terms, the industry is the expert;
- economic: tourism is as beneficial as other industries, use of tourism to create economic change, development defined in economic terms, planner is expert;
- spatial: tourism is a resource user, development defined in environmental terms, regional phenomenon, preservation of genetic diversity; and
- community: local control asserted, search for balanced development and alternatives to 'mass' tourism, development defined in socio-cultural terms, and the planner is facilitator not expert.

These of course are not mutually exclusive (Getz, 1986), nor are they necessarily sequential, so there will be a range of approaches and results in any particular economy with respect to regional and national tourism development; however, boosterism is the approach most used in regional development and this applies especially to regional tourism in Japan (Sorensen, 2002).

Turning now to the theory and process of local development through tourism, the development of particular tourist facilities typically begins with an investment concept based on preliminary analyses of demand (Cooper and Flehr, 2006). Normally, the developer then obtains capital from lending institutions, secures land, hires architects and engineers to formulate physical plans, employs consultants to conduct various surveys regarding the characteristics of the land and of the projected demand, and begins to seek development approval from relevant authorities. For major projects a developer may incur substantial debt in this early development phase, often spending significant amounts of money before any actual or implied development approval can be gained. In the Japanese as in other contexts this situation can produce a climate of uncertainty for investors, as local authorities might enact zoning or other ordinances that render the development financially impossible. Alternatively, administrators responsible for environmental protection and building codes, for example, might react negatively to a politically desirable local development by hedging it with conditions that again make it impossible for the developer to carry through on the project. In both of these situations the developer is subject to a local approving authority's discretion and may be left stranded once initial work and financing has been arranged but before the right to develop land has been secured, if planning approval is refused or unduly delayed. In addition, the extent to which such problems conflict, or are perceived to conflict, with resource management and development policy derived after due process at higher-levels of government can constitute a political difficulty at the local level. This is why in Japan, as in other countries, the power of the state may be invoked to ensure desired outcomes for public sector policymaking through private investment, especially where regional development is perceived to be at stake. Under this situation higher-level (higher than the local community) government approval then provides the developer with vested rights, often by invalidating local zoning regulations applicable to a property because the higher public benefit of the development, economically and/or socially, is said to override such local considerations (ibid.).

In Japan, one such prescriptive framework for development was the Law on the Development of Comprehensive Resort Areas 1987 (the Resort Areas Law) which took tourist resort development outside the Japanese local land use control system, and led to massive national government investment in local tourism projects designed to influence the pattern of regional economic development. This law was seen as a way of promoting certainty for developers of resorts and golf courses, which were considered at that time at the national level to be ideal bases for rural regeneration and regional economic development, and also a way to promote the effective use of leisure time and stimulate domestic tourism demand (Hebbert, 1994; Klamann, 1990). While this centralizing process has been proven to reduce uncertainty for major developments and their proponents by enabling developers to protect their investment, it has also given rise to the slogan *fukoku hinmin* (enrich the country, impoverish the people; McCormack, 1996). Under this system, a (usually) small group of chosen developers received an almost unfettered right to develop resorts, and local zoning regulations were frozen, allegedly in exchange for public benefits. Payment for sites quite often also in part came from the public purse, again allowing developers to reduce their risks and gain cheap land and finance.

The net effect of state involvement in tourism development planning is thus a form of boosterism of the economy, rather than the fostering of a community-oriented approach to tourism development. When a higher-level government can promote the idea that a particular tourism development will provide social and economic benefits to a local community, with negligible disadvantages, and should therefore be supported by state policy even if such policy effectively results in public loss for private gain, the mechanisms discussed in this paper allow for this to happen. From the perspective of the state, continued capital accumulation is necessary and in the twenty-first century this depends largely on private investment. The state therefore needs to encourage private investment, while private investors need to find a home for their money, and such mutual interdependence necessitates bargaining as both sides would otherwise be able to frustrate each other's policy initiatives. While this does not mean that state initiatives will always be implemented by individual businesses, or that all proposed developments by private developers will be designated as major, it does mean that the planning agenda for major tourism investment will be dominated by state and business concerns rather than local community objectives (Cooper and Flehr, 2006).

Tourism development and life in provincial and rural Japan

So what has been the recent pattern of tourism development in regional and local areas of Japan in the prevailing economic and social climate of the recent past? This section reviews some of the studies of local and regional economic and social trends that have been carried out in what we might call peripheral Japan, that is to say in the *mura* (villages), *machi cho* (towns) and smaller *shi* (cities) over the last few years, projects forward the observed trends and compares them with similar trends in other parts of the world, notably Europe. The classic responses to these kinds of pressure have been the amalgamation of communities to pool their resources and services, together with attempts to raise their profiles through various types of *machizukuri* (literally "making the town"; Knight, 1994; Traphagen, 1998) and bring back jobs and people through the aegis of tourism.

As is often the case in Japan, some of these attempts were not spontaneous but reflected national policies such as the *furusato sosei undo*, or home town campaign, of the late 1980s, and the finance provided under the Law on Comprehensive Development of Resorts 1987 (Cooper et al., 2007; Funabiki, 1992; Thompson, 2003). These were in the main bubble economy extravaganzas, in which communities were given large sums of money to shore up their local identities and attract visitors. Despite the excesses of some communities in the ways in which they invested the money – one mayor bought a lump of gold and put it on display as a tourist attraction, while another invited two American artists to construct a dune out of 29,700 tons of sand, which was, alas, soon blown away (Funabiki, 1992) – two broad themes emerged from these policies: the encouragement of specialized niche agriculture, and the promotion of local tourism.

This discussion starts first with a case study based on John Knight's work in a town he calls Hongu in Wakayama (Knight, 2003a). Knight has noted that many Japanese writers see the depopulation of Japan and the return to nature as a national disaster, the loss of a national resource. His research was carried out in a town formed through the amalgamation of 5 villages after the Second World War. In the 1950s, the population had stood at over 10,000 but by the 1990s this had fallen to under 5000, with 20 percent of the population leaving during 1965–70 alone. Most of the emigrants were of course younger people, resulting in a drastic fall in births and marriages, and bachelors finding it increasingly difficult to find wives. Some migrants do return every year at the time of the Bon festival, but return to the cities immediately after (in the same way, the graves in the deserted villages of Shiga sport a few fresh flowers in the summer, but these soon wither). The rural depopulation is in a perverse way in line with central government policy; particularly with attempts to reduce the acreage of rice under cultivation. Some villagers have planted their fields with trees, effectively helping extend the boundaries of the forest. The community's self-image is not surprisingly one of terminal decline, to which the town hall has attempted to respond; they have tried to stimulate return migration, promoted *furusato* ties with migrants to the big cities so that they want to return to their roots regularly, and tried to attract new settlers and/or tourists.

As with other communities around the world, these are recurring themes. Interestingly, one initiative has been to try and attract the elderly, through the concentration of care and medical services. Clearly, with growing numbers of elderly, this is not a bad strategy for the Japan of the next generation or so. They have also tried to stimulate more marriage and reproduction, through setting up marriage consultancies, young people's clubs, making marriage awards to young couples, and incentive schemes for go-betweens (some individuals have given up and made their own arrangements to import brides from Thailand and the Philippines). They have also tried to lure 'Uturners' back from Tokyo, by providing lists of empty houses which could provide accommodation for them on their return. *Furusato* ties have also been encouraged by a mail order service of local products being sent to migrants throughout the country (Knight, 1998). In addition to the elderly, some of those who have been attracted back are counter-cultural types with an interest in the arts, traditional industries and culture, or organic agriculture. Needless to say, not all of them manage to put down roots, and they become serial settlers as they move on to the next community in their quest for rural authenticity. But Knight's gloomy conclusion is that none of these initiatives has reversed the trend, and his alternative scenario is for wild animals such as macaques, bears and wolves moving in, making life seemingly even more insecure and thus hastening the rural–urban exodus (Knight, 1999; Knight, 2003b).

As a second case study, John Traphagen's work on the town of Kanagasaki (Tohoku Prefecture; Traphagen, 1998, 2000) is of interest to the thesis advanced in this chapter. Much of the town in the 1980s and 1990s still relied on agriculture, though there was some local industry in the form of semi-conductors and pharmaceuticals. Farming was part-time, and agricultural cooperatives were significant for marketing, producing and providing inputs and machines. By the mid-1990s, the town had been trying for 15 years to modernize itself through a *machizukuri* campaign. The local people had organized lectures, meetings, and campaigns to create a "living environment," and they had reinvented tradition in the form of festivals and celebrations of public holidays (15 September, Respect the Elderly Day, was an important day in the local calendar). Generally the discourse was one of lifelong education, a healthy environment, and good social relations, everything that an elderly population could want. Other new initiatives included improved home help, a Center for Life-Long Education, meeting rooms, classrooms, computer training facilities, kitchens and fitness facilities, improved sports facilities, better sewage systems, promotion of local ecotourism, and a new town hall.

Another Tohoku city on a similar scale is Tono, famous from the collection of weird stories collected there by Yanagita Kunio in the Meiji period, *Tono Monogatari (Stories About a Place)* (Yanagita, 1910). The city hall found Yanagita's book useful in its *machizukuri* campaigns, and over the years it has tried to bring the landscape of the town in line with the book. Otherwise there is something of an image problem, in that Tono looks much the same as other Japanese settlements of comparable size. So, instead of the fetching Taisho period bronze nudes in the style of Degas or local warlords in the style of Tom Cruise which seem to grace the exterior of many provincial Japan Railway stations, Tono has a *kappa*, a water spirit vaguely reminiscent of Sesame Street.

Tono now projects itself as a rural museum (tourist) city, the city of myth, and the *furusato* of folklore. The original manuscript of Yanagita's book is prominently displayed in the museum, while the study in which he wrote it has been brought up from Tokyo and reconstructed in Tono. At the center of the town's regeneration is the Tonopia theme park project, with a complex of facilities including the city museum, the folklore village, and a heritage park. The museum offers information on the world of *Tono Monogatari*, the natural environment of the region, and the rest of the city's folklore. The folklore village features recitations of Yanagita's tales in Tono dialect by local storytellers. Or rather it is something that sounds like Tono dialect to the visitors – the storytellers themselves admit that the Tono dialect has all but gone, so they try to produce something which is at least *Tonorashii* (a facsimile). The heritage park includes surviving buildings in traditional style which have been restored, and other sites around the town which feature in Yanagita have also been incorporated into the tourist circuit. Old people have revived local crafts to service the tourist market, while 1992 saw the staging of a world folklore exhibition, with performers from a number of other countries. There is something of an irony in the fact that Yanagita himself was a Tokyo bureaucrat; given that the regions of Japan often see their own decline as the corollary of the growth of the capital. Yanagita has been localized, however, through the appropriation of his study and his manuscript, to create a mythic landscape that probably never was, using a combination of local *machizukuri* and the tourist gaze (Urry, 1990) backed up by the tourist Yen. How far these factors will be sufficient to sustain the industry in future if the population of the region as a whole suffers meltdown is anyone's guess, but certainly Tono City is making a concerted try. It may be that in the long run the only way to sustain this kind of tourism is to give it the full theme park experience, as has happened in the examples of national and literary tourism described by Joy Hendry (2000); whether Tono is close enough to major urban centers (or between major urban centers) to allow this to happen is an interesting empirical question for the future.

As a final example of provincial life and the construction of scenarios for its future, the next section briefly discusses Beppu, the home of Ritsumeikan Asia Pacific University. Beppu is currently a city of 160,000 people and the largest hot spring resort in Japan. It has well over 2,000 hot springs within the city limits, around three times the number of any of its rivals. It is sandwiched between two other sizable cities, Oita City itself and Hiji, and the total population around Beppu Bay is in excess of 700,000. There are good air services and ferry services with the rest of Japan, in addition to road and rail, so it is quite accessible. Even though the schools excursion market has more or less collapsed, tourism is still the basis of the local economy with demand in the overnight stay and excursion sectors still fairly buoyant (12 million visitors a year, 140,000 of them international). However, the local population is aging and the nature of the tourism market (heavily weighted to domestic use of *onsen*, or hot springs, and *ryokan*, or traditional inns) tends to attract mainly older people, by definition. Also, the trendier resort of Yufuin 24 kilometers away is competing for custom (3.5 million domestic tourists a year), so there are concerns for the future of the area, not just Beppu but Oita prefecture as a whole.

Enter the colorful ex-governor of Oita, Hiramatsu Morihiko, who retired in 2004. He became governor in 1979 after a successful government career in charge of information technology, and he set out to use his connections in the electronics industry to transform the fortunes of Oita, at that time one of the poorest prefectures in Japan. The strategy had two foci (Broadbent, 1989): the first was the launching of the One Village One Product campaign. This was reminiscent of the kinds of *machizukuri* initiatives noted above, and involved the same promotion of local products and local tourism, though in the Oita case it involved a coordinated campaign over an entire prefecture. The focus was on local agriculture (greenhouse tangerine oranges, or *mikan*, available throughout the year, shitake mushrooms, and *kabosu*, the local lime), and local handicrafts (baskets in the case of Beppu). The campaign has had its critics, but it was widely imitated in other countries of the region, notably Thailand and Malaysia, and this gave Hiramatsu a support network of civic leaders spanning the Asia-Pacific. The second initiative was the Oita Technopolis project, one of the 20 or so technopoles planned by the Japanese government in the early 1980s (Castells and Hall, 1993). This was a bold attempt at decentralizing Japanese research and industry away from the major cities by imitating the Silicon Valley model, a collaboration between local government, private industry and major research universities. The most successful of these schemes was Tsukuba Science City (Dearing, 1995); many of the others lacked the local research base necessary for this kind of project to work, and Oita was no exception. But the Oita Technopolis scheme did have some interesting features. First, many of the facilities were to be established outside the main cities of Beppu and Oita, mainly along the road out to the new Oita airport (Castells and Hall, 1993). This airport is situated to the north-east of Beppu on reclaimed land, far away from Oita itself by road, though there is a high-speed hovercraft link. Second, Hiramatsu decided he would establish his own local university. This was a period in which many prefectures were establishing prefectural universities (there are now over 20). However, Hiramatsu decided on a different strategy, basically to buy in the Ritsumeikan brand name. So APU was established in 2000 at a cost of 27 billion yen, 24 of which came from the prefecture. Unfortunately for the Silicon Valley model, Ritsumeikan had already decided to locate its high-tech teaching and research on its new Biwako campus at Kusatsu in Shiga prefecture. The fallback position was to exploit Hiramatsu's and Ritsumeikan's Asia-Pacific networks, and set up a regional international university to concentrate on the social sciences and management in 2000. By this time, however, the bubble economy had long-since burst, and the technopolis scheme itself seemed to be on the back burner. Hiramatsu staged a few last extravaganzas, such as the construction of the state-of-the-art Big Eye football stadium to host three World Cup matches in 2002, before he retired in early 2004. Now the word in the prefectural government is that the new governor wants to establish his own policies, and One Village One Product is no longer being given the prominence it once was. But the technopolis project did provide an interesting blueprint of an alternative Japan, one in which the provinces would have their day in terms of development, with an attempt to siphon capital and research away from the major urban centers.

This leaves Beppu and the surrounding areas with the competitive advantage they possessed before the Hiramatsu era, a lot of hot water and not much else apart from that current rarity in Japanese higher education, an international university. Given the density of aging hotels and the aging population, one obvious way forward is to establish the city as a silver service center, which will attract both the silver tourists and silver retirement capital. There are developmental models elsewhere; some of the European spas, starting with Baden Baden and Monte Carlo in the nineteenth century, managed to establish themselves on the tourist map with a combination of facilities for aging aristocracies and gambling facilities (Turner and Ash, 1975), where they could deposit some of their wealth for the benefit of urban development. Whether Beppu will sprout a casino, hot water theme park, and the entertainment facilities to persuade the silver excursion and overnight crowd to stay a little longer is of course a matter for much debate, but something needs to be done to counteract the aging of both the local population and the types of tourist that have traditionally visited Beppu for the *onsen*. However, a revitalized health and wellness campaign based on *onsen* is currently a successful strategy in many parts of Europe, and would probably appeal to the kinds of clientele that cities like Beppu already attract.

Discussion and conclusion

As has frequently been pointed out (e.g. by Hendry, 2000), Japan as a whole has an extraordinary concentration of theme parks and other tourist facilities based on notions of cultural identity, landscape, and heritage, and financed through past mainly national efforts in regional development. These range from the fantasy world of Tokyo Disneyland, through the imported Otherness of the various Spanish, Dutch, Canadian, Russian, and other theme parks found throughout the country, to local manifestations of cultural identity in city and prefectural museums, *machizukuri* (local renewal) initiatives, and archaeological sites.

Part of the background to this situation is the nature of the Japanese leisure industry as a whole and the methods of regional promotion outlined above. Despite the image of Japan as a country of dour salary-persons with no leisure time or desire to use it if they did have it, the internal tourist and leisure industry is alive and well. The fact is that the Japanese do enjoy themselves, but that the pattern of work lends itself to short bursts of leisure rather than long leisurely holidays involving international travel (Japanese travel for longer periods, but this is most typical of specific age groups, such as younger unmarried women and seniors, rather than the nuclear family). The short break leisure pattern is encouraged by the proliferation of one-day national holidays, many of which turn into long weekends. Therefore, the one-day or half-day attraction, especially the theme park experience, is the staple of the Japanese domestic tourist industry for good economic and lifestyle reasons.

A second factor is the history and nature of Japanese urbanism. With the high-speed growth of the post-war period, Japan rapidly became one of the most urbanized countries in the world. This has several results that are important for the nature and marketing of tourism. First, many people still have a sense of belonging to one or other of the rural areas of the country, which they or their parents left. This creates a sense of rural nostalgia, which the travel and tourist industry has been quick to exploit through images of the *furusato*, or home village excursion. Also, Japanese cities are uniformly new and rather characterless in their planning and architecture as a result of extensive renewal schemes after the destruction of the Second World War. Traditional wooden buildings do not last well, unless they are periodically renovated as major national cultural resources, so older buildings are surprisingly few even if they were not destroyed in the war. But even Kyoto, the one major city to be spared, is largely indistinguishable from other major cities in its concrete and steel landscape, apart from the main temple and palace sites (as is Beppu which was not bombed). This means that city hall planners of *machizukuri*, the recreation of urban identity, have to be highly innovative in exploiting any historical monuments or associations that can mark out their community from others (Sorensen, 2002). There is also a dramatic contrast in landscapes between the cities on the country's few large plains and the mountain landscapes now largely depopulated, which the travel industry has also been quick to exploit.

Third, there are the factors of the population density and the looming population decline of Japan, coupled with the advanced state of its economy. Japanese consumers are among the most prosperous and healthy in the world, with comparatively large disposable incomes. The concentration of this population into relatively few large cities whose economies are dominated by a relatively small number of integrated manufacturing, retailing, transport, and leisure industry companies (Seibu of Tokyo is a classic example), means that both consumer tastes and economic development strategies are fairly uniform throughout Japan. One feature of expressions of Japanese local identity throughout the country is that the same means are employed in almost every place to express this identity. *Ryokan* (traditional hotels), *onsen* (hot springs), Japanese restaurants, and *omiyage* (souvenir) shops throughout the country sell a remarkably uniform range of goods, with minor local variations. The packaging of the goods is what sells local identity, not the nature of the goods themselves, which tend to be found everywhere, and are in any case increasingly manufactured abroad in South-east Asia or China. The media is also dominated by a small group of companies, so that the information and images available to both developers and consumers are also remarkably uniform throughout the country. When this is combined with an aging population it is not surprising that current regional development initiatives favor *furusato*, hot water-based wellness and theme park tourism.

Fourth, the cultural and social homogeneity that this pattern of geographical concentration produces means that any dramatically different cultural repertoires have to be imported from outside to exist at all. This may explain the popularity in Japan of the exotic national theme parks mentioned above; despite the Japanese interest in and desire to consume different cultures, the prevailing lifestyle and aging population makes prolonged overseas travel difficult for many, so a compromise is to import these cultures and market them within Japan itself.

In other words, much of the so-called distinctiveness of the Japanese domestic leisure industry is perfectly rational within the parameters of Japan's geography, population size, and culture and its experience of urbanization and economic growth. In many ways, Japanese tourism is not dissimilar to that of countries of similar size and relatively dense population in Europe. The main difference between Japan and, say, Italy or France, however, is that, for historical and architectural reasons, the sheer density of heritage sites to be found in western Europe is lacking in Japan. This results in creative efforts by local communities and leisure companies to exploit any meaningful symbols of local or suitable international identity that can be found, and to recreate or invent them where they are lacking. Are these efforts a sign of an increasing Japanese tendency to welcome Otherness or an irrational love of pastiche as a cultural pastime? The chapter suggests that they may simply be a creative response to Japanese geography, demographics, and the parameters of the Japanese consumer market in the postmodern phase of advanced capitalism.

To sum up, then, what has been presented here is a series of vignettes based on recent research of a continuum of settlements outside the major urban centers in Japan, and their attempts to adapt to the changing demographic landscape in innovative ways. They are all beset by the same problem, aging population and the decline of traditional industries, particularly agriculture, in the face of globalization. They are all responding in broadly similar ways, trying to promote a feeling of local community identity through *furusato* imagery, trying to promote tourism through boosterism, and reviving local agriculture to meet high-value niche market demands – as former Governor Hiramatsu delighted in reminding his audiences, in terms of value for weight, shitake mushrooms are much more valuable than BMW cars! Some of these settlements are able to exploit the local landscape for visitors, either for sports purposes as in the skiing villages described in the classic studies by Okpyo Moon (1989, 1997), or the literary and imaginary landscape, as in the case of Tono. There are other examples: the exploitation of historical sites, traditional industries, ceramics (Moeran, 1997), papermaking, wood carving and other decorative arts (Eades et al., 2000; Eades et al., 2002), sake production, lacquer (Rausch, 2003), traditional buildings (Carle, 2003), traditional furniture and so on. The variety of local resources available for these projects is wide, though most of them center round a few particular themes which are extremely widespread, particularly nostalgia, or *furursato* imagery (Moon, 1997, pp. 191–2). These are then propagated through images disseminated on national television, travel brochures, guidebooks (which in Japan seem to concentrate disproportionately on food, souvenirs, and *onsen* facilities), and publicity literatures from city, town, and village halls all over the country.

But if current trends continue, there is still the problem that Japan will soon be running out of people. We can discount the idea that it will ever attract large numbers of overseas tourists: it is seen as too expensive, too isolated, and climatically too cool for that; and *Nihonjinron* is a very effective tool for cultural separateness. Therefore the markets for both tourists and permanent residents will have to rely on a declining pool of clients who also have the option of spending their time and money overseas. The growth of a low-cost airline network in east Asia could have the same kind of devastating effects on traditional Japanese holiday destinations that cheap trips to places like Benidorm had on the seaside holiday industry in the UK, and an increasing number of Japanese pensioners might well decide at some point to spend most of their lives in warmer climes outside Japan (Yamashita, 2003).

So what will be the effect of all this on provincial Japan? Here are some broad hypotheses based on developmental theory and actual experience, and it would be interesting to see how far they are supported by the regional experience of other countries:

- In the new slim-line geriatric Japan, communications will be vital. Many rural communities will survive, but they will only do so if they are easily accessed and have local attractions. So increasingly those that can compete will be located along the main motorway or railway lines, particularly the Shinkansen in the case of the latter, or near airports. Perhaps the past enthusiasm for local airports which are not justified by market demand will, in the fullness of time, appear to have been a rational strategy should an east Asian low-cost air network eventually take off.

- Settlements which are on the periphery of the major cities could do quite well, following the British new town or American "edge city" model (Garreau, 1991). These towns are often attractive to live in, are within easy commuting distance of major city centers by rail, and even provide attractive locations for new businesses wanting to provide good living environments for their employees. As one example, the towns on the eastern side of Lake Biwa in central Japan from Otsu to Nagahama are thriving as dormitory suburbs for Kyoto, Osaka and Nagoya, thanks to good rail and motorway links with all three.

- Settlements away from these main transport arteries will have a much more difficult time. The rural settlements described by Knight and Thompson appear to be pretty much doomed. The Tonos of this world may have a better chance of survival because they are larger, they appear to be attracting some new industry, and, in the case of Tono, there is a plausible basis for a tourist industry. But to really make it work as a regional hub, it will probably need the Disney treatment (Raz, 1999), and that is increasingly unlikely because of the failure of those constructed under the Resorts Act of 1987. The most successful theme parks in Japan are those near the major urban hubs. Others, like Huis Ten Bosch (Hendry, 2000), which are more peripheral, are already in trouble. So a Tonopia Disneyland, however appealing a project, is probably not going to happen, and in the longer term Tono-size settlements and their parochial attractions may also be doomed. The Gifu villages with their surviving thatched houses as described by Ron Carle (2003) are clearly on the tourist route – but mainly because they lie close to the major population centers of Kansai, Aichi and Hokuriku. If they were in Aomori Prefecture for example they would probably have long since disappeared.

- The Beppus of this world may be able to compete better, but only if they take full advantage of their competitive advantages and pour all their resources into those. Beppu actually has the communications infrastructure and hot water to become the Baden Baden or Monte Carlo of Japan – but it will need the cultural and recreational facilities to go with them. The disjointed set of regional development policies of the last twenty years, focusing on distractions such as house mikan growing in silicon valleys, high-cost resorts, or even attractive universities located on local mountains should not detract from the central aim of repositioning Beppu and Oita in the national tourist market. A major arts festival, Spa Park, a casino complex, or a good quality symphony orchestra able to make more effective use of the venues which already exist in the area might be projects which could be considered. What is needed is something which will not only bring the tourists, but keep them around spending money over a longer period, and keep them coming back.

As for the rest of Japan, if the population implodes at the rate of over a million people per year huge areas will become deserted and the problem will remain of what to do with them. Luxury hotels serving the eco-tourism industry, massive expansion of the national parks system, and good feeder roads into them so that the SUV owners of the future can enjoy the green life are probably the best that can be hoped for. Just as in parts of Italy (Palmer, 1978), today's impoverished farming sector is tomorrow's unspoiled national park (until you spot the old terracing under the trees along the hiking trails), the same could easily happen in Japan. Some rural areas on the periphery of the large conurbations could see commuter development, along the lines of the UK where the old farming villages have become bijou residences for the business and academic elite (Strathern, 1981), but most of them will remain increasingly under-populated or even deserted.

This is going to be a transformation on a national scale, so some kind of nationally proactive policy is clearly needed, given the speed of the decline which will soon be upon Japan. Otherwise, the Darwinian struggle for community survival using whatever resources the local landscape can provide will simply use up scarce resources fruitlessly, given that for many if not most communities it is a struggle that can no longer be run. Of course there is an alternative scenario already suggested by the UN – massive immigration to offset the population decline (Buckley, 2004) – but it is difficult to see this happening given the current attitudes of Japanese politicians and communities. Currently, therefore, rapid depopulation partially offset by national regional investment programs creating more theme parks remains the only scenario in town, and the implications are well worth thinking about, for planners and tourism developers/managers alike.

References

Appadurai, A. (1995) 'The production of locality'. In R. Fardon (ed.) *Counterworks: Managing the diversity of knowledge*. London: Routledge, pp. 204–25

Bhaba, H. K. (1994) *The location of culture*. London: Routledge

Broadbent, J. (1989) 'Strategies and structural contradictions: Growth coalition politics in Japan'. *American Sociological Review*, 54(5), 707–21

Buckley, S. (2004) 'Japan mulls multicultural dawn'. BBC News, 5 October. Retrieved 2 November 2011, from http://news.bbc.co.uk/1/hi/world/asia-pacific/3708098.stm

Carle, R. (2003) 'The development and social impact of heritage tourism in Ogimachi'. *Ritsumeikan Journal of Asia Pacific Studies*, 12, 31–60

Castells, M. and Hall, P. (1993) *Technopoles of the world*. London: Routledge

Cooper, M. J. and Flehr, M. (2006) 'Government intervention in tourism development: Case studies from Japan and South Australia'. *Current Issues of Tourism*, 9(1), 69–85

Cooper, M. J., Eades, J. S. and Jankowska, J. (2006) 'The Politics of exclusion? Japanese cultural reactions and the Government's desire to double inbound tourism'. In P. Burns and M. Novelli (eds) *Tourism and politics: Global frameworks and local realities*. Oxford: Elsevier Science, pp. 71–82

Cooper, M. J., Ogata, M. and Eades, J. S. (2007) 'Heritage tourism in Japan'. In B. Prideaux, K. S. Chon and D. Timothy (eds) *Cultural and Heritage tourism in Asia and the Pacific*. London: Routledge

Dearing, J. W. (1995) *Growing a Japanese science city*. London: Routledge

Dower, J. (1979) *Empire and aftermath*. Cambridge, MA: Harvard East Asian Monographs

Eades, C., Eades, J. S., Nishiyama, Y. and Yanase, H. (2000) 'Houses of everlasting bliss: Globalization and the production of Buddhist altars in Hikone'. In J. S. Eades, T. Gill and H. Befu (eds) *Globalization and social change in contemporary Japan*. Melbourne: Trans Pacific Press, pp. 159–79

Eades, C., Nishiyama, Y. and Yanase, H. (2002) 'Tradition and recession: Strategies for coping with economic change in a Japanese craft industry'. *Ritsumeikan Journal of Asia Pacific Studies*, 10, 109–42

Funabiki, T. (1992) 'From rice to money: The communal and the social in Japan with reference to a village, Kurokawa'. *Japanese Review of Cultural Anthropology*, 96(6), 47–66

Garreau, J. (1991) *Edge city: Life on the new frontier*. New York: Doubleday

Getz, D. (1986) 'Models in tourism planning: Towards integration of theory and practice'. *Tourism Management*, 7(1), 21–32

Hebbert, M. (1994) 'Sen-biki amidst Desakota: Urban Sprawl and Urban Planning in Japan'. In P. Shapira, I. Masser and D. W. Edgington (eds) *Planning for Cities and Regions in Japan*. Liverpool: Liverpool University Press, pp. 70–92

Hendry, J. (2000) *The orient strikes back: A global view of cultural display*. Oxford: Berg

Johnson, C. (1982) *MITI and the Japanese Miracle*. Palo Alto, CA: Stanford University Press

Klamann, E. (1990) 'Can mouse ears fit steel hats?'. *Japan Economic Journal*, 28 April

Knight, J. (1994) 'Town making in rural Japan: An example from Wakayama'. *Journal of Rural Studies*, 10(3), 249–61

—— (1995) 'Municipal matchmaking in rural Japan'. *Anthropology Today*, 11(2), 9–17

—— (1998) 'Selling mother's love: Mail order village food in Japan'. *Journal of Material Culture*, 3(2), 153–73

—— (1999) 'Monkeys on the move: The natural symbolism of people–macaque conflict in Japan'. *Journal of Asian Studies*, 58(3), 622–47

—— (2003a) 'Repopulating the village?'. In J. W. Traphagen and J. Knight (eds) *Demographic change in Japan's aging society*. Albany, NY: State University of New York Press, pp. 107–24

—— (2003b) *Waiting for wolves in Japan: An anthropological study of people-wildlife relations*. Oxford: Oxford University Press

Knight, J. and Traphagen, J. W. (2003) 'The study of the family in Japan: Integrating anthropological and demographic approaches'. In J. W. Traphagen and J. Knight (eds) *Demographic change in Japan's aging society*. Albany, NY: State University of New York Press, pp. 3–23

McCormack, G. (1996) *The emptiness of Japanese affluence*. New York: Sphere

Moeran, B. (1997) *Folk art potters of Japan*. London: Curzon

Moon, O. (1989) *From paddy field to ski slope: The revitalization of tradition in Japanese village life*. Manchester: Manchester University Press

—— (1997) 'Tourism and cultural development: Japanese and Korean contexts'. In S. Yamashita, K. H. Din and J. S. Eades (eds) *Tourism and cultural development in Asia and Oceania*. Bangi, Malaysia: Penerbit UKM, pp. 178–94

Murphy, P. E. and Price, G. G. (1994) 'Tourism and sustainable development'. In W. F. Theobald (ed.) *Global Tourism: The next decade*. Oxford: Butterworth-Heinemann, pp. 167–93

Palmer, R. (1978) 'The Italians: Patterns of migration in London'. In J. L. Watson (ed.) *Between two cultures: Migrants and minorities in Britain*. Oxford: Basil Blackwell

Rausch, A. (2003) 'Place, process and product: A research framework for assessing territorially-signified cultural commodities in local development'. *Ritsumeikan Journal of Asia Pacific Studies*, 12, 75–94

Raz, A. E. (1999) *Riding the black ship: Japan and Tokyo Disneyland*. Cambridge MA: Harvard East Asian Monographs

Sorensen, A. (2002) *The making of urban Japan: Cities and planning from Edo to the twenty-first century*. London: Routledge

Strathern, M. (1981) *Kinship at the core: An anthropology of Elmdon, a village in north-west Essex in the nineteen-sixties*. Cambridge: Cambridge University Press

Thompson, C. S. (2003) 'Depopulation in rural Japan: "Population politics" in Towa-cho'. In J. W. Traphagen and J. Knight (eds) *Demographic change in Japan's aging society*. Albany, NY: State University of New York Press, pp. 89–106

Traphagen, J. W. (1998) 'Emic weeds or etic wild flowers? Structuring "the environment" in a Japanese town'. In K. Aoyagi., P. Nas. and J. Traphagen (eds) *Towards Sustainable Cities*. Leiden: Leiden Development Studies No. 15, pp. 37–52

—— (2000) *Taming oblivion: Aging bodies and the fear of senility in Japan*. Albany, NY: State University of New York Press

Turner, L. and Ash, J. (1975) *The golden hordes: International tourism and the pleasure periphery*. London: Constable

Urry, J. (1990) *The tourist gaze: Leisure and travel in contemporary societies*. London: Sage

Wahab, S. and Cooper, C. (2001) 'Tourism, globalization and the comparative advantage of nations'. In S. Wahab and C. Cooper (eds) *Tourism in the globalization age*. London: Routledge, pp. 3–21

Waters, M. (1995) *Globalization*. London: Routledge

Yamashita, S. (2003) *Bali and beyond: Explorations in the anthropology of tourism* (trans. J. S. Eades). Oxford and New York: Berghahn Books

Yanagita, K. (1910) *Tono monogatari (Stories About a Place)*. Tokyo: Yamato Shobo

26

Interviews with mainland Chinese seniors on their motivations for leisure travel

Cathy H. C. Hsu, Kevin K. F. Wong, Liping A. Cai

Introduction

Evidence abounds that the world population, particularly in the developed world, is ageing, a process which appears to be slow enough to encourage excuses for delaying prompt actions in some societal areas, but which is now fast enough to render costly consequences if planning is not undertaken with understanding and foresight. Like elsewhere, where birth rates have significantly slowed down coupled with a decline in death rates, the mainland Chinese population has been ageing with a proportion of the mature population growing ever steadily. The Fifth National Census of China documents that citizens of China over the age of 60 years (which is the generally accepted criterion for designating an ageing population) totalled 132 million or approximately 10 per cent of the population and people aged over 65 years totalled 88 million or 7 per cent of the total population (China.org, 2005). Urban cities, such as Beijing and Shanghai, have shown even stronger trends in the numbers of ageing people. For example, in Beijing, those over the age of 60 totalled 1.7 million in 2000 accounting for 12.54 per cent of the city's population (China.org, 2005) while in Shanghai this figure reached 2.4 million accounting for 18.3 per cent of the population (Zhang and Zhang, 2001). By 2007, there will be 200 million Chinese aged 65 or older, making up 14 per cent of the total population (China Daily, 2004).

As part of this significant trend, mature travellers have important implications for China's growing travel and tourism industry. The emerging and growing numbers of Chinese senior travellers may be attributed to the notable changes in societal values as well as economic and cultural conditions in China in the past decade. Unobligated time and discretionary income available to China's seniors are among some of the motivating factors prompting a rise in domestic travel. In addition, the improvement in physical well-being and the influence of Western culture and values (e.g. knowledge acquisition and self-enhancement) play an important role in raising the frequency and propensity to travel among the ageing population. The continuing trend towards more "empty nest" families especially in the cities, further promotes more travel. In particular, Chen (2001) pointed out that the emerging urban senior traveller market in China may be attributed to more leisure time, strong financial support and the change in value and lifestyle.

In 1999, the number of senior travellers in China reached 5 million, accounting for 20 per cent of Chinese travellers. A survey conducted in Beijing by the Beijing ShenZhou International Travel Agency estimated that 44 per cent of senior travellers paid their travel expenses out of their own annuities or deposits while the remaining 56 per cent were financed by their children and relatives (Wang, 2000). A better understanding of the motivations of this significant market segment will create a win–win situation for both the travellers and the travel industry in that travellers' needs will be better met and travel businesses will be rewarded with more customers and higher spending by their clients.

Seniors citizens in China have been through different periods of the country's contemporary history. The older ones witnessed the Second World War, the Civil War, and the founding of the New China in 1949. Their lives were all affected by the Cultural Revolution, and the open-door policy and economic reforms. To varying degrees, they all experienced hardships and poor living standards when they were young, and their ideology is rooted in Chinese traditions. Influenced by the mixture of Confucianism, Taoism and Buddhism, these traditions place high values on family harmony, frugality and abstention from indulgence. To them, leisure travel would have been a luxury reserved for the rich and powerful. Yet, these traditions have converged with modernity brought about by the phenomenal development of the country's economy since the adoption of the open-door policy and economic reforms in 1978. Some traditions began to give way to the demand for modern pleasures, including leisure travel. Domestic tourism in China was officially endorsed by the government in 1984. Even seniors, who are typically in the vanguard of old traditions, now embrace travel as an acceptable form of leisure.

The extant literature on senior travellers is abundant, but research on their motivation is relatively scarce and mostly in the context of developed economies and Western cultures. The sum of the values, customs and learned beliefs of non-Western tourists which drive their travel behaviour are purportedly different from those from the Western countries. American tourists, for example, tend to be active and adventurous in nature (Pizam and Jeong, 1996; Pizam and Sussmann, 1995) in contrast to Saudi Arabian tourists, who are more insular in their travel behaviour. Chinese social behaviour, which is profoundly influenced by Confucianism, manifests itself in areas of trust, association and authoritarianism. Importantly, Chinese people are more group-oriented in their pursuit of activities (including travel) and they seek harmony in their interactive environment (Bond, 1986; Ge et al., 1996).

The relationship between the seniors' income and travel motivation has been well established in developed countries. For example, Zimmer et al. (1995) found that higher income level was significantly associated with a higher tendency to travel. Such relationship is applicable to China's senior tourism as well. What is unique about the relationship in China is the mediating effects of the notion of family and intergenerational relationship. Numerous studies on seniors in developed countries concur that seniors have generally made their financial and time investment in home and family, have become free from their children's dependency, and possess a relatively large share of all discretionary dollars (Anderson and Langmeyer, 1982; Blazey, 1992; Javalgi et al., 1992). The Western concept of financial independence between the seniors and their adult children is remote in China. To most seniors, their family always includes married children and the grandchildren, and they usually live with one of the married children. The intergenerational financial relationship is reciprocal both in the long term and the short term, and continues throughout the lifespan.

The intergenerational reciprocity between Chinese seniors and adult children also extends to the use of time. Most Chinese seniors are committed to taking care of their offspring even after they have grown up. They do whatever they can for their children as well as grandchildren.

They are willing to sacrifice everything they have to maintain the family's well-being. If there is any time conflict between travelling and their family, in most cases they would give up travelling.

Numerous studies conducted in developed countries identified indulgent relaxation as an important factor of motivations for seniors (e.g. Backman et al., 1999; Cleaver et al., 1999; Guinn, 1980; Kim et al., 1996; Sellick, 2004; Stone and Nicol, 1999). Travel, especially in the form of luxury vacation, is a means of rewarding themselves for dealing with present-day demands and boredom associated with staying home. It is almost an instant gratification. Chinese seniors reward themselves too through leisure travel, although not necessarily in the form of luxury vacation. However, the reward is not for coping with the present-day routine demands, but rather for the hardships and tough times they have experienced throughout their lifespan.

Before motivations can be instrumental in influencing tourists' behaviours, it is important to understand what influences motivations and what are travellers' primary motivations. Since Western theories and empirical findings may or may not be relevant to the Chinese context, this study used a qualitative approach to explore the complex issue of senior travel motivation. Specific objectives of the study are to identify senior travellers' in-depth motivation, analyse the motivation data integrating the examination of Western theories' applicability in the Chinese setting, and suggest issues for future research in the area of Chinese senior travellers. A qualitative approach was particularly appropriate considering the rich life experiences of the study population and the nature of the study – a first attempt to explore Chinese senior travellers' motivation of leisure travel.

Methodology and data

A total of 27 personal interviews were conducted between 3 and 15 October 2004 in the capital city, Beijing, and the largest metropolis of Shanghai. A pre-designed interview record sheet was used. The questions were both semi-structured and open-ended to encourage free expressions of interviewees' thoughts and feelings. The interviewer applied probing and paraphrasing to facilitate recalls and allow delayed responses. Questions were organized in the categories of attitudes towards and motivations of leisure travel, factors influencing the realization of their travel, and their actual travel behaviours/trip characteristics. Some basic demographic information was also gathered.

All of the interviews were conducted in Chinese; 16 interviews were conducted in Beijing and 11 in Shanghai. One native Shanghai dialect speaker was recruited to help translate for the interviewer, who has some Shanghainese skills, as needed. Most of the interview sessions took 40–50 minutes, with a few lasting more than one hour. All the interviews were recorded by a digital recorder and the facial expressions and gestures of the interviewees were noted by the interviewer. Some potential respondents were approached in public areas, such as community common areas and public parks. An attempt to obtain permission from the community committee was made; the person in charge indicated that the researcher could approach the seniors directly. A total of 10 seniors in Beijing and 11 in Shanghai were approached in public areas; 4 and 8, respectively, didn't want to participate. The other senior interviewees were referred by friends. Since in mainland China, the official retirement age is 55 for females and 60 for males, the interviewees were selected according to these age criteria.

Digital recordings of the interviews were transcribed into text for data analysis. An indexing method was used to organize the data. The analysis of the data involves disaggregating the mass of text into meaningful and related parts or categories, which allowed the researchers to rearrange and analyse these data systematically. Guided by the structure of the interviews and the research aim of the project, data were categorized into main themes and sub-themes. Some of the expressions by seniors were directly quoted to provide a trail of evidence to support the categorization pattern.

The analysis was undertaken and completed by two researchers independently and the results were compared to provide inter-analyst reliability. The resulting categories and sub-themes were further reviewed by a third researcher. Several runs of recategorization were conducted before a final structure was accepted. Because all researchers involved in the analysis are bilingual, the Chinese transcripts were analysed and themes and results were recorded in English. Direct quotes were translated into English by the researchers.

Results

Of the interviewees 12 were females and 15 were males. The age range was 55–90, with 13 in the 55–69 age group, 11 in their 70s, 2 in their 80s and one aged 90 (see Table 26.1).

All of the 27 interviewees have had some experience of travel for leisure, business or visiting relatives or friends: 10 of them travelled for leisure frequently at the time of the survey; 14 used to travel for leisure from time to time, but had by then stopped travelling due to constraints of health, housework or financial conditions; 3 had only travelled for business prior to retirement.

Results of the analysis were classified into two themes: intrinsic desires and supporting external conditions. Data in each of the two themes were further categorized into several sub-themes.

Intrinsic desires

Patriotism and pride. Some of the comments made about travel revealed the seniors' pride in China's development over the years. They talked about the great accomplishments of the country and said they would like to see the progress themselves. For example:

> Since we don't know very much about other places of our motherland, we can view the development and construction of our country after the open-door policy and the economic reforms through travelling, and that also makes us feel happy. (No. 1, 66-year-old male, retired, catering staff)

Improving mental and physical wellbeing. Many seniors indicated that the most important thing for them to do is to enhance health and improve life expectancy; 15 mentioned that they travelled for physical and mental health. They emphasized that travelling made them feel active and happy. As one of them put it:

> After we view the scenery, we feel happy and we know about another place. Meanwhile, for example, we all have heart disease or coronary heart disease, but when we go out to travel, we feel recovered even though we don't take medicine! We feel happy and broad-minded. We don't feel tired while walking and talking with each other. I think it is necessary to travel. If you always sit at home, in low spirit, you have nothing to talk even you sit with others. You cannot really open your eyes and know the outside world only by watching TV and reading newspapers. (No. 4, 63-year-old female, retired, shop manager)

Table 26.1 Profile of the senior interviewees

No.	Age	Gender	Occupation	Year of Retirement	Education	Marital Status	No. of Children	Monthly income in RMB (Individual / Family)	Income Sources	☺
1	66	Male	Catering	1998	Secondary School	Married	2	1,600/3,000	Pension	☺
2	58	Female	Sales Clerk	1996	Junior College	Married	2	900/Not Available	Pension	☺
3	59	Female	Manager	2000*	High School	Married	2	1,500/6,500	Pension	☺
4	63	Female	Shop Manager	1991*	Secondary School	Married	2	1,500/400	Pension	☺
5	68	Female	Mechanical Engineering	1992	Bachelor	Married	2	1,000/2,300	Pension & children	☺
6	62	Male	Hospital Administration	2002	Bachelor	Married	3	1,500/3,000	Pension & children	☺
7	64	Male	Engineer	1995*	Junior College	Married	2	1,700/7,000	Pension & business	☺
8	74	Male	Gas Company	1990*	Vocational School	Married	2	2,400/3,000	Pensions	¥H
9	78	Female	Farming	-----	Not-educated	Widowed	7	NA	Children	AD
10	70	Male	Mechanical Engineering	2001*	Bachelor	Married	3	1,500/Not Available	Pension	?D
11	59	Female	Accountant	Not Retired	Vocational School	Married	2	1,500+1,200/6,700	Pension & salary	HD
12	61	Male	Academic	Not Retired	PHD	Married	2	4,000/6,700	Salary	T
13	74	Male	Sales Clerk	1990	Primary School	Married	3	1,000/2,000	Pension	ID
14	73	Male	Bus Driver	1990	Primary School	Married	1	1,000/1,800	Pension	四¥
15	90	Female	Pharmacy	1968	Not-educated	Widowed	6	1,000+	Pension	A
16	72	Male	Mechanical Worker	1982*	Not-educated	Widowed	3	1,000+	Pension	¥四
17	69	Female	Government Staff	1991*	Primary School	Married	2	1,000/2,000	Pension	¥四H☺
18	60	Female	Manufacturing Worker	1993*	Primary School	Married	2	900/2,000	Pension	☺

19	71	Male	Manufacturing Worker	1995	Secondary School	Married	2	1,000/2,000	Pension	☺
20	68	Male	Factory Manager	1996	High School	Married	2	1,000/2,000	Pension	IH
21	77	Male	Technician	1997*	Primary School	Widowed	3	800	Pension	□
22	70	Male	Mechanical Worker	2002*	Primary School	Married	2	1,000/2,000-	Pension	¥D
23	89	Male	Secretary of Workers' Union	1974	Secondary School	Married	5	1,000/2,000	Pension	A□
24	80	Male	Technician	1981	Primary School	Married	5	9,00/1,600	Pension	□A
25	78	Female	Community Worker	1984	Secondary School	Widowed	1	800	Pension & children	□☺
26	67	Female	Nurse	1982*	Vocational School	Married	2	1,300/2,500	Pension	H□D
27	74	Female	Accountant	1980	Junior College	Married	2	800/1,900	Pensions	□A

Note: Nos. 1–16 interviewees were interviewed in Beijing and Nos.17–27 in Shanghai from 3 to 15 October 2004.

"*" means that the interviewee had continued to work for a period of time after retirement age but has now completely retired.

☺ means that at the present time the interviewee has the conditions to travel and does travel relatively often.

□ means that a health problem prevents travelling; ¥ - money, T - time, A - age, H – housework, I - interest, D means they accept day trips. ___means they travelled before when their age and health permitted.

411

Knowledge seeking. The desire to know the outside world and observe new things were noted strongly in the interviews; 14 said that they wanted to obtain more knowledge through travelling. They believed that travelling helps them enrich themselves, and thus makes them feel mentally healthy. The following comment was shared by many others:

> For instance, when travelling in Xinjiang I would like to see the local people's costumes and to know what clothing is for the unmarried, married and different ages. I can also learn some local dialect. All these help me to enrich my knowledge and enlarge my field of vision. It makes me happy and I don't even feel tired after coming back. (No. 4, 63-year-old female, retired, shop manager)

Escaping daily routine. Escaping the daily routine and experiencing different things in another environment were the motivation for 7 of the interviewees. Though most of them are very satisfied with their current living conditions, they still need some stimulation to make them feel energetic and active after retirement. As one retired accountant put it:

> I feel very bored if I always stay at home. Going out makes me feel happy. The views of other places are different from those of Shanghai. (No. 27, 74-year-old female, retired, accountant)

Socializing. For 7 of the interviewees travel was an opportunity to meet and communicate with others. They felt that socialization enriches life, and communication with others is good for their health. Below is a sample comment:

> Travelling…enables people to communicate with each other and keep up with the current society. If you reach this age and always stay at home, you will feel very lonely. (No.10, 70-year-old male, retired, mechanical engineering)

Reward for hard work. For 6 of the interviewees enjoyment and relaxation associated with travel was a reward for hard work in their early years. Travel is regarded as a compensation and entitlement by some. After years of thrifty living and hardships, they felt it was time for them to reward themselves and enjoy the good things in life. One senior expressed her feelings like this:

> I feel that I should not treat myself too unfairly. I should not always have to work so hard and live frugally. It is not necessary to be frugal any more, and I don't need to. I had to be frugal when my two children went to school. (No. 5, 68-year-old female, retired, mechanical engineer)

Nostalgia. For 2 of the seniors, travelling was a means of reliving past experiences and bringing back memories. They would like to go back to places where they grew up, experienced a significant life event, or witnessed events of historical significance. One of them indicated:

> I want to see the changes of the country. For example, when I was in my teens, I walked on the Xiaobei Road of Guangzhou. I still remember what it looked like at that time. Some of the Liberation Army soldiers were killed there. Is it the same as it was before? I want to have a look. (No. 16, 72-year-old male, retired, mechanical worker, widowed)

Supporting external circumstances

Improved living standards. Several seniors attributed their ability and desire to travel to the improvement in living standards of society in general. For example:

> Meanwhile, you cannot deny that nowadays people's living standards have improved and they get higher income than ever before. People want to go out and travel. We didn't have the chance to travel when we were young because of the limited living conditions. We all had to live a frugal life at that time. (No. 11, 59-year-old female, not retired, accountant)

Personal financial resources. Several seniors related their interest in leisure travel directly to the personal and family affluence. Interestingly, to some the affluence results from the freedom of not supporting their children anymore; to others the affluence comes from the support from their children, as indicated in the comments listed below.

> Now the children have grown up and have jobs. We don't need to take care of them anymore. We have more than 3,000 Yuan per month and we cannot eat much since we are old. (No. 1, 66-year-old male, retired, catering staff)

> Now both of them have graduated with graduate degrees…I didn't have the financial resources at that time since all of my money had been spent on them…We spent almost 10,000 Yuan for our last trip….So we have to be funded by our children to travel. Why should I decline their filial behaviour? (No. 5, 68-year-old female, retired, mechanical engineer)

To some seniors, however, their ability, or inability, to travel was limited by the lack of personal financial resources. For example:

> Most of the people earn only around 1,000 Yuan per month and the commodity prices are so high now. You see, we have to be frugal and practical. We can just meet the basic living needs for things like food but not go out to travel and have entertainment. (No. 22, 70-year-old male, retired, mechanical worker)

Time resources. Not all of the interviewed seniors have retired although they have reached the retirement age. Among the 27 seniors, 2 have not retired. Meanwhile, 11 reported that they were engaged in some sort of part-time job or continued to work for their previous companies for a period of time after their retirement arrangement. They feel that they are still capable of working and want to contribute as much as possible.

Their time was also constrained by their commitment to caring for their spouses and families of their children; 5 said that housework prevented them from travelling. In China, some grown-up children still live with their parents. The seniors like to live with their children and are very willing to take care of them even at the expense of their own time. These are reflected in the following comments.

> People in our generation lived in difficulty and we have got used to it. Now in order to contribute to the society, although not to the society as a whole, we would like to do our duty for the family. (No. 8, 74-year-old male, retired, gas company)

Originally I planned to participate in the senior tour groups of the Red Setting Sun the year before last year, but I didn't go because my granddaughter was not in good health that time. She has asthma. My son and daughter-in-law work in the airlines and they are very busy. I really cannot go travelling. If conditions allowed me to travel, however, it would be wonderful! [laughter] (No. 18, 60-year-old female, retired, manufacturing worker)

Health conditions. Even though many seniors perceived leisure travel as a means of improving both physical and mental health, as discussed earlier, poor health is also a condition that inhibits their travel. Some of them were interested in travelling, but as they get older, their interest is dimmed by the inconvenience caused by age and poor health. Health problems prevented 10 of them from travelling. Most of them do not want to take the risk. For example:

I cannot travel because of my health...now I don't want to travel because my health is not good. Travelling is, of course, a good thing...If I could, I would like to do so. However, there is no way for me now. My daughter's family often travels, but my health condition does not allow me to do so. (No. 23, 89-year-old male, retired, secretary of workers' union)

Observations and discussion

Based on the results reported above, sentiments observed during the interviews and reviewed literature (both in English and Chinese), several observations were made and are discussed here.

China's phenomenal economic development since the late 1970s has brought about tremendous improvements in living standards for society in general. As the majority of the population has grown out of poverty with basic needs of subsistence met, the pursuit of higher-level needs such as leisure travel becomes possible financially. Progress towards modernity modifies Chinese traditional values such as the virtue of being frugal. However, the effects of both improved living standards and value changes on the seniors' motivation for leisure travel vary from cohort to cohort.

Respondents in the 55–69 age group tended to be more enthusiastic when expressing their opinions about travel than those who were in their 70s and over; 8 of the 10 interviewees who still travelled were aged 55–70, and only 2 of them were over 70. Those who were above 75 seldom travelled. Cohort effects were observed in studies on seniors in developed economies as well. For example, Moschis (1992) indicated that cohorts of seniors were influenced by different environments, both in their formative years, as well as during their advanced years. However, the cohort effects observed in this study are uniquely Chinese due to the drastic societal transformation in present-day China.

The youngest of the senior respondents in the survey were born in the late 1940s and early 1950s. That would imply that all of them experienced different stages of the Korean War, the Great Leap Forward Movement, the Anti-Rightist Campaign, the three-Year 'Natural' Disaster, and the most infamous Cultural Revolution. While the description of each of these historical periods is beyond the scope of this study, it is important to point out that, to most Chinese, these prolonged events were disastrous to the national economy and delayed, if not pulled back, the improvement of living standards for most Chinese.

Those in their late 50s and 60s were recent retirees, who have benefited from the 25 years of the country's economic reforms. They might have earned more and accumulated more for their retirement than the 70 and over age group. Having directly participated in the country's economic reforms and open-door policy, they are more receptive to the social and cultural changes. The older group might reveal more profoundly the Chinese traditional value of being frugal. One 74-year-old male identified himself as too conservative to consider leisure travel, while a 70-year-old male simply regarded leisure travel as "entertainment", and therefore unacceptable. The association of leisure travel with "entertainment" implied a somewhat derogative connotation in the way it was used. A 90-year-old female suggested spending on leisure travel was irresponsible and wasteful.

Sellick (2004) identified a unique senior segment of Australians who travelled for nostalgic reminiscences. Nostalgic seeking as a motivation of senior travellers was also examined in Cleaver et al. (1999). In a study by Szucs et al. (2001) of educational travel programmes in the United States and some European countries, the desire to visit one's ancestral home was found to motivate participants who stayed at elder hostels. Numerous other studies report the phenomenon of emotional tourism (Jordan, 1997; Smith, 1998) to explain the desires of the American veterans and their relatives to relive past memories by visiting Germany, South Korea and Vietnam. The term "dark tourism" has also been used to describe "travel to a location wholly, or partially, motivated by the desire for actual or symbolic encounters with death" (Seaton, 1996, 1999).

The rich life experiences of the Chinese seniors, albeit mostly bitter, give them a strong motive to travel for nostalgic purpose. Although not necessarily "dark", it is certainly emotional and they have much to reminisce. Cohort effects are expected, as different age groups of seniors went through different historical events at various stages of their adult life. To most Chinese seniors, visiting their ancestral or birth places can be positively emotional. The Chinese saying of "returning home in glory" is often quoted to describe those who left home humbly in their youth but are returning home wealthy and with achievements. Results of the interviews supported the view that Chinese peolpe have strong emotional attachments to their roots and strong nostalgic desires that motivate their travel.

The two strong phenomena which emerged from the results of the study, cohort effect and nostalgic sentiment, have been reported in previous studies on senior travellers in other countries. However, the unique Chinese historical and culture background gives special meanings to these two phenomena for the interviewees. A casual observation of the themes derived from the data analysis may indicate similarities between the Chinese and Western senior travellers' motivations and barriers. Some elements of the push and pull motivation model (Crompton, 1979; Dann, 1977, 1981) and social psychological model of tourism motivation (Iso-Ahola, 1982, 1984) surfaced in the concepts identified in the study. However, as discussed at the beginning of this chapter, intergenerational reciprocity and the forms of relaxation and reasons for reward have different meanings for the Chinese and the Western senior travellers. Thus, existing Western-oriented models may not be able to fully represent seniors' travel motivation in the Chinese setting. A more comprehensive model is needed to incorporate unique cultural aspects such as family support and responsibility, respect for the elders and other important values which may influence seniors' views and motivations of travel.

Conclusion

This study was undertaken against the backdrop of an increase in the numbers of seniors as a viable segment of China, which itself is experiencing phenomenal growth in both domestic and outbound tourism. Like most senior travellers, the mature mainland Chinese set, today, have the discretionary income and time to travel domestically and with improved health and heightened curiosity, and their frequency of travel has not only increased but become more diversified.

Beyond the basic desire to enrich themselves in knowledge of the "outside world" which makes up their pride and joy, these seniors revealed a genuine desire to improve both their physical and mental health and, in the process, aspired to refresh their social links with other members of society to ease their loneliness and relive their youthful experiences.

The results of this study further underscores the need to steer away from an inaccurate and misunderstood stereotype view of mature travellers and to seek a more comprehensive understanding of the heterogeneity and variegations of their travel behaviour so that tourism products and services can be customized to match their special needs. While the findings of this study are by no means representative or conclusive, it rightly opens a thought-provoking window for scholars to progressively understand and appreciate the travel motivation of this steadily growing market segment in mainland China that has hitherto been manifestly ignored.

Future studies on this population are needed to continue the inquiry initiated in this exploratory research. The often-called 'young–old' (i.e. those between 55 and 75 years old) (Abdel-Ghany and Sharpe, 1997; Goard and Hardy, 2004; Lago and Poffley, 1993) segment of the Chinese seniors warrants particular attention because, among all seniors, this is the most active travel market and the relatively young age indicates many more years of future travel, which represents great market opportunities for the tourism industry. The proposal of a conceptual model based on existing knowledge of travel motivation and distinctiveness of the Chinese seniors would be a logical next step to provide directions for additional empirical studies.

Acknowledgments

The authors wish to thank The Hong Kong Polytechnic University for funding this research project (A-PE89).

References

Abdel-Ghany, M. and Sharpe, D. L. (1997) 'Consumption patterns among the young-old and old-old'. *Journal of Consumer Affairs*, 31(1), 90–112
Anderson, B. and Langmeyer, L. (1982) 'The under-50 and over-50 traveller: A profile of similarities and differences'. *Journal of Travel Research*, 20(4), 20–24
Backman, K. F., Backman, S. J. and Silverberg, K. E. (1999) 'An investigation into the psychographics of senior nature-based travelers'. *Tourism Recreation Research*, 24(1), 13–22
Blazey, M. A. (1992) 'Travel and retirement status'. *Annals of Tourism Research*, 19(4), 771–83
Bond, M. H. (ed.) (1986) *The Psychology of the Chinese People*. New York: Oxford University Press
Chen, J. (2001) 'Trend analysis of China's domestic travel consumer in the 21st century'. *Social Scientist*, 16(5), 21–4
China Daily (2004) 'Ageing population challenges China'. China Daily, 9 June. Retrieved 31 October 2011, from http://www.chinadaily.com.cn/english/doc/2004–06/09/content_337985.htm
China.org (2005) 'China faces up to ageing population'. China.org, 7 January. Retrieved 31 October 2011, from http://www.china.org.cn/english/2005/Jan/117070.htm
Cleaver, M., Muller, T. E., Ruys, H. F. M. and Wei, S. (1999) 'Tourism product development for the senior market, based on travel-motive research'. *Tourism Recreation Research*, 24(1), 5–11
Crompton, J. L. (1979) 'Motivations of pleasure vacation'. *Annals of Tourism Research*, 6(4), 408–24
Dann, G. M. S. (1977) 'Anomie, ego-enhancement and tourism'. *Annals of Tourism Research*, 4(4), 184–94
—— (1981) 'Tourist motivation: An appraisal'. *Annals of Tourism Research*, 8(2), 187–219
Ge, G., Toomey, T. S. and Gudykunst, W. (1996) 'Chinese social interaction: Harmony and hierarchy on the good earth'. In M. H. Bond (ed.) *The Handbook of Chinese Psychology*. New York: Oxford University Press, pp. 309–21

Goard, L. M. and Hardy, J. (2004) 'When does someone attain old age?' (Senior Series No. SS-101-R04). Retrieved 31 October 2011, from http://ohioline.osu.edu/ss-fact/pdf/0101.pdf

Guinn, R. (1980) 'Elderly recreational vehicle tourists: Motivation for leisure'. *Journal of Travel Research*, 14(1), 9–12

Iso-Ahola, S. E. (1982) 'Toward a social psychological theory of tourism motivation: A rejoinder'. *Annals of Tourism Research*, 9(2), 256–61

—— (1984) 'Social psychological foundations of leisure and resultant implications for leisure counseling'. In E. T. Dowd (ed.) *Leisure counseling: Concepts and applications.* Springfield, IL: Charles C. Thomas, pp. 97–125

Javalgi, R. G., Thomas, E. G. and Rao, S. R. (1992) 'Consumer behaviour in the US pleasure travel marketplace: an analysis of senior and nonsenior travellers'. *Journal of Travel Research*, 31(2), 14–19

Jordan, M. (1997) 'War and remembrance: Germany targets the power and popularity of nostalgic tours'. *Outbound Traveler*, 4(1), 12–14

Kim, Y., Weaver, P. and McCleary, K. (1996) 'A structural equation model: The relationship between travel motivation and information sources in the senior travel market'. *Journal of Vacation Marketing*, 3(1), 55–66

Lago, D. and Poffley, J. D. (1993) 'The ageing population and the hospitality industry in 2010: Important trends and probable services'. *Hospitality Research Journal*, 19(1), 30–45

Moschis, G. (1992) *Marketing to older consumers: A handbook of information for strategy development.* Westport, CT: Quorum

Pizam, A. and Jeong, G. (1996) 'Cross-cultural tourist behaviour: Perceptions of Korean tour guides'. *Tourism Management*, 17(4), 277–86

Pizam, A. and Sussmann, S. (1995) 'Does nationality affect tourist behaviour?'. *Annals of Tourism Research*, 22(4), 901–17

Seaton, A. V. (1996) 'From thanatopsis to thanatourism: Guided by the dark'. *Journal of International Heritage Studies*, 2(2), 234–44

—— (1999) 'War and thanatourism: Waterloo 1815–1914'. *Annals of Tourism Research*, 26(1), 130–58

Sellick, M. C. (2004) 'Discovery, connection, nostalgia: Key travel motives within the senior market'. *Journal of Travel and Tourism Marketing*, 17(1), 55–71

Smith, V. L. (1998) 'War and tourism: An American ethnography'. *Annals of Tourism Research*, 25(1), 202–27

Stone, G. and Nicol, S. (1999) 'Older, single female holidaymakers in the United Kingdom: Who needs them?'. *Journal of Vacation Marketing*, 5(1), 7–17

Szucs, F. K., Daniels, M. J. and McGuire, F. A. (2001) 'Motivations of elder hostel participants in selected United States and European educational travel programs'. *Journal of Hospitality and Leisure Marketing*, 9(1/2), 21–34

Wang, B. (2000) 'Senior citizens love to travel'. People.com, 8 November. Retrieved 31 October 2011, from http://www.people.com.cn/GB/channel3/25/20001108/305299.html

Zhang, J. and Zhang, M. (2001) 'Senior traveler market in Shanghai is getting popular'. People's Daily (overseas version), 11 January. Retrieved 31 October 2011, from http://unn.people.com.cn/GB/channel335/336/823/200101/11/28846.html

Zimmer, Z., Brayley, R. and Searle, M. S. (1995) 'Whether to go and where to go: Identification of important influences on seniors' decisions to travel'. *Journal of Travel Research*, 33(3), 3–10

Index

Page numbers in **bold** refer to figures, page numbers in *italic* refer to tables.